*THE HISTORY OF AMERICAN WEATHER*

# Early American Winters
# 1604–1820

## David M. Ludlum

American Meteorological Society
45 Beacon Street
Boston, Massachusetts 02108
1966

1966
Copyright by David M. Ludlum
of Princeton, New Jersey

Jacket design by Eric Sloane
of Warren, Connecticut

Printed by Lancaster Press, Inc.
of Lancaster, Pennsylvania

Published and sold by the
American Meteorological Society
45 Beacon Street, Boston,
Massachusetts 02108

The design of THE HISTORY OF AMERICAN WEATHER is to relate the facts concerning the development of the science of meteorology in the Americas and to describe the principal weather events in our climatic past by means of a series of historical monographs.

---

*Early American Hurricanes 1492–1870*
*Early American Winters 1604–1820*
*Early American Winters 1821–1870* (In press—1967)
*Early American Tornadoes* (In research)

---

The task of assembling the record of our early weather history is a monumental one due to the multiplicity and diversity of sources. All references to the location of meteorological records or descriptions of weather events, either in manuscript or in printed form, will be most welcome. Address: Historian, American Meteorological Society, 45 Beacon Street, Boston, Massachusetts 02108.

A great thunderstorm; an extensive flood; a desolating hurricane; a sudden and intense frost; an overwhelming snowstorm; a sultry day,—each of these different scenes exhibits singular beauties even in spite of the damage they cause. Often while the heart laments the loss to the citizen, the enlightened mind, seeking for the natural causes, and astonished at the effects, awakes itself to surprise and wonder. *A Snow Storm as it Affects the American Farmer.* St. John de Crèvecoeur.

IN HONOR OF

St. John de Crèvecoeur, 1735–1813 of France and America

Henry David Thoreau, 1817–1862 of Concord and Walden Pond

Charles Franklin Brooks, 1891–1958 of Harvard
and Blue Hill Observatory

All shared a professional and personal interest in this subject

# CONTENTS

Foreword ................................................... viii

The American Colonies in the Seventeenth Century ............   2

The Northeast in the Eighteenth Century ....................  38

Winters of the Revolution ..................................  88

The Old South in the Eighteenth Century .................... 138

The Early Nineteenth Century in the Northeast .............. 164

The Old South in the Early Nineteenth Century .............. 198

Early Winters in the Old Northwest ......................... 218

A Winter Anthology ......................................... 240

The Sources of Wintry Data ................................. 279

Index ...................................................... 282

# FOREWORD

The purpose of this work is to set down in chronological order and in proper geographical setting the meteorological details attending the occurrence of extreme winter conditions over the eastern portion of the United States from its first settlement to 1820. When Henry David Thoreau sought to learn more about the details of the Great Snow of 1717 or the circumstances making Cold Friday of 1810 so memorable, he could find no satisfactory answers to his innate curiosity about such matters despite a diligent search of historical literature at Harvard and personal inquiries about Concord. A similar first quest by this writer a hundred years later was likewise unrewarding since the subject of winter weather in the United States had never been the object of an organized study. There have been historical works on a national scale about hurricanes, tornadoes, hailstorms, and floods, but none concerned primarily with the cold season of the year. Thus, the extremes of cold and snow experienced in the past and the limits of such climatologically possible, now and in the future, have remained largely unknown.

The plan of the work is to present a series of studies of the highlights of weather events of the winter season with emphasis on the prevalence of cold and frozen precipitation. Only the major storm events of the period and summaries of particularly extreme seasons can be presented in the space available, though much additional material has been gathered on other contemporary weather events. It is hoped that this form of presentation will accomplish the main purpose of determining the limits of the extremes of the past. Where narrative chronologies are available, they have been repeated in full, so that comparisons can be made between succeeding seasons. After 1781 the New Haven temperature record became available so that a quantitive comparison can be made as to relative coldness. No continuous precipitation record nor complete snowfall measurements have been uncovered for this period. Chronological lists of outstanding cold days and accounts of unusually early or late snows have been compiled. Extensive quotations by witnesses of the major events have been included to show how contemporaries viewed the storms and seasons.

The divisions as to time have been made on the conventional method of centuries though climatic trends do not recognize man's calendar. The first wintering-over season on the northern Atlantic Coast adjacent to the present United States came in the early Seventeenth Century in 1604. Thenceforth, there were some Europeans in what is now northeastern United States during each winter season. The first century of settlement during which almost all of the Atlantic seaboard was occupied is treated in the first section. The Eighteenth Century witnessed the independent growth of the colonies and also brought the introduction of weather instruments and the commencement of regular meteorological observations by individuals. The second main division is devoted to these hundred years, broken down geographically into separate sections dealing with the Northeast, the Old South, and the Old Northwest, for the climatic conditions and historical material of these varied greatly. With the turn of the 19th Century the flow from pen and press increased markedly, so the first 20 years to 1820 are treated in a third section, again following the same geographic divisions into Northeast, South, and Northwest. It was during these two decades that first attempts were made to establish a national weather observing system by the Medical Corps of the United States Army. Following 1820 our sources of data are greatly enriched by records from all sections of the country. A knowledge of the extremes of winter conditions is much easier to come by. A final section of the work has been entitled: A Winter Anthology. Here a number of contemporary descriptions of winter events by witnesses have been assembled, to give local color to particular occurrences or to expand accounts of the events described in the main body of the text.

# PREVIOUS STUDIES OF AMERICAN WINTERS

There have been many weather-watchers of varying literary ability on the American scene since the first John Winthrop observed and described some winter events on the shores of Massachusetts Bay. But the first American who was in a position to take a historical view of the subject of winter weather was Ezra Stiles, a weather observer of long standing and the president of Yale College during the Revolution and afterwards. An avid collector of Americana, his massive diary and his manuscript thermometrical register contain many references to severe storms and occurrences of severe winters in the colonial period.[1] Perhaps his most famous student, Noah Webster, sharing his mentor's interest in meteorological events, prepared a lengthy study of the character of past winters by a wide-ranging survey of historical material from classical, European, and American sources. Later in his life, after the occurrence of a particularly cold period in 1835, Webster assembled a listing of similar periods in past American history.[2]

Another contemporary seeking to define the limits of the severity of past winters was Samuel Hazard of Philadelphia who searched the local newspaper files for details of winter seasons on the Delaware. The "Effects of Climate," published in his *Register of Pennsylvania* in 1828, provided references to almost every winter season for more than a century and a quarter.[3] A somewhat similar, though briefer, account appeared for the Hudson River Valley in an 1832 newspaper article.[4] But the material in these was thin and confined to a limited area.

Of the almanac material, the best historical summary appeared in the *American Almanac and Repository of Useful Knowledge for the year 1837* (Boston).[5] This contained data on the winters of 1717, 1740–41, 1779–80, as well as available statistics on 19th Century winters. Apparently this provided a source for many later newspaper articles as the facts presented here appear again and again in the American press. The almanacs, in general, are a very disappointing source for contemporary weather stories; they confine themselves to a few sayings of dubious weather wisdom and some vague forecasts for unprecise dates.

When Lorin Blodget prepared and issued his impressive, 536-page *Climatology of the United States* in 1857, he was able to compile historical accounts of American hurricanes and tornadoes, but his listing of winter storms was limited by the lack of material to the recent past.[6] Even the Smithsonian period of collecting contemporary weather records and data from 1849 to 1872 did not produce any compilation of winter storms although much useful information was gathered into its depository and now resides in the National Archives.

Since the establishment of a Federal weather service in 1871 no such compilation has appeared. The *Monthly Weather Review* in the 1880's and 1890's published extensive summaries of past temperature and precipitation data, and Cleveland Abbe, its guiding light and able editor after 1893, expressed the hope that someone would make use of these and produce an organized study of historical weather events, but no one came forward to do so.[7] The nearest approach to such a study appeared in 1891, but confined its attention to a single region only. Sidney Perley's *Historic Storms of New England* contained a number of interesting accounts of big snows and cold winters.[8] Perley, culling most of his material from contemporary newspapers, made no attempt to introduce any meteorological data into his accounts, so his work contains little of scientific value today. In 1914 Prof. Charles F. Brooks published his monograph, *Snowfall in Eastern United States,* but his main purpose was not to probe the historical past. His references to big snows of early America were confined to several brief paragraphs.[9]

The reason for the lack of any coordinated study in depth on a national scale became readily apparent when a first survey of the nature of the source material was made. It was diverse in type of written record and greatly scattered in geographical location. During the period under current survey, 1604 to 1820, there were no organized meteorological services and even few instrumental records by individuals of substantial length or value. Nor was there any collecting agency to gather together existing data. Much rested in what could not be considered strictly scientific sources without adequate bibliographical guides. Thus, Henry Thoreau had no means of knowing the whereabouts of manuscript diaries covering his periods of interest in 1717 and 1810, nor of locating files of contemporary newspapers which might have supplied the answers to his questions.

During the course of the present century much of the source materials has been gathered into depositories such as the Library of Congress, the National Archives, and the National Weather Records Center, as well as in numerous university libraries. These have been cataloged, indexed, and guides prepared, though the task is far from complete.[10] The recent introduction of rapid and inexpensive photoduplication methods at even small libraries has made these available to all seekers, and has to a large extent eliminated the necessity for time-consuming travel. One seeking the answers to Thoreau's questions now can search the basic documents and data in his own library or study. A listing of the general sources to wintry data employed in the preparation of this study will be found in a concluding section. References to sources employed in describing specific storm occurrences will be found in the footnotes at the conclusion of each individual study.

[1] *The literary diary of Ezra Stiles.* Franklin B. Dexter, ed. New York, Scribner's Sons, 1901. 3 vols.
Ezra Stiles. Ms. Thermometrical Register. Yale University Library.

[2] Noah Webster. A dissertation on the supposed change in the temperature in winter (1799); Supplementary remarks (1806). *Trans. Conn. Acad. Sci.* 1-1 (1810), 1–46; 47–68. Reprint: Noah Webster. *A collection of papers on political, literary and moral subjects.* New York, Webster & Clark, 1843. 119–62.

———. Notices of extraordinary seasons of cold. *Amer. Jour. Sci.* (New Haven). **28** (July 1835), 185.

[3] Samuel Hazard. Effects of climate on navigation. [Delaware River 1681–1828]. *The Penna. Register* (Phila.) **2**-1 (July 1828), 23–26; **2**-6 (Dec 1828), 379–386.

[4] Notices of the winters. New York for forty-two years, and of the dates on which the river was frozen, or obstructed or closed by ice at Albany. *New York Daily Advertiser,* Dec 1832.

[5] Notices of remarkably cold winters. *American Almanac and Repository of Useful Information for the year 1837.* Boston, Charles Bowen, 1836. 169–73.

[6] Lorin Blodget. *Climatology of the United States and of the temperate latitudes of the North American continent. Embracing a full comparison of these with the climatology of the temperate latitudes of Europe and Asia. And especially in regard to agriculture, sanitary investigations, and engineering. With isothermal and rain charts for each season, the extreme months, and the year. Including a summary of the statistics of meteorological observations in the United States, condensed from recent scientific and official publications.* Philadelphia, J. B. Lippincott and Co., 1857. 536 pp.

[7] *Monthly Weather Review* (Washington), 1872–. Published successively by the Signal Corps. U.S. Army; Department of Agriculture; and Department of Commerce.

[8] Sidney Perley. *Historic storms of New England. Its gales, hurricanes, tornadoes, showers with thunder and lightning, great snow storms, rains, freshets, floods, droughts, cold winters, hot summers, avalanches, earthquakes, dark days, comets, auroraborealis, phenomena in the heavens, wrecks along the coast, with incidents and ancedotes, amusing and pathetic.* Salem, Mass., The Salem Press, 1891. 341 pp.

[9] Charles F. Brooks. The snowfall of the eastern United States. *Monthly Weather Review* (Wash.). **43**-1 (Jan 1915), 2–11.

[10] *List of climatological records in the National Archives.* Lewis J. Darter, ed. Washington, The National Archives, 1942. 160 pp.

Ms. Inventory of packages among unpublished hydrologic data in attic of Smithsonian Institution observed and listed by Mr. C. S. Jarvis, Mr. H. S. Schrieber, and Mr. R. W. Ellis, May 3, 1937. 54 packages listed; also note: "Lost in fire of January 24, 1865, at the Smithsonian Institute." (sic).

James M. Havens. *An annotated bibliography of meteorological observations in the United States, 1731–1818.* Tallahassee, Fla., Dept. of Meteorogy, Florida State Univ., 1956. 31 pp.

# THE HISTORICAL PERIOD: 1604–1820

The period under study extends from the first season that a group of Europeans wintered on the northern Atlantic coastline and survived to leave a definite record of their experiences. The French spent the three winters from 1604–05 to 1606–07 in the vicinity of the Bay of Fundy, and thereafter some white men with the ability to record passing events were to be found from Virginia northward as each winter solstice approached and passed. There were, however, no sizable permanent establishments in the area of normally severe winter conditions until the founding of Plymouth Plantation on the shores of Cape Cod Bay late in 1620. For the next 200 years there exists an evergrowing body of historical literature which upon close examination sheds light on the nature of the North American winter. Half way through this 200-year period the thermometer was introduced to America. The first such instrument to be employed for meteorological purposes, according to the evidence now at hand, was the property of Dr. Cadwallader Colden, then of Philadelphia, who employed a combined thermometer-barometer in the winter of 1717–18, apparently brought to this country by the scientifically-trained Colden when he returned from England either late in 1715 or early in 1716 accompanied by his bride. Colden had studied medicine at London and science at Edinburgh before first coming to America in 1710.[11]

Another hundred years would pass before any systematic effort was made to establish a group of observation points which would make a start toward the objective measurement and description of the American climate. Thus, the year 1820 provides a convenient cut-off date for the present study—afterwards the records of the U.S. Army Medical Corps provide some crude scientific data upon which a quantitative, meaningful comparison of winter seasons can be made. A second volume covering the next 50 years, 1821–70, will be devoted to this period in the meteorological development of our country.

[11] ". . . I thank you for your account of the state of the Barometer and Thermometer at Philadelphia part 1717 and part 1718. I continue to keep a journal of the winds and weather and shall yearly transmit you the same." William Douglass to Cadwallader Colden, Boston, *July 28, 1721. Coll. Mass. Hist. Soc.* 4th ser., **2**, 166.

## GEOGRAPHICAL LIMITS

The geographical area of the study has been limited to the section now comprising the eastern half of the United States. On several occasions materials relating to events in southern Canada have been included since the atmosphere knows no nationalistic boundaries and the Canadian data greatly illuminates the description of events in the United States. A rich store of meteorological data of the early period exists for the Canadian region, and this awaits its historian who is familiar with the main channels of his country's historical material.

In general, the geographical region has been confined to the colonies, territories, or states east of the Mississippi River since the area of settlement had hardly passed the east bank of that river by 1820. Accounts of two main exploration expeditions into the Louisiana Purchase Territory are treated in an appendix since a study of climate conditions to be encountered were high on the agenda of each mission, and both occurred during a winter having interesting meteorological conditions. The bulk of the study is, of necessity, heavily weighted toward the Northeastern part of the colonies or states. The center of population of the United States in 1820 still lay in western Virginia near present-day Moorefield, West Virginia, only 100 miles almost due west of Washington, D. C. Not only were winter conditions in the Northeast, and especially in New England, normally more noteworthy as to extremes, but the populace had a long tradition of weather-watching and were of a literary bent with a disposition toward recording what they saw and felt. This imbalance is a situation confronting all aspects of historical research in this period.

The geographical divisions of the work into Northeast, South, and Northwest are general in nature. Moving cyclones and anticyclones do not respect man-made boundaries, and it is often necessary for a better understanding to describe a storm's antecedent history in another section. The general boundaries have been observed, for the most part, as a convenience to the reader who wishes to study a particular area. The Northeast has been considered as comprising the Atlantic coastal plain and the eastern slopes of the Appalachians north of the Potomac River. The South includes the area from Virginia southward to Florida and southwestward to Louisiana. The Northwest makes up the area west of the crest of the Appalachians from Kentucky to the Great Lakes as far as the Mississippi River.

## THE CALENDAR

The dating of events in the period under study was complicated by the use of two calendar systems. Until 2 September 1752 the Julian calendar was employed in the English colonies, though the French and Dutch had adopted the reformed system or Gregorian calendar before our period commenced. Thus, in most of the colonies the next day after 2 September 1752 was designated 14 September, 11 days having been skipped to bring man's reckoning and solar position into accord. The dating of a meteorological event must be transposed into the calendar in current use so that it may be viewed in its proper climatological setting and valid comparisons made with current occurrences.

In the 17th Century 10 days have been added to Old Style dates, and in the first 52 years of the 18th Century 11 days have been added for this purpose. Some dates in quoted material and in newspaper datelines must be left in their original form, and these appear in italics to indicate they are Old Style. Other dates have been corrected to New Style and appear in regular type. This also applies to the naming of a month since *January 1752* (Old Style) actually would be the equivalent of January 12th to February 11th (New Style).

Another difficulty arose from the use under Old Style of March 25th as the first day of the new year. Many employed a double designation for naming of years of events in January, February, or March to the 25th. Thus, the Great Snow commenced *16 February 1716/17,* or 27 February 1717 as it would now be written.

Italics have been employed again for Old Style dates, and the double designation has been dropped in an effort toward uniformity. A further complication arose through the Quaker usage of the term "first month" standing alone when meaning March—the practice continued through the "twelfth month" for February. This quaint calendar reckoning has also been corrected to modern usage.

## THE SOURCES

After some fifteen years of occasional searching the sources of American historical literature for meteorological references, it is realized that only a start has been made—the surface has been scratched, some shafts have been sunk in obviously promising territory and have yielded rewards, yet there remain many enticing areas for prospecting new finds. No doubt, some scholarly digging at the state or local level will uncover a wealth of meteorological data revealing many important details about winter weather of the past for particular localities. Probably many fine weather records lie buried in the manuscript archives of local historical societies, inadequately cataloged, and many files of local newspapers remain unscanned by weather-conscious eyes. Let us hope that each region or state will ultimately have its historian of atmospheric events so that the complete story of our meteorological past can be reconstructed. Only if we have knowledge of the extremes of the past, can we prepare to cope with the future onslaughts of Nature.

# Early American Winters

# THE AMERICAN COLONIES IN THE SEVENTEENTH CENTURY

New France: 1604–1607 .................................... 3

Early New England: 1607–1619 ............................ 6

Plymouth Plantation: 1620–21 .............................. 7

Massachusetts Bay Colony: 1629–1649 ...................... 12

The Three Landmark Winters of the Century:

    1641–42: Winthrop's Severe Winter ..................... 15

    1680–81: Increase Mather's Severe Winter .............. 16

    1697–98: The Terriblest Winter ........................ 16

The Winthrop Chronicle of Winter Events in New England: 1631–1653 ................................................. 18

John Hull's Winter Chronology: 1654–1678 .................. 22

John Pike's Winter Chronology: 1682–1700 .................. 24

New Netherland: 1609–1664 ................................ 27

New Sweden: 1683–1663 .................................... 29

Pennsylvania: 1682–1700 ................................... 31

Virginia: 1607–1700 ....................................... 32

The Carolinas: 1660–1700 .................................. 35

When the wintry sun rose out of the Atlantic Ocean on New Year's morning of 1601, there were no Europeans living on the northern Atlantic coast of America to record the nature of the weather that day or to describe the character of the ensuing winter. In fact, no European had ever spent a winter on the coastline north of Cape Hatteras and survived to leave a record for his contemporaries. The native population, of course, had experienced countless centuries of varying climatic conditions in the post-glacial period, but they had no means of preserving a record of such or of communicating their innate weather knowledge to others. The true nature of the North American winter in these latitudes remained a great unknown.

It was general knowledge that Jacques Cartier had wintered near Quebec in 1535–36, but this was at a relatively high latitude, toward the interior, where Europeans assumed winter conditions might be rigorous.[1] Some English had spent the winter season of 1585–86 on Roanoke Island in coastal North Carolina where year-round conditions are generally mild. Thomas Hariot afterwards referred to "the excellent temperature of the ayre there *at all seasons,* much warmer than in England." He also spoke of trips taken in winter when he slept on the bare ground without covering.[2] A second group of colonists planned to spend the winter of 1587–88 in the same locality, but whether they did so is unknown to history as all had disappeared when a much-delayed relief expedition finally arrived in 1590—the intriguing Lost Colony of Roanoke.

The explorers who coasted our shores in the great century of discovery in the 1500's were mainly summer visitors who never felt the frigid bite of a northwester nor the snow blast of a northeaster. Estevan Gomez of Portugal did cruise Maine waters without landing in January and February of 1525, but he had no unusual weather experiences which would provide a clue to the potential of a northern winter.[3] No others have left any winter documentation in the Sixteenth Century.

It is possible that some European fishermen or traders, who were accustomed to come to Newfoundland and the Gulf of St. Lawrence, had wintered on Cape Cod or Maine when driven thence by storms or adverse winds, but there is no written record of such. The Spanish in Florida, of course, had maintained permanent settlements at St. Augustine since 1565, but this area does not concern us at this time since cold and frost were the least of the problems facing His Most Catholic Majesty's outpost there.

## NEW FRANCE: 1604–1607

The Seventeenth was the century of colonization. The pace of exploration quickened among all nations with the immediate view of establishing permanent settlements. The English and French sent exploratory thrusts into the North Atlantic area in the summer of 1602 and 1603, and in 1604 the latter sought to establish the first settlement to winter over in the northern area. Under Pierre du Guast, Sieur de Monts, the French spent the rugged winter of 1604–05 on St. Croix Island, a small spot of land in the estuary of the St. Croix River which now separates the State of Maine from the Province of New Brunswick.[4]

Perhaps forgetful of the winter experiences of Jacques Cartier near Quebec in 1535–36 and deceived by the familiar latitude, the French thought the Canadian weather would be no more severe than known in their native France. The winter of 1604–05 proved exceedingly rigorous—commencing early with snow the first week of October, approaching in its depth the extremes possible for the region with river and bay icebound and the ground covered with a very deep snow, and continuing unusually late to the end of April. It was so cold that all beverages except Spanish wine froze—cider was given out by the pound! Thirty-five of the 79 colonists died in that bitter winter, mainly from scurvy, and many more barely survived. Samuel de Champlain (1567–1635), who served as geographer of the expedition, maintained a diary of the major events with a keen eye to the weather:

> Snow fell on the sixth of October. On the third of December we saw ice passing, which came from some frozen river. The cold was severe and more extreme than in France, and lasted much longer. I believe this is caused by the north-west winds, which pass over mountains continually covered with snow. This we had to a depth of three or four feet up to the end of the month of April; and I believe also that it lasts much longer than it would if the land were under cultivation.[5]

"It was difficult to know this country," declared Champlain later, "without having wintered there; for on arriving in summer everything is very pleasant on account of the woods, the beautiful landscapes, and the fine fishing for the many kinds of fish we found there. There are six months of winter in that country." [6]

When summer came, Champlain accompanied an expedition southward on what was a climatologically-motivated, exploring trip to seek a more hospitable site for settlement. When on Cape Cod near Nauset in mid-July of 1605, the French quizzed the Indians as to the nature of the winter there:

> We asked them if they had a permanent abode in this place, and whether there was much snow. But we were unable to ascertain this fully from them, not understanding their language, although they made an attempt to inform us by signs, by taking some sand in their hands, spreading it over the ground and indicating that it was the color of our colors, and that it reached the depth of a foot. Others made signs that there was less, and gave us to understand also that the harbor never froze; but we were unable to ascertain whether the snow lasted long. I conclude, however, that this region is of moderate temperature and the winter not severe.[7]

The expedition visited both Plymouth and the north shore of Massachusetts Bay, the future sites of Pilgrim and Puritan settlements, but the French were not very favorably impressed with what they saw. Champlain prepared and published a very usable map of Plymouth Harbor some 15 years before the famous landing in 1620. His observations concerning the areas visited and his concern with the winter season appeared in a diary entry:

> Such is a true statement of everything I observed both in regard to the coasts and peoples, as also to the river of Norumbega (Penobscot); but they are not the wonders described by some. I believe this region is as disagreeable in winter as is that of our settlement, in regard to which we were greatly deceived.[8]

Upon the return northward in August, the diary showed the same obsession with winter:

> The Sieur de Monts decided to remove elsewhere, and to build another settlement to escape the cold and the dreadful winter we had experienced at Ste. Croix island . . . searched for a suitable site for our residence, with shelter from the north-west wind, which we dreaded on account of having been greatly distressed thereby.[9]

A location on the Annapolis Basin directly across the Bay of Fundy in Nova Scotia was determined on. This had been previously explored; it was known to contain a good anchorage and suitable soil. In addition, it had, from the climatological view, the desired features of hills to the northwest and north to protect against frigid winds and a predominately maritime exposure. Fortunately, the two succeeding winters were much less severe than that of 1604–05. A southerly and easterly flow of mild air conditioned over the Atlantic Ocean replaced the continental circulation which had brought Arctic air masses to the region constantly during the first winter. The record of Champlain described the outstanding events of the winter of 1605–06:

> On the twentieth of December it began to snow, and some ice passed in front of our settlement. The winter was not so severe as it had been the year before, nor was the snow as deep or of such long duration. Among other occurrences, on the twentieth of February 1605/06 it blew so great a gale that a large number of trees were blown down, roots and all, and many broken off. It was a strange sight to behold. The rains were quite frequent, which was the cause of the mild winter in comparison with the preceding, although from Port Royal to Ste. Croix the distance is only twenty five leagues.[10]

Champlain made a trip in March back to the old settlement at St. Croix, "this place of misfortune," and on the vernal equinox he found "a great quantity of snow" still laying at the old site, again demonstrating the differing climatological character possessed by these two nearby sites, one backing on the continent, the other almost wholly exposed to maritime influences.

The French made a second trip southward in 1606 when summer came. This time they explored Martha's Vineyard and put into Stage Harbor at Chatham on Cape Cod. They left Nauset to begin the northward voyage on 28 October 1606, "that day was quite cold and there fell a little snow."[11] Three days later they beached their vessel on Great Wass Island on the central Maine Coast, and Champlain again made a judgment of the differing conditions between continental and maritime exposures:

> On the first of November we went to a place we thought suitable for beaching our vessel and repairing our helm. That day I went ashore, and there saw ice two inches thick which had been frozen some eight or ten days. I noticed clearly that the temperature here differed greatly from that at Mallebarre or Misfortune harbour; for the leaves of the trees were not yet dead, nor had any fallen when we left those places. Here they all had fallen and it was much colder than at Misfortune Harbour.[12]

The character and some of the events of the winter of 1606–07 at Port Royal were described:

> The snow was not long as in the preceding years, nor did the snow remain so late upon the ground. It rained pretty often, on which account the Indians suffered a severe famine, because of the scarcity of snow. (They could not capture moose by running them down in deep snow.) [13]
> On the night of the twenty-sixth of December, a wind from south-east blew down a number of trees.
> The last day of December it began to snow, and continued to do so until the next morning.
> On the sixteenth of January following, in the year 1607, the Sieur de Poutrincourt, wishing to go to the head of the Equille River, found it closed with ice some two leagues from our settlement, and had to return since he could not go farther.

On the eighth of February some ice-floes began to come down from the head of the river into port, which only freezes along the shore.

On the tenth of May following it snowed the whole night, and toward the end of the month there were several heavy white frosts which lasted as late as the tenth and twelfth of June, when all the trees were covered with leaves, except the oaks which do not put out theirs until the 15th.[14]

Among those wintering at Port Royal was Marc Lescarbot, a Parisian lawyer and a man of considerable literary skill. His *History of New France*, first published in 1609, ran through several editions in the next decade, both in French and English.[15] The work had a deserved popularity as it presented many previously unknown facts about the New World in an entertaining style. Lescarbot's remarks on the weather and climate of New France comprised the ablest climatological discussion about American conditions in the entire century:

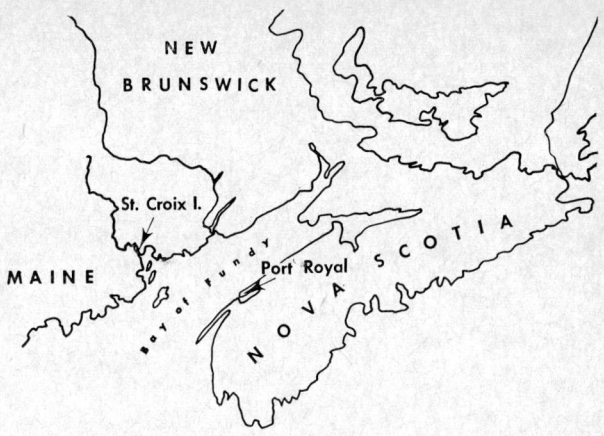

We had fair weather almost during all the winter. For neither rains or fogs are so frequent there as here (France), whether it be at sea or on the land. The reason is because the sunbeams, by the long distance, have not the force to raise up vapours from the ground here, chiefly in a country all woody. But in summer it doth, both from the sea and the land, whenas their force is augmented and those vapours are dissolved suddenly or slowly, according as one approacheth to the equinoctial line. For we see that between the two tropics it raineth in more abundance both at sea and on the land, specially in Peru and Mexico, than in Africa, because the sun by so long space at sea, having drawn up much moistness, from the main ocean, he dissolveth them in a moment by the great force of this heat; where contrawise towards the Newfoundlands they maintain themselves a long time in the air before they be turned into rain or be dispersed: which is done in summer (as we have said) and not in winter, and at sea more than on the land. For on the land the morning mists serve for dew, and fall about eight o'clock; and at sea they dure two, three, and eight days, as oftentimes we have tried (experienced).

Seeing then we are speaking of winter, we say that rains being in those parts rare in that season, the sun likewise shineth there very fair, after the falls of snows, which we have had seven or eight times, but it is easily melted in open places, the longest abiding have been in February. Howsoever it be, the snow is very profitable for the fruits of the earth, to preserve them against the frost, and to serve them as a furgown. Which is done by the admirable providence of God for the preservation of men, as the Psalm saith (Psa cxlvii. 16):

> He giveth snow like wool, hoar-frost
> Like ashes he doth spread,
> Like morsels casts his ice.

And as the sky is seldom covered with clouds towards Newfoundland in winter-time, so are there morning frosts, which do increase in the end of January, February, and in the beginning of March, for until the very time of January, we kept us still in our doublets.[4] I remember that on a Sunday, the 14th day of that month, in the afternoon, we sported ourselves singing in music on the river l'Equille, and in the same month we went to see the corn two leagues off from our fort, and did dine merrily in the sunshine. I would not for all that say that other years were like unto this. For as that winter was as mild in these parts (France), these last winters of the year 1607, 1608 have been the hardest that ever was seen; it hath also been alike in those countries, in such sort that many savages died through the rigour of the weather, as in these our parts many poor people and travellers have been killed through the same hardness of winter-weather. But I will say that the year before we were in New France (1605–06), the winter had not been so hard as they which dwelt there before us have testified unto me.

Let this suffice for that which concerneth the winter season. But I am not yet fully satisfied in searching the cause why in one part and the selfsame parallel of the season is in those parts of New France more slow by a month than in these parts, and the leaves appear not upon the trees but toward the end of the month of May; unless we say that the thickness of the woods and the greatness of forests do hinder the sun from warming the ground; item, that the country where we were is joining to the sea, and thereby more subject to cold, as participating of Peru, a country likewise cold in regard of Africa; and besides that, this land having never been tilled is the more dampish, the trees and plants not being able easily to draw sap from their mother the earth. In recompense whereof the winter there is also more slow, as we have heretofore spoken.

The cold being passed, about the end of March the best disposed among us strived who should best till the ground, and make gardens to sow in them, and gather fruits thereof.[16]

---

[1] *Early English and French Voyages chiefly from Hakluyt 1534–1608*. Henry S. Burrage, ed. New York, Charles Scribner's Sons, 1906. 75.

[2] Thomas Hariot. *A briefe and true report of the new found land of Virginia, &c. discovered by the English Colony there seated by Sir Richard Greinville, Knight, in the yeere 1585*. London, 1588. Reprint: *The Roanoke Voyages*. London, The Hakluyt Society, 1955. 2d ser., 104. 1, 383.

[3] Henry F. Howe. *Prologue to New England*. New York, Farrar & Rinehart, 1943. 25.

[4] *Les Voyages du Sieur de Champlain.* Paris, 1613. Reprint: *The works of Samuel de Champlain.* H. P. Biggar, ed. Toronto, The Champlain Society, 1922. 1, 302.
[5] *Ibid.*, 302–03.
[6] *Ibid.*, 307.
[7] *Ibid.*, 352.
[8] *Ibid.*, 300.
[9] *Ibid.*, 367.
[10] *Ibid.*, 377.
[11] *Ibid.*, 485.
[12] *Idem.*
[13] *Ibid.*, 447.
[14] *Ibid.*, 446–47.
[15] Marc Lescarbot. *Histoire de la Nouvelle France contenant les navigations decouvertes et habitations faites par les François és Indes Occidentales et Nouvelle France sous l'avoeu et authorité de noz Rois Tres-Chretiens et les diverses fortunes d'iceux en l'execution de ces choses depuis cent ans jusques à hui.* Paris, 1609.
[16] Marc Lescarbot. *Nova Francia: or the description of that part of New France, which is one continent with Virginia.* London P. Erondelle, trans. London, 1609. Reprint: *Nova Francia. A description of Acadia, 1606.* New York, Harper & Brothers, 1928. 120–22.

# EARLY NEW ENGLAND: 1607–1619

The first northern winter about which there exists a definite record as to its severity within the present United States followed the establishment in the warm season of 1607 of two English colonies: one destined to be permanent at Jamestown in Virginia; the other, short-lived, at Sagadahoc in Maine. Disease incurred on shipboard and aggrevated by semi-starvation ashore took a sad toll among the settlers at both sites during the summer and fall months that followed. As the days shortened and the frosts came, little did the colonists suspect what the North American winter had in store for them. For no Englishman at this time had experienced a northern winter in America and left an account to warn his successors as to its possible rigors.

## SAGADAHOC COLONY: 1607–08

The prevailing winter circulation of the atmosphere again returned to a predominance of northerly flow in 1607–08 when representatives of the London Company sought to found a permanent colony to the southward of the St. Croix River on the central Maine Coast at the mouth of the Kennebec River. This was the ill-fated Sagadahoc Colony established in August 1607 under the command of George Popham and Raleigh Gilbert in the same colonizing impulse that had sent an expedition to Jamestown in Virginia a few months earlier. A brief reference to the first English winter in Maine was contained in a manuscript history of the enterprise by William Stratchey, who was more closely associated with the Virginia Colony:

> Many discoveries had likewise been made both to the Mayne and unto the neighbour rivers, and the frontier nations fully discovered, by the diligence of Captain Gilbert, had not the winter proved so extreme unseasonable and frosty; for it being in the year 1607, when the extraordinary frost was felt in most parts of Europe, it was here likewise as vehement, by which no boat could stir upon any business.[1]

Both new colonies suffered many casualities from the rigor of the climate for which they were unprepared. In the north, Popham along with others died at Sagadahoc during the long winter. In summer Raleigh Gilbert received news of the death of his older brother, Sir John Gilbert, and felt the call to return home and assume his inherited rights. "The fear that all the other winters would prove like the first, the company would by no means stay in the country," so the entire colony embarked with Gilbert and "this was the end of that northerne colony upon the river Sachadehoc," a victim of the North American winter.[2] Sagadahoc might have been as famous as Jamestown and have taken symbolic precedence over Plymouth had the winter of 1607–08 been of a different nature.

## INTEREST IN MAINE

Activity in the area picked up considerably in 1611 when no less than six different groups of vessels were at one time on the coasts of Nova Scotia and Maine, and three of them spent the winter. "We have no knowledge that any Englishmen had wintered on these coasts up to this period, with the single exception of the Sagadahoc Colony. But Frenchmen had wintered on the Bay of

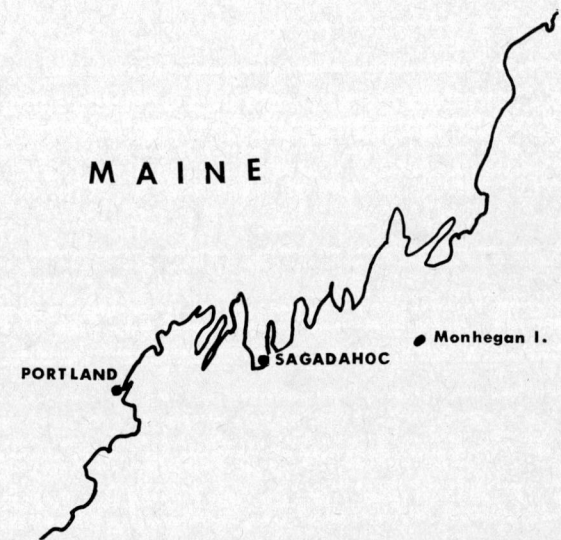

Fundy through the seasons 1604 to 1607 inclusive, and again here in this season of 1611–12," summarized Henry F. Howe in his survey *Prologue to New England*.[3] These were groups bent on fur trading or fishing, not seeking permanent settlement; nor were they concerned with preserving records of conditions experienced.

The popularity of the area received great impetus when Captain John Smith (1579/80–1631) explored the Massachusetts and Maine coasts in 1614. He gathered much valuable information about the face of the country and its natural resources, publishing his findings in 1616 in *The Description of New England*.[4] Smith labeled his glowing account of the bountiful fisheries, fertile soil, and varied products with a paragraph subhead: "a proof of an excellent climate."[5] The book soon stimulated great interest about Maine, and there were many summer visitors in the following years seeking wealth in the fur trade and in fishing. The area was now completely dominated by the English who had driven out the remnants of the French in Maine and initiated one hundred and fifty years of colonial strife on land and sea.

Smith was especially pleased with what he saw around Massachusetts Bay that summer. In noting, "the moderate temper of the air," he asked: "who can but approve this a most excellent place, both for health and fertility? And of the four parts of the world that I have yet seen not inhabited, could I but transport a colony, I would rather live here than any where."[6] His writings, which read like a real estate brochure and were probably intended as such, were given credit for exerting considerable influence in the selection by the Puritans of Massachusetts Bay as their settlement site. But Smith at this time had no knowledge or experience with the New England winter to pass on to his countrymen.

Interest in the area continued. In 1615–16 some English fishermen wintered on Monhegan Island off the coast of Maine, and in 1618–19 several mutineers stayed the winter at the same place; "with bad lodging and worse fare," but survived and were taken to Virginia the next summer by a passing boat. In 1622 a pamphlet giving an account of the region appeared from a London press: *A Brief Relation of the Discovery and Plantation of New England*. This comprised a pre-Plymouth appraisal of the New England scene, and included a brief mention of the Maine climate. Like most contemporary documents of the type, it contained more propaganda than fact:

> But this country, what by the general and particular situation, is so temperate, as it seemeth to hold the golden mean, and indeed is most agreeable to the nature of our own, which is made manifest by experience, the most infallible proof of all assertions; in so much as our people that are settled there, enjoy their life and health much more happily, than in other places; which can be imputed to no other cause, than the temperature of the climate.
> Now, as the clime is found to be so temperate, so delicate, so healthful, both by reason and experience. . . .

[1] William Strachey. *The Historie of Travaile into Virginia Britannia* (1612?). London, The Hakluyt Society, 1849. 1st. ser., no. **6**. 179.

[2] *Ibid.*, 180.

[3] Henry F. Howe. *Prologue to New England*. New York, Farrar & Rinehart, 1943. 192, 279, 284.

[4] John Smith. *Travels and Works of Captain John Smith President of Virginia and Admiral of New England. 1580–1631*. Edward Arber and A. G. Bradley, eds. Edinburgh, John Grant, 1910. **2**, 695.

[5] *Ibid.*, **2**, 708.

[6] *Idem.*

[7] *A brief relation of the discovery and plantation of New England*. London, 1622. Reprint: *Coll. Mass. Hist. Soc.* 2d. ser., **9**, (1832), 18.

## PLYMOUTH PLANTATION: 1620–21

The decision of the Pilgrims to land on the shores of Massachusetts was a happenstance largely induced by the current meteorological situation, and it was a decision of great importance to the immediate well-being of the expedition and also for the subsequent flavor of American history. It resulted from an untimely combination of tide, wind, and waves at the very time the *Mayflower* was passing a particularly dangerous oceanographic feature of the North Atlantic continental shelf at the southeastern tip of Cape Cod.

After more than two months at sea, a landfall had been made soon after daybreak of 19 November on the central headlands of Cape Cod near Nauset. Then the *Mayflower* with "wind and weather fair" headed southward, according to original plans, for the lands of the Virginia Company in the vicinity of New York Harbor where a patent of somewhat dubious legality had been secured. But late in the afternoon when near the notorious shoals area east of Monomoy Point, "contrary winds" and an adverse tide buffeted the small 180-ton ship. A sector of shallows, now designated Pollock Rip, is well known to coasting boats, large and small, for its treacherous waters. William Bradford (1589/90–1657), the historian and later governor of Plymouth Plantation, told of the experiences that day:

> After some deliberation had amongst themselves and with the master of the ship, they tacked about and resolved to stand for the southward (the wind and weather being fair) to find some place about Hudson's River for their habitation. But after they had sailed

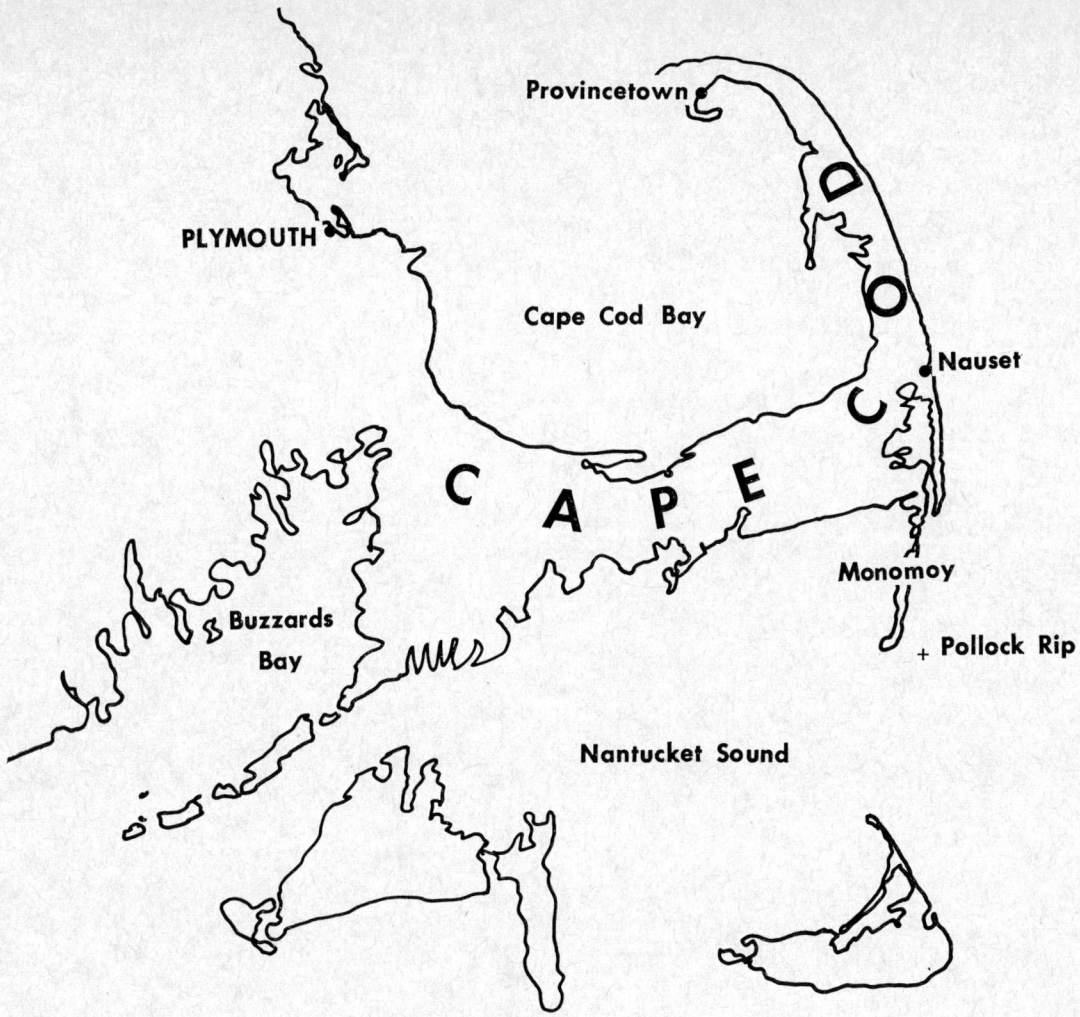

that course about half the day, they fell amongst dangerous shoals and roaring breakers, and they were so far entangled therewith as they conceived themselves in great danger; and the wind shrinking upon them withal, they resolved to bear up again for the Cape and thought themselves happy to get out of those dangers before night overtook them, as by God's good providence they did. And the next day they got into the Cape Harbor where they rid in safety.

The Pilgrims were fortunate in having clear weather with good visibility from the time of their landfall and on the two following days. This not only aided in the identification of the land area they happened on, but greatly assisted in the intricate navigation that followed. The weather map situation on the morning of the 19th would probably show a ridge of high pressure covering the New England coastal area with barometers at their peak for the current atmospheric wave. The wind on the morning of the 19th blew from a westerly or a northerly quadrant, at gentle to moderate force, as is normal just to the east of the ridge line of an anticyclone. This enabled the *Mayflower* to approach the unsounded shore safely and then tack about easily to take a southerly course, aided by following winds. But by afternoon the ridge line or backbone of the anticyclone had passed to the eastward, pressure commenced to fall off gradually, and the wind shifted to a southerly component on the backside of the anticyclone. This "contrary" flow, of course, would greatly impede farther southward progress of the vessel just when it was entering the dangerous shoal waters.[3]

The master of the *Mayflower* was experienced in American waters having made several trips to Virginia previously and in doing so had coasted New England waters. He knew the character of such shallows, the danger of adverse winds, and the possibility of a rising storm in view of the advanced season of the year. No doubt, in view of the sea-worn condition of the *Mayflower*, he concurred, weatherwise, in the decision of the ship-weary Pilgrim fathers to turn back northward, take the advantage of the south wind, and seek safety by rounding the northern tip of Cape Cod into the protected waters of the bay beyond. The clear weather and favorable wind held on the 20th and 21st, speeding the ship northward while skirting the back of Cape Cod. The *Mayflower* dropped anchor early on the morning of the 21st in Provincetown Harbor after 65 days at sea.[4]

To describe the predicament facing the Pilgrim band at Provincetown, Bradford later composed one of the most moving passages in all American history, his "back-to-the-wall" document:

> Being thus passed the vast ocean, and a sea of troubles before in their preparation (as may be remembered by that which went before), they had now no friends to welcome them nor inns to entertain or refresh their weatherbeaten bodies; no houses or much less towns to repair to, to seek for succour . . . And for the season it was winter, and they that know the winters of that country know them to be sharp and violent, and subject to cruel and fierce storms, dangerous to travel to known places, much more to search an unknown coast.[5]

The immediate problem was to seek a suitable site for settlement with celerity. "For summer being done, all things stand upon them with a weatherbeaten face, and the whole country, full of woods and thickets, represented a wild and savage hue."[6] Practically all writers on the subject maintain that the first winter of 1620–21 on Cape Cod and at Plymouth was mild as to temperature, though the season did commence with some hard winter weather in late November and early December just at the time the Pilgrims were exploring the unknown land.

The sandy areas of Cape Cod immediately to the southward were first visited on foot, then with the assistance of a shallop which had been brought over in the hold of the *Mayflower* for such occasions. Bradford accompanying these expeditions, wrote of conditions on 7–8 December: "for the ground was now all covered with snow and hard frozen."[7] And the *Relation* confirmed that "it blowed and did snow that day and night, and froze withal." On the 8th their progress was impeded by the condition of the ground "which lay half a foot thick with snow."[8] On this leg of the expedition they found little which met their requirements for a combination of good soil, adequate water, and a safe harbor for ships.

On the 16th of December the shallop set out again "in very cold and hard weather" to sound the southern shore of Cape Cod Bay. Next day being windy, "the weather was very cold and it froze hard as the spray of the sea lighting on their coats, they were as if they had been glazed."[9] On the afternoon of the 18th there commenced a storm of snow and rain. These were early winter conditions that eventually gave way to a milder temperature regime when the winds shifted out of the northeast to a southerly flow, but at this crucial time the elements added greatly to the difficulties attending the search for a settlement site in an unknown country.

The exploring party then shifted to the western shore of the Bay where one of the mariners remembered having visited a large harbor on a previous voyage. Actually, Samuel de Champlain had visited this harbor in 1605, made a usable navigation chart of the area, and published this in 1612. Thus, the Pilgrims were not the earliest to visit Plymouth harbor when their "first" landing took place on the wild night of 18–19 December 1620. Bradford has graphically described the meteorological éclat attending the landing:

> After some hours' sailing it began to snow and rain, and about the middle of the afternoon the wind increased and the sea became very rough, and they broke their rudder, and it was as much as two men could do to steer her with a couple of oars. But their pilot bade them be of good cheer for he saw the harbor; but the storm increasing, and night drawing on, they bore what sail they could to get in, while they could see. But herewith they broke their mast in three pieces and their sail fell overboard in a very grown sea, so they had like to have been cast away. Yet by God's mercy they recovered themselves, and having the flood with them, struck into the harbor. But when it came to, the pilot was deceived in the place, and said the Lord be merciful unto them for his eyes never saw that place before; and he and the master's mate would have run her ashore in a cove full of breakers before the wind. But a lusty seaman which steered bade those which rowed, if they were men, about with her or else they were all cast away; the which they did with speed. So he bid them be of good cheer and row lustily, for there was a fair sound before them, and he doubted not but that they should find one place or other where they might ride in safety. And though it was very dark and rained sore, yet in the end they got under the lee of a small island and remained there all that night in safety. But they knew not this to be an island till morning, but were divided in their minds; some would keep the boat for fear they might be amongst Indians, others were so wet and cold they could not endure but got ashore, and with much ado got fire (all things being so wet); and the rest were glad to come to them, for after midnight the wind shifted to the northwest and it froze hard.[10]

More favorable conditions followed the storm. The company took two days in drying out, in exploring the small island, and in sounding the harbor. Then on the 21st of December, the equinox new style, the celebrated landing took place, though from the small shallop and not from the larger ship, probably on the sandy beach and not on a "rock," by only 10 men and not with women and children, and without any ceremony as the party was fearful of meeting hostile natives as soon as they stepped ashore. After a reconnaissance showed the site to have some advantages over the other places recently surveyed, the shallop returned to Provincetown and the entire company came over in the *Mayflower* on the 26th. After considerable debate the decision was made to found the colony on the surveyed site at Plymouth.

There were more suitable places for a permanent colony known to be within reasonable distance both to the north in Massachusetts Bay and the southward of Cape

Cod in Buzzards Bay and the Narragansett area. But again the fateful decision to stay at Plymouth was largely dictated by prevailing meteorological conditions, as was set down by one of those present:

> But the last and special reason was, that now the heart of winter, and unseasonable weather, was come upon us, so that we could not go upon coasting and discovery, without danger of losing men and boat; upon which would follow the overthrow of all, especially considering what variable winds and sudden storms do there arise. Also cold and wet lodging had so tainted our people (for scarse any of us were free from vehement coughs) as if they should continue long in that state, it would endanger the lives of many, and breed disease and infection amongst us." [11]

The winter of 1620–21 was "a calm winter, such as was never seen here since," wrote Thomas Dudley of Massachusetts Bay in 1630 when comparing conditions in the founding of the two settlements. Edward Winslow, one of the most active and articulate of the Pilgrims, also testified as to the "remarkable mildness" of the first winter in *Good Newes from New England*, published in 1624.[12] And William Wood, who was there in 1633, wrote in *New England's Prospect*: "the year of New Plymouth men's arrival was no winter in comparison."[13] As to actual conditions, there was negative evidence in the writings of Bradford in that, after the first days on the Cape, he made no mention of subsequent snowstorms or particularly severe cold-weather experiences. On the positive side there existed the testimony of others that it was an "open" winter with a mild close of December, a moderate January, a brief cold spell with sleet and some snow in early February, followed by definitely mild conditions and an early spring. We hear of no snow that lay except for the early December occurrences.

The only document approaching a diary of day-to-day conditions during the first winter of settlement was *Mourt's Relation*, a pamphlet published in London in 1622. It consisted of extracts of letters and communications, probably written mostly by Bradford and Winslow, to the London Adventurers, as the stay-at-homes designated themselves. The section entitled, "The Journal of the Plantation," showed the writer to be very weather conscious and did reveal certain significant characteristics of the winter of 1620–21:

> Thursday, 31 December: Next morning it was stormy and wet, that we could not go ashore; and those that remained there all night could do nothing, but were wet, not having daylight enough to make them a sufficient court of guard, to keep them dry. All that night it blew and rained extremely. It was so tempestuous that the shallop could not go on land as soon as was meet, for they had no victuals on land. About eleven o'clock the shallop went off with much ado with provisions but could not return, it blew so strong; and was such foul weather that we were forced to let fall our anchor, and ride with three anchors ahead.
>
> Friday, 1 January: The storm still continued, that we could not get aland, nor could they come to us aboard.
>
> Monday, 4th: That night we had a sore storm of wind and rain.
>
> Tuesday, 5th: It was foul weather, that we could not go ashore.
>
> Wednesday, 6th: We went to work again.
>
> Friday and Saturday, 8 and 9th: We fitted ourselves for our labour; but our people on shore were much troubled and discouraged with rain and wet that day, being very stormy and cold.
>
> Monday, 18th: Was a very fair day, and we went betimes to work.
>
> Tuesday, 19th: Was a reasonable fair day. . . . Frost and foul weather hindered us much. This time of year seldom could we work half the week.
>
> Thursday, 21st: It was a fair day.
>
> Friday, 22d: We went to work; but about noon it began to rain, that it forced us to give over work.
>
> Saturday, 23d: It was an extreme cold night. . . . They wandered all that afternoon, being wet; at night it did freeze and snow . . . but in frost and snow, were forced to make the earth their bed and the element their covering.
>
> Sunday, 24th: In the morning about six of the clock, the wind being very great. . . .
>
> Monday, 25th: It rained much all day, that they on ship could not go on shore, nor they on shore do any labor, but were all wet.
>
> Tuesday, Wednesday, Thursday, 26, 27, 28th: were very fair, sunshiny days, as if it had been in April; and our people, so many as were in health, wrought cheerfully.

## FEBRUARY 1621

> Monday, 1st: Was a fair day.
>
> Monday, 8th: In the morning cold, frost, and sleet, but after reasonable fair.
>
> Tuesday and Wednesday, 9 and 10th: Cold frosty weather and sleet, that we could not work in the morning.
>
> Sunday, 14th: Was very wet and rainy, with the greatest gust of wind that ever we had since we came forth; that though we rode in a very good harbour, yet we were in danger, because our ship was light, the goods taken out, and she unballasted; and it caused much daubing of our houses to fall down.
>
> Friday, 19th: Still the cold weather continued, that we could do little work.
>
> Friday, 26th: Was a fair day; but the northerly wind continued, which continued the frost.

## MARCH 1621

> Saturday, 13th: The wind was south, the morning misty, but towards noon warm and fair weather. The birds sang in the woods most pleasantly. At one of the clock it thundered, which was the first we heard in that country. It was strong and great claps, but short; but after an hour it rained very sadly till midnight.
>
> Wednesday, 17th: The wind was full east, cold, but fair. . . . This day some garden seeds were sown.

Friday, the 26th: A fair warm day towards (noon?).
Saturday and Sunday, 27 and 28th: Reasonable fair days.
Monday and Tuesday, 29 and 30th: Proved fair days. We digged our grounds and sowed our garden seeds.
Wednesday, 31st: A fine warm day.[14]

For the first winter season many lived aboard the *Mayflower* anchored about a mile-and-a-half offshore and went to the land each day, weather permitting, to the task of building adequate shelters. Bradford described the winter weather as "blustery" with "much rain." The testimony from the *Relation* has given adequate evidence as to the occurrence of wind storms. A winter's northeaster can kick up troublesome seas in this sector of Massachusetts Bay, but the natural harbor affords considerable protection from wave and surf. Nothing appeared in Bradford or the *Relation* about a cold storm from the northeast, often accompanied at this time of year with sleet or snow. On the other hand, a southeaster has a short fetch thanks to the protective configuration of the curving shore of Cape Cod to the south and east of Plymouth, but the harbor is open to the southeast and choppy conditions result when a southeaster continues long. A southerly or southwesterly wind blows from the land and is not a serious concern to ships in Plymouth Harbor.

A surmise as to the meteorological situation during this winter is that a combination of high pressure over Quebec and southeastern Canada and a low pressure trough off the New England coast in late November and early December, at times, induced a northeasterly flow of cool, maritime air which produced the subfreezing conditions with mixed rain and snow as described by Bradford. This gave way in later December and January to a predominance of ridge or anticyclonic conditions offshore with the trough of low pressure having migrated well to the west inland over the continent.

The main storm track of travelling cyclones now lay well to the north, in the St. Lawrence Valley or northward, so that the Massachusetts coastal area often was located in the warm sector of these storms with southerly flow prevailing. Storms under this regime were of the southeasterly type as fronts approached from the west, gave hard rains and gusty winds, but brought moderate thermal conditions as the air flow had been tempered by passage over or near the Gulf Stream offshore to the southeast. The passage of such fronts can be succeeded by a west or south-westerly flow carrying a well-modified air mass rather than by the fresh, piercing blasts from the Northwest or North out of Canada which usually follow the passage of a northeasterly disturbance along the coastal storm track. Despite the generally warmer than normal conditions, almost half of the original passengers and crew of the *Mayflower* succumbed to disease during the first winter of the stay on the shores of Massachusetts and Cape Cod bays.

Naturally, the Adventurers and others in London were interested in the type of weather and climate that existed in the New World. Edward Winslow in a letter dated 21 December 1621, after one year of observation, tried to compare weather types of the Old World and the New:

> . . . for the temper of the air, here it agreeth well with that in England, and if there be any difference at all, this is somewhat hotter in summer, some think it to be colder in winter, but I cannot out of experience so say; the air is very clear and not foggy, as hath been reported, I never in my life remember a more seasonable year, than we have here enjoyed.[15]

Two years later our first climatologist of New England produced a pamphlet of some 67 pages, *Good Newes from New England,* in which he elaborated on his early views after experiencing two, more normal American winters:

> Then for the temperature of the air, in almost three years' experience, I can scarce distinguish New England from Old England, in respect of heat, and cold, frost, snow, rain, winds, &c. Some object, because our plantation lieth in the latitude of 42 it must needs be much hotter. I confess, I cannot give the reason of the contrary; only experience teacheth us, that if it do exceed England, it is so little as must require better judgments to discern it. And of the winter, I rather think (if there be a difference) it is both sharper and longer in New England than Old: and yet the want of those comforts in the one which I have enjoyed in the other, may deceive my judgment also. But in my best observation, comparing our own condition with the relations of other parts of America, I cannot conceive of any to agree better with the constitution of the English, not being oppressed with extremity of heat, not nipped with biting cold, by which means, blessed be God, we enjoy our health, notwithstanding, those difficulties we have undergone, in such measure as would have been admired, if we had lived in England with the like means.[16]

Most early writers touched briefly on the subject of climate and weather in early New England, but we cannot expect them to dwell at length in chronicling the hardships of a bitter winter season or in describing the severity of a particular northeaster. They were essentially propagandists intent on sending favorable reports to influence their sponsors in England or in trying to induce other settlers to make the hard decision to come to America. There is no detailed information as to the character of subsequent winters during the first decade of settlement at Plymouth. Bradford did not keep a running account of daily events; his history was produced at a much later date, probably in the mid-1640's. Life was hard on the scraggly shore where circumstances and the near approach of winter led the Pilgrims to make a settlement. It was always a marginal existence. Starvation remained an ever-present threat, with the weather more a foe than a friend. Each winter was a season to be dreaded.

[1] William Bradford. *Of Plymouth Plantation 1620–1647.* Samuel E. Morison, ed. New York, Alfred A. Knopf, 1952. 60.
[2] *Idem.*
[3] Warren S. Nickerson. *Land Ho!* Boston and New York, Houghton Mifflin Co., 1931. 101.
[4] *Ibid.,* 143.
[5] Bradford, 61–62.
[6] *Ibid.,* 62.
[7] *Ibid.,* 66.
[8] *Mourt's Relation or Journal of the Plantation at Plymouth.* Henry M. Dexter, ed. Boston, John Kimball Wiggin, 1865. 39.
[9] Bradford, 68.
[10] *Ibid.,* 70–71.
[11] *Mourt's Relation,* 39.
[12] Edward Winslow. *Good Newes from New England.* London, 1624. Reprint: *Coll. Mass. Hist. Soc.,* 2d ser **9**, (1822), 100.
[13] William Wood. *Wood's New England's Prospect.* London, 1634. Reprint: Publications of the Prince Society. Boston, John Wilson and Son, 1865. 5.
[14] *Mourt's Relation,* 65–90.
[15] *Ibid.,* 61.
[16] Winslow, 100.

# MASSACHUSETTS BAY COLONY: 1629–1649

The Massachusetts Bay area, with its intriguing complex of islands, harbors, and coves, enticed an occasional settler during the 1620's. These were mainly men who found the restrictive atmosphere at Plymouth uncongenial or a few who were dropped off by various ships coming from England. In 1626 a colony of Dorsetshire men established a settlement on Cape Ann and later moved to Salem. In 1628 another group from the same locality arrived. In that year the Massachusetts Bay Company, as successor to the London Company, received a royal charter for lands between the Merrimac and Charles rivers. Plans then went forward to found a settlement and establish a government.

The first ships of the new company were dispatched in April 1629 and settlements commenced in early summer along the north shore of Massachusetts Bay. Among the colonists was Thomas Higginson who sent home his first impression of the cold season in New England: "In the winter season for two months space, the earth is commonly covered with snow, which is accompanied with sharp biting frosts, something more sharpe than is in Old England, and therefore we are forced to make great fires."[1] Higginson later added the fillip: "a sup of New England air is better than a whole draught of Old England ale."[2]

The winter season of 1629–30, according to William Wood who accompanied the 1629 migration, was not severe:

> It is observed by the Indians that every tenth year there is little or no winter, which hath twice been observed of the English; the year of new Plymouth men's arrival was not winter in comparison; and in the tenth year after likewise when the great company settled themselves in Massachusetts Bay, was a very mild season, little frost, and less snow, but clear serene weather, few northwest winds, which was a great mercy to the English coming over so rawly and uncomfortably provided, wanting all utensils and provisions which belonged to the well being of the Planters.[3]

The usual death toll occurred during the winter, though Wood attributed this more to the shipboard diet than to the rigors of the climate.

The main effort of the Massachusetts Bay Colony came in the spring of 1630 when eleven ships transporting men, women, and children left English ports for the New World. Most of the vessels arrived in June, and these included the *Arbella* carrying John Winthrop, (1587/88–1649), the elected governor and the strong man of the group. Winthrop had been educated at Trinity College, Cambridge, and later practiced law in London. He was a man of substance and experience in handling the affairs of men and also of women, having been married thrice. He proved an able leader in organizing the expedition on land, and was firmly in command on the voyage over. His abilities did much to stabilize the colony during the first difficult years.

Winthrop also had a keen interest in scientific matters of the day. On the voyage across the Atlantic he maintained a daily log in which he noted the direction of the wind, its force, the general temperature conditions, and the type and duration of storms encountered.[4] From his account of the voyage of the *Arbella,* it would be easy today to reconstruct daily weather maps showing the sequence of troughs and ridges, cyclones and anticyclones, encountered during the voyage. Later on in his *Journal* or "History of New England," as it has been generally known, he would describe many geophysical facts of the land and sea and chronicle natural and physical events that took place in Massachusetts during his lifetime there from 1630 to 1649. In addition to describing all the principal weather happenings, such as cold winters, droughty summers, hurricanes, and tornadoes, he recorded the occurrence of earthquakes, meteors, unusual tides, and optical phenomena. In the field of meteorology, he made a special study of snowflakes on several occasions, drawing a figure to represent their six-pointed shape, and noting some of extraordinary size.[5]

There is evidence that Winthrop actually kept, or intended to keep, a daily diary of weather events at Boston. In late 1634 he wrote his son, then in London and planning to return soon to Boston: "I wish that, in your return, you will observe the winds and weather, every day, that we may see how it agrees with our parts."[6] Such a record for Boston, if Winthrop actually did maintain one, has not survived. In his *Journal,* however, are many passages about all aspects of the weather of the 1630's and 1640's which provide much of interest and worth for the historical climatologist. These are presented in the chronology at the conclusion of this section.[7]

The second winter of the Massachusetts Bay settlement, 1630–31, rated as severe, according to Winthrop's testimony. The Puritan band was much better prepared to meet such conditions than had been their predecessors at Plymouth in 1620–21 or their immediate forerunners in 1629–30. Not only was the terrain better known and more hospitable along the shores of Massachusetts Bay, but the potential of the North American winter was now a well-known fact, so adequate preparations could be made. Their well-planned arrival in June 1630 enabled houses to be constructed, fuel gathered, and some late grain raised, though many of the less provident were still housed in tents made of ship sails when winter closed down. Winthrop has described some of the winter events and incidents of 1630–31, mixing sound meteorological wisdom with some spurious weather lore:

Dec. 7. Bitter frost and snow for 3 days preceding.
Jan. 3. Till this time there was (for the most part) fair, open weather, with gentle frosts in the night; but this day the wind came N.W., very strong, and some snow withal, but so cold as some had their fingers frozen, and in danger to be lost. Three of the governor's servants, coming in a shallop from Mystic, were driven by the wind on Noodle's Island and forced to stay there all that night, without fire or food; yet through God's mercy, they came safe to Boston next day, but the fingers of two of them were blistered with cold, and one swooned when he came to the fire. The rivers were frozen up, and they of Charlestown could not come to the sermon at Boston till the afternoon at high water.
Jan. 7. They were put to sea, and the boat took in much water, which did freeze so hard as they could not free her . . . where some got on land, but some had their legs frozen into the ice, so as they were forced to be cut out . . . and were forced to lie in the open air all night, being extremely cold . . . they were so weak and frozen, as they could not stir . . . the ground being so frozen as they could not dig his grave . . . not able to launch their boat, (which with the strong N.W. wind was driven up to the high water mark . . . where another member of their company died, his flesh being mortified with the frost; and the two who went towards Plymouth died also, one of them not being able to get thither, and the other had his feet so frozen as he died of it after.
Feb. 15. The ship *Lyon* arrived at Nantasket . . . She had a very tempestuous passage.
Feb. 19. The *Lyon* came to an anchor before Boston, where she rode very well, notwithstanding the great drift of ice.
Feb. 20. The frost brake up; and after that, though we had many snows and sharp frost, yet they continued not, neither were the waters frozen up as before. It hath been observed, ever since this bay was planted by Englishmen, viz., seven years, that at this day the frost hath broken up every year.[8]

It did not take Winthrop long to learn the weather ways of the Massachusetts coast. In April he noted: "The beginning of this month we had very much rain and warm weather. It is a general rule, that when the wind blows twelve hours in any part of the east, it brings rain or snow in great abundance."[9]

Though the early New Englanders were prolific in producing letters and documents on the political and theological affairs of the colony, little was written about the weather and climate that has value for meteorologists and climatologists today. Of course, the lack of instruments and the crude knowledge of climatology mitigated against the production of worthwhile treatises. Two writers did attempt the subject. These were William Wood whose *New England Prospect* was published in London in 1634 and John Josselyn, "Old Josselyn," as some later writers called him, who was in Massachusetts and Maine on two occasions: in 1638 and 1663.

*Wood's New England Prospect*
Chap. II

Of the seasons of the year, Winter and Summer, together with the Heat, Cold, Snow, Rain, and the effects of it.

For that part of the country wherein most of the English have their habitations: it is for certain the best ground and sweetest climate in all those parts, bearing the name of New England, agreeing well with the temper of our English bodies, being high land, and sharp air, and though most of our English towns border upon the sea-coast, yet they are not often troubled with mists, or unwholesome fogs, or cold weather from the sea, which lies east and south from the land. And whereas in England most of the cold winds and weathers come from the sea, and those situations are counted most unwholesome, that are near the sea-coast, in that country it is not so, but otherwise; for in the extremity of winter, the northeast and south wind coming from the sea, produces warm weather, and bringing in the warm-working waters of the sea, looses the frozen bays, carrying away their ice with their tides, melting the snow, and thawing the ground; only the northwest wind coming from the land, is the cause of extreme cold weather, being always accompanied with deep snows and bitter frost, so that in two or three days the rivers are passable for horse and man. But as it is an axiom in Nature,

Nullum violentum est perpetuum, No extremes last long, so this cold wind blows seldom above three days together, after which the weather is more tolerable, the air being nothing so sharp, but peradventure in four or five days after this cold messenger will blow a fresh, commanding every man to his house, forbidding any to out-face him without predjudice to their noses: but it may be objected that it is too cold a country for our English men, who have been accustomed to a warmer climate, to which it may be answered, (Igne levatur hyems) there is wood good store, and better cheap to build warm houses, and make good fires, which makes the winter less tedious; and moreover, the extremity of this cold weather lasteth but for two months or ten weeks, beginning in *December,* and breaking up the twentieth day of February; which hath been a passage very remarkable, that for ten or a dozen years the weather hath held himself to his day, unlocking his icy bays and rivers, which are never frozen again the same year, except there be some small frost until the middle of *March*. It is observed by the Indians that every tenth year there is little or no winter, which hath been twice observed by the English; the year of new Plymouth men's arrival was no winter in comparison; and in the tenth year after likewise when the great company settled themselves in Massachusetts Bay, was a very mild season, little frost, and less snow, but clear serene weather, few northwest winds, which was a great mercy to the English coming over so rawly and uncomfortably provided, wanting all utensils and provisions which belonged to the well being of planters: and whereas many died at the beginning of the plantations, it was not because the country was unhealthful, but because their bodies were corrupted with sea diet, which was naught, their beef and pork being tainted, their butter and cheese corrupted, their fish rotten and voyage long, by reason of cross winds, so that winter approaching before they could get warm houses, and the searching sharpness of that purer climate, creeping in at the crannies of their crazed bodies, caused death and sickness; but their harms having taught future voyagers more wisdom, in shipping good provision for sea, and finding warm houses at landing, find health in both. It hath been observed, that of five or six hundred passengers in one year, not above three have died at sea, having their health likewise at land. But to return to the matter at hand, daily observations makes it apparent, that the piercing cold of that country produces not so many noisome effects, as the raw winters of England. In public assemblies it is strange to hear a man sneeze or cough as ordinarily they do in old England: yet not to smother anything, lest you judge me too partial in reciting good of the country, and not bad; true it is, that some venturing too nakedly in extremity of cold, being more foolhardy than wise, have for a time lost the use of their feet, others the use of their fingers; but time and surgery afterwards recovered them: some have had their overgrown beards so frozen together, that they could not get their strong water bottles into their mouths; I never heard of any that utterly perished at land with cold, saving one English man and one Indian, who going afowling, the morning being fair at their setting out, afterwards a terrible storm arising, they intended to return home; but the storm being in their faces, and they not able to withstand it, were frozen to death, the Indian having gained three flight-shot more of his journey homeward, was found reared up against a tree with his aquavitae bottle at his head. . . .

The country is not so extremely cold, unless it be when the northwest wind is high, at other times it is ordinary for fisherman to go to sea in January and February, in which time they get more fish, and better than in summer, only observing to reach some good harbors before night, where by good fires they sleep as well and quietly, (having their main sail tented at their backs, to shelter them from the wind) as if they were at home. . . .

The hard winters are commonly the fore-runners of pleasant spring-times, and fertile summers, being judged likewise to make for the health of our English bodies: It is found to be more healthful for such as shall adventure thither, to come towards winter, than the hot summer; the climate in winter is commonly cold and dry, the snow lies long, which is thought to be no small nourishing to the ground. For the Indians burning it to suppress the under-wood, which else would grow all over the country, the snow falling not long after, keeps the ground warm, and with his melting conveys the ashes into the pores of the earth, which doth fatten it. It hath been observed, that English wheat and rye proves better, which is winter sown, and is kept warm by the snow, than that which is sown in the spring.

John Josselyn: *Two Voyages*

Cold weather begins with the middle of November, the winter's perpetually freezing, insomuch that their Rivers and salt-Bayes are frozen over and passable for Men, Horse, Oxen and Carts: Aequore cum gelido zephyrus fert xenia Cymbo. The North-west wind is the sharpest wind in the Countrie. In England most of the cold winds and weathers come from the Sea, and those seats which are nearest the Sea-coasts in England are accounted unwholsome, but not so in New-England, for in the extremity of winter the North-east and South-wind coming from the Sea produceth warm weather, only the North-West-wind coming over land from the white mountains (which are always (except in August) covered with snow) is the cause of extream cold weather, always accompanied with deep snowes and bitter frosts, the snow for the most part four and six foot deep, which melting on the superficies with the heat of the Sun, (for the most part shining out clearly every day) and freezing again in the night makes a crust upon the snow sufficient to bear a man walking with snowshoes upon it. And at this season the Indians go forth on hunting of Deer and Moose twenty, thirty, forty miles up into the Countrie.[11]

[1] Francis Higginson. *New Englands Plantation*. London, 1630. Reprint: Publications of the Essex Book and Print Club. Salem, 1908. 9.
[2] *Ibid.,* 10.
[3] William Wood. *Wood's New England's Prospect*. London, 1634. Reprint: Publications of the Prince Society. Boston, John Wilson and Son, 1865. 5.
[4] John Winthrop. *Winthrop's Journal "History of New England 1630–1649."* James K. Hosmer, ed. 1908.

Reprint: New York, Barnes & Noble, Inc., 1959. **1**, 23, 50.
[5] *Ibid.,* **1**, 330; **2**, 263.
[6] *Winthrop Papers.* J. Winthrop to J. Winthrop, Jr., Boston, 12 Dec. 1634. Boston, The Mass. Hist. Soc., 1943. **3**, 176.
[7] See Chronology at end of section.
[8] Winthrop, **1**, 58.
[9] *Ibid.,* 61.
[10] Wood, 3–6.
[11] John Josselyn. *An account of two voyages to New-England, made during the years 1638–1663.* London, 1675. Reprint: Boston, W. Veazie, 1865. 45–48.

## THE THREE LANDMARK WINTERS OF THE CENTURY

Three winters during the first century of settlement of the New England coastal area were employed to compare and judge all others. These came in 1641–42, 1680–81, and 1697–98. The first person to establish these facts was Noah Webster (1758–1843), who was well qualified to be our first historian of American winters since in 1790 he had been editor of the original publication of *Winthrop's Journal,* the basic document on which much of early New England history rested.[1]

In the first years of the New England colonies the winter of 1632–33 stood out as rigorous, for in January the snow lay very deep and the rivers and ponds in the Boston area were closed with ice. The winter of 1637–38 rated "unusually severe" with snow about Boston standing 18 inches deep; beyond the Merrimac River it was said to be 36 inches, and even greater in southern Maine.[2]

## 1641–42: WINTHROP'S SEVERE WINTER

The first landmark winter in 1641–42 received extended coverage in the *Journal:*

> The frost was so great and continual this winter, that all the bay was frozen over, so much and so long, as the like, by the Indians' relation, had not been these 40 years, and it continued from the 28th of this month (January) to 3d of March, so as horses and carts went over in many places where ships have sailed. Capt. Gibbons and his wife, with diverse on foot by them, came riding from his farm at Pullen point, right over to Boston, the 27th of February, when it had thawed so much as the water was above the ice half a foot in some places; and they passed with loads of wood and six oxen from Muddy river to Boston, and when it thawed it removed great rocks of above a ton or more weight, and brought them on shore. The snow likewise was very deep, especially northward about Acomenticus, above three feet, and much more beyond. It was frozen also to sea so far as one could well discern.
>
> To the southward also the frost was as great and the snow as deep, and at Virginia itself the great bay was much of it frozen over, and all their great rivers, so as they lost much cattle for want of hay, and most of their swine.
>
> There was a shallop with eight men to go from Pascataquack to Pemaquid about the beginning of the frost, they would needs set forth upon the Lord's day, though forewarned, etc. They were taken with a N.W. tempest and put to sea about 14 days: at length they recovered Monhigen. Four of them died with cold, the rest were discovered by a fisherman a good time after, and so brought off the Island.
>
> There was great fear lest much hurt might have been done upon the breaking up of the frost, (men and beasts were grown so bold), but by the good providence of God, not one person miscarried, save one Warde of Salem, an honest young man, who going to show a traveller the safest passage over the river, as he thought, by the salthouse, fell in, and, though he had a pitchfork in his hand, yet was presently carried under the ice by the tide. The traveller fell in with one leg while he went to help the other, but God preserved him. He had about him all the letters from England which were brought in a ship newly arrived at the Isle of Shoals, which sure were the occasion of God's preserving him, more than any goodness of the man. Most of the bridges were broken down and divers mills.[3]

With Winthrop's demise in 1649 there came a lapse of five years for which there was no regular source of data about New England winters until John Hull (1624–1683) of Boston took up his weather watching in 1654. Hull was an early custodian of the colony's mint and achieved lasting fame as a silversmith. His personal diary ran from 1647 to 1682 and during part of this period he also maintained a series of "notes of publick occurrences."[4] His special interest in winter weather conditions extended from 1654 to 1678, so for almost a quarter-century there existed some indication as to the relative severity of almost every season. Though several hard winters occurred in this span of years, Hull's testimony did not indicate any standout seasons. In his observation the winters of 1654–55 and 1665–66 were the most rigorous, but neither of these had the combination of bitter cold, long-continued freeze, and deep snow to match those of 1641–42. Curiously, Hull omitted any reference to 1656–57, which from other sources was known to have been very severe. In Hull's record there prevailed many "temperate" seasons. In fact, such outnumbered severe ones. The impression from his data leads to the conclusion that the third-quarter of the century in the Boston area enjoyed a relative freedom from extreme winter conditions.

John Hull's last accounting of a winter came in the season of 1677–78. Again there came a short lapse of four years before our next winter historian took up the task in the person of Rev. John Pike (1653–1710) who lived at various places on the coastal plain of southeastern New Hampshire, mainly at Dover. This was still frontier country at the turn of the century; his personal diary of local events makes exciting reading and reveals him as a fighting parson, having Indian massacres and retaliatory expeditions interspersed with routine church activities. His written observations, covering the years 1678 to 1710, were divided into three main sections: personal, providences, and weather.[5] A critic has described the manuscript as "impersonal and disjointed," and that it was, but it did contain an important section for our study entitled: "Observable Seasons." When the diary was published by the Massachusetts Historical Society in 1876, this section was omitted, but, fortunately, in an earlier edition of the manuscript some weather-minded antiquarian, probably John Farmer of Concord, had prevailed upon the New Hampshire Historical Society to include the "Observable Seasons" section in the first edition published in 1832.

John Pike has the honor, to our knowledge, of being the first "snow-watcher" of a long line of such distinguished personages who have graced the New England scene. From 1682 to 1710 he noted the occurrence and date of each snowstorm, and thus provided a good accounting of the "number of days" with snow falling, and also the dates of the first and last snowfall each season. Though the record in the early years was rather sketchy, in the last half of the period he extended his comments to note extremely cold periods and the advance or retardation of a season, greatly enhancing the data's value for present-day climatologists. Pike's record revealed the cluster of snowstorms in January and February of 1698 making that season so memorable. He also witnessed the 9–10 October snowstorm in 1703 which stood for a century as the outstanding example of an early season snow. It proved valuable also for tracing and confirming the dating of several hurricanes occurring in this period. From Pike's record there existed little doubt that 1697–98 was the snowiest, if not the coldest, winter in his span of records.[6]

## 1680–81: INCREASE MATHER'S SEVERE WINTER

"The coldest winter that has been known these 40 years." This was the opinion of Rev. Increase Mather who took a deep interest in all things, natural and supernatural.[7] His comment provided contemporary evidence about the season, and he reiterated the statement when he published his volume—*Remarkable Providences*—in 1686.[8] Webster also included this in his list of severe winters of the century. The span of approximately forty years in the spacing of extreme winter conditions has probably already struck the reader, and this will become a notable singularity of the American climate in the 18th and 19th centuries. The decade of the 1680's produced other cold winters in America as in Europe, but only a very few details have been preserved.

Samuel Sewall, the eminent Boston diarist whose some fifty years of comments on the Boston scene included many valuable weather notes, took notice of the severe winter under consideration:

Jan. 20. Charles River frozen over, so to Noodle's Island.
Mar. 10. Coragious south wind breaks ice between Boston and Dorchester Neck. Hath been a very severe winter for snow and a constant continuance of cold weather; such as most affirm hath not been for many years.[9]

No additional information has been uncovered about this standout winter which occurred during a seeming literary hiatus in New England. Unfortunately, only fragments of the Sewall diary for these years have survived. Cotton Mather would not take up his pen until a year later to commence his famous diary which he would continue for almost 50 years. John Hull of Boston had ceased his winter chronology two years previous, and John Pike of New Hampshire would not commence his winter-watching for another two years.

## 1697–98: "THE TERRIBLEST WINTER"

The climactic winter of the first century of settlement came in the season of 1697–98. It served as a comparison piece for over 40 years until the next outstanding severe season struck in 1740–41.[10] In the words of the town records of Sudbury, Massachusetts, it was "the terriblest winter for continuance of frost and snow, and extremity of cold, that ever was known."[11] Judge Samuel Sewall of Boston in one of his letters referred to "the prodigious length and strength of this winter."[12] Down at New York in the fall of 1698 the Earl of Bellomont, in excusing some of his official shortcomings, classified the previous winter as "the severest that ever was known in the memory of man."[13]

We do not have satisfactory information as to the details of the succession of snowstorms and cold waves supplying the frigid ingredients of the season. There were no newspapers published in English in America at this date. Our best source was the *Journal of John Pike* who kept a watch on the weather at Dover, New Hampshire, from 1678 to 1709.[14] His diary indicated that the first snow of the season of 1697–98 came on the 20th of November and the last on April 9. The first heavy snow occurred on 24 December, and thereafter hard winter held the New England countryside in its icy grip. November produced one snowy day, December five, January nine, February nine, March three, and April four—for a total of 31 days with snowfall. The major storm happened just prior to Christmas, old style. On the 30th Cotton Mather noted in his diary: "This day, there being a violent storm arisen . . . preached Refuge from the storms of the Wrath of God."[15] The next day Samuel Sewall noticed: "A very great snow is on the ground."[16] This storm was also mentioned in old Swedish records along the Delaware as occurring toward the last of December 1697.[17]

The middle two weeks of February had a concentration of eight snowy days—similar to the seasons of 1717 and 1802, which would later produce remarkable snow cover at this time of year. It was during the last of February 1698 that the depth on the ground at Cambridge reached a reported figure of 42 inches—if reliable, certainly an historic depth for the Boston area.[18] This comprised the only linear estimate of snow depth in New England for this season that has been uncovered.

In the St. Lawrence Valley at Montreal the depth was estimated "at the height of a man."[19] The period of deep snow coincided with the days of greatest cold extending from early February to the equinox in March. Thereafter, a thaw set in, though on March 25th Sewall observed the snow still remained a foot deep in coastal Boston.[20] Very likely, it was the continuance of hard winter conditions through most of March that added much to the season's unsavory reputation.

The best summary of the general conditions this winter season has been found in the records of the First Church of Cambridge:

> Anno 1697. The winter of this year (1697–98) was a very severe winter for cold and snow. The ground was covered with snow from the beginning of *December* to the middle of *March*. Many snows fell one upon another, in February it was judged to be 3 feet and a half deep on a level.
>
> March 3 a pleasant afternoon, spring weather for 4 or 5 days which settled the snow; it turned into a drizzling rain which continued all the next day, and at night about 8 o'clock it thundered and lightninged and rained hard in showers. The next day was windy and fair, the snow much wasted. Mr. Cook's Hill in the Neck was bare of snow and many spots of ground now appeared.

> Charlestown Ferry was frozen up so that the boat did not go over once from January 27 to March 10—six weeks complete. In which time I rode over upon the ice from the ferry to Mr. Broughton's warehouse three times, and twice back. The river was frozen up two weeks before the ferry boats ceased going so that people went over on foot, only in that fortnight's time for three days the ice was so broken that people did not venture to walk over.
>
> April 3. In the morning a storm of snow three or four inches deep. It turned into rain which carried away all the snow. People were much straitened for want of hay this spring. March 27th was a public fast.[21]

Judge Samuel Sewall embellished his famous diary with many references to events and conditions during the season:

> Jan. 17. Went over Charles River on the ice—lecture and came back on ice.
> 22. By reason of the severity of the weather and a great cold. . . .
>
> Feb. 1. Extreme cold.
> 2. Very cold . . . very thin assemblies this Sabbath and last; and great coughing; very few women there; Mr. Willard prayed for mitigation of the weather; and the South Wind begins to blow with some vigor. My clock stood still this morning, and yesterday morn, which has not done for many years.
> 4. Ride over Charles River on the ice.
> 5. Ride over Charles River on the ice which had much water on it by the thaw, the south wind having blown hard all night. I considered Mr. Gee before I ventured; and in the morn looked out and found that the ice between us and the Castle was not broken.
> 12. I ride over the ice to Charlestown.
> 13. I saw water a little below the Castle.
> 24. Very fair and large paths were shoveled by great pains and cost for funeral of Col. Shrimpton.
> 25. Remarkable sun-dogs and a rainbow were seen.
>
> Mar. 1. I go over the ice and visit.
> 2. A very cold day. He preached from these words, he sends forth his word and thaws them; which began the 21st and especially the 22d, and has thawed much yet moderately.
> 3. I ride over the Charlestown on the ice, then over to Stoweris, go to Mr. Wigglesworth, could go but a foot pace on Mystick River, the snow was so deep. Mr. Wigglesworth preached Feb. 2 from those words: Who can stand before His cold? Then by reason of his own and peoples sickness three Sabbaths passed without public worship.
> 7. A considerable quantity of ice went away last night: so that now there is a glade of

water along by Governor's Island. Easterly wind all this day.

9. A guard is set upon Charles River to prevent persons venturing over on the ice for fear of drowning; and the Ferryman are put upon cutting and cleaving the ice, which they do so hapily, that I think the boat passeth once this day. March 10, I walk on purpose and see the wharf at Henchman's clear, and the Ferryboat passing very comfortably.

21. My horse floundered in a bank of snow and threw me off.[22]

Southward of New England the same rigors of winter were experienced. The Earl of Bellomont, governor of New York, gave testimony as to conditions in his area:

> If by providence the last winter had not been the severest that ever was known in the memory of man, the French would have certainly destroyed both Albany and Schenectady. . . . The French were supposed to have 1500 pairs of snowshoes at Mt. Royal, but the snow was deeper than the height of a man, so invasion plans of the Hudson Valley settlements had to be abandoned.[23]

In the Philadelphia area a sleigh was driven on the Delaware from the Quaker City down to Chester, an exceptional event. The reputation of the severe winter remained long in the minds of the colonists. Some 50 years later Peter Kalm, when gathering his store of data about the geography and social conditions of the Atlantic Coast settlements, included the following in his *Travels*:

> I likewise found everybody agreed in asserting, that the winter betwixt the autumn of the year 1697 and spring of the year 1698 was the coldest and severest which they had ever felt.[24]

[1] Noah Webster. *A collection of papers on political, literary, and moral subjects.* New York, Webster and Clark, 1843. 119–162.
[2] *Winthrop's Journal "History of New England" 1630–1649.* James K. Hosmer, ed. New York, 1908. Reprint: N. Y., Barnes & Noble, Inc., 1959. **1**, 269.
[3] *Ibid.*, **2**, 55.
[4] John Hull. Public Journal. *Trans. and Coll. Amer. Antiq. Soc.* (Worcester, Mass.). **3**, (1857), 141–64.
[5] Journal of the Rev. John Pike. Observable Seasons. *N. H. Hist. Soc. Coll.* **3**, (1832), 62–67.
[6] *Ibid.*, 64.
[7] Diary of Increase Mather. *Proc. Mass. Hist. Soc.* 2d ser., **13**, (1900), 409.
[8] Increase Mather. *Remarkable Providences.* London, 1684. Reprint: London, J. R. Smith, 1856.
[9] Diary of Samuel Sewall. 1674–1729. *Coll. Mass. Hist. Soc.* 5th ser., **5**, (1878), 49.
[10] Records of the First Church, Cambridge. *The Genealogical Magazine* (Boston). **1**, (March 1906), 359.
[11] William Barry. *History of Framingham.* Boston, James Monroe and Co., 1847. 35.
[12] S. Sewall, *Diary,* **1**, 195, 198.
[13] Earl of Bellomont to Board of Trade, *28 Oct 1698. Documents relative to the colonial history of New York.* **4**, 409.
[14] J. Pike, *Journal,* **3**, 64.
[15] Diary of Cotton Mather. *Mass. Hist. Soc. Coll.* 7th ser., **8**, (1912).
[16] S. Sewall, *Diary,* **1**, 442.
[17] *Peter Kalm's Travels in North America.* London, 1770. Reprint: New York, Wilson, 1937. **1**, 277.
[18] First Church, *Geneol. Mag.,* **1**, 359.
[19] Earl of Bellomont, *Doc. Col. Hist. N.Y.,* **4**, 409.
[20] S. Sewall, *Diary,* **1**, 475.
[21] First Church, **1**, 359.
[22] S. Sewall, *Diary,* **1**, 466–75.
[23] Earl of Bellomont, 409.
[24] Peter Kalm, **1**, 277.

## THE WINTHROP CHRONICLE OF WINTER EVENTS IN NEW ENGLAND: 1631–1653

The following entries are taken from John Winthrop's *Journal* unless otherwise noted. Though not strictly meteorological information, they do give some hint as to existing conditions so that some judgment as to the nature of each winter can be made. In addition, they illustrate the eternal problems that winter brings to those exposed to its forces. All dates are corrected to New Style; when the month is italicized, it appeared in the original text in old style—thus *January* would equal 11 January to 10 February, New Style.

### 1631–32

Oct. (late). And partly because of the season, (it being then frost and snow).

Feb. 17. They went all about it upon the ice (Spot Pond) . . . but it being then close and rainy, they could see but a small distance.

### 1632–33

Dec. 14. At a meeting of all the assistants, it was agreed, in regard that the extremity of the snow and frost had hindered the making ready of the bark . . . to defer any further expedition against the pirates.

Dec. 15. Accordingly, the governor despatched away John Gallopp with his shallop. The wind being very great at S.W., he could reach no farther than Cape Ann harbor that night; and the winds blowing northerly, he was kept there so long, that it was January 12th before he returned . . . and about forty men, who, coming to Pemaquid, were there wind-bound about three weeks.

*Jan.* A maid servant of Mr. Skelton of Salem, going toward Saugus, was lost seven days, and at length came home to Salem. All that time she was in the woods,

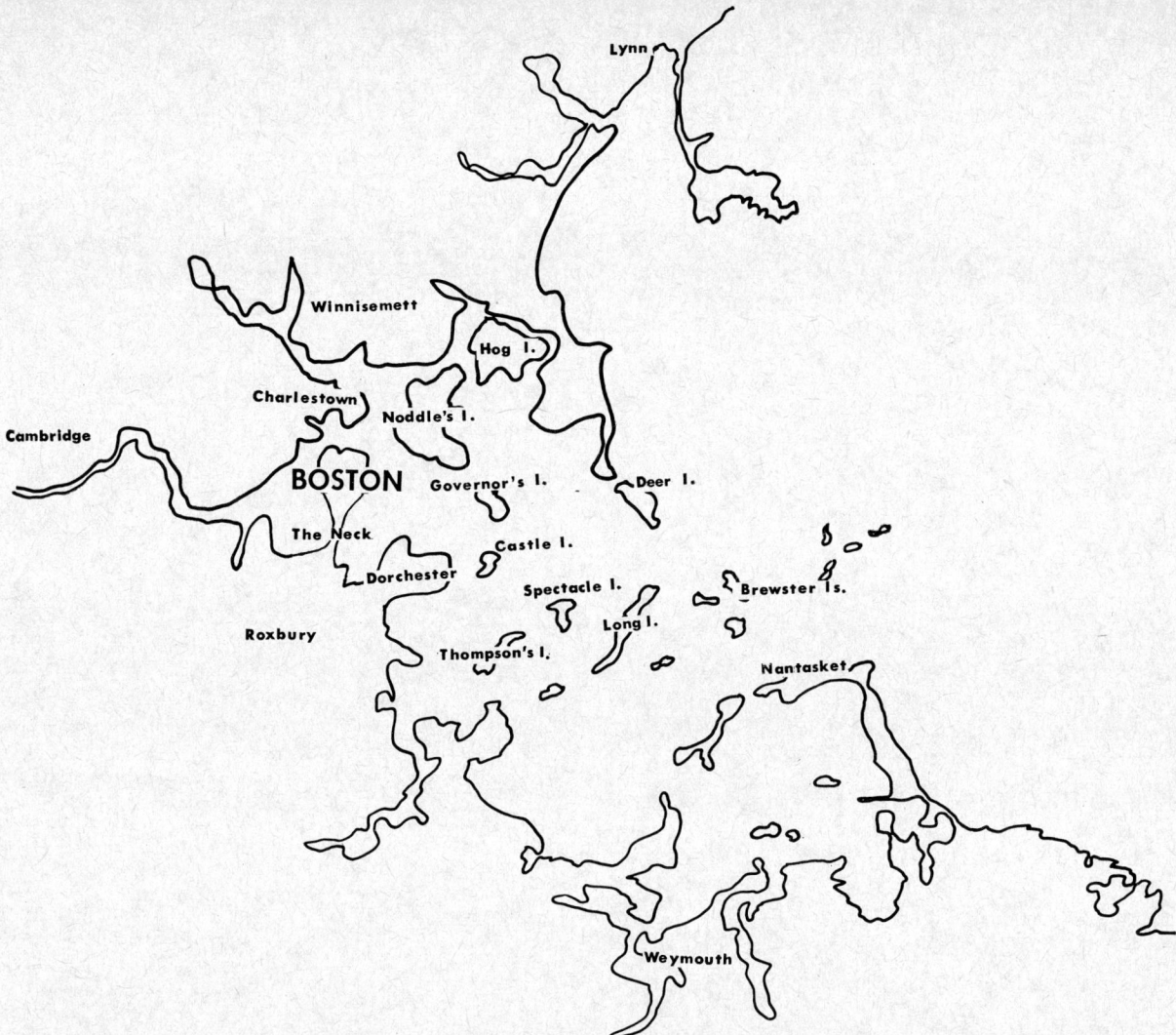

having no kind of food, the snow being very deep, and as cold as at any time that winter. She was so frozen into the snow some mornings, as she was one hour before she could get up; yet she soon recovered and did well, through the Lord's wonderful providence.

About the beginning of this month of *January* the pinnaces, which went after pirates, returned, the cold being so great as they could not pursue them. . . .

March 3. The governor and four of the assistants, with three of the ministers, and others, about twenty-six in all, went, in three boats, to view Natascott the wind W., fair weather; but the wind arose at N.W. so strong, and extreme cold, that they were kept there two nights.

### 1633–34

Dec. 6. Mr. Wilson (by leave of the congregation of Boston, whereof he was pastor) went to Agawam to teach the people of that plantation, because they had yet no minister. Whiles he was there, December 14, there fell such a snow (knee deep) as he could not come back for (blank) days, and a boat, which went thither, was frozen up in the river.

This winter was very mild, little wind, and Most S. and S.W. but oft snows, and great. One snow, the 25th of this month [Feb.] was near two feet deep all over.

### 1634–35

*Nov.* For by reason of the great snows and frosts, we used not to keep courts in the three winter months. [Reference to next session to be held in March.]

Nov. 29. We have had the greatest snow fall the 29th of November that I have seen yet since I came into the land. *Winthrop Papers.* 131.

Dec. 1. In a small boat over to Noddle's Island . . . were cast away in a N.E. tempest.

Dec. 4. About the same time one was twenty-one days upon Plumb Island, and found by chance frozen in the snow, yet alive, and did well. He had been missing twenty days, and himself said he had no food all that time.

Dec. 14. Was an extraordinary tempest of wind and snow, at N.N.E. which continued twenty-four hours, and after that such frost as, within two days, the whole bay was frozen over, but free again before night.

Dec. 21. The lectures at Boston and Newtown returned again to their former courses, because the weather was many times so tedious as people could not travel. etc.

Dec. 22. Winter hath begun early with us. The bay hath been frozen all over, but is now open again; and we had a snow last week of much depth in many places. It came with so violent a storm, as it put by our lecture for that day. I wish that, in your return, you would observe the winds and weather, every day, that we may see how it agrees with our parts. *Life and Letters of John Winthrop.* Robert C. Winthrop, ed. Boston, Tichnor and Fields, 1867. 126.

### 1634–35

Jan. In the end of this month, three men had their boats frozen up at Bird Island, as they were coming from Deer Island, so as they were compelled to lodge there all night; and in the morning they came over the ice to Noddle's Isle, and thence to Molten's Point in Charlestown, and thence over the ice, by Mr. Hoffe's, to Boston. At the same time six others were kept a week at the Governor's Garden; and in the end gate with their boat to Mattapan Point; for, near all that time, there was no open place between Garden and Boston, neither was there any passing at Charlestown for two or three days, the wind about the N.W. three weeks, with much snow and extreme frost. About the middle of *February,* a proper young man, servant to Mr. Bellingham, passing over the ice to Winnesemett, fell in, and was drowned. Divers others fell in, in that and other places, but, by God's providence, were saved.

### 1635–36

Nov. 19. About this time an open pinnace, returning from Connecticut, was cast away in Manemett Bay; but all the men (being six) were saved, and came to Plymouth, after they had wandered ten days in extreme cold and deep snow, not meeting with any Indian or other person.

Dec. 6. There came twelve men from Connecticut. They had been ten days on their journey, and had lost one of their company, drowned in the ice by the way; and had been all starved, but that, by God's providence, they lighted upon an Indian wigwam. Connecticut River was frozen up the 25th of November.

Dec. 8. A great shallop, coming from Pascataquack in a N.E. wind with snow, lost her way, and was forced into Anasquam; and going out with a N.W. wind, through the unskilfulness of the men, was cast upon the rocks, and lost £100 worth of goods.

Dec. 12–13. The 12th and 13th of this month fell a snow about knee deep, with much wind from the N. and N.E.

Dec. 20. The ship *Rebecka* . . . was frozen twenty miles up the river [Connecticut], but a small rain falling set her free.

April 10. Those of Dorchester, who had removed their cattle to Connecticut before winter, lost the greatest part of them this winter; yet some, which came late, and could not be put over the river, lived very well all the winter without hay. The people were also put to great straits for want of provisions. They ate acorns, and malt, and grains. They lost near £2000 worth of cattle.

### 1636–37

Feb. 16. A young man of Weymouth . . . leaped out at a high window into the snow, and ran about seven miles off, and being traced in the snow, was found dead next morning.

### 1637–38

Nov. 11. A young man, coming alone in a skiff from Newtown, in a N.E. storm of wind and snow, was found dead in his boat, with a half-crown piece in his mouth.

Jan. 23. About thirty persons of Boston going out in a fair day to Spectacle Island to cut wood, (the town being in great want thereof,) the next night the wind rose so high at N.E. with snow, and after at N.W. for two days, and then it froze so hard, as the bay was all frozen up, save a little channel. In this twelve of them gate to the Governor's Garden, and seven more were carried in the ice in a small skiff out at Broad Sound, and kept among Brewster's Rocks, without food or fire, two days, and then the wind forbearing, they gate to Pullin Point, to a little house there of Mr. Aspenwall's. Three of them gate home the next day over the ice, but their hands and feet frozen. Some lost their fingers and toes, and one died. The rest went from Spectacle Island to the main, but two of them fell into the ice, yet recovered again. In this extremity of weather, a small pinnace was cast away upon Long Island by Natascott, but the men saved, and came home upon the ice.

Feb. 1. I can write you no news only we had letters from Connecticut, where they were shut up with snow about a month since; and we at Boston were almost ready to break up for want of wood, but it pleased the Lord to open the Bay (which was so frozen as men went over it in all places) and mitigate the rigor of the season blessed be his name. *Winthrop Papers,* 4, 10.

Some died of the frost at Boston. *Ibid.*, **4**, 4.
Bay froze over to carry men. Opened so that wood could be obtained. One man frozen to death. *Ibid.*, 2, 218.

May 3. This was a very hard winter. The snow lay, from November 14th to April 2d, half a yard deep about the Massachusetts, and a yard deep beyond Merrimack, and so the more north the deeper, and the spring was very backward. This day (May 3d) it did snow two hours together, (after much rain from N.E.) with flakes as great as shillings. This was in the year 1637 [1637–38]. The spring was so cold, that men were forced to plant their corn two or three times, for it rotted in the ground; but, when we feared a great dearth, God sent a warm season, which brought on corn beyond expectation.

### 1638–39

*October.* About this time was very much rain and snow, in six weeks together; scarse two days without rain or snow. This was observed by some as an effect of the earthquake.

Dec. 25. The wind at N.E., there was so great a tempest of wind and snow all the night and the next day, as had not been since our time. Five men and youths perished between Mattapan and Dorchester, and a man and a woman between Boston and Roxbury. Anthony Dick, in a bark of thirty tons, cast away upon the head of Cape Cod. Three were starved to death with the cold; the other two got some fire and so lived there, by such food as they saved, seven weeks, till an Indian found them, etc. Two vessels bound for Quinipiack were cast away at Aquiday, but the people saved. Much other harm was done in staving of boats, etc. and by the great tides, which exceeded all before.

March 26. There was so violent a wind at S.S.E. and S. as the like was not since we came into this land. It began in the evening, and increased to midnight. It overturned some new, strong houses; but the Lord miraculously preserved old, weak cottages. It tare down fences, people ran out of their houses in the night, etc. There came such a rain withal, as raised the waters at Connecticut twenty feet above their meadows, etc.

### 1639–40

In this winter, in a close, calm day, there fell divers flakes of snow of this form *, very thin, and as exactly pointed as art could have cut them in paper.

### 1640–41

*April.* And though it be but six miles, yet they lost their way, and wandered two days and one night without food or fire, in the snow and wet.

Not long before a godly maid of the church at Linne, going in a deep snow from Meadford homeward, was lost, and some of her clothes found after among the rocks.

### 1641–42

Nov. 22. A great tempest of wind and rain from the S.E. all the night, as fierce as an hurricane. It continued very violent at N.W. all the day after. Divers boats and one bark cast away in the harbor, but (which was a wonder to all) no dwelling house blown down, nor any person killed; and the day after it came to S.E. again, and continued all the night with much wind and rain; and thereupon (it being about the new moon) followed the highest tide we have seen since our arrival here.

[For account of winter 1641–42, see page 15]

### 1642–43

This winter was the greatest snow we had, since we came into the country, but it lay not long, and the frost was more moderate than in some other winters. [Passage at the end of December 1642].

### 1643–44

There was little rain this winter, and no snow till 13th of March, the wind continuing W. and N.W. near six weeks, which was an occasion that very many houses were burned down, and much chattels (in some of them) to a greater value than in 14 years before.

### 1644–45

Feb. 26. The winter was very mild hitherto, and no snow lay, so as ploughs might go most part of the winter, but now there fell so great a snow in several days, as the ways were unpassable for three weeks, so as the court of assistants held not (the magistrates and juries not coming to Boston March 14th being the usual day for that court). And withal the weather was cold, and frost as fierce as is at any time of the winter; and the snow was not off the ground till the end of *March*.

Feb. 27. Mr. Allerton coming from New Haven in a ketch, with his wife and divers other persons, were taken in a great storm at northeast with much snow, and cast away at Scituate, but the persons all saved.

### 1645–46

Dec. 25. There appeared about noon, upon the north side of the sun, a great part of a circle like a rainbow, with the horns reversed, and upon each side of the sun, east and west, a bright light. And about a month after were seen three suns, about the sun-setting; and about a month after that two suns at sun-rising, the one continued close to the horizon, while the other (which was the true sun) arose about half an hour. This was the earliest and sharpest winter we have had since we arrived in the country, and it was as vehement cold to the southward as here. Divers of our ships were put from their anchors with the ice and driven on shore on January 4th, and one ketch carried out to sea, and wrecked on Lovell's Island. At New Haven a ship bound for England was forced to be cut out of the ice three miles. And in Virginia the ships were frozen up six weeks.

At Ipswich there was a calf brought forth with one head, and three mouths, three noses, and six eyes. What these prodigies portended the Lord only knows, which in his due time he will manifest.

There was besides so sudden a thaw in the spring, (the snow lying very deep,) and much rain withal, that it bare down the bridge at Hartford upon Connecticut, and brake down divers mills to the southward about New Haven, and did much other harm.

### 1646–47

Roxbury. This winter was one of the mildest we ever had; no snow all winter, nor sharp weather. We never had a bad day to go preach to the Indians all this winter. Praised be the Lord. Rev. John Eliot.

### 1647–48

No references to winter conditions located.

### 1648–49

Jan. 21. About eight persons were drowned this winter, all by adventuring upon the ice, except three, where of two (one of them being far in drink) would needs pass from Boston to Winisemett in a small boat and a tempestuous night. This man (using to come home to Winisemett drunken) his wife would tell him, he would one day be drowned, etc., but he made light of it. Another went aboard a ship to make merry the last day at night, (being the beginning of the Lord's day,) and returning about midnight with three of the ship's company, the boat was overset by means of the ice, they guided her by means of a rope, which went from the shore. The seamen waded out, but the Boston man was drowned, being a man of good conversation and hopeful of some work of grace begun in him, but drawn away by the seamen's invitation. God will be sanctified in them that come near him. Two others were the children of one of the church of Boston. While their parents were at lecture, the boy, (being about seven years of age,) having a small staff in his hand, ran down upon the ice towards a boat he saw, and the ice breaking, he fell in, but his staff kept him up, till his sister, about fourteen years old, ran down to save her brother (though there were four men at hand, and called her not to go, being themselves hastening to save him) and so drowned herself and him also, being past recovery ere the men could come at them, and could easily reach ground with their feet. The parents had no more sons, and confessed they had been too indulgent towards him, and had set their hearts over much upon him.

*Jan.* Hartford: Vessel could not go to the Dutch because the weather being unseasonable and the vessel frozen in. *Winthrop Papers,* **5**, 301.

### 1649–50

Salem. We have had a mild winter until the beginning of *January,* and then fell snow upon snow which lay until the latter end of *March*: and then a pleasant and not backward spring. *Winthrop Papers,* **5**, 75.

### 1652–53

Connecticut: Snow sometime in Feb.–March 1653 made travel difficult between New London and New York. *Winthrop Papers,* **5**, 523.

## JOHN HULL'S WINTER CHRONOLOGY: 1654–1678

The first systematic analysis of the New England climate over a span of years appeared in the "Notes of Publick Occurrences" of John Hull (1624–1683). Hull had come from England to Boston in 1635. He prospered in his trade as a goldsmith and merchant, but it was as mint master of the young colony that he won lasting fame. He coined the first Massachusetts shillings, and his early designs in working precious metals into useful objects are now highly prized as examples of early American art. His diary entries contained the usual religious introspections of the age, but also much about the weather scene. His period of winter weather notes covered the span from 1654 to 1677, very conveniently filling the interim between John Winthrop's demise and the commencement of John Pike's record.

### 1654–55

About 26th December, the frost was extreme, and suddenly froze the Bay over, that, in very few days, it was firm to pass between the town and Long Island, and a constant passage to Charlestown and Noddle's Island, and so continued above a month. The other part of the winter was as usual; only the month of *April* was cold.

### 1655–56

This winter was very little cold weather—not above seven very cold days until the 12th of February; nor scarse any snow at all until the 15th of said month, whereon there fell a pretty deep snow. And it continued cold weather all *February,* and the 10th of March very cold; but after that the weather grew very moderate again, and the spring came on forwardly.

### 1656–57

No entry

### 1657–58

This winter was very temperate. The month of *November* was pretty cold, and the beginning of *February*: else very moderate weather and very little snow. By the 20th of March, the frost was generally out of the ground; and only in the latter end of *February* and in *March,* there was two or three times much thunder and rain.

In the latter end of *March,* and in the month of *April,* very much wet weather, that husbandmen doubted opportunity for sowing their corn, and so continued until the latter end of *April.*

Upon the 23d of April, there came a storm of snow, about two inches deep, and in the night following a hard frost. In the latter end of the month the skies cleared, and warm weather and dry, that it proved suddenly a very forward spring and comfortable seed-time.

### 1658–59

We had much cold weather for three weeks before, Jan. 7, but very little snow; yet the river was not quite frozen over. The cold continued sharp until about the middle of *January;* then we had fine, warm, pleasant weather till the midst of *February;* after that, we had wet, stormy weather, both snow and rain, until *March*: then fine moderate weather, only the frost not full out of the ground till about the 20th of April. It was a pretty cold spring.

### 1659–60

We had a sharp frost the latter end of *December,* all our Bay frozen over; but the ice continued not in the channel but a few days. We also had much snow; and it continued until the 25th of February, and then the weather grew very temperate: no frost for many nights together, that it soon wasted. . . . The frost out of the ground when *February* ended.

March 26. There was a very great storm of wind and snow, such as none went beyond it all winter. All *March* very cold. A snow, April 16th.

### 1660–61

Feb. 2. We have had very little snow hitherto, and not much frost: a few pretty cold nights in the beginning of *November* and the latter end of *December,* otherwise hitherto very little frost.

Feb. 17. There fell a snow, about a foot deep, and pretty sharp frost so far on to this month; but about the 20th day of February, it began to be very moderate, and the snow every day wasted apace.

### 1661–62

No entry

### 1662–63

Jan. 1. Fell a pretty deep snow; and so several times, both in *January* and *February.* The snow was generally two feet deep. About March 8th, and beginning of *March,* it wasted gently from day to day.

### 1663–64

Very little cold weather until the beginning of *January,* and then sundry great snows, though intermixed with many moderate seasons and thaws. The spring proved cold and dry.

### 1664–65

Most of *January* and *February* was very temperate; little frost, only not much clear sunshine. On the 1st of March, the winter did, as it were, begin again. A cold spring: no trees budded until the 10th of May.

### 1665–66

The first week of *January* the frosts were violent. Charles River was passed on foot, and only the channel open before Boston. About 22d January, all open again, and on Feb. 4th all frozen again and Boston channel, all down to the Castle, passable to any. February 9th, all open again. Feb. 16 all froze again down to the Castle. 21st Feb. began to open to the channel, and so gradually.

### 1666–67

Upon a sabbath morning, the ice cut the cables of above eight ships, four whereof were ready to sail for England. All forced on shore; and get off they could not until January 12th, which was three days after the spring tides in ordinary course.

The spring pretty forward. April 22 the apple trees put forth their leaves.

### 1667–68

This winter was exceeding moderate, scarse one extreme cold day, and a great part of it, very little frost. The sheep, in most places, scarse eat any hay; and the spring came on very forward. Apple trees began to blossom April 28.

#### 1668–69

Very temperate winter.

#### 1669–70

No entry

#### 1670–71

The winter very moderate.

#### 1671–72

About the 25th of December, the weather was very moderate, and so continued till 30 of January.

Jan. 31, Feb. 1. The winter returned in severity; the bay full of ice in two nights; cut Master Greenough three cables, sent his ship adrift and another ketch, but continued not, but became pretty moderate again.

#### 1672–73

A very moderate winter, excepting two weeks of cold.

#### 1673–74

The winter very moderate as to frost; pretty much snow and wet weather.

#### 1674–75

Dec. 25. The weather began this month cold, but grew pretty temperate for three weeks together.

Much snow in *January,* and several cold fits most of this month; yet the harbors, nor Charles Ferry, scarse shut up from passage any one day.

From Jan. 25th to Feb. 1st—very cold; 19th, 29th–31st, as cold a time in many years, and so dry and windy that the dust blew like snow.

All *March* pretty cold; *April* very raw and cold until May 1st; then began to be a little warm, and the sun to shine which it had done but now and then a day for a month together; wind had been constantly easterly.

#### 1675–76

Winter came in exceeding sharp in beginning.

*December.* The soldiers conflicting with much cold and snow.

*April* and *May* months were very sickly through this Colony.

#### 1676–77

No entry

#### 1677–78

This winter was mostly moderate weather.

## JOHN PIKE'S WINTER CHRONOLOGY: 1682–1700

John Pike of New Hampshire was the first of a long line of self-appointed snow-watchers in New England. Perhaps others preceded him, but their accounts have not been preserved, and even Pike's record might have been unpublished at this date if another snow-watcher, probably John Farmer, had not insisted that the "Remarkable Seasons" be published along with Pike's diary of religious and political events when the New Hampshire Historical Society first put the diary into print in 1832.

John Pike was born at Salisbury, Massachusetts, on *15 May 1653*. He was graduated from Harvard College in 1675 at the head of his class. Ordained a minister on *31 August 1681* at Dover, New Hampshire, he served several towns during the next 30 years. This was still frontier country and subject to Indian attack. In 1689 he was forced to remove to the protection afforded by Portsmouth, and then served a term at Fort Pemaquid, a defensive outpost nearby on the central Maine coast. In 1698 he again settled at Dover, and spent most of his remaining years there until his death on *10 March 1710*. According to a distinguished New Hampshire historian, Jeremy Belknap, Pike was "a grave and venerable person and generally preached without notes." In the words of one of his contemporaries, he was "a person of great humility, meakness, and patience, much mortified to the world, and without gall or guile."

Pike's weather notes were of the sketchiest kind in the early years, but later on he did add some illuminating notes so that one can judge the relative severity of the winters he experienced. Pike's main interest centered in the winter, leaving few notes about other seasons. All winter references follow. All dates have been corrected to New Style; and Old Style references to whole months are italicized.

To supplement the rather bare statistical data of Pike's record, extracts have been made from *The Diary of Samuel Sewall* where they relate to the weather scene. Judge Sewall (1652–1730) played a prominent role in Massachusetts affairs as merchant and colonial magistrate. His just fame rests upon his voluminous diary which vividly reproduces life and times in colonial Boston. Extracts from Sewall's diary supplement the material from Pike's record and generally follow in the concluding paragraphs of each year's account.

#### 1682–83

First snow Oct. 29, which issued in a great rain.

Snows: Nov. 26, 30; Dec. 2, 7, 16, 22, 30; Jan. 7, 16, 20; Feb. 1, 12; March 2, 20, 28, 30.

Feb. 19. A considerable deal of snow being on the ground, there falls such plenty of warm rain as that the water swell so as to do much damage. Ipswich dam and bridge is carried away by the flood and ice violently coming down; so that they now go over in a boat, horse and men. Rowly Mill Dam also spoiled, and generally much harm done in Dams and bridges, so tis judged many thousands will scarse repair the loss. Woburn hath suffered much, Roxbury Bridge carried away just as persons on it; so that a woman was near drowning.

### 1683–84

Snows: Nov. 5, 14; Dec. 1, 25; Jan. 9, 24, 30; Feb. 6, 8, 21, 25; April 1, 7.

April 1. There was an extraordinary high tide, which did much hurt at Boston and Charlestown coming into houses and Warehouses that stood low. All I hear of at Cambridge, Charlestown, and here, say tis higher than ever any has known before.

### 1684–85

Snows: Nov. 22, 23; Dec. 3, 24; Jan.; 4, 16, 19; Feb. 3, 7, 14, 27; March 7, 19, 27.

Jan. 27. Boston harbor frozen over down to the Castle, and nine hundred men on the ice at once.
Jan. 30. Was fine moderate weather though had been very severe for near a week together before.
Feb. 6. Day was louring after the storm, but not freezing.

### 1685–86

Snows: Nov. 30; Dec. 15, 22, 28, 29; Jan. 3, 9, 14, 17, 19, 21, 27; Feb. 5, 24; March, 3, 21; April 24.

Nov. 30. A very rainy and dark day, and in the afternoon turns to a storm of snow . . . ground quite covered with snow when Court was done.
Jan. 3. Considerable snow this night.
    4. A great snow fell last night so this day and night very cold.
    19. A very great storm of snow and wind.
    23. Very cold day.
    24. Thursday exceeding cold . . . it being night and excessive cold.
    26. Notwithstanding the three very severe nights last past and snow in abundance lately fallen, yet, by reason of the Spring Tides, and wind 2 of the nights, the Harbour remains fairly open, and the Chanel between the Castle and Dorchester Neck; though much loose ice floating up and down. Isaiah Tay told me yesterday, that the 27th of January last year he went on the ice to the Castle, and nine hundred were told by their Company going and coming on the ice, and at the Island.
    27. Rain and thaw all day.

Feb. 2. Friday night and Saturday were extreme cold, so that the Harbour frozen up, and to the Castle. This day so cold that the Sacramental Bread is frozen pretty hard, and rattles sadly as broken into the plates.
Feb. 4. Though the snow extreme deep by reason of this day's snow and what was before.
    9. Gallant warm thawing weather.
    11. In the afternoon a great cake of ice comes from Cambridgeward and jostles away the body of ice that lay between the outward Wharfs and Noddle's Island: so now our Harbour open again.
    12. Several ships sail.
    22. Ice breaks up from Gill's Wharf.
    23. Pretty well clear our dock of ice by a passage cut open. Shut up about 7 weeks.

### 1686–87

Snows: Dec. 4, 31; Jan. 16, 18, 21, 29; Feb. 3, 10, 12, 16; March 12, 19, 31.

Feb. 13. Spring tides shake ice and carries away part; near night it suddenly breaks away to the outward wharfs more suddenly than hath usually been known.

### 1687–88

Snows: Dec. 28; Jan. 8, 16; Feb. 1, 13, 21; March 4. This winter was productive of few snows and those very shallow. It seldom fell above an inch at a time, and perhaps altogether would not have amounted to above a foot or a foot and a half deep; but many rains in lieu thereof.

### 1688–89

Snows: Nov. 19; Dec. 26; Jan. 7, 14, 18, 29; Feb. 1, 7; March 5, 6, 7, 16, 22.

Nov. 18. There is a considerable snow on the ground which fell last Thursday night and Friday, near half a foot deep.

### 1689–90

Snows: Dec. 1, 5; Jan. 7, 14, 30; Feb. 3, 18; March 15, 22—continuing with some intermission to 26. But this year, by reason of my absence and illness, some snows are omitted.

### 1690–91

Snow: Nov. 3; Dec. 14, 24, 27, 29; Jan. 2, 11, 13, 24, 27; Feb. 1, 11, 17, 19; March 3, 5, 6, 13, 16.

Jan. 31. Very cold.
Feb. 27. Passage has been open for about a week, and Crooked Lane a 14 night.

### 1691–92

Snows: Nov. 27; Dec. 3, 7, 12; Jan. 5, 9, 13, 17, 31; Feb. 3; March 1.

Dec. 12. Very stormy day of snow and rain.

Jan. 4. Cold and snowy.

    22. This week's rain and sun have thawed the ways as if it were March.

March 9–10. Exceeding high wind this day at Northeast.

### 1692–93

Snows: Oct. 18; Nov. 30; Dec. 11, 28; Jan. 13, 16, 21, 27, 30; Feb. 1, 4; March 7; April 15.

Feb. 1. A very extraordinary storm by reason of the falling and driving of the snow. Few women could get to meeting.

    8. A very sunshiny, hot, thawing day.

### 1693–94

Snows: Nov. 18; Dec. 17, 24, 27; Jan. 5, 9, 13, 17, 31; Feb. 3; March 1.

Dec. 4. The first snow falls.

    25. Very pleasant weather.

    30. There is a great snow on the ground, most of it fallen within these 7 days.

    31. Very moderate comfortable weather.

Jan. 25. The ice is clear gone out of the docks as in March.

March 26. A great snow falls.

### 1694–95

#### Fort Pemaquid

Snows: Nov. 7; Dec. 22, 25, 29; Jan. 1, 22, 26; Feb. 1, 7, 8, 19; March 5, 27; April 2—very stormy, 3—very cold.

Dec. 30—extreme cold and windy; Jan. 4—rain, after which very cold, 21—very rainy day, 31—very cold; Feb. 2–7—continued rain, with little intermission, 16—very rainy, 21, 22, 23, 26, 27—very cold; March 4, 10—very wet, 22–23—very cold; April 9—fine morning, 11, 12, 26—very cold, 27—fine; May 8—very cold, rain, 30, 31—very cold; June—early very warm, 17—very warm day; rest of summer hot and cold by turns.

Feb. 19. This day there is a very extraordinary storm of snow.

Feb. 22. The last night and this day the weather is extreme cold.

March 27. A very sore storm of snow.

April 2. Very sore storm of rain.

April 20. When I rise this morn I find the ground and houses covered with snow. Be it that Lewis the 14th be indeed dead &c. yet we have had a sharp, though short winter in New England still.

### 1695–96

Snows: Dec. 2—moderate, 14, 17, 23; Jan. 5, 11, 19, 26, 28; Feb. 4, 8, 19; March 7, 16; April 2, 7.

Nov. 21, 23, 24—very cold and windy; Dec. 13, 14, 19—extremely cold and windy; Jan. 17, 21, 25—very cold; Feb. 20—very windy, 23—very cold, 27, 28—very cold and windy; March 3—extreme cold and windy, 4—very cold, black, stormy, 5—cold and northwest wind, 13, 14—very cold and windy, 17, 18, 19—fair moderate weather, 27, 28—very stormy; April 2, 7—very stormy, 11, 13, 14 very fine.

Mar. 8. There had been great snow storms. The roads were so filled, that there was no travelling. J. B. Felt. *Hist. Salem,* 2, 115.

April 22. About 8 m. it begins to snow; by noon the houses and grounds were covered, and at 5 p.m. I saw an Isicle seven inches long. This new snow was plentifully to be seen on the ground for about three days apace.

### 1696–97

Snows: Dec. 2, 4, 10, 12, 13, 22, 30, 31; Jan. 8, 12, 30; Feb. 1, 7, 28; March 4, 5, 7; May 2.

Nov. 11—sabbath very fine, 12—very foul, 13, 14—very cold, windy, squally; Dec. 3—very cold, clear, windy, 6, 7, 8, 9—very cold storm, 18, 19, 20—cloudy, foggy, wet, 22 windy, 29—cold, black; Jan. 4—very cold, 7—very cold still, 9 wet, 10 windy, 12 rain, 20 warm, wet. Feb. 1—bitter cold northwest storm, 2 bitter cold, 3 clear; most of this month moderate; Feb. 11, 12 fine, 13 rainy, 14–21 very cold, 21—very fine. March 11, 12, 13—very fine; 18 fine; 21 March–April 5—windy, cold; April 8—cold, windy.

Dec. 30. This day, there being a violent storm arisen . . . preached Refuge from the storms of the wrath of God. C. Mather. *Diary,* 1, 212.

    31. A very great snow is on the ground.

Feb. 15. Extreme cold.

March 23. Weather was extreme cold.

April 15. Last night and this morning were very cold, possibly that might be the reason. Street of earth and water was hard frozen.

### 1697–98

Snows: Nov. 20—issued in great rain; Dec. 2 and 8—moderate, 14—pretty deep, 21, 29; Jan. 4, 5, 9, 12, 14, 16, 18, 21, 29; Feb. 7, 11, 12, 14, 16, 18, 20, 23; March 1, 9, 24 issued in rain; April 1, 3, 7, 9.

[See page 16 for Sewall entries for 1697–98]

### 1698–99

Snows: Nov. 5; Dec. 9; Jan. 4, 12, 15, 17, 28; Feb. 1, 5, 9, 16, 19, 24—bitter cold and stormy, 28; March 21; April 3, 9.

Cambridge. The winter after [1698–99] moderate little snow. Only Feb. 24 a violent Searching storm of snow. Records of First Church, Cambridge. *Genealogical Magazine,* 1, (March 1906), 360.

Newbury, Mass.: "This year, says the reverend Richard Brown, in his diary, "has been famous for three things, namely: 'First, for that the winter was turned into summer, or at least we have had very little or none, the ground being bare for the most part, though we have had snow at times, yet very shallow, not exceeding above twelve inches and that by an advance of southerly gales faded away speedily." Joshua Coffin, *Hist. Newbury,* 167.

### 1699–1700

Snows: Dec. 1, 4, 9—very stormy, 17, 22; Jan. 5, 12, 19, 21, 23; Feb. 5—issued in rain, lightning and thunder, 9, 10, 15, 19—very cold, 21, 22; March 4, 20; April 1, 6, 8. From April 5 to 9 was a continued storm of snow, rain, hail, thunder and extreme wind. It began with snow and ended with snow. [Dates after 19 February 1700 have 11 days, instead of 10, added to conform with New Style].

Dec. 8. Trees laden & many broke down by ye Ice & Mr. Eliot came to board. *Records of the First Church,* Cambridge, 360.

Dec. 10. The rain freezes upon the branches of the trees to that thickness and weight, that great havock is thereby made of the wood and timber. Many young and strong trees are broken off in the midst; and multitudes of bows rent off. Considerable hurt is done in orchards. Two of our apple trees are broken down, Unkles Tree, two thirds of it are broken down. Peach trees at Mrs. Moodeys are almost all spoiled. And my little cedar almost quite mortified. Some think that spoil that is made amounts to thousands of pounds. How suddenly and with surprise can God destroy! *Diary of Samuel Sewall,* 506.

Feb. 11. A pretty deal of thunder, rain, hail the last night.

12. Tis so very cold that none of us venture to go out.

16. High wind and very cold at NW.

16, 17, 18. Were reputed to be the coldest days that have been of many years. Some say brooks were frozen for carts to pass over them, so as has not been seen these ten years.

22. A considerable snow falls.

26. Pleasant weather.

Mar. 6. Wednesday and Thursday were extravagantly stormy. On Friday Mr. Cooke come home but the wind was strong in my face, and cold that I durst not venture. Saturday was also very cold.

April 24. I saw and heard the swallows proclaim the spring.

## NEW NETHERLAND: 1609–1664

The magnificent harbor afforded by New York Bay and the beautiful inland water route provided by the Hudson River Valley were first fully explored in September of 1609 when Henry Hudson and crew ascended the majestic river in the *Half Moon* to a point near Troy. Aboard ship as mate was Robert Juet of Limehouse, England, who maintained a daily log which included an account of the weather and winds on that historic voyage. So to Juet has been accorded the title of "New York's First Weatherman." [1]

But it was not until five years later that any Dutch or other Europeans spent a winter in this vicinity. Adriaen Block in the cold season of 1614 cruised the chill waters of the East River through "Hellegat" into Long Island Sound, but no daily record of the prevailing weather conditions has survived.

With the permanent occupation of Manhattan Island in 1624, officials in the homeland, anxious for an accounting of the climate of the new settlements, requested such information be included in reports to the West India Company and also to the Estates-General. All seemed agreed that conditions resembled those in Holland except for the greater extreme of cold in winter and the longer duration of heat in summer.

David de Vries experienced some wintry conditions on the Delaware River to the southward in the early 1630's in territory that the Dutch claimed and sought to occupy:

> They did not imagine that we had been frozen up in the river, as no pilot or astrologer could conceive, that in a latitude from the thirty-eighth and a half to the thirty-ninth, such rapid running rivers could freeze. Some maintain that it is because it lies so far west; others adduce other reasons; but I will tell how it can be, from experience and what I have seen, and that it is thus: inland, stretching towards the north, there are high mountains, covered with snow, and the north and northwest winds blow over the land from these cold mountains, with a pure clear air, which causes extreme cold and frost, such as is felt in Provence and Italy, which I have experienced often when I was at Genoa, when the wind blew over the land

from the high mountains, making it as cold as it was in Holland. I have found by experience in all countries, during winter, that when the wind blows from the land, the hardest frosts makes. It is so in New Netherland also, for as soon as the wind is southwest, it is so warm that one may stand naked in the woods and put on a shirt.[2]

Certainly the longest attempt to depict the climate of the Dutch possessions appeared in Adriaen van der Donck's *A description of the New Netherland*. This lengthy document, composed in 1656, summarized the prevailing opinion about the climate. The following are the sections dealing with winter conditions:

> We will now notice the winters of New Netherlands, which are different at different places. Above the highlands, towards Rensselaerwyck, and in the interior places extending towards New England, (which we still claim), there the winters are colder and last longer than at New Amsterdam, and other places along the sea coast, or on Long Island, and on the South River (Delaware). At the latter places, there seldom is any hard freezing weather before Christmas, and although there may be some cold nights, and trifling snows, still it does not amount to much, for during the day it is usually clear weather. But at Rensselaerwyck the winters begin earlier, as in 1645, when the North River closed on the 25th day of November, and remained frozen very late. Below the highlands and near the sea coast, as has been observed, it never begins to freeze so early, but the cold weather usually keeps off until about Christmas, and frequently later, before the rivers are closed; and then they frequently are so full of drifting ice during the northwest winds, as to obstruct the navigation; and whenever the wind shifts to the south or southeast, the ice decays, and the rivers are open and clear. This frequently happens two or three times in a winter, when the navigation will be free and unobstructed again. Much rainy weather, or strong winds which continue to blow from one quarter a long time, are not common, or to be expected in the country.
>
> It is probable, (and many people support the position with plausible reasoning), that the subtlety and purity of the atmosphere changes the water before it comes to the earth, or whilst it is still retained in the clouds, or in its descent to the earth, into hail or snow. The latter is sooner to be credited, for during the winter much snow falls, which frequently remains weeks and months on the earth, without thawing away entirely. But below the circle of the highlands, the southerly winds are powerful; there the snow cannot lay long, but is removed by the southerly weather.
>
> It frequently happens once or twice in a winter, that the trees are silvered over with sleet, which produces a beautiful and speculative appearance when the sun shines on the same, particularly on the declevities of the hills and mountains. Many persons say the sleets and heavy hail are signs of good fruit seasons in the succeeding year.
>
> It is strange and worthy of observation, and surpasses all reasoning, that in the New Netherlands, without or but with little wind, (for when the weather is the coldest, there seldom is much wind), although it lies in the latitude of Spain and Italy, and the summer heat is similar, that the winters should be so much colder, as to render useless all the plants and herbs which grow in those countries, which will not endure the cold weather. The winter weather is dry and cold, and we find that the peltries and feltings are prior and better than the furs of Muscovy. For this difference several reasons are assigned, which we will relate, without controverting any, except in remarking that in most cases wherein many different reasons are assigned to establish a subject, all are frequently discredited. Some say that the New Netherlands lie so much further west on the globe, and that this causes the difference; others who compare the summer heat with Spain and Italy, deny this position; others declare that the globe is not round, and that the country lies in a declining position from the sun. Other assert that the last discovered quarter of the world is larger than the other parts, and ask, if the world was formerly considered round, how that theory can be supported now, when about one-half is added to it? Some also say that the higher a country is situated, the colder it is. Now, say they, the New Netherlands lie in a high westerly position; ergo, it must be colder there in winter, and as warm in summer. Many remark, and with much plausibility also, that the country extends northerly many hundred miles to the frozen ocean, and is accessible by Davis Straits, (which by some is doubted), and that the land is intersected and studded with high mountains, and that the snow remains lying on them and in the valleys, and seldom thaws away entirely' and that when the wind blows from and over those cold regions, it brings cold with it. Receiving the cold from above and from beneath (both being cold), it must of course follow that the cold comes with the northwesterly winds. On the contrary, they say, that when the wind blows from the sea, if it be in the heat of the winter, then the weather becomes sultry and warm as in Lent.
>
> The cold weather, however, is not so severe as to do much injury, or to become tedious; but for many reasons it is desirable for the benefit of the country, which it frees from insects and every other kind of impurity of the air, and fastens firmly in their positions all the plants, and screens the same from the effects of the cold, against which nature has thus carefully provided.
>
> There is everywhere fuel in abundance, and to be obtained for the expense of cutting and procuring the same. The super-abundance of this country is not equalled by any other in the world. The Indians do not cloth as we do, but frequently go half naked and withstand the cold, in fashion, and fear it little. They are never overcome with the cold, or injured by it. In bitter cold weather, they will not pursue their customary pleasures, particularly the women and children; for the men do not care so much for the cold days in winter as they do for the hot days in summer.[4]

[1] David M. Ludlum. New York's first weatherman. *Weatherwise* (Boston), 12–3, (June 1959), 95–97.

[2] David Pietersz. De Vries. Korte historiael ende journaels aenteyckeninge. 1630–33. "David de Vries's Notes." Reprint: *Narratives of Early Pennsylvania*. 26.

[3] *Documents relative to the colonial history of the State of New York.* Albany, Weed, Parsons & Co., 1856. 1, 14, 40, 179, 275.

[4] Adriaen van der Donck. *A description of the New Netherland.* Amsterdam, 1656. Reprint: *Coll. New York Hist. Soc.* 2d ser., 1, 1841, 183–84.

## NEW SWEDEN: 1638–1663

The distinction of being America's first weatherman is generally accorded Reverend John Campanius, or John Campanius Holm (of Stockholm), (1601–1683), as he was interchangeably called. Certainly he was the first resident of present-day United States to maintain a systematic record of daily weather sequences.[1] Others may have kept such, but the whereabouts of their manuscripts, if they survived, has not been revealed. Today the United States Weather Bureau honors outstanding observers with the John Campanius Holm Award.

Campanius was a Lutheran clergyman who arrived in New Sweden on Delaware Bay in February 1643 in the midst of a considerable meteorological disturbance:

On the 13th we had a great storm in the Western ocean until Sunday, the 15th. Then it abated, but immediately afterwards, on the Monday, it stormed again mighty hard and continued over a period of 14 days, so that we had never had such a violent storm, with heavy snow, which was the 26th and the 27th of January, that we then in the Bay off the Hornkill lost three large anchors, the breakhead, a spritsail, and the mainmast. The ship, the *Swan,* ran aground and lost some apparel as we did in the same storm, but on the 15th of February we came, however, God be praised, safely to Ft. Christina in New Sweden near Virginia, in the afternoon at 2 o'clock.[2]

Campanius remained in the New World for five years, and during this period he kept an account of affairs and conditions in the small colony on the Delaware. He was a man of wide interests, with a definite intellectual bent. His translation of Luther's *Catechism* into the local Indian dialect, completed in 1647, antedated any similar accomplishment by the New England divines who had preceded Campanius to the New World by a score of years.[3]

Campanius also exhibited an intense interest in the natural history of the new country. His observations in this field supplied much data to those in the Old World who were eager for such information about the New. He made astronomical observations of an elementary sort. One of his chief concerns centered in the weather. He wished to compare the day-to-day changes of New Sweden with those in the homeland, so for at least two years, 1644 and 1645, he maintained a written account of local Delaware weather conditions. His observations were made "every day and night of every month." The original manuscript has not survived, but fortunately, his grandson, Thomas Campanius Holm, published an account of New Sweden at Stockholm in 1702 which included an abstract of the original Delaware weather records along with a chapter on the climate:

### CHAPTER III.

Of the Climate and Temperature of Virginia and New Sweden.

The climate and temperature in Virginia and New Sweden are variable, as with us; some years are colder and others are warmer. In the year 1657, the same in which the winter was so cold in our country, that the belt was frozen over, and our brave hero, King Charles Gustavus, of glorious memory, crossed over it, with his army, into Funen, Laland, Falster, and Sealand, the river Delaware, as I have been informed, was entirely frozen up in one night, so that a deer could run over it, which, as the Indians relate, had not happened within the memory of man. Otherwise, the climate is moderate, the air is pleasant and very wholesome, moderately moist and warm, so that every thing that is planted and sown grows very fast, and produces abundant crops; and, although the weather is sometimes damp and rainy, yet it does not last so long as in this country; in two or three hours it is over, and the sun shines again as bright as ever.

The severity of winter lasts, at most, two months; it begins in January, when it is somewhat cold, and then it increases, so that before Christmas there is very little cold, but only wind and rain: the end of January, and the beginning of February are the coldest parts of the winter.

Spring is very fine and pleasant, without any stormy or rigidly cold weather, but only small soft rains and a clear sky.

The summer is, for the most part, pleasant and moderately warm, except in August and September, which are the hottest parts of the year, and in some years it is so warm that people long for rain and wet weather, by which the air is immediately cooled.

The autumn is pleasant and dry, and sometimes a little cold, as was observed by John Campanius in the year 1645.[4]

Campanius, of course, did not possess any instruments as only in the previous year, 1643, had Torricelli announced the principle of the barometer, and this instrument and the thermometer did not come into general use, even in the highest scientific circles in western Europe, until the decade of the 1660's. James M. Havens has made a study of the Campanius weather record and reproduced the language into graphic form employing modern weather symbols. Havens commented:

The weather of the months, divided approximately into thirds and corresponding to Old Style, or Julian dating, is given in diagramatic form in figure 1. It cannot, of course, be interpreted strictly and in de-

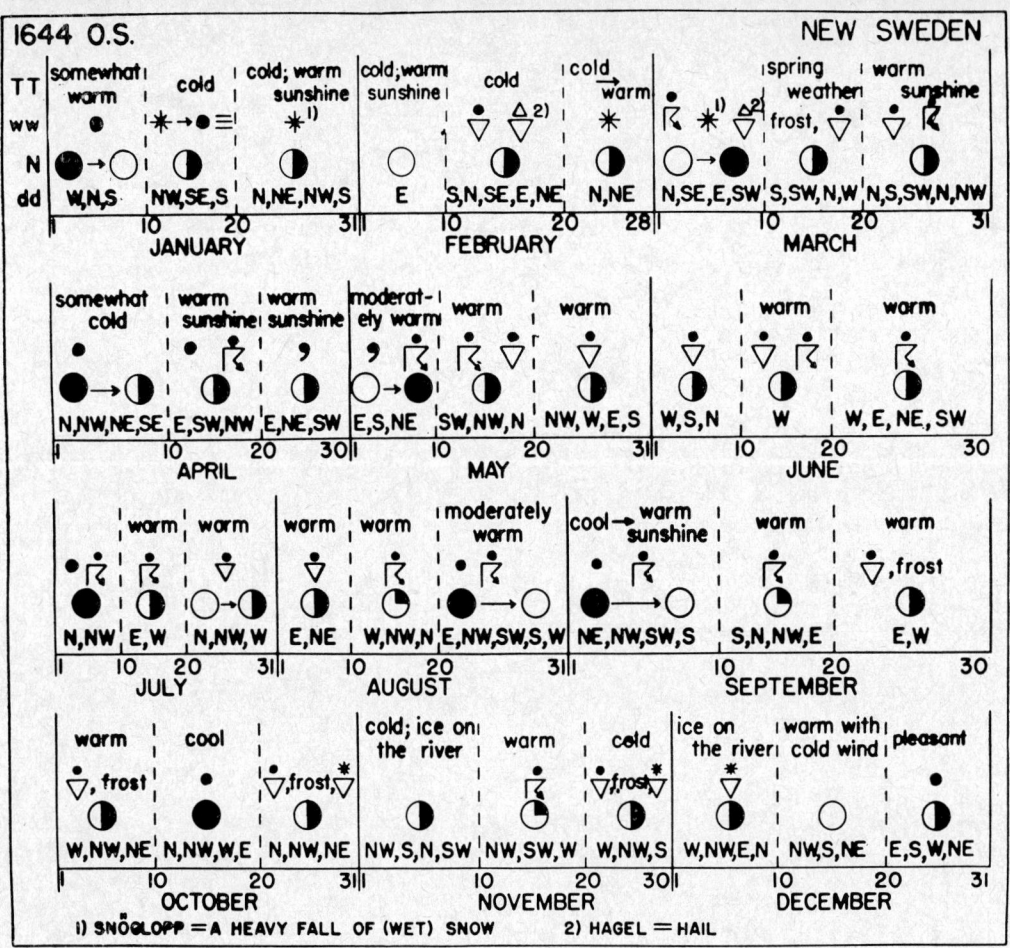

The weather for the year 1644 at New Sweden in the present state of Delaware, using conventional weather code symbols. By James M. Havens, *Weatherwise*, 1955.

tail. At best it gives a general view of the year's weather. Each component, whether the general temperature TT, characteristic weather ww, cloud cover N, or wind direction dd, is generally represented as a function of time."[5]

The grandson had the entire manuscript records at hand when he was composing his book. He stated that they were much too long to be inserted in full, but he did give an abstract of those for 1644, "by which the reader will be enabled to judge of the temperature of the country":

### 1644

*January*—The winter began about the 21st, with severe cold, and then much snow. Afterwards came rain and a thick fog, with occasional sunshine, until the end of the month. During this time the winds were NW, ESE, SE, S.

*February*—At first high and cold wind, then snow and sleet, with intervals of warm sunshine, until the 11th; winds N, NE, WNW, S. From the 11th to the 21st, cold and clear, sometimes pretty warm, wind generally E. The residue varied with rain, hail, clear and cold; winds S, N, SW, E, NW.

*March*—In the first week cold and clear, with some snow, winds N, NE; in the second, calm, pleasant; in the third, rain, with thunder and lightning, sometimes hail and wet snow; winds N, NE, SE, SW; in the remainder clear and pleasant, sometimes rain, high winds, and night frosts, winds S, SW, N, W, SE, SW, WNW.

*April*—Blustering until the 11th, with rain, hail, thunder and lightning, sometimes warm sunshine, winds ranging from N to S on the west side; until the 21st generally cloudy, rainy, and raw cold, with occasional sunshine; winds N, NW, WNW, ENE, SE; afterwards generally clear and warm, with some white frost at night; but sometimes cloudy and rainy, with thunder and lightning, winds E, W, SW, WNW.

### 1644

*November* had generally clear sunshine; the first ten days also some clouds and rain, a little snow, and white frost some nights, winds N, NW, ENE; the next third part, clear cold, that made a little ice on the water, occasionally somewhat cloudy, winds WNW, S, N, SW; afterwards mostly warm sunshine, sometimes rain, thunder and lightning, no violent gales, winds WNW, SW, W.

*December* had until the 11th, clear weather, but cold and frosty, sometimes rain and snow, winds W, WNW, S; from thence until the 21st clear sunshine and cold that made ice on the shores, now and then snow, winds W, NW, E, N; during the residue warm, and sometimes clear sunshine.

The only other contemporary description of the climate came from Peter Lindstrom, a Swedish engineeer serving in the colony in the mid-1650's. It shed little light on actual weather conditions, but was climatologically quaint:

> The winter begins in *December,* and ends in *January,* continuing only seven, eight, or at most nine weeks; but it is, while it lasts, equal in cold to any in Sweden. It sometimes comes with such violence, that the rivers would be covered with thick ice in three or four nights, if the billows of the sea were not so forcibly driven into it. When departing, it suddenly breaks up in all the creeks, and the ice drives with the ebb tide to the sea like mountains, and with such a roaring crash, as if a great number of large cannon were discharged. Soon after this the weather becomes quite warm.

> It doth not often rain, but when it does, it is generally with lightning and thunder, tremendous to the sight and hearing. The whole sky appears to be on fire, and nothing can be seen but smoke and flames.[6]

[1] Nicholas Collin. Observations made at an early period, on the climate of the country about the River Delaware. *Trans. Amer. Philo. Soc.* Ns. 1, (1818), 341.

[2] Amandus Johnson. *The instructions for Johan Printz.* Phila., The Swedish Colonial Society, 1930. 23.

[3] Amandus Johnson. *The Swedish Settlements on the Delaware.* New York, D. Appleton & Co., 1911. **1**, 372; **2**, 678. Also *Dictionary of American Biography.* New York, Charles Scribner's Sons, 1929. **3**, 445.

[4] Thomas Campanius Holm. *Kort beskriftning om Provincien Nya Swerige uti America.* Stockholm, 1702. Reprint and trans., Peter S. du Ponceau. *Memoirs Hist. Soc. Penna.* (Phila.). **3**, (1834), 55–62.

[5] James M. Havens. The "first" systematic American weather observations. *Weatherwise* (Boston), **8**–5, (1955), 116–17.

[6] T. C. Holm, 56.

## PENNSYLVANIA: 1682–1700

The Delaware Valley with its broad bay gradually narrowing into a spacious river remained the last of the northern areas to attract a large settlement. It had been occupied and fought over by the Dutch, Swedes, and English, but only small groups resided there when William Penn (1644–1718) arrived on 27 October 1682 to direct personally the establishment of his "Holy Experiment."

Penn, an active propagandist eager to see his Quaker lands prosper, sent home glowing letter extolling the richness of the country. The chief descriptive document of the early years formed part of a long letter sent in August 1683 to the Free Society of Traders in London. Penn described the winter climate through which he had recently passed:

> For the seasons of the year, having by God's goodness now lived over the coldest and hottest, that the oldest liver in the province can remember, I can say something to an English understanding.
>
> Of the fall, for then I came in: I found it from the 3d of November, to the beginning of *December,* as we have it usually in England in *September*, or rather like an English mild spring. From *December* to the beginning of the month called *March,* we had sharp frosty weather; not foul, thick, black weather, as our northeast winds bring with them in England; but a sky as clear as in summer, and the air dry, cold, piercing and hungry; yet I remember not, that I wore more clothes than in England. The reason of this cold is given from the Great Lakes that are fed by the fountains of Canada. The winter before was as mild, scarce any ice at all; while this for a few days froze up our great River Delaware. From that month to the month called *June,* we enjoyed a sweet spring, no gusts, but gentle showers, and a fine sky. Yet this I observe, that the winds here as there, are more inconstant spring and fall, upon that turn of Nature, than in summer or winter. From thence to this present month (*August*), which ends the summer (commonly speaking) we have had extraordinary heats, yet mitigated sometimes by cool breezes. The wind that ruleth the summer season, is the southwest; but spring, fall, and winter, 'tis rare to want the wholesome northwester seven days together: and whatever mists, fogs or vapours foul the heavens by easterly or southerly winds, in two hours time are blown away; the one is always followed by the other: a remedy that seems to have a peculiar providence in it to the inhabitants; the multitude of trees, yet standing, being liable to retain mists and vapours, and yet not one quarter so thick as I expected.

Since no day-to-day record of activities in the Quaker community in diary form has survived, we have no information about the major weather events until after the turn of the century. Nor are the various descriptive pamphlets about the new province of much assistance; they merely echo what Penn had to say earlier. The only shred of 17th Century climatic information came from publications aimed at prospective German settlers who were soon to flood the colony after the turn of the century. Among these was Falckner's *Curieuse Nachricht,* a sort of catechism about the new land. The 13th question read: "How the climate is constituted there in summer and winter":

> The climate is almost the same as here, according to the season, only that everywhere it is much more

subtle and penetrating. Although the sun has greater power, yet the breezes temper its rays. In summer it is warmest from nine o'clock in the morning until the clock strikes two, particularly during the months of July and August. Two hours before nightfall it generally begins to get cool and damp. During the night the dew falls heavily. Whenever the dew fails to fall, it is a sign that it will soon rain. Strong winds blow from the west and northwest, of which the latter brings the same kind of weather as the northeast winds do with us. On the contrary, the northeast winds and easterly winds bring us a two days' driving rain; southeasterly winds, a twelve hour storm and rain; and the south wind, sudden and heavy showers and down pours of rain. During the winter the sun has greater strength than here; consequently snow gradually disappears. Another advantage is that the shortest day with us is two hours longer,[15] while the longest is so much shorter. The greatest cold comes with the northwest wind, when it freezes harder in one night than otherwise in two.

[1] Edwin B. Bonner. *William Penn's 'Holy Experiment'. The founding of Pennsylvania 1681–1701.* New York, Columbia Univ. Press, 1962. 78.

[2] A letter from William Penn, Proprietary and Governour of Pennsylvania in America, to the Committee of the Free Society of Traders in that Providence, residing in London. 16 *August* 1683. London, 1683. *Narratives of early Pennsylvania, West New Jersey and Delaware 1630–1707.* Albert C. Cook, ed. New York, Charles Scribner's Sons, 1912. 226–27.

[3] *Curieuse Nachricht von Pennsylvania.* The German American Society (Lancaster, Pa.). **14**, (1905), 101.

# VIRGINIA: 1607–1700

The climate of the Jamestown area played a dominant role in compounding the difficulties that beset the first year of the troubled Virginia colony on the tidewater of the Chesapeake Bay region. The main factor, of course, was the long, hot summer of 1607, with its enervating heat and subsequent death-dealing, autumnal fever. Arriving in May and weakened by the usual ills attending a long sea voyage in that era, the emigrants had little resistance to these twin scourges of the climate. By mid-winter of 1607–08 when the first supply vessel arrived, the band of colonists, now existing on a very uneven diet, had been reduced by death from the original 105 to only 32. It soon became a Virginia axiom that, if one could live through his first year, he was "seasoned" and would probably survive for many winters and summers to come.[1]

The winter climate, too, struck a heavy blow at the struggling colony in its first season and again four years later. William Strachey, who spent these years in Virginia, related in his historical account: "In the year 1607–08 was an extraordinary frost in most of Europe, and this frost was as extreme in Virginia." [2] Captain John Smith in his *General History* referred to "the extreme frost of 1607" and "the extremity of the bitter cold." [3] George Percy, who authored the only semblance of a diary of the first year, also blamed the cold winter for being chiefly responsible for the deaths of more than half the colony.[4] No details as to the occurrence of snowfall or the duration of the bitter cold have been left. This season was also severe in Maine where the tiny Sagadahoc Colony struggled through an exceptional northern winter.

The next two winters were more temperate. Strachey continued: "but the next following, and so ever since (he left in 1611), for 8 or 10 days ill weather, we have commonly 14 days fayre and sommery weather." [5] Strachey failed to mention the cold month which came during the crisis winter of 1609–10—the famous starving time—when the population was again decimated by many deaths. The cold of that one unspecified month was thought by Percy to be the equal for severity of any in the first winter of 1607–08.

The most detailed account of the climate in the early days of Virginia came from the pen of Captain John Smith in *A Map of Virginia* published in 1612. Practically the same wording also appeared in *The Historie of Travaile into Virginia Britannia,* a manuscript by Strachey also written about 1612. It is not known who composed the original text. The Smith version follows:

## VIRGINIA

The temperature of this country doth agree well with English constitutions, being once seasoned to the country; which appeared by this, that by many occasions our people fell sick; yet did they recover by very small means, and continued in health, though there were other great causes, not only to have made them sick, but even to end their days.

The summer is as hot as in Spain; the winter cold as in France or England. The heat of summer is in *June, July,* and *August,* but commonly the cool breezes assuage the vehemency of the heat. The chief of the winter is half *December, January, February* and half *March.* The cold is extreme sharp, but here the proverb is true, that no extreme long continues.

In the year 1607–08 was an extraordinary frost in most of Europe, and this frost was found as extreme in Virginia. But the next year for 8 or 10 days of ill weather, other 14 days would be as summer.

The winds here are variable, but the like thunder and lightning to purify the air, I have seldom either seen or heard in Europe. From the Southwest comes the greatest gusts with thunder and heat. The Northwest wind is commonly cool and brings fair weather with it. From the North is the greatest cold, and from the East and Southeast as from the Bermudas, fogs and rains.

> Sometimes there are great droughts, other times much rain.[6]

Smith, who had made journeys into the interior, added an additional climate note:

> ... those mountains. For in the winter they are covered with much snow, and when it dissolves the waters fall with such violence, that it causes great inundation in some narrow valleys, which is scarce perceived being once in the rivers.[7]

Though a number of pamphlets came from the English presses concerning the state of affairs in Virginia during its first score years, nothing new was added concerning the natural history or climate of the region. Smith again republished his Virginia climate material in *The Generall Historie of Virginia, New England, and the Summer Isles* in 1624.[8] His information about New England and Virginia circulated widely for the day. In fact, Smith achieved more for the advancement of British America with his pen than he ever did with sword or political activity.

No consecutive data from a local source as to the nature of individual Virginia winters have been uncovered. The Cavaliers were of a different disposition and intellectual bent than their New England countrymen, mainly as a result of their dissimilar religious and cultural backgrounds and these were perhaps encouraged by the softer nature of their new climate, hence diary-keeping and weather-watching were not the imperative they assumed in New England. There existed a large literature about the unending political wrangles of the Virginia governors, company, and crown, but surprisingly little on everyday life. Philip A. Bruce in his exhaustive two-volume study, *Economic History of Virginia in the Seventeenth Century,* could locate only a few scattered references to the basic subject of climate, and these were of little significance.[9]

In fact, we can learn more about Virginia winters from a New England source, *Winthrop's Journal,* than elsewhere. The Puritan governor noted the simultaneous occurrence of severe conditions in Virginia with those in New England in 1641–42 and in 1645–46. In regard to the first landmark winter, he wrote: "To the southward also the frost was as great and the snow as deep, and at Virginia the great bay was much of it frozen over, and all the rivers, so they lost much cattle for want of hay, and most of the swine." As to 1645–46, he continued: "And in Virginia the ships were frozen six weeks."[10] The close occurrence of the two severe winters in Virginia would be duplicated one hundred and forty years later in 1780 and 1784 when again Chesapeake Bay congealed solidly twice at a similar four-year interval.

That severe winters were not considered common in this portion of the 17th century we learn from the testimony of Sir Thomas Gates who wrote in 1610: "The soil is favorable for the cultivation of vines, sugar canes, oranges, lemons, almonds and rice—the winters are so mild that the cattle can get their food abroad, and swine can be fatted on wild fruits."[11] The practice of not providing for the emergencies that a severe winter season could bring would occasionally cause great hardship in Virginia, as Winthrop pointed out, but this became a Southern way of agricultural life. It would again cause much comment when the two cultures next mixed in the settlement of the Ohio Country toward the close of the 18th century.

Nor were later Virginians much given to worthwhile climatological analysis of their surroundings. Captain John Smith wrote of conditions as he knew them in 1607–09, but none improved on his knowledge till fourscore years had passed. Near mid-century in *A Perfect Description of Virginia* (1649), the author could muster only the following words on the subject of weather and climate: "Our spring begins the tenth of *February,* the trees bud, the grass springs, and our autumn and fall of leaf is in *November,* our winter short, and most years very gentle, snow lies but little, yet ice some years."[12] And in 1676 Thomas Glover, "an ingenious Chiruigion who hath lived some years in that country", forwarded *An Account of Virginia* to the Royal Society of London. He did devote a paragraph to describing the Great Virginia Hurricane of 1667, but failed to include mention of any other weather event and devoted only one line of doubtful validity to describing winter conditions: "Their winter is usually *November, December,* and *January.*[13]

After some eighty years of settlement Virginia did produce a full-scale consideration of the climate written in accordance with the descriptive tenets of the day. Rev. John Clayton's account of the *Air of Virginia* stands with John Josselyn's *Two Voyages* about New England as the only worthwhile climatological documents of the period in English.[14] Clayton was rector of Crofton at Wakefield in Yorkshire, England. He had come to Virginia in the early 1680's at the behest of the Royal Society of London with the specific purpose of making a scientific survey of the natural history of the colony. He was equipped with the latest scientific equipment available. For meteorological observations, he had a thermometer and barometer, and these were dispatched in a second ship to follow him to Virginia. Unfortunately for meteorological posterity, this vessel foundered in a storm and down to the bottom of the sea went thermometer, barometer, and all. Thus, the New World was deprived of the opportunity of having its atmosphere sounded scientifically, and the initiation of instrumental records of the American weather received a postponement for a quarter-of-a-century during which many interesting weather events passed by unmeasured.

Clayton's letter opened with an account of his purpose and methods:

> By sea I lost all my books, chymical Instruments, glasses and Microscopes, which rendered me incapable of making those remarks and observations I had designed, they were all cast away in Captain Win's ship, as they were to follow me; and Virginia being a country where one cannot furnish ones self again with such things, I was discouraged from making so diligent scrutiny as otherwise I might have done. So that I took very few minutes down in writing. And therefore since I have only my memory to rely on, which too has the disadvantage of its own weakness, and of the distance of two years since I now left the country, if future relations shall in some small points, make out my mistake, I thought this requisite to justify my candor. . . .

Concerning the weather and winter climate, Clayton wrote:

> The air and temperature of the seasons is much governed by winds in Virginia, both as to heat and cold, dryness and moisture, whose variations very notable, I the more lament the loss of my barometers and thermometers, for considerable observations might have been made thereby, there being often great and sudden changes.
>
> The Nore and Nore-west are very nitrous and piercing; cold and clear or else stormy. The Southeast and South hazy and sultry hot: their winter is a fine clear air, and dry, which renders it very pleasant. Their frosts are short, but sometimes very sharp, and it will freeze the rivers over three miles broad; nay, the Secretary of State assured me, it had frozen over Potomac River, over against his house, where it is near nine miles over. I have observed it freeze there the hardest, when from a moist Southeast, on a sudden the wind passing by the Nore, a nitrous sharp Nore-west blows; not with high gusts, but with a cutting brisk air; and those vales then that seemed to be sheltered from the wind, and lie warm, where the air is most stagnant and moist, are frozen the hardest and seized the soonest; and there the fruits are more subject to blast than where the air has a free motion. Snow falls sometimes in pretty quantity, but rarely continues there above a day or two. Their spring is about a month earlier than in England. . . .[15]

Just after the turn of the century there appeared the first survey of Virginia affairs written by a native. Robert Beverley's *The History and Present State of Virginia* (written in 1703; published in 1705) has been called the first literary work that is "self-consciously American."[16] In the section dealing with the natural history of the Old Dominion, Beverley portrayed the natural beauty, fertility, and benevolence of the climate in much the same intimate terms that Crevecoeur and Thoreau would do later. He devoted a chapter to the climate and the following were his subheadings:

Chap. XIX. Of the Temperature of the Climate, and the Inconveniences attending it.
77. Of the Natural Temper and Mixture of the Air.
78. Of the Climate, and Happy Situation of the Country in respect to latitude.
79. Of the occasions of its general ill character.
   Of the Rural Pleasures natural to the place.
80. Of all the natural Annoyances, or Occasions of Uneasiness.
   Of the loud Thunders.
   Of the Heat of Summer.
   Of the troublesome Insects, wherein of the Frogs, Snakes, Musketa's, Chinches, Seed-ticks, and Red-worms.
81. Of the Winters.
   Of the sudden Changes of the Weather.

Their winters are very short, and don't continue above three or four months, of which they have seldom thirty days of unpleasant weather, all the rest being blest with a clear air, and a bright Sun. However, they have very hard frosts sometimes, but it rarely lasts above three or four days, that is, till the wind change: for it blows not between the northeast, and northwest points, from the cold Appalachian Mountains, they have no frost at all. But these frosts are attended with a serene sky, and are otherwise made delightful, by the tameness of the wild fowl and other game, which by their incredible number, afford the pleasantest shooting in the world.

Their rains, except in the depth of winter, are extremely agreeable and refreshing. All the summer long they last but a few hours at a time, and sometimes not above half an hour, and then immediately succeeds clear sunshine again; but in that short time it rains so powerfully, that it quits the debt of a long drought, and makes everything green and gay.

I have heard that this country is reproached with sudden and dangerous changes of weather; but that imputation is unjust: For tho' it be true, that in the winter, when the wind comes over those vast mountains to the northwest, which are supposed to retain mightly magazines of ice, and snow, the weather then is very rigorous; yet in spring, summer, and autumn, such winds are only cool and pleasant breezes, which serve to refresh the air, and to correct those excesses of heat, which the situation would otherwise make that country liable to.[17]

---

[1] John Smith. *Travels and works of Captain John Smith President of Virginia and Admiral of New England. 1580–1631.* Edward Arber and A. G. Bradley, eds. Edinburgh, John Grant, 1910. **1**, 48.
[2] William Strachey. *The historie of travaile into Virginia Britannia* (1612?). London, The Hakluyt Society, 1849. Ser. 1, **6**, 30.
[3] Smith, **1**, 103, 104.
[4] Alexander Brown. *The first republic in America.* Boston & New York, Houghton, Mifflin and Co., 1898. 113.
[5] Strachey, 38.
[6] Smith, **1**, 344.
[7] *Ibid.*, 345.
[8] *Ibid.*, **2**, 407.
[9] Philip A. Bruce. *Economic history of Virginia in the Seventeenth Century.* New York, The Macmillan Co., 1907. **1**, 131n.

[10] Winthrop. *Journal.* 2, 73, 311.
[11] Samuel Purchas. *Purchas His Pilgrims.* Glasgow, James MacLehose and Sons, 1905. 19, 72.
[12] *A perfect description of Virginia.* London, 1649. Reprint: *Coll. Mass. Hist. Soc.* (Boston). 2d ser., 9, (1821), 119.
[13] Thomas Glover. An account of Virginia, its scituation, temperature, productions, inhabitants and their manner of planting and ordering tobacco &c. Royal Society of London. *Phil. Trans.* 9–126, June 20, 1676. 633, 635. Reprint: Oxford, H. Hart, 1904.
[14] John Clayton. An account of several observables in Virginia, more particularly concerning the air. May 12, 1686. *Phil. Trans.*, 17, (1693), 784–85.
[15] *Idem.*
[16] Robert Beverly. *The history and present state of Virginia.* London, R. Parker, 1705, 1722. Reprint: Louis B. Wright, ed. Chapel Hill, Univ. North Carolina Press, 1947. xxi.
[17] *Ibid.*, 303–04.

# THE CAROLINAS: 1660–1700

In the first half of the 17th Century when New England, New Netherland, New Sweden, Maryland, and Virginia were receiving settlers, the Carolina coastline remained unoccupied. The proximity of the Spanish in Florida, no doubt, had much to do with this, and its reputation for heat and hurricanes also played a part. But soon after 1650 Virginians commenced to filter southward overland and small communities grew on the northern reaches of Albemarle Sound. In fact, North Carolina in these days was called Albemarle.

The shoreline to the southward was thoroughly explored by the mid-1660's, and by 1670 two settlements were in being: one at Cape Fear in extreme southeastern North Carolina, the other on the Ashley River called Old Charles Town. The South Carolina capital was moved to the junction of the Ashley and Cooper rivers in 1680, and Charleston became the principal settlement of the area. By 1700 several other settlements were established on the many bays and rivers that make up the plantation country.

The Carolina climate played a role both in attracting and in repelling settlers. Visitors from the North or England who arrived only for a brief stay in summer took away a rather disparaging view of the local weather. But again, as in Virginia, anyone "seasoned" to the climate, *i.e.,* immune to the prevailing fevers, found it livable and pleasant. Though no day-to-day account of weather conditions in diary form for early Carolina has come to light, several interesting climatological documents, written mainly in defense of the questioned salubrity of the region, have survived, and these do make passing mention of winter conditions. In lieu of more detailed data, these are presented in full so far as they concern winter:

## CAROLINA: ROBERT HORNE?

Last of all, the Air comes to be considered, which is not the least considerable to the well being of a Plantation, for without a wholsom Air, all other considerations avail nothing; and this is it which makes this Place so desireable, being seated in the most temperate Clime, where the neighborhood of the Glorious Light of Heaven brings many advantages, and his convenient distance secours them from the Inconvenience of his scorching beams. The Summer is not too hot, and the Winter is very short and moderate, best agreeing with English constitutions.[1]

## CAROLINA: THOMAS ASHE

The air so serene and excellent a temper, that the Indian natives prolong their days to the extremity of old age. And where the English hitherto have found no distempers either epidemical or mortal, but what have had their rise from excess or origine from intemperance. In July and August they have sometimes touches of agues and fevers, but not violent, of short continuance, and never fatal. English children there born, are commonly strong and lusty, of sound constitutions, and fresh ruddy complexions. The seasons are regularly disposed according to natures laws; the summer not so torrid, hot and burning as that of their Southern, nor winter so rigorously sharp and cold, as that of their Northern neighbors. In the evenings and mornings of December and January, thin congealed ice, with hoary frosts sometimes appear; but as soon as the sun elevates herself, above the horizon, as soon they disappear and vanish; snow having been seen but twice in ten years, or from its first being settled by the English.[2]

## CAROLINA: SAMUEL WILSON

The eastern shore of America, whether it be by reason of its having the great body of the continent to the westward of it, and by consequence the northwest wind (which flows contrary to the sun) the freezing-wind, as the northeast is in Europe, or that the frozen lakes which lie-in, beyond Canada, and lie north and west from the shore, impregnate the freezing wind with more chill and congealing qualities, or that the uncultivated earth, covered for the most part with large shading trees, breathes forth more nitrous vapors, than that which is cultivated; or for all these reasons together, it is certainly much more cold than any part of Europe, in the same degree of latitude of thirty nine and forty, and England and those parts of America about the latitude of thirty nine and forty, and more north, though about six hundred miles nearer the Sun than England; is notwithstanding many degrees colder in the winter.

The author having been informed by those that say they have seen it, that in those parts it freezeth above six inches thick in a night, and great navigable rivers are frozen over in the same space of time; and the country about Ashley River, though within nine degrees of the tropic, hath seldom any winter that doth not produce some ice, though I cannot yet learn that any hath been seen on rivers or ponds, above a quarter of an inch, which vanishes as soon as the Sun is an hour or two high; and when the wind is not at northwest, the weather is very mild. So that the December and January of Ashley River, I suppose to be of the same temperature with the latter end of March, and beginning of April in England. This small winter causes a fall of the leaf, and adapts the country to the production of all the grains and fruits of England, as well as those that require more Sun; in so much that at Ashley River the apple, the pear, the plum, the quince, apricot, peach, medlar, walnut, mulberry and chestnut thrive very well in the same garden together with the orange, the lemon, olive, the pomgranate, the fig and almond; nor is the winter here cloudy, overcast or foggy, but it hath been observed that from the twentieth of August to the tenth of March, including all the winter months, there have been but eight overcast days; and though rains fall pretty often in the winter, it is most commonly in quick showers, which when past, the Sun shines out clear again.

The summer is not near so hot as in Virginia or the other Northern American English Colonies, which may hardly gain belief with those that have not considered the reason; which is its nearness to the tropics, which makes it in a greater measure than in those parts more northward partake of those breezes, which almost constantly rise about eight or nine of the clock, within the tropics, and blow fresh from the east till about four in the afternoon; and a little after the sea breeze dies away, there rises a north wind, which blowing all night, keps it fresh and cool. In short, I take Carolina, to be much of the same nature with those delicious countries about Aleppo, Antioch, and Smyrna: but hath the advantage of being under an equal English Government.[3]

## NORTH CAROLINA: JOHN LAWSON

Lastly, as to the climate, it is very healthful; our summer is not so hot as in other places to the eastward in the same latitude; neither are we ever visited by earthquakes, as many places in Italy and other summer-countries are. Our northerly winds, in summer, cool the air, and free us from pestilential fevers, which Spain, Barbary, and the neighboring countries in Europe, &c. are visited withal. Our sky is generally serene and clear, and the air very thin, in comparison of many parts of Europe, where consumptions and catarrhs reign amongst the inhabitants. The winter has several fitts of sharp weather, especially when the wind is at N.W. which always clears the sky, though never so thick before. However, such weather is very agreeable to European bodies, and makes them healthy. The N.E. winds blowing in winter, bring with them thick weather, and, in the spring sometimes, blight the fruits; but they very seldom endure long, being blown away by westerly winds, and then all becomes fair and clear again. Our spring in Carolina is very beautiful, and the most pleasant weather a country can enjoy. The fall is accompanied with cool mornings, which come in towards the latter end of August, and so continue (most commonly) very moderate weather till about Christmas; then winter comes on apace. Though these seasons are very piercing, yet the cold is of no continuance. Perhaps you will have cold weather for three or four days at a time, then pleasant, warm follows such as you have in England, about the latter end of April or beginning of May. In the year 1707, we had the severest winter in Carolina, that ever was known since the English came to settle there; for our rivers, that were not above half a mile wide, and fresh water, were frozen over, and some of them, in the north part of this country, were passable for people to walk over.[4]

## OF THE AIR OF CAROLINA: MARK CATESBY

. . . The Winter-Months are so moderate, and the Air so serene, that it sufficiently compensates for the Heats in Summer, in which it has the Advantage of all our other Colonies on the Continent; even in Virginia, tho' joining to Carolina, the winters are so extreme cold, and the Frosts so intense, that James River, where it is three Miles wide, is sometimes frozen over in one Nighe, so as to be passed. The coldest winds in Carolina usually blow from the North west, which in December and January produce some Days of Frost, but the Sun's Elevation soon dissipates and allays the Sharpness of the wind, so that the Days are moderately warm, tho' the Nights are cold; after three or four Days of such weather usually follow warm Sunshiny Days, thus it continues many Days with some Intervals of cloudy weather, which is succeeded by moderate soaking Showers of Rain, continuing not often longer than a Day, then the Air clears up with a sudden shift of wind from South to North-west, which again usually brings cold Days, and so on.

Tho' in the beginning of February some few Trees and smaller Plants decorate the woods with their Blossoms, yet the Spring makes but slow Progress till the Beginning of April, when it advances suddenly with frequent Rains.[5]

\* \* \* \* \*

The Northern Continent of America is much colder than those Parts of Europe which are parallel to it in Latitude; this is evident from the mortal Effects the Frosts have on many Plants in Virginia, that grow and stand the Winters in England, tho' 15 Degrees more North; and what confirms this is the violent and sudden freezing of large Rivers, as before mentioned.

Admitting these Circumstances, that in the northernmost part of our Island the Frosts are not more intense than in Virginia, it will then appear that the Winters in Virginia, tho' in the Latitude of 37 Degrees North, and parallel with the South Part of Spain, are as cold as in the North Part of Scotland, which is in the Latitude of 57, that is, 20 Degrees more North.

This great Disparity of Climate holds throughout our Northern Colonies: Newfoundland, and the South of Hudson's Bay being not habitable for Cold, tho' in the Latitude of the South Parts of England.

The Frosts of Carolina and Virginia continue not long without Intervals of warmer Weather, yet by their ill Effects cause a Deficiency of many useful Productions, which Countries in the same Latitude in Europe are blessed with, such as Wine, Oil, Dates, Oranges, and many things impatient of hard Frost.

There has indeed of late been some Efforts toward the making of Wine in both Virginia and Carolina, the Success of which, time will discover.

Some Oranges there are in Carolina, but in the Maritime Parts only. I never saw or heard of one produced ten Miles from Salt Water. Such is the great Difference of Temperature between the Maritime Parts, and those distant from the Sea, as the following instance may serve to illustrate.

Accomack is a narrow Slip of Land in Virginia, having the Sea on one Side, and the Bay of Chesapeck on the other, here I saw Fig-trees, with Trunks of a large Size, and of many Years standing, without any Injury received by hard Weather. On the opposite Shore were only Fig-trees of a very small Size, occasioned by their often being killed to the Ground.

Yet this is not so remarkable as that the same Kind of Tree will not endure the Cold of Carolina five Miles distant from the Sea, so well as at Acomack [sic], tho' five or six Degrees North of it.

Many, or most Part of the Trees and Shrubs in Carolina, retain their Verdure all Winter, tho' in most of the low and herbacious Plants, Nature has required a Respite; so that the Grass, and what appears on the Ground, looks withered and rusty, from October to March.[5]

[1] Robert Horne? *A brief description of the province of Carolina.* London, 1666. Reprint: *Narratives of early Carolina 1650–1708.* Alexander S. Salley, ed. New York, Charles Scribner's Sons, 1911. 70.

[2] Thomas Ashe. *Carolina, or a description of the present state of that country.* London, 1682. Reprint: *ibid.,* 141.

[3] Samuel Wilson. *An account of the province of Carolina.* London, 1682. Reprint: *ibid.* 167–69.

[4] John Lawson. *History of North Carolina.* London, 1709 and 1714. Richmond, Va., Garrett and Massie, 1951. 88–89.

[5] Mark Catesby. *Natural history of Carolina, Florida, and the Bahama Islands.* 2 v. London, 1731 and 1743. **2**, i–iii.

# THE NORTHEAST IN THE EIGHTEENTH CENTURY

The Three Landmark Winters of the Century .................. 39

John Pike's Winter Chronology: 1701–1710 .................. 40

Two Severe Winters Back-to-Back: 1704–05 & 1705–06 ........ 41

The Great Snow: February/March 1717 ..................... 42

The Severe Winter of 1719–20 ............................ 46

The Severe Winter of 1732–33 ............................ 47

Hard Winter in 1740–41 .................................. 48

Winter of the Deep Snows: 1747–48 ....................... 55

The Severe Winter of 1764–65 ............................ 60

Snowy March in 1772 .................................... 63

The Long Winter of 1783–84 .............................. 64

Winter Comes Late in 1785 ............................... 67

Triple Big Snows in Early December 1786 .................. 68

A Severe January in 1792 ................................ 73

The Long Winter of 1798–99 .............................. 74

Cold Days of the Century ................................ 76

Early Snows of the Century .............................. 80

Late Snows of the Century ............................... 82

Samuel Lane's Chronology of New Hampshire Winters: 1737–1799 83

# THE THREE LANDMARK WINTERS OF THE CENTURY

During the second century of settlement, two winters stood out above all others, and these were employed by contemporaries to judge the degree of severity of those coming before or after. At the close of the previous century, the season of 1697–98 had made an indelible impression upon all. Peter Kalm found old people employing it as a reference even at mid-century of the 1700's.[1] But for those born after that memorable season, the winter of 1740–41 assumed the role of the most talked about "old-fashioned winter."

For the next 40 years this season held first place unchallenged when one wished to evoke the memory of a long and severe winter. Not until 1779–80, when the Nation was deep in its War of Independence, did an equal come along to usurp the revered role held by 1740–41. Then several mature historians, who had experienced the rigors of both, gave the nod to the more recent.[2] Long afterward it was referred to as "The Hard Winter"—and this appellation seemed well deserved since no season to the present day has produced such a long continuance of unbroken cold conditions preceded by such a combination of heavy snowstorms. Some weather-watchers believed that the first winter following the close of the war, 1783–84, had a more rigorous character in their particular sections, but this had a much different type of climatic conditions with alternate periods of cold and thaw, deep snow cover and bare ground, but lacking the complete domination of Arctic conditions that The Hard Winter of 1779–80 produced over the entire eastern half of the now United States.[3]

The classification of winters of the Eighteenth Century as to their relative severity or mildness prior to the commencement after 1780 of regular weather observations with accurate thermometers, proper exposure, stated hours, and uniform methods of reduction must remain on a subjective basis. There is always the chance that some historical detail has been overlooked, especially in the first half of the century, which would radically alter our opinion of the season. In the main, the best criteria to follow are the freezing over of bodies of water usually open all winter to navigation, or the long continuance of deep snow cover, or an unusual postponement in the normal date of the spring break-up. The following paragraphs attempt to list the winters outstanding either for severity or mildness.

The winters of the century qualifying for the *very severe* classification were: 1704–05, 1705–06, 1719–20, 1732–33, 1740–41, 1747–48, 1764–65, 1779–80, 1783–84, and 1798–99.

Among those which might deserve a *severe* designation were: 1707–08, 1711–12, 1725–26, 1726–27, 1727–28, 1734–35, 1751–52, 1756–57, 1760–61, 1761–62, 1763–64, 1771–72, 1776–77, 1781–82, 1784–85, and 1791–92.

On the other hand, there were a number of open winters which should be placed in the *very mild* category: 1706–07, 1708–09, 1733–34, 1737–38, 1739–40, 1742–43, 1744–45, 1745–46, all four from 1752–53 to 1755–56, 1769–70, 1770–71, 1774–75, 1778–79, 1780–81, most from 1786–87 to 1794–95 with the exception of 1791–92. Among the latter, 1789–90 and 1794–95 were outstanding for continued warmth.[4]

[1] *Peter Kalm's travels in North America.* London, 1770. Reprint: New York, Wilson, 1937. **1**, 277.

[2] *The literary diary of Ezra Stiles.* Franklin B. Dexter, ed. New York, Scribner's Sons, 1901. **2**, 402.

N. Webster. Notices of extraordinary seasons of cold. *Amer. Jour. Sci.* (New Haven). **28**, (July 1835), 185.

Ebenezer Hazard to Jeremy Belknap, 10 Mar 1780. The Belknap Papers. *Coll. Mass. Hist. Soc.* 5th. ser., **2**, (1877), 36.

Thomas Jefferson. *Notes on the state of Virginia.* London, 1787. Reprint: William Peden, ed. Chapel Hill, Univ. of North Carolina Press, 1955. 78.

[3] *The journals of Henry M. Muhlenberg.* Phila., The Muhlenberg Press, 1945. **3**, 574.

William D. Williamson. *The history of the State of Maine.* Hallowell, Glazier, Masters & Co., 1832. **1**, 100.

[4] See chronology for further details.

# JOHN PIKE'S CHRONOLOGY OF WINTERS: 1701-1710

### 1700-01

Snows: Nov. 22; Dec. 5, 10, 14, 25; Jan. 12, 17, 24—issued in warm rain, 27, 31—very stormy, issued in rain; Feb. 4, 10—both very stormy, 19, 21—issued in rain, 23, 26, 28; March 8, 14, 25, 28; April 3, 7.

### 1701-02

Snows: Nov. 8; Dec. 4, 5, 30, 31; Jan. 9, 14, 18, 22, 23, 24, 29; Feb. 1, 2, 4—issued in rain, 8, 9, 10, 15, 17; March 1, 6, 14, 17, 20; April 3.

### 1702-03

Snows: Dec. 1—issued in rain, 11, 18, 19—very cold and stormy; Jan. 2, 25, 26, 30, 31; Feb. 3; March 17, 23, 26.

### 1703-04

First snow Oct 9—very cold. Oct. 17, 18, 19—very cold storm of rain; Nov. 4—very fine warm sabbath, 11—very cold, windy sabbath.

Snows: Nov. 13, 21, 25, 30; Dec. 2, 9, 14; Jan. 6—very cold, windy, stormy, 14, 21, 27, 30; Feb. 11, 18; March 2, 12, 18.

Winter began Nov. 11 and ended March 18. Dec. 3 a poor man lost his life going after his team in the night between Boston and Roxbury. That day and the next were extremely cold and windy.

### 1704-05

Nov. 9—extreme northwest wind, cold and black—sabbath day.

Snows: Nov. 21, 22, 23—very cold, windy sabbath, 24—very cold, issued in a great rain, 28 mild; Dec. 7—very stormy, 28—sabbath, very cold; Jan. 2—cold, 5—cold, 16, 22, 26—very stormy and searching, 29; Feb. 4, 19; March 14—issued in great rain, 15 and 22; April 23, 27—very cold windy storm.

Winter began Nov. 21 and began to break up March 1.

*March* was for the most part fine and dry; *April* cold and windy; *May* very wet; the summer following we had very often wet weather on the sabbath day.

### 1705-06

Snows: Nov. 2—very cold, windy, stormy; Dec. 5, 7, 10, 29—next day very windy and cold; Jan. 2—very cold, windy, stormy, 9, 14, 16; Feb. 3, 7, 10—very stormy, drifty, and cold; March 1, 3—extreme windy, hail, rain, 7—issued in rain, 9—followed with cold, 27—issued in rain, 31; April 7, 23—very cold.

This year the winter began to set in hard about Nov. 21—began to break up Candlemas Day (Feb. 13).

Most part of *April* and *May* was stormy, wet, cold, cloudy weather. The summer following pretty hot. The coldest was Jan. 5, the hottest day was July 10.

### 1706-07

Snows: Nov. 28, 29; Dec. 9—issued in rain; 17, 19, 23—cold, windy; Jan. 9—cold, 22, 23, 24, 25, 26—great storm began 22, last day was very stormy; Feb. 4—stormy, 9, 13, 18, 25, 28; March 7, 16; April 6.

This year the winter began to set in hard about Dec. 15—began to break up about the 13th of March. No deep snows—many rains and thaws. A moderate winter, and fine spring. Summer following very fruitful. Fall very dry. Coldest day of the winter was Jan. 17. The summer passed without any extreme hot day. Sept. 5 was one of the hottest.

### 1707-08

Snows: Nov. 22; Dec. 15, 16, 17; Jan. 5, 16—very stormy, 18—with high, cold northwest wind, 27, 28—very black, cold, N.E. wind; Feb. 21, 22, 23-24—very cold, black, N.E. wind; March 1, 20, 22—very stormy; April 5—followed with violent cold, high N.W. winds.

This winter began to set in hard about 30th December—began to break about February 7th (though we had some winter-like weather till the later end of *March*). Snows not so deep nor so many this winter as formerly, but the weather extreme cold. *Spring* cold, wet, backward. *Summer* following very hot and dry—so likewise was the *fall*: by which means hay and corn were cut exceeding short. Coldest day in the winter was the 13 January if the April 6 did not exceed it. Hottest day in the summer was July 13.

### 1708-09

Snows: Dec. 10, 15, 20—extreme cold, N.E. wind—next day very high N.W. cold and squally, 24; Jan. 5—followed with fine weather, 11—issued in rain, 27—very stormy, 30—moist; Feb. 2, 4, 9, 13—followed with fine evening, 14—dreadful stormy, high N.E. wind, next day N.W., 16—very still, calm, 13—very cold, stormy; Apr. 14—sabbath morning.

*Winter* began Nov. 16. *November* and *December* very cold and hard. *January* very moderate. Greatest snow fell February 14. Snow not extreme deep this winter. *Spring* somewhat cold and backward. *Summer* and fall very dry. Coldest day in the winter was December 6. Hottest day in the summer following was the 30th of July.

### 1709–10

This year an extraordinary cold storm of rain fell out about the midst of August; next day very warm and fine.

Flits of snow Dec. 2 and 5, 13—harsh, 17—flit, moist; Jan. 2, 16, 29—issued in rain; Feb. 4, 19; March 1, 7—very stormy.

(Rev. John Pike died on 21 March 1710.)

## TWO SEVERE WINTERS BACK-TO-BACK: 1704-05 & 1705-06

Winter commenced on November 21st, according to Rev. John Pike's record, when snow fell in southeastern New Hampshire for three consecutive days with "very cold" days following on the 23d and 24th—a situation which would be repeated in 1798. In December very stormy conditions prevailed on the 6th and very cold on the 28th. January produced the stormiest month of the winter with snows on the 16th, 22d, 26th, and 29th. The snow on the 26th was described by Pike as "very stormy and searching." February had only two snows. March was "for the most part fine and dry," but then the circulation changed with April "cold and windy." [1]

This season was long remembered at Philadelphia for its deep snows. The Pennsylvania post arrived at New York on March 1st, apparently after a long delay, with the report that there had been very deep snows to the westward and no traveling for weeks.[2] Peter Kalm, the Swedish visitor and author, who took an avid interest in the history of the American climate, later wrote: "many stags, birds, and other animals died, and that the snow was nearly a yard deep." [3] This later found its way into many histories and was construed to the effect that the snow fell in a single storm to the depth of a yard. It would seem that Kalm meant the maximum snow cover "was nearly a yard deep." Further evidence came from the diary of Isaac Norris: "We have had the deepest snow this winter, that has been known by the longest English liver here. No travelling; all avenues shut; the post has not gone these six weeks; the river fast; and the people bring loads over it as they did seven years ago [1697–98]." [4] Rev. Sandel in his reminiscences corroborated Norris: "In 1704, in the later part of November and December, and in January, 1705, we had many great and lasting snow-storms. Few persons could remember such a severe winter." [5]

The major storm of the season occurred on January 25–26th. This was Pike's "very stormy and searching" day. The history of the event can best be followed in the press dispatches appearing in America's first successful newspaper in English, the *Boston News-Letter*, then in its initial year of publication:

Boston: Jan. 26
 On sabbath the 25th instant at noon began a great storm of snow, the wind being at North-East, and continues still at the printing on Monday morning.[6]

Newport: Feb. 5.
 On sabbath the 25th instant, began here a great storm the wind at S.E. and continued till next day which caused a tide to rise here two foot higher than ever was known, which has done near 1400£ damage to this place and drowned 17 sheep of Connonicut's.[7]

Salem: Jan. 31
 No travelling—tide on 26th "at least 14 inches higher than has been known in 20 years past—much damage—nobody has come from Boston since the storm (five days).[8]

John Pike in his regular diary also made special mention of the storm:

Jan, 26—Happened the highest tide that ever was observed in these parts of the country. Did great damage to warehouses and cellars; carried away some houses and many stages at Isle of Shoals; transported many hay stacks, and in some places tore up great quantities of marsh and removed it far off into other places.[9]

A final note from Samuel Sewall's diary indicated that the wintry conditions continued into April over a month after the spring equinox:

April 23 1705. Thanksgiving Day. The night was so cold that was a very great frost, thick ice, and the street frozen like in winter. Remained frozen at noon in shady places of the street. Mr. Melyen had a great tub of water frozen so hard, that it bore two men standing upon it in his sight.[10]

[1] John Pike, Observable Seasons, *N. H. Hist. Coll.,* **3**, 66.
[2] New York 11 Mar, in *Boston News-Letter, 12 Mar 1705.*
[3] *Peter Kalm's travels,* **7**, 311.
[4] Logan Ms. in John F. Watson. *Annals of Philadelphia and Pennsylvania in the olden time.* Phila., Elish Thomas, 1856 & 1860. **2**, 349.
[5] Nicholas Collin. Observations made at an early period, on the climate of the country about River Delaware. *Trans. Amer. Philo. Soc.* ns. **1**, (1818), 351.
[6] *Boston News-Letter, 15 Jan 1705.*
[7] *Ibid., 5 Feb 1705.*
[8] *Ibid., 12 Feb 1705.*
[9] J. Pike, **3**, 66.
[10] S. Sewall, *Diary,* **2**, 128.

Following on the heels of the cold winter of 1704–05, came a second severe season that combined extreme cold with frequent and deep snows. John Pike at Dover, New Hampshire, has given a capsule comment on the season:

> Snows, Nov. 2, very cold, windy, stormy; Dec. 4, 6, and 9; Dec. 30, next day very windy and cold; Jan. 2, very cold, windy, stormy, 9, 14, 16; Feb. 3, 7, 10, very stormy, drifty, and cold; 29, 31, extreme windy, hail, rain; Mar. 8, issued in rain, 10, followed with cold; 27, issued in rain, 31; Apr. 7, 23, very cold.
> This year the winter began to set in hard about November 30th—began to break up *Candlemas Day* (Feb. 13). Most part of *April* and *May* very stormy, wet, cold, cloudy weather. Coldest day Jan. 5.[1]

The Boston press mentioned the heavy snow on January 2–3. This was followed by a cold *Christmas Day*, and then on the 6th "there fell a pritty deal of snow."[2] Rev. Cotton Mather noticed: "there came upon us a very cold season."[3] Alternate snows and thaws followed during January and February, but the deep snow cover was not entirely carried off the streets of Boston until early March.[4]

Down at New York City the frigid wave at *Christmastime* was thought by contemporaries to have been the coldest ever felt there. Hudson River froze over completely and continued fast for "several days."[5] The severest part of the cold wave lasted three days. The onset of the Arctic regime on Dec. 30th was made memorable by *A Winter Tragedy* when a "private ship of war" grounded in the northwest gale when trying to clear Sandy Hook and 132 members of the crew froze to death before assistance arrived.[6] See A Winter Anthology at end of volume.

## SAMUEL SEWALL: 1705–06

Dec. 5. Snow falls and covers the ground. Has been very cold weather this week.
29. Great rain.
Jan. 2. Very great snow.
5. [*Christmas Day*] Very cold day but serene morning. Sleds, sleighs, and horses pass as usually, and shops open.
30. Very cold weather.
Feb. 3. Storm of snow.
9. Extraordinary storm; yet at noon I rode to John Russell's with very great difficulty by reason of the snow and hail beating on my forehead and eyes hindering my sight, and the extravagant banks of snow the streets were filled with.
12. Much ice in River.
Flood in late *February* when rivers broke up.
Mar. 27. A storm of snow.[7]

[1] J. Pike, **3**, 66.
[2] *Boston News-Letter*, 31 Dec 1705.
[3] Cotton Mather, *Diary*, **1**, 529.
[4] *News-Letter*, 18 Feb 1706.
[5] *Ibid.*, 21 Jan 1706.
[6] New York, *4 Jan,* ibid., *7 Jan 1706*.
[7] Samuel Sewall, *Diary*, **2**, 142–156.

# THE GREAT SNOW: *FEBRUARY/MARCH 1717*

There is probably no event of a non-political nature in New England's history that has acquired such a reverential status as the Great Snow of 1717. Accounts appear in many local, state, and even national histories written in the 1700's and 1800's. Over the years it provided a conversation piece whenever a heavy snowstorm came along. Certainly, newspaper editors created a lot of copy by comparing its legendary reputation with contemporary storms. In this connection, Henry Thoreau took another swing at his favorite ideological punching bag, Rev. Cotton Mather, who in a much-published, contemporary letter had described some of the unusual events that took place during the Great Snow. "He little thought," wrote Thoreau chidingly, "that his simple testimony to such facts . . . would be worth all the philosophy he might dream of."[1]

The commencement of winter 1716–17 had been fairly severe with snow and ice at an early date. But an earlier-than-normal January thaw introduced three weeks of spring-like weather and this extended on into February.[2] It looked as though there would be an early spring. Some even hopefully planted beans and peas. At New London in Connecticut the season was described as "very moderate," and people were "comforting themselves on having gotten through the winter."[3] But, as New Englanders have learned over the years, winter

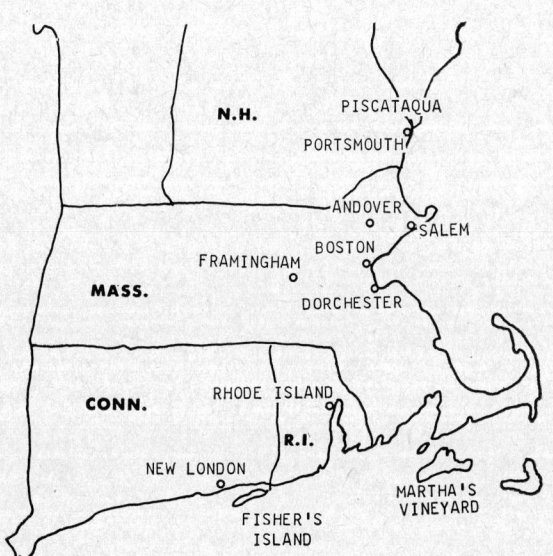

takes a reluctant leave of the region. Early March often brings "the crown of winter storm."

The basic pattern of the Great Snow is well told in the entries of Judge Samuel Sewall, the eminent Boston diarist of the period, who noted most of the major weather events from 1675 to his death in 1730. The dates are corrected to New Style to conform with our present seasonal calendar:

Feb. 27. Is a great storm of Snow and Sleet.
28. Serene.
March 1. Great Storm of Snow; yet good going under foot.
2. Serene. Cold. Snow blows.
3. Another snow coming on.
4. Extraordinary storm of snow.
5. It was terribly surprising to me to see the extraordinary banks of Snow on the side of the way.
6. Serene and pleasant.
7. Violent storm of snow.[4]

Rev. Cotton Mather, as usual, saw some theological significance in the current adversities of Nature, in that they caused his flock to miss two Sabbath assemblies in a row. His diary entries at this time convey some of the essence of the snow scene:

Mar. 11. As mighty a snow, as perhaps has been known in the memory of man, is at this time lying on the ground; and as mighty a thaw must be looked for.
Mar. 18. This a time of much rebuke from Heaven upon us, in the season. Such storms and heaps of snow, visit us in the approach of spring, as were hardly ever known in the depth of winter. A great part of the assemblies in the country have been interdicted their public sacrifices. A multitude of cattle have perished. The business of the country has an uncommon stop upon it. Many difficulties grow upon us. I would procure a day of humiliations and supplication to be kept upon these occasions.
Mar. 19. Many people are thrown into straits and wants, by the difficulty of the season; I would both express and excite all suitable expression of charity on these occasions.[5]

The storms were northeasters and also affected areas along the coast to the southward. At Philadelphia the river was full of floating ice at this time, and reports to the Boston press described "a great snow upon."[6] At New London, Joshua Hempstead, who maintained a famous farmer's diary of terse, daily entries, made note of the series of storms:

### February 1717

13. Much Snow last night & Rain. Misty & Cloudy till about 3 aftern yn fair. it was warm in ye forept & Colder toward night.
14. fair moderate till near night yn Cold. SW. Mr. ad pr al d. [Mr. Adams preached all day].
15. fair & Bitter Cold.
17. Snow in ye foren.
18. Snowy.
19. fair.
20. fair.
21. fair. Mr. ad. pr al day. A Thawing day.
22. Lowering till toward night it Rained hard.
23. Cloudy & Windy fair Cold.
24. fair Cold.
25. fair Cloudy.
26. Stormy.
27. Rainy Snow al d. a Stiddy Rain & Snow.
28. fair.

### March 1717

1. Snow in ye forept of the day.
2. fair Cold.
3. fair till the Evening & yn Snow.
4. A great Storm of Snow. itt is said to be 4 foot deep in ye woods on a Level. itt Snowed al last Night. knee deep in ye Morning. itt Continued Snowing al. day tht the drifts were So high thr was no passing to an fro for man or beast. ye wind blew very hard the drifftts in Some places higher yn a mans head. I was att home al day. Ben fox & Jno Pendall broke through from Dennis's hiether & lodged here.
5. fair very windy. ye Snow is drove in Some places 10 or 12 foot deep. a Cold day. Wm Lathams New Sloop is drove a Shore in his Coave bilged filled & overset. Woostters open Sloop is drove out of ye harbour Bound for Easternpoint. got into ye Coave Recd no Damage. I was at home al day.
6. fair more Moderate. I was at home al day.
7. it Snowed Smartly last night & this morn windy & Cold. No Meeting. I kept house al day. many horses & Cattell are dead wth ye Storm.
8. fair. I was at home al day. more Moderate.
9. fair. I was in Town Most of the day. Moderate.
10. fair Pleasant. I was at home al d.
11. Snow last night & most of ye day. a moist Snow. I was at home al day.
12. fair Pleasant. I was at home & up Town most of ye day.
13. Rainy. I was at home al day. it Snowed last night & ys morn.
14. fair Moderate. Mr. Adams pr. al. d. a thin appearance.
15. fair.
16. fair most of ye d. it drifted in ye morn & Snowed Last night.
17. fair ye foren. Storm of Snow & Rain aftern.
18. Cloudy Cold & Windy. Ensign George Way was buried brought by men on Snow Shoes, he hath been dead 10 or 12 days.

19. fair Most of ye day some Snow Squalls.
20. Cold & windy.
21. pleasant.
22. Cloudy.
23. fair.
24. fair.
25. fair.
26. fair.
27. fair. Cold.
28. fair. mr adams Pr al day.
29. fair. Moderate.
30. Misty & Rainy.
31. Cloudy. little Wind.

### April 1717

1. Cloudy.
4. Mr ad. pr. al. d. Moderate.
5. Rain.
6. fair till Near Night & yn Snow.
7. fair.
8. fair.
9. fair Most of ye day Scatering Rain. little wind.
10. fair.
11. fair. Mr. adams Pr al day.

## THE *BOSTON NEWS-LETTER* REPORTS THE GREAT SNOW

(Dates are corrected to New Style)

New York, 5 March: We have now severe winter, our river full of ice and have had a hard Northeast since Thursday last (1 March) which still continues.

New London, 3 March: We have had a great storm of snow, two sloops were forced from their anchors ashore upon the Rockes.

Rhode Island, 5 March: On Monday last (1 March) we had a violent Northeast storm of wind and snow: and on Wednesday night till this morning (5 March) we had another extraordinary storm of wind and snow, the deepest snow that has been seen for several years past.

Boston, 8 March: Besides several snows, we had a great one on Monday, the 1st currant; and on Wednesday the 3d it began to snow about noon, and continued snowing until Friday the 5th, so that the snow lies in some parts of the streets about six foot high.

Saturday last (6 March) was a clear sunshine, not a cloud to be seen till toward the evening. And the Lord's Day the 7th a deep snow.

No vessels are arrived this week.

The extremeity of the weather has hindered all the three posts from coming in; neither can they be expected until the roads (now impassable with a mighty snow upon the ground) are beaten.

Piscataqua, 12 March: The deep snow hindered our post from coming in till yesterday; the snow is said to be five feet deep on a level up in the country: we travel here altogether on snow shoes, horses not being able to pass.

Boston, 15 March: *February* ended with snow, and *March* begins with it, the snow so deep there is no travelling.

The great snow on the ground has still hindered any of the posts coming in.

Ships cleared this week, but there were no arrivals.

Philadelphia, 16 March: Our river has been full of ice again, and we have as winter like weather as any we have had, and a great snow upon.

Boston, 22 March: The bad weather and the deep snow upon the ground hindered all three of our posts coming in, on Saturday the 6th; and also on Saturday the thirteenth of this instant March; and with great difficulty the Southern post came in on Wednesday noon (17 March) on foot, no travelling for horses, who also brought the Western posts Mayle; and in order (if possible) to regain part of the lost time, the Southern and Western Mayles were sent out again on Thursday the 18th currant to return on Saturday the 27th instant.

The Eastern post went out on the (2d of March), and with snow shoes got to Piscataqua the eleventh, he came from thence the 12th at noon: and got hither with his Mayle and snow shoes on Friday noon the 19th: He says that in the woods the snow is five feet deep, and in some places between 6 and 14 feet deep; he sets out again on Monday night the 22d instant at five o'clock, to return in course.

Rhode Island, 25 March: Such a violent storm of deep snow as has been here of late, was never known before, by the Oldest Livers.

New London, 29 March: The weather has been very severe here; and travelling yet very bad.

Boston, 5 April: The deep snow upon the ground hindered the Eastern posts coming till Monday night last the 29th, who was dispatched out again on Tuesday noon, in order if possible to return in course on Saturday, the 3d April. The Southern post came in late on Saturday night, who also brought the Western Mayle, in return of that sent out on Thursday night the eighteenth currant, being hindered by the deep snow on the ground.

The Eastern post not yet come in, but expected hourly.

Boston, 12 April: On Tuesday morning (6 April) the Eastern post came in, the roads still being very deep with snow and bad travelling, and was dispatched out again that afternoon, in order, if possible, to return in course.

The Western post not yet come in, on Monday morning the twelfth April, but hourly expected; in order to set out at six o'clock at night, with the Southern and Eastern post to return in course.

Boston, 19 April: All three posts are in and set out on Monday night at six o'clock.

### HOW DEEP?

How deep did the snow fall during the nine-day period from 27 February to 7 March when the four storms, two of them of major stature, occurred? The *News-Letter's* report that "the snow lies in some parts of the streets about six foot high," no doubt was a reference to drifts and piles of snow which had fallen off roofs.[8] Another much-quoted account told of snow 15 to 20 feet deep and piled up against buildings over the second story window.[9] These indicated the severe drifting in the high winds accompanying the northeasters and must be discounted as trustworthy meteorological measurements.

There were two contemporary references that are now helpful in arriving at a reasonable figure. The Blanchard manuscripts described the snow as "four feet deep, very close and hard" at Andover, some 15 miles north of Boston.[10] An account from Dorchester, immediately south of Boston, told of drifts 25 feet high, but stated "in the woods a yard generally on the level." [11] The latter figure would seem reasonable, well within what is known to be meteorologically possible in the Boston area for a series of such storms if concentrated in a like nine-day period. But such a depth has not been achieved in the 95-year history of the Boston Weather Bureau.

Further evidence was given by Dr. William Douglass. Though not a witness to the actual event (he arrived in Boston a year after the occurrence of the storms), Douglass took a keen interest in the meteorological scene, and, no doubt, questioned many people concerning the Great Snow. In the early 1750's, probably in 1751, he composed a full-scale treatise on the history and present condition of the American colonies. In a brief section on the New England climate, he made the following statement: "1716–17, *February 20 to 22,* (March 3 to 5), wind at N.E. northerly, fell a very deep snow upwards of 3 feet upon a level." On the following page, he added: "the greatest snow in my remembrance was 1716–17, third week of *February.*" [12]

Another indirect reference came from Martha's Vineyard where Rev. William Homes took notice: "The storm did much damage in the country. The snow was said to be in the woods where it did not drive about 3 feet and a half deep generally on the mainland." [13] The total accumulation in the Boston area from the four storms might reasonably be placed at a minimum of 36 inches and a maximum of perhaps 42 inches. The mention of sleet mixed with the snow would indicate a solid pack, one which probably settled into a compact mass most difficult to travel through. North of Boston, where there probably was less of mixed precipitation and more snow, the accumulations could have been even greater—a figure of five feet in the woods was mentioned by the northerly post rider. Such depths have been achieved in southern Maine within the present century.

Eastern New England was paralyzed for many days and weeks by the great body of snow. The post took nine days to accomplish the 40 miles from Salem to Portsmouth in New Hampshire, even when employing snow shoes. He reported the snow depth to be five feet in the woods and drifting to 14 feet in the erstwhile roads.[14] In Boston there were no meetings for two Sabbaths in a row at Cotton Mather's church as people could not move about—an unheard of event in that church-going community.[15] The *News-Letter* reported on March 15th: "the snow is so deep that there is no travelling." [16] Dr. Edward Holyoke was detained at Cambridge for two weeks or more before conditions permitted his setting out for home at Salem.[17] Down on Cape Cod the burial of Rev. Samuel Treat, who died on 18 March, was delayed for several days; finally an arch was dug in a huge drift through which he was borne to his grave. A local historian in describing the scene tells us: "The wind blew with violence; and whilst the ground around his home were left entirely bare, the snow was heaped up in the road to an uncommon height." [18] At Framingham all public meetings were postponed until the end of the month so difficult was the travelling, first in the deep snow and then in the bottomless slush when melting set in.[19]

Down at Fishers Island in Long Island Sound a letter from John Winthrop told of one farm losing 1,100 sheep during the snowstorms; about 100 more fortunate ones, huddled in a drift, were buried for 28 days before being dug out alive.[20] Among the animal population, the deer, unable to move about in the deep cover, fell frequent victims of bears and wolves. Estimates were made that 95 per cent of the deer population perished. This caused several New England towns to appoint deer-reeves to conserve the much-valued game animals.[21]

The psychological effect of the Great Snow on the people of New England received attention in a sermon preached by Rev. Eliphalet Adams of New London soon after the first storm. He took his theme from a passage in Nahum: "The Lord hath his way in the whirlwind and in storm, and the clouds are the dust of his feet." Joshua Hempstead described the congregation that snowbound day of 14 March as "a thin appearance." The sermon was later published in a 32-page pamphlet, *A discourse occasioned by the late distressing storm,* thus securing for this meteorological event a permanent shrine in the body of New England theology.[22] *

---

[1] *The Journal of Henry D. Thoreau.* Bradford Torry and Francis H. Allen, eds. Boston, Houghton Mifflin Co., 1949, **8**, 165.
[2] *Boston News-Letter, 21 Jan 1717.*
[3] Eliphalet Adams. *A discourse occasioned by the late distressing storm. February 20, 1717, delivered March 3.* New London, T. Green, 1717. 27.
[4] Diary of Samuel Sewall. *Coll. Mass. Hist. Soc.* 5th ser., **7**, (1882), 120–21.
[5] Diary of Cotton Mather. *Mass. Hist. Soc. Coll.* 7th ser., **8**, (1912), 439.
[6] Phila., 5 March, in *Boston News-Letter, 1 April 1717.*
[7] Diary of Joshua Hempstead of New London, Connecticut, covering a period of forty-seven years

from September, 1711, to November, 1758. *Coll. New London County Hist. Soc.* **1** (1901), 64–65.
[8] *Boston News-Letter, 25 Feb 1717.*
[9] Joshua Coffin. *A sketch of the history of Newbury, Newburyport, and West Newbury from 1635 to 1845.* Boston, Samuel G. Drake, 1845. 209–10.
[10] Abiel Abbott. *History of Andover from its settlement to 1829.* Andover, Flagg and Gould, 1829. 188.
[11] Account of Dorchester. *Coll. Mass. Hist. Soc.* **9**, (1804), 196.
[12] William Douglass. *A summary, historical and political, of the first planting, progressive improvements, and present state of the British settlements in North America.* Boston, New England, printed London, 1755. 2, 212–13.
[13] Diary of Rev. William Homes of Chilmark. *New Eng. Hist. & Gen. Soc.* **49**, (1895), 414.
[14] *Boston News-Letter, 11 March 1717.*
[15] C. Mather, *Diary,* 506.
[16] *Boston News-Letter, 15 March 1717.*
[17] Abiel Holmes. The history of Cambridge. *Coll. Mass. Hist. Soc. for the year 1800.* **7**, 58.
[18] History of Eastham. *Coll. Mass. Hist. Soc.* **8**, (1802), 176.
[19] William Barry. *History of Framingham.* Boston, James Monroe & Co., 1847. 64–65.
[20] *Coll. Mass. Hist. Soc.* **1–2**, (1793), 13.
[21] Sidney Perley. *Historic Storms of New England.* Salem, Mass., The Salem Press, 1891. 34.
[22] E. Adams, *Discourse.*
\* See A Winter Anthology at end of volume.

## THE SEVERE WINTER OF 1719–20

William Douglass, a Bristol physician, had migrated to Boston about 1718 with one of the avowed purposes being to study the meteorological conditions of the area. He maintained a daily record of sky and wind conditions, though at this time he did not possess any instruments. He wrote his frequent correspondent, Cadwallader Colden of Philadelphia and New York, about the winter under study: "No snow continued laying above 24 hours till January 10 and almost gone from the streets by March 4, tho' to the N Eastward good logging the week of March 19–25th." Douglass, echoing a press opinion, thought the cold on January 18th had not been equaled since 1697–98.[1] This "great frost" sealed up Boston Harbor "several leagues beyond anything known before," according to Thomas Lechmere.[2] A major snowstorm, raging for 16 hours on February 10th, did great damage at Boston, and also at Piscataqua in New Hampshire to the northeast and at Newport in Rhode Island to the southwest.[3]

The mid-January cold also closed New York Harbor as a dispatch to the Boston press informed:

On 20th, 21st, 22d, and 23d instant great numbers went over Hudsons River upon the ice, from New York to New Jersey, since which the weather has been very warm, like the Spring, and all the ice gone.[4]

Trouble developed with ice again at New York in mid-February: "our rivers are full of ice and have been so for a great while."[5] By the first of March, however, a thaw had set in freeing the waterways about New York and also at Philadelphia where the Delaware River opened to navigation on March 3d after having been closed since early January.[6]

### JUDGE SEWALL'S DIARY: 1720

Jan. 10. Great storm of snow.
    14. Comfortable Sabbath overhead and under foot.
    18. Extreme cold.
    21. Very cold, yet serene and good going.
    27. By a wonderful thaw the ferry boat goes again.
    28. Serene in the morning and comfortable weather all day.
    29. Very dirty going.
Feb. 1. Very moderate weather.
    6. Very good going to Charlestown over Ferry: ground dry, and no troublesome ice.
    9. A very pleasant day.
    10. In the afternoon a sore storm of snow began, grew so violent in the night, that several ships were driven from their fasts at the Wharf, on to Dorchester Neck. Much snow fell.
    14. Great rain.
    16. This is a very cold day.[7]

### THE PRESS REPORTS THE WINTER OF 1719–20

#### New England

Boston: On Wednesday last (Jan. 9) we had a deep snow and very cold weather last week. *Boston News-Letter, 4 Jan. 1720.*

Harwich: Great storm on Jan. 9. *Ibid., 10 March 1720.*

Boston: Last week especially on the last three days (Jan. 18–20) was very cold weather, which has froze Charlestown River, that man and horses go over on the ice. Thursday Last (18th) was so extreme cold that it is thought we have not had so cold a day these twenty years past. Our harbor is also froze to Winnisinet and the Castle. The first day of the week (21st) was also as cold as the last three days of last week. *Ibid., 11 Jan. 1720.* . . . has been the reverse of the former for moderation, the 2d, 3d, and 4th days of the week (22–24) moderate frosty weather, hundreds of people going and coming on the ice to and from Nantasket, the three last days almost like Spring weather, the snow and ice thawed and our river and harbor all open again. *Ibid, 18 Jan. 1720.*

Harwich: Thursday the 18th was the severest cold day that was ever known in these parts. *Ibid., 10 March 1720.*

Boston: Last week was very moderate weather for the season of the year. *Ibid, 25 Jan. 1720.*

Boston: Most violent northeast snow storm commenced at 1000 on 10th—continued until 0200 on 11th—considerable damage to shipping and wharves. *Weekly Mercury* (Phila.), *1 March 1720.*

Piscataqua: Northeast snow storm did damage on Saturday last (10th).

Rhode Island: Northeast snow storm did damage on Saturday last (10th).

Boston: Last week was moderate, thawy weather. *News-Letter, 22 Feb. 1720.*

Rumney Marsh: Sheep buried in snow of Feb. 10th found alive this Saturday night (March 8th). *Ibid., 7 March 1720.*

### To the Southward

Philadelphia: Jan. 9. Our river is full of ice and it is extreme cold. *News-Letter, 25 Jan. 1720.*
Jan. 12. Our river is fast with ice.

New York: Jan. 30. On the 20th, 21st, 22d, and 23d great numbers went over Hudson's River upon the ice from New York to New Jersey, since which the weather has been very warm, like spring, and all ice gone. *Ibid., 1 Feb. 1720.*

New York: Feb. 27. Trouble with ice in New York harbor—no arrivals—our rivers are full of ice and have been so for a great while.

Philadelphia: March 6. Our river is now clear of ice. *Weekly Mercury, 23 Feb. 1720.*

Virginia: It has been extreme cold in Virginia last winter, the coldest that was ever known. *News-Letter, 17 March 1720.*

[1] William Douglass. Colden Papers. *Coll. N.Y. Hist. Soc.* **50**, (1917), 119.
[2] Thomas Lechmere. *Coll. Mass. Hist. Soc.* 6th ser. **5**, (1892), 391.
[3] *Boston News-Letter, 8 Feb 1720.*
*Weekly Mercury* (Phila.), *1 Mar 1720.*
[4] *News-Letter, 1 Feb 1720.*
[5] New York, 27 Feb, in *Weekly Mercury, 23 Feb 1720.*
[6] Samuel Hazard. Effects of climate on navigation. *The Penna. Register* (Phila.). **2–1**, (July 1828), 23.
[7] S. Sewall, *Diary,* **3**, 238–243.

## THE SEVERE WINTER OF 1732–33

Several contemporary authorities agreed that the winter of 1732–33 rated among the hardest of memory. In Maryland the season proved "one of the most severe in Chesapeake history" as ships had to wait at Annapolis until the beginning of March in order to put to sea.[1] In the Delaware Valley, Rev. Eneberg remarked: "1732 in the latter part of *November,* ice made the river impassable: 1733 there was much snow in *January.*"[2] On January 1st so much ice filled New York Harbor that vessels could not venture through the bay and reach the sea. Ice blocks also clogged Long Island Sound.[3] At Boston in early *January* the harbor froze over so that people could pass to Castle Island and to Charlestown with loaded sleds.[4] Dr. William Douglass in his historical account of the New England colonies made special mention of the season: "1732, the rivers froze up the middle of *November,* and continued froze until the end of *March,* many cattle die for want of provender."[5] Rev. Thomas Smith in Maine remarked that Casco Bay became solidly frozen in *January* and *February* and that the snow remained four feet deep in the woods as late as April 9th.[6]

Though our two longtime guides to daily weather in Boston had passed from the scene, Cotton Mather in 1729 and Samuel Sewall in 1730, Rev. Thomas Smith at Falmouth and Rev. Ebenezer Parkman at Westborough, Massachusetts, had already taken up their weatherwise pens. Unfortunately, neither was too verbose in describing conditions in 1732–33. Newspapers of the day, however, did supply some details. At Philadelphia as early as December 5th the river "was fuller of ice than has been known at this time of year, for many years past, so that no vessel can come in or out till a favorable opportunity offers."[7] Early in January there were 11 ships at Lewis Town waiting to proceed up the bay and river.[8] The ice did not break at the Quaker City until early March, and it was the 15th before the river was fully open and vessels could come up.[9] A great snowstorm occurred on the 29th of January, driving great blocks of ice upon the south shore of Delaware Bay.[10]

Boston Harbor froze over early in *January* and remained so until early in *February.* On the 9th of the second month a mild spell had opened the harbor, yet the ice remained fast around the wharves—men were set to work to cut away the shore ice so that vessels might load and unload.[11]

The severe cold also took its toll at sea. A ship arriving at Newport, Rhode Island, from Barbados had several men with frozen extremities, and another brought ashore a sailor who had succumbed to frostbite when approaching the port.[12]

Rev. Thomas Smith left the following comments about the season at Falmouth, now known as Portland, in Maine:

Jan. 19. Cold.

24. This whole week has been a spell of warm weather.

Feb. 5. It does not seem to be very cold, yet it was froze over to Purpoodoc all last night.

19. Prodigious blustering and cold.

26. It thawed all last night.

Mar. 5. Ice still as far as North Yarmouth. A man may walk over to Hog Island.

10. It is melancholy to see so much snow as has fallen so late in the year.

21. There has been but little of the snow consumed yet.

Apr. 2. Snow mostly consumed.

9. The snow in the woods is near four feet deep.[13]

Another Down East historian has related that the York River in extreme southern Maine remained frozen over on April 27th and that it snowed all day on May 4th.[14]

[1] Arthur P. Middleton. *Tobacco Coast*. Newport News, Va., Mariners Museum, 1953. 45.
[2] *Trans. Amer. Phil. Soc.* ns. **1**, (1818), 352.
[3] *New England Weekly Journal, 12 Feb 1733.*
[4] *Boston News-Letter, 4 Jan 1733.*
[5] William Douglass. *A summary, historical and political.* **2**, 211.
[6] T. Smith, *Journal*, 266.
[7] S. Hazard. Effects of climate. *Penna. Reg.*, **2**, 23.
[8] Phila., 6 Jan, *N.E. Jour.*, 22 Jan 1733.
[9] S. Hazard, **2**, 23.
[10] John F. Watson. *Annals of Philadelphia.* **2**, 326–27.
[11] *Boston News-Letter, 18 Jan, 1 Feb 1733.*
[12] *N.E. Jour., 1 Jan 1733.*
[13] T. Smith, *Journal*, 266.
[14] C. E. Banks. *History of York, Maine.* 15–16.

# HARD WINTER IN 1740–41

There were several severe winters in the first half of the 18th Century, such as 1704–05, 1719–20, and 1732–33, when on each occasion New York harbor froze over and stopped navigation completely, but none served as a landmark for past and future generations in the minds of contemporary diarists and newspaper editors until the season of 1740–41 came along. Rev. Nathaniel Appleton of the First Church at Cambridge, Massachusetts, left the following pertinent memorandum in his church records:

> The winter in ye year 1740 is agreed by those yt are in years amg us was Considerably a more Severe Winter then that of 1697. there were large quantities of Snow and ye Ferry was froze over for a longer space. People thro' ye Country put to Extreme difficulty to get wood. Hay Extremely Scarse in ye Spring & Multitudes of Cattle dyed.[1]

The early cold, deep snows, frozen harbors, and the late continuance of these into spring made an indelible impression on all who experienced their rigors. Ezra Stiles was old enough to remember the season, and would make comparisons later with the Hard Winter of 1780 and the Long Winter of 1784.

## START OF WINTER

The snow season commenced early in New England with some biting cold on 15 November and a 6-inch snowfall in central Connecticut.[3] Equally heavy amounts fell over other parts of the region. There followed another noteworthy storm on the 24–25th bringing a foot of snow to localities in eastern Massachusetts. Rev. Ebenezer Parkman at Westborough in central Massachusetts commented: "it continues to snow, and is a very difficult time." He noted the 26th and 27th as very cold, and on the 29th: "a great storm of snow. Very cold and tedious."[4] Up in Maine at Falmouth, Rev. Thomas Smith, the veteran weather-watcher, declared: "I believe that no man knew so winter-like spell so early in the year."[5]

## STORMY DECEMBER

A major circulation change occurred with the opening of December. At Westborough, December 2d was a "very fine pleasant day. Such as we have not had for a long time," and the following day was "moderate weather." But this warm spell served only as the introduction to an unusually protracted rainy period of 14-days duration.[6] The melting snows with rain day-after-day raised the greatest floods experienced in the lower Connecticut Valley in 50 years, or since the memorable spring overflows in 1692.[7] The freshets were particularly severe in eastern Massachusetts and New Hampshire along the Merrimac River where flood crests were thought to be the highest ever known.[8] The shipbuilding industry suffered the heaviest losses as hundreds of cords of fine wood floated downstream. In Maine mills were swept away, bridges carried off, and highways ruined.[9] Severe floods are not unknown at this season; another major December flood would occur in 1784. It takes a combination of early heavy snows plus a sustained thaw with continuous rains to raise the rivers and streams to their greatest heights.

The weather pattern shifted again toward the end of December and a regime favorable for the development of a series of northeasters took over. "A prodigious storm out of the north and northwest" on the 28th buried the interior under a knee-deep snow, and severe gales on the coast along with rain and snow caused unprecedented havoc to shipping.[10] A combination of huge waves and great tides cast more than 50 sail on the shores of Massachusetts Bay alone. This storm must rate as one of the major coastal storms of the century, but unfortunately we lack meteorological details and even wind sequence data. Its influence, however, was widespread.

It was marked as particularly severe at Philadelphia where a heavy snowstorm struck Delaware Bay and Delaware River. Much timber was floated away at high tide along the surrounding bodies of water. At New York City the boisterous storm brought the first mention of wintry conditions in the press: "Our streets are confused with heaps of snow, so that the lovers of sledriding can scarsely use them without danger. The whole mass fell in one nights time and now the cold is so excessive, that while I am writing in a warm room by a good fireside, the ink freezes in the pen."[11] From late December on, persistent trough conditions prevailed along the Atlantic seaboard just as would occur in December of 1839 when a series of devastating northeasters pounded the Atlantic seaboard with conditions resembling 1740–41.

A second disturbance on January 6th swept up the coastline. At Westborough, well inland, the storm raged "exceeding vehement" with the snow falling on an already deep layer "to make extraordinarily difficult passing."[12] A third coastal storm of wind and snow came on the 13th. At Newport, Rhode Island, the local press reported the easterly winds so strong "that no person could walk well in the streets."[13] Unfortunately for our story, the very informative diary of Rev. Parkman had a lapse following *31 December 1740* (old style), so we do not have his day-by-day account of the events during the remainder of this exceptional winter season.

## COLD MID–JANUARY, THEN A THAW

Cold blasts out of Canada followed the passage of each of these northeasters. After the first storm on the 28th of December, a cold regime of some three weeks duration featured Arctic air masses without any intervening mild spells. The 17th and 18th of January at Philadelphia were thought to have been the coldest for many years; these probably featured advective cold with strong, biting winds as the lack of continuous thermometer records precluded a precise judgment by scientific measurement.[14] Drifting snow soon brought an end to regular travel by highway over New England and the Middle Colonies, and the continuance of penetrating cold soon closed all the rivers and inland waterways with solid ice. Many salt water bays and channels, seldom before frozen, congealed solidly, and even the ocean shore along southern and eastern New England became ringed with an unusual icy surface.

Boston harbor froze over solidly soon after Christmas to halt all shipping for 30 days.[15] It remained firm enough in many places so that people could come over from the islands dotting the harbor in sleighs to Dorchester for church services on 15 consecutive sabbaths. Charlestown ferry remained frozen for more than 10 weeks. The ocean front along the South Shore from Point Allerton southward for 20 miles almost to Plymouth Bay was reported frozen, a most exceptional occurrence. Ice at Deer Island was 30 inches thick.[16] The strength of the cold was well attested by the tendency of tidal bays and estuaries to freeze and remain solid. Narragansett Bay supported sleighs to go back and forth between Newport and Providence, an event unknown before.[17] People could drive from New London up to Newport over the shore ice, and Fishers Island in eastern Long Island Sound was joined to the mainland by an ice highway.[18] The most publicized event of the winter, and one told many times afterwards, took Francis Lewis, later destined to be a signer of the Declaration of Independence, on a sleigh ride all the way from Barnstable on Cape Cod to New York City, the entire journey of some 200 miles being made on ice along the shore where ocean waves erstwhile had broken.[19]

Rev. James MacSparran, pastor of Trinity Church at Newport, thought he saw a warning from the Almighty in "the uncommon inclemencies of a cold and long winter." In a sermon preached on 26 March 1741 and later published, he tried to describe the wintry scene about him and to sound its theological significance:

> The elements have been arm'd with such piercing cold and suffocating snows, as if God intended the Air that he gave us to live and breath in, should become the instrument to execute his vengence on us, for our ingratitude to his goodness, and our trangression of his law. . . . Boreas has so far entered into the

chambers of the South, that he has sealed up the sun, and intercepting his dissolving influence; and Southern snows are signs of the planets impotent efforts to regain his usurped dominions.[20]

Farther south at New York City the Hudson River was shut to navigation by ice on two occasions: (1) following the storm of 28 December until the 21st of January, and (2) during the second and third weeks of February when an editor wrote: "We now have a second winter more severe than it was some weeks past." Six vessels in Long Island Sound were reported frozen in, and another was "likewise driving there with the ice, whose sails are set, but no person on board."[21]

At Philadelphia the Delaware River received an icy covering on 27 December and this continued for three months until 27 March. All navigation at the Quaker City ceased on 30 December and did not resume until 24 March, a period of 12 weeks cessation of commerce. In January ice extended from Lewes near the entrance to Delaware Bay seaward as far as the eye could see.[22]

At Annapolis the winter was considered the hardest ever known in the Chesapeake Bay area. The Severn River froze over where a mile wide so that heavy loads could go back and forth.[23] York River near Williamsburg was crossable and would not freeze as solidly again until 1780.[24] Down at Charleston, South Carolina, the month of December 1740 proved the coldest calendar month in the thermometer records of Dr. John Lining who had commenced his pioneer instrumental record in 1737.[25] His observations, published by the Royal Society of London, covered the period 1737–1753, and were the first continuous series of meteorological records of which details have been preserved. Lining's thermometer averaged 42° in December with a maximum of only 69° and a minimum of 21°.[26]

The exact degree of cold in the North was not recorded with any precision. The Hollis thermometer was still at Cambridge and would soon be employed for meteorological purposes when Prof. John Winthrop commenced his series of observations in 1742. At this time, however, it hung indoors in the president's house.[27] At New Haven, President Clap also had a thermometer attached to a barometer and exposed in the southeast corner of his living room. "I do not know what thermometer this was, but believe it was of Florentine construction," wrote his successor, Ezra Stiles, 40 years later. Stiles considered the mercury in 1740–41 as descending to about eight below, according to his conversion scale, a figure which would be greatly exceeded in 1765 and 1780.[28]

A January thaw came about on schedule in 1741, and must have been most welcome. On January 30th Rev. Smith at Portland declared: "the whole week has been a spell of charming weather." The 6th of February he described as "a charming pleasant day," but the following twenty-four hours brought an end to the thaw.[29] Boston Harbor, at least the shipping lanes, was reported open for navigation on the 5th of February, though the shore and rivers remained locked up.[30] This mid-winter interlude proved only temporary, much like the mid-December thaw, and emphasized the changing circulation patterns which prevailed in this severe, but variable winter—the most difficult portion of the season was yet to come.

## SNOWY FEBRUARY

We do not have an actual day-by-day measurement of the many snowfalls occurring in February of 1741, but two were of sufficient stature to receive mention in the columns of the *Boston News-Letter:*

Boston:
Last night and this day [8–9 Feb.] we have a very great N.E. storm of wind and snow. All this morning, the wind comes in sudden gusts, and is prodigious high. The snow is also higher than has been known among us since the vast snow we had the *19th of February, 1716, 17*. It is to be feared that we shall have further melancholy accounts of the losses of lives, vessels, and cargoes upon our coasts.[31]

Rhode Island:
On Monday, Wednesday, and Thursday last, we had here a great storm of snow and wind at N.E., which no doubt has done a great deal of damage to man and beast: and ever since, we have had the most severe season for cold, frost and snow, that ever was known in the memory of the oldest man living here.[32]

John Bissell, then serving as town clerk of Bolton, Connecticut, left the following summary record in the town minutes. Bolton is situated about 12 miles east of Hartford in hilly country; conditions prevailing there can be considered representative of southern New England localities away from the immediate shoreline:

In memory of the cold and hard winter, A.D. 1740 and 41, never to be forgotten.—The preceding summer was short and cold; *October* was as cold as ordinarily *November* is, and the Little River at Windsor was shut and people passed it on ice in *October*. In the beginning of *November* fell a snow about six inches deep, and winter-like weather succeeded it, the Dec. 5th, and then the cold something abated, and a rain succeeded, which continued ten days successively, which produced the biggest flood in the Connecticut River that had been known in fifty years before, doing damage to bridges, fences, hay, &c. and the Indian corn chambers, cribs, &c. being much ruined by the long continuance of wet weather; then the weather clearing up moderately, but soon grew extreme cold. About the middle of *December* came a prodigious storm of snow out of the north and north west, which was full knee deep, attended in said storm with violent cold weather, which continued steadily so extreme that the eaves were not seen to drop for thirty days. Travelling was almost wholly suspended by reason of the extreme cold and deep snow, and God had sealed up the hand of every man. *We had a very sensible consideration of that Who can stand before his cold?*

January 28th, the cold abated, and a considerable thaw followed, it continued moderate for about ten days, and violent cold succeeded, and *January* went out like a Lion. Another snow fell about the latter end of *January* about seven inches deep. About the beginning of *February,* there was a terrible and violent storm of snow, which continued for near three days together, which, with what snow was before, was more than three feet deep. The weather grew somewhat more moderate, and the snow settled considerably; but March 8th fell another snow about seven inches deep, and 14th another about as deep; so that notwithstanding the settling of the snow, the snow on the 17th day of March was three feet deep. The weather continued cold and the snow wasted but slowly, so that there was considerable quantity of snow the *middle of April.*

The great river was crossed upon the ice above Scantick on the 11th day of April, and the Sound between the Main and Long Island was frozen over that winter so they passed it on ice. At Guilford a sheep was, in the winter, buried in a storm of snow and lay there ten weeks and three days and came out alive! The spring came on very slowly; the beginning of *March* about half the people of the government had spent all their hay, and subsisted them by falling trees, giving out their Indian corn, and by reason of which scarcity a great number of cattle and horses died, and near half the sheep, and about two thirds of the goats. Exceeding scarcity followed, partly by reason of abundance of Indian corn being ruined by the long rains in *December,* and partly by people giving their corn to their creatures to save their lives.[33]

## NEWBURY, MASSACHUSETTS

Another composite picture of the winter season of 1740–41 was compiled by Joshua Coffin, the historian (1845) of Newbury in coastal northeastern Massachusetts, who always had a facile pen when weather events were to be considered:

The summer and fall of this year, were as remarkable for the rain, which fell and flooded the country, as the subsequent winter was, for the severity of the cold. It was probably the most severe winter ever known, since the settlement of the country. Reverend Mr. Plant, Stephen Jaques, honorable Nathaniel Coffin, and many others, recorded some of the most remarkable events that occurred, from which I shall make a few extracts.

The summer of 1740 was a wet summer. In *October* gathered our corn, one third very green. We could not let it stand by reason of rain. On November 15th the winter set in very cold. On the 26th a foot of snow fell, about Dec. 3rd it began to rain and it rained three weeks together. The stars in the evening seemed as bright as ever, but the next morning rain again, which occasioned a freshet in Merrimack River, the like was not known by no man for seventy years. It rose fifteen feet at Haverhill and floated off many houses. It was said that a sloop might pass between Emery's mill and his house, and that the water was twelve feet deep on Rawson's meadow at Turkey hill.

It washed away all the wood and timber for building of ships so that for fourteen days every inhabitant was fishing for wood in the river. It was commonly supposed that upwards of two thousand cords were taken up on Plum Island.

'Our corn,' says Stephen Jaques, 'moulded as fast as six hogs could eat it.'

December 23. The river was shut up again by the severity of the weather. Before the *first of January* loaded teams passed from Haverhill, Newbury, Newtown, Amesbury, sometimes twenty, thirty, forty in a day having four, six, eight oxen in a team and landed below the upper long wharf nigh to the ferry. People ran upon the ice for several days to half tide rock. Shipping was all froze in and this severity extended to New York government. On December 25th about thirty-five minutes past six there was a loud noise of the earthquake.'

## 1741

January 21st there was a thaw, which held three days. January 29th about four A.M. and on February 5th about ten minutes before four P.M. there was an earthquake. February 14th about a foot more of snow fell, February 20th another great snow, and on February — another. In *February* the streets were full of snow to the top of the fences and in some places eight or ten feet deep. The river all the time was frozen over to colonel Pierce's farm. April 8th the sleighing was good on Pierce's farm, and Plum island. April 18th there fell about a foot of snow so there now lay about four feet deep in the woods. From December 16, 1740 till April 7th, 1741 Plum island river was frozen over. On the 30th and 31st of March the river was frozen to the lower end of Seal island. In Plum island river the ice broke about the 10th of April. There were twenty-seven snows this winter, the hardest winter that ever was known. The people of Newbury had the principal part of their corn ground at Salisbury mills. From February 14th till April 11th—Pearson's mill was stopped by the ice. March 11th, the ice at Deer island the strongest place of the tide was thirty inches thick.[34]

A letter to the *Boston News-Letter* from a resident of Dorchester, located on the Bay just south of Boston, dated 8 April, summarized the season there:

We have had the severest winter that has been known in memory of the oldest among us. Our river has been so hard and long frozen, that people from Thompson's Island, Squantum, and the adjacent neighborhood have come 15 Sabbaths successively upon the ice to our meeting, viz. from the 25th of December to April 1st. We have had 30 distinct settled snows this winter, which cannot be equaled, even by the remarkable cold season we had in 1697–98 in which winter were 26 snows, as some elderly people say; and also that persons then passed on the ice over the above said river to Dorchester Meeting 13 Sabbath Days.[35]

## LATE SPRING

The grip of ice and snow on rivers and land broke up at an almost record late date. New Haven harbor was crossed by a wagon load of oysters as late as 23 March.[36] The Thames River at New London did not break up at Winthrop's Neck until 26 March.[37] The Hudson River at Esopus proved strong enough for loaded teams to traverse on 1 April.[38] The Connecticut River was crossed by a man on horseback from Hadley to Northampton as late as 11 April as related in another letter to the weather-conscious editor of the *Boston News-Letter*:

> The winter passed has been long and hard, the like has not been known, we suppose, by the most aged men now living on Connecticut River; corn and hay are now grown as scarce as has been known for many years; Connecticut River has been so long and so hard frozen, that in this month of *April* there was safe passing over the river from Hadley to Northampton upon the ice, not only for footmen but for horses. We whose names are underwritten, on the *first day* of this instant, passed over the said river, in the company of Dr. Porter, who had with him a large horse, which he first lead, and then mounted him, and then crossed the river on the ice. We suppose the like has never been known in any age.
>
> Taban Grant
> David Moodey [39]

On April 10th Richard Hazen was running the Massachusetts-New Hampshire border survey. When just north of Ashburnham, Massachusetts, he found "the snow for the most part was two and a half feet deep and more." [40] At Weare, New Hampshire, the depth on the 22d covered the fences.[41] Down East at Falmouth, Rev. Smith gave eloquent testimony as to the lateness of the season: "April 21: Melancholy time, the snow lying, little hay. May 6: The snow has now consumed wonderfully. May 11: The roads now settled surprisingly; the reason is, there has been no frost in the ground the winter past." [42]

Joshua Hempstead of New London, Connecticut, who had described in detail the occurrence of the Great Snow of 1717, again was on hand as he would be in the Winter of the Deep Snows in 1748 to pen a journal of the daily weather events:

### December 1740

4. Cloudy moist weather. mr. adams pr all Day.
5. a grt Rain.
6. Rainy day. ye foren being Rainy.
7. Cloudy & Some Rain.
8. Cloudy.
9. fair & moderate.
10. Rainy.
11. Cloudy & some wt.
12. Some Rain Some fair but warm for the Season. a great Rain. night misty & miry abundance of.
17. Rain hath fallen (   ). the flood hath been great in Connecticut & (   ).
18. a great Storm of wind at E & N E & much Rain. mr ads pr.
19. wind N E Some Rain.
20. fair. a very high wind at night it got about to N W.
21. it began to Snow in the morning & wee came home a Cold time & very windy not much Snow or 3 Inches.
22. fair & windy.
23. fair & cold.
24. fair & Cold.
25. fair & very Cold. mr adams pr. al Day.
26. fair & very Cold.
27. fair & not quite so Cold.
28. it began to Snow & blow in the night & held al Day & Some of ye night very Cold & much Snow Drifted.
29. fair & Cold. I was at home al Day windy.
30. I was at home al day.
31. fair & Cold.

### January 1741

1. fair & Cold. Mr adams pr. all Day.
2. all fair & Cold.
3. all fair & Cold.
4. all fair & Cold.
5. all fair & Cold.
6. a very bad Storm of Snow & wind all Day after 10 or 11 of the Clock & most of the night Some Small matter of Hail & Rain which Crusted the Snow and (   ) Slead paths which were with much difficulty broke & used (   ) Days are all filld up again.
7. Some Snow & Cold. wee all kept house. a Severe time of Cold.
8. fair & more moderate tho Cold Enough. mr adams pr all Day.
9. fair & a Southwest wind tho Raw cold.
10. fair & moderate for the Season but an Exceeding close time (   ) have broke the way again over the fresh medows & (   ) Joseph Harris's mr Coits Six acres & John Coits Lot the (   ) Town being So full of Snow banks yt there is no passing.
11. I was out to my Island in the Swamp with (   ) Joshua Cutting Rail Timber & Wood adm a Sleading (   ).
12. fair & very Cold. I was at home all Day.
13. a Cold Snow Storm. I was at home all Day the Sleading (   ).
14. fair & moderate for ye Season.

15. fair & windy which Drifted the Snow that fell Last night about ( ) made the Snow fly as if it came from the Clouds. mr adm ( ).
16. fair in the foren & Cold. aftern Some Snow.
17. fair & very Cold but not windy. Son John Led my Horse a Cross the River on the ( ) at Mr Winthrops neck in order to prove the ( ) because I was about to drive over Some Horsekind & Cattel.
18. fair. drove all a Cross the River. it began to Snow ( ) of the clock at night & Snowed all night & untill ye ( ).
19. a Snowy Day.
20. fair.
21. fair.
22. Snow in the foren. aftern. Rain a Little & giving ( ).
23. wind S W a Thaw. Some Rain like a fogg or Scottish mist. Exceeding Slippry & ( ).
24. Wind S W a Thaw Some Rain Some fair like yesterday. Sunday it was full 2 foot high in ( ) it was not drifted & now the hills & high land bare ( ).
25. Cloudy & Some Snow Showers out of the N E till aftern ( ) wind backt to N & N N W. I was at home all day.
26. fair.
27. Cloudy & Snow before night 4 or 5 Inches.
28. fair.
29. fair. mr adams pr all Day.
30. fair. In the foren I went to the Island & broke in the Ice & Snow to make it fitt to bear.
31. ( ) F. wind fair S— weather.

## February 1741

1. Misty morn & yn fair.
3. Wet misty.
4. Small flight of Snow in the morn Early & yn fair & Cold at N W.
6. Snowy Day.
8. Cold Snowy Day. I was at home all Day.
9. Snowy day & cold & windy much drifted.
10. Cloudy the Snow flies Exceedingly.
11. fair & Cold. I was at home all Day. James Larabee Set out in the morn about 9 Clock for Norwich a foot. a Tuff time of it.
12. fair & Cold. mr adams pr all Day to a Thin Congregation.
13. it Snowed all Day till night & thn Rain at N E wind high.
14. Cloudy in the morning & yn Sunshine & Soon Snow fast. aftern the wind came from N E to No West & grew Cold.

17. fair & Remains Exceeding Sharp Cold. the harbour ( ) below that people Cross on the Ice below the fortt ( ).
18. Cold but not quite So violent. I was at home all Day.
19. fair & moderate a Southerly wind but a very Little to be Seen in the South a few breathing holes generally ( ) up to fishers Island & as far as we can See towards ( ).
20. Snowed Last night & this morn a Considerable & much drifted again & afternoon Rain.
21. fair & moderate.
22. a Rainy Day. Sloppy weather but ( ).
23. fair but not Exceeding cold.
24. fair & Colder pretty Sharp.
25. fair. I Rid from the fort to ye ferry Nattee behind me. there is a Tent on the River about 10 or 12 Rod below the Island of Rocks ( ) are Barbaqueing a Shoat.
26. it Rained Last night ye Latter part of it & all Day a bad ( ).
27. fair.
28. fair & Thawing a S W wind toward night Cloudy & in ye night Some Snow.

## March 1741

1. fair & very Cold & windy at N W. In the morning I went to ( ) with Josh. Natt & adam Drove the 4 oxen & 2 farrow Cows (over) on the Ice from the fort streight to ferry wharf. I was at Court all Day after ( ) wee Sat at Mr Curtises by Reason of the Cold.
2. fair & very Cold night & foren. aftern more moderate but Still Cold.
3. Snow at night 2 Inches fair & moderate. 2 Sloops & a Scooner have Layd at ( ) wharff froze in 3 weeks or more. have in 2 days time Cutt out from Powder Island but now the wind is come at S W & keeps the ( ).
4. fair & moderate.
5. fair in the foren. about 3 or 4 Clock it began to Snow at S E & Some ( ).
6. fair & warm. it Thawd much. wee measured a Cross the River on a Line from the Lower Side ( ) Lot at highwater mark to the Cornner of the fort & found it to wan ( ) of half a mile. 154 Rod across ye River ferry.
7. fair till near noon & then it Snowed Smartly & held till ni(ght I was) at home all Day.
8. fair.
9. fair & Cold.
10. fair & Cold.
12. ( ) & very Cold.
13. a great Storm of Snow from ( ) in ye Morn to Dark 6 inches.

14. Rainy.
15. fair & very windy & Cold.
16. fair Cold & windy.
17. fair.
18. a Snow Storm. it began about Sunrise & Snowed Smartly till ( ) afternoon. wind S E & back to N E & thn moderated. wind got back to N W and Snowed again till night 8 or 9 Inches. I was at home al day.
19. fair. Sacramt Day. mr adams all Day.
20. fair. I Rid over on the Ice from mr Winthrops Neck to Capt. Starrs Landing place ye old building yard.
21. fair.
22. fair & warm. a Little Scatering Snow in the night Something like Hail.
23. fair & cold in the foren wind at N W. I was home in the Evening. over in ye Boat ye River being now open at the ferry but fast above from Mr Winthrops point to his Land at Groton & ( ).
24. fair in the foren. aftern it Rained a Little.
25. it Rained Smartly a while & yn moderately. ye Snow Run briskly. I was about home all Day very miry & wet.
26. fair. mr. ad. pr al Day. it Thawd much in the aftern.
27. fair. I went to Stonington & Crost ye ferry in the Boat tho the Ice is fast above mr Winthrops neck to norwich.
28. fair & warm. it Thawed Some So that it was Sloppy & Miry in the path & where ye Snow is gone.
29. foren Cloudy. it Rained in the aftern & most of the night with Thunder & Lightning.
30. fair Cold & windy N W. I finisht ye Ladder & it was too Cold to prune Trees.
31. fair & very Cold.

### April 1741

1. fair & not Quite So Cold.
2. fair & moderate. Joshua went home a foot ys morn ( )ing Early and Crost the River on the Ice from Mr Winthrops ( ) to the Neck. & Some Groton people came over to meeting & ( ) the Last of the Ice Bearing on monday it began to break up.
3. Snowy Day al Day & in the night about 7 or 8 Inches not very Cold.
6. fair a pleasant morning. I went from mr Dea( ) a Cross ye Hills to the Road with Dificulty by Reason of the great Quantity of ( ). I Left my ( ) the ferry by Reason the ferryman was afraid of the Ice that wee ( ) the River in great Cakes. I got over in a Long boat yt hapned there.
7. fair.
8. fair.
9. fair. mr adams pr aftern. his Son Wm foren.
10. fair Cold windy.
11. fair & prety Cold.
12. fair.
13. fair.
14. fair.
20. fair & windy Snowd night Some Rain.
22. Some Rain Some Snow & Some Hail not very much of Either.

---

[1] Records of the First Church, Cambridge. *The Genealogical Magazine* (Boston). **1,** (1890), 361.
[2] Ezra Stiles. *The Literary Diary of Ezra Stiles.* Franklin B. Dexter, ed. New York, Scribner's Sons, 1901. **2,** 401.
[3] John Bissell. A Hard Winter 1740–1741. Ms. Memorandum, Bolton, Conn. Poulson's *Amer. Daily Adv.* (Phila.), 3 March 1820.
[4] The Diary of Ebenezer Parkman. *Proc. Amer. Antiq. Soc.* (Worcester). **72**-1, (1962), 140–41.
[5] *Journals of the Rev. Thomas Smith, and the Rev. Samuel Deane.* William Willis, ed. Portland, Joseph S. Baily, 1849. 268.
[6] E. Parkman, *Diary,* 142–43.
[7] J. Bissell, Ms. Memo.
[8] *Boston News-Letter, 27 Nov & 4 Dec 1740.*
[9] *Ibid., 18 Dec 1740.*
[10] *The General Magazine and Historical Chronicle for all the British Plantations in America* (Phila.). 1-1, (Jan 1741), 73.
[11] *Penna. Gaz.* (Phila.) *28 Dec 1740; N. Y. Weekly Jour., 22 Dec 1740.*
[12] E. Parkman, *Diary,* 146.
[13] Newport dispatch, *3 Jan,* in *Boston Post Boy, 12 Jan 1741.*
[14] *Penna. Gaz., 8 Jan 1741.*
[15] Boston *Evening Post, 12 & 26 Jan 1741.*
[16] *Ibid., 12 Jan 1741; Boston News-Letter, 2 April 1741.*
[17] Newport dispatch, *30 Jan,* in *Boston News-Letter, 19 Feb 1741.*
[18] Frances M. Caulkins. *History of New London, Conn.* New London, H. D. Utley, 1895. 411.
[19] *Boston Post Boy,* in Charles W. Elliott. *The New England History.* N. Y., Charles Scribner, 1857. 1, 464.
[20] James MacSparran. *A sermon preached at Naraganset, March 15th A.D. 1740,* 1. Newport, printed by the Widow Franklin, under the Town School House, 1741. 16.
[21] *N. Y. Weekly Jour., 5 Jan & 16 Feb 1741.*
[22] *Gen. Mag.,* 216.
[23] *Ibid.,* 145.
[24] *Idem.*
[25] Lionel Chalmers. *An account of the weather and diseases of South Carolina.* London, Edward and Charles Dilly, 1776.
[26] *Idem.*
[27] J. Winthrop. Ms. Met. Jour, 9 March 1744.
[28] E. Stiles, *Diary,* **2,** 401.
[29] T. Smith, *Journal,* 268.
[30] *Boston Eve. Post., 26 Jan 1741.*
[31] *Boston News-Letter, 29 Jan 1741.*

[32] *Ibid.*, 19 Feb 1741.
[33] John Bissell, Ms. Memo.
[34] Joshua Coffin. *A sketch of the history of Newbury, Newburyport, and West Newbury from 1635 to 1845*. Boston, Samuel G. Drake, 1845. 209–10.
[35] *Boston News-Letter*, 2 April 1741.
[36] E. Stiles, *Diary*, **2**, 401.
[37] F. Caulkins, *New London*, 411.
[38] Diary of Col. Abraham Hasbrouck (extracts), *The New York Times*, 18 Jan 1893.
[39] *Boston News-Letter*, 24 April 1741.
[40] Helen C. Nutting. *To Monadnock*. New York, Stratford Press, 1925. 33–37.
[41] William Little. *History of Weare*, 1735–1888. Lowell, Mass., S. W. Huse & Co., 1888.
[42] T. Smith, *Journal*, 268.

## WINTER OF THE DEEP SNOWS: 1747–1748

*The snow lay deep in drifts upon the ground.*
*The roads unbroken no one could discern*
*'Twas hill and vale in deep untrodden snow.*

Thus some unknown poet of Newbury described the scene on Christmas morning of 1747. Sidney Perley in *Historic Storms of New England* has written: "The winter of 1747–48 was one of the memorable winters that used to be talked about by our grandfathers when snow whirled in deep drifts around their half-buried houses."[1]

This winter season was the standout in the colonial period for production of snowstorms and heavy snow cover. The snow came relatively early, fell at frequent intervals throughout the height of the season, and remained as a very deep cover unusually late.

There were two contemporary witnesses who attempted to summarize the wintry conditions in a brief statement. The records of the First Church of Cambridge contain the following memorandum:

> The winter of 1747 was very severe, not so much for the extremity of the cold as for the great quantity of snow. We had about 30 snows and less thawing weather than usual, so that the snows lay upon the ground till it came to be 4 or 5 feet deep. So that it was exceeding difficult passing from place to place. The 5th of April there was 2 to 3 feet of solid snow on a level, on that day the snow was on the back side of my house about 4½ feet high, was up to the middle of the window.
> But God so ordered the seasons that in a few days of South wind without any rain it went off, so that on the twelfth day of April I had my garden sowed and planted with onions, carrots, parsnips, peas, beans, &c.

The second summary came from the diary of Samuel Lane at Stratham in coastal New Hampshire:

### 1748

> We had a tedious hard Cold and Most Difficult Winter, by reason of much Snow & bad passing ('tis said) ever known by Any person now Living. The Cold began Severe about ye 8th of December & held Constant 26 Days and on ye 14th of December 1747 the Deep Snows began to come; and held near 4 months, so Exceeding Deep; that there was Scarcely any passing in Roads: and with great difficulty throu' fields, on Rivers, and any where that people co'd get along. I counted 25 Snows this Winter, & that in all, they Contain'd about 12 feet in Depth. the 9th Day of April Men & Horses Broke the Way from my House to Esqr Leavits in the Road; where had been no passing 2 or 3 Months.
> This large Body of Snow went away Strangely, without any rain or Land flood; the ground not being froze, it Soak'd into the Earth as it melted.—this is ye 2nd hard Winter together.

The snow season commenced with a great storm on December 14th. Its impact at Boston was described by the *News-Letter*:

> Last Thursday night we had a most violent storm of wind, about N Est (attended with a great snow) by which damage was done onshore, as well as to shipping in the harbor. Several chimneys were blown down, and the roofs of sundry buildings in town tore up, and carried to a considerable distance by the violence of the wind, several old buildings thrown down, and in the harbor, the Massachusetts frigate was driven from her moorings, and received much damage, and several other vessels drove ashore, and two or three were overset and sank at the wharves. [Other vessels reported ashore at Nantasket and on Cape Cod].[4]

Snow upon snow followed as the *Diary of Rev. Ebenezer Parkman*, which is appended at the end of this article, clearly demonstrated.[5] The meteorological

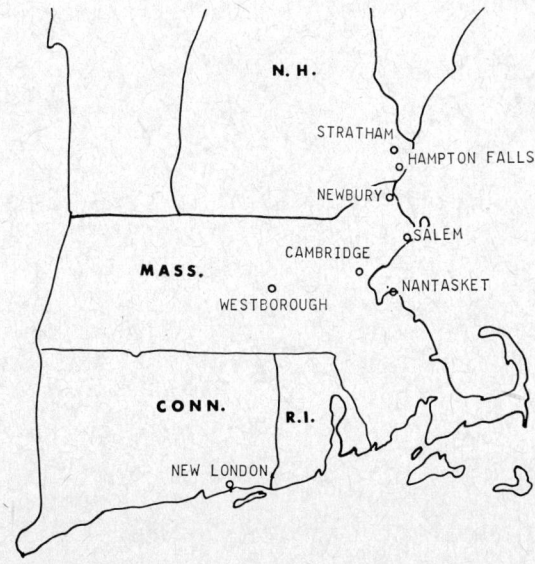

question remains as to how deep the snow cover mounted in coastal Massachusetts, New Hampshire, and Maine? Dr. Edward Holyoke at Salem in his diary on March 4th wrote: "snow on a level 30 inches and in the woods 4½ feet." And on March 10th: "No travelling about the country except on rackets."[6] This was in line with the estimate in the records of the First Church of 4 to 5 feet depths. Deacon David Batchelder of Hampton Falls, New Hampshire, referred in his diary to the snow in February as being "four feet deep."[7] But up in Maine at Falmouth, Rev. Thomas Smith told of accumulations of 66 inches on the ground during the period of maximum cover at the conclusion of the first week in April.[8] These depths may have been equaled in the Great Snow of 1717, but that came under a different climatic situation, being the results of a nine-day concentration of storms rather than the long accumulation of numerous snows attended with little melting. The snow depths in the winter of 1748 stand unrivaled in the colonial period. John Preston at Salem expressed the contemporary view: "it was thought there was more snow this winter than there had been any winter since the country was inhabited."[9]

Rev. Smith up at Falmouth kept a close tab on the character of the months this winter Down East in Maine, and "snowy" was the only adjective he could find to describe the season:

Jan. 4 The snow, though settled considerably, is full three feet deep.
  10. This *December* has been a very unpleasant *month*.
*January*. A cold, snowy *month*.
*February*. A cold, snowy, uncomfortable *month*.
*March*. Comes in smiling; the rest of the *month* generally cold and snowy.
April 11. Comes in joyfully (*April*).
  19. The snow is all gone except a few drifts.
May 31. It is but seven weeks since there were five and a half feet of snow on the ground.

Two almost day-by-day accounts of the winter's events of 1747–48 are available. One comprised the meteorological record maintained by Prof. John Winthrop on the Harvard campus. Though his temperatures were not representative of outdoor conditions, his wind observations and general comments were of significance in documenting this extraordinary winter. The other record consisted of the weather entries in the diary of Rev. Ebenezer Parkman of Westborough, located between Framingham and Worcester, who recorded his suffering from adverse weather conditions when not giving space to his mental turmoil caused by the spiritual waywardness of his flock:

---

## METEOROLOGICAL EXTRACTS FROM THE DIARY OF EBENEZER PARKMAN OF WESTBOROUGH, MASSACHUSETTS

### December 1747

1. Grows cold, yet it is a pleasant bright day.
2. Bright and pleasant but cold and blustering.
10. Comfortable day tho somewhat cold.
11. A cold, windy, but bright day.
14. A snow storm to go home in. The storm increased very much, both the snow and wind. The night was very tempestuous. The house shook exceedingly. But God safely preserved us.
15. A very difficult morning. The snow deep.
16. The cold increases.
17. A pritty cold day, but few at meeting . . . It was so cold that I finished the exercises early about 3.
19. Cold day.
20. Last night it snowed; this morning very cold, but bright more moderate and pleasant afterwards.
21. The cold continued.
22. Snowed again.
23. Very cold.
24. A very cold day.

## METEOROLOGICAL EXTRACTS FROM THE DIARY OF JOSHUA HEMPSTEAD OF NEW LONDON, CONNECTICUT

### December 1747

12. fair.
13. fair.
14. Cloudy till about 2 Clock & then it began to Rain & Snow & held a violent Storm at E or E N E. it Snowd all night half Leg deep & more.
15. Cloudy & Sometimes Snow all day.
16. fair & prety cold.
17. fair and cold. mr adams was not well not out & his Son Mr Wm adams pr. all day.
18. fair & cold. I was att home all day till near Sunset I went to visit Mr adams who is not well. hath only a bad Cold.
19. Cloudy. I was all day with adam looking Sheep & found but one.
20. Some Small matter of Snow & cold in the foren & in the aftern fair & moderate.
21. fair & cold.
22. Snow in the foren & then Some Rain & then Snow til night but not very much.
23. fair very cold.
24. Mr adams pr all day. very cold in the night & Cloudy for Snow.

25. A very cold storm of snow.
26. Bright and pleasant but cold. A very tight severe season.
27. A cold storm of snow again.
28. Exceeding cold and stormy some hail and rain and forms a crust. Ceased storming p.m. but very cold; as almost any weather that comes . . . Winds exceeding high.
29. A very severe night we have passed through, but God's mercys are new this morning which is bright without clouds, and silvered by the icicles everywhere shining and the trees glistening. But it is still cold. As the day gets up the wind rises. 'Tis as much as we can do to take care of ourselves and the children, provide for and tend the fires, and the cattle. But our eyes should be to the Lord our never failing support. Benjamin Whipple came, and got wood out of the snow and cut it for me. The evening somewhat moderate.
31. It snowed again last night—but today very bright and comfortable.

### January 1748

1. A moderate day.

3. But the weather was such as I could not venture out in.
4. Cloudy and rainy.

7. Snowy day.
8. Snow storm.

9. A bright pleasant day.

12. So slow riding that it was near night when I got home, the weather being thick fogg, southerly wind and warm.
15. The Day was a very cold day, yet many attended the meeting.
16. Snow storm.
17. Rained last night, and a thaw ensues. Thunder and lightning.
19. Snowy again.

21. Snowed and stormed especially at night.

25. a very Cold Storm of Snow att N E held all day. I kept att home all day.
26. fair. I was at home all day.
27. Cloudy in the morn Rain & S— wind in the aftern & at night. I was att home all day. a great Storm of Rain most of the night.
28. N W. Snow & high wind. in the aftern it left Snowing & grew cold & windy. the Snow flew like a fog all day. I was at home all day.
29. fair & very cold & windy. I was att home all day.
30. fair & calm in the morning & then all day moderate & toward night Cloudy & in the Evening It Snowed.
31. fair but last night it Snowed in the last of ye night & then Rained very much. Raised ye Brook & Ran over the Bridge & Exceeding windy. Mr adams pr all Day.

### January 1748

1. fair till night & then a little Rain & Snow in the Evening & Rain in ye night Carried of ye Snow & was very Slippery. the ground all covered with it.
2. Cloudy.
3. Thawing Drisley & cloudy all day. I was at home all day.
4. fair.
5. Cloudy.
6. fair & moderate.
7. fair.
8. Rain moderately. in the morning I Set out for Newlondon & the Rain Increasing I Stopt at Mr Rossiters put my mare in the Stable & toward night it began to Snow & held it till 8 or 9 &c.
9. fair & moderate.
10. fair.
11. Rainy. I was at home all day. had ye flux very much. wee killed my Red Hogg. Weighed—226lb.
12. Rainy.
13. fair.
14. Snowy Squally & Some fair not very cold.
15. fair N W cold & windy.
16. fair. Rain at night.
17. Rainy Last night & ys morning & Some Large hail. aftern fair.
18. fair.
19. fair.
20. fair.
21. Cold & windy Rainy & toward night Hail & Snow. Mr adams pr. all day.

22. It was a rugged day—the snow deep, the air somewhat sharp, the wind blew about the snow.
27. Moderate and pleasant.
28. It snowed this Sabbath also. . . . When we came home at evening, it snowed very hard and was very windy and cold—the night a windy, cold night.
29. And such a day followed as the night was which rendered a tedious time.

### February 1748

1. A fine day.

2. It being a very fine, warm day.

3. A somewhat cold day. . . . The snow was so deep before we got to Deacon Jonathan Keyes that I was obliged to dismount several times, my mare worrying sometimes pritty much to surmount or get through the banks.
4. It snowed all day.

8. Snowed.

11. It was a bright day which we have not had for public assembling this very great while.

15. Snow hard when we returned home.

17. The extremest cold day, I think that we have had this year.
18. Cold day.
19. Bright and comfortable.
20. Snowed again.
22. Snowy day.

27. Snowed p.m.
28. The snow storm continues.

22. fair.
23. fair & pleasant Thawing ye Snow.
24. fair.
25. fair.
26. Rain in the morn & then misty.
27. fair.
28. Rainy in the foren that I did not go to Meeting. aftern fair. I went & Mr adams pr all day.
29. fair & very cold & windy.
30. Snow in ye night ancle deep.
31. fair.

### February 1748

1. fair warm Thawing ye Snow toward dark & in the night itt Rained.
2. fair & warm very dirty Travelling. very windy & Sloppy & Rain about 9 at night.
3. fair in the foren.
4. Snowy last night & most of ye day fine & not much 2 or 3 Inches deep. prety cold. Mr. adams pr. all day.
5. fair.
6. fair & moderate.
7. fair.
8. Rainy tho moderately.
9. fair warm Thawing Dirty weather.
10. Cloudy.
11. fair. Mr adams pr. all day.
12. Rainy in the middle & Latter part of ye day.
13. fair & clear & moderate.
14. very cold & windy & fair N W. a very cold night.
15. fair in the morning wind South & got back to S. E & very cold & Soon aftern it began to Snow & held while after bedtime wind N E.
16. fair.
17. fair & Sharp cold.
18. fair & cold. Mr adams pr all day.
19. fair & not So cold as yesterd.
20. Snow in the foren. aftern fair.
21. fair. aftern it Snowed a Little.
22. Snowy all day but a little in ye Morn.
23. fair.
24. fair.
25. fair. Mr adams pr all day. very warm Thawing weather.
26. fair Southerly weather. it Thawed away the Snow So as to Spoil Sleading.
27. a Snowy day. it began before Sunrise & held all day & Late in ye night.
28. Rainy all day. ye great Quantity of Snow knee deep yt fell yesterday is much of it melted & very Sloppy.
29. fair & very cold.

## March 1748

1. A very great storm of snow. The greatest that has come, perhaps these seven years. Now 31 years since the Great Snow.
3. It was better coming when the way was brake. But 'tis a very tedious time.
4. A fine day though the snow is deep.
5. Snowstorm again and snowed fast for great part of the day. A great body of snow on the earth: the ways are very much blocked up; little stirring but neighbor Ebenezer Maynard here most of the afternoon.
6. It being a pleasant day tho the snow was deep, I attempted to ride over to the South Road.
7. The deep snows prevent my going to Worcester to preach Mr. Maccartys lecture tho tis fine weather overhead.
11. Bright a.m. Thawy toward eve. Rain at night.
12. It being a pleasant day, my wife rode with me in the new slay. I find the snow very deep.
18. Mr. John Brainard . . . designing to have come to me if he could have got here, but the snow is so deep, no horse (I suppose) can pass between here and Mr. Eagers Tavern.
19. I walked out in the morning on the snow to visit divers of my neighbors . . . The day was so bright and pleasant and the sun so warm that I had bad slumping in the snow some times.
20. Snow melts a great pace.
27. It snowed and hailed in the night.
30. Very heavy riding and breaking through the deep snow from Marlboro home.

## March 1748

1. fair & warm a S W wind in the aftern.
2. a violent Storm att N E wind & a great Snow from before Sunrise to near Sunset. I was at home all day. Adm fetched al the Cattle home (from Gilbert Lot) for Shelter. the Sno drives furiously.
3. fair & windy. the Snow drives much. Mr adams pr all day. a Thin Congregation. No weomen.
4. fair & moderate. I went with Joshua to break the way thro ye Snow banks. two Horses backward & forward before the Slead wch adam drove to our Island & then adam drew out the Sleepers as I cut them off while Joshua Cut a Ld of wood & then Adam brot home 5 Sleepers in the Slead &c.
5. Snow in the morning about 2 or 3 hours & then moderate Rain & a little Snow toward night. I was att home all day.
6. Cloudy & warm. I was most of ye day att the Cornfield Shoveling away the Snow in 2 places in order to Thrash Barley & oats.
7. fair.
8. fair most of ye day a Little Snow. Not to hinder business. I was at home all day.
9. fair & cold.
10. fair & moderate. mr adams pr all day.
11. fair. ye English Hay Stack about ¾ left.
12. fair & warm. I was most of the Day on the Island Endeavoring to Split Some posts & Rayls but the frost was so much in ye Timber that I left of.
13. fair Snow at night.
14. fair & moderate. it Thawed Snow Run plentyfully.
15. fair & warm. it froze hard last night.
16. fair.
17. a Small flight of Snow in the morning & then fair. Mr adams pr all day.
18. fair & prety cold.
19. fair.
20. fair & warm.
21. fair & warm.
22. fair & Raw cold at N E & cloudy.
23. fair Raw cold till Sun near Set & then Snow.
24. fair & moderate. a Sacramt day. mr adams pr all day.
25. fair but cloudy.
26. Cloudy in the morning & Soon Rain Hail & Snow a Cold Storm at N. E.
27. fair but cloudy.
28. Cloudy & Raw cold.

## EXTRACTS FROM THE METEOROLOGICAL JOURNAL OF PROF. JOHN WINTHROP, CAMBRIDGE, MASSACHUSETTS

### December 1747

14. At 1600 begins to snow—great storm of wind and snow all night—NE.
15. Continues snowing all day—N.
17. At 1600 a flight of snow.
18. Snow in the night—W.
20. Snow in the night—N.
22. Snows all the afternoon.
25. Snow—N—at 1400 great storm of snow all day—at 1900 continues.
27. Afternoon snows a little—SE.
28. Much rain in the night—0815 now snows—N—great storm of snow until 1300—NW.
30. Evening snows.

### January 1748

1. Snows all the evening.
7. Snows all the afternoon and a little in the evening—ESE.
8. Hails till noon—NNE—snow all afternoon—evening snows a little.
11. At 1600 begins to rain—rains gently all evening.
14. From 0900 till 1000 snows—at 1300 hails a little—SW—a flight or two of snow later—NW.
16. From 1430 till 1730 snows—SE.
17. Rains in the morning—S—at 1000 very dark and rains hard with some thunder—noon fair—SW.
21. Soon rains—at 1100 begins to snow and snows very fast all the afternoon and evening—N.
24. Snows all the afternoon—NNW.
26. Rains till 1000—SE.
28. Begins to snow at 0845—E—continues snowing till 1445—then clears up—W.
31. Snow in the night—NW.

### February 1748

1. At 2000 begins to rain—SW.
4. About 0800 begins to snow and continues.
8. Snows till 1400—NW.
15. Afternoon snows a little—snows very fast all the evening.
18. Excessive cold—NW.
22. At 1100 begins to snow—continues till 2100—N.
27. At 1430 begins to snow—E.
28. Great storm of snow—all night—at sunrise hail—NE—evening snows—N.
29. Snows till 0900—snows a little all day—NW.

### March 1748

2. At 1030 begins to snow—great storm of snow till late in the evening—E to N.
5. At 0900 begins to snow—snows all the afternoon and evening—NE.
22. Snows a little 1000 to 1100—NW.
23. Snows all day and evening—NE.
25. Evening snows a little—E.
26. Hails from 1615 till late in night—ENE.
27. Hails and snows till 1000—N.
28. Afterwards snows and hails—E.

### April 1748

3. At 1000 begins to snow—continues all day—NE.
4. Evening snows a little—SE.

---

[1] Sidney Perley. *Historic storms of New England.* Salem, Mass., The Salem Press, 1891. 54.
[2] Records of the First Church, Cambridge. *The Genealogical Magazine* (Boston), **1**, (1890), 361.
[3] Samuel Lane. *A journal for the years 1739–1803.* Charles L. Hanson, ed. Concord, N.H. Hist. Soc., 1937. 68.
[4] *Boston Weekly News-Letter, 10 Dec 1747.*
[5] The diary of Ebenezer Parkman. *Proc. Amer. Antiq. Soc.* (Worcester). **73-1**, (1963), 45.
[6] Edward A. Holyoke. Ms. Met. Jour. (Harvard).
[7] Journal of Deacon David Batchelder. Warren Brown. *History of Hampton Falls, N.H.* Concord, The Rumford Press, 1900. 476.
[8] *Journals of the Rev. Thomas Smith, and the Rev. Samuel Deane.* William Willis, ed. Portland, Joseph S. Baily, 1849. 270.
[9] Diary of Lt. John Preston. *Essex Inst. Hist. Coll.* (Salem). **9**, (1872), 258.
[10] T. Smith, *Journal,* 270.
[11] E. Parkman, *Diary,* 115–20; 386–404.

# THE SEVERE WINTER OF 1764–65

The winter of 1764–65 was the snowiest since 1748 and the coldest since 1741. The season featured two notable northeasters: one introduced the snow season to the Middle Colonies and southern New England on Christmas night, and the other concluded the season in late March with a mighty coastal storm. There had been some snows in late October, November, and early December across northern New England resulting in a 15-inch blanket at Portland, Maine, on the 17th of December.[1]

The storm on Christmas night and the following day swept the entire coast. Described at Philadelphia as "a violent windstorm and snow," it commenced at 2000 Christmas night and continued through the next day, although changing to rain toward the end.[2] The Delaware River, which had been clogged with much floating ice, was cleared out by the northeasterly gales. At New York City, too, the wind blew strong and much snow fell—on the same day of the month that storms of equal status would occur in 1872 and in 1947.[3]

Along the Massachusetts coast the heavy northeaster did much damage, especially at Salem, and a deep snow fell both on the coast and inland. At Bedford, New Hampshire, the snow cover measured "more than two feet" and at Portland, Maine, Rev. Smith judged there were between two and three feet. "It has thus far been a severe winter; nothing like it since 1747 and 1748, then it was more so," he commented.[4]

A cold Arctic outbreak came at the turn of the year as a northwesterly air stream rushed into the trough of the northeaster. On the 30th Dr. Muhlenburg, then at Germantown, Pennsylvania, declared: "Today we had such penetrating cold as we have not had in many years."[5] The mercury at New York City dropped to zero; after three days of such conditions the rivers and harbor became clogged with ice. On one day the Narrows between the Upper and Lower Bays were jammed with ice floes so that even small boats could not pass.[6] Large ships were still detained at their docks as late as January 23d, unable to put to sea during the first three weeks of the month. The Delaware closed during the New Year's cold spell, and even as far south as Annapolis ice covered Chesapeake Bay so as to prevent all communication by boat.[7]

Another major snowstorm swept up the coast on the 5-6th to raise snow depths to unusual early January figures. At Germantown in suburban Philadelphia the depth was reported at two feet.[8] At New York City, James Watts, the secretary of the New York Historical Society, who also kept a watchful eye of the weather, noted in his interesting *Letter Book* that on the 10th there was "snow and sleighing in abundance, more than has been known for this twenty years."[9]

A circulation shift took place about January 10th with a westerly flow moderating the wintry weather prevailing since before Christmas. Sleighing conditions remained good even though the melting reached as far north as Maine. Rev. Smith observed on the 22d: "the heart of winter seems broken; incomparable sledding." And on the 23d, during the traditional January thaw period, he noted: "it was a charming day."[10]

The northerly blasts soon renewed their attack. Temperatures plunged to the lowest figures reached since the introduction of the thermometer. At Kings College in New York City an instrument of an undocumented exposure dropped its mercury into the ball, *i.e.*, zero, on January 26th. According to contemporary press reports, the fluid remained in that depressed state for 57 hours until 1400 on the 28th. It was estimated that the lowest point reached was −6°, though just how this interpolation arose was not explained. If the thermometer was accurate, the exposure correct, and the observation properly made, this certainly would constitute the longest duration of below-zero temperatures in the meteorological history of New York City. In the light of subsequent events, the authenticity of this early measurement of thermometric nadirs must be viewed skeptically. Since fairly continuous records commenced in 1788, on only one occasion, 9-10 January 1859, has the temperature remained below zero for more than 24 hours. The extreme degree of cold on this 1765 occasion may be judged by the reading of −4.75° at Newport, Rhode Island, the lowest there since thermometer watching commenced in 1752—the previous lowest had been only −3° in the bitter winter of 1751-52.[12] At Cambridge, Prof. Winthrop had a low reading of −9°, but this was not necessarily the minimum as he did not have a registering thermometer, and the Boston press also carried the same figure of −9°.[13] Down in Pennsylvania Dr. Muhlenberg's diary for the 27th read: "Last night and today we had penetrating cold, the like of which we had not had in many years, with the exception of that which I experienced in Upper Lausitz in the year 1740."[14] (This was the famous cold season of the 18th century in Europe.)

The Hudson River at Manhattan Island again froze over almost solid to the Jersey shore. This blocked the usual communication routes forcing the southern mail for a few days to cross from Staten Island over the Narrows, and then reaching Manhattan via the East River ferry. There was an account of a Philadelphia-bound traveller who decided to take the direct route across the North River ice to Jersey on foot to speed his journey homeward. When 350 yards from the shore, he fell through a weak place, but was hauled to safety by several on shore who were watching his progress and saw his plight.[15] There were no reports of mass crossings of the ice at this time such as would occur during the cold cycles in 1780, 1805, 1821, and 1836.

The Delaware River at Philadelphia had closed on 31 December and continued solid until near the end of February. To celebrate the event an ox was roasted on the ice midway between the city and Camden, amidst the dispensation of warming liquids.[16] Out at Pittsburgh the two rivers were passable on foot for a period of six weeks.[17]

Snow cover throughout the northern colonies reached a maximum about mid-February. John Watts in New York City related on the 11th: "for this six weeks we have been in Greenland, the ground covered near three feet with snow, a few months again will hurry us into the torrid zone."[18] Up at Hartford in Connecticut the press furnished an account of a dispute that arose at a town meeting on 19 February as to the depth of the snow cover. A participant went outside with a stick and after several measurements concluded the mean snow depth to be 38 inches.[19] Press estimates in eastern Massachusetts at this period mentioned depths from three to four feet on the level. Reports from Down East in Maine spoke of 60-inch cover.[20]

February turned somewhat milder after mid-month. At Portland the 18th was "fine, warm weather," and Smith noted that no snow had fallen in February. It is not unusual for coastal Maine to miss snowstorms which may drop deep cover along the southern New England shore. At Philadelphia a thaw commenced on the 14th and the ice soon rotted sufficiently to permit vessels to come up to Reedy's Island below the city, and by the 28th the shipping column informed: "our navigation is now quite clear and several vessels have come up."[21] At Portsmouth, New Hampshire, the whole of Great Bay remained frozen on the 25th sufficiently strong to permit a ship of 200 tons to be hauled on the ice by 80 yoke of oxen. Some thousand persons thronged the ice to witness the spectacle.[22] Connecticut River opened by the 11th of March after having been shut up for three full months.[23]

The northeaster of 24 March 1765 deserves top ranking in the list of destructive coastal storms of our period. It caused shipwrecks from North Carolina to Maine, raised a mighty tide which did great damage to wharves and harbor installations, and dropped a very deep snow in the range of two feet and more from Pennsylvania to Massachusetts.

The *Pennsylvania Gazette* at Philadelphia gave full notice to the storm:

> On Sunday night last there came on here a very severe snow storm, the wind blowing very high, which continued all the next day, when it is believed there fell the greatest quantity of snow that has been known (considering the advanced season) for many years past; it being generally held to be two feet, or two feet and a half, on the level, and in some places deeper. A great number of trees were destroyed by it, some torn up by the roots, others broken off; and the roads are rendered so bad and dangerous, that there has hardly been any travelling since.[24]

In the back country on the Maryland-Pennsylvania border, Charles Mason and Jeremiah Dixon were surveying the famous Line. Their journal contained the following significant entry:

> March: 12–20 observations interrupted by clouds and rain; 21, 22, 23 snow; 24 at 9 a.m. snow was near 3 feet deep; 25, 26, 27, snow so deep we could not proceed.[25]

The editor of the *Massachusetts Gazette & Boston News-Letter* took notice of the great storm in the issue of 28 March 1765. His account is presented *verbatim et literatim* to show how a colonial editor handled a weather story:

> Friday last we had here a severe Wind at about E.N.E. accompanied with Rain and Snow, which encreased, excepting at some Intervals, until Saturday Night, when a very violent Storm began, and continued until the Next Day in the Afternoon: The Full Sea was about Two o'Clock; after which Time the Tide, or rather the Sea, drove in higher than it had done for many Years past: almost all the Wharves in Town, (excepting Hancock's, which has lately been raised and repaired) and several Streets near them, were laid under Water; the Cellars and lower Floors of many Stores, Shops, and Houses were also overflowed, and the Goods that were therein much wet: But the greatest Damage which accrued was by the Violence of the Waves that rushed in like a Flood, and beat up a great Part of many of the Wharves, carrying off the Ship-Timber, Cord-Wood, Boards, Shingles, and almost every other Thing that lay thereon; the Vessels in the Harbour were scarcely holden by their Anchors and Fasts, several of them drove up to the Heads of Docks, beating against each other and against the Shops, &c. near which they were driven, and being surrounded with the floating Timber, they received great Damage, some losing their Booms, Bowsprits, Masts, &c. and two or three were sunk: At the Time of the greatest Difficulty, the Wind was extreme high, the Rain and Snow fell in Abundance, and the Sea flowed in with such Impetuosity, that scarce any were able to give Assistance, until the Storm abated, which was at the Ebbing of the Tide, about 3 o'Clock, P.M. —but the Storm did not subside until the next Morning. We are not able to make a Computation of the Loss hereby sustained to many of the Inhabitants of the Town; certainly it must take considerable Sums (to) repair the Wharves, Vessels, Stores, Shops, &c. that have greatly suffered, besides the Loss of Salt, Rice, and other Articles, which were in Warehouses that the Tide came into, and the floating away the Lumber, which has been drove promiscuously to all Parts of the Harbour, and left where the Waves carried it. We don't learn that much Sugar has been damaged at this Time, this is attributed to the prudential Care of those who had any of that valuable Article, by their storing and timely laying the Hogsheads on Skids, to a Heighth above an extraordinary Tide.—This Precaution we mention that others who are often exposed, may take the like Method.
>
> The Wharves, Stores, &c. at Charlestown, have suffered considerably by the above Storm.
>
> We hear that in the Country-Towns great Damage has been done also by the blowing down of Apple and other Fruit-Trees, Fences, Sheds, &c. There was not much Rain with them, but the Snow fell in many Places in the Roads above a Foot high.
>
> We hear that much Damage was sustained at Marblehead, one Schooner belonging to Piscataqua outwardbound, was stove to Pieces, and another drove up so high on the Shore as not to be got off again.
>
> At Newbury Port we hear that vast Damage was done there, by the Sea beating into the Stores, and washing away vast Quantities of Salt, Sugars, &c. and damaging the Wharves and Vessels that lay in the Harbour; we also hear, that the Hulls of several

Vessels building there, were drove from off their Stocks, and carried to Places from whence it will be very difficult to remove them.

As there are many Vessels expected about this Time on the Coast, we are not without Fears of some of them having been too near the Shore in this Storm.

From Portsmouth in New-Hampshire, we hear the Storm was extreme violent there, carrying all before it where the Tide came, destroying vast Quantities of Goods that were in Warehouses near the Water-Side; but that some Judgment may be made of the Damage sustained there, we shall insert the Account as published in the *Portsmouth Mercury,* viz.

### PORTSMOUTH, MARCH 25.

Yesterday we had the most violent storm of Wind and Snow, that has been known for many Years past; The Damages sustained by this Storm is very great, having blown down several Wharves and Warehouses entirely to Pieces, broke sundry Vessels from their Fasts, &c. The Damage sustain'd by the above Storm to the Wharves, &c. of this Town, is suppos'd to amount to some Thousands.

[1] T. Smith, *Journal,* 275.
[2] S. Hazard, *Effects of climate,* 2, 25.
[3] *N. Y. Gaz.,* 7 Jan 1765.
[4] *The Diary of Matthew Patten of Bedford, N. H.* Concord, The Rumford Printing Co., 1903. 146.
[5] *The Journals of Henry Muhlenberg.* Phila., The Muhlenberg Press, 1945. 2, 160–61.
[6] *N. Y. Gaz.,* 7 Jan 1765.
[7] *Md. Gaz.* (Annapolis), 10 Jan 1765.
[8] H. Muhlenberg, *Journal,* 2, 163.
[9] Letter Book of John Watts. *Coll. N. Y. Hist. Soc.* 61, (1928), 326.
[10] T. Smith, *Journal,* 275.
[11] *N. Y. Mercury,* 4 Feb 1765.
[12] *Newport Mercury,* 28 Jan 1765.
[13] *Mass. Gaz.,* 4 Feb 1765.
[14] H. Muhlenberg, *Journal,* 2, 172.
[15] *Penna. Gaz.,* 7 Feb 1765.
[16] S. Hazard, *Effects of climate,* 2, 25.
[17] *Idem.*
[18] J. Watts, *Letter Book,* 331.
[19] E. Stiles, Ms. Thermo. Reg. (Yale).
[20] *Mass. Gaz.* in J. Felt. *Annals of Salem.* 2, 464.
[21] S. Hazard, *Effects of climate,* 2, 25.
[22] Portsmouth dispatch, 25 Feb, in *Penna. Gaz.,* 21 March 1765.
[23] *Conn. Courant* (Hartford), 11 March 1765.
[24] *Penna. Gaz.,* 28 March 1765.
[25] Charles Mason's Daily Journal, Ms. in National Archives, quoted in *Maryland Weather Service.* Baltimore, The Johns Hopkins Press, 1899. 1, 343–44.
[26] *Mass. Gaz.,* 28 March 1765.

## SNOWY MARCH IN 1772

The winter season of 1772 was often recalled in later days mainly for the deep snows which fell over the Northeast during the month of March and in early April. In 1807 an editor in central New York State, when writing about the great snowstorm of March 31st of that year, remembered March 1772 as a particularly snowy month in his region. Joseph Felt, the historian of Salem, included 1772 among the six most memorable winters of the 18th Century when he made his compilation in the 1840's.[1]

Midwinter in 1772 had been cold in the Northeast, but not particularly snowy. The Washington and Jefferson Snowstorm of late January, dropping over 30 inches over Virginia and Maryland, did not develop more than a modest snowstorm along the New England coast and its influence reached only a short distance inland.[2] But with the commencement of March the storm track shifted closer to New England, and a series of coastal storms successively piled snow upon snow, even at tidewater Boston, maintaining a level approaching 24 inches at times throughout March and into the first days of April!

The sequence of storms at coastal Newport in Rhode Island was carefully noted by Ezra Stiles both in his regular diary and in his thermometrical register. The following comprised a composite of the weather comments from both:

March 5. Snow storm—4″—31° and 35°—SE.
    9. Snow—29.5° and 32°—NE.
  10. Measured snow 8″ on a level.
  11. Snow storm.
  12. Snow knee deep in Warwick Woods.
  13. Noon—snow.
  14. Snow storm last night—measured whole depth of snow on a level, 10½″ or 11″.
  15. Very cold—9.5° at morning.
  16. Snow 2″ at 1800.
  20. A violent snow storm all day—snow high round 5″—32°—NE.
April 2. Snow at 1200—34°—NE.
   3. Snow—very stormy—high wind—32°—NE.[3]

The same sequence of snowstorms was noticed at Salem in the weather observations of Edward A. Holyoke—on the 5th, 9th, 11th, 13th, 16th, 19–20th, and April 2–3d. The storm of the 5th was attended by "very high wind," on the 19th there was "very high wind and much snow on the ground," and the storm of April third was rated as "a great storm of snow," a phrase he reserved for only the biggest storms.[4] Professor Winthrop kept watch on his barometer during these days and noticed three major depressions: 28.87″ on the 5th, 28.95″ on the 12th, and 28.97″ on the 21st. These may not have been corrected for sea level as his total range of barometric readings during the month varied from 28.87" to 30.15". Winthrop rated March colder than February, one of the few times that this has occurred in eastern Massachusetts.[5]

Indicative of the deep snow cover were the diary entries of Edward P. Sparhawk of Lynnfield near Boston. These appear in Alonzo Lewis' *History of Lynn* (1844). A search for the manuscript diary has been unrewarding so that one cannot judge the writer's reliability at firsthand. If authentic, these March snows certainly were the greatest such ever experienced in the area:

> An amazing quantity of snow fell in the month of March, such as I never knew in the time that I have lived. On the fifth of March, the amount of snow which fell, was 16 inches; on the ninth, 9 inches; on the eleventh, 8 inches; on the thirteenth, 7 inches; on the 16th, 4 inches, and on the twentieth, 15 inches. Thus the whole amount of snow, in sixteen days, was nearly five feet on a level.[6]

Though Boston press accounts do not wholly substantiate the above, they do indicate a very deep snow on the ground. After the final big storm on April 2–3d, an editor commented: "as severe a snow storm as any during the past winter—the snow two feet deep."[7]

The storms also covered inland areas with a very deep cover. On March 24th the *Connecticut Courant* at Hartford took notice:

> Since the first of March instant, there have been no less than four heavy storms of snow which is very much drifted and has rendered travelling almost impracticable. The snow upon the level in these parts is upwards of three feet. It is said the winter past has been the most severe of any since the year 1740.[8]

The paralysis of communications as a result of the heavy snow cover prevented any mails arriving at Hartford during the first week of April. On the 7th no Boston or New York newspaper had come in since those of March 28th. The Connecticut River broke up on the last day of March, a relatively late date for this annual event.[9]

Up in southern New Hampshire Matthew Patten at Bedford also had a tale of heavy snows to fill his diary:

> March 5. There fell the deepest snow that fell this winter at one times falling. It was a foot deep.
> 9. Snowed this day.
> 11. A heavy storm of snow from the NE.
> 20. Was a NE storm of snow and blowed very hard.[10]

Around Hampton Falls in southeastern New Hampshire the surveyors were called out on April 8th to break out the roads as the late storm had filled them three feet deep.[11] In Maine the season of March was "a cold blustery month."[12]

The March snows affected the Middle Colonies also. At Philadelphia there had been some very mild weather in late February with the mercury soaring to 65°, the navigation of the river open, and shad appearing in the market. But March proved cold and snowy. There were snowstorms on the 9th, 11th, 15–16th, and 18–19th: these accumulated to a depth of "about two feet deep on level," according to the local press.[13] Ice commenced to run in the river again after having been clear. A final storm on April 2d dropped an additional six inches of new snow, but this soon melted and by the 5th winter had ended its hold on the region.[14]

---

[1] *Otsego Herald* (Cooperstown, N. Y.), 2 April 1807. *Salem Gazette* in *N. Y. Tribune*, 5 Feb 1844.
[2] See pages 144–46.
[3] E. Stiles, *Diary*, 1, 216–20.
———, Ms. Thermo. Reg.
[4] E. Holyoke, Ms. Met. Jour.
[5] J. Winthrop, Ms. Met. Obs.
[6] Alonzo Lewis. *The history of Lynn, including Nahant*. Boston, Samuel N. Dickinson, 1844. 211.
[7] Boyle's Journal. *New Eng. Gen. Hist. Reg.* (Boston). 84 (1930), 358.
[8] *Conn. Courant* (Hartford), 24 March 1772.
[9] *Ibid.*, 31 March & 7 April 1772.
[10] M. Patten, *Diary*, 281.
[11] Warren Brown. *History of Hampton Falls, N. H.* Concord, The Rumford Press, 1900. 476.
[12] T. Smith, *Journal*, 278.
[13] *Penna. Gaz.*, 19 March 1772.
[14] *Ibid.*, 6 April 1772.

## THE LONG WINTER OF 1783–84

### A Very Hard Close Winter

The winter of 1783–84 earned the reputation of being the longest such season in our period of study, and in addition ranked close to the top for extremes of deep snow cover and low temperatures. Here were some of its achievements: produced the greatest seasonal snowfall ever known in northern New Jersey, the longest spell of below-zero readings of record in southern New England, shut up the harbors and channels of Chesapeake Bay longer than any other interruption, and received recognition by the dean of early historians of Maine as the longest and coldest winter since the area had been settled by white men. Coming so closely on the heels of the Hard Winter of 1780, people were able to make a comparison, and many thought the Long winter of 1783–84 more "tedious" since the severe conditions continued well into spring.

After a "strange warm day" serving as a traditional weather-breeder, winter clamped down with an early-season snowstorm on 12–13 November which swept the Atlantic seaboard with two to three inches of snowfall from New Jersey to Maine. Another November storm on the 28–29th commenced the sleighing season by dropping 11 inches in northern New Jersey and 10 inches in southern New Hampshire.[1]

There were periods of alternate cold and warmth throughout December and January. The major snowstorm of the winter, reminiscent of 1779–80, came at the end of the year. On December 30th and 31st a coastal storm deposited 20 inches at Morristown, New Jersey, almost on the same date that four years earlier General Washington's camp there had been similarly buried.[2] At Trappe, Pennsylvania, on New Year's Day the snow piled up "uncommonly deep so that one can scarsely get out of the house," noted Rev. Muhlenburg.[3]

A complete thaw followed toward the end of the first week of January which melted much of the snow, put the rivers in flood, and greatly weakened harbor ice. In eastern Massachusetts and Rhode Island much damage to bridges and dams resulted.[4] But with a change of the circulation snows again came to New Jersey with measurable falls on the 10–11th and 18–19th.[5] Then the traditional January thaw followed, again putting the rivers in flood along the coastal plain as snows melted and ice fields broke up. An ice jam in the James River at Richmond gave way on the night of January 24th. The rush of water and ice swamped the boats tied up at the head of navigation below the falls and carried away an important bridge over a creek nearby.[6] In eastern New England the great January freshet destroyed part of the much-traveled Watertown bridge cutting communication with the north from Boston.[7] Winter, returning with a vengeance after the week of mild weather, brought 18 inches of fresh snow to Morristown and 15 inches to New Haven. The events of this so far in-and-out winter were caught in the diary of Joseph Lewis of Morristown, New Jersey:

Nov. 12. 2.5" snow.
    27–28. 11".
Dec. 2–3. 2".
    4. 3".
    8. Indian summer began.*
    11. No snow now appears.
    18. 5".
    24. 2".
    25–26. 1".
    27. Most excellent sledding.
    29. 1".
    30–1. Snow began at 0300/30th—continued to 0400/1st—it fell about 20 inches deep and drifted considerably.
Jan. 11. 5".
    14. Good sledding continues.
    18–19. 10".
    20. 3".
    26–27. From 2100/26th to 2100/27th—18".

The snow cover laid down in the last days of January remained for many days and prepared the scene for the most spectacular event of the winter. Arctic air masses, which had been permitted only temporary hold on the Middle Atlantic and New England area so far, drove southward during the second week of February, the time climatologically suited for the greatest development and refrigeration of the Hudson Bay type anticyclone. On eight consecutive mornings from 10 to 17 February the mercury at Hartford, Connecticut, stood at −12° or lower. This was on a reliable thermometer which was to remain in service for fifty years. At New Haven the reading was at −2° or lower on six consecutive mornings on Ezra Stiles' long-trusted instrument. His minimum of −10° came at sunrise on the 10th. The readings at Hartford, which may be taken as representative of interior southern New England, exceeded any other period for duration of intense cold. The records were preserved by Noah Webster and later published in the *American Journal of Science*:

Feb. 10 −19°    Feb. 14 −20°
      11 −12           15 −12
      12 −13           16 −16
      13 −19           17 −16 [9]

Most river and harbors, if not already shut up in January, now closed to navigation. 1784 would long remain in the memories of mariners as their toughest ice season. Baltimore harbor had been sealed on January 2d and did not open until March 25th, 16 days later than in 1780![10] Chesapeake Bay was reported frozen nearly to its entrance. Thomas Jefferson, then at Annapolis, remarked on the severity of the season in his correspondence, and James Madison wrote from Orange, Virginia: "We had a severer season and particularly a greater quantity of snow than is remembered to have distinguished any preceding winter."[11] The Delaware River at Philadelphia stopped on 26 December and remained so until March 12th.[12] Newport harbor in Rhode Island closed during the mid-February cold spell so that people could cross to the mainland, only the third time in the century that this could be accomplished.[13] The western end of Long Island Sound also congealed permitting sleds and wheeled vehicles to cross from Long Island to the mainland where now the mighty Whitestone Bridge spans the narrow waterway.[14] But the most spectacular news was made at New York City where the Narrows between Staten Island and Long Island became choked with ice and remained

---

* This is the first use of the term Indian Summer in a weather diary as noted in this research. St. John Crèvecoeur's employment of the term in his essay antedated John Lewis' by about five years. It is significant to note that both had lived in close proximity: Lewis in northern New Jersey and Crèvecoeur in southeastern New York.

so for ten days preventing ships sailing from Manhattan Island through the Upper and Lower Bays to the open ocean past Sandy Hook. Harbor and weather conditions in New York City were described by General Josiah Harmar who was awaiting passage to Europe:

### February 1784

7. Very cold—fine fair NW wind—The Narrows chocked with the ice, no sailing.
8. Glorious very cold wind—The Ice, The Ice still prevents our sailing—Clear all to the Narrows.
9. Very cold—yesterday & today extremely so.
10. The weather colder than in the Hard Winter of 1780—A prodigious quantity of Ice made.
11. Snow all day & night but more moderate than yesterday—Mr. Lacase one of our passengers this day set off for Philadelphia expecting to return & sail with us in the pacquet.
12. Fine snow—freezes still out of the sun.
13. Very cold still—the North River frozen.
14. Very cold weather.
15. Such a severe close spell of weather has scarcely ever been known.
16. Very cold.
17. More moderate weather—a Brig sailed today—but ships cannot yet.
18. Thawing weather.
19. Moderate—In hopes the river will now be soon cleared of Ice.
20. Thaw'd all day.
21. Fine weather—Wind W.N.W. Set sail from the wharf at 10 o'clock A.M.—left the Hook with a gentle fair wind at 1 o'clock—almost out of sight of the High Lands of Neversink [Navesink] by night.[15]

Another severe cold spell came in late February, as it would at the end of the famous cold month of February 1934, to insure that the period would qualify among the memorably cold months of recorded American meteorological history. At Philadelphia the mercury went below zero on the 29th and also dipped below on the first two days of March.[16] At New Haven Leap Day of 1784 was the coldest daylight period of the entire winter as Stiles' thermometer remained close to the zero mark all day and a strong wind blew throughout.[17] The month of February 1784 ranked as the fifth coldest February in the New Haven summary covering the years 1781–1870.[18]

Though March 1784 did not average as great a departure from normal as February, it ran colder than normal. The snow cover in Connecticut and New Jersey was increased by two moderate falls early in the month. "The dreadful winter is setting in afresh," Muhlenburg dolefully wrote in his diary, but by the 13th a definite thaw commenced. A return to wintry conditions came after the vernal equinox.[19] Little did people suspect that another month of hard weather lay ahead. Noah Webster, declaring "such a winter and spring are seldom known in this climate," left a chronicle of the backward April weather he experienced at Hartford:

April 1. A small fall of snow.
  3. A storm of snow.
  9. A fall of snow.
  11. A fall of snow.
  21. Hail and cold.
  22. This is the first pleasant day.
May 1. At home. Cold, cloudy, disagreeable weather.[20]

At Dover in New Hampshire the snowfall on 3–4 April measured 7 inches, and this fell on drifts standing three feet deep. On the 14th Jeremy Belknap noted in his diary: "snow goes off very slowly, travelling extremely bad." There remained patches of snow on the ground as late as May 8th where there had been deep drifts. His apple trees did not bloom until May 30th, a full 18 days later than his earliest recorded blossoming in 1759.[21] Down in North Carolina, the *Moravian Diary* summed up the effect of the long winter: "The present lack of grain oppresses the land, so that men and cattle are suffering. . . . Because of the hard winter, which lasted unusually long, most of the farmers used all their feed before they could turn the cattle out to graze."[22]

It was Down East in Maine that the winter lingered longest and made the greatest impression on contemporaries. William Williamson in his impressive *History of Maine,* published in 1832, devoted considerable space to the unusual season.[23] Rev. Smith's *Journal* read:

November 12. A strange warm day. 13. A deep snow. 28. A great storm.
December. The first half moderate, the latter cold and stormy.
January 31. The first week of this month was moderate, but the rest horrid cold, stormy, snowy weather.
February. A cold month, and indeed a cold winter through the whole; the longest and coldest ever known.
March has been moderate, and not so very windy as usual.
April 6. It snowed yesterday and went away today. 17. This is the third day of cold, rainy, snowy weather. 29. Raw, cold; the spring is very backward.[24]

## DR. MUHLENBERG'S WINTER AT TRAPPE: 1783–84

### December 1783

14. The weather was pleasant.
19. Snow and cold weather.
20. Snow.
22. We had a violent wind storm the whole day and night.
23. Calm, clear weather after a violent storm last night.
24. Much snow and bitter cold.
25. We had snow and bitter cold.

27. Extreme cold.
29. The severe cold continues.

### January 1784

1. The New Year set in with an uncommonly deep snow, so that one can scarsely get out of the house.
7. This severe winter season.
14. It snowed hard the whole day.
16. The cold is more severe and continuous than it has been for many years.
19. Last night a violent snow and rainstorm arose and continued throughout the whole day with such force that everything must be broken to pieces. The rolling sounds like many wagons threshing about the sky, and along with it there is cold in extreme degree.
23. Heavy rain which is melting the deep snow and making the roads icy and impassable.
25. He could not get across the Schuylkill because the streams are too high and full of ice floes.
27. Last night we had another deep snow, followed today by a continued wind storm from the northwest and dreadful showers of snow. Never have I experienced such winter weather in this country.
29. Our children would be glad to be back home, but they must wait until there is a path made on the road, for the windstorm has piled up the snow as high as six to eight feet in many narrow places on the road.

### February 1784

7. The cold is so continuously severe that it is not to be compared with previous winters.
13. The severe cold continues still.
14. The severe cold still continues.
26. Snow again and rough cold winds.
29. Today it is cold in the extreme, with a strong wind from the northwest, as it was in 1740 in Upper Lusatia when in some places the fir trees cracked with the sound of cannon shots from the cold.

### March 1784

1. The severe cold still continues.
7. Thawing weather, half rain, half snow.
9. Another deep snowfall. . . . The dreadful winter is setting in afresh.
20. Cold weather and frost again, as in winter.
21. Bitter cold.
29. Tolerable weather.

### April 1784

2. Last night a deep snow fell, but it was all melted today.
7. Cold storm, wind and frost.
8. Cold storm, wind and frost.
9. Some snow and frost.
10. Raw cold weather.
11. Stormy windy weather.
15. Storm wind and rain.
16. The storm wind continued unabated.
26. First thunder and lightning storm.[25]

[1] Diary of Joseph Lewis. *Proc. N. J. Hist. Soc.* 59-3, (July 1941), 159.
[2] *Ibid.*, 160.
[3] H. Muhlenberg, *Journal,* 3, 574.
[4] *The Boston Magazine for January 1784.* 1-4, 122.
[5] J. Lewis, *Diary,* 161.
[6] Richmond, 31 Jan, in *Penna. Packet* (Phila.), 21 Feb 1784.
[7] Boston, 9 Feb, *ibid.,* 28 Feb 1784.
[8] J. Lewis, *Diary,* 165.
[9] N. Webster. Notices of extraordinary seasons of cold. *Amer. Jour. Sci.* (New Haven). 28-1 (July 1835), 186.
[10] J. Thomas Scharf. *The chronicles of Baltimore.* Balto., Turnbull Bros., 1874. 235.
[11] James Madison to Thomas Jefferson, Orange, Feb. 11 1784. *The Papers of Thomas Jefferson.* Julian P. Boyd, ed. Princeton, Princeton University Press, 1952. 6, 537.
[12] S. Hazard, *Effects of climate,* 2, 380.
[13] *Newport Mercury,* 14 Feb 1784.
[14] *Conn. Jour.* (New Haven), 18 Feb 1784.
[15] Harmar Mss. (Clements Library, Univ. of Michigan).
[16] S. Hazard, *Effects of climate,* 2, 380.
[17] E. Stiles, *Diary,* 3, 109.
[18] Elias Loomis and H. A. Newton. On the mean temperature, and the fluctuation of temperature, at New Haven, Conn. *Trans. Conn. Acad. Arts & Sci.* 1-1, (1866), 194.
[19] H. Muhlenberg, *Journal,* 3, 584.
[20] N. Webster, *Notes,* 1, 73–76.
[21] Jeremy Belknap. Ms. Met. Obs. (Mass. Hist. Soc.).
[22] *Records of the Moravians in North Carolina.* 5, 2016.
[23] William D. Williamson. *The History of the State of Maine.* Hallowell, Glazier, Masters & Co., 1832. 1, 100.
[24] T. Smith, *Journal,* 282–83.
[25] H. Muhlenberg, *Journal,* 574.

## WINTER COMES LATE IN 1785

*We had a Close Winter, Especially after January; when the Snow was Exceeding Deep & Drifted, & Difficult passing, as almost ever known—very Cold and backward Spring; Scarcely any Spring work done 'till the latter end of April.*

It was "Annus Memorabilis." Among the noteworthy events of the year, Nathan Taylor of Sanbornton, New Hampshire, listed a diary entry of April 20th relating how he drove his team of oxen over the fences on a hard crust of snow to the saw mill, but upon his return the sun had softened the surface and the oxen fell through frequently.[1] This marked the culmination of a winter that was outstanding for late and great snowstorms. The last major fall occurred as late as April 19th, on the 10th anniversary of the Battles of Lexington and Concord.

There had been a series of heavy storms in February. From the 24th to 26th there raged "an exceeding great driving snow storm" from southern Pennsylvania to Maine.[2] Additional snows fell in March and into the first part of April. The combination of low maximum temperatures and frequent new snows kept the cover at near record depths throughout the first 30 days of the normal spring season.

The sequence of snowstorms at Bedford, New Hampshire, appeared in the diary of Matthew Patten:

Feb. 1. A very tedious storm of snow from the northeastward the wind high.
  2. Lay by all day. The snow 16 or 18 inches deep & drifted much. No paths.
  12. Twelve inches. Northwest.
  24. Snow greater part of day from the N.E. The wind high and the storm constantly increasing. It stormed all night and drifted much.
  25. A very heavy storm all day and all night following.
  26. I set out for home after 12 o'clock and had hard work to get home by dark. Much drifted at all places where the wind could do it.
Mar. 30. Heavy storm snow and hail, 8 to 10 inches.
Apr. 3. Snow storm from N.E.
  8. Snow.
  10. Snow N.E.[4]

Jeremy Belknap, then at Dover, New Hampshire, had much the same story:

Feb. 24. A violent driving NE snow storm begins this evening and holds till the 26th—the deepest snow we have had & very much drifted.
Mar. 30. A violent snow storm. Wind began, went around to N.E.—snow very deep & solid mixed in hail—measured one foot deep.
Apr. 1. Snow drifts about my house 6 feet deep and in many places level with the fences—it is as deep everywhere as after the great snow of Feb. 24th.
Apr. 19. A snow storm with hail.[5]

The final storm of the season on April 19th made a great impression on all. It was long remembered—as late as 1843 when another backward spring came along, it called forth reminiscences from many editors. The storm of the 19th produced a massive precipitation and covered a vast geographical extent. In most places along the coast there fell a dense mixture of snow and sleet. New Haven had 2.5 inches and Hartford 3.0 inches of a solid mass, but in the hills of western Connecticut snow prevailing over sleet and glaze piled up to depths of 24 inches in Litchfield County.[6] At Salem, Massachusetts, snow and sleet covered the streets to a depth of four inches with the mercury reading 34° at noon of the 19th.[7] At Harvard the barometer dropped to 29.16″ early on the 20th as a northeaster at force 6 swept the area.[8] At Waltham nearby there had been eight snows in March and six in April to contribute to a total of 38 individual storms during the winter.[9]

It was also snowy Down East in the District of Maine. Rev. Smith at Portland commented: "March 31—True winter weather. April 10—Back street the snow is high as the fences; no sleighs can pass. 13–14th—Very cold. 24th—The snow consumes surprisingly, but it is two to three feet deep in the woods."[10] At Gardiner on the lower Kennebec River near the coast a total of 36 inches of snow fell during the first 20 days of April—a figure not to be approached again until 1843.[11]

[1] Moses T. Runnels. *History of Sanbornton, New Hampshire*. Boston, A. Mudge & Sons, 1882. **1**, 134.
[2] S. Hazard, Effects of climate, *Penna. Reg.* **2-6**, (Dec 1828), 380.
[3] H. Muhlenberg, *Journal*, **3**, 654–59.
   T. Smith, *Journal*, 283.
[4] M. Patten, *Diary*, 503.
[5] J. Belknap, Ms. Diary.
[6] E. Stiles, *Diary*, **3**, 156.
   N. Webster, *Notes*, **1**, 127.
[7] E. Holyoke, Ms. Met. Jour.
[8] *Boston Magazine*, April 1785, 160.
[9] Jacob Cushing, Ms. Met. Obs.
[10] T. Smith, *Journal*, 283.
[11] John W. Hanson. *History of Gardiner, Pittston, and West Gardiner*. Gardiner, Me., W. Palmer, 1852. 139.

## TRIPLE BIG SNOWS IN EARLY DECEMBER 1786

Winter struck early in the late fall of 1786, bringing some of the coldest weather ever experienced at the end of November and following with the heaviest early-season snowfalls of record. This was all the more surprising to residents of the Northeast since the autumn had been remarkably mild and pleasant. "A wonder of a fall this, hitherto; almost constantly one uniform course of moderate weather. It has been as dry and hot as summer; no rain but one day," wrote Rev. Smith at Portland, Maine, on 30 October.[1] Thereafter, it was a different matter as the circulation pattern changed and northerly air streams replaced the southerly flow.

Snow fell at Morristown, New Jersey, on 30 October for one-and-a-half hours and again on 1 November for two hours. There were no accumulations from these, but the cold regime continued. Four inches of snow fell on the 18th, and there was sleighing in the Morris County hills on the 19th and 20th.[2] Up in Maine, Rev. Smith described the latter part of November: "12th—

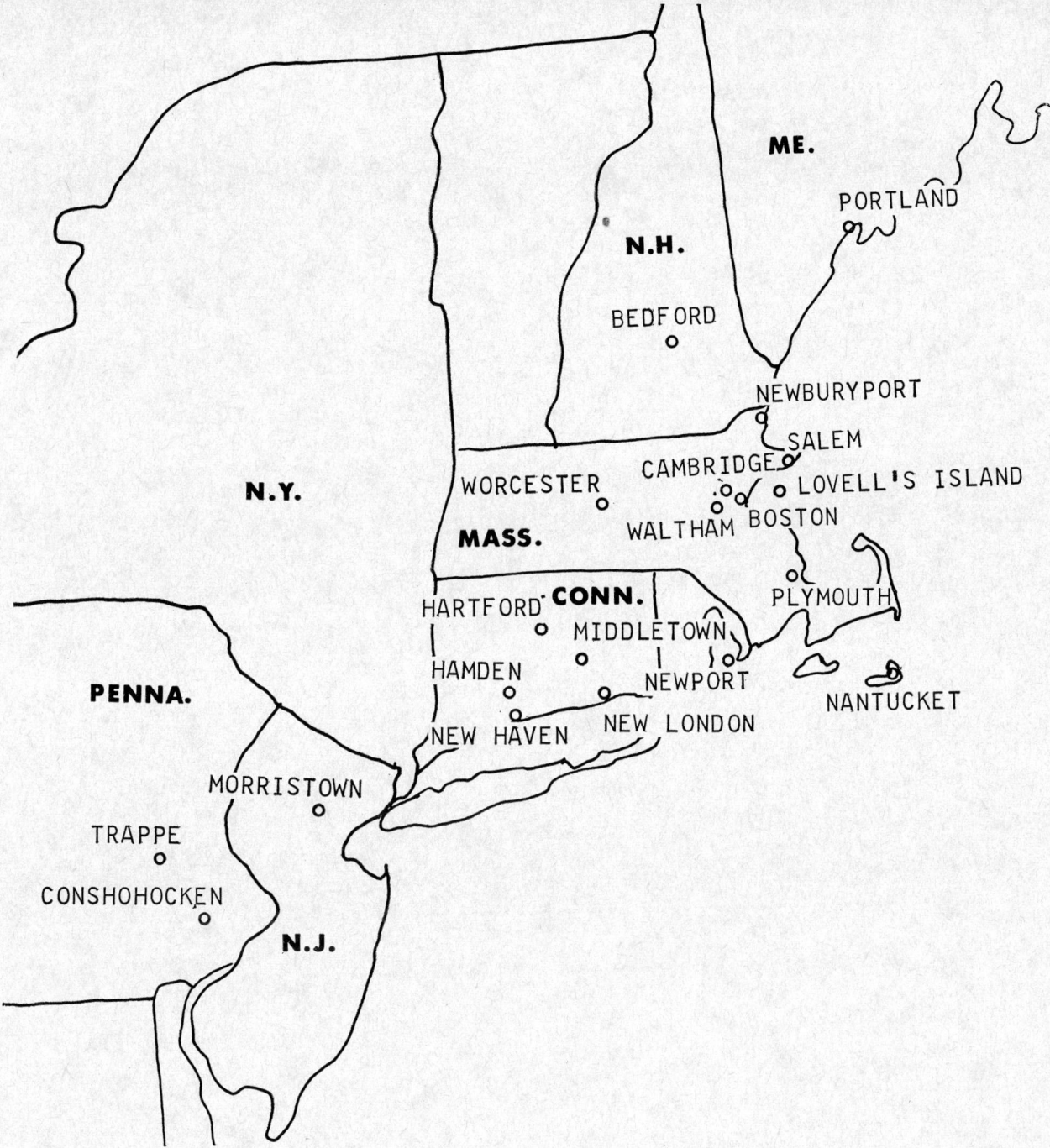

raw and cold. 17th—It snowed, and came up windy and cold. 20th—cold. 25th—Fine sledding; true winter since the 17th."[3]

The closing days of November brought on a cold wave of record severity for so early in the season. Ezra Stiles' thermometer at New Haven was down to 19° on the 25th, to 9° on the 28th, and on the 29th to +4°.[4] At Hartford the mercury read 0° at sunrise of the 29th. The extreme cold froze the Connecticut River.[5] At Middletown 30 to 40 boats were locked in and navigation ceased at an unexpected early date.[6]

The Delaware at Philadelphia also congealed unusually early to hinder shipping interests anticipating another four weeks of free navigation.[7]

## THE FIRST STORM

The first major snowstorm of the season came on the 4–5 Dec. Its origin was lost in historical obscurity, though probably originating in the South Atlantic States area. It was definitely a northeaster as winds at all check points along the coast were from east to north, and it was a cold storm in that the ground was previously frozen and the mercury remained well below freezing throughout, to insure an all-snow condition and not the usual mixture of snow, sleet, and rain so common at this season of the year. Exact timing for the onset of the storm was not available. The snow commenced at Morristown during the day of the 4th; at Hamden, Connecticut, in the afternoon; at Salem, Massachusetts, at sundown.[8] All points had continuous snowfall for about 24 hours, long enough to provide a heavy snow cover.

The storm at Conshohocken, Pennsylvania, left "a very deep snow."[9] At Morristown, Joseph Lewis measured 18″ on the 4–5th.[10] Jeremiah Alling at Hamden, Connecticut, had 20″ in a "driving snow."[11] Noah Webster described a "violent snowstorm" at Hartford.[12] Newport, Rhode Island, reported: "a prodigious quantity of snow fell, much drifted, the wind being excessive."[13] Prof. Wigglesworth at Harvard described the storm as "nivia vehemens."[13] At Salem, Dr. Holyoke recorded in his diary: "4th—Cloudy, cold, snow storm. 5th—Violent snow storm—extreme high tides—snow about 12 inches—aurora borealis." His barometer read 29.28″ at sunrise of the 5th.[14] The snowfall also reached into southern New Hampshire where Matthew Patten at Bedford had "a violent snowstorm."[15]

Our Harvard meteorological observer made the following observations during the storm period:[16]

|        | 0800   | 1300   | 2100   |
|--------|--------|--------|--------|
| Dec. 4.| 10°    | 21°    | 25°    |
|        | 30.25″ | 30.22″ | 29.96″ |
|        | W      | NW     | N      |
|        |        |        | Snow   |
| 5.     | 21°    | 16°    | 15°    |
|        | 29.30″ | 29.31″ | 29.59″ |
|        | Snow   | Snow   |        |

At Hartford the mercury exhibited the same range: on the 4th, 28°/12° and on the 5th, 17°/16° with little variation during the period of heaviest snow. On the morning of the 6th it dropped to −9°, a very low mark for so early in December.[17] At New Haven the Yale thermometer was as low as −4° on the 6th.[18]

The storm of the 4–5th at Boston was described in the *Independent Chronicle*:

> On Monday evening last came on, and continued without intermission until Tuesday evening, as severe a snow storm as has been experienced here for several years past. The wind at east and northeast, blew exceeding heavy, and drove in the tide with such violence on Tuesday, as overflowed the pier several inches. . . ."[19]

This snowstorm also had political consequences. This was the crucial year of "the critical period" of American history when economic and social hardships following the Revolution took form in threatened rebellion of certain dissident elements mainly on the agrarian frontier. The 5th of December had been selected as the day for a rally at Worcester of the followers of Daniel Shays, the leader of the rebellious farmers of central and western Massachusetts. On the date of the rendez-vous the heavy snow prevented many from reaching Worcester and definitely dampened the fighting ardor of those who did assemble there, so no armed uprising took place at this time as was feared by the authorities.[20]

## THE SECOND STORM

A second northeaster of much less physical size and portent moved northward up the coast on the 7th and 8th. It brought "more snow" at Lancaster, Pennsylvania, and eight additional inches at Morristown, New Jersey. Hamden in Connecticut had a nine-inch fall during a snowy morning, then cloudy. At Newport "another considerable snow fell, wind N.E., then calm." Prof. Wigglesworth at Cambridge reported snow at his 0700 observation on the 8th with wind west, and at Salem only a "flight of snow" was mentioned.[21] Apparently this disturbance affected only the Middle Atlantic States and the immediate southern New England coast.

## THE THIRD STORM

Another major disturbance, developing out of the same elements that had spawned the first two northeasters, swept up the coast on the 9th and continued to rage in eastern sections most of the 10th. This was the greatest atmospheric upheaval of the three, with central barometric pressure falling well below 29.00″, its wind force reaching gale force and more, and creating great tides along the entire shoreline. Snowfall amounted to slightly less than on the 4–5th, but there were reports of sleet and small hail being mixed with the snow as often occurs in cyclones which develop great intensity, pursue a slower than normal course, and draw into their circulations winds conditioned over the warmer waters of the central Atlantic Ocean.

In Pennsylvania our observers at Trappe and Conshohocken both emphasized snow and great winds in their entries for the 9th.[22] Joseph Lewis at Morristown made a measurement of 15 inches this time, to bring his week's total to 39 inches. At Hamden eight inches of "driving snow—some hail," for a week's fall of 37 inches. At Newport snow began early in the morning of the 9th, continuing to noontime when a change to hail took place, and this lasted well into the night. At Salem, Dr. Holyoke had a 'violent snowstorm" which began "very early, before day" on the 9th and continued until about 1000/10th. About 10 inches of snow fell—"much drifted."[23] Prof. Wigglesworth this time noted, "temp. vehemens," in his meteorological notes:

|         | 0800    | 1300    | 2100    |
|---------|---------|---------|---------|
| Dec. 8. | 27°     | 33°     | 24°     |
|         | 29.88"  | 29.87"  | 29.90"  |
|         | West    | West    | West    |
|         | Snow    |         |         |
| 9.      | 17.5°   | 18.5°   | 9.5°    |
|         | 29.87"  |         | 29.38"  |
|         | North   | NE      | North   |
|         | Snow    | Snow    | Snow    |
| 10.     | 11°     | 13°     | 12.5°   |
|         | 28.91"  | 29.13"  | 29.55"  |
|         | NW 4    | NW 4    | NW 4    |
|         | Snow    |         |         |

Again the editor of the *Independent Chronicle* thought the event newsworthy:

On Saturday morning began, and continued 24 hours, a snow storm equally severe and violent with that which we experienced on Monday and Tuesday preceding. The quantity of snow is supposed to be greater, now, than has been seen in this country at any time since that which fell about 70 years ago, commonly termed *the great snow*. The traveling is extremely difficult, and in many places impractical.[24]

Reports from all over told of roads blocked with huge drifts. One Boston press estimated the depth of the snow after the last as "nearly four feet deep upon a level."[25] Jacob Cushing at Waltham made this note: "On the 5th and 9th of December were unusual storms for quantity of snow—cold and wind—which occasioned difficult traveling, perhaps as known in this part of the country."[26] At Newburyport the roads were never known to have been so blocked by snow.[27] Up in New Hampshire Matthew Patten summarized: "the wind very high both storms and the snow drifted very much—it was between two and three feet deep."[28] Rev. Smith's report from Portland read: "The roads all blocked up with snow."[29]

From New London the *Connecticut Journal* reported: "The roads leading to this city have been so filled with the repeated falls of snow since the 5th that there has been but little communication with the country during that time, and most of the inhabitants are distressed for want of fuel, and many of them for provisions."[30] In Windham County in northeastern Connecticut roads were filled with three to four feet of snow.[31] Clogged roads prevented a supply of paper from reaching the *Middlesex Gazette* at Middletown, so the post-storm issue appeared with a single sheet.[32] At New Haven, Ezra Stiles noted: "Snow above knee deep in the woods—very much drifted—equal to two feet on the level."[33] Noah Webster mentioned his difficulties in the storm: "stuck in snow drift—break the sleigh."[34]

## AT SEA

The series of storms also struck savagely at sea. The town clerk of Nantucket made the following entry in his record book for 1786:

A dreadful high tide and storm Dec. 5th 1786 swept the wharves, washed away shops, vessels, tryhouses, wood, etc. On Dec. 7 a town meeting was convened and a committee appointed to salvage the wreck and return property to owners.[35]

The two major storms battered Boston Harbor with very high tides. That on the 10th at Salem was thought to have been higher than any since the hurricane tide of 20 October 1770 and within four inches of that memorable mark.[36] A number of vessels were caught in Massachusetts waters by the storms. The press carried many accounts of losses including the story of the wreck of a Boston-to-Plymouth sloop and the miraculous rescue of the 16 persons aboard, to balance the other tragic losses.[37] A sloop from Penobscot went ashore on Lovell's Island on the 5th with 13 out of the crew of 15 perishing.[38]

The best summary of the storm situations uncovered came from the press at Newport, Rhode Island, the most exposed southern New England point at that time possessing a press. Later on in our storm history Nantucket will replace Newport as a point of vantage to judge the intensity and character of passing northeasters:

On the night of the 4th inst. came on a violent snow storm from N.E. and continued till near sunset the next day, when the wind shifted to N.—A prodigous quantity of snow fell, much drifted, the wind being excessive. On the night of the 7th, and the morning of the 8th, another considerable snow fell, wind N.E. then calm.—Early on the morning of the 9th it began to snow again, wind N.E.—Wind and snow increasing to a violent storm till about noon, when the snow somewhat abated, but a considerable quantity of hail supplied the abatement of the snow, and continued with a high wind all the ensuing night. In short, there has scarsely been known by the oldest inhabitant living, so stormy a week as the last, or so much snow on the ground, at one time as at the present. Ten or twelve ships, brigs &c. were driven from the wharves and forced on shore in Brenton's Neck &c and a considerable number of small craft dashed to pieces, and a large quantity of sugar, salt and rum destroyed.[39]

A cold wave of severe proportions followed the passage of the final northeaster up the coast. The Hartford *Connecticut Courant* carried daily temperature figures for the period. The following sunrise readings were noted: 10th +6°, 11th +4°, and 12th −21°. The latter was the coldest day with three readings throughout the day: −21°, +10°, and +7°. Down at New Haven the Yale thermometer stood at −5.5 at 0800/12th. The *New Haven Gazette* published these figures with the note: "the severity of the weather this week past must be our excuse for publishing but half a sheet." About the same degree of cold was reached in eastern Massachusetts: Waltham −3° and Salem −5°.[40]

A thaw soon followed the cold. The daily maximum at Hartford from the 13th to 18th ran 37°, 45° 40°, 41°, 38°, and 37°. A rain fell on the night of the 13–14th at New Haven and half the snow melted away, according to Stiles. Another fall, however, came on the 19–20th, though of moderate depth, and still another on the 23d. Nevertheless, the great body of snow soon commenced to dissolve rapidly as another warm spell came after Christmas. At Morristown the ground appeared for the first time in many places on January 3d and on the 5th Lewis could report "but a few banks left." Even up northeast at Portland, Rev. Smith observed on the 31st: "the weather moderates."[41]

## WINTHROP SARGENT IN NEW JERSEY

Sunday 3d 36°. . . . Fair weather & moderate wind from N West all Day—Dined with his Excellency Governor Franklin who still appears in very extraordinary Vigor of Mind & Body for a man of his advanced time of life. On the morrow I propose quitting this Town by the stage for the City of New York.

Philadelphia is the largest & handsomest City of N. America. It consists of between six & seven thousand dwelling Houses & many very elegant Public Buildings.

Monday December the 4th 25°. . . . Thick cloudy morng, & small N E wind—at 10 oClock some light snow, & by 12 we had a severe storm which continued through the day.

Left Philadelphia in the stage at 3 oClock in the morng, but obliged to halt at Brunswick a little after noon on account of the weather. Crossed the Delaware just above Trenton Falls, the River below for six miles being shut up by the ice—at Bristol was much floating in the River, tho' at the City it was quite clear. The stage waggon is now rendered a very easy conveyance in *even* Tolerable Roads—it is hung on steel springs somewhat after the manner of coaches—cushions & sides stuffed &c &c.

Tuesday the 5th. All the last night the snow storm raged & to a very violent degree—this morng at 10 oClock it abated & the wind backened in to N W from which quarter it blew in force all Day—it ceased to snow after noon but here are drifts of more than four feet in Height which very much impedes our travelling.

Left Brunswick by the way of the Bridge, the Ferry being impassable, & came to Elizabeth Town Point distant from the Town just two miles—crossed the water to Bergen Point two miles more, where we were detain'd all night from the state of the Roads—but not without one *unsuccessful* essay for Paulus Hook. We lodged at Grummons Tavern, Bergen Point. It is a House of *only* tolerable accommodations, but the People are obliging & civil.

Wednesday the 6th 12°. . . . Moderate western wind & fair weather all Day. Left Bergen Point this morng at sunrise, but from the badness of the Roads it was 1 oClock before we reached Paulus Hook—Distance of nine miles only—we had one or two overturns in our waggon, broke it & finished our journey in a miserable wood sled.

Thursday 7th cloudy weather all Day & a bleak chill air from the N. East.

Friday the 8th calm & cloudy all Day. In the last night there fell five or six inches of snow at very least, which may make tolerable sleigh'g.

Saturday 9th. A N East wind last night, which was this morng increased to a violent gale attended with a great fall of snow—A continuation of the storm through the Day.

Sunday the 10th. The storm of yesterday continued all last night & until this morng, & the tide was higher than has been known for many years. Strong N W wind & clear cold weather all Day—Full two feet of snow on a level over the whole country.

Monday the 11th. The mercury in the Thermometer this morng stood at 18 a few minutes before sunrise & the weather was colder than since the last Day of its being noted—whenever there appears but a single observation of the mercury, it is to be understood as made just at sunrise. Strong N W wind & fine clear weather all Day.

Tuesday the 12th 18°. Calm cloudy weather all Day & appearances of more snow—or rain.

Wednesday 13th 24°. Light winds from the S E all Day, & cloudy with small rain at sundry times in the morng & evening.

Thursday 14th 33°. Small S E wind with gentle showers last night—wind from W S W, very light all Day, & snow fast dissolving.

Friday 15th 33°. Light easterly wind & fair warm weather all Day.

Saturday 16th 32°. Small easterly wind and fair weather all Day.

Sunday 17th 34°. Continuation of the easterly wind blowing moderately all Day, & the atmosphere hazy with some small showers of rain in the eveg.[42]

[1] T. Smith, *Journal*, 284.
[2] Diary of Joseph Lewis. *Proc. N. J. Hist. Soc.* 61-1, (Jan 1943), 49.
[3] T. Smith, *Journal*, 284.
[4] Ezra Stiles. Ms. Met. Reg. (Yale).
[5] *Conn. Courant* (Hartford), 4 Dec 1786.
[6] *Middlesex Gazette* (Middletown), 4 Dec 1786.
[7] *Penna. Jour.* (Phila.), 9 Dec 1786.
[8] Jeremiah Alling. *A register of the weather, or an account of the several rains, snow-storms, depth of each snow,—hail and thunder; with some account of the weather each day, and some other events worthy of notice for the last twenty-five years, ending March 31, 1810—at Hamden*. New Haven, Oliver Steele 1810. 10; J. Lewis, Diary, 51; W. Bentley, *Diary*, 1, 47.
[9] *The Journals and Papers of David Shultze*. Andrews Berky, ed. Pennsburg, The Schwenkfelder Library, 1953. 2, 198–99.
[10] J. Lewis, *Diary*, 51.
[11] J. Alling, *Register*, 10.
[12] N. Webster, *Notes*, 1, 170.
[13] *Newport Mercury*, 14 Dec 1786.
[14] Edward Wigglesworth. Ms. Met. Reg. (Harvard).

[15] E. Holyoke, *Met. Journal*, 120.
[16] E. Wigglesworth.
[17] *Conn. Courant*, 11 Dec 1786.
[18] E. Stiles, *Diary*, 3, 250.
[19] *Ind. Chron.* (Boston), 7 Dec 1786.
[20] *Boston Gaz.*, 8 Dec 1786.
[21] See locality references above.
[22] H. Muhlenberg, *Journal*, 3, 724; D. Shultze, *Journals*, 2, 199.
[23] See locality references above.
[24] *Ind. Chron.*, 15 Dec 1786.
[25] Boston, 15 Dec, in *Penna. Jour.*, 27 Dec 1786.
[26] Jacob Cushing. Ms. Met. Reg. (Harvard).
[27] Newburyport, 13 Dec, in *Ind. Chron.*, 12 Dec 1786.
[28] M. Patten, *Diary*, 530.
[29] T. Smith, *Journal*, 284.
[30] *Conn. Jour.* (New London), 15 Dec 1786.
[31] *Conn. Courant*, 1 Jan 1787.
[32] *Middlesex Gaz.*, 11 Dec 1786.
[33] E. Stiles, *Diary*, 3, 250.
[34] N. Webster, *Notes*, 1, 170.
[35] Alexander Starbuck. *The history of Nantucket*. Boston, C. E. Goodspeed & Co., 1924. 336n.
[36] W. Bentley, *Diary*, 1, 48.
[37] *Mass. Gaz.*, 22 Dec 1786.
[38] *Mass. Centinel* (Boston), 13 & 16 Dec 1786.
[39] *Newport Mercury*, 14 Dec 1786.
[40] See locality references above.
[41] *Idem.*
[42] Ms. Diary of Winthrop Sargent. (Mass. Hist. Soc.).

## A SEVERE JANUARY IN 1792

The winter of 1791–92, unlike those preceding and following, featured some noteworthy winter events: unusually early snowstorms after mid-October and in early November—a normal December—a very warm turn of the year—a frigid period in January featuring record duration of below-freezing temperatures—a severe cold wave on the 23d and 24th with very low daily means—and two heavy northeasters producing fine sleighing along the seaboard. The East River at New York City froze so as to permit people to cross on foot, and the entrance to the harbor became clogged with ice impeding navigation.[1] The Delaware River at Philadelphia closed on 23 December, opened in the New Year's warm spell, and closed again with the onset of the cold wave on January 7th to remain solid for eight weeks until March 6th.[2]

The South also felt the sting of the January cold. The Elizabeth River at Norfolk froze over for the first time since 1784, solidly enough for crossings to be made on foot,[3] and down in North Carolina the Moravians described January: "There was much snow during this month, and unusually continuous cold weather."[4]

The early snows fell in the Middle Atlantic States on October 17–18th. A short distance from Philadelphia as much as three inches covered the ground,[5] and in north-central New Jersey enough remained for sleighing at this record early date.[6] Less than a week later another general snow spread along the coast with sufficient to whiten roofs, but inland at Rutland in the Green Mountains of Vermont a full 10 inches descended.[7] A third early season storm again covered coastal locations on November 2–3d. It was noted as far south as the Winston-Salem area of North Carolina: "Nov 3. It snowed heavily from morning to night, as it seldom does even in winter, and it looked the more strange as the leaves were nearly all green."[8] Northward Ezra Stiles reported a six-inch fall at New Haven,[9] and at nearby Hamden there were four inches.[10] Rev. William Bentley of Salem in the Bay State entered in his diary for the 3d: "Nivis Tempestatas per totum diem."[11]

Both November and December at New Haven averaged about one degree above normal and did not produce any noteworthy weather events, but January 1792 proved a different story. After a very mild first week which witnessed the break-up of many rivers, a cold wave, striking on the 7th, brought the longest duration of severely cold weather since the Hard Winter of 1780. [In fact, New Yorkers agreed that all-around the winter of 1791–92 had been the most rigorous since the string of famous winters occurring during the Revolution.][12] Despite the warm first week January at New Haven earned 8th place among the coldest 1st month in the 90-year record there.[12]

The mercury on Henry Laight's thermometer in downtown New York City did not rise above 30° at any of his three daily observations from January 7th through the 30th. The lowest came on the 23d with +2° and the highest on the 15th with 30°.[13] His instrument's location in a door entry at ground level did not indicate the influences of nocturnal radiation, nor did it show any serious radiative influence in daytime—its readings were conservative. Other thermometers in the city, according to the press, dropped as low as −5°.[14]

In New England the mercury dropped as low as −29° at Rutland and −28° at Bennington, without any of the real cold pockets having thermometers to report at this time.[15] At Cambridge the mercury in President Webber's glass remained below zero all day on the 23d to produce the lowest daily mean in his and Prof. Farrar's records spanning the years from 1790 to 1821.[16] The three readings on the Harvard thermometer were: −11.5° at 0700, −2° at 1400, and −5° at 2100—for what appeared to have been an authentic zero day. Dr. Holyoke at Salem had −12.5° in the morning and a +1° at 1500 on his instrument which was admittedly subject to daytime radiative effects.[17] Down at Philadelphia the reading at 0700 on David Rittenhouse's thermometer was −5°—close to the lowest ever experienced in downtown locations. "During the week of extreme cold," he noted, "the air was generally clear, and always calm."[18]

The Eastern seaboard's greatest snowstorm since the triple blitz in December 1786 struck in the middle of the cold period and probably set in motion the cold air masses which soon engulfed the region. From Philadelphia to Salem, weather observers on the 18–19th noted a heavy snowfall of 12 inches or more attended by very high northeasterly winds and gales. Noah Webster at Hartford, who had complained about the lack of sleighing on the 11th, described the storm as raising the depth to two feet with much drifting.[19] Wind and drift were mentioned in reports from Providence and New Haven. Rev. William Bentley observed the storm at Salem and entered in his diary:

> Last evening it began to snow, & in the night a very violent storm arose, which continued with unabating fury through the night, & was stifling in the morning ... drifts 8 to 10 feet deep. After three the snow began to cease.[20]

February at New Haven continued the cold regime with an average of 1.8 degrees below normal. The movement of the mercury showed great conservatism: a minimum of +8° and a maximum of only +46°.[21] A second heavy snow fell on the 7th with ten inches measured at Hamden.[22] Noah Webster remarked on the "fine sleighing" following this storm. Temperature conditions favored the continuance of sleighing, even at the seaboard, throughout most of the remainder of the month. At Salem the Holyoke thermometer rose above 40° on only two days during February.[23]

But Old Sol began to take charge in the first days of March. The Delaware River at Philadelphia opened on March 6th,[24] and the Connecticut at Hartford was fully free for navigation by the 16th.[25]

[1] Henry Laight. Ms. Met. Obs. (N. Y. Hist. Soc.); *New York Journal*, 28 Jan 1792.
[2] S. Hazard. Effects of climate. *Penna. Reg.*, 3, 380.
[3] *Va. Gaz.* (Richmond), 27 Jan 1792.
[4] *Records of the Moravians in N. C.* 5, 2357.
[5] *Amer. Museum* (Phila.), Nov 1791, 207.
[6] Scudder Family Jottings. *Proc. N. J. Hist. Soc.* 63-3, (July 1945), 174.
[7] Samuel Williams. Ms. Met. Obs. (Harvard).
[8] *Moravians in N. C.*, 5, 2328.
[9] E. Stiles, *Diary*, 3, 440.
[10] J. Alling. *Register of the Weather*. 25.
[11] W. Bentley, *Diary*, 1, 320.
[12] Elias Loomis and H. A. Newton. On the mean temperature and on the fluctuations of temperature, at New Haven, Conn. *Trans. Conn. Acad. Arts and Sci.* 1-1, (1866), 200.
[13] H. Laight. Ms. Met. Obs.
[14] E. Stiles. Ms. Thermo. Reg.
[15] *Idem*.
[16] *Mem. Amer. Acad. Arts and Sci.* 3-2, (1815), 361.
[17] Edward A. Holyoke. A meteorological journal from the year 1786 to the year 1829, inclusive. *Mem. Amer. Acad. Arts and Sci.* ns. 1, (1833), 131.
[18] David Rittenhouse. Ms. Met. Obs. (Amer. Phil. Soc.).
[19] N. Webster, *Notes*, 1, 353.
[20] W. Bentley, *Diary*, 1, 340.
[21] E. Loomis, 200.
[22] J. Alling, 26.
[23] E. Holyoke, 131.
[24] S. Hazard, 3, 380.
[25] N. Webster, 1, 353.

## THE LONG WINTER OF 1798–99

The famous Long Winter of 1798–99, generally considered the severest since 1784, formed part of the series of "backward springs" which featured many of the years from 1779 to 1819. The season of 1798–99 opened in a spectacular manner with a five-day snow period in the Northeast culminating in the Long Storm of 19–21 November. This spread a deep mantle of white from Maryland to Maine and easily won the title of the heaviest November snowstorm in the recorded meteorological history of the coastal Northeast. After this start the Long Winter had a *much below* December and a *much below* March, to fortify the impression of exceptional duration. In the 90-year span of early records at New Haven, the season of 1798–99 rated as fifth coldest on a December–February basis and third coldest on a December–March basis.

After two November days of intermittent rain, thunder, and lightning at New York City, the wind, with a shift to north about 2200/19th, mounted high and brought on a heavy snowfall. "The gale abated much in the morning, but continued to snow all day, until near eleven at night, in which time not less than eighteen inches of snow fell," according to a New York observer. The barometer at the height of the storm dropped at least to 29.02″—to indicate the intensity of the disturbance. A north wind drove the temperature down to 22° on the 22d, a very low figure for the date.[2] It was the city's deepest snow in the 12 years since the heavy falls in early December 1786.

After a rainy November 19th, "at night it began to snow and continued through the 20th, a violent gale, snow fell on the earth when not frozen, a foot deep," Noah Webster related in his diary at New Haven. His thermometer went down to +12° on the morning of the 22d, also an extreme figure for the commencement of the last week in November.[3]

Farther north along the coast the storm raged even more savagely. At Salem a mixture of rain and snow, then sleet and snow fell from the 19th to the 21st, piling up a total depth of 10 inches.[4] But inland and northward it was all snow. Many town histories of southeastern New Hampshire and southern Maine described this storm as exceptional. Joseph Philbrook of Weare, New Hampshire, entered in his diary: "Nov. 19, 1798—snow fell for three days, in the whole about three feet deep, a tremendous storm."[5] At York, Maine, Jeremiah Weare, Jr. mentioned a five-day snowfall from the 17th to 21st: "the snow is near 3 feet deep on a level."[6] This snow was destined to remain all winter. At coastal Hampton Falls in New Hampshire the ground was covered from 17 November to 5 April.[7] Inland at Keene in the southwestern corner of the state the mail stage passed through the town on runners for 18 consecutive weeks, according to an April 16th report.[8]

The November storm also struck hard at sea, taking a human toll that would not be equaled for 100 years until the tragedies attending another November blow, the Portland Storm of 1898. Many vessels were wrecked on the shores of Cape Cod as cemetery tombstones will testify. At least seven vessels went to pieces on that sandy promontory with the loss of all aboard, and the bodies of 25 sailors later were taken from bilged ships and buried ashore.[9]

The snowy regime continued through a cold December at Salem, Massachusetts, with additional falls on the 2d, 8–9th, 11th, and 19th.[10] At Philadelphia it was thought that so much snow had not fallen prior to January 1st in any previous year.

One of the coldest days of the century occurred in this penultimate year, on January 5th. At Salem the mercury did not get above zero all day from its low point of −8°.[12] Charlestown across from Boston reported a low reading of −11°.[13] There were frequent light to moderate snows thereafter, but no truly severe winter event until early March when an exceptional late-season cold spell set in. Temperatures on March 5th dropped well below the zero mark even at coastal points in New England. At New Haven a reading of −4° was reported by Noah Webster, just a degree higher than the previous March low registered in 1784.[14] The deep cover continued in the Middle Atlantic States.[15] A sizable amount still lay on the ground at Philadelphia on March 12th, and in the western part of the state the depth reached three feet in Washington County in the southwest and five feet in the northwestern counties near Lake Erie.[16] Northward in Maine such a severe winter had not been known since

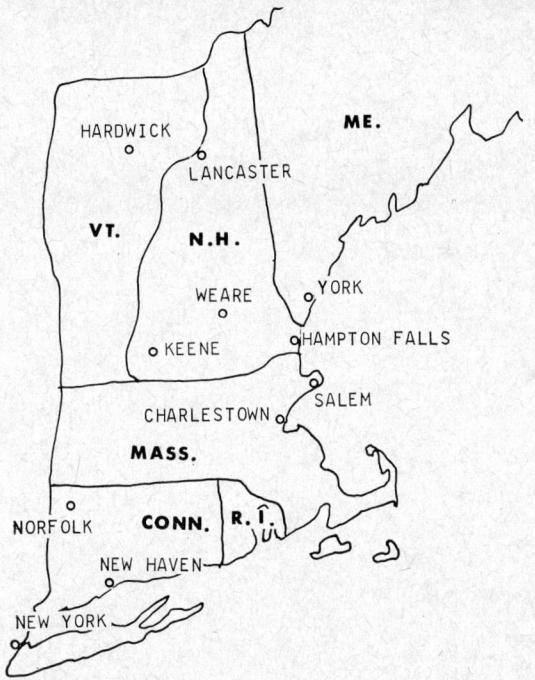

1784, it was thought—forty snows were counted at Portland this winter.[17]

The snow season continued well into spring. There were more April and May falls in the Northeast than any other season under survey. On April 7th William Bentley reported three feet of snow still covering the back streets of Salem and on the Neck.[18] White flakes fell all day on April 24th in sufficient quantity, four inches, to make sleighing possible.[19] At Keene in southwestern New Hampshire the streets were still ice covered on April 18th, and the snow lay deep all about in the sheltered valleys.[20]

May also brought flurries even to coastal New England. At New Haven and Salem some snow fell on both May 2d and 8th.[21] At Norfolk in the hills of northwestern Connecticut the ground became white on the morning of May 8th.[22]

Up in northern Vermont at Hardwick in Caledonia County, the snow lay four feet deep on the last day of March when all was ready for sugaring; but a fall of two feet additional in early April prevented farmers from getting out to tap their trees until April 15th.[23] Around Keene in southwestern New Hampshire, the local Sentinel report on May 11th: "The snow in many parts of this town is 2 or 3 feet deep."[24] In eastern New Hampshire the white banks finally disappeared from the east side of Mt. Odione on May 22d.[25] Drifts were still visible in protected spots in northern Vermont as late as June 9th.[26]

The conclusion of this distressingly laggard season can be visualized through the eyes of a New Hampshire resident of Lancaster in Coos County in the northern Connecticut Valley:

April 12. Snow lies 3 feet on ground.
    24. Six inches snow fell.
    25. One sleigh at meeting—snow lies two feet deep.
    29. River entirely free of ice.
May 5. Snow a foot deep on level in woods.
    10. Some snow came today.
    15. Began to plow on meadow.
June 1. Quite cold.[27]

[1] Elias Loomis and H. A. Newton. On the mean temperature, and on the fluctuations of temperature, at New Haven, Conn. *Trans. Conn. Acad. Arts & Sciences.* 1-1, (1866), 194.

[2] *Medical Repository* (New York). 2-3, (1799), 320. Hugh Gaine, *Journal,* 2, 211.

[3] N. Webster, *Notes,* 1, 488.

[4] Edward A. Holyoke. A meteorological journal for the year 1786 to the year 1829, inclusive. Enoch Hale, ed. *Mem. Amer. Acad. Arts & Science.* (Boston). ns. 1, (1833), 107.

[5] Diary of Joseph Philbrook. William Little. *History of Weare.* Lowell, Mass., S. W. Huse & Co., 1888. 370.

[6] Diary of Jeremiah Weare, Jr. C. E. Banks. *History of York, Maine.* 181.

[7] Warren Brown. *History of Hampton Falls, N. H.* Concord, The Rumford Press, 1900. 407.

[8] William Bentley, *Diary,* 2, 300.

[9] Edward R. Snow. *A pilgrim returns to Cape Cod.* Boston, The Yankee Publishing Co., 1946. 122; *Salem Gaz.,* 30 Nov 1798.

[10] W. Bentley, *Diary,* 2, 291–92.

[11] S. Hazard, *Effects of climate,* 2, 382.

[12] E. Holyoke, *Met. Jour.,* 145.

[13] Joseph Barrell. Account of the first and last snow. *Mem. Amer. Acad. Arts & Science.* 3-1, (1809), 105–06.

[14] N. Webster, *Notes,* 1, 490.

[15] S. Hazard, 2, 382.

[16] W. J. McKnight. *History of Northwest Pennsylvania.* Phila., J. B. Lippincott, 1905. 375; Alfred Creigh. *History of Washington County, Penna.* A. Creigh, Washington, Pa., 1870. 349.

[17] Portland press, 6 April 1799, in *Portsmouth Gazette* in *Niles National Register* (Balto.), 7 Jan 1832.

[18] W. Bentley, *Diary,* 2, 302.

[19] *Ibid.,* 2, 300.

[20] *N. H. Sentinel* (Keene), 18 April 1799.

[21] N. Webster, *Notes,* 1, 489; W. Bentley, *Diary,* 2, 302.

[22] *Diary of Thomas Robbins, D.D. 1796–1854.* Increase N. Tarbox, ed. Boston, Beacon Press, 1886. 1, 82.

[23] Samuel French. *News and Notes* (Montpelier). Vt. Hist. Soc. (March 1954). 51.

[24] *N. H. Sentinel,* 11 May 1799.

[25] W. Little, *Hist. of Weare,* 370.

[26] S. French, 51.

[27] *History of Coos County, New Hampshire.* G. D. Merrill, ed. Syracuse, N. Y., W. A. Fergusson & Co., 1888. 278.

## COLD DAYS OF THE CENTURY

The best contemporary authority on the history of 18th Century winter weather in New England was Rev. Ezra Stiles (1727–1795). As pastor at Newport from 1749 to 1775 and later at New Haven as president of Yale College from 1778 to his death in 1795, he maintained a daily weather watch.[1] Stiles also served as an active collector of early Americana. His keen interest in affairs meteorological led him to preserve many notices of weather events from both the past and present. In addition to carrying on his meteorological observations faithfully, Stiles also compiled a massive diary of contemporary affairs which contained much additional information pertinent to this study.[2]

Stiles made special mention in his diary of three notable cold days in his lifespan. These occurred on 26 February 1732, 22 February 1773, and 5 February 1789.[3] An examination of contemporary accounts revealed these as days of advective cold when severe Arctic outbreaks accompanied by bitter winds swept the New England countryside with a stinging chill factor. The mercury remained at low levels near zero for 24 hours or more. These were "Cold Friday" types when the arrival of the core of the intensely cold air mass in daylight nullified the warming effects of Old Sol.

The first twenty-five years of the 1700's in New England appear to have been without thermometrical record. A revealing statement to this effect was made in 1721 by Dr. William Douglass of Boston in a letter to Cadwallader Colden who had brought a combined barometer-thermometer to Philadelphia previously:

> According to my promise I sent you inclosed the History of the winds and weather in Boston for last year. I keep a diary of the same, and from thence have extracted those Tables and Observations; for the next year I hope to contrive a better method. I have no other instruments than the naked eye, pen, ink, and paper, I know of no thermometer or barometer in this place.[4]

In the early 1730's Superior Court Justice, Paul Dudley, maintained a daily weather record, and this was considered worth mentioning in the *Transactions of the Royal Society,* though it contained no instrumental observations other than that of the weather vane.[5]

No mention of a barometer or thermometer at Harvard College has been uncovered until 1728 when a combined instrument was included in the Hollis gift of scientific apparatus by a London benefactor.[6] An instrument of this type was known to be in the possession of President Edmund Holyoke later, though no meteorological use of the barometer-thermometer has been mentioned until Professor John Winthrop commenced his series of faithful observations in 1742—the first set of regular instrumental records known to have been made in New England.[7] President Clap of Yale College at New Haven also had a combined barometer and thermometer in his front room during the Hard Winter of 1740-41 from which Stiles was able to deduct an approximate of the extremity of cold reached in that season.[8] Until this period our knowledge of temperature conditions must be based on non-scientific opinion, and even for the next 40 years, until after the conclusion of the War of Independence, the multiplicity of scales employed, the disregard of regular stated hours of observation, and the indifference to proper outdoor exposure greatly lessened their value for an evaluation of 18th Century temperature conditions.[9]

[1] Ezra Stiles. Ms. Thermometrical Register. (Yale).
[2] *The literary diary of Ezra Stiles.* Franklin B. Dexter, ed. New York, Charles Scribner's Sons, 1901. 3 vols.
[3] E. Stiles, Ms. Thermo. Reg., 5 Feb. 1788.
[4] William Douglass to Cadwallader Colden, Boston, *20 Feb 1721.* Colden Papers. *Coll. N. Y. Hist. Soc.* **50,** (1917), 115.
[5] *Trans. of the Royal Society of London.* No. 445, **40.** (1737), 160.
[6] Josiah Quincy. *The history of Harvard University.* Boston, Crosby, Nichols, Lee & Co., 1860. **2,** 482-83.
[7] John Winthrop. Ms. Meteorologic Observations at Cambridge in New England. (Harvard). A description of his instruments and methods of observation, dated *9 March 1744,* follows his annual summary for 1743.
[8] E. Stiles, Diary, **2,** 401; *Extracts from the itineries and other miscellanies of Ezra Stiles. 1755-1794.* Franklin B. Dexter, ed. New Haven, Yale Univ. Press, 1916. 221.
[9] *Life, journals, and correspondence of Rev. Manasseh Cutler.* William P. Cutler and Julia P. Cutler, eds. Cincinnati, R. Clarke & Co., 1888. **1, 73.**

Perhaps it would be best to present in full all pertinent evidence as to cold days in the century under study:

### 1705-06

Boston: Last week, Tuesday, Wed.. & Thurs, were extream cold.—*Boston News-Letter, 14 Jan 1706.*

New York, 7 Jan: Christmas Day was the coldest that was ever felt here; Hudson River was froze over and continued fast several days, the severe cold lasted three days. *News-Letter, 21 Jan 1706.*

### 1708

Boston: Tuesday the 25th of December was remarked the coldest day ever known in the country from its first settlement. Thomas Hutchinson. *History of the Colony of Massachusetts Bay.* Lawrence S. Mayo, ed. **2,** 131n. Hutchinson gave the year as 1709, but this appears to have been in error. Hutchinson also was one year off in his assignment of the severe winter of 1697-98.

Boston: Dec 25th. Had a very serene and very cold Aer." S. Sewall, *Diary,* **2,** 246.

### 1715-16

Lords Day. Jan 26. An extraordinary cold storm of wind and snow. Blows much worse as coming home at noon, and so holds on. Bread was frozen at the Lord's table: Mr. Pemberton administered. Came not out to the afternoon exercise. Though twas so cold, yet John Tuckerman was baptised. At six a-clock my ink freezes so that I can hardly write by a good fire in my Wive's Chamber. Yet very comfortable at meeting. Laus Deo. S. Sewall, *Diary,* **3,** 231. Spiritous liquors are scarse proof against the frost, thus Sunday middle of Jan 1715/16 our Parson had his Thumbs froze in handeling of the word, & an old Woman froze dead a bed. . . . William Douglass to Cadwallader Colden, 20 Feb 1720-21. *Coll. N. Y. Hist. Soc.,* **50,** (1917), 118.

### 1720

Boston: 18 Jan. A very high N Wester the coldest of days, a thick vapor-like smoak from the water, chimneys smoak, the best water dogs would not take the water, at night tho' serene not so many stars visible as usually frosty nights, No weather so cold since 1697; in 24 hours Charles Town ferry froze over and People cross over on the ice. William Douglass.

Boston: 18 Jan. Thursday last was so extreme cold that it is thought we have not had so cold a day these twenty years past. *Boston News-Letter, 11 Jan 1720.*

Harwich: Thursday 18th [Jan] was the severest cold day that was ever known in these parts. *Boston News-Letter, 10 March 1720.*

### 1730

Swanzey, R. I., 26 Jan: This day for ye extremity of cold may deserve to be chronicled. Diary of John Chromer. *Coll. R. I. Hist. Soc.,* **8,** (1893), 121.

### 1732

Boston: In the middle of February 1731-32, called the cold Tuesday (the most intense insupportable cold I ever felt) the wind was at N.W.

1731-32, Feb 25 and 26, tinctura sacra froze, the coldest weather ever felt, after a flight of hail and snow, the wind from the south came suddenly to northwest. William Douglass. *A summary, historical and political.* **2,** 208, 210.

Boston: The remarkable cold Tuesday in New England was on the 26th day of February 1731–32—No snow, or very little on the ground. Wind W by S or WSW. Ezra Stiles. Ms. Thermo. Reg. (Yale).

Boston: Tuesday last [26 Feb] was reckon'd as cold a day as has happened here in the memory of the oldest man among us. *New England Weekly Journal (Boston), 21 Feb 1732.*

## 1741

New Haven, Conn.: Hence Pres. Clap's observation in 1740/41 of 5° to the extreme of cold agreeing to Fahrenheit cypher, being as he told me, made in the house, it is just to allow several degrees for the temperature of the air abroad. And with this correction we may nearly determine the cold of that winter 1741 abroad to have been Eight Deg. below 0 of Fahrenheit." E. Stiles, *Diary*, 2, 401.

## 1748

Salem, Mass., 18 Feb: Ther. 115 degrees abroad (Hauksbee scale). (+5.5° F.) *Holyoke Diaries*, 44.

Westborough, Mass, 17 Feb: The extremest cold day, I think we have had this year. E. Parkman, *Diary*.

Boston, Mass.: Last Saturday 17th and the day following the weather was extreme cold and the wind high. *Boston News-Letter, 11 Feb 1748.*

## 1752

Boston: We have had a cold winter. The first of January was the sharpest day when my glass reached 100 which is three and a half degrees colder than any since I had it being 7 or 8 years. John Perkins to Benjamin Franklin, 17/28 Feb 1752. *The Papers of Benjamin Franklin.* 4, 267.

Cambridge, Mass.: John Winthrop recorded +0.5° on 23 Jan 1752. *Mass. Gazette,* 4 Feb 1765.

## 1754

Stratham, N. H.: A moderate winter, remarkable for an uncommon cold day, cuming up suddenly the 22 of Jan. in which many people out a fishing and otherwise exposed perished. Samuel Lane, *Journal,* 70.

Cambridge, Mass.: John Winthrop included 22 Jan in his list of cold days: 1748–65—he recorded +3° at 0745. *Mass. Gazette,* 4 Feb 1765.

Salem, Mass.: It is very remarkable that Monday the 21st of Jan 1754 was a very fine pleasant fair day and so warm that the thermometer was at 48°, but very suddenly about 7 or 8 o'clock in the evening after a small shower of rain, the wind chopped about from south, went to the northwest and was most intensely cold, so that it sank the thermometer tho in the old entry before morning to 12° which is perhaps nearly as cold as in this climate it is possible to be when there is no snow on the ground; which was the case here. So cold a night after so warm a day was never known in this country before, ie. about 34° or 35° in less than 12 hours. Edward A. Holyoke, Ms. Met. Jour.

## 1765

Newport, R. I.: Yesterday −4 ¾°, two degrees colder than in 1752. *Newport Mercury,* 28 Jan, in *Penna. Gaz.,* 14 Feb 1765.

New York City, 26 Jan: 1700 mercury sank into ball and remained there until 1400 Tuesday—a period of 57 hours—believed to be −6°. *New York Mercury,* 4 Feb 1765.

Boston, 27 Jan: −9° abroad at Boston. *Mass. Gaz.,* 4 Feb 1765.

## 1766–67

Salem, Mass: The last day in the year 1766 was the coldest that has been known for a long course of years. My thermometer never sank so low. E. Holyoke. Ms. Met. Obs. (Harvard).

Salem, Mass: −9°.

Boston, Mass: Dec 31, −5°; Jan 1, −6°; Jan 2, −5°; another thermometer Dec 31, −7°, Jan 1, −5°. Four years previous never lower than −3.5°. *Mass. Gaz.*

New Haven, Conn: The weather hath been two or three degrees colder here than hath been known for thirty years past. *Conn. Gaz.* (New Haven), 12 Jan 1767.

Brandywine Creek, Penna., 2 Jan 1767: Mercury at −22°. Royal Society of London. *Trans. for the year 1768.* 58, (1769), 332.

## February 1773—Memorable Cold Sabbath

Dover, N. H., 21 Feb: Fair, high wind & extreme cold—coldest day I ever felt—41 degrees below freezing point (−11°). We both froze our ears and I my cheek coming from meeting J. Belknap. Ms. Met. Obs. (Mass. Hist. Soc.).

Ipswich, Mass., 21 Feb: A remarkable cold day. But few people at meeting, and most of them were frozen in some of the extremities of the body.

Feb. 22. Extreme cold last night. *Essex Gazette* states temp. yesterday at 1400 was −5°—today at half hour after sunrise mercury at −9.5°—six inches snow on ground—cracked with great noise. Manesseh Cutler, *Life,* 1, 41.

Salem, Mass: Feb. 21, 1773 was remarkable for a most severe, cold, piercing wind at N. West, the sky for the most part cloudy. 1000 −4°, 1200 +4°, sunset −6°, 2100 −7°; Feb. 22 −9.5°. E. Holyoke. Ms. Met. Obs. (Harvard).

Bradford, Mass., 22 Feb: −9.5° at 0815. Rev. Samuel Williams. *Trans. Amer. Phil. Soc.,* 2, (1786), 136.

Cambridge, Mass:

| | | | | |
|---|---|---|---|---|
| Feb. 21 | 0900 | +2° | Feb. 23 0700 | −1° |
| | 1415 | −2° | 1700 | +21° |
| Feb. 22 | 0645 | −11° | Feb. 24 0730 | +9° |
| | 1615 | +8.5° | | |

J. Winthrop, Ms. Met. Jour.

Newport, R. I.: −7°, two degrees colder than in 1752. Sermon only 25 minutes due to cold. E. Stiles, *Diary*, 1, 352.

New York City: Sunday, Feb. 21. it is supposed was the coldest day that has happened in this Part of the World for half a century and that the cold on Monday morning more intense by at least two degrees and a half than it had been known during that time. *New York Gazette and Weekly Mercury*, 1 Mar 1773.

Philadelphia, Pa., 22 Feb: 0600, 0° east side of city (Thomas Pryor), −4° west side (Daniel Wister). J. Hiltzheimer, *Diary*, 24.

New England: Ezra Stiles collective from press—Portsmouth—20°, Salem −9.5°, Providence −10°, New London −12°, Newport −7°, and New Haven −7°. Ezra Stiles, Ms. Thermo. Reg. (Yale).

### 1780—The Hard Winter

Salem, Mass., 29 Jan: −17° E. Holyoke. *Holyoke Diaries*. 102.

Hartford, Conn., 29 Jan: −22°. E. Stiles. Ms. Thermo. Reg.

New Haven, Conn., 22 Jan:—$3\frac{1}{3}$°. *Idem.*

New York City, n.d: −16°. *N. Y. Gazette* (Fishkill, N. Y.), in E. Stiles.

Albany, n.d: −20°. E. Stiles.

Philadelphia, Pa., 20 Jan: 0°. D. Rittenhouse. Ms. Met Obs. (Penna. Hist. Soc.).

Williamsburg, Va., +6°. *Va. Gaz.*, 29 Jan 1780.

### 1783

New Haven, Conn., 3 Feb: −13° at sunrise. Coldest February reading 1780–1825. Met. of New Haven. *Trans. Conn. Acad.*, 1–1, (1866), 202–03.

### 1784

Hartford, Conn:

| | | | |
|---|---|---|---|
| Feb 10 | −19° | Feb 14 | −20° |
| 11 | −12° | 15 | −12° |
| 12 | −13° | 16 | −16° |
| 13 | −19° | 17 | −16° |

N. Webster. Notices of extraordinary seasons of cold. *Amer. Jour. Sci.*, 28-1, (July 1835), 186.

New Haven, Conn., 10 Feb: −10°. E. Stiles.

### 1786

Salem, Mass: Jan 17 −11°
18 −8
19 −8
20 +1

Hartford, Conn: "In the severe winter 1780 the mercury descended to 22 below 0. In the winter of 1784 the mercury fell to 21 below 0. Tuesday morning last (19 Jan 1786) was two degrees colder than was ever observed in this place (−24°), and the whole day proportionally more extreme. The thermometer with which the above observations were made hath been verified at the points of freezing & water boils." Nathan Strong.

| | | | | |
|---|---|---|---|---|
| Jan 17 | Sr. | −14° | 19 Sr. | −24 |
| | 1200 | +10 | 0900 | −18 |
| | 2100 | −7 | 1200 | 0 |
| 18 | Sr. | −20 | 2100 | −12 |
| | 1400 | +6 | 2300 | −14 |
| | 2100 | −8 | 20 Sr. | −17 |
| | 2300 | −14 | 1000 | −5 |
| | | | 1400 | +18 |

Nathan Strong in E. Stiles, *Diary*, 2, 201.

### 1788

| | 0800 | 1300 | Ss | 2200 |
|---|---|---|---|---|
| Salem, Mass: Feb 5 | +1 | +2 | −2 | −2 |
| 6 | 0 | 11 | 8 | 11 |

E. Holyoke. *Met Obs.*

New Haven, Conn., 5 Feb: One of the coldest days in New England for 70 years.

0800 −4°    1400   0
0930 −6.5   1530 +2.5
1230 −4.75  2200 −3

E. Stiles. Ms. Thermo. Reg.

Morristown, N. J., 5 Feb: This day the cold was so severe that it must be called the cold Tuesday. Joseph Lewis. *Proc. N. J. Hist. Soc.*, 62, (1944), 37.

Philadelphia, Pa., 5 Feb: −6°, fell from 38° in 17 hours. S. Hazard. *Penna. Reg.*, 2, 380.

### 1789

Hartford, Conn., 2 Feb: 28 below 0 at sunrise; four degrees lower than ever known there before. *Columbian Magazine* (Phila.), (Feb 1789), 134.

New Haven, Conn. Feb. 1—A very severe clear cold day, the thermo. 5° above zero in morning. Snow half a foot deep, fell chiefly last Friday night. Feb. 2—At sunrise Fahr. Th. 12 deg. below Cypher at Y. C. E. Stiles. *Diary*. 3, 340.

Albany, N. Y., 2 Feb: −24°, colder by 6° than ever known. Weather book kept at the museum opposite Denniston's tavern on Green Street. *The Annual Register* (Albany), 1849, 329.

Philadelphia, Pa., 2 Feb: −5° at 0600. D. Rittenhouse.

Spring Mill, Pa., (13 miles NNW of Phila.) 2 Feb: −17.5° (coldest in records from 1785–1827). Peter Legaux, Ms. Met. Obs. (Amer. Phil. Soc.).

Lancaster, Pa., 2 Feb: Colder than anyone living can recall 21° below zero at 0700. Ms. notes of Elizabeth Kieffer (Lancaster Hist. Soc.).

### 1792

Salem, Mass., 23 Jan: Dr. Holyoke had −12.5° in morning, and only +1° at 1500—clear and NW wind —no example of freezing (humans) in 1792. W. Bentley, *Diary*, 1, 344.

New Haven, Conn., 23 Jan: At sunrise Fahr, Th 8 below cypher. E. Stiles, *Diary*, 3, 440.

Cambridge, Mass., 23 Jan: −11.5° at 0700, −2° at 1400, −5° at 2100. Mean −8°, lowest daily mean in Harvard series 1790–1821. *Mem. Amer. Acad. Arts & Sci.*, 3–2, (1815), 361.

New York City, 23 Jan: +2° at Sr, +9° at 1400. H. Laight. Ms. Met Obs. (N. Y. Hist. Soc.).

Philadelphia, Pa., 23 Jan: −5° at 0700. During this week of extreme cold, the air was generally clear, and always calm. D. Rittenhouse in *Nat. Gaz.* (Phila.), 30 Jan 1792.

United States: Ezra Stiles collective from press:

| | | | |
|---|---|---|---|
| Rutland, Vt. | −29° | Norfolk, Conn. | −20.5° |
| Bennington, Vt. | −28° | New Haven, Conn. | −8 |
| Westfield, Mass. | −13° | New York City | −5 |
| Hartford, Conn. | −12 | Philadelphia | −6 |
| Boston, Mass. | −10 | | |

### 1796–97

Salem, Mass., 24 Dec: −5° at 0800, +8° at noon, +5° at Ss, +2° at 2200. E. Holyoke. *Met. Jour.* 140.

Cambridge, Mass., 24 Dec: −6.5°. *Mem. Amer. Acad. Arts & Sci.*, 3–2, (1815), 361.

Williamstown, Mass, 24 Dec: −28°—The greatest cold ever known 1796–1834. C. Dewey. Ms. Met Obs. (Williams College).

Northhampton, Penna., 24 Dec: −13°. Joseph Priestly.

Cambridge, Mass., 8 Jan: −12.5° at 0700, +6° at 1400, −3.5° at 2100. *Mem. Amer. Acad.*, 361.

Poughkeepsie, N. Y., 8 Jan: −19°—seven degrees colder than for the past 20 years by a thermometer. *Medical Repository* (New York), 1–1, (1797), 112.

Nine Partners, N. Y., 8 Jan: −20°. *Idem.*

Philadelphia, Pa., 9 Jan: −13°
              10 " −10°

New Haven, Conn., 8 Jan: −10°—coldest in January 1781–1825. Met. of New Haven. *Trans. Conn. Acad.* 1–1, (1866), 200.

### 1799

Cambridge, Mass., 5 Jan: −6° at 0700, +2° at 1400, −5° at 2100. *Mem. Amer. Acad. Arts & Sci.*, 3–2, (1815), 361.

Salem, Mass., 5 Jan: −8° at 0800, 0° at 1200, −2° at Ss, −6° at 2200. E. Holyoke. *Met. Jour.* 145.

Charlestown, Mass., 5 Jan: −11°. *Mem. Amer. Acad.* 3–1, (1809), 105.

## EARLY SNOWS OF THE CENTURY

### 1673

Hampton, Mass, Oct. 4: "There was a storme of raine and snow so that the ground was covered with snow, & some of it continued to Oct. 6th." C. W. Chase, *Hist. of Haverhill*, 118.

### 1692

Dover, N. H., Oct. 18: "First snow." Jour. John Pike, *N. H. Hist. Coll.*, 3, 63.

### 1703

Philadelphia, Pa., Oct. 8: "We have had a fall of snow, and now the northwest wind blows very hard." Isaac Norris quoted in Watson, *Annals Phila.*, 2, 349.

Boston, Mass., Oct 9: "Very cold and snow to cover the ground." Oct. 10: "The snow is now three or four inches deep and a very cold Norwest wind. A sad face of Winter, to see the Houses and Ground so covered with snow, and to see much Ice." Samuel Sewall, Diary, *Mass. Hist. Soc. Coll.*, 46, 89.

Salem, Mass., Oct. 9: "The storm of snow and the cold days which followed were such as I never knew the like of for the time of year." J. Felt, *Annals of Salem*, 2, 116.

Braintree, Mass., [*September*]: "I shall only remark of the above month. the storm of snow which was on the 28th day [Oct. 9th] and the cold days that followed was such as I never knew the like for the time of the year. John Marshall's Diary. *Proc. Mass. Hist. Soc.* 14, (1900–1901), 33.

Dover, N. H., Oct. 9: First snow, very cold. J. Pike, *Journal*, 65.

### 1746

Salem, Mass., Oct. 21: "Last night and this morning: a flight of snow."

Salem, Mass., Oct. 29: "Last night and today a snow fell, deep 5¾ inches." *Holyoke Diaries*, 41.

Salem, Mass., Oct. 29: "The snow a foot deep." Jour. of John Preston. *Essex Inst. Hist. Coll.* 11, (1872), 258.

Newbury, Mass., Oct. 28: "Friday about nine A.M. it began to snow and continued snowing until three P.M. the next day. I and my wife went to church in the sleigh and it was good sleighing, the snow being two feet on the level and lasted four days." M. Plant in *Hist. of Newbury*, 217.

## 1749
Portland, Me., Oct. 29: "Snow." T. Smith, *Journal*, 271.

## 1755
Salem, Mass., Oct. 18: "Snowed considerably, very cold weather." Oct. 25: "Snow again." Oct. 30: "Snowy stormy day as you shall know in the winter time." J. Preston, *Journal*, 261.

Salem, Mass., Oct. 30: "NE. Very cold. Stormy. Snow. Moist Air. Some wind. Fair. (3 or 4 inches snow). Holyoke, Ms. Met. Obs.

Bedford, N. H. Oct. 25: "Fell a considerable snow." Oct. 30: "Fell a snow about ankle deep." Matthew Patten, *Diary*, 22.

## 1764
Bakers River, N. H. (north of Plymouth one day's journey), Oct. 26: "Snow fell 7 inches deep." *ibid.*, 144.

## 1765
Rutland, Mass., Oct. 27: "The Lords Day october 27 a Very Remarcable Storm of Snow with a Very high wind. the Snow fell twenty two Inches Deep." *Journal of Seth Metcalf*, 20.

Salem, Mass., Oct. 27: "Rain. Cold. Stormy. Snow." Holyoke, Ms. Met. Obs.

## 1769
Dover, N. H., Oct. 9: "Raw, chilly, cloudy—P.M. Rain mixed with snow." J. Belknap, Ms. Met. Obs.

Bristol, N. H., Oct. 9: "Two feet snow fell." R. W. Musgrove, *Hist. Bristol*, 470.

Philadelphia, Pa., Oct. 3: "Snow this morning covered houses." Dairy of Benjamin Horner. *Amer. Daily Adv.*, in *Penna. Reg.*, 1 Dec 1832, 352.

## 1777
Dighton, Mass., Oct. 21: "N.E. storm, rain, hail, snow." E. Stiles, *Diary*, 2, 220.

Bedford, N. H., Oct. 28: "Hail covered ground—N.E.—violent storm." M. Patten, *Diary*, 374.

## 1786
Salem, Mass., Oct. 30: "Snow two to three inches." *The Diary of William Bentley*. Salem, The Essex Institute, 1905. **1**, 44; William Currie. *An historical account of the climates and diseases of the United States of America*. Phila., T. Dobson, 1792. 20.

Charlestown, Mass., Oct. 30: First snow. Joseph Barrell. Account of rain, &c. that fell at Charlestown, Massachusetts, in ten years. *Mem. Amer. Acad*, 3-2, (1815), 115.

New Haven, Conn., Oct. 30: "Snow two inches." *Trans. Conn. Acad.*, **1**-1, (1866), 241–42.

## 1789
Salem, Mass., Oct. 26: "2200—snowing 46°"; Oct. 27: "0800—raining 36°." *Holyoke Diaries*, 126.

## 1791
Philadelphia, Oct 17–18: "Snow fell to the depth of 3 inches within 20 miles of the city." *American Museum*, Nov 1791, 207.

Philadelphia, Oct 18: "Rain, sleet, snow. 36.7° max./ 32.0° min." Oct 22: "Cloudy, snow. 43.9° max./ 34.5° min. *Idem*.

Springfield, N. J., Oct 17: "At night fell a considerable snow fit for sledding." Scudder Family Records. *N. J. Hist. Soc. Proc.*, (1945), 174.

New Haven, Conn., 17: "Snow at night." Oct 22: "Chiefly cloudy, some snow." J. Alling, *Register of the Weather*, 25.

Charlestown, Mass., 23 Oct: Snow noticed. *Mem. Amer. Acad.*, Rutland, Vermont, Oct. 22–23: Snow storm all day—10″. S. Williams, Ms. Met. Obs. (Harvard).

## 1793
Thompson, Conn., Oct 29: "Snowed all day; very cold." Ellen Larned, *Mon. Wea. Rev.*, 22, 418–19.

Hamden, Conn., Oct 29: "Snow one inch." Oct 31: "Some snow." Jeremiah Alling, *Register of the weather*, 31.

Blue Hill, Me., Oct 29: "A severe snow storm." Oct 31: "Snow north of East Machias 20 inches on level and fairly up to the waist band of my Breeches in Swamps. I do not think the oldest man on earth ever saw such a snow the first that came." Nov 1: "The snow is so thick on the trees and so very deep on the ground, that we can do nothing at present." Notes of John Peters, *The Bangor Historical Magazine*, 2, 18.

Gardiner, Me.: "Snow in October 1793 covered potatoes in field." J. W. Hanson, *Hist. Gardiner*, 163.

Salem, N. C., Oct 27: "Yesterday's storm brought such piercing cold this evening it began to snow. . . . The snow storm lasted until morning, and the snow was several inches deep, which is most unusual for this time of year in Carolina." *Moravian Diary*, 6, 2474.

Bethabara, N. C., Oct 28: "Last night and this morning the first snow fell, several inches deep. The afternoon sunshine melted most of it. Snow is unusual in this part of the country at this time of year." *Ibid.*, 6, 2488.

## LATE SNOWS OF THE CENTURY

### 1638

Boston, Mass., May 3: "It did snow two hours together, (after much rain from N.E.) with flakes as great as shillings." *Winthrop's Journal,* **1**, 269.

### 1659

Hampton, Mass., May 10: "April thirtieth, old style, there was a great storme of snowe, which lay three or four inches thick upon May-day in the morning." Hampton Records in *History of Newbury,* 62.

### 1696

Dover, N. H., May 2: "Last snow." John Pike, *N. H. Hist. Coll.,* **3**, 64.

### 1733

York, Me., May 4: "Snowed all day." C. E. Banks, *Hist. of York, Me.,* 15–16.

### 1758

Ft. Augusta (Sunbury), Pa., May 26: "It is snowing here and the ground is covered." S. Pearce, *Annals of Lucerne,* 477.

### 1761

Bedford, N. H., May 5: "It snowed all day. It abated in the evening. It fell about 3½ inches deep at my house. It is said it fell 10 inches deep at William MacDoles and midleg deep in Chester and at one o'clock in the afternoon and was then snowing hard. It fell 15 inches deep in Starkstown."
May 6: "The snow went mostly off about my house." M. Patten, *Diary,* 94.

Dracut (near Lowell), Mass., May 4: "Cold storm began about noon with rain, turned to snow, snows all night and the next day—snow 5 inches deep by noon, then mixed with rain." S. R. Coburn, *History of Dracut,* 341.

Cambridge, Mass., May 4: "May storm. Rain & snow." May 5: "Rain and snow storm." J. Belknap, Ms. Met. Reg.

Salem, Mass., May 5: "NE. Very high wind. Some snow." *Holyoke Diaries.*

Ashford, Conn., May 5:
> On the fifth of May, 1761, a very
> Stormy day of snow—an awful sight—
> The trees green and the ground white;
> The sixth day the trees on the blow
> And the fields covered with snow.

Ebenezer Byles, Town Clerk. Ms. Ashford Town Book, quoted by E. D. Larned, *Mon. Wea. Rev.* (Wash., D. C.), **35**-5, (May 1907), 221.

### 1765

Rutland, Mass., May 8: "Snow 3 inches deep followed by hard frost." Seth Metcalf, *Journal,* 20.

Central Mass., May 8: "Much snow fell between Springfield and Boston." Ezra Stiles, Ms. Thermo. Reg.

### 1769

Salem, Mass., May 11: "Snow for 12 hours—six inches." S. Perley, *Historic Storms of New England,* 74.

Boston, Mass., May 11: "Last Thursday afternoon and night we had a considerable fall of snow in this town and neighborhood." *Va. Gaz.,* 8 June 1769.

Goffstown, N. H., May 11: "Snow fell two inches deep and covered apple blossoms." G. P. Hadley, *History of Goffstown,* **2**, 554.

Hereford Twp., Bucks Co., Pa., May 1–2: "Rain and snow." *Journals and papers of David Shultze,* **2**, 38.

Worcester, Mass: On Wed 10th of May 1769 the mercury at 84° in shade, on May 11th it fell to 36° and snowed that afternoon. Letter of Mr. Stuart Bell, Peabody, Mass., to WBO, Boston, 1955.

### 1773

Newbury, Vt., June 10: "Great frost." June 11: "This night there fell a snow two inches deep." Frederic P. Wells, *Hist. of Newbury,* 259.

Salem, Mass., May 11: N.E. Cold, rain, snow, hail, a.m. Some wind, rain, p.m. E. Holyoke, Ms. Met. Jour.

### 1774

Nominy Hall, Va., May 4: "Last night and this morning fell a considerable snow, so much I imagine had it not melted after it fell it would have been six inches deep." *Diary of Philip Vickers Fifthian,* 138.

Philadelphia, Pa., May 4: "The houses this morning are all covered with snow." Jacob Hiltzheimer, *Diary,* 30.

Goshenhoppen, Pa., May 4: "A snow several inches at night, heavy frost and ice. . . . Snow four to six inches, icicles eighteen inches long formed and continued several days and nights." D. Schultze, *Journal,* 68–69.

Germantown, Pa., May 4: "Heavy rain on night of May 3–4 which turned to snow toward morning and fell 4 inches deep." *Germantown Zeitung,* 19 May 1774.

New York, N. Y., May 4: "I remember that on May 4, 1774 a considerable quantity of snow fell." S. L. Mitchill. *American Magazine,* (Jan 1790), 38.

New Jersey and New York, May 4: "Snow fell in Jersey and New York on May 4, 1774—commenced latter part of night and continued most of forenoon." *Poughkeepsie Barometer* in *Amer. Adv.* (Phila.), 17 May 1803.

Bedford, N. H., May 4: "A very cold rain and sleet, the wind at north or northeasterly." M. Patten, *Diary*, 322.

Mt. Vernon, Va., May 4: "Very cold all day with spits of snow and the wind blowing hard at NoWest. G. Washington, Ms. Weather Diary.

Dumfries, Va., May 4: "Snow fell on May 4th." *Va. Gaz.* (Williamsburg), 12 May 1774.

Monticello, Charlottesville, Va., May 4: "The blue ridge of mountains covered with snow. 5th—a frost which destroyed almost everything. . . . At Monticello near half the fruit of every kind killed; and before this no instance had ever occurred of any fruit being killed here by frost. Thomas Jefferson, *Garden Book*, 55.

Philadelphia, Penna., May 4–5: Snow on the 4th—on the 3d mercury at 1500 was 61°—on the 5th at sunrise at 31.5°—grain and fruit hurt. N. Collin. Ms. Weather Notes. (Swedish-American Hist. Soc., Phila.).

### 1777

Ipswich, Mass., May 1: "Annual fast. Few people at meeting. A very remarkable day for this season of year. It might properly be called a N.E. snow-storm." M. Cutler, *Life*, 1, 61.

Waltham, Mass., May 1: "Snow about one inch deep. More melted." J. Cushing, Ms. Met. Reg.

Dover, N. H., May 1: "NE snow storm all day—three inches—hard & wet." J. Belknap, Ms. Met. Reg.

Hampton Falls, N. H., May 1: "Snow storm on May 1, 1777." W. Brown, *Hist. Hampton Falls*, 477.

Salem, Mass., May 1: 43° a.m., 46° p.m. N.E. Stormy, rain, snow, moist air. E. Holyoke, Ms. Met. Jour.

### 1780

Hampton Falls, N. H., May 1: "Snow on May 1, 1780." W. Brown, *Hist. Hampton Falls*, 477.

Salem, Mass., May 1: 33° a.m., 34° p.m. East. Stormy, rain, some snow, moist air. E. Holyoke, Ms. Met. Jour.

### 1789

Tinmouth, Vt., May 8: "Heavy snow." N. Perkins, *Narrative of a Tour*, 15.

### 1799

New Haven, Conn., May 3: "Snow & rain. 39°." May 8: "Violent squalls with thick snow. 35°." J. Day, Ms. Met. Obs.

Norfolk, Conn., May 8: "In the morning the ground was covered with snow. Very cold for the season." Thomas Robbins, *Diary*, 1, 84.

Charlestown, Mass., May 12: "Snow—a shower only." *Mem. Amer. Acad.*, 3-1, 106.

Salem, Mass., May 12: "This morning we had a flight of snow in all the forms of winter, large, driving, steady." W. Bentley, *Diary*, 2, 302.

Salem, Mass., May 12: "0800—snowing—37°." E. Holyoke. Met. Jour. *Mem. Amer. Acad.*, ns. 1, 145.

Lancaster, N. H., May 5: "Snow a foot deep on level in woods." May 10: "Some snow came today." *Hist. Coos. Co.*, 278.

## SAMUEL LANE'S CHRONOLOGY OF NEW HAMPSHIRE WINTERS: 1737–1799
## STRATHAM, NEW HAMPSHIRE

*Digest II—Events of General Interest*
*Samuel Lane's Journal from 1737*
*Extracted from my Daily Journals*

A Brief Account of Some Remarkable Events, relating to the Seasons of the year, Such as verry Cold Difficult Seasons in Winter; Droughts in Summer; Scarcitys, Plentys, times of Remarkable Sickness, Health, Wars &c Since the year Anno. 1737, taken from my Daily Journals.

(Only events of meteorological significance have been extracted)

### 1736–37

This year, we had an Exceeding hard Winter, and backward Spring: Hay Exceeding Scarce; (Some Sold for 8s old Tenr a Hundred) Creatures were verry poor, and Abundance Died.

### 1737–38

We had this year a Moderate Winter, so that Hay was but about half so dear this Spring as it was last fall.

### 1738–39

An Exceeding Hard Winter; Hay Scarce and Dear.

### 1739–40

Moderate Winter.

### 1740–41

We had this year, a terrible hard Winter; Deep Snows; Scarcely Any passing; Except throu' fields, on Snowshoes &c Difficult getting Meal; Hay verry Scarce.

#### 1741–42

We have a Moderate Winter.

#### 1742–43

We had a Moderate Winter.

#### 1743–44

Hard Winter.

#### 1744–45

An Uncommon Moderate Winter.

#### 1745–46

Moderate Winter.

#### 1746–47

We have a tedious hard Winter, drifted Snows, difficult passing (so that we were oblig'd to go round by Greenland, to get to Hampton) and in Dec and Jan Exceeding cold, for more than 30 Days together.

#### 1747–48

We had a tedious hard Cold and Most Difficult Winter, by reason of much Snow & bad passing ('tis Said) ever known by Any person now Living. The Cold began Severe about y$^e$ 27$^{th}$ of Nov. & held Constant 26 Days, and on y$^e$ 3$^{rd}$ of Dec. 1747, the Deep Snows began to come; and held near 4 months, so Exceeding Deep; that there was Scarcely any passing in Roads: and with great difficulty throu' fields, on Rivers, and any where that people co'd get along. I counted 25 Snows this Winter, & that in all, they Contain'd about 12 feet in Depth. the 29$^{th}$ Day of March 4 Men & Horses Broke the Way from my House to Esq$^r$ Leavits in the Road; where had been no passing 2 or 3 Months.

This large Body of Snow went away Strangly, without any rain or Land flood; the ground not being froze, it Soak'd into the Earth as it Melted.—this is y$^e$ 2$^{nd}$ hard Winter together.

#### 1748–49

a Comfortable Winter.

#### 1749–50

a hard Winter, which made it difficult keeping cattle alive, (Hay being cut Short last year) which was done chiefly by Corn Brouse &c—great Quantities of Bass fish are Caught in our River this Winter.

#### 1750–51

an Uncommon Moderate Winter; so that the ferry Boat, Cross'd the Salt River every month in y$^e$ Winter.

#### 1751–52

We had a more than common Cold close hard Winter; the Cold Continuing verry Extraordinary, for two full Months; and froze so hard that it was the Common practice to go with Sleds & Sleighs from Boston to Castle William; and Vessels all froze in, as Appears by the Publick prints.

#### 1752–53

An open Winter, so that in Febr. gundeloes pass'd from Exeter to Portsm$^o$. great Scarcity of provisions by reason of the frost last year.

#### 1753–54

A Moderate Winter, Remarkable for an Uncommon Cold Day, cuming up Suddenly the 22 of Jan. in which many People out a fishing, & otherwise Expos'd perished.

#### 1754–55

A Moderate Winter (which is y$^e$ 3$^{rd}$ Successively).

#### 1755–56

a fourth Open Winter Successively; many people Plow'd and fenc'd in the Month of February: and as good Carting as in Summer.

#### 1756–57

A hard Winter, much Snow; great Scarcity of Hay.

#### 1757–58

A verry hard Winter, Deep Snows, and the Most difficult passing we have had for 10 years. the latter end of March the Snow being 3 or 4 feet Deep, was hard like ice; and people Sleded upon it, over fences &c Hay Scarce.

#### 1758–59

we had a Comfortable Winter.

#### 1759–60

Another Comfortable Winter.

#### 1760–61

we had a pretty hard Winter.

#### 1761–62

we had the most hard Severe, cold long Winter (I believe) ever known; which began the first of December; and held late and backward in the Spring: and many people having large Stocks of Cattle, and but few of them fit to kill; presum'd to keep them over, on a little Hay; trying to keep them alive by Corn Brouse &c hoping for a Moderate Winter: but the Winter proving verry hard, Many Cattle, Horses, Swine, and abundance of Sheep and Lambs died.

#### 1762-63

We have a third hard difficult Winter Successively; Deep Snows, & difficult passing; Hay Scarce, 120L a Ton.

the Beginning of March 1763, the Snow was so Deep, there was no passing, Except on Snowshoes—and about the Middle of the Month, there was Such a Crust on the Snow, that People Rode & Sleded over fences, and any where they wanted to go; about 10 Days.

#### 1763-64

a Comfortable Winter, & provisions plenty.

#### 1764-65

a hard Cold Difficult Winter, Deep Snows & Difficult passing as ever was known.

#### 1765-66

A Moderate Winter.

#### 1766-67

Midling Winter.

#### 1767-68

a Moderate Winter.

#### 1768-69

Verry Cold weather after the Middle of Jan. this Winter; which held more than a Month; and froze harder than has been known for Many years. pass'd from Portsmouth with Sleighs & teems over Newbury & Charlestown ferries; to Boston on the ice.

#### 1769-70

Pretty Moderate Winter.

#### 1770-71

we have an open Winter; Several great freshets which Carried away many Mills Bridges &c. Hay Scarce.

#### 1771-72

a hard Winter, and Difficult passing; held late and backward in the Spring: the Latter part of the Winter we had verry Drifted Snows, which laid in Drifts till the latter End of April.

#### 1772-73

A Comfortable Winter, & much good Sleding.

#### 1773-74

a favourable Winter.

#### 1774-75

A Moderate Winter.

#### 1775-76

A pretty Comfortable Winter.

#### 1776-77

Not a hard Winter, and but little Sleding.

#### 1777-78

A pretty Close Winter; & but little good Sleding.

#### 1778-79

A pretty Close Winter; Several remarkable Deep Snows, toward the latter end of March—Hay verry Scarce.

#### 1779-80

This year has been Remarkable on Many Accounts, which as they are of a Publick Nature I think worthy to be observ'd.

We had the Most hard Difficult Winter, by reason of Violent cold weather, beginning Early in the year; tedious Storms of Deep Drifted Snows, and Difficult passing, even from Neighbour to Neighbour, in Case of Sickness or otherwise, ('tis Said) that ever was known by any Person now Living.—The violent weather began about the 13th of Dec. 1779, and Continued about Nine weeks; in all which time there was not more than a Day or two, So moderate as to thaw on the Suney Side of a House: and the Snow So Deep & Drifted, that People could not possibly keep the Roads open; tho' it was a Considerable part of their Business to break them with oxen and Shoveling by men, untill they were quite Discouraged, and gave up the point; and Endeavoured to pass (tho' with great Difficulty) on the top of the Snow, and through fields, on Rivers, and any where that they could get along.—Many Suffered for want of Wood; and were obliged to cut down Apple trees, and other Trees that Stood near the path, for firewood. Many oblig'd to hall Wood, & go to Mill on handsleds &c.

the Cold weather so froze up the Water, that People were put to great Difficulty for want of Meal in most of our Towns far and Near; Mr. Pottles Malt Mill Supply'd many People grinding with 2 Horses for Double toll.

The Roads were so Block'd up with Snow, that the Members of the General Court, as well as other People, were oblig'd to travel on the River, the greatest part of the way, from Portsmouth to Exeter, for a long time.

the bad traveling held in many places, till the latter end of March: and the beginning of April it was so cold, that there was Some pretty good Sleding on the top of the Snowbanks.

#### 1780-81

We had a pretty favourable Winter; but little verry Cold weather; Considerable Snow and rain, and Changable weather—Much good Sleding. Abundance of Corn & grain brought down out of the Country.

### 1781–82

We had a pretty cold Winter after y<sup>e</sup> 20<sup>th</sup> of January; Deep Snows, good Sleding in the path, but no turning out.

### 1782–83

We had a pretty broken Winter.

### 1783–84

We had the year past a verry hard Close Winter and backward Spring.

### 1784–85

We had a Close Winter, Especially after January; when the Snow was Exceeding Deep & Drifted, & Difficult passing, as almost ever known—verry Cold and backward Spring.

### 1785–86

We had this year, a comfortable Winter; pretty backward Spring.

### 1786–87

. . . we had Several Violent cold Driving Storms of Snow the beginning of December & Difficult passing.
We have had this year, a pretty Comfortable Winter.

### 1787–88

We have had a Midling Winter, pretty Deep Drifted Snows.

### 1788–89

This Winter has been the Most Agreeable Winter, that ever I Knew; but little verry cold weather; and yet full cold Enough for good Sleding and Business: and the most Sleding, Slaying, & other Such Business done this Winter, that ever I knew in any Winter; for the 28<sup>th</sup> of Dec 1788 there came 8 or 9 inches of Snow & Hail, which all froze together like a Solid Body of ice, which lasted all Winter, to Sled upon; and wo'd bare Cattle out of the path & in the Woods; So that there is no difficulty in turning out of the path, or in the Woods with a load; no Drifted Snows; but when the path began to wear up, by the Abundance of passing; there wo'd Come 2 or 3 inches of Snow frequently, and Mend it.—abundance of provisions Bro't down out of the Country & Sold verry cheap.

### 1789–90

We had this year, a Comfortable Winter: not much verry Cold weather (Except 1 week in February) nor verry Deep Snows; but abundance of Remarkable good Sleding and Sleighing.

### 1790–91

We had a pretty hard Winter; Deep Drifted Snows, & difficult passing. Especially turning out of the path: but Notwithstanding there has abundance of Business been done by Sleding, especially by Sleighing: Families Removing into the Country; Visiting friends: bringing down Country produce: Carrying up Salt, goods, &c &c So much of Such like Business Seldom or never known to be done in any Winter before—We have had but little high Winds or Storms; and tho' there was much Snow on the Earth; it went away without much Land flood, this Spring; but Soak'd into the Earth as it Melted: and we had not a Storm of Wind or rain this Spring.

### 1791–92

We had a verry cold difficult Winter: and altho' I have Lived to see many Winters of difficult passing, yet I think this rather exceeds them all; the Snow being deep & verry much Drifted; and Weather Exceeding cold; notwithstanding many people to drive through & over the Drifted Snows, & do a great Deal of business.

### 1792–93

We had the year past, a pretty open Winter; verry changable weather—in February, 5 freshets in 10 Days.

### 1793–94

the Winter past was pretty moderate favourable weather in general; so that Hay was plentier & cheaper this Spring than it was last fall.

### 1794–95

A pretty Moderate Winter, the 3<sup>rd</sup> Moderate Winter Successively—but little Sleding.

### 1795–96

The Winter past has been in general Comfortable weather, and may be called the 4<sup>th</sup> Moderate Winter Successively: little Snows so as to mend the Sleding & Sleighing, of which there has been abundance up and down the Country, carrying produce & goods forth and back all this Winter.

### 1796–97

The Coming Winter Sits in verry Early & Severe from the 23 of Nov.
The former part of last Winter was verry cold Setting in Early: Deep Snows: verry dry in Wells and Brooks; difficult getting Water for Cattle & House work &c the latter part open.

### 1797–98

This Winter has been pretty Close weather Hay pretty Scarce, Especially up Country.

### 1798–99

We had a tedious long Cold Winter, beginning about the 17th of Novr & Continuing near 6 Months; near all which time Cattle were Confined to our Barns: and Hay Exceeding Scarce in every part of the Country, as we hear by the News papers, and Many creatures have Died.

Corn is pretty plenty, tho' much has been given to our Cattle to keep them alive.

The Spring is verry Cold and backward: many people don't finish planting till June.

[Weather entries end with the year 1799]

# WINTERS OF THE REVOLUTION

Pre-Lexington and Concord: 1774–75 ....................... 89

The Quebec Expedition: 1775–76 .......................... 90

The Winter Siege of Boston: 1775–76 ...................... 96

Trenton, Princeton, and Morristown: 1776–77 .............. 98

Valley Forge: 1777–78 .................................... 100

New Jersey Again: 1778–79 ................................ 107

The Hessian Storm of December 1778 ...................... 109

The Hard Winter of 1779–80: Morristown .................. 111

Watching New York City: 1780–81 ......................... 134

Post-Yorktown, New Jersey Again: 1781–82 ................ 135

The Final Winter: 1782–83 ................................ 137

# PRE-LEXINGTON AND CONCORD: 1774-75

## *A Moderate Winter**

The first significant military action of the War of Independence came at the very end of an extraordinary winter. The New England militia had been mobilized in 1774 and throughout the cold season had been keeping an eye on the British in anticipation of an incursion into the countryside by the King's troops in Boston. The Americans had a good time of it, weatherwise. "It has been the most moderate winter in the memory of man," wrote Ezra Stiles on March 31st. "The water from Charlestown to Boston has not been frozen over this winter, which is seldom the case thro' a whole winter. The Army [British] has been in great jeopardy lest the country should rush in upon them over a bridge of ice: and since the time of freezing has elapsed, have become rather more insolent than before."[1]

Up at Portland in the District of Maine, Rev. Thomas Smith declared: "It has been a wonder of a winter, so moderate and unfreezing." On February 7th he noted: "There has been no snow, and but little rain since December 29th; wonderful weather, we saw two robins."[2] At Dover, New Hampshire, Jeremy Belknap recorded in his weather notes a prize example of the January thaw when from 20 to 28 January there was no freezing weather, not even during nighttime.[3]

The Delaware River remained open all winter, an unusual occurrence; at Philadelphia the only seasonal weather came at the end of January with some snow and floating ice noticed in the river, but no freeze-up.[4] January, according to the records of Thomas Coombe, averaged 35.6°, or 8.6 degrees above the previous January; and February, 41.2°, or 9.4 degrees above the previous February.[5]

Thomas Jefferson at Monticello in west-central Virginia lent his testimony to the mildness of the season: "We have had the most favorable winter ever known in the memory of man. Not more than three or four snows to cover the ground, of which two might lie about two days and the other one. The only weather which could be called anything cold was for about a week following the frost before noted Nov. 17."[6] And the Moravian diary in west-central North Carolina also took note of the season: "The weather this year was unusual, especially in January and February, when it was constantly warm as spring, so that by the end of February the peaches began to blossom."[7]

One must always pay for a moderate winter, however. In March and early April the circulation pattern shifted, and cold northerly air streams swept the New England countryside replacing the balmy southerly currents. In southern New Hampshire the "most tedious" storm of the winter, according to Matthew Patten, came on April 12th with a combination of snow, hail, and rain carried by a cold northeast wind.[8] The wintry conditions extended into the Boston area where our meteorological observers at Cambridge and Salem reported a mixture of snow, sleet, and rain on the 11–12th.[9]

If the British were waiting for the end of wintry conditions to launch their foray into the countryside, the proper weather commenced to unfold on the 16th at the conclusion of the cold spell as the polar air mass was replaced by a more moderate one. Wind flow went into the southwest as a low pressure trough approached from the interior of the continent. The cold front of the storm system moved across eastern New England during mid-day of the 18th when the British were putting plans into final shape for the sortie. Steady rain fell early on the 18th (1.08 inches on Prof. Winthrop's gage), but this was followed by westerly winds and rapid post-frontal clearing during the afternoon and evening. Visibility, no doubt, was good late in the evening of the 18th when the signal lamps were hung in the steeple of Old North Church.

The general meteorological conditions during the night of the famous Ride of Paul Revere, the British advance into the countryside, and the skirmishes at Lexington Common and at Concord Bridge can best be deduced from the observations made that day by Prof. John Winthrop whose location at Harvard College in Cambridge was close both to the line of advance and withdrawal of the British. His thermometer at 0600 on the morning of April 19th read 45.7° F., his barometer 29.56" and rising, wind at west at only force 1, and a "very fair" sky—in all, a cool, fresh spring morning. This observation was close to the time of the skirmish at Lexington Common soon after daylight. Winthrop made his next observation at 1300 on the 19th after the embattled farmers had made their early morning stand at Concord Bridge and the British had commenced their painful withdrawal from Concord back through Lexington and Cambridge on the road to Boston. The wind, with the barometer continuing to rise, had picked up to force 2, still blowing from the west, bringing cool, dry air across the area. The thermometer had risen only to 51.7° and the sky was "fair with clouds"—probably fair weather cumulus—

---
* Descriptive captions are from *Samuel Lane's Journal*.

an ideal day for outdoor activity! Winthrop's entry immediately following the above: "Battle of Concord, will put a stop to observing."[10] A break in his records followed until May 1st when the series was resumed at Andover, some 20 miles to the north away from the battle zone.

The general conditions existing on Lexington-Concord day were confirmed by the contemporary observations of Dr. Edward A. Holyoke at Salem, some 25 miles east-northeast of Concord. The passage of the storm system had been noted there on the 18th with "moist air and rain" in the morning, followed by "fair and some wind" in the afternoon and evening. Holyoke's morning thermometer reading on the 19th was 51°, but this was a sheltered location.[11] His comments for the 19th were: "serene, dry air, pleasant, cool."—apparently the shot heard round the world took some time in reaching staid Salem.

[1] *The literary diary of Ezra Stiles.* Franklin B. Dexter, ed. New York, Scribner's Sons, 1901. **1**, 529.
[2] T. Smith, *Journal,* 279.
[3] J. Belknap. Ms. Diary. (Mass. Hist. Soc.).
[4] S. Hazard. Effects of climate on navigation. *Register of Penna.* (Phila.). **2**-1, (July 1828), 26.
[5] Thomas Coombe. Ms. Met. Obs. near Philadelphia. (Amer. Phil. Soc.).
[6] Thomas Jefferson. *Garden Book 1766–1824.* Edwin M. Betts, ed. 66.
[7] *The records of the Moravians in N. C.* **2**, 855.
[8] M. Patten, *Diary,* 34.
[9] J. Winthrop, Ms. Met. Obs. (Harvard). E. Holyoke, Ms. Met. Jour. (Harvard).
[10] J. Winthrop.
[11] E. Holyoke.

## THE QUEBEC EXPEDITION: 1775–76

### *A pretty comfortable winter*

The main military action in the first full winter season of the war took place in northern climes where snows were deep and the cold severe. It commenced early with snow and freezing conditions in late October across northern New England, at the very time when Col. Benedict Arnold was leading the famous Quebec expedition over 350 miles of most difficult terrain from tidewater in central Maine, over the height of land at the boundary mountains, and down again to tidewater on the St. Lawrence River opposite the citadel of Quebec. Most of the time very adverse weather conditions, extreme for the season, were experienced. The first group of the force of 1,100 men left the Down East base at Fort Warren (Augusta) on the Kennebec River on 24 September, but only about 600 arrived some 46 days later, on November 8–9th, at Point Levis across the river from their objective.[1]

When deep in the Maine woods, the varied array of colonial troops experienced the wind-lashing of a storm of hurricane strength and suffered a cruel drenching from a cold three-day rain. This filled to overflowing the bogs and swamps which had to be traversed near the main portage from the headwaters of the Kennebec to those of the Chaudiere. When in this most difficult part of the journey, the now poorly-clothed, ill-shod, and under-nourished troops were subject to an unusually early onset of winter with late October cold, ice, and snow adding to the twin hardships of semi-starvation and physical exhaustion. The Rev. Thomas Smith has summarized conditions in southern Maine quite similar to those facing the troops in the northern reaches of his district in late October and throughout November: "The whole of this month has been one spell of severely cold, windy, winter-like weather."[2]

Probably no military expedition in American history possessed a greater percentage of diary keepers than Arnold's soldiers who marched, apparently with pad and pencil in hand, to Quebec in 1775. Kenneth Roberts, as a supplement to his exciting novel *Arundel,* collected and edited many of these into a single volume.[3] Though of uneven quality and often contradictory as to military facts, the collection did present a vivid picture of the meteorological additive to the heartbreaks and hardships attending the historic march. The following excerpts from the diaries have been selected to portray the weather conditions encountered en route.

Consecutive diary entries are by the same author whose name is appended until a new name is mentioned.

### October 1775

7. It rained very heavy all night. (Dearborn).[4]
8. It rained some part of the morning. . . . P.M. the weather proved very rainy.
9. It rained the biggest part of this day.
12. We have had remarkably fine weather since we left Cambridge (Arnold).[5]
12. But we cannot cross it by reason of the winds blowing very hard. (Dearborn).
13. The wind so high that the boats could not cross the pond. (Meigs).
14. Last night a tree blown down by the wind, fell upon one of our men and bruised him in such a manner, that his life is despaired of.
14. A high chain of mountains . . . covered with snow, in contrast to the others adds greatly to the beauty of the scene. (Arnold).
15. Thick weather and calm, with some rain, but not very cold. (Thayer).[6]

19. Small rains the whole of this day—at 3 P.M. the storm abating.

    N. B. rained very hard all night. (Arnold).
20. Rainy morning—at noon major Meig's Division came up, & being very wet & the storm continuing, they proceeded on, intending to encamp early. Continues rainy the whole of this day—wind to the So wd.
21. Storm continues tho' somewhat abated, a Prodigious fall of rain for 2 days past—has raised the river upwards of three feet. . . It was now quite dark so that we had little time to encamp, & it was near 11 o clock before we could dry our Clothes & take a little refreshment, when we wrapped ourselves in our blankets, & slept very comfortably until 4 o clock in the morning, when we were awakened by the freshet which came rushing in on us like a torrent, having rose 8 feet perpendicular in 9 hours, and before we could remove wet all our Baggage & forced us from our comfortable Habitation very luckily we had a small hill to retreat to, where we conveyed our baggage & passed the remainder of the night in no very agreeable situation.
21. Found it necessary this morning to decamp as early as possible. Wind S.S.W. The storm increased excessively, and now raised the river to a quick running current. . . . The wind increased to an almost hurricane the latter part of the day. The trees tumbling on all quarters that rendered our passage not only difficult, but very dangerous. (Senter).[7]—As not desiring to be in the tent on account of the falling trees. Storm abated about 12 o'clock, and the weather became fair.
22. This morning presented us a very disagreeable prospect, the Country round entirely overflowed, so that the course of the river, being crooked, could not be discovered.
22. The river has risen eight or nine feet. (Meigs).[8]
22. The rise of the waters was computed at ten feet. (Senter).
22. The storm abated, the river rose 6 feet perpendicular, and ran exceeding rapid. The sun rose with a little rain, but soon grew fair. (Thayer).
23. The stream by reason of the freshet very quick. (Arnold).
24. We proceeded about 1 mile higher up, when night coming on, & the rain increasing, which had begun about an hour before, we encamped—It continued raining and snowing all night. At 4 in the morning the wind shifted to North & it cleared up—About two inches of snow now on the ground.
25. Snowed and blowed very hard—the wind at north. All this day in the last Lake the sea ran so high

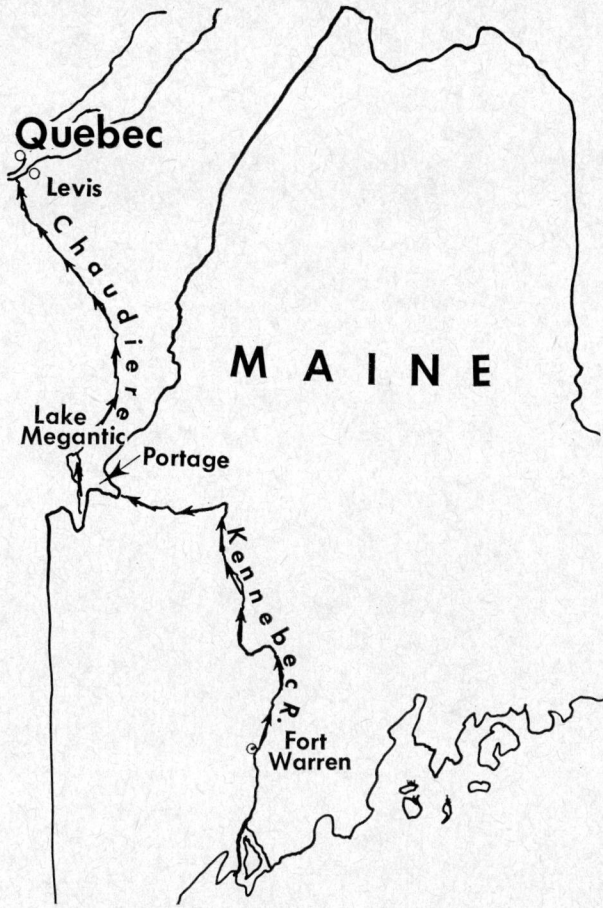

we were obliged to go on shore several times to bail our Battoes, which was with difficulty kept above the water—Night coming on & we being much fatigued and chilled with the cold.
25. A storm of snow had covered the ground nigh six inches deep, attended with very severe weather. (Senter).
28. Capt Goodrich was almost perished with the cold, having waded several miles backwards and forwards, sometimes to his arm-pits in water and ice.
29. The wind at East & some snow renders it very cold. (Arnold).
30. Proceeded through a swamp above 6 miles, which was pane glass thick frozen. (Thayer).
30. We immediately forded, although much frozen on each side. This Balneum Frigidum served to exercise our motion in order to keep from freezing. (Senter).

[Arnold's journal ended on 30 October; the remainder has not been located]

### November 1775

3. Our men proceeded down the river, tho, in poor circumstances, for traveling, a great number of them barefoot, and the weather cold and snowy,

many of our men died within the last three days, from here to Quebec is seventy miles.
3. A snow storm; the going exceedingly miry. (Haskell).[9]
4. We set out early this morning; had bad travelling by reason of the late snow.
4. The weather snowy. (Dearborn).
5. The weather is clear and very pleasant for this time of year.
6. Bad travelling almost knee deep in mire. (Haskell).
7. A snow storm; very bad stirring.
9. A thick cloudy morning. We have not had a fair day since we have been in the country [Canada].

The invading forces, resting on the banks of the St. Lawrence River, were not prepared to launch aggressive operations until late December. Their number slowly increased to about 800 as some Canadians joined the cause and a few stragglers came up. This ill-equipped group of independent battalions, operating hundreds of miles from their home bases, sought to dislodge a force of well-equipped and coordinated troops from the bastion of Quebec. A direct assault was decided upon by General Montgomery although several of the battalion leaders expressed serious misgivings as to the wisdom of such a course. It was decided to launch the operation of "storming Quebeck as soon as a good opportunity offered," *i.e.*, when the desired weather conditions unfolded. "It was a hard chance, but the only one; and even that hung upon the favor of the weathercock," an historian of the period has commented.[10]

The documents relating to the storming of Quebec were not in agreement as to the sequence of military events and the accompanying weather conditions. In fact, there existed a long-standing argument as to whether the assault occurred on the early morning of December 31st or January 1st. The military reports of Col. Arnold and Sir Guy Carleton, however, agreed on the earlier date, and this is definitely corroborated by the meteorological evidence at hand.[11]

Our best weather authority for the preliminaries to the assault and for the ensuing winter events during the "siege" was Thomas Ainslie, an officer of the British garrison who was well aware of the often decisive influence that weather elements played in military affairs, both large and small. He noted the following weather conditions at Quebec as General Montgomery was waiting for the proper situation to unfold[12]:

### December 1775

25. Mild day, wind at S.W. . . . Last night everything was remarkably quiet.
26. Last night it was clear and inconceivably cold; the wind is N.W. today, freezing beyond expression. No man can handle his arms in this weather, nor is it possible to scale walls.
27. Hazy cloudy night the last, the wind at W.N.W. this morning with snow.
28. The weather was clear and mild in the night. The wind is soft at S.W. today.
29. Last night the weather was clear,—no alarm: this morning is serene, with sunshine.
30. Wind westerly, very mild. In the night a deserter came in from the rebels. . . . He warns us to be on our guard, for that we shall be attacked the first dark night.

There was no hour-by-hour weather log of the weather sequence on the night of the 30–31st. Most writers agree with Thayer that the night was "very dark and it snowed"—the conditions desired by Montgomery. Apparently, there was a let-up in the intensity of the snowfall soon after midnight as the possibility of canceling the operation had been considered, but "as the storm grew furious again," plans went ahead for the five o'clock zero hour.[13] Some diarists and later commentators refer to a "tempest"—"a tremendous storm"—and even a "blizzard" on that night. Nothing in the contemporary documents sustains this. Carleton did state: "an assault was given on the 31st of December between four and five of the morning, during a snowstorm from the northeast." But Arnold in communicating the news of the defeat in letters written on the very day of the event and again on January 2d made no mention of the weather as being an adverse factor.

The visibility at zero hour (about five o'clock), when the rockets were sent aloft from Cape Diamond to coordinate the advance of the two main parties, must have been above the minimum desired by Montgomery as they were clearly seen by the British officer in charge of the sentries in the Lower Town. Then the flashes of gunshot that followed were visible to those on the heights of the Upper Town so that they could add their fusilade with effect. And as far away as three miles across the river other Americans perceived the shooting in the town before dawn. Probably much more adverse than the overhead conditions on the morning of the 31st were those underfoot where a deep snow cover had frozen into a slippery icy mass. This along with piled-up shore ice impeded efforts of the troops to move ahead along the narrow river path with any precision toward their objectives. Lost was the advantage of surprise and resulting confusion that the Americans had counted on. Street fighting in the Lower Town continued from about five o'clock until about ten, but the fate of the venture had been sealed in the first minutes when General Montgomery's initial thrust had been repulsed and the American troops scattered in front of their prime objective.

The intermittent snow, varying from light to moderate, on the morning of the 31st did develop into a very heavy fall during the afternoon and evening of the 31st as one of the two major storms of the winter came on.[15] At its conclusion about noon of New Year's Day the snow lay "six feet deep in drifts."[16] It was this heavy snowfall following the conclusion of the battle that stood out in the minds of many diarists when setting down their recollections at a later date. They confused the weather events on the nights of the 30–31st and 31–1st, and this probably greatly contributed to the uncertainty among later writers as to the actual date of the assault.

Over half of the attacking force were casualities, either killed or captured. General Montgomery lay dead in a snowdrift, and Colonel Arnold had hobbled back to the hospital with a crippling bullet through his leg. Certainly, no army had a less cheerful prospect than that facing the Americans before Quebec on New Year's Day of 1776. Justin Smith has succinctly described the situation:

> The army, already small, was now a shred; and there it lay, buried in the drifting snows of a Canadian winter, beaten and broken-backed, its friends far away and the enemy close at hand, mutely asking in a half-conscious way what the fate of it was to be.[17]

The small American force remained on the banks of the St. Lawrence River all winter, laying siege to the much larger British army comfortably quartered in the city, throughout what proved to be a bitter season even for that northern latitude. Rev. Thomas Smith down in Maine described local conditions: "January—this month, like the two past, has been constantly and severely cold. The wind has been westerly all winter. February—a dismal cold snap of weather. 29th—the past winter has been the coldest, in the whole, that has been known. The ground has been constantly covered with snow."[18] Some militia on their way to Canada found the snow five feet deep at Joe's Pond in northern Vermont on February 3d.[19]

The meteorological rigors endured by the besiegers of Quebec have been related by Lt. Ainslie in a day-to-day military diary containing sufficient weather data to permit one to judge for himself as to the nature of the current Canadian season. Some pertinent excerpts from Caleb Haskell's diary have been inserted in Ainslie's entries and marked by Haskell or H:

### January 1776

1. A very great snow fell last night.
3. Soft cloudy weather.
4. Soft drizzly weather today—wind at S.W.
5. Wind S.W. with a great thaw.
6. Wind N.W. It began to freeze early this morning —as the sun rose the cold encreased.
7. Wind at W. very cold.
8. Wind at N.E. cloudy, raw, blowing weather.
9. Wind N.E. soft snowy weather. There fell a very great quantity of snow before morning.
    A bad snow storm today. (Haskell)
10. Wind N.W. very cold . . . the snow drifted much; many people walked in the streets this morning on snow shoes, and some folk dug themselves out of their houses, the snow having filled up their doors.
    Severely cold and uncomfortable. (Haskell)
11. Wind W. by N. very cold and very clear. It drifted in the afternoon, encreasing so as to fill the streets.
    Continues cold. At night a bad snow storm. (Haskell)
12. Wind S.W. fine morning; afternoon dirty.
    The snow deep and bad storming. (Haskell)
13. Bad weather last night.
    Cold and squally. Little stirring. (Haskell)
14. The wind is at W. today, the cold excessive.
15. It froze very hard last night; wind S.W. today, blowing, drifting, cold weather.
    A bad snow storm, and so cold that a man can scarce get out without freezing. (Haskell)
16. It froze hard in the night.
17. Wind N.E. mild and snowy.
    A cold snow storm; the snow deep. (Haskell)
18. Wind S.W. but cold.
    Clears off pleasant in the afternoon. H.
19. Cold clear westerly wind.
20. Wind S.W. with showers of snow.
    Moderate but some snow. H.
21. Wind S.W. mild with snow.
    A pleasant day. H.
22. Wind N.E. drifty, cloudy, not cold.
23. S.W. wind, mild weather.
    A pleasant day. H.
24. Mild fine weather, wind S.W.
    Moderate weather. H.
25. Wind S.W. clear and mild weather.
26. Easterly wind, with a little snow, mild air, heavy sky.
27. Wind S.W. very cold.
    Exceeding cold weather. H.
28. Wind S.W. excessively cold.
29. Wind west, clear and intensely cold. It froze exceedingly hard last night; if this weather continues but a few days, it is feared that our river will freeze up.
    It continues cold, but something more moderate in the evening. H.
30. Easterly and cold morning. High wind with snow in the evening, weather milder.
31. East wind, dark and soft.

## February 1776

1. Cold, blowing, with drift.
2. Clear and cold with a west wind.
3. Wind W. excessively cold.
   The weather almost unendurable by reason of the cold. H.
4. Wind W. clear and cold. By the appearance of the river, it is probable that it is frozen over at the Chaudiere, six miles above.
5. Wind W. milder than yesterday, with squalls, a circumstance against the freezing over the river.
6. Wind high at W. with drift.
   It continues cold as ever. There is little stirring by reason of the cold. H.
7. Wind S.W. clear and cold.
8. The morning is soft and clear.
   A pleasant day. H.
9. A heavy wind at N.E. with much snow; the storm hourly increased until evening, it blew a mere hurricane—nobody could hold his face against it a minute. A sailor is missing; if he attempted to desert, he must be lost in the snow; in the spring he may be found under the snow in the street; in some places it has drifted 20 feet high.
   A severe snow storm came on this afternoon, increasing this evening. H.
10. Wind still at N.E. and very little moderated; the streets are absolutely impassable in many places without snow shoes. The first stories of many places are under the snow; the windows of the second level with the streets, and serve as doors. About eight at night the wind fell suddenly and it ceased snowing.
10. The storm continues. Such a storm, I believe, never was known in New England. Two of our men nearly perished going after provisions. H.
11. Cold westerly wind.
    It clears off pleasant. H.
12. Wind S.W. a fine moderate day; great working parties employed in clearing the ditch and ramparts of snow; one could walk through the embrasures into the ditch on snow shoes, although the foot of the wall is in these places 30 feet below the guns, which lay entirely buried.
13. A fine moderate day.
14. Wind at S.W. with fine weather.
    A pleasant day, and the sun is so warm that snow gives a little on the roofs of the houses, which is something remarkable. H.
15. A dark lowering morning, with a cold wind at N.E.
16. Wind westerly, a fine day and mild; a very numerous party clearing away the snow from the foot of the wall near Cape Diamond; even after this day's labour, ladders of 14 feet would reach from the top of the bank of snow to the embrasures in some places.
17. Westerly wind, a little cold, with fine clear weather. A cold, sharp air. H.
18. Exceedingly cold westerly wind.
    We had a severe cold night and it continues cold today. H.
19. Fine moderate weather, wind S.W.
20. Westerly wind, clear and cold.
21. A cloudy lowering mild morning, with westerly wind.
22. The weather was mild last night and very clear; the northern lights were equal to a moon; all was quiet; in the morning the wind got to the N.E. and brought cold.
23. West wind, lowering cold weather.
    Cold, uncomfortable weather. H.
24. Wind S.W. fine moderate weather.
25. Wind at N.E. warm and pleasant.
26. Wind N. dark sleety moderate weather.
27. Wind at S.E. close and sultry.
    A warm pleasant day; the snow beginning to thaw; at night we had some rain.
28. S.E. wind with soft snow—a thorough thaw.
    Continues rainy; the going is exceedingly bad. H.
29. High wind at S.W. with hard frost.

## March 1776

1. Cold N.W. Wind.
2. Thick weather, and some snow; clears off pleasant in the afternoon. H.
3. West wind, clear and excessively cold.
4. It thaws very much today; the wind is easterly.
   Uncomfortable weather; in the evening we had a heavy rain.
5. Strong wind at N.E. with heavy sky and cold rain.
6. It rained in the night. The wind is S.W. and it rains still; there is no walking in the streets, the risings are covered with ice, and in every hollow there is a pond of water.
7. Wind S.W. variable weather.
8. Wind at S.W. a mild morning.
9. Wind to the northward of west, cold and clear. About two inches of light snow fell last night; the river is not very full of floating ice; the outermost vessels in Cul de Sac have their sterns free.
12. Last night there fell near a foot of snow, with a N.E. wind; it blew hard at N.W. in the afternoon and cleared up.
13. Fine clear day, sharp air, wind N.W. . . . When the wind is from the west, the river is quite clear of ice on the Quebec side.
14. Easterly wind, heavy snow.

15. Much thaw—a fine day.
16. Wind N.E. There fell about two inches of snow last night; nothing remarkable today except the very heavy rain.
17. It rained all the night. This morning the wind shifted to S.W. and it rains still.
18. Wind S.W. thawing mild weather; in the evening, the wind changed to N.E. raw and dark.
19. Wind N.E. with snow and rain; in the evening it cleared up at W.
20. A gentle easterly wind, rather cloudy.
21. Wind N.W. It Froze last night very hard, and it still continues.
24. It was very dark last night; today it is cold, with a gloomy hard sky, though the wind is N.W.
25. Wind N.W. excessively cold, clearing up.
26. It was exceedingly cold last night.
31. Wind S.W. with snow; thawing.

### April 1776

4. It rained all night, the wind is about to S.W.
6. Wind easterly, with a heavy sky; it thaws much.
7. Rain, hail, sleet and N.E. wind.
10. Wind westerly; a very soft fine day, but the streets almost impassable, from the great runs of water; the remaining snow is porous and rotten; if one steps aside from the sleigh track, he sinks above the knees.
11. Heavy rain with a strong wind at N.E.
    Bad stirring. The snow goes away fast; the ground overflowed with water. H.
13. Lowering weather, wind W, cold and freezing.
    It is bad travelling by reason of the water being in many places three feet deep; the ground begins to appear on the top of some hills. H.
17. Wind N.E. there fell two inches of snow in the night.
18. Wind S.W. showers of snow. The ice of Lake St. Peter passed the town today.
19. It froze hard, and was clear last night.
21. Fine weather, wind S.W. swallows seen today.
22. At daybreak snow with N.E. wind.
23. There fell three inches of soft sloppy snow since yesterday morning.
25. It did not freeze last night. St Charles's River clear of ice.
26. The last night was the worst we have had for many months; the wind was violent at N.E. with a very heavy rain; it cleared up in the afternoon.
30. A small breeze at E. with soft rain in the morning; fog with heavy rain in the afternoon.

### May 1776

1. At four o'clock this morning it began to snow, and by eight there lay three inches in depth on the ground—the wind is northerly and cold—it began to clear up in the afternoon.
2. The last night was very clear and very cold—standing water froze a third of an inch—it freezes still with W.N.W. wind.
3. Last night was delightfully clear and serene; this morning the air is easterly, with hot sunshine.

[1] Justin H. Smith. *Our struggle for the fourteenth colony. Canada and the American Revolution.* New York, G. P. Putnam's Sons, 1907. **1**, 605.
[2] T. Smith, *Journal,* 279.
[3] *March to Quebec. Journals of the members of Arnold's Expedition.* Kenneth Roberts, ed. New York, Doubleday, Doran & Co., 1938.
[4] Capt. Henry Dearborn Journal of the Quebec Expedition, *ibid.,* 134.
[5] Col. Arnold's Journal of his expedition to Canada, *ibid.,* 50.
[6] Journal of Capt. Simeon Thayer's march through the wilderness to Quebec, *ibid.,* 254.
[7] Journal of Dr. Isaac Senter, *ibid.,* 208.
[8] A journal of occurrences within the observation of Return Jonathan Meigs, *ibid.,* 179.
[9] Caleb Haskell's Diary, *ibid.,* 478.
[10] J. H. Smith, *Our struggle,* **2**, 124.
[11] B. Arnold to General Wooster, Montreal. General Hospital (near Quebec), December 31, 1775. K. Roberts, *March to Quebec,* 102.
Guy Carleton to General Howe, Quebeck, January 12, 1776. *American Archives.* Peter Force, ed. Washington, U. S. Government, 1843. 4th ser., **4**, 656.
[12] Thomas Ainslie. Journal of the most remarkable occurrences in Quebec, from the 14th of November, 1775, to the 7th of May, 1776. By an officer of the garrison. *Coll. N. Y. Hist. Soc. for the year 1880.* **13**, 175–236.
[13] J. H. Smith, *Our struggle,* **2**, 126–27.
[14] *ibid.,* 129. George M. Wrong. *Canada and the American Revolution.* New York, The Macmillan Co., 1935. 302.
[15] T. Ainslie, *Journal,* 190.
[16] I. Senter, *Diary,* 236.
[17] J. H. Smith, *Our struggle,* **2**, 147.
[18] T. Smith, *Journal,* 279.
[19] Col. Frye Bayley's reminiscences. *Proc. Ver. Hist. Soc.,* (1923–25), 31.
[20] T. Ainslie, *Journal,* 175–236.

## THE WINTER SIEGE OF BOSTON: 1775–76

### GUNS FROM TICONDEROGA

The snow-covered terrain and wintry conditions hampering the Americans before Quebec in late December 1775 proved a boon to the forces of George Washington then besieging the British Army in Boston. One of the great prizes of the victory at Ticonderoga in May 1775 consisted of numerous cannon, howitzers, and mortars, types of military hardware of which the Continentals had few. It was impossible to move such cumbersome pieces over the primitive roads in summertime, but with the coming of winter and snow-covered terrain the artillery could be sledded to the seacoast if a determined effort were mounted.

Washington selected for the job young Henry Knox, in civilian life a bookseller. His efficient accomplishment of the difficult task earned him a high place in the esteem of his commander.[1] Knox reached Ticonderoga on 5 December 1775 and immediately set to work selecting the pieces and arranging to haul them to the northern end of Lake George where they could be ferried by raft 30 miles to the southern end. In a letter to General Washington from Fort George on 17 December, Col. Knox gave a vivid picture of the difficulties encountered on the first stages of the trip:

"I returned to this place on the 15th, and brought with me the cannon, it being nearly the time I computed it would take us to transport them here. It is not easy to conceive the difficulties we have had in transporting them across the lake, owing to the advanced season of the year and contrary winds; but the danger is now past. Three days ago it was very uncertain whether we should have gotten them until next spring, but now, please God, they must go. I have had made 42 exceeding strong sleds, and have provided 80 yoke of oxen to drag them as far as Springfield, where I shall get fresh cattle to carry them to camp. The route will be from here to Kinderhook [New York], from thence to Great Barrington [Mass.], and down to Springfield. I have sent for the sleds and teams to come here, and expect to move them to Saratoga on Wednesday or Thursday next, trusting that between this and then we shall have a fine fall of snow, which will enable us to proceed farther, and make the carriage easy. If that shall be the case, I hope in sixteen or seventeen days' time to be able to present to your Excellency a noble train of artillery."[2]

The weather situation during the first stages did not favor the enterprise. No continuous meteorological register has been uncovered for a locality closer than Concord, Massachusetts, where Professor John Winthrop of Harvard had finally set up his barometer and thermometer following the opening of hostilities in April 1775. There had been a thermometer at Albany in the pre-Revolutionary days and also references were made to one during the Hard Winter of 1780, but a record for the intervening critical war years has not survived.[3] Winthrop's observations in eastern Massachusetts, however, can be studied as indicative of the general type of air masses that overlay the upper Hudson Valley and western Massachusetts at this time. His thermometer would probably be on the conservative side running a bit higher, especially at night, than the general conditions some 150 miles to the west along the trail of the expedition. But as to precipitation, the Winthrop record cannot be employed as a guide to the conditions met by Knox since the precipitation regime between the Hudson Valley and the seacoast can vary greatly, not only as to amount, but also as to type, whether frozen or liquid, snow or rain.[4]

The Winthrop record, and these are backed up by Dr. Holyoke's contemporary observations at Salem, indicated a mild period until December 20th with five afternoon thaws and no severely cold mornings. From the 20th to the 30th conditions were generally favorable for the formation and the maintenance of ice. The 21st was "extreme cold and wind high from the northwest" as an Arctic air flow swept the countryside. At this period Knox made good progress southward along the Hudson River which had to be crossed four times. A Christmas Eve snowstorm raised the level to nearly two feet. This was apparently part of the storm system

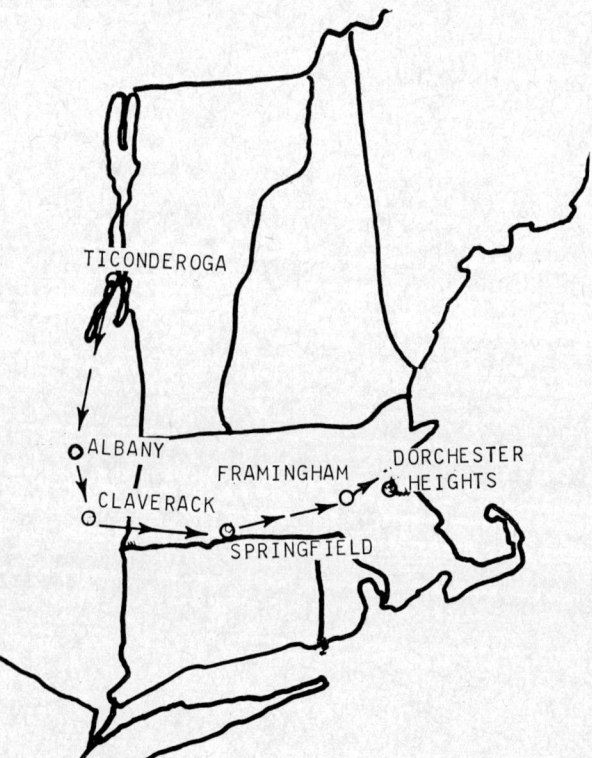

which, dumping similar amounts on South Carolina during the "Snow Campaign," had brought hostilities to a halt in the South.

The ten days of cold weather came to an end on the 30th. A heavy rainstorm drenched eastern Massachusetts on the 30–31st at the same time that the fateful snowstorm was approaching the Quebec area, perhaps the two regions were in different quadrants of the same disturbance. The soft weather in the Northeast delayed the Knox expedition in their attempts to get the heavier cannons across the Hudson River for the final time at Albany. Knox wrote to Washington on January 5th of his difficulties:

> "I was in hopes that we should have been able to have the cannon at Cambridge by this time. The want of snow detained us for some days, and now a cruel thaw hinders from crossing the Hudson River, which we are obliged to do four times from Lake George to this town. The first severe night will make the ice sufficiently strong; till that happens, the cannon and mortars must remain where they are. These inevitable delays pain me exceedingly, as my mind is fully sensible of the importance of the greatest expedition in this case." [5]

A spell of almost continuously freezing weather set in on the 10th of January, and this greatly accelerated the progress of the unusual caravan as it turned eastward toward its final destination. The route ran from Claverack on the old Albany–New York Post Road eastward over hill and valley following the old trail through the Berkshire Mountains in southwestern Massachusetts, along present Route 23, in the general region where on a typical January day cars now speed along the Massachusetts Turnpike at a sixty-mile clip between ploughed snowbanks. Only on the 12th and 16th did the mercury rise above freezing at the early evening observation at Salem, indicative of almost uninterrupted ice conditions at inland points.

When Springfield was reached in the floor of the Connecticut Valley, the snow had worn thin, and the New Yorkers wished to return home with their teams. Massachusetts groups were then hired for the final trek across relatively flat territory eastward. Framingham was reached by January 25th, and the prize of Ticonderoga was then within reach of George Washington to employ as he wished.[6] The journey of some 260 miles from the head of Lake George to the vicinity of Boston had taken 40 days, and probably a cargo of more political and military import never traversed the New England countryside. If the military situation a year earlier had demanded that this task be performed, during the mild winter of 1774–75, there would not have been enough snow or cold to furnish the necessary icy surface, and if the mission had been delayed a year until the severe winter of 1776–77, it could have been accomplished with much greater ease.

## THE EVACUATION

General Washington, ever conscious of the weather factor, wished to take military advantage of the severer than normal winter conditions prevailing. In mid-February he drew up a daring tactical plan of attacking the British Army in Boston over the frozen surface of the inshore harbor, while the enemy's naval vessels in the outer harbor were prevented from coming in close to lend support by existing ice conditions.[7] But with the Ticonderoga artillery now in hand, a more strategic plan prevailed. The guns would be mounted on Dorchester Heights, just south of Boston on a peninsula jutting out into the bay, where they could command the harbor and approaches to the town. By a prodigious effort on a dark night, the feat was accomplished by early morning of March 5th, taking the British by surprise. General Howe immediately realized the difficulty of his position and planned a counterattack the succeeding night to seize and occupy the commanding position, and he had the forces to do so if resolutely led. But "a hurrycane or terrible sudden storm" arose to thwart the launching of his plan. "About midnight the wind blew almost a hurricane from the south," William Heath recalled. "Many windows were forced in, sheds and fences blown down and some vessels drove on shore."[8] The impact of the unexpected storm disrupted the initial stages of the planned assault. High surf prevented any flat boats from landing in the choppy waters as the storm accompanied by torrential rains continued into the next day.[9]

Both our weather observers in the vicinity, John Winthrop at Concord and Edward Holyoke, noted southeast winds prevailing at the height of the storm, having shifted from southwest through south, indicating the arrival of a deep trough from the westward rather than a coastal disturbance moving up from the south.[10] Dr. Holyoke wrote on the 6th: "SE. Very high wind. Stormy. Rain. Temperature 53° morning, 48° evening."[11]

General Howe, in view of the strength of the American position and cognizant of the adversity of the weather elements at this season, had already made up his mind to evacuate Boston, so plans for a renewal of the attack were abandoned and the celebrated evacuation commenced on March 17th, leaving Bostonians far from the front line in a war destined to continue seven more long years.

[1] Noah Brooks. *Henry Knox. A soldier of the Revolution.* New York, G. P. Putnams' Sons, 1900. 38–44.
North Callahan. *Henry Knox, General Washington's general.* New York, Rinehart, 1958. 39–55.

[2] N. Brooks, 40.
[3] *Albany Gazette,* 13 Jan 1772, in *Albany Annual Register* (1850), **2**, 192.
[4] John Winthrop. Ms. Met. Obs. (Harvard); Edward A. Holyoke. Ms. Met. Jour. (Harvard).
[5] N. Brooks, 41.
[6] Henry Knox. Ms. Diary. (Mass. Hist. Soc.).
[7] Allen French. *The first year of the American Revolution.* Boston & New York, Houghton Mifflin Co., 1934. 656.

Christopher Ward. *The War of the Revolution.* John R. Alden, ed. New York, The Macmillan Co., 1952. **1**, 126.
[8] Walter N. Lacy. Weather influences preceding the evacuation of Boston, Mass. *Monthly Weather Review* (Washington). **36**-5, (May 1908), 128–29.
[9] William Heath. *Memoirs of Major-General Heath.* Boston, 1798. Reprint: N. Y., A. Wessells Co., 1904. 50.
[10] J. Winthrop, Ms. Met. Obs.
[11] E. Holyoke, Ms. Met. Jour.

## TRENTON, PRINCETON, AND MORRISTOWN: 1776–77

*Not a hard Winter, and but little Sledding*

The early part of this winter continued mild until December 20th. The scene of military activity now centered in the Middle Colonies. The British, having occupied the New York Harbor area and part of New Jersey after routing the Americans in the battles of Long Island and White Plains, went into winter quarters by official order on December 14th. They held a number of strong points across central New Jersey from Perth Amboy at the southwest corner of New York Bay to Trenton on the east bank of the Delaware River.[1]

General Washington withdrew his men to the western side of the Delaware with the forces divided into three corps guarding the main ferry crossings from Yardley to Bordentown. Fearful of a strong attack once the river surface was frozen solidly, the American leader decided he might "under the smiles of Providence effect an important stroke."[2]

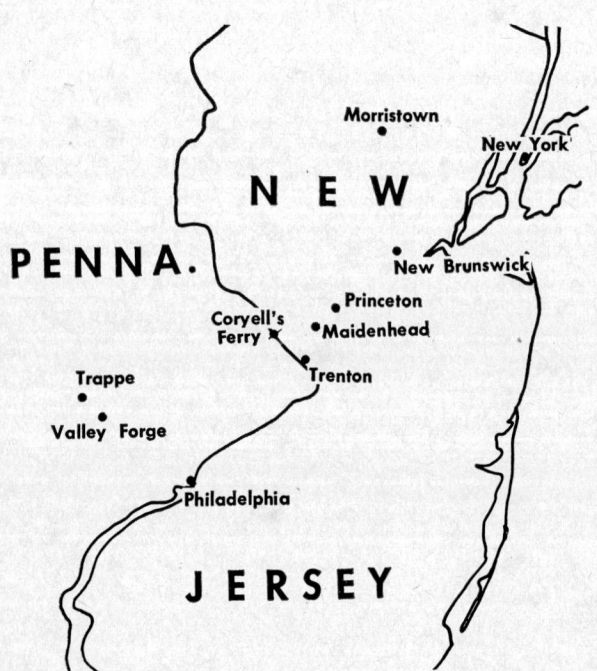

Probably no winter scene in our history is more indelibly impressed on the American mind than the dramatic picture of Washington crossing the Delaware on the stormy evening following Christmas Day of 1776. No doubt the adverse meteorological conditions contributed to the surprise of the Hessian garrison at Trenton early the next morning, but these also made the crossing and the eight-mile march extremely difficult. One of Washington's staff has left the following account:

> "Christmas, 6 p.m. . . . It is fearfully cold and raw and a snowstorm setting in. The wind is northeast and beats in the faces of the men. It will be a terrible night for the soldiers who have no shoes. Some of them have tied old rags around their feet, but I have not heard a man complain."[3]

The middle Delaware Valley stood on the northern fringe of a great coastal disturbance that Christmas night and on the following day. From as far south as central North Carolina, there was "shoe-top" snow at Salem on Christmas night and at Friedberg the fall amounted to "more than a foot deep."[4] Thomas Jefferson at Monticello related in his manuscript Weather Book that a deep snow was deposited there on Christmas night, and later on referred to this storm which "fell in one night 24 inches" deep, though he also once gave the depth as 22 inches.[5] Another observer of this storm was Nicholas Cresswell, a British prisoner passing his captivity at Pennroyal Hill, Frederick County, in northwesternmost Virginia. His journal for December 26th noted: "The snow fell last night two feet thick and level. This is the greatest fall of snow I have seen in this country."[6]

The storm area appeared to have been somewhat similar to the great Knickerbocker Storm on 27–28 January 1922 which left a very deep snow mantle of 24 to 30 inches over Virginia and Maryland, but with much lesser amounts in Pennsylvania and New Jersey. The center of the disturbance probably remained off the Carolina coast and moved off east-northeastward rather than on the usual northeastward course.

Close to the important military action, we have a full meteorological report at Philadelphia where Phineas Pemberton, a member of the American Philosophical Society, kept a watch on the weather. On Christmas morning the area was enjoying pleasant anticyclonic conditions with the barometer at the high level of 30.50″, the wind light out of the north. The sky, though decked with some clouds, had a bright sun shining. The mercury stood at 32°.[7]

During the day a falling barometer and a shift of wind into northeast heralded a coming storm. By evening snow and "hail" (more correctly sleet) set in as the southern disturbance spread its precipitation canopy northward. The Philadelphia and Trenton areas remained on the northern edge of the heavy precipitation sector of the storm and did not receive the deep snowfall which covered North Carolina and Virginia. Pemberton described the 26th, as "a very stormy day with much rain & hail & snow at times. Cleared about 5 p.m." At mid-afternoon his barometer had dropped to 29.53″, probably close to the low point as the wind had already shifted into northwest. His thermometer stood at 33°.[8]

About 35 miles west of Trenton at Trappe, Dr. Muhlenberg in speaking of the 25–26th recorded: "Last night and today we had violent windstorm with snow, so that it is imposssible to come or go, and yet little groups of provincial militia keep marching by through this weather on their way to Philadelphia."[9] At Trappe on the morning of the 27th the snow lay "a foot deep and it is bitter cold." By this time Washington's troops had recrossed the Delaware with their bag of prisoners and captured equipment.

The British soon sought to retaliate. Under the energetic leadership of General Cornwallis, 8,000 regulars advanced from New Brunswick, through Princeton, to Maidenhead (Lawrenceville) on the 1st and 2d of January. An early January thaw had set in on New Year's Day with the mercury soaring to 51° at Philadelphia in the afternoon.[10] Melting snows and a hard rain at night turned the erstwhile roads into bottomless tracks making movement of men and vehicles most difficult.

The advancing British met the outposts of the Americans, who had for the third time crossed the river, at the lower end of Maidenhead and drove them back after some sharp skirmishing on the 2d. That afternoon the Continental forces guarding Trenton were also forced back to prepared positions along the southern bank of Assunpink Creek. The British made some efforts to cross the little stream, but met stout opposition. As the daylight waned, Cornwallis believed he had Washington trapped and decided to wait until morning to launch a fullscale assault and "bag the fox."[11]

Washington now found his troops in a desperate position—outnumbered—a well-equipped and disciplined enemy in front—confined to a small maneuver area by muddy roads on each flank, and an ice-clogged river behind sealing off retreat. A council of war was held late on the 2d from which an audacious plan emerged. "A providential change in the weather" was in the making.[12] A cold front had moved through the area early on the 2d. The day was described by Pemberton as fair and windy in the morning, and cloudy with sunshine and still windy in the afternoon—a typical post-frontal day in wintertime. But the weatherwise Washington noticed the wind holding to the northwest all day and the temperature not rising during the day, but remaining steady near 39° as a continued flow of cold air poured into the area.[13] Surely, this meant a freeze that night, a freeze that would harden the roads into a tractable surface and permit the army, now immobilized by General Mud, to move. While seemingly preparing to defend the defensive position on the morrow, with huge camp fires blazing and much moving about, Washington's entire force packed their equipment and supplies after midnight in preparation for an end run around the left flank of the British camped across the creek. A recently hewn-out secondary road, now part of civil defense highway 533, provided an escape route. This ran east-northeastward, three or four miles southeast of the main post road in British hands, through present Mercerville, Clarksville, and Port Mercer, then converging to join the main post road near Stoney Brook just south of Princeton. After sunset the mercury had dropped below the freezing point, as Washington had anticipated, to 31.5° at 2100.[14] When the army commenced to move about 0400/3d, it was still lower and the new road was frozen solid, though progress was hindered by a badly rutted surface with here and there numerous unremoved stumps providing stumbling blocks.

"The day dawned beautifully: clear, cold, and still"— a typical anticyclonic morning in wintertime. The first rays of the sun found Washington and his troops well in the rear of the main body of Cornwallis' force which was still looking forward to the decisive frontal assault on the erstwhile American position south of Trenton. The advance guard of the forward detachment of Americans, when approaching Princeton from the southwest, came in contact with an equally small column of British regulars moving southward on the Trenton Post Road to join the main body at Trenton. A clash took place between Stony Brook and Frog Hollow, astride present Mercer Road, southwest of Nassau Hall, on "a clear frosty morning." The Philadelphia thermometer at this hour read 21°, so the desired freeze had taken place overnight making open fields as well as roads tractable for military operations.

The Battle of Princeton was a hotly-fought, but brief affair, the entire fire-fight lasting only about 45 minutes from start to finish, with the outcome in doubt between the disciplined British and the American militia until the main force of seasoned Continentals came on the scene. The successful outcome of the clash cleared the way for Washington to move across Cornwallis' main supply route and to threaten to occupy his main base at New Brunswick. Such a prize, however, was beyond the ability of the leg-weary Americans. Washington wisely selected his secondary objective: the strategic Watchung range of hills in north-central Jersey, a safe lair from immediate pursuit and a vantage point for keeping watch on the British. The army went into winter quarters around Morristown, 20 miles west of New York City, the first of five memorable winters to be spent in the general area.

There was no more military activity during the winter of 1776–77. The British outposts withdrew to New Brunswick and Amboy with the main forces quartered in New York City. The ensuing winter followed an in-and-out course with plenty of snow but few severely cold periods. The 0800 thermometer readings out-of-doors at Philadelphia descended only to +14° in January and to +13° in February.[16] The second month of the year, however, featured several snowstorms. A major fall occurred on 24 February. At Trappe Dr. Muhlenberg described "an extraordinary snow storm. Perhaps as much as two feet fell."[17] Pemberton's Philadelphia weather record carried the entry: "stormy & a very deep snow, having continued near 24 hours without interruption (15 inches deep)."[18] At Bound Brook on the outskirts of Washington's defensive line in New Jersey the fall also measured 15 inches, this on top of previous snows.[19] Hugh Gaine on the 24th at New York City witnessed: "a very heavy snow all day, and considerably deep."[20] In southeastern Massachusetts at Dighton the storm brought 18 inches of new snow to raise the level in Dighton Woods to 30 inches, according to Ezra Stiles' statements.[21] This concluded the snowy phase of the winter. There remained deep snow on the ground at Trappe, Pennsylvania, on March 1st, but by the 9th a warm spell set in making "bottomless roads since the ground had thawed."[22]

In the Far North where the British were assembling a large force to invade through the Lake Champlain gateway, it was a snowy, but not cold winter, favorable for such operations. The *Journal of Du Roi the Elder,* a German mercenary from Brunswick, supplied a pertinent comment: "It was said that this winter has been very mild and that there had not been one like it for the last twenty years."[23]

[1] C. Leonard Lundin. *Cockpit of the Revolution; the War for Independence in New Jersey.* Princeton, Princeton University Press, 1940.
[2] William S. Stryker. *The Battles of Trenton and Princeton.* New York, Houghton, Mifflin & Co., 1898. 362.
[3] *The writings of George Washington from the original manuscript sources 1745–1799.* Wash., Gov't Printing Office, 1932. **6**, 372–73.
[4] *Records of the Moravians in North Carolina,* **3**, 1109.
[5] Thomas Jefferson. Ms. Weather Book. (Library of Congress).
[6] *The Journal of Nicholas Cresswell 1774–1781.* Lincoln MacVeaugh, ed. New York, The Dial Press, 1924. 178.
[7] Phineas Pemberton. Ms. Met. Obs. (Amer. Phil. Soc.).
[8] *Idem.*
[9] *The Journals of Henry Muhlenberg.* Phila., The Muhlenberg Press, 1945. **2**, 767.
[10] P. Pemberton.
[11] Alfred H. Bill. *The Campaign of Princeton, 1776–1777.* Princeton, Princeton University Press, 1948. 88.
[12] *Ibid.,* 92.
[13] P. Pemberton.
[14] *Idem.*
[15] A. Bill, *Princeton,* 96.
[16] P. Pemberton.
[17] H. Muhlenberg, *Journal,* **3**, 16.
[18] P. Pemberton.
[19] Revolutionary diary kept by George Norton of Ipswich, 1777–1778. *Essex Inst. Coll.* (Salem), **74**, (1938), 338.
[20] *The Journals of Hugh Gaine.* New York, Dodd, Mead & Co., 1902. **2**, 19.
[21] E. Stiles, *Diary,* **2**, 128–31.
[22] H. Muhlenberg, *Journal,* **3**, 16.
[23] *Journal of Du Roi: the elder, lieutenant and adjutant in the service of the Duke of Brunswick, 1776–1778.* Charlotte S. J. Epping, ed. University of Penna. Press—New York, D. Appleton & Co., 1911. 65.

# VALLEY FORGE: 1777–78

*A pretty Close Winter; & but little good Sledding*

Valley Forge has become a term in our language synonymous with hard suffering of ill-housed, ill-clad, and ill-nourished soldiers whom circumstances had forced to encamp in the open countryside during the depth of winter. We are all familiar with the portrayal of George Washington praying out-of-doors with the stark winter terrain in the background and bloody footprints visible in the foreground snow. This eloquently conveys both the circumstances and the spirit of Valley Forge.

Yet on the basis of cold statistics, the winter of 1777–78 in the latitude of Philadelphia was not a severe one. Of the seven winters during the period of the War of Independence when the contending armies were in the field, two (1779–80 and 1781–82) were severe, and two were notably mild (1778–79 and 1780–81) the others (1775–76, 1776–77, and 1777–78) were moderate. If Valley Forge had occurred a year earlier, there would have been much greater suffering; and, if a year later, conditions would have been much less harsh. None-the-less one needs only to read the contemporary testimony of those who endured the winter at Valley Forge to realize that spending even a mild winter in the field without proper equipment, food, and shelter would constitute an ordeal for a human in the best of health.

In reconstructing the meteorological situation at Valley Forge we are fortunate in having two excellent sources that provide a running account of day-to-day conditions. Complete weather records were maintained at this time by Thomas Coombe at his residence only "two miles west of Philadelphia," probably that distance west of the Schuylkill River, approximately in the 63d St. and Market St. area of present West Philadelphia.[1] Coombe had commenced his records at least as early as 1767, and they have been carefully preserved in the library of the American Philosophical Society. His equipment included a barometer and two thermometers: one located inside and the other outside. He has left a record of two daily observations, usually at 0800 and 1500, times of day which would give an approximate of the maximum and minimum temperatures in wintertime. He included sky conditions and wind direction with mention of precipitation and other unusual phenomena. The records were kept very diligently and appear trustworthy. His outdoor thermometer was exposed on the casement of an open window facing northwest. His barometer showed good movement though it never registered above 30.50" despite his location being very close to sea level. The West Philadelphia observation point lay about 17 miles southeast of the encampment at Valley Forge. Average winter temperatures would vary about 1.5 to 2.5 degrees under ordinary situations; but, under special circumstances when optimum radiation conditions obtained, a temperature differential of 5 to 10 degrees might obtain for limited periods. Winter precipitation amounts would not vary in any significant degree, but under critical conditions, when the mercury was hovering close to the 32-degree mark, Valley Forge might experience sleet or wet snow while the lower-lying city area might have a cold rain. Modern records show that snowfall in the Valley Forge area runs about 20% above that experienced in the present urban area at tide water.[2]

In addition to this fine record, we have the daily journals of Rev. Henry Melchior Muhlenberg living at Providence, now Trappe, close to the Perkiomen River in Montgomery County.[3] Muhlenberg stated that his homestead lay just 10 miles distant from the encampment at Valley Forge, in a north-northwesterly direction. Meteorological conditions at the two locations would be quite similar. Rev. Muhlenberg had been a life-long observer of the weather, both in Europe and in America, and most every change or unusual phenomenon was mentioned in his voluminous diary covering the years 1742–1787. In his declining years he grew quite weary of severe winter weather and thus expressed himself vehemently during the period of extreme conditions which characterized the early 1780's. There was no evidence that Muhlenberg had a thermometer or access to one during the period under study. He limited himself to general comments on the day's weather and on travel conditions. These are most helpful in reconstructing the weather story of these turbulent times.

Generally speaking, the winter of 1777–78 was an in-and-out affair. There were two periods of relatively severe cold: at the end of December (a +6° reading at West Philadelphia at 0800) and at the commencement of March (+8°). Two periods of moderate cold came in mid-winter: January's lowest was +12° and February's, +16°.[4]

There were only three continued snowstorms, and these were all of the moderate-to-heavy, not excessive, variety. Four inches fell at Philadelphia on 28 December, with more indicated for the Valley Forge area; a "deep snow" came on February 8th which was washed away by a heavy rain on the 10–11th; and on 2–3 March "enough for sleighing" in downtown Philadelphia concluded the snow season. A camp diarist indicated as much as a foot of snow on the ground early in January, and Dr. Muhlenberg thought the snow of February 8th "deeper now than we have had the whole winter." In January the ground appeared to have been snow-covered a good part of the time, though in February there seemed to have been more days with bare ground than not. Throughout the season there were frequent thaws, creating muddy fields and putting the roads in atrocious shape for travel or movement.

The Delaware River was closed to navigation by ice during the first cold spell from 30 December to 8 January, and again for a short number of hours around January 19th.[7] There was floating ice seen on 23 January, 9 February, and 5 March.[8] But no long-continued freeze-up took place such as blocked the river for many days in a row in the winters of 1776–77 and 1779–1780. There were several distinct, warmer-than-normal periods: from 20–26 December, 3–12, 18–22, 29–31

January, 1–8 and 25–27 February—when overnight thaws predominated.[9]

The first snow of the season fell on 12 December when the American Army was camped at Whitemarsh to the east of Valley Forge. But real winter conditions did not commence until 27 December when the deepest single snow of the season fell and the severest cold followed.[10] The winter began to break up on 9–10 March as overnight thaws became regular. The 12th brought the first true spring weather.[11] These dates are close to the normal for the onset of favorable spring conditions in the Philadelphia area.[12]

The Americans moved into the camp site at Valley Forge on December 19th, a day described ominously by Muhlenberg as having "stormy winds and piercing cold."[13] The condition of the troops at this time has been vividly described by an historian of the period:

> It is impossible to exaggerate the misery of the troops at this time. General Greene wrote: "One half of our troops are without breeches, shoes and stockings; and some thousands without blankets." A quarter of the whole number were reported unfit for duty, "because they are barefoot and otherwise naked." The quartermaster's department, as well as the commissariat, had completely broken down. "While the army was suffering . . . want of shoes &c., hogsheads of shoes, stockings and clothing were at different places upon the road and in the woods, lying and perishing, for want of teams and proper management.

\* \* \*

Even then their shelters were but apologies for dwelling places. They were far from weatherproof. The cold winter winds blew through their crevices. The ill-designed fireplaces filled them with eye-stinging, throat-choking smoke. Few had wooden floors. For the most part the men lay on the damp earth, padded by a thin coating of scarse straw. Yet there was some warmth within them and shelter from snow and rain.[14]

It is not within the scope of this work to describe the daily activities at Valley Forge. This has been ably done recently by John J. Stoudt in *Ordeal at Valley Forge,* but the complete meteorological record of Thomas Coombe follows along with pertinent excerpts from the *Journals of Henry M. Muhlenberg* and the *Journals of Capt. John Montresor.*

---

## PHILADELPHIA, 2 MILES WEST

(Thomas Coombe)

(Two daily observations were usually made: at 0700 and 1500.)

### December 1777

| Day | Temp | Pressure | Wind | Conditions |
|---|---|---|---|---|
| 18. | 37° | 29.87″ | NE | Cloudy. Rain last night |
|  | 42 | 29.70 | SW | Cloudy p.m. |
| 19. | 29 | 29.90 | NW | Fair. Rain last night |
|  | 30 | 30.00 | NW | Fair |
| 20. | 25 | 30.10 | W | Fair |
|  | 31 | 29.90 | WSW | Fair |
| 21. | 31 | 30.10 | W | Cloudy |
|  | 33 | 30.10 | W | Fair |
| 22. | 33 | 29.90 | SW | Sunshine & clouds |
|  | 36 | 29.80 | SW | Fair |
| 23. | 32 | 30.05 | NW | Clouds & sunshine |
|  | 36 | 30.05 | NE | Cloudy |
| 24. | 23 | 30.02 | NE | Fair |
|  | 28 | 30.00 | NE | Sunshine & clouds |
| 25. | 27 | 30.05 | NE | Cloudy. Fair at noon |
|  | 34 | 29.87 | SW | Cloudy. A little snow last night |

## TRAPPE, PENNSYLVANIA

Based on *The Journals of Henry Melchior Muhlenberg* at his homestead located about 10 miles north-northwest of the encampment. Supplementary material in italics has been added: for December 1777 and March 1778 from "The Journals of Capt. John Montresor" at Philadelphia; and for January and February 1778 from *Ordeal at Valley Forge* by John J. Stoudt which contains a series of extracts from soldiers' diaries at Valley Forge. Montresor's journal for January and February 1778 has never been located.

### December 1777

18. Dark, cloudy, and cold rain.

19. Today we have stormy winds and piercing cold; it it very hard for the poor destitute people! *Snow begins.*

20. *Snow ceased.*

21. *Snow on ground and cold.*

22. *Excessive cold and uncomfortable. Great smoke from many campfires.*

23. *Cold and uncomfortable.*

24. *A flurry of snow.*

25. The weather was bitter cold. Had snow during the night.

| | | | | | |
|---|---|---|---|---|---|
| 11. | 34 | 29.67<br>29.35 | NE | Rain<br>A thick fog & thawing stormy &<br>snow the following night | 11. Last night a heavy rain fell upon the deep snow, and it continues to rain today, which will result in high waters and impassable roads. *Rained so hard we could not stir out. Wet and sloppy.* |
| 12. | 35 | 29.45 | NW | Windy & sunshine<br>Same, flying clouds | 12. During the night we had a violent windstorm which continues today and is carrying away much that cannot resist it. *Cold and raw.* |
| 13. | 32 | | NW | Fair & windy<br>Sunshine & flying clouds | 13. The stormy, penetrating northwest wind continued throughout the whole day and made both men and cattle shiver. |
| 14. | 22 | 29.92 | NW | Fair & windy<br>Sunshine & clouds | 14. |
| 15. | 31 | 30.02 | NE | Cloudy & sunshine<br>Cloudy | 15. Thawing weather. |
| 16. | 29 | 29.77 | NE | Cloudy. Hail & snow last night.<br>Fair from 1200 to 2 p.m.<br>Cloudy p.m. | |
| 17. | 20 | 30.32 | NW | Fair & windy<br>Fair & windy | |
| 18. | 20 | 30.42 | SW | Fair<br>Sunshine & clouds | |
| 19. | 27<br>38 | 30.17 | NE<br>Calm | Sunshine & Cloudy. Rain the following night | |
| 20. | 36<br>29 | 29.75 | NE | Cloudy & foggy<br>Cloudy—snow a.m. | |
| 21. | 24 | 30.30 | NE | Fair<br>Fair | |
| 22. | 26<br>34 | 30.20<br>29.85 | NE<br>E | Cloudy. Snow this afternoon<br>Cloudy. Hail evening | 22. Snowed the whole day. |
| 23. | 34 | 29.77 | SW | Flying clouds & sunshine<br>Windy & flying clouds | |
| 24. | 35 | 30.05 | W | Fair<br>Clouds & sunshine | 24. *Uncommonly severe and cold. Sleet.* |
| 25. | 36 | 30.10 | SW | Hasey & sunshine<br>Sunshine & clouds | 25. *Freezing.* |
| 26. | 43 | 29.82 | SE | Rain & foggy<br>Cloudy | 26. It began to rain heavily in the morning, and this made the roads utterly impassable. |
| 27. | 49<br>37 | 29.72 | NW | Much rain last night and continued most of day with snow in the afternoon | 27. The rain continued unabated last night. Today both snow and rain are falling together. |
| 28. | 30<br>39 | 30.00<br>29.92 | SE<br>SE | Fair & frost<br>Cloudy a little snow in the afternoon | 28. *A thaw has set in.* |

## March 1778

| | | | | | |
|---|---|---|---|---|---|
| 1. | 33° | 29.97" | SW | Clouds & sunshine<br>Rain & snow last night<br>A squall of wind at NW with snow about 9 this eve. | 1. But the Schuylkill was so high and the roads so deep that he was unable to come. *Cold and frosty. Winds boisterous at N.W. Fall of snow in the night.* |
| 2. | 17 | 30.02 | | Windy & fair<br>Windy, sunshine & cloudy | 2. Again it was colder than ever before this winter. During the night the snow fell again. *A fall of snow at night. Wind at N.N.W.* |
| 3. | 22 | 29.95 | NE | Snow the preceding night till 11 a.m. Begun again about 3 p.m. & continued part of the night | 3. A deep snow fell again today. *Snowed all day. Wind at N.N.E.* |
| 4. | 8 | 30.07 | NW | Fair<br>An intense frost<br>Fair | 4. During the past night, and up to now, the cold has been still more severe than heretofore this winter. *Intensely cold. Wind at NW. Good sleighing.* |

| | | | | | |
|---|---|---|---|---|---|
| 5. | 23 | 30.12 | SW | Cloudy. Ice in Delaware | 5. The severe cold continues unabated. *Wind NNW and cold. River Schuylkill frozen over.* |
| | | | | Fair | |
| 6. | 26 | 30.47 | NE | Sunshine | 6. *Moderate weather. Wind northerly. Floating ice on the river.* |
| | | | | Sunshine | |
| 7. | 32 | 30.32 | E | Cloudy | 7. Again dark and cold weather in the realm of nature and morals. *Wind E S E. Foggy and moist weather. Ice on the edge of the River.* |
| | | | | Cloudy. Rain this afternoon | |
| 8. | 35 | 30.15 | NW | Fair | 8. The roads and weather are bad. |
| 9. | 34 | 30.50 | NE | Cloudy. Snow most of the day | 9. Today deep snow is falling again. *Wind N E and snowy weather.* |
| | 38 | 30.55 | E | | |
| 10. | 36 | 30.45 | NE | Rain | 10. We have rain, snow, bad roads, and high water. *Wind at N E and snow.* |
| | 40 | 30.30 | NE | Cloudy & foggy | |
| 11. | 40 | 30.20 | NE | Cloudy & foggy | 11. Now we are having rain and thaw, which is opening up the frozen ground, making the roads to be knee-deep in mud, and causing high water. *Rained all day. Weather unsettled for the past several days.* |
| | 44 | 30.10 | NE | Cloudy & rain | |
| 12. | 43 | 30.05 | NE | Foggy & drizzling | 12. Thawing weather, and the roads are so deep and impassable that neighbors are scarcely able to get to each other. *Weather continues hot rather than warm; first spring-like day.* |
| | | 29.97 | SW | Rain most of last night | |
| | | | | Sunshine & cloudy p.m. | |
| | | | | Lightning evening | |
| 13. | 54 | 30.05 | SW | Thick fog in a.m. | 13. Today was the first day of spring we have had; heard the turtle doves and frogs. *Weather warm. The verdure has begun to appear. Some birds have come.* |
| | | | SE | Cloudy with intervals of sunshine | |
| 14. | 53 | 30.00 | SW | Hasey & Sunshine | 14. *Very warm for the season. Laylock and Gooseberry leaves sprouting.* |
| | | 30.05 | SW | Flying clouds. Windy in the forenoon | |
| 15. | 53 | 30.30 | N | Cloudy | 15. It rained steadily from midnight on. *Uncommonly warm; wind S E. Roads better.* |
| | 58 | 30.35 | N | Cloudy | |
| 16. | 45 | 30.13 | NE | Cloudy. Much rain the preceding night. | 16. *Easterly winds and damp.* |
| | 49 | 29.80 | NE | Cloudy | |
| 17. | 49 | 29.73 | SW | Cloudy | 17. *Fine weather. Frogs croak in the swamps.* |
| | | 29.95 | W | Wind & fair | |
| 18. | 34 | 30.33 | NW | Fair | 18. *Fine weather. Frogs still croak in the swamps.* |
| | | 30.35 | NW | Fair | |
| 19. | 36 | 30.27 | SW | Sunshine & cloudy | 19. *Fine weather.* |
| | | 30.05 | SW | Sunshine & cloudy | |
| 20. | 36 | 30.05 | NW | Fair | 20. Our womenfolk began the first work in the garden today. *Fine weather.* |
| | | 29.87 | SW | Sunshine & clouds | |
| 21. | 39 | 30.03 | NW | Windy & fair | 21. Today we had a strong northwest wind and frost. *The false spring is over. Wind today was at N W and extremely cold. Ice on the River. Windy.* |
| | | 30.20 | NW | Windy & fair | |
| 22. | 23 | 30.35 | NW | Fair. Cloudy A.M. | 22. Cold raw northwest wind. *Ice an inch thick and very cold.* |
| | | 30.20 | NW | Fair | |
| 23. | 28 | 30.20 | NE | Sunshine | 23. *Quite raw. Wind N E. Roads dry.* |
| | | 30.10 | NE | Overcast | |
| 24. | 35 | 30.13 | NE | Fair | 24. *Very fine weather.* |
| | | 30.15 | SW | Cloudy | |
| 25. | 41 | 30.07 | SW | Cloudy | 25. *Very fine weather.* |
| | | 29.93 | SW | Cloudy | |
| 26. | 43 | 29.70 | SE | Cloudy & drizzling | 26. It commenced to rain. The rain kept up all day and night. *Damp morning. Wind at N E.* |
| | 44 | 29.60 | NE | Rain at different times of day | |
| 27. | 38 | 29.67 | NW | Sunshine & flying clouds | 27. *Very fine weather. Wind at N W.* |
| | | 29.83 | NW | Rain last night. Cloudy P.M. | |
| 28. | 43 | 29.95 | SW | Fair | 28. *Wind S S W.* |
| | | 29.85 | S | Fair afternoon, cloudy | |

| | | | | | | |
|---|---|---|---|---|---|---|
| 29. | 42 | 29.55 | ENE | Stormy & rain with hail today without intermission & most of evening and night. | | 29. Stormy wind and rain and snow. |
| | 37 | 29.37 | ENE | | | |
| 30. | 36 | 29.65 | NE | Cloudy | | 30. The ground is covered with snow. |
| | 42 | 29.77 | N | Cloudy | | |
| 31. | 38 | 30.00 | NW | Fair. High clouds A.M. | | 31. Cold raw weather. |
| | | 29.97 | NW | Fair & windy | | |

### April 1778

| | | | | | |
|---|---|---|---|---|---|
| 1. | 38° | 30.02″ | NW | Fair | 1. Lovely weather. |
| | | 29.92 | SW | Sunshine & cloudy | |

[1] Thomas Coombe. Ms. Met. Obs. near Philadelphia. (Amer. Phil. Soc.).
[2] U. S. Weather Bureau. Local climatological data. Phoenixville, Penna.
[3] H. Muhlenberg, *Journal,* 3, 113–143.
[4] T. Coombe.
[5] Journals of Capt. John Montresor. *Coll. N. Y. Hist. Soc.* 13, (1881), 480, 482.
[6] John J. Stroudt. *Ordeal at Valley Forge.* Phila., Univ. of Penna. Press, 1963. 77.
[7] S. Hazard. *The effect of climate,* 2, 379. N. J. Gaz. (Burlington), 31 Dec 1777.
[8] T. Coombe.
[9] *Idem.*
[10] H. Muhlenberg, 3, 117.
[11] T. Coombe.
[12] U. S. Weather Bureau. Local climatological data. Philadelphia.
[13] H. Muhlenberg, 3, 114.
[14] Gen. Nathaniel Greene quoted in Christopher Ward. *The War of the Revolution.* New York, The Macmillan Co., 1952. 2, 543–45.
[15] H. Muhlenberg, 3, 114–143.

# NEW JERSEY AGAIN: 1778–79

### *A pretty close winter*

The commencement of winter in 1778–79 found the troops in much the same relative positions they had occupied twelve months earlier. In mid-November Washington established a number of strong points in a 50-mile semi-circle around New York City, stretching on the south from Middlebrook in central New Jersey, northward to West Point on the Hudson River, and eastward to Danbury in Connecticut. The British held only the major ports of New York City and Newport. The little active fighting that took place during the winter of 1778–79 occurred in the South where weather conditions this season did not constitute an important military factor.

The most interesting meteorological event took place along the southern New England shore where a great coastal storm struck at Christmastime and ever after was referred to as the "Hessian Storm" for reasons to be related.[1] This season, like 1772, also endured a very late winter with March snow piling upon March snow. Sandwiched between the cold storm of late December and the snowy March came a period of exceptionally fine winter weather in January and February. Surgeon Thacher with Washington's army in New Jersey referred to the "remarkable mild & temperate" conditions in mid-winter.[2] In Maine our authority stated there was no sledding on January 8th and the whole month of February appeared mild: the 4th was described as a "hot, thawy day—7th, fair and moderate—10th, thawy —22d, moderate—March 2d & 3d, delightful days."[3]

At the end of February, Elizabeth Drinker of Philadelphia wrote:

It is many years since we have known a season so forward as this—ye weather has for several days past been very moderate; we have Crocuses blown in our garden for a week past, and this day Persian Irises are also blown. Ye Apricot trees are in blossom.[4]

The *New Jersey Gazette* took notice of the warmth of February as bringing out buds on the trees: "Some early fruit trees to vegetate to a greater degree than has been remembered at this season by the oldest men in the neighborhood."[5] On the last day of February Ezra Stiles' thermometer at New Haven soared to 62°, weather fair and warm.[6]

This was the period toward the end of February that George Rogers Clark and his men made an amazing march across southern Illinois and Indiana to seize Vincennes from the British by surprise. It occurred during the winter break-up when streams were out of their banks and the marshy land overflowing.[7]

But, as usual, March extracted the price of a warm February. Dr. Muhlenberg at Lancaster noted the following wintry turns of the weather:

March 7. Last evening and during the night we had a deep snowfall.
14. It snowed last night and still continues.

19. Last night we had another heavy snowfall and it is still snowing.
21. I was able to walk over the snow and ice to Augustus Church.
24. Last night we had a snowfall deeper than any we have had the whole winter, and the snow is still falling heavily today.
25. Deep snow is now lying on the ground, and we have as severe cold as in the middle of winter.
April 24. The frost has killed the buds of the fruit trees in the gardens and the common trees in the woods, and they have lost all their green, as in autumn and winter, and it has also injured the rye in the fields.
30. Last night we had snow and rain, followed by cold wind. Everything is behind in the gardens and fields that is necessary for the nourishment of the body, and what came up was killed by the recent three-day frost.
May 1. The cold wind still continues.[8]

At Ipswich, Massachusetts, Manasseh Cutler, witnessed the late March storms:

March 22. A very hard snowstorm—more snow on the ground than at any other time this winter.
March 24. A remarkable thick snow storm the whole day and part of the preceding and succeeding nights. A great quantity fell, so it is judged there is more snow on the ground now than there has been at a time for several years. Snow banks exceedingly high. In both these remarkable storms, though the wind was very high, it was not at all cold.

The same conditions prevailed inland at Bedford in south-central New Hampshire:

March 22. A very heavy snowstorm out of the northeast.
24. Came about 9 or 10 O'clock an exceeding storm of snow from the N.E. It fell upward of a foot deep.
25. It snowed all day. The snow is 3 feet 10 inches deep and in some places 4 feet. The last 3 snows that fell is 26 inches deep.[10]

Dr. James Thacher summarized the past winter conditions on April 13th as they had appeared to him in New Jersey:

We have passed a winter remarkably mild and moderate. Since the 10th of January, we have scarcely had a fall of snow, or a frost, and no severe weather. At the beginning of this month the weather was so mild that vegetation began to appear; the fruit trees were budded on the first, and in full blossom on the 10th.[11]

This was an exceptionally mild winter in Virginia, also, as we learn from the *Journal of Du Roi, the Elder,* a lieutenant in the service of the Duke of Brunswick, who had been captured at Saratoga and made the long treck to Charlottesville with many of his fellow soldiers, to spend the rest of the war in relative freedom in the Old Dominion. He related the climatic conditions along with many other perceptive details of the American scene:

The weather since our arrival is considered extraordinarily good, and everybody says that it never was like this before. The month of January ended with very pleasant days, and almost all through February we had the most delightful spring weather. (This month is generally very cold with plenty of snow.) I saw peach-trees in full bloom in the open fields during February, also cherry trees. On many trees the leaves are already out (March 16th), and it is uncomfortably warm for walking. If cold weather should set in, or snow fall, as everybody expects, it is certain that the branches of the peach trees will not break this year from too heavy a load of fruit. The beginning of spring is much more beautiful here than in New England, where spring is hardly noticeable. There the hot weather commences immediately after the cold. The warm days, which are so delightful here, are entirely missing. The spring here is as pleasant as it ever can be in Germany.

\* \* \*

In regard to the particularly good weather during February, I wish to add that the same changed suddenly. We had some hard frost at night in April, which ruined all the fruit. After that, the weather became warm again, and the trees have all their foliage now. The days are often as hot as in July at home, but towards the end of April it turned cold again. The leaves of many trees, and in fact the whole trees were frozen. Green peas, strawberries, all fruits, cabbage, and green vegetables, are dead. This cold spell did not, however, include the whole province, but covered about twenty miles in the direction of Williamsburg. Some of the higher situated plantations near Charlottesville were not touched in the same degree. We have now nice warm weather. It is, however, very dry and nothing will grow in the gardens.[12]

[1] See page 109.
[2] James Thacher. *A military journal during the American Revolutionary War from 1775 to 1783.* Boston, Richardson and Lord, 1823. 192.
[3] T. Smith, *Journal,* 280.
[4] *Extracts from the Journal of Elizabeth Drinker from 1759 to 1807 A.D.* Henry D. Biddle, ed. Phila., J. B. Lippincott Co., 1889. 115.
[5] *N. J. Gaz.* (Burlington), 24 Feb 1779.
[6] E. Stiles, Ms. Thermo. Reg.
[7] Major Bowman's Diary. Zachariah F. Smith. *History of Kentucky from its earliest settlement to the present date.* Louisville, The Prentice Press, 1895. 137–38.
[8] H. Muhlenberg, *Journal,* 3, 222–26.
[9] M. Cutler, *Life,* 1, 74.
[10] M. Patten, *Diary,* 397.
[11] J. Thacher, *Journal,* 192.
[12] *Journal of Du Roi the elder.* Charlotte S. J. Epping, trans. Phila. & New York, Univ. of Penna. & D. Appleton, 1911, 156–57, 160–61.

## THE HESSIAN STORM OF DECEMBER 1778

The cold storm of 26 December 1778 combined all the elements that make up the severest type of winter disturbance known to the North Atlantic seaboard. Dr. Edward A. Holyoke at Salem listed its features: "A very great storm. Snow. Very high wind. Excessive cold." [1] These are the characteristics of what would now be designated an Eastern blizzard. Holyoke added: "The storm of the 26th was one of the coldest known." No other atmospheric upheaval since the introduction of meteorological instruments to New England in the early 1740's had measured the grand combination of extremes of weather elements that prevailed on the Day after Christmas of 1778, though there would be others of equal stature through the next century: on 24 December 1811, 19 January 1857, 12–13 March 1888, and 12–13 February 1899.[2]

The scene had been set for the development of the disturbance by the arrival of an Arctic air mass in New England at the winter solstice. A light snow fell on the 21st followed by a piercing cold northwest wind the next day. On the 23d and 24th a "very hard frost" chilled the British and Hessian troops occupying the seaport of Newport in Rhode Island. On the 25th occurred an "extreme hard frost," so frigid that "the harbor and all the rivers smoked from the intenseness of the cold, so that it appeared like fog in summer." [3] (This was Arctic sea smoke formed when an intensely cold stream of air with low vapor content passes over a relatively warm body of water). At Ipswich in Massachusetts cold air masses featured an ice fog with tiny needles of frozen vapor floating in an otherwise clear sky—an inversion phenomenon common in the Arctic on clear, calm days when stable air is present, but relatively rare in windy New England where much mixing in the lower layers usually takes place.[4]

The prime requisite for the great winter storms of the North Atlantic seaboard is a strong anticyclone over the Quebec-Labrador area. This serves three purposes: it slows the normal swift movement of a coastal low northeastward, so that the precipitation period continues longer than usual; it feeds southward a stream of air from the northeast sufficiently cold to keep temperatures well below freezing; and the tight barometric pressure gradient between the blocking anticyclone and the deepening depression off the Middle Atlantic and New England coasts creates gale force winds to intensify the severity of the storm. On Christmas morning such a blocking anticyclone with intensely cold air was present as the weather observation at Montreal clearly indicated: temperature −21°, sky clear, and wind out of the northeast. It was a bitterly cold day at the Canadian military post with the mercury at −18° at the early evening observation.[5]

Christmas Day in 1778 rated with the coldest such holidays in New England history.[6] Professor John Winthrop's thermometer in the Harvard Yard read −8° at 0800 on Christmas morning, and down at New Haven President Ezra Stiles noticed a −3° that morning on the Yale campus.[7] Neither of these probably represented the absolute minimum that cold morning. At Newport port wine froze in bottles inside a house, as did all weaker liquors, also mustard, and all sorts of pickles![8]

With the extremely cold air mass overlying the Northeast, a depression formed on the frontal zone somewhere in the Southern Colonies or in the Gulf of Mexico, as often occurs during such severe polar outbreaks. On Christmas Day the coastal depression made steady progress northeastward. The mantle of snow reached eastern Pennsylvania in the afternoon, New York City by evening, New Haven by 2200, and Newport by midnight. Dr. Muhlenberg in Pennsylvania noted on the 25th: "In the afternoon it began to snow heavily and continued throughout the night." On the 26th: "Snow and wind storm the whole day." And on the 27th: "Deep snow and bitter cold." [9] At New York City, Lt. Col. Kemble's Journal read: "A violent snow storm, great quantities of ice. Several vessels lost with some lives." [10] The New York press reported the mercury four degrees lower than it had been for the past seven years. There were "monstrous bodies of ice floating in our bay." The northeast gales attending the arrival of the Arctic front on the 24th and the great snowstorm on the 26th and 27th drove 28 vessels onto the beaches of Staten Island which forms a lee shore in such an air flow.[11]

At New Haven, President Stiles was having difficulty in maintaining classes in view of the threat of British raids and the onslaughts of Old Boreas:

Dec. 22. Snow storm last night; snow 3 inches—This is the first of notice this winter.
24. Excessively cold—yesterday +1°—this morning +2°, rose at 1100 to +13°, by noon fell to +9° and at 1800 to +6°.
25. −3°.
26. A most severe snowstorm—wind high NE.
27. Excessive cold—a very severe cold day, wind high, snow blowed a hurricane all day.
28. The Steward being unable to uphold Commons in the Hall, I found it necessary, and according with the Advice of the Tutors I dismissed College, & the students this afternoon begun to return home. [Vacation regularly commenced on the 2d Thursday of January].[12]

The storm reached its greatest development in the vicinity of coastal Rhode Island. The center probably passed close to Block Island and may have hesitated in that area for six to 10 hours as often happens in a blocking situation. Fortunately for our account, Lt. Frederick Mackenzie of the Royal Engineers was stationed with the British at Newport at the entrance to Narragansett Bay exposed to the full sweep of the northeasterly gales from the Atlantic Ocean. He described the onset of the developing storm and its destructive effects most vividly:

> Dec. 26. It began to blow hard, and to Snow with great violence about 12 last night; the Wind N. and a Severe frost. It continued all this day. Toward Evening the wind encreased greatly, the Snow drifted to such a degree, and the frost was so severe, that it was with the utmost difficulty and danger any person could pass the Streets. The Snow was blown about, in the town, in all directions, and was so thick that the houses on the opposite side of the Street could not be discerned during most of the day. About 18 inches of Snow had fallen, by Six this Evening.
> It is feared that the Tender which sailed yesterday will be lost.
> Dec. 27. The Snow continued most part of last night. Strong Gale of wind at N. all this day, with a severe frost.
> The Snow drifted yesterday and last night to a Surprising degree: in Some places it was thrown up to the height of 20 feet; in others there was not the least appearance of it. It was so dry and Small, that wherever the Wind found a passage, it carried the Snow with it—So that very few houses could keep it out.
> Most of the Inhabitants were obliged to cut passages thro the Snow this Morning, in order to get out of their houses. Several men lost their lives yesterday, and many were frost bitten. No damage done among the shipping.
> The Inhabitants say they never remember so severe a storm as that of yesterday.
> Three soldiers of Bunau's Regt., one of the Artillery, one of Brown's are lost, and above 30 different regiments are frost bitten.
> The roads are so entirely filled up by the drifting of the snow that all communication with the country is at present cut off.
> Dec. 28. Very hard frost. Wind N.
> Parties of the troops were employed yesterday and this day in clearing away the snow, and making passages to the different magazines, and from thence to the bakery, and to the windmills, in order to get rice ground.[13]

In the Boston area the barometer fell steadily all Christmas Day with the first flakes commencing to fall during the early night. Next morning "a great snow storm" had developed: wind, a gale from the northeast —mercury, $+6°$—barometer, 29.47″. The winter tempest continued for about 24 hours then passed off to the northeast. The 27th turned "very fair" according to Winthrop, but the temperature did not rise above the freezing mark until the 30th, a very cold Christmas week. The full Harvard weather log follows:

| | | | | | | |
|---|---|---|---|---|---|---|
| Dec. 22 | 0945 | 30.05″ | $+9°$ | NW | 2 | Very fair |
| | 1415 | 30.08 | 12 | NW | 3 | Very fair |
| 23 | 0815 | 30.23 | 3 | W | 2 | Very fair |
| | 1430 | 30.00 | 10 | W | 2 | Covered |
| 24 | 0830 | 30.08 | 0 | NW | 2 | Clear |
| | 1515 | 30.07 | 5.5 | NW | 2 | Very fair |
| | 2230 | 30.15 | $-2$ | NW | 2 | Very fair |
| 25 | 0800 | 30.10 | $-8$ | NW | 2 | Very fair, excessive cold 8 days |
| | 2245 | 29.82 | $+5$ | N | 1 | Evening snows |
| 26 | 0815 | 29.47 | 6 | NE | 2 | Great snow storm |
| | 1415 | 29.24 | 7 | NE | 2 | Violent snow storm |
| 27 | 1030 | 29.66 | 6 | NE | 2 | Covered |
| | 1500 | 29.66 | 10.5 | NW | 2 | Very fair[14] |

Our last meteorological check-point for the fury of the storm came at Ipswich, northeast of Boston on Cape Ann, where Rev. Manasseh Cutler maintained a weather observing post at this time:

> Dec. 23. The cold extreme. The air exceedingly full of ice particles; sometimes cloudy, but not so dense as to obscure the sun.
> 24. The last night the coldest I can remember. Froze in places never known to freeze before. The well froze over near two inches thick. The whole day exceedingly cold, but the air much clearer. Rode to town. The stars very bright and twinkling in the evening.
> 25. Still exceedingly cold, but not so extreme. Cloudy. At evening began to snow. Wind N.E.
> 26. A most violent snowstorm, such as I do not remember. Wind very high at N.E.
> 27. Clear and cold, the snow much drifted.

The great storm struck all coastal New England a heavy blow. At Newport, appropriately, it was long called "The Hessian Storm." Colonel Popp, a German mercenary from Hesse-Cassel, has related in his diary that nine men in one regiment alone were frozen to death at their posts during the storm period, and that a woman resident of Newport and her two children suffered a similar fate.[16] One historian of Revolutionary Newport estimated that at least 50 persons in the vicinity, military and civilian, died of freezing or the results of frostbite.[17]

Around Massachusetts Bay the event ever since has been called "The Magee Storm" in memory of the brave captain of the armed brig *Arnold*.[18] His ship had sailed from Boston into the teeth of the storm and was subsequently cast on the shore of Plymouth Bay after a desperate struggle with the mighty northeast gales which created an overwhelming wave surge. Of a crew of over 100 men, only 34 survived the rigors of the elements that wintry night though many had gained the shore, but were unable to find adequate shelter on the bare, sandy beaches.[19] Out at Nantucket the sloop *General Stark* ran ashore with the loss of 20 hands. Many reports of wrecks came from points on the southern New England shore, Long Island, and New Jersey.[20]

At Kittery in southern Maine a prominent pastor, Rev. Chase, fell victim to the numbing cold and was later discovered frozen to death in a field.[21] In another instance at Boston Neck, a driver with his team of four oxen and a horse were found after the winds subsided, solidly congealed and still standing rigidly upright.[22] Rev. Cutler at Ipswich, a weather observer of experience, could truthfully say: "Such a storm has not been known in the memory of men."[23]

[1] E. A. Holyoke. Ms. Met. Jour.
[2] See page 182; and *Monthly Weather Review* (Wash.), **16**-3, (March 1888), 59–62 and **27**-2, (Feb 1899), 41–44.
[3] F. Mackenzie, *Diary*, **2**, 434–35.
[4] *Life, journals, and correspondence of Rev. Manasseh Cutler*. William P. Cutler and Julia P. Cutler, eds. Cincinnati, R. Clarke & Co., 1888. **1**, 73.
[5] Mr. Barr. A journal of the weather at Montreal by Mr. Barr, purveyor to his Majesty's Hospital in Canada. *Phil. Trans. Royal Society of London for the year 1780*. **70**-1, 272–77.
[6] J. Winthrop. Ms. Met. Obs.
[7] E. Stiles, Ms. Thermo. Reg.
[8] F. Mackenzie, *Diary*, **1**, 73.
[9] H. Muhlenberg, *Journal*, **3**, 211.
[10] Journals of Lieut.-Col. Stephen Kemble. *Coll. N. Y. Hist. Soc. 1883*. **16**, 168.
[11] *N. J. Gaz.* (Burlington), 27 Jan 1779.
[12] E. Stiles, *Diary*, **2**, 315.
[13] F. Mackenzie, *Diary*, **2**, 437.
[14] J. Winthrop, Ms. Met. Obs.
[15] M. Cutler, *Life*, **1**, 73.
[16] *A Hessian soldier in the American Revolution; the diary of Stephen Popp*. Reinhart J. Pope, trans. Racine, Wis. (?), private print, 1953.
[17] Samuel G. Arnold. *History of the State of Rhode Island and Providence Plantation*. New York, D. Appleton & Co., 1860. **2**, 434.
[18] Edward R. Snow. *Great storms and famous shipwrecks of the New England coast*. Boston, The Yankee Publishing Co., 1943. 65–72.
[19] *Mass. Gaz.*, 7 Jan, in *N. J. Gaz.*, 20 Jan 1779.
[20] *Mass. Gaz.*, 11 Jan, in *N. J. Gaz.*, 27 Jan 1779.
[21] T. Smith, *Journal*, 239.
[22] *Idem*.
[23] M. Cutler, *Life*, **1**, 73.

## THE HARD WINTER OF 1779–80: MORRISTOWN

*The most hard difficult winter . . . that ever was known by any person living.*

There has been only one winter in recorded American history during which the waters surrounding New York City have frozen over and remained closed to all navigation for weeks at a time. This occurred during the Hard Winter of 1780, a critical year during the War of Independence, when General Washington and his poorly-quartered, ill-clad, and under-nourished troops at Morristown in the Jersey hills were keeping a watchful eye on the British comfortably stationed in New York some 20 miles distant.

By mid-January General Boreas had taken complete command of the military situation by spreading an icy sheath over the erstwhile watery moat protecting the British around Manhattan Island, thus opening the way for surprise incursions from the mainland. This novel situation also shut off supplies and reinforcements coming from seaward. But the extreme depth of the snow and the frigid combat conditions largely limited action, nullifying the opportunities that nature had seemingly given the Continentals. There were a few raids and skirmishes on and near Staten Island, but when spring finally arrived neither side had gained an advantage.

The severity of the 1780 season reached all parts of the colonies. Reports from Maine southward along the seaboard to Georgia, and from Detroit down through the interior waterways to New Orleans, all chronicled tales of deep snow, severe cold, and widespread suffering. Historians of our climate seem agreed that the 17th Century had featured milder conditions than the latter part of the 18th Century, and that a "Little Ice Age," commencing in America about 1750, continued for some 100 years.[1] The evidence presented in this work largely sustains this view, and definitely indicates that the season of 1779–80 in the eastern United States comprised the extreme winter of the "cool hundred years" and well deserved its contemporary appellation: *The Hard Winter*.

There are adequate comparisons that can be made with the two previous landmark winters of 1697–98 and 1740–41, mainly in the length of time that waterways remained solidly frozen. All seem agreed that the combination of severe weather elements attending the Second Winter at Morristown topped both of the previous contenders for the title. Ezra Stiles, along with the weatherwise father of Noah Webster, both of whom had lived through the rigors of 1740–41, gave their nod to the more recent.[2] Two other weather-watching correspondents in different areas, Ebenezer Hazard of Philadelphia and Jeremy Belknap of Boston and New Hampshire, added their affirmative for 1780.[3] In the South Thomas Jefferson in Virginia and Col. William Fleming in Kentucky thought there had been nothing similar in the American experience.[4] At the conclusion of the unusual season a committee of the American Philosophical Society was formed "to make and collect observations on the effects of the severe and long-continued cold of last winter."[5]

Since this remarkable season occurred during a war year, we are fortunate in having a considerable number of diaries of Revolutionary figures whose descendants have proudly published their accounts for posterity. These often provide an excellent source of eye-witness accounts of weather phenomena. Contemporary newspaper pages during a normal war year were usually too taken up with the exciting military action to take notice of passing meteorological events; but in this case, so outstanding were the weather happenings and so restricted the military operations due to inclement conditions, that considerable space was devoted to presenting thermometrical journals and accounts of damage caused by the principal storms. The *Connecticut Courant* at Hartford supplied the most complete and authentic temperature record, but the editor deemed it necessary to explain the nature of a thermometer and what its readings meant. Worthwhile meteorological data also appeared in the *New Jersey Gazette* and the *Virginia Gazette* among others.[6]

## WINTER COMMENCES

The snow season in the Northeast commenced with a light fall on November 2d and another on the 17th, indicating the presence of polar air in the area of sufficient frigidity to cause frozen precipitation. Real snowstorms followed on 26 November and 5 December with falls of approximately nine inches on each occasion at New Haven, leading Ezra Stiles to note in his diary that "an excessively rigorous season" had already commenced.[7] This snowfall at New York City was "a very great fall" and lay for a week despite moderate weather on the 8th and 9th. Severely cold conditions, however, did not set in until mid-December, on the 14th, when a cold front swept down out of Canada, the forerunner of a series of invading Arctic air masses which were to dominate the general atmospheric circulation and the local weather scene for the next 13 weeks. A visitor to the newly-occupied Morristown winter quarters in the hills of northern New Jersey on 18 December remarked: "I rode out today on purpose to take a view of our encampment. I found it excessively cold. . . ." In the same issue the *New Jersey Gazette* informed: "the weather has been intensively cold for many days past, which has entirely stopped the navigation between this place [Burlington] and Philadelphia."[8]

## SNOWBOUND

The opening phase of the Hard Winter centered in a series of heavy snowstorms. Each was followed by colder and colder, gale-force blasts out of the northwest which drifted the previous snow into mountainous piles and further intensified the already rigorous wintery conditions. After the introductory snowstorms, a major fall on the 18th of December laid down a permanent snow cover which lasted until the winter break-up in mid-March. This storm deposited 17 inches of new snow at New Haven.[9] There followed at the turn of the year an outstanding series of three major northeasters which ravaged the entire coastal plain from Virginia northward. These came in quick succession in a 10-day period on 28–29 December 1779, 2–3 January, and 5–7 January 1780.

The three major snowstorms at the turn of the year 1779–80 rank with the greatest such combinations in our meteorological history. The depth of snow laid down by the triple snow blitz may be compared favorably with three snows of early March 1717, the three early December storms of 1786, and winter's triple strokes in December 1839—to consider the outstanding events of our period only.

The storms under consideration raged equally severe on land and at sea. They struck particularly hard at British war vessels which were engaged in a major regrouping of troops, some sailing southward to reinforce the effort at Savannah and others heading homeward in the normal supply runs to Great Britain. It so happened that Generals Clinton and Cornwallis had sailed from New York City on Sunday afternoon, 26 December, for the Southern colonies. Monday was calm, but the next day the first of the three struck a savage blow at the fleet off Delaware Bay; and the offshore seas continued very rough for the duration of the voyage. The diary of Hessian General Von Huyn noted the occurrence of the three storms on 28–29 December, 2–3 January, and 5–6 January when his transports were severely battered by the succession of coastal northeasters.[10]

Our southernmost land checkpoint for Storm No. 1

was at Trappe in eastern Pennsylvania where Rev. Henry Muhlenberg told of a heavy snow commencing early on the 28th accompanied by high winds. This changed later to an equally heavy rain that penetrated through buildings during the night and continued well into the next day. At New York City, tory Hugh Gaine, a local editor, reported snow and rain mixed during the day of the 28th, and about 1800 in the evening "a most violent storm of rain and wind set in from the N.E. and continued at least six hours; it did little or no damage in the harbor, but many are uneasy about the fleet, I hope it is safe." [12]

To the north and east, the precipitation was all snow. The fall commenced in the evening at New Haven, according to Ezra Stiles, and mounted to a depth of 18 inches.[13] The flakes made good progress up the coast as Dr. Holyoke at Salem, Massachusetts, had cloudy skies on the morning of the 28th, but a storm set in by evening with snow. The 29th at Salem was described as "a great storm—snow—moist air—wind northeast." [14]

The first flakes of the second storm commenced to fall in eastern Pennsylvania during the early afternoon of January 2d: "After service it began to snow heavily again, accompanied by a stormy northeast wind." Rev. Muhlenberg continued his entry on the 3d:

> Since yesterday afternoon and throughout the night, there was such a snowstorm that the house and yard are so circumvallated that one can scarcely get out or in, and the snow is still falling. Had some time for reading and writing. The cold wind still continues. It kept up its frightful howling the whole night.[15]

The northeaster lashed savagely at the New Jersey shoreline, raising a very high tide and casting several ships on the beaches. There were the usual early rumors of large British warships high and dry, defenseless against an attack by the militia. But upon investigation these reports were considerably scaled down; the Philadelphia press finally stated that a brig of 12 guns was ashore near South Amboy in New York Bay and a ship of 20 guns near Squan Beach.[16] A British transport went ashore on Long Island, probably in the Sound where a northeaster makes the north shore of Long Island a lee shore.[17] Ezra Stiles clocked a "violent snowstorm" as commencing about sunset of the 2d, raising the highest tide known by two or three feet.[18]

> New London, Conn: On Last Sabbath night (Jan. 2) hard gale of wind, attended by snow. In four hours the wind went around the compass and threw the highest tide by two or three feet ever known—large quantity of sugar lost—boats driven from moorings—one warehouse full of sugar floated away—several houses flooded.[19]

> Newport, Rhode Island: Sunday night violent storm of wind, snow, rain from NE to E and SE at which last point the gale was supposed to have been as heavy as any which has happened in 20 years and caused as high a tide in this harbor as has been seen within said period. Out of the very few vessels remaining at our wharves, several broke their masts, and were driven on Goat Island.[20]

> Boston: Considerable damage has been done to the shipping here, in the three severe storms the week past. Several vessels have been drove ashore and much damaged. (The *Independent Chronicle* was limited to only one sheet in its issues of the 13th and 20th, and thus gave only brief notice of local news).[21]

Storm No. 3 was of a different variety. In the Middle Colonies it came mainly as a northwester whose gale force winds raised a storm of blowing snow attended with great drifting, but with only intermittent falls from the clouds. It was likely that the center of the disturbance stalled in the vicinity of the Gulf of Maine and deepened there to set up a strong pressure gradient across all the Northeast. A strong northerly flow prevailed over New England for the next five days.[22] The snowfall in Storm No. 3 ran heavier over eastern New England than farther west or southwest.

Muhlenberg's records for eastern Pennsylvania indicated the snow commenced on the night of the 4–5th, with the wind on the 5th out of the northwest and a tumbling thermometer; on the 6th: "Violent storm from the northwest the whole day with intermittent snow."[23]

Washington at Morristown had much the same conditions with a cloudy morning on the 5th and some sunshine in the afternoon, but on the 6th: "snowing and sunshine alternately—cold with the wind west and northwest and increasing—night very stormy." On the 7th: "very boisterous from the west and northwest and sometimes snowing, which being very dry drifted exceedingly." [24]

> New Haven: 5th: Severe winter weather—snowing still and snow blowing and drifting. 6th: Severe weather. Snow storm continues with some intermission. 7th: Snow over the fences. . . . This day extremely cold, high winds, snow blows a storm.[25]

> Salem: Snow. Cold. Some wind. Stormy. Fair. A vast quantity of snow.[26]

> Westborough: 6th: It is very stormy again, and the snow deeper, and though the sun was visible a little while in the afternoon, yet it was soon clouded, and the storm rages at night. 7th: An astonishing morning—for the dreadful storm rather increases. Besides snowing and blowing with violence the cold is very intense. This is thought to be the most tedious of any that has come hitherto.[27]

> Bedford, N. H.: 6th—a very tedious storm of snow. 7th—it snowed and blowed hard all day & drifted. 8th—drifted very much no stirring out these days.[28]

How deep was the snow cover after the series of exceptional falls? At New Haven, where we have what appear to be trustworthy snow measurements, the first of the series of three deposited 18 inches; the second, by far the most violent for wind and tide, brought 12 inches; and the third, consisting mostly of blow rather than snow, increased the drifts to amazing depths but added little to the total seasonal depth. At the conclusion of the 10-day storm period, the general accumulation in the fields of southern Connecticut covered fence tops and in the woods lay 42 to 48 inches deep. Drifts were estimated by Stiles at 6 to 10 feet high. Fifty-two inches of new snow, as measured by Tutor Atwater, had fallen at New Haven during this period. "It is judged there is a greater quantity of snow than in the hard winter of 1740/41 which I well remember," declared Stiles.[29]

General Washington at Morristown found time in this troubled period to resume his weather diary which he maintained off and on for the greater part of his life. On the 6th of January he wrote: "The snow which in general is eighteeen inches deep is much drifted—roads impassable." [30] He must have referred to the new snow cover at this time which had just fallen. His surgeon-general, James Thacher, related that the snow cover at this time reached a depth of four feet generally.[31] Later historical accounts from New York City usually placed the depth at four feet on the level, though this figure is nowhere substantiated by an actual measurement.[32] The Somerset militia were called out to break a road from Hackettstown to Princeton at this time: "The whole face of the country lay buried from three to five feet deep; roads, fences, and frozen streams were obliterated, and as the storm had been accompanied by a very high wind, in places the drifts were piled ten to twelve feet high." [33] It was the same situation in Pennsylvania in Lancaster County where Rev. Muhlenberg declared on the 23d: "the snow is over three feet deep." [34] And a report from the Wilkes-Barre area in northeastern Pennsylvania also mentioned the snow as three feet deep.[35]

The three major snowstorms of the winter expended their greatest force in southern and eastern New England, closing all main roads for the duration of the winter with the exception of the Boston-Hartford route via Worcester, which was broken out and became passable by January 20th.[36] Side roads, however, generally awaited the March thaw before they were passable. Ezra Stiles took a keen interest in the snow statistics. He believed that the snow in his vicinity lay "three and a half feet on level in the woods," and at nearby Waterbury Woods it was "four feet on a level."[37] At Salem on coastal northeastern Massachusetts, Dr. Edward A. Holyoke, a weather observer of long experience and veracity, recorded that the snow measured two to three feet deep on a level there.[38] Rev. Ebenezer Parkman at Westborough thought there had not been so much since the Great Snow of 1717. Jeremy Belknap, writing from Jamaica Plain just outside Boston, remarked: "for the depth of the snow is so great that I think the post cannot come in for a day or two yet. I do not remember having ever seen so much snow on the ground at once before." [39]

Ebenezer Miller, who lived at Braintree immediately south of Boston, provided a succinct account of the snow and cold in his diary:

Jan 1. The ground has been covered with snow from 26 Nov'r and this day set in violent cold. 10. it has snowed almost every day from the first of this month. the snow over the tops of many fences.
Feb 7. Supposed to be 3½ feet deep if leavel. It has been fair for about 4 week but extrem cold but very few days from 1 Jan'y that it has Dropt off the house till to Day.[40]

## DEEP FREEZE

"Frigidissime" was the diary entry of David Shultze of Goshenhoppen near Philadelphia on the morning of the 19th as the Hard Winter entered its coldest phase.[41] January 1780 rated as the most persistently cold calendar month in the history of eastern United States. At the latitude of Philadelphia the mercury in the Ritten-

---

Tutor Atwater's observations of snow at Yale College taken within 10 miles from the sea side

1779–80

| | | | | | |
|---|---|---|---|---|---|
| Nov. 17 | 2″ | Jan. 2–3 | 12″ | March 12 | 2″ (Hail) |
| 26 | 9″ | 10 | 5″ | 16 | 4″ |
| — | | 17 | 1″ | 31 | 4″ |
| | 11″ | 27 | ½″ | | — |
| Dec. 2 | 1″ | | — | | 10″ |
| 5 | 9″ | | 18½″ | Season: 1779–80 | 95″ |
| 12 | 1″ | Feb. 7–8 | 7″ | Season: 1780–81 | 25″ |
| 16 | 2″ | 23 | ½″ | | |
| 18 | 17″ | | — | | |
| 27–8 | 18″ | | 7½″ | | |
| | 48″ | | | | |

house thermometer rose above freezing at an observation time only once, and that for only a short time.[42] At Hartford, Connecticut, and at Waltham, Massachusetts, trusted thermometers also were above the freezing mark on only one day, both at 37° on the 30th.[43]

The coldest periods occurred during the blowing snowstorm on the 6–8th, on the 13–16th, and from the 19th through the 29th. During the last period all sunrise readings at Hartford, Connecticut, were +6° or lower, with five consecutive mornings below zero from the 25th to 29th. Thermometers throughout the Northeast reached the season's nadir at sunrise of the 29th of January: Hartford −20° and Salem, Mass., −17°.[44] A figure of −16° was attributed to a New York City thermometer by the *New York Packet* of Fishkill, N. Y., but this cannot be verified since no complete file of this Revolutionary journal has been preserved. The −16° figure for New York City received mention in the diaries of both Rev. Ezra Stiles and Lt. Frederick MacKenzie.[45] There were no registering thermometers in use at this time—readings were taken at sunrise as this was assumed to be the coldest hour, though this was not necessarily so.

## ICEBOUND

The continuance of cold through January eventually shut up every seaport along the North Atlantic Coast, even those not ordinarily susceptible to an ice blockade. Philadelphia, always an early closer, was frozen solid by 21 December and did not open for large ships until March 4th—an interruption of 75 days.[46] Baltimore harbor remained closed until the 9th of March, and Chesapeake Bay could be crossed at Annapolis with people walking to Poplar Island and Kent Island, an event "never known before," according to the *Maryland Gazette*.[47] To the southward, the broad bay congealed to the mouth of the Potomac, and around Norfolk much of the lower bay was solid almost to the Virginia Capes. Albermarle Sound in North Carolina permitted troops to cross on the ice by foot for several days.[48] Thomas Jefferson in his *Notes on the State of Virginia* related that York River near Williamsburg froze completely and this had not occurred previously, to his knowledge, not even in the famous freeze in 1741.[49]

Conditions in New York Harbor were the most exceptional. Though both the Hudson and the East Rivers were accustomed to freeze solidly from time to time in the olden days, there was no record of the entire Upper Bay congealing so that sleighs could go back and forth from Staten Island to Manhattan Island for a number of days and cross the ice-clogged Narrows to Brooklyn. Hugh Gaine, the editor of the *New York Mercury*, kept a close tab on ice conditions since the safety and reinforcement of the British forces there were

Sunrise temperatures at Hartford, Connecticut

January 1780

| Jan. | |
|---|---|
| 1 | 2 |
| 2 | −7 |
| 3 | 14 |
| 4 | 16 |
| 5 | 6 |
| 6 | 10 |
| 7 | 9 |
| 8 | −1 |
| 9 | 5 |
| 10 | 19 |
| 11 | 26 |
| 12 | 11 |
| 13 | 8 |
| 14 | 9 |
| 15 | 15 |
| 16 | 10 |
| 17 | 17 |
| 18 | 12 |
| 19 | −13 |
| 20 | 5 |
| 21 | −6 |
| 22 | 5 |
| 23 | −9 |
| 24 | 6 |
| 25 | −16 |
| 26 | −6 |
| 27 | −2 |
| 28 | −8 |
| 29 | −22 |
| 30 | 15 |
| 31 | −4 |

thought to depend on free navigation of the surrounding waterways. Gaine's diary related that by January 7th all navigation on the rivers was stopped by the jam of ice cakes and that vessels inside Sandy Hook were unable to come up the bay. By the 14th the floes had consolidated so the East River could be crossed on foot, and by the 20th the mighty Hudson also was traversed by pedestrians.[50] William Dunlap, an early historian of New York who lived through this period, confirmed that people walked on the ice all the way from Staten Island to Manhattan Island, a distance of five miles, on the 29th, that sleighs crossed on the 1st of February, and that heavy loads and even large cannon were dragged across the iceways to fortify the British position on Staten Island which had been subject to cross-the-ice forays from Washington's outposts in Jersey. As many as 86 sleighs went from Manhattan on the 6th with provisions and ammunition.[51]

The first general thaw set in on the 11th of February when the mercury soared to 48° at New Haven, and by the 15th it had reached 54°. The ice commenced to rot.[52] On the 17th some rain fell at New York City, the first since December 29th. Small boats could come through the Narrows on the 20th and on the next day, the ice having been cut between Governors and Bedloes Islands, they could reach the docks of Manhattan. The

*Galatea* from Jamaica came up from the Lower Bay on the 22d, and by the 25th the first vessels sailed down the Bay and through the Hook, after six weeks of total stoppage of maritime traffic![53]

Throughout the bays and harbors of New England it was the same icy story. Ezra Stiles with a group of students was able to measure the width of New Haven harbor on 7 February by walking a chain across its frozen surface.[54] Long Island Sound was almost completely clogged with ice, and people were able to cross from Long Island to the vicinity of Stamford on the Connecticut shore for several days; some Hessian soldiers took advantage of this route in order to escape from their regiments.[55] The Thames River, an estuary especially subject to strong tidal movement, closed early in January and was shut tight until the second week of March.[56]

Conditions at Nantucket were recalled by Obed Macy, writing fifty-five years later of events "during the winter of that year, designated the hard winter":

> The harbor was closed with ice about the twentieth of the twelfth month, 1779, and continued frozen, without intermission during the winter. The inhabitants soon began to feel the effects of this severity: for the cold increased and the ice was formed on all sides, so that there was no water to be seen from the highest eminences, for the space of several weeks. There was also much snow and ice on the ground.[57]

A sailing ship when about 12 miles south of Block Island in the open Atlantic Ocean encountered "a very large body of ice."[58] A vessel from Europe was turned away from Boston Harbor as late as February 14th by the ice blockade.[59] Down East in Maine the tidal waters of Casco Bay and Penobscot Bay were frozen, "the like was never known by any living," in the words of the contemporary authority on Maine weather, Rev. Thomas Smith.[60]

## ECONOMIC CONSEQUENCES

The economic consequences of the great snow and ice blockade added more woes to a country already strained to the breaking point by the hardships of five years of warfare. The deep snow put an end to most travel and interrupted social intercourse; only the great road from Boston via Worcester to Hartford was said to be open in late January.[61] The cover proved too deep for traveling across country or into the woods. Sleighing could not be pursued due to the huge snowbanks which prevented turning out to pass. The posts were carried by men on snow shoes as horses were unable to make progress. The conduct of normal wintertime chores around the farm became increasingly difficult.

Communication with the rest of the world by ship ceased as even the harbors least susceptible to freezing, such as New York and Portsmouth, were sealed tight. A ship arrived at Boston on February 14th, but was prevented by great ice fields from coming into the harbor to unload. The supply of wood, so vital at this season, was also cut off as the commodity was normally transported in small boats down rivers and along coastal waterways. Foraging parties had to be organized in a cooperative effort to beat paths through the deep snow to adjacent woodlots.[63]

The long continued cold retained all the precipitation that had fallen since November in a great frozen mass. Ground water supplies without a thaw dropped to very low levels as did stream flow. A farmer at Shirley in southeastern Massachusetts complained: "the coldest month I ever knew, no thaw, no stirring with oxen or horses; the springs low, some wells no water, the streams so low but a little grinding, a great many mills entirely still for want of water; dull time for news."[64]

With the mills out of operation, no paper for newsprint could be manufactured, and deliveries of the dwindling stock were made only with great difficulty. The weekly *Boston Gazette,* usually a four-page affair, was restricted to one sheet for the edition of January 10th, and this format repeated on the 17th and 24th. The *Independent Chronicle* also issued a one-page edition on January 13th. The week previous no southern, eastern, or western mails had arrived with fresh news, so the editor filled the columns with the *Narrative of Col. Ethan Allen's Captivity,* a current best seller. The paper mills in New Jersey, too, experienced difficulties—the *New Jersey Journal* appeared in two-thirds size on February 9th. As late as March 16th the Boston *Chronicle* complained of the lack of paper. A writer in the *Norwich Packet* urged Connecticut farmers to hire additional help to dig flax out of the snow so that the crop would not be lost through spoilage.[65]

## THE BACKWARD SPRING

The back of winter was broken in southern New England on February 11th when the temperature at New Haven soared to 48°, the first real thaw in over eight weeks. On the 15th a general rainstorm, the first since late December, spread over the Northeast, being noted from Pennsylvania to New Hampshire. Thereafter, the snow commenced to dissolve. George Washington noticed bare spots by the 20th, though at Springfield, New Jersey, some of the snow which had come on December 5th still remained in huge banks on March 7th. Benjamin Scudder measured some of them on that date and found them 20 inches deep.[66] Ebenezer Miller at Braintree near Boston noted in his diary: "Feb 15. It began to thaw and kept thawing gradually till 15 March when the roads in some places was passable with carts."[67] Edward Holyoke stated that no serious flooding accompanied the transformation of some eight inches of water from solid to liquid form, so gradual was the melting process. The main casualty of the run-off was the Great Bridge at Hartford, much of which was carried away on March 7th by an ice jam in the flood-swollen river.[68]

But winter was not over yet. As often happens, a warm early March is succeeded by a cold last half. On the 16th Ezra Stiles complained: though the earth was almost cleared of former snows at New Haven, yet "snow again today."[69] On the 31st a northeast snowstorm brought ankle-deep depths to the Atlantic seaboard. Charles Carroll down in Maryland had a 4 to 5-inch snow on April 5th.[70] A final visitation of the Hard Winter swept across the interior of the Northeast on May 1st from Columbia County in New York to New Hampshire, though accumulations were insignificant.[71]

Frost formed throughout New England on June 4th, 5th, and 6th, the dates of the damaging June frosts in the "Year Without A Summer," to come in 1816. At Waltham, Massachusetts, just outside Boston, Jacob Cushing reported the frosts on June 6th and 9th had killed the beans and some corn.[72] Up in central Vermont at Barnard water froze on grindstones the mornings of June 4th and 5th, and another frost occurred in low lands nearby on 12 July 1780.[73]

## POSTVIEW

The unusual meteorological conditions excited great curiosity among scientific gentlemen, so the American Philosophical Society appointed a committee "to make and collect observations on the effects of the severe and long continued cold of last winter." Those with pertinent data were urged to send them to Col. Lewis Nicola at Philadelphia. This request received wide publicity in the press of the country. A search of the files of the Society has revealed only one communication that can be definitely related to the appeal. It came from Delaware and concerned the effect on the following summer crops, especially in regard to the dearth of insects as a result of the Hard Winter.

---

How did the mean temperature in January 1780 compare with other cold months in the meteorological history of the Northeast? We cannot arrive at a precise figure from the original data since no record of maximum and minimum readings was made on a registering instrument, and many of the records made in that year are suspect due to improper exposure of the instrument.

The best thermometer record was made at Hartford, Connecticut, but only the sunrise readings have survived for the full 31 days. If it is assumed that sunrise represents the actual minimum, we obtain a sunrise average for January 1780 of +4.1°.

When these are compared with the presently accepted 30-year climatological mean for Hartford (Bradley Field), the month of January 1780 assumes real stature as probably the coldest calendar month in recorded American meteorological history. Bradley Field is a rural exposure some 10 miles north of downtown Hartford, now in surroundings probably quite similar to those existing in 1780 around the residence of Rev. Nathan Strong. The present Hartford mean minimum for January is 17.6°, or 13.5 degrees higher than the January 1780 sunrise mean. The present monthly mean at Hartford is nine degrees greater than the mean minimum. So by adding nine degrees to the 1780 figure, we arrive at 13.1° for a comparable monthly mean for January 1780.

The coldest month in an early set of records for Hartford (1837–57) was January 1857 with 13.9°, and the closest approach in the modern records (1904-present) was February 1934 with 16.5°. In the long period of records at New Haven (1781–1965) no month was colder than January 1857. Thus, it appears quite certain that no other month was colder than January 1857 with the exception of the month under study: January 1780. Due to the imprecise nature of the readings and the varying methods of compiling means, it would be reasonable to place January 1780 and January 1857 in a class by themselves, as co-holders of the title of the coldest month in history. January 1857 probably produced greater extremes, but January 1780 stands preeminent for duration of cold without a break.

[1] C. E. P. Brooks. *Climate through the ages. A study of the climatic factors and their variations.* New York, McGraw-Hill Book Co., 1949. 307, 375.
Victor Conrad. Climatic changes or cycles? *Climatic change. Evidence, causes, and effects.* Harlow Shapley, ed. Cambridge, Mass., Harvard Univ. Press, 1953. 233.
[2] E. Stiles, *Diary,* **2**, 402.
N. Webster. Notices of extraordinary seasons of cold. *Amer. Jour. Sci.* (New Haven), **28**, (July 1835), 185.
[3] Ebenezer Hazard to Jeremy Belknap, 10 Mar 1780. The Belknap Papers. *Coll. Mass. Hist. Soc.* 5th ser., 2, (1877), 36.
[4] Thomas Jefferson. *Notes on the state of Virginia.* London, 1787. Reprint: William Peden, ed. Chapel Hill, Univ. North Carolina Press, 1955. 78.
[5] American Philosophical Society, 21 Mar 1780, in *Penna. Jour.* (Phila.), 22 Mar 1780.
[6] *Conn. Courant* (Hartford), 11 Jan, 8 Feb 1780; *N. J. Gaz.* (Burlington), 23 Feb 1780; *Va. Gaz.* (Williamsburg), 15 Jan 1780.
[7] E. Stiles, *Diary,* **2**, 400–01.
[8] *N. J. Gaz.,* 22 Dec 1780.
[9] E. Stiles, *Diary,* **2**, 401–02.
[10] Diary of General Von Huyn. *The Siege of Charleston.* B. A. Uhlendorf, ed. Ann Arbor, Univ. of Michigan Press, 1938, 369.
[11] H. Muhlenberg, *Journal,* **3**, 277.

[12] *The Journals of Hugh Gaine Printer.* Paul L. Ford, ed. New York, Dodd, Mead & Co., 1902. **2,** 74.
[13] E. Stiles, *Diary,* **2,** 528.
[14] E. Holyoke, Ms. Met. Jour.
[15] H. Muhlenberg, *Journal,* **3,** 282.
[16] *N. J. Jour.* (Chatham), 11 & 18 Jan 1780.
[17] *Conn. Gazette* (New London), 19 Jan 1780.
[18] E. Stiles, *Diary,* **2,** 400.
[19] *Conn. Gaz.* (New London), in *Mass. Gaz.* (Boston), 31 Jan 1780.
[20] *Newport Mercury,* 5 Jan 1780.
[21] *Independent Gaz.* (Boston), 13 Jan 1780.
[22] E. Holyoke, Ms. Met. Jour.
[23] H. Muhlenberg, *Journal,* **3,** 283.
[24] George Washington. Ms. Account of the weather begun 1st Jan 1780. (Lib. Congress).
[25] E. Stiles, *Diary,* **2,** 401.
[26] E. Holyoke.
[27] Ebenezer Parkman. *Diary.* Harriette M. Forbes, ed. Westborough, Mass., The Westborough Historical Society, 1899. 203–05.
[28] M. Patten, *Diary,* 410.
[29] E. Stiles, *Diary,* **2,** 401–02.
[30] G. Washington, Ms. Account.
[31] James Thacher. *A military journal during the American Revolutionary War from 1775 to 1783.* Boston, Richardson and Lord, 1823. 221.
[32] *New York Evening Post,* 5 Jan 1832.
[33] Andrew Mellick, Jr. *The story of an old farm or life in New Jersey in the eighteenth century.* Somerville, The Unionist-Gazette, 1889. 514.
[34] H. Muhlenberg, *Journal,* **3,** 286.
[35] Oscar J. Harvey. *A history of Wilkes-Barre.* Wilkes-Barre, private print, 1909. **2,** 1225.
[36] *Mass. Spy* (Worcester), 20 Jan 1780.
[37] E. Stiles, *Diary,* **2,** 398–402; also Stiles, Ms. Thermo. Reg.
[38] *Holyoke Diaries,* 102; also E. Holyoke, Ms. Met. Jour.
[39] *The Belknap Papers,* 30.
[40] Diary of Ebenezer Miller. *Proc. Mass. Hist. Soc.* 2d. ser. 8 (1893), 114.
[41] *The journals and papers of David Shultze,* **2,** 110.
[42] David Rittenhouse. Ms. Height of Fahrenheit's thermometer at Philadelphia, 1780. (Penna. Hist. Soc).
[43] *Conn. Courant* (Hartford), 8 Feb 1780; Jacob Cushing. Ms. Met. Obs. at Waltham. (Harvard).
[44] *Conn. Courant,* 8 Feb 1780; *Holyoke Diaries,* 102; E. Stiles, Ms. Met. Obs.
[45] *New York Packet* (Fishkill, N. Y.) in E. Stiles; F. MacKenzie, *Diary,* **2,** 469.
[46] S. Hazard, *Effects of Climate,* **2,** 379.
[47] *Md. Gaz.* (Annapolis), 28 Jan 1780; *Va. Gaz.* (Williamsburg), 22 & 29 Jan, 5 Feb 1780; J. Thomas Scharf. *The Chronicles of Baltimore.* Baltimore, 1874. 184.
[48] James Long to Governor Caswell, Tyrell County, Jan 17, 1780. *The State Records of North Carolina.* Goldsboro, Nash Bros., 1898. **15,** 318.
[49] T. Jefferson, *Notes on Va.,* 78.
[50] H. Gaine, *Journal,* **2,** 75–81.
[51] William Dunlap. *History of the New Netherland, province and state of New York, to the adoption of the Federal Constitution.* New York, Carter & Thorp, 1839–40. **2,** App. ccxxx.
[52] E. Stiles, *Diary,* **2,** 415.
[53] H. Gaine, *Journal,* **2,** 80–81. Major-General Patterson to Lord George Germain. New York, 22 Feb 1780. *N. J. Archives,* 2d ser., **4,** 466–68.
[54] E. Stiles, *Diary,* **2,** 411.
[55] *Conn. Gaz.* (New London), 9 Feb 1780.
[56] Frances M. Caulkins. *History of New London, Conn.* New London, H. D. Utley, 1895. 411.
[57] Obed Macy. *The History of Nantucket.* Boston, Hilliard, Gray & Co., 1835. 107.
[58] *Mass. Gaz.,* 28 Feb 1780.
[59] *Ibid.,* 14 Feb 1780.
[60] T. Smith, *Journal,* 281; History of Bath. *Coll. Maine Hist. Soc.* **2,** (1847), 218.
[61] *Mass. Spy,* 20 Jan 1780.
[62] *Mass. Gaz.,* 14 Feb 1780.
[63] E. Stiles, *Diary,* **2,** 401.
[64] Diary of James Parker. *New Eng. Gen. Hist. Mag.* (Boston). **69,** (1915), 217.
[65] *Norwich* (Conn.) *Packet* in *Mass. Gaz.,* 28 Feb 1780.
[66] Marginal jottings from the Scudder family. *Proc. N. J. Hist. Soc.,* 63-3, (July 1945), 153.
[67] Diary of Ebenezer Miller. *Proc. Mass. Hist. Soc.* 2d. ser. 8 (1893), 114.
[68] *Conn. Courant,* 14 March 1780.
[69] E. Stiles, *Diary,* **2,** 418–19.
[70] Carroll Papers. *Md. Hist. Soc.* v, vi, 93–94.
[71] Warren Brown. *History of Hampton Falls, N. H.* Concord, The Rumford Press, 1900. 477.
[72] J. Cushing, Ms. Met. Obs. (Harvard).
[73] William M. Newton. *History of Barnard, Vermont.* Montpelier, Vermont Historical Society, 1928. **1,** 284.
[74] American Philosophical Society, 21 March 1780, in *Penna. Jour.,* 22 March 1780.

March 22, 1780.        T H E        Numb. 1332.

# PENNSYLVANIA JOURNAL
### AND
# WEEKLY ADVERTISER

*WEDNESDAY,* MARCH 22, 1780.

Philadelphia, March 21, 1780.

The Committee appointed by the Philosophical Society, to make and collect observations on the effects of the severe & long continued cold of last winter, request the curious in every part of the continent, to communicate to them such remarks as they have already made, or may hereafter make on this subject, particularly such as may properly come under the following heads.

First, Meteorological observations, accurately made with good instruments.

Secondly, The effects of the cold on the earth and waters; such as the depth of earth frozen, the thickness of ice, &c. together with such remarkable circumstances, as may attend either freezing or thawing. Also its effects on spiritous, vinous and other liquors.

Thirdly, The effects of the cold, during and after the winter on animals, birds, reptiles, insects and their chrysalsies.

Fourthly, The same on vegetables, distinguishing the indigenous from foreign, the spontaneous from the cultivated.

Fifthly, What diseases prevailed most in the extreme cold weather, and after it.

Accurate observations made on former winters, remarkable for cold will be accepted.

As the comparing together different climates and different seasons is not a matter of mere speculative curiosity, but real benefits may be derived to mankind, by improving this branch of natural knowledge, the Committee promise themselves the assistance of the ingenious, whether Members of the Society or otherwise, in their endeavours to unite in one common stock many valuable fragments of Philosophy, which must otherwise perish with individuals.

The Committee do not propose to make their report before the close of next summer. In the mean time such gentlemen as chuse to favour the Society with their observations, will please to direct their letters to Col. Lewis Nicola, of Philadelphia.

(The Printers of News-Papers on the continent, are requested to give the foregoing a place in their respective Papers.)

## WESTBOROUGH, MASSACHUSETTS

Extracts from *The Diary of Ebenezer Parkman* supplemented in italics by wind directions from the meteorological journal of Edward A. Holyoke of Salem.

## NEW HAVEN, CONNECTICUT

Extracts from *The Literary Diary of Ezra Stiles* supplemented in italics by Tutor Atwater's snowfall record at New Haven and by Rev. Nathan Strong's temperature record at Hartford: sunrise readings from 1 to 8 January and both sunrise and afternoon readings from 9 January to 5 February.

### November 1779

28. A considerable snow last Friday (26th). *9".*

### December 1779

### December 1779

2. I had no lecture this day it being stormy snow, & at night rain & violent thunder. *1".*

5. Excessively rigorous season: severe snowstorm. *9".*

8. The steward at great difficulty in upholding Commons.

10. Ride in the sleigh to Col. Brigham's. . . . The weather prevented my visiting. *SW.*
11. *SW.*
12. Cold, stormy. Few at communion. *SW/W.*
13. It was too stormy for me to venture. *NW.*

14. *NE.*

15. *NE.*
16. *NE.*
17. Breck [his son] to Sutton in the sleigh to get paper. Succeeds but in part. *NE/NW.*
18. It is exceedingly stormy, snowing, blowing and very cold. *NE.*

16. Broke up College & dismissed the students till the end of the winter vacation, viz. till Feb. 1, 1780.

18. Terrible snowstorm. Half a leg deep or more. *17".*

19. Difficult to get to meeting, but few there. *N/NW.*

20. A very cold season, & continues so. *SW.*
21. NW/W.
22. *NW.*
23. *NW/W.*
24. *N.*

27. A terrible snowstorm began last evening. *18".*

*Continued on page 122*

## NEW YORK CITY AND MORRISTOWN

*The Journals of Hugh Gaine* at New York City for November and December 1779 and the Ms. Account of the Weather by General George Washington at Morristown, New Jersey, for January to April 1780.

### New York City

### November 1779

26. Snow and rain, the first this season.

29. Snow.

### December 1779

5. Nothing stirring but snow, of which we have a very great fall this day.

6. The snow continues.
7. The weather still cold, and the snow lies on the ground.
8. The weather more moderate and the wind at S.W.
9. It continues pretty moderate, and the snow wears away fast.
12. Wet, dirty, and cold.

14. Very cold.

15. Cold and snow continues.

19. Very cold indeed.

20. The weather continues cold.

## TRAPPE, PENNSYLVANIA

*The Journals of Henry M. Muhlenberg* supplemented in italics by the January and early February minimum temperatures from the record of David Rittenhouse of Philadelphia.

### November 1779

26. Today we are having a dreadful wind and snowstorm.
28. Since the snow was deep and the roads hard to travel.

### December 1779

2. Heavy rain and raw, stormy wind the whole day.
3. Piercing, raw wind and severe cold . . . Our expected guests did not come this week on account of the bad weather and roads.
5. But it began to snow so hard early in the morning, and continued thus throughout the whole day, that the snow lay a foot and a half deep and there was no going out of doors.
6. It was bitter cold today.

12. But since there was a violent rainstorm last night.
13. The heavy rain continued last night. Now we are having dark and melancholy days and long nights.
14. Since last evening, all through the night and today, we have had such a terrible and bitterly cold windstorm as we have not had in a long time. Men and beasts tremble.
15. The severe cold still continues.
16. Last night another snow fell.
17. Bitter cold.
18. Rain and snow last night, severe cold today, which has formed a crust on the snow and makes the going hard for travelers. . . . Severe cold and terribly stormy northwest wind.
19. The northwest wind was violent, and the cold penetrating, as it has not been in many previous winters.
20. The severe cold continues.
21. The severe cold continues.
22. The severe cold continues.

*Continued on page 123*

## Westborough

25. I rode up to Shrewsbury—to Mr. Nathan Goddard's who has persuaded me to take this cold ride. *E.*

28. A close time for study, but a great storm abroad. *NW.*
29. A very dismal morning. Storm continues until about noon. *NE.* Snow-banks very high one nigh my saddle-horse 6 feet high. Roads blocked up.
    My son Breck had also designed to go in a double sleigh to Ashburnham, but no team nor sleigh can stir. How wonderful the Works of the Great God!
30. I keep close to my study. . . . Enough to do to keep warm. *E.*
31. *NE.*

### January 1780

1. And in special in so difficult a season, of so much cold and snow and tedious stirring, I am favoured in Divine Providence, with the necessaries and so many of the comforts of life. *NW.*
   People are chiefly employed in making roads, providing for the fires, taking care of cattle, &c. But the Lord pitty the poor and exposed!
2. Exceeding difficult in getting to meeting. . . . At night another snow storm. *N.*

3. The storm is very severe, much more snow has fallen. It was higher than the red fence before my house by the storm last week: it is now higher, and the front gate is not to be seen. *E.*

4. God has his Treasures of Snow and Hail and Wind. Power belongeth unto God. How distressing to the poor. *NW.*
5. Thro' Divine Favour this was a bright, pleasant day. Both my sons and my steers join with a number of the street neighbors with cattle and shovels to break the roads. Tis difficult to compute the height or depth of it. I am almost ready to conclude that there has not been so much snow on the ground at a time since the Great Snow in year 1717. *NW/S.*

## New Haven

### January 1780

1. $+2°$

2. Excessive cold, snow a foot & half on level & hardens to walk & ride on. (About sunset came a violent snowstorm & highest tide ever known by two or three feet. Wind for four hours blew almost every point of compass). $-7°$.
3. Violent snowstorm, drifted over fences. $+14°$. $12''$.

4. $+16°$.
5. Severe winter weather—snowing still and snow blowing and drifting, nearest like the year 1740–41, which I well remember. This day 50 men with horses, sleighs, and two sleds beat a path out six miles to Goodyear's farm for wood. The poor in distress! $+6°$.

*Continued on page 124*

### New York City

25. The sailing has been some days put off in consequence of the ships being drove in shore by the ice.
26. The whole fleet with the troops sailed out of the Hook this day at 4 o'clock, with a fair wind.
27. The wind and weather much in favor of the fleet.
28. Rain and snow today, but the wind still fair for the fleet.
29. About 6 o'clock last evening a most violent storm of rain and wind set in from the N.E. and continued at least six hours; it did little or no damage in the harbour, but many are uneasy about the fleet, I hope it is safe.
30. Pleasant fair weather for the fleet to join in case they separated in the gale of wind last night.
31. Very cold indeed, but the wind still hangs to the eastward, which is very fair for the fleet.

### Morristown

#### January 1780

1. Clear—cold—& freezing with little wind.
2. Very cold—about noon it began to snow, & continued without intermission through the day & night.—The wind high and variable, but chiefly from the west and northwest.
3. The same weather as yesterday—to wit, cold & stormy—wind from the same point.
4. Very cold with high winds from the west & northwest—and intermittent snow.
5. Cloudy till afternoon—when the sun appeared.

### Trappe

25. The bitter cold still continues.
28. Upon the severe cold followed a deep snow which changed to a northeast storm of wind and rain, the like of which there has not been in many years, penetrating all places in the buildings.
29. The storm has ceased. In the afternoon my two oldest sons came back from New Hannover in the company of the third. Heinrich lamented that he had suffered much damage to his furniture and books from the storm yesterday since the old parsonage is too full of holes to withstand snow and rain.
30. It will doubtless be impossible to get through because of the high water and ice floes in the streams.

#### January 1780

1. Extremely cold weather . . . with great trouble they first had to break an opening through the river, which was full of ice. Winter travel is dangerous and laborious. *17°*.
2. After the service it began to snow heavily again, accompanied by a stormy northeast wind. *23°*.
3. Since yesterday afternoon and throughout the night, there was such a snowstorm that the house and yard are so circumvallated that one can scarcely get out or in, and the snow is still falling. Had some time for reading and writing. The cold wind still continues. It kept up its frightful howling the whole night. *22°*.
4. *22°*.
5. Last night it started to snow again upon the already deep snow, and it still continues. . . . Today the northwest wind brought the temperature several degrees lower than before. *22°*.

*Continued on page 125*

## Westborough

6. The great God has his Treasures of snow and has supreme command of all the meteors. It is very stormy again, and the snow deeper, and tho the Sun was visible a little while in the afternoon, yet it was soon clouded, and the storm rages at night. *NW/W*.
7. An astonishing morning—for the dreadful storm rather increases. Besides the snowing and blowing with violence the cold is very intense. This is thought to be the most tedious of any that has come hitherto. *NW*.
8. Hardly ever was the Sun more welcome—but yet the cold is so sharp and the wind so high, it is very difficult to undergo the hardships we are called to. *NW*.
9. I was in doubt whether there would be a meeting. But a few came on rackets. *NW*.
10. ... but I cannot get to him by reason of the deep snow, and difficult stirring. *W/S*.
11. Mr. Forbes still alive, but no horse can go in the deep snow, but I have no rackets nor strength to go far as to visit him. *N*.
12. Fair, but too rough and severe for me to go abroad. *N*.
13. A very cold day—we think the severest of any that has come. *NW*.
14. It was sharp cold, the wind piercing, the sled goes over the tops of walls and fences. ... There were so many people with snow shoes that there was a good path. ... It was too tedious for me to stay at the grave. *NW*.
15. It holds an uncommon cold, difficult season. *NW*.
16. *NW/S*.
17. *S*.

## New Haven

6. Severe weather. Snowstorm continues with some intermission. *+10°*.
7. Snow over the fences—drifts high—in woods at Amity, Carmel and Chesire 3½ feet and four feet deep on level. It has the nearest resemblance to the hard winter of 1740–41 which I perfectly remember. The snow and severe weather set in then about Dec. 10th O.S. or about our present Christmas [rather Dec. 17th first great snow], and lasted 13 weeks. This day extremely cold, high winds, snow blows a storm—Distressing time for want of wood. *+9°*.
8. Snowing over. Excessive cold. *−1°*.
9. *+5°/+28°*.
10. Snow this night half a foot. *+19°/+32°. 0.5″*.
11. Arrived at Southington this evening and found only two of the ministers of the Ordaining Council convened. The ways are impassable on account of the quantity of snow, which is 3, 4, 6 and ten feet deep, estimated at four and a half on the level. It is judged there is a greater quantity of snow than in the hard Winter of 1740/41 which I well remember. The high winds fill up paths. *26°/M*.
12. But through the severity of the season, and high winds blowing the snow and filling up the paths. ... In the evening Mr. Newell arrived having been all day in coming seven miles and 40 men employed in opening the way. *+11°/29°*.
14. Very blustering. *+8°/19°*.
15. *+15°/32°*.
16. *+10°/27°*.
17. *+17°/32°. 1″*.

*Continued on page 126*

## Morristown

6. Snowing & sunshine alternately—cold with the wind west and northwest & increasing—night very stormy—The snow which in general is eighteen inches deep, is much drifted. Roads almost impassable.

7. Very boisterous from the west & northwest & sometimes snowing, which being very dry drifted exceedingly—Night intensely cold and freezing—Wind continuing fresh.

8. Morning cold & windy from the northwest—Midday and afternoon more moderate and less windy—Weather clear—after sunset it again turned very cold, the wind freshning from the northwest.

9. Morning clear and cold the wind (though not high) from the northwest—Mid-day moderate with but little wind—the evening cold though the wind had shifted to the southward.

10. Morning clear and mild—wind at southeast—before noon it clouded & about two began to snow & continued to do so all the afternoon and evening.

11. Clear and moderate with little or no wind in the forenoon but rather cloudy—variable wind in the afternoon.

12. Variable weather with a little snow in the day & more in the night.—In the whole a fall of about three inches.—In the afternoon it turned very cold.

13. Wind fresh at northwest and exceedingly cold—Weather clear and frost very severe.

14. Clear & cold—Wind steadily from the west—but not hard.

15. Wind at northwest—Weather clear but not cold.—of a sameness through the day.

16. Fine morning, and pleasant day though cool—but little wind & that southerly.

17. Morning cloudy and great appearances of snow. Mid-day clear with a disposition to thaw, but the wind shifting to northwest it turned exceeding cold and froze hard.

## Trappe

6. Violent storm from the northwest the whole day with intermittent snow and such severe cold that the fires are of no help at all. Moreover, the firewood is frozen under the snowdrifts and hard to get at. *10°.*

7. The storm lasted the whole night and still continues today, more violent than ever . . . the wind has piled up the snow higher than a man's head. *12°.*

8. But will probably not get far on account of the deep snow and continuing windstorm and penetrating cold. *10°.*

9. I had promised to preach in Augustus Church, but the snow was so deep, the cold so severe, and the roads so unbroken that I was unable to get there. *18°.*

10. The cold grows even more severe. *25°.*

11. I had spent a miserable night, partly because of the severe cold and windstorm. . . . *26°.*

12. *23°.*

13. Though with this severe cold and deep snow the means of sending the packets are scarce. *5°.*

14. Yesterday, last night, and up to now the cold has been more fierce than it has been for many years. *7°.*

15. The severe cold still continues. Our firewood is gone, and it is hard to get more because it is everywhere buried under the snow and frozen fast. *16°.*

16. But the preacher was unable to get through on account of the deep snow. *11°.*

17. The weather is milder. *25°.*

*Continued on page 127*

## Westborough

18. As no team of oxen or horses can pass, people are obliged to go to mill with hand sleds. *W*.
19. *NW/SW*.
20. *NW*.
21. *SW*.




22. A newspaper of Dec. 30 is the last. *NW/W*.


23. A considerable congregation, tho very cold. *NW/W*.




24. I went, but with great difficulty, by reason of the deep snow. *NW*.

25. Elias [his son] leaves his studies and helps those who are breaking the roads with a yoke of cattle. *NW*.
26. Squire Baker is so engaged in breaking roads that he has got Elias & a yoke of my cattle, on the road again. *SW*.
27. Elias is gone again with the cattle today to break and shovel the road. *SW/W*.

28. The latter part of this was the most remarkable cold day that we have had (as every body is free to allow) and Elias goes again with Squire Baker, and drives two pair of my steers, to breaking the road down to Taplin's in Southboro; The evening and night were so extremely severe that I was much concerned for him till he returned; and did survive though he had been in danger of being overcome with cold & fatigue. *W/WSW*.
29. The morning was the most severe and sharp—Elias thinks some of his limbs are froze, but (God be thanked) he is about with usual currency. *NW/WSW*.

30. *SW/W*.

## New Haven

18. Returned to New Haven. Snow very deep. *+12°/ 21°*.
19. *−13°/+14°*.
20. *+5°/+8°*.
21. *−6°/+26°*.

22. My thermometer was broken 5th July last day of the enemy's taking New Haven. I procured Professor Strong's thermometer which I received this evening, when at 1900 the mercury stood at +6—2000 it was at zero—at 2100 it had descended to −3¾. Clear and cold. Wind N.W. *+5°/+29°*.

23. At sunrise Friday mercury in Fahrenheits thermometer stood at zero—at noon 17 above.... Excessive cold ... the highest altitude of the day 18½ above. at 2100 at zero. *−9°/+16°*.

24. *+6°/+30°*.

25. *−16°/+19°*.

26. Still cold. Thermometer 7 this morning. Frozen out two miles beyond 5 mile point. They pass in sleighs from Long Island to Horseneck. *−6°/ +28°*.
27. *−8°/+18°. 0.5"*.

28. The highest altitude of the mercury this day was 15 above at 1500; it descended to 7 by 2100 and to 3½ at 2200 with an increasing cold.




29. Sunrise thermometer −1. At noon 7; at 1500 11½. at 2000 in evening 10. I rode over to East Haven across the harbor on the ice. Wind high S.W. *−20°/+7°*.

30. The S.W. wind has broken up some ice beyond the beach and off the mouth of the harbor. *+15°/ +37°*.

*Continued on page 128*

## Morristown

18. Clear & cold. Wind at northwest but not very fresh.
19. Clear. Morning tolerably pleasant—evening cold—wind at northwest but not very fresh.
20. Intensely cold & freezing—wind very fresh from the northwest the whole day.
21. In the night the wind shifted to the southwest & the severity of the cold abated. The day pleasant with but little wind & that about southwest till the evening when it got more to the westward blew fresh & grew colder.
22. Tolerably pleasant with but little wind from the westward. At night it grew cold & froze severely.

23. Wind easterly & little of it—air keen & no thawing even in the sun—south of the houses.

24. Clear in the forenoon and cloudy afternoon—cold but little or no wind—but that westerly—no thaw.
25. Clear and pleasant, yet cold—wind continued to the westward.

26. Wind for the most part of the day southerly—but cold and sharp air notwithstanding—weather clear.

27. Cold in the morning with a little snow—clear midday and afternoon with the wind at west.
28. Very cold—the wind being fresh from the northwest—froze severe.

29. Clear and cold without much wind which in the forenoon was westerly & in the afternoon to southwest.

30. Warm and clear in the forenoon with the wind at south & thawing fast—afternoon cold & freezing. Wind getting to the northwest and blowing fresh particularly in the night.

## Trappe

18. Last night we had a heavy wind and snowstorm. *18°.*
19. *6°.*
20. Last night a stormy northwest wind arose, and the cold of the steady windstorm is so severe that men and beasts can hardly live. *0°.*
21. The severe cold continues. *4°.*

22. The severe cold still continues. *8°.*

23. There was no public service here because of the severely cold weather and the deep snow. . . . In the evening Gen. Muhlenberg returned from Tolpehaken because he was unable to proceed (L.C. on his journey to Virginia) owing to the fact that the snow is over three feet deep and there is no possibility of getting through with the wagon. *8°.*
24. Last night another snow fell on the already deep and hardened snow. Firewood is hard to get and becoming increasingly so. *14°.*
25. The fierce cold continues. *7°.*

26. Still severer cold. . . . The wagons were to come from Lancaster to fetch Heinrich's things had not yet arrived. There is still no track broken on the road to make it possible to get through.
27. The cold is still more severe than before (L.C. indeed, more severe than I experienced forty years ago at Hennersdorf, in Upper Lusatia). *8°.*
28. The severe cold still continues. The roads are gradually becoming more passable because they are being used by many sleighs. *12°.*

29. Last night there was a violent windstorm, and the severe cold still continues. The newspaper reports many accidents, people frozen to death, dying of hunger, and perishing in the ice of inland streams. *7°.*
30. He came over on foot because the Schulkiel is frozen solid. *17°.*

*Continued on page 129*

### Westborough

31. Hear that Sue Bimeleck was lately frozen to death. This whole month has been cold to admiration. We have scarce ever known its equal. The cold of this day is to high degree of extremity. *NW*.

### February 1780

1. We walked on the top of the snow, which was many times as high as the top of the fence. *NW/SW*.

2. It was too cold for me to go out. *NW*.

8. Providence further frowns upon us in sending another snowstorm, which covers the racket tracks & fills the roads again. *E*.

9. Elias goes with Breck & others to break the roads to Southboro.

15. The air is exceeding thick. P.M. it rains, the snow wastes. . . . At eve a storm of wind and rain which beat vehemently. *S*.

### New Haven

31. Cold. Thermometer at 7 at 1030 and 16 at 1400 and 6½ at 2200. *−4°/+12°*.

### February 1780

1. *+2°/+26°*.

2. *+3°/+16°*.

3. Thermometer 36° at noon, mild, pleasant. *0°/+30°*.

4. *+15°/+22°*.

5. Cold day. Thermometer 6 lowest, 17 highest. *+8°/+15°*.

7. This day being pleasant, thermometer 33°, I surveyed the harbor of New Haven upon the ice, accompanied by Mr. Tutor Atwater and five of the senior class.

8. A terrible snowstorm, snow fell half a foot. . . . The Worcester paper of 20 January says the road from Hartford to Boston is passable, but no others except on snowshoes. Nothing like it these forty years.—Rev. Mr. Trumbull of Westbury tells me the Hard Winter 1740/41 was not equal to this in quantity of snow, in early beginning, and perhaps in intenseness of cold; that now Feb. 8, the snow in Waterbury Woods is four feet on level. Mr. Trumbull says in Hard Winter 1740/41 he and his people had no difficulty in getting to meeting without making paths, not so now. *7"*.

11. Mild warm weather. Thermometer 48. Thaw.

13. Pleasant day.

15. Thaw.

*Continued on page 130*

## Morristown

31. Very cold & freezing—wind being fresh from the northwest the whole day.

### February 1780

1. More mild especially in the forenoon—wind variable but mostly southerly—afternoon chilly with appearance of snow.
2. Clear & tolerably pleasant in the morning. In the afternoon a keen air from the westward.
3. Moderate—rather warm & thawing—wind for the most part of the day southerly—evening cold.
4. Clear and cold—wind westerly—little or no thawing.
5. Wind at northwest & cold—frost very severe. In the evening the wind shifted to the southward & moderated.
6. Clear and tolerably pleasant—wind rather south of west—snow melting.
7. Clear, mild and moderate in the forenoon—but little wind—afternoon rather lowering and cooler.
8. A fall of nine or 10 inches of snow in the night from the northeast. Wind continuing in the same quarter all the forenoon with a little snow and some rain. In the afternoon the wind got westerly & in the evening cleared.
9. Wind fresh in the night from the westward—day clear and not very cold—the wind continued westerly all day.
10. Wind southerly—weather moderate—but somewhat lowering.
11. Wind at southwest and pretty fresh—forepart of the day very lowering & dropping rain—snow much softened & beginning to dissolve—afterwards clear & pleasant.
12. Clear and pleasant with but little wind—rather cooler than yesterday—snow dissolving a little—frost at night.
13. Clear and pleasant with but little wind & that at northeast thawing a little in the middle of the day.
14. Air keen, though but little wind—forenoon clear, afternoon a little lowering.
15. A kind of sleet in the morning, & moderate rain in the remaining part of the day with but little wind. Snow much dissipated.

## Trappe

31. The high wind and severe cold continue. *11°*.

### February 1780

1. The wind has abated and the weather is pleasant. *10°*.
2. *18°*.
3. *20°*.
4. The cold still continues. *28°*.
5. The severe cold still continues. *10°*.
6. There should have been a Reformed service but there was none. (L.C. The weather would not permit.) *18°*.
7. *13°*.
8. Last night we had a violent windstorm, with snow from the northeast which made the snowdrifts still higher, and it continued the whole day. . . . The violent storm kept up to midnight. *31°*.
9. Clear weather and high northwest wind. *23°*.
10. *23°*.
11. *32°*.
12. Somewhat milder weather, but the snow is still on the ground. *28°*.
13. *19°*.
14. *18°*.
15. Today a cold rain is falling on the deep snow, which has been on the ground so long that it will cause floods if the rain continues. *32°*.

*Continued on page 131*

### Westborough

16. A fine day after such a violent storm. The snow is much sunk, but it is so pervaded by the rain that the creatures slump very deep, and no horse can pass the road.

17. Our lowest and best well has been ever since the great storm, froze up and filled with snow that we have not been able to use it, till today, when we got it open.

22. But today it is very difficult passing by reason that the snow is exceeding soft. It is foul weather P.M. The rain spoils travelling.
23. Very bad travelling.

26. Mrs. Lamson about 3 P.M. attempts to go home, but the rain prevailed so that she turned back and tarrys with us.

### New Haven

16. Mild pleasant day, thermometer 54. Snow dissolving.

17. Mild weather. Thermometer 41. Snow sinking away.

19. Snow greatly dissolving. Dr. Dexter from Boston last week says the snow four and a half deep there on a level, froze out to Nantasket's Lighthouse.
21. They lately crossed over Narragansett Bay on the ice from the ferry at South Kingston to Newport. The winter has been severe beyond memory. A gentleman from Virginia informs that Chesapeake Bay has been frozen, so that men have passed over from York Town to Accomack side 32 mile on the ice, drawing after them a light birch canoe.
22. Rain, wind SE.

23. *0.5".*

26. For several days a thaw.

28. Mild and thawing. Snow gone off the hills, and farmers taking up flax.

*Continued on page 132*

## Morristown

16. Clear & quite warm in the forenoon—snow yielding fast to the sun—much water in the roads and brooks—and the thick beds of snow over which good sleighing had been were now too soft to bear—and too difficult and dangerous to horses to pass. Afternoon lowering.
17. Clear and pleasant with but little wind—thawing all day pretty considerably.
18. Wind fresh from the northwest but moderate with respect to cold, notwithstanding it continued to blow from that quarter all day.
19. In the morning it was a little cool. In the afternoon somewhat raw, but upon the whole pleasant. Wind at west & northwest but not fresh.
20. Clear & pleasant morning. Wind about southwest in the forepart of the day, but shifted to the west & northwest afterwards & though pleasant got a little cooler.
21. Ground where bare, and top of the snow pretty hard frozen. But little wind in the morning or any part of the day, the first part of which was clear, the latter part lowering.
22. Wind at northeast and raining moderately all day, beginning about 7 o'clock with fine hail. In the night the wind freshened from the same quarter.
23. Lowering morning with a little snow in the forenoon. Wind at southwest, but shifting to the northwest about 3 o'clock & blowing hard it cleared and grew cold and began to freeze very hard.
24. Hard frost—flying clouds in the forenoon but clear afterwards. Wind fresh from the northwest & very cold. No thawing even in the sun at midday though the roads & fields in many places were uncovered.
25. Perfectly clear. Wind westerly, fresh & cool, but thawing nevertheless.
26. Hazy & lowering in the morning. Clear about noon, but moderately raining by intervals afterwards till eight o'clock at night when it cleared & the wind blew pretty fresh from the westward. There was but little wind in the day and that southerly.
27. Clear and pleasant morning with the wind at west. The day much of a sameness throughout—thawing pretty considerably.
28. A great hoar-frost—quite clear—wind still westerly and pleasant—thawing—the snow having dissipated very considerably in the course of the last two or three days.
29. Clear, warm and exceeding pleasant with but little wind & that southerly. Snow almost gone off the fields & roads, the latter of which is beginning to get deep.

## Trappe

16. Fair weather. *36°*.

17. Clear weather, but with a wind that forebodes snow or rain. *36°*.

22. Steady rain.

23. Today the northwest wind is again bringing the same severe storms and cold that we have already had several times this winter.

24. The cold is so severe and continuous that both men and beasts are shivering.

25. The bitter cold and the cold northwest wind still persist.
26. The weather is somewhat milder and inclines toward snow or rain.

*Continued on page 133*

## Westborough
### March 1780

1. Notwithstanding the rain and very difficult travelling, I went A.M. to the funeral of old Mr. Jonah Warren . . . the snow and ice made it dangerous to ride . . . the weather rough and the roads very bad.

9. Elias went with me again at evening—and we returned safely, notwithstanding the badness of the way—the horse breaking into the snow banks, oftentimes and the sleigh tossing uncomfortably, being also in the rain.
11. The weather is still so rough and the roads so unfit for travel . . .
12. It was so great a storm of snow and rain that there were but few at meeting—especially in the afternoon.

14. We are much reduced as to wood, but the weather is still too cold to be indifferent about it. No going to the ministerial lot.
15. Elias sows hay seed upon the snow.
16. We have such another winter by the storm of snow, which came today as makes us think of the value of wood, and pity such as are destitute.
24. It is so rugged weather that I am much afraid Elias will be put to difficulty, and be obliged to buy [wood] at the excessive Cambridge price.

30. We cannot but remark how uncommon the cold has been and continued.

### April 1780

3. The earth is as yet partly covered with snow, and where it is open, is froze.

## New Haven
### March 1780

1. An exceeding foggy day, thermometer 46.
6. Fine day. Thermometer 57. Snow dissolving apace. Flax less damnified than was feared.

7. Great rain—snow much gone.
9. Rain. N.E. storm.
10. The snow generally carried off about New Haven, and the ground bare.

12. N.E. storm, hail, snow, sleet, rain. *2"*.

16. Though the earth almost cleared of former snows; yet snow again today. *4"*.

31. For several days the snow generally gone. But a N.E. snowstorm all this day has covered the earth again with snow ankle deep. *4"*.

### April 1780

1. For several days raw and cold, although the snow is gone off. An aurora borealis night before last. Yesterday a violent N.E. snowstorm cloathed the earth again with snow ankle deep.

## Morristown
### March 1780

## Trappe
### March 1780

1. It rained hard last night and still continues, which is melting the snowdrifts and raising the streams.
2. Cold windstorm.
5. The weather is pleasant but the roads are still muddy and bad.
7. Rainy weather.
8. Today the weather is clear again and there is a cold northwest wind.

12. Snowing & hailing in the night, with the wind fresh from the northeast. In the morning the ground was covered about two inches deep.

12. Beginning last evening, and continuing through the whole night, we had a strong windstorm with cold, heavy showers of rain and they have not let up.
13. The weather is again alternately clear and dark.
14. Stormy wind again today, and as cold as winter.

15. Still cold.

16. Ground was frozen again—about sunrise it began to snow from the north or north a little westerly and continued without intermission the whole day—at the same time cold—snow about 9 inches deep.
25. Morning fine, being clear, warm, pleasant—the trees and earth being glazed looked beautiful.

16. Snow fell again during the past night and continued the whole day.
17. The snow is still on the ground and the cold penetrating.
19. Another heavy snowstorm in the evening.
20. Bitter cold.
26. Last night it was as cold as in the middle of winter.
27. In the evening a mighty windstorm arose and kept up the whole night.
28. The wind still continues.

31. Snowing more or less all day & generally pretty fast—wind though not much of it about northeast.

31. Last night it began to snow again, and it is still continuing to snow hard today.

### April 1780

### April 1780

1. The snow which fell yesterday and last night was about 9 or 10 inches deep upon a level. The morning and remainder of the day clear & pleasant overhead. Wind westerly but thawing nevertheless. Pretty good sleighing in the forenoon.
2. Hard frost—clear & very cold—wind fresh from the northwest & continued so all day. Towards evening it began to freeze hard. The snow but little dissipated.

1. The snowstorm continued through the night, and the snow is very deep. The northwest wind and the snow cause a degree of cold like that of midwinter.
2. Bitter cold from the snow, and violently stormy northwest wind.
3. The extreme cold still continues.
9. Last night we had a violent rain and thunderstorm. Beautiful sunshine today.
10. Today we have a strong and cold northwest wind again.
21. The weather is still cold and windy, and it almost seems that the fruit tree blossoms will again suffer injury as they did last year.
26. Since last night, and throughout the whole day, a heavy cold rain, mingled with snow and stormy wind, has been falling.

## WATCHING NEW YORK CITY: 1780–81

*A pretty favorable winter*

Washington's troops were strung out from Morristown to West Point and down into Connecticut during this winter as they had been for the previous two seasons. No military action took place. The main news concerned the attempted mutiny of the Pennsylvania Line and a later similar attempt by the New Jersey Line. Scanty provisions and pay in arrears caused the principal dissatisfaction. The weather proved quite mild in the first half of the winter after an unseasonable cold snap had brought a deep snow on November 1st over the Middle States and a freeze-up of the Hudson River at Albany on the 11th, an unusually early date.[1] Lt. Mackenzie of the Royal Engineers at New York City commented that the mildness of December and January rendered the roads so soft that Washington would have a hard time moving to an attack. Also, unlike the previous winter, the lack of ice in the rivers and harbor provided an additional defensive moat for the British.[2] On the 19th of January, there had been no snow at New Haven, though the interior had good sleighing.[3]

The principal weather event of the season centered in a great coastal storm which raked the Middle Atlantic coast and then cut across eastern New England. Its influence also encompassed Virginia where a "hurricane" was reported on the 22d.[4] Points as far inland as Trappe, Pennsylvania, experienced very high winds "which shook our whole house."[5] At most coastal points the first phase of the storm was attended by heavy rain, and then, with a wind shift, snow came on the wings of a northerly blow. New Haven had southeast gales on the night of the 22d; these shifted to north about 0200/23d with snow and sleet falling until mid-morning.[6] The temperature during the snow period at New Haven ran about 35°, but farther inland it was below freezing and a great snowfall took place over northern Connecticut and central Massachusetts.[8] Full details are not available as to the actual depths. Matthew Patten in southern New Hampshire, probably well north of the heavy precipitation belt, experienced "a tedious storm of snow from the northeast. It fell a foot deep. It drifted much."[9]

The observant Frederick Mackenzie caught the storm at New York:

> Jan. 22. Slight frost last night. Clear weather till 12 this day with the wind at S.W., soon after which it changed to E, and at 3 began to rain, which continued heavy till night.
>
> Jan. 23. Heavy rain and high wind 'till 2 o'clock this morning, after which it began to snow, and the wind encreased to so great a degree by 5 this Morning, that several Chimneys and the trees were blown down, and a great deal of damage done. Slight frost in the morning, which fixed the snow wherever it touched. The wind which was laterally at N.N.E. & N. did not abate till after 3 in the afternoon. Some persons were killed by the fall of Chimneys among the ruins, where many poor people have built themselves huts. About 9 inches of Snow fell.
>
> The *Grantham Packet,* bound for England, was the only vessel in the Hudson, and she rode out the gale without any accident. Several vessels in the East River were driven ashore near Brooklyn. Much damage we fear has been done by this storm, as it was the severest that has been felt here for many years.[10]

The storm struck a blow at the British fleet all along the coast. In Hampton Roads, Virginia, seven British ships of undetermined size were forced ashore by the gale on the night of the 22d. A New London dispatch related that four naval vessels were caught by the storm at Gardiners Island near the eastern end of Long Island: one drove on a reef, one rode out the gale but lost masts, a third rode it out but sprung her masts, and a fourth broke cable and had not been heard from since. At Newport a mighty 74-gun ship cast away on Brinton's Reef with the reported loss of all hands.[11]

The mild conditions existing prior to the great storm gave way to a wet and cold February. Snow covered the ground at Ipswich, Massachusetts, throughout the whole month, and the temperature dipped to zero on the 9th.[12] Next day another storm swept up the coast, depositing 10 inches at New York City and 16 inches at Ipswich. The lowest temperature at New York City this winter, according to Mackenzie, reached only +12°, or 26 degrees above the mark of the previous Hard Winter.[13] New Haven noticed a zero on the 12th. Snow cover along the coast, however, did not lay for many days, but inland apparently prodigious amounts piled up. In northeastern Connecticut, a report by J. A. Wheelock, whose family maintained a temperature record for 100 years, mentioned 15 days with snow in February 1781 and incredible depths of "eight feet on the level."[14] Confirmation of this cannot be found in any other source. Rev. Smith up in Maine had the following February notes: "1st, snow again. 5th, severe cold storm of snow. 9th extreme cold. 17th great storm of snow. 20th blustering and very cold. 24th the streets is brim full of snow, we are buried up."[15]

March continued cold and blustery. There was another "tedious storm of snow" on the 7th in southern New Hampshire,[16] and Rev. Smith commented on the 10th: "cold month thus far, good sleighing." And the snowy regime continued into April when Smith had "a great storm of snow" on the 3d.[17] This dropped another foot of new cover in New Hampshire.[18] At the commencement of April a traveller reported no snow in the Connecticut Valley south of Northampton, but from there to Bennington Pass (Wilmington, Vermont) it increased to three to four feet and was so hard that a horse could travel on it without making an impression.[19] Sleighs crossed the Connecticut River at Deerfield as late as April 10th.[20] The town historian of Goffstown, a hill location in central New Hampshire, wrote of snow being five feet deep on April 24th, so deep in the open fields that fences could not be seen.[21] If true, this would place 1781 in a class with the famous backward springs of 1785 and 1799. The final snow report of the season in this area was filed on May 9th by Matthew Patten at Bedford: "it snowed in the afternoon. It fell very fast and fell an inch or two deep."[22]

There was some minor military action in the South this winter as Cornwallis with the assistance of local Tories tried to clear eastern North Carolina of the rebels. The weather proved not a significant factor in this operation. The Moravians in central North Carolina related that the first snow of the season did not fall until the unusually late date of April 16th. A killing frost followed. The spring continued raw and cold into May—a cold front thunderstorm occurred on May 9th with rain and then some snow in its concluding phase—apparently the southern sector of the same front bringing snow to New England that May day.[23]

## NEW YORK CITY—HUGH GAINE'S JOURNAL

### December 1780

22. Some snow.
23. Still dull weather and dirty.
24. Pretty moderate, but very dirty, and like to continue.
25. Foggy.
26. Cleared up with cold weather.
27. Continues very pleasant.
28. The weather still pleasant.
29. Still uncommonly mild.
30. Very fine weather indeed.
31. Pleasant and mild.

### January 1781

1. The weather continues fine.
3. Still soft and pleasant weather.
   [no more on weather until 23d]
23. Last night a most violent gale of wind, attended with rain and snow, but did little damage besides blowing down some old walls, by which one or two women were killed and some wounded.
24. The snow extreme deep indeed!
30. Pleasant weather.

### February 1781

2. Dull foggy weather.
3. The weather dull and dirty indeed.
5. Extreme cold.
6. Frost continues, but moderate.
7. Changeable weather.
8. Moderate.
   [No more references to winter weather in Feb. or March]

---

[1] E. Stiles, *Diary*, 2, 476.
[2] F. Mackenzie, *Diary*, 2, 447, 472.
[3] E. Stiles, 2, 498.
[4] *Virginia Gaz.* (Richmond), 27 Jan 1781 ?, in E. Stiles, Ms. Thermo. Reg.
[5] H. Muhlenberg, *Journal*, 3, 394.
[6] E. Stiles, Ms. Thermo. Reg.
[7] *Conn. Gaz.* (New London), 30 Jan 1781.
[8] Ellen Larned. Ms. Weather Records. (Conn. State Lib.).
[9] M. Patten, *Diary*, 426.
[10] F. Mackenzie, 2, 469.
[11] Baltimore, 2 Feb, in *N.J. Gaz.*, 14 Feb 1781. *Conn. Gaz.*, 30 Jan, in *N.J. Gaz.*, 14 Feb 1781. Newport, 27 Jan, in *N.J. Gaz.*, 7 Feb 1781.
[12] Manasseh Cutler. *Mem. Amer. Acad. Arts Sci.* (Boston), 1, (1785), 337–39.
[13] F. Mackenzie, 2, 469.
[14] Press clipping in Ellen Larned. Ms. Weather Records 1852–1911. (Conn. State Lib.).
[15] T. Smith, *Journal*, 281.
[16] M. Patten, 428.
[17] T. Smith, 281.
[18] M. Patten, 428.
[19] E. Stiles, Ms. Thermo. Reg.
[20] *Idem.*
[21] George P. Hadley. *History of the town of Goffstown*. Concord, The Rumford Press, 1922–24. 1, 554.
[22] M. Patten, 430.
[23] *Moravians in N.C.*, 5, 1692.
F. Mackenzie, *Diary*, 2, 460.
H. Gaine, *Journal*, 2, 109.

## POST YORKTOWN, NEW JERSEY AGAIN: 1781–82

### *A pretty cold winter*

After the surrender of Cornwallis at Yorktown in October, Washington transferred his army back to the vicinity of Morristown where he watched for an opportunity to launch a strike against the long-held British base of operations in New York City. The chance never came, and no military action took place this severe winter.

The first snow of the season fell in eastern Pennsylvania on November 11th.[1] Hard winter conditions struck Down East in Maine by the 25th.² The ground in northeastern Massachusetts remained snow-covered throughout all December, an unusual circumstance, though never exceeding 3 to 4 inches.³

January produced an outstanding snowy month in eastern Massachusetts. Manasseh Cutler at Ipswich measured a total fall of 44 inches. The big storm came on the 23d when 20 inches piled up.⁴ Both these figures, if representative, were in excess of anything recorded by the Weather Bureau at nearby Boston in the modern period for a single storm or a monthly total. At Lancaster in Pennsylvania the same storm dropped 18 inches, and it is likely that similar amounts fell all along the coastal plain.⁵

A severe cold wave descended on the Northeast in the closing days of January. At Philadelphia the mercury went down to −4° on the 29th, "the coldest day in many years."⁶ Hugh Gaine at New York City made special mention of the cold that day.⁷ Hartford caught a low reading of −22° at this time, though Ezra Stiles' minimum at New Haven read only −5°.⁸

The cold and snowy regime received the attention of Dr. Muhlenberg at Trappe, Pennsylvania.

Jan. 23. It snowed the whole day today, one and a half feet deep.
   27. A fresh snow is falling on that which is already on the ground.
Feb. 2. Snowed almost the whole day.
   9. Extreme cold and cutting northwest wind.
   12. Last night we had a frightful wind storm, followed by unusually severe cold today.
   17. Good weather overhead, but thawing, bottomless slush underfoot.
   19. During the night we had a deep snowfall on the slushy ground.
Mar. 11. Six inches snow.
   22. Cold as in the middle of winter.
   28. Bitter cold as in winter.⁹

Rev. Smith's diary agreed with Dr. Muhlenberg's: "Feb. 28—A long, close, stormy and severe winter as perhaps ever was known."¹⁰

## NEW YORK CITY—HUGH GAINE'S JOURNAL

### December 1781

9. Snowy weather.
10. Dirty weather.
12. Disagreeable weather.
26. Much ice.
30. Much ice in river.

### January 1782

1. Very pleasant for the season.
3. Dirty, dull weather.
6. Foggy this day and dull indeed.
7. Still foggy weather.
12. Extreme cold indeed, with some snow and dirty weather.
13. Still very cold, with snow, hard frost and bad walking.
15. The cold continues with snow and wind.
16. Vessel drove on Robert's Reef by the ice and a sloop sunk.
20. Disagreeable weather.
24. Deep snow and very cold. Fine sleighing weather indeed.
25. The snow continues and is very cold.
27. So much snow fell today that the packet could not sail.
29. A remarkable, severe, cold day indeed, insomuch, that we have experienced nothing like it since the winter of 1779. [1779–80?].
30. The cold continues as yesterday, very severe indeed.
31. A little more moderate but not much.

### February 1782

1. Much the same weather as the day before.
2. Rather colder today.
3. Snowy weather.
4. The snow continues to lay on the ground, but not so cold as it was.
5. Very pleasant and looks for falling weather.
6. Continues uncommonly pleasant.
7. Pleasant indeed for the season.
8. Weather like for a change.
9. Very cold today, the weather having changed suddenly.
10. This day also cold, and raw weather.
17. The weather moderate.
20. The wind being easterly.
23. A very cold day indeed.
24. The cold continues with a severe frost.
25. Cold weather still continues.

### March 1782

10. Very cold.
11. Snow this day about 10 o'clock and much rain.
17. Dull and dirty weather.
18. Disagreeable weather.
19. Extreme cold indeed, with some little snow and hard frost.
20. The cold weather continues.
27. Very cold with thunder and snow!
28. Colder than yesterday, hard frost indeed.
29. Still very cold with frost.
30. So cold that I wear an overcoat.
31. Pretty pleasant and the weather becomes agreeable again.¹¹

[1] H. Muhlenberg, *Journal,* **3,** 458.
[2] T. Smith, *Journal,* 282.
[3] M. Cutler, *Mem. Amer. Acad.,* **1,** 350.
[4] *Idem.*
[5] H. Muhlenberg, **3,** 470.
[6] *The journals and papers of David Schultze,* **2,** 143.
[7] H. Gaine, *Diary,* **2,** 142.
[8] E. Stiles, *Diary,* **3,** 5.
[9] H. Muhlenberg, **3,** 470–76.
[10] T. Smith, *Journal,* 282.
[11] H. Gaine, *Dairy,* **2,** 14.

## THE FINAL WINTER: 1782–83

*A pretty broken winter*

The only military action along the Atlantic coastal plain in 1782 occurred during a skirmish in South Carolina in August. The British were occupied in evacuating Wilmington, Charleston, and Savannah. By the end of the year New York City remained the only port still in the King's hands.

In eastern Pennsylvania some snows came in December, but a rainy Christmas night melted much of the cover causing floods.[1] January ran in-and-out with a snowstorm on the 10th providing the main event of the winter.[2] This dropped a foot of snow at New Haven, and gave eastern Massachusetts its principal cover—Ipswich received most of the 23 inches measured in January in this storm.[3]

February continued the variable regime of January. An early February cold wave produced a −8° reading at Ipswich at 0800 on the 3d. After the 18th it turned quite warm. Farmers in Essex County, Massachusetts, were plowing their bare fields as early as February 21st.[4]

[1] H. Muhlenberg, **3,** 520.
[2] E. Stiles, *Diary,* **3,** 55.
[3] M. Cutler, *Mem. Amer. Acad.,* **1,** 350.
[4] *Idem.*

# THE OLD SOUTH IN THE EIGHTEENTH CENTURY

The Climate of Early Winters ............................... 139

Dr. John Lining at Old Charles-Town: 1737–1760 ............ 139

Hard Winter in 1740–41 ...................................... 140

The "Sudden Change" in 1745 ............................... 141

The Coldest Colonial Day .................................... 141

Cold Waves in 1766 and 1768 ............................... 143

Citrus Freezes of Winter 1771–72 in the Deep South ........... 144

The Washington & Jefferson Snowstorm ...................... 144

Snowy March in Maryland: 1772 ............................ 146

Cold Sabbath in February 1773 ............................. 146

White Rain in Florida During 1774 ......................... 147

The Snow Campaign of December 1775 ...................... 147

Winter of Independence: 1776–77 ........................... 148

The Hard Winter of 1780 in the South ...................... 148

The Long Freeze-up of 1784 ................................ 151

The Snowy Turn of the Century at Charleston and Savannah .... 154

Two Legendary Snowstorms: 1790 and 1798 ................. 155

Cold Waves in 1796–97 ..................................... 157

Record Southern Snows of 1800 ............................. 158

The Close of the Century—Climate Change? ................. 162

# THE CLIMATE OF EARLY WINTERS

Our knowledge of early weather conditions in the Southern Colonies in the 18th Century will always remain inadequate, tantalizingly so in view of the many spectacular winter events that occurred. There were few continuous meteorological observations over substantial periods, and no voluminous personal diaries of residents exist such as serve in the New England area to highlight the flow of major weather events. The newspapers of the early period, the *South Carolina Gazette* (1732—), the *Virginia Gazette* (1736—), and the *Maryland Gazette* (1745—), prove disappointing in the discussion of local events, though they occasionally featured happenings elsewhere in North America garnered from exchange papers. Most historical information for the period must be gathered from letters and reports of public officials, and these seldom contained meteorological intelligence. Thus, only certain outstanding events with a minimum of detail can now be reconstructed.

An early mention of severe winter conditions came from the work of John Lawson in his *History of North Carolina,* published at London in 1714:

> The fall is accompanied with cool mornings, which come in toward the latter end of August, and so continue (most commonly) very moderate weather till about Christmas then winter comes on apace. Though these seasons are very piercing, yet the cold is of no continuance. Perhaps you will have some cold weather for three or four days at a time, then pleasant, warm weather follows such as you have in England, about the latter end of April or beginning of May. In the year 1707, we had the severest winter in Carolina, that ever was known since the English came to settle there; for our rivers, that were not above a half mile wide, and fresh water, were frozen over, and some of them, in the north-part of this country, were passable for people to walk over.[1]

Lawson, as did most colonial publicists, took a most favorable view of the Carolina winter clime:

> The winter, most commonly, is so mild that it looks like an autumn, being now and then attended with clear and thain northwest winds, that are sharp enough to regulate English constitutions, and free them from a great many dangerous distempers, that a continual summer afflicts them withal, nothing being wanting as to the natural ornaments and blessings of a country, that conduce to make reasonable men happy.[2]

Another reference to an early hard winter appeared in John Brickell's work, *The Natural History of North Carolina,* though again the details were scanty:

> The weather is generally pretty moderate till after Christmas; then the winter comes on apace and continues variable 'till the middle of February, according to the winds, sometimes warm and pleasant, at other times Rain, Snow, or Frost, but the ice is seldom so strong as to bear a Man's weight.
>
> In the year 1730, we had the most agreeable and pleasant summer that has been known for many years, and the winter most severe.[3]

The first reference uncovered as to actual snowfall at Charleston, South Carolina, in the 18th Century, was contained in a letter of Charles Hart to Governor Nicholson, dated Charleston, 18 February 1726: ". . . . and the inclemency of the weather, we having more frost and deeper snow, than ever I knew since my being here."[4] A severe winter season prevailed in the Northern Colonies at this time—ice blocked the Delaware River so that no vessels could come up from the sea, and the month of *February* 1726 in eastern Massachusetts was judged a "hard" winter period.

In the next decade the *South Carolina Gazette* on *22 January 1737* carried notice of extremely cold conditions for the latitude:

> We have had so cold weather here that in one night between Tuesday and Wednesday the water in the creeks and ponds in and about Town, was frozen near three inches thick.

[1] John Lawson. *The history of Carolina.* London, 1714. Reprint: *Lawson's History of North Carolina.* Richmond, Garrett and Massie, 1937, 89.
[2] *Ibid.,* 176.
[3] John Brickell. *The natural history of North Carolina.* Dublin, 1737. Reprint: J. Bryan Grimes, ed. Raleigh, Trustees of the Public Library, 1911.
[4] Charles Hart to Governor Nicholson, 2 Feb. 1726. *Colonial Papers.* 30 (1726–27), 21.

## DR. JOHN LINING AT OLD CHARLES-TOWN: 1737–1760

The distinction of being the first person in the British North American Colonies to take a series of regular observations with meteorological instruments over a substantial period has generally been accorded to Dr. John Lining (1708–1760), a Scottish physician who came to South Carolina about 1730. A man of wide scientific interests, he published accounts of contemporary yellow fever epidemics, studied the effects of climate on his own metabolism, and conducted experiments with electricity while corresponding with Benjamin Franklin in Philadelphia.[1]

Dr. Lining's records, along with those of his successors, cover an extended period of more than 20 years, and much of the general results have been preserved, unlike many long-lost and lamented colonial meteorological records. Others did precede Lining in taking records for short periods, but none was made regularly over a long period and in such a sophisticated manner that they would be of scientific value today.

These valuable instrumental records included temperature, barometric pressure, humidity, wind direction, and precipitation. Lining's chief interest lay in human physiology and not in an attempt to describe and explain meteorological causes and events. The regular records commenced as early as April 1737 and continued at least until February 1753 and probably longer. Though the original daily manuscripts have not been preserved, adequate summaries in sufficient detail were sent to London at the time and extracts published, so that some data on comparative winter conditions can now be deduced. Lining's summaries appeared in the *Philosophical Transactions of the Royal Society of London* in 1748 and 1753.[2]

A second set of Charleston observations ran from 1750 to 1759. These were published in 1776 through the pages of Dr. Lionel Chalmers' *Account of the Weather and Diseases of South Carolina*.[3] They were generally attributed to the author who served as an associate of Dr. Lining in the apothecary trade. It cannot now be firmly established whether part of these were cooperative or wholly the work of Chalmers. Nevertheless, the two combined series gave more than twenty years of climatological data in much better form than any other American location possessed at that time.

Weekly and monthly reports appeared from time to time in the *South Carolina Gazette* in the 1750's, but these ceased in March 1761.[4] Though it was known that thermometers continued to be read and rain gages occasionally checked for the next 30 years, this most likely was not done on a regular basis as no such records remain except a scattering of reports in the press in the late 1780's. Not until 1791, when the Medical Society of South Carolina initiated a new series, has a set of regular daily temperature observations been preserved.[5]

[1] Robert C. Aldredge. Ms. Weather observers and observations at Charleston, South Carolina, 1670–1871. (Library, U. S. Weather Bureau, Wash., D.C.)

[2] Extracts of two letters from Dr. John Lining, physician at Charles-Town in South Carolina, to James Jurin, M.D., F.R.S., giving an account of statistical experiments made several times a day upon himself for one whole year, accompanied with meteorological observations, to which are subjoined six general tables, deduced from the whole year's course. Charles-Town, Jan. 22 1740/41. Read May 19, 1743. Royal Society. *Phil. Trans. Vol. 42 for the years 1742 and 1743*, 491–509.
A letter from Dr. John Lining to C. Mortimer M.D. Sec. R.S. concerning the weather in South-Carolina; with abstracts of the tables of his meteorological observations in Charles-Town. Read May 6, 1748. *Trans. Royal Society for the year 1748*. 45, 336–44.
A letter from John Lining, M.D. of Charles-Town, South-Carolina, to Rev. Thomas Birch, D.D. Secr. R.S. concerning the quantity of rain fallen there from January 1738, to December 1752. Charles-Town, April 9, 1753. Read July 8, 1753. *Trans. Royal Society of London for the year 1753*. 48–1, 284–85.

[3] Lionel Chalmers. *An account of the weather and disease of South Carolina*. London, Edward & Charles Dilly, 1776.

[4] R. C. Aldredge, Ms. Weather observers, 58.

[5] *Ibid.*, 62.

## HARD WINTER IN 1740–41

The two standout winters of the 18th Century in the North occurred in 1740–41 and 1779–80, and these had their counterparts in the South.[1] From the records of John Lining, commenced three years previously, there were temperature data as to the extremities of cold reached during the first of these severe winters. Cold waves reached Charleston in both December 1740 and in February 1741, following the general pattern of the winter in the North—a severe start and ending with a changeable January intervening. In December the minimum as noticed by Lining was 21°, in January only 34°, and in February 25°. The month of December averaged 42°, according to his calculations, or a depression of 10 degrees from the 24-year normal averaged from 1738 to 1761. This figure equaled the coldest December in the span and also equaled the mark as the second coldest month of any name. January had an average 4.2 degrees below normal, and February relapsed with a 7.0-degree minus departure.[2] The three winter months in 1740–41 comprised the coldest season in the early Charleston records. There would be colder single months and more extreme readings on a single day, but the prolonged cold continued in the South as in the North this winter, to mark it as a standout in the century.

Severe weather prevailed as far south as Savannah

## OLD SOUTH—EIGHTEENTH CENTURY

SYMBOLS

| | |
|---|---|
| + + | Much above normal, 12.5% |
| + | Above normal, 25% |
| N | Near normal, 25% |
| − | Below normal, 25% |
| − − | Much below normal, 12.5% |

| | Dec. | Jan. | Feb. | Season |
|---|---|---|---|---|
| 1737–38 |  | + + | N |  |
| 38–39 | − | N | N | − |
| 39–40 | + | − | + | + |
| 40–41 | − − | − | − − | − − |
| 41–42 |  | + | − − |  |
| 42–43 | N | − | + | − |
| 43–44 | − | + | + | N |
| 44–45 | − | − − |  | − − |
| 45–46 | − | − | N | − |
| 46–47 | N | + + | − | + |
| 47–48 | + + | − − | N | N |
| 48–49 | + + | N | + | + |
| 49–50 | + | + | + | + + |
| 50–51 | N | − | N | N |
| 51–52 | + | − − | + + | N |
| 52–53 | N | + | + + | + + |
| 53–54 | + | + + | + | + + |
| 54–55 | + | + | − − | N |
| 55–56 | − | + + | + + | + + |
| 56–57 | N | − | N |  |
| 57–58 | + | + | − | + |
| 58–59 | − − | − − |  | − − |
| 59–60 | − | N | + | N |
| 60–61 | N | N | − | − |

Source: *World Weather Records.* H. H. Clayton, ed.

this winter. Colonel William Stephens left an important meteorological document in his official records relating both of deep snow and severe cold:

Dec. 6. Tuesday—A great snow began falling early this morning before day, which continued to do so till near ten o'clock, by which time it was four or five inches thick on the ground; but notwithstanding that, though the Sun did not shine, towards mid-day it began to waste and before noon it was all gone suddenly, without any mark of it being left.[3]

Jan. 4. In the evening the rigour of the weather seemed to abate, and a change was expected, after eight or nine days of continuance of the severest frost that has been known by any person now living here.[4]

During the next two decades there were only two winters in a class with the low average of 44.3° achieved in 1740–41. These came in 1744–45 (47.6°), rating third among early winters for coldness, and 1758–59 (45.0°), rating second.[5] But the winter of 1752 had the distinction of producing the coldest single calendar month with a January figure of 41°, or 8.2 degrees below normal. The coldest two consecutive months came in December 1758–January 1759. This winter definitely put an end to the series of mainly mild seasons prevailing since 1751–52. The middle years of this decade in the North, too, ran notably mild, i.e., from 1752–53 to 1755–56.

A graphic representation of the relative cold for each winter month for which records were available is presented in the accompanying table.

[1] See pages 48–54, 111–133.
[2] J. Lining, *Phil. Trans. 1742–43, No. 42,* 491.
[3] Journal of Col. William Stephens. *The colonial records of Georgia.* 4, supplement (1908), 36.
[4] *Ibid.,* 61.
[5] *World Weather Records.* H. H. Clayton, ed. Smithsonian Miscellaneous Collections No. 79. Reprint: Wash., D.C., The Smithsonian Institution, 1944. Pub. No. 2913, 823–24.

### THE "SUDDEN CHANGE" IN 1745

Governor Glen devoted considerable space in his *Description of South Carolina* (1761) to instances of extreme cold and its influence on the health and comfort of residents of Charleston.[1] While maintaining his own records from 1738 to 1741, the lowest reading noticed was 21°. The same figure appeared in the Lining records for December 1740. But since that time, Glen related, "I have frequently seen the thermometer much lower."[2] He referred to the "sudden change" in January 1745 and the extreme freeze in February 1748.

Of the first instance in 1745, Dr. John Lining wrote:

It frequently happens that one day is ten or more degrees warmer than the preceding day. But the decrease of heat are always greater & more sudden than its increase. On the 10th of January at 2 p.m. the mercury in the thermometer was at 70. Next morning it had sank to the 26th degree. On the 12th in the morning it was at 15, which was the greatest and most sudden change I have seen.[3]

[1] James Glen. *A description of South Carolina.* London, 1761. Reprint: *Colonial South Carolina.* Chapman J. Milling, ed. Columbia, S. C., Univ. of South Carolina Press, 1951, 17.
[2] *Ibid.,* 17.
[3] J. Lining, Ms., 30 Sept 1746. (Aldredge 143.)

### THE COLDEST COLONIAL DAY

The second instance of intense cold in the 1740's received notice in another letter which Dr. Lining later addressed to the Royal Society:

Since I sent the abstract of my meteorological tables to the Royal Society, I have seen Fahrenheits thermometer in the shade once down at 10th degree.[1]
Charles Town, 9 April 1753

Governor Glen also made reference to this coldest of colonial days and apparently relied on Dr. Lining's instrument for his data:

> In my table of thermometrical observations, 21 degrees is the lowest station of the thermometer but since that time for which that table was formed [1738–41], I have frequently seen the thermometer much lower; particularly on the 6th of February 1747, at 8 o'clock in the morning, it was at the tenth degree, and no doubt had been lower some hours before that, as the spirits in the thermometer were then rising, the air being warmed by the sun.[2]

Governor Glen's statement that the coldest period in his experience occurred in 1747 has left a false impression among later writers as to the correct dating of this most important event in the early meteorological history of winters at Charleston. The event occurred on either 17 or 18 February 1748, according to our present calendar reckoning. It was the custom under Old Style, prior to 1752, to commence the new year on March 25th. Some wrote the year as 1747/48 when discussing events in January, February or March, but others neglected to use the double indication of years, resulting in great confusion. Later Carolina historians have repeated Glen's dating without questioning its correctness.

We cannot be sure of the exact date as Governor Glen in one place referred to the 17th and in another paragraph to the 18th. Dr. Lining made no statement as to the exact day or year.

There existed good meteorological evidence that the extreme cold in the South could have occurred only in 1748. The 17th of February 1748 in the North received notice in newspapers and had been mentioned in diaries as an extremely cold day with strong northerly winds blowing. On the other hand, 17 February 1747, in the Winthrop temperature record at Cambridge, Massachusetts, seemed a mild winter's day.[3] No other thermometer record for these two years has been located, though such instruments were in use in Philadelphia and New York City.

It would be meteorologically improbable to have a +10° reading at Charleston, South Carolina, on the same day that Cambridge, Massachusetts, stood above 32°. The only circumstance for such a latitudinal inversion would be the presence of a very marked storm system off the Middle Colonies with a strong warm front over northern New England and a sharp cold front over the Middle Colonies separating warm, maritime air over southern New England from an Arctic air stream reaching the West and South. But this situation did not exist on 17 February 1747 as the Winthrop records clearly indicated. A year later in 1748 a very cold period did occur at Cambridge in February, characteristic of those prolonged cold spells when frigid air occupies the entire Atlantic seaboard from New England to Florida.

In view of the above, the date for Charleston's coldest weather of the 18th Century must be placed in February 1748. Additional evidence existed in the inclusion of 1748 among the list of cold winters traditionally repeated by Louisiana historians when intensely cold weather caused the orange trees to perish.[4]

The +10° or lower achieved in February 1748 at Charleston ranked with the +7° obtained by the U. S. Weather Bureau in February 1899 and takes second place only to the near-zero readings indicated on various local thermometers in the Great Arctic Outbreak of 1835 at Charleston.[5] The lowest figure of the 20th Century (1901–1964) at the Weather Bureau's downtown location at the edge of the harbor reached +12° in December 1917.[6]

In the first period of records at Charleston, the mercury descended below 20° on four occasions: January 1739 to +19°, January 1745, +15°, February 1748, +10°, and January 1752, +18°.[7]

Later colonial writers in Carolina made mention of low temperatures of their experience. Both Chalmers and Milligen had witnessed a low of +18° in January 1752: "the lowest station of the thermometer for these ten years was 18°."[8] Alexander Hewatt, publishing in 1779 though probably composing his material prior to the war, mentioned a low of +16°.[9] Perhaps this occurred in 1766 during the citrus freeze in northern Florida, or in another damaging cold period in 1771–72. During the Hard Winter of 1780 the mercury went at least as low as +17°, and this mark received acceptance by David Ramsay from his personal meteorological experiences at Charleston in the 1790's as the lowest generally reached for the area.[10]

Governor Glen added some interesting details to illustrate the degree of severity of the cold in 1748:

> The first instance of intense cold that I shall mention, relates to a healthy young person of my family, who at the time was two or three and twenty years of age and usually slept in a room without a fire: that person carried two quart bottles of hot water to bed, which was of down and covered with English blankets; the bottles were between the sheets but in the morning they were both split to pieces, and the water solid lumps of ice.
> In the kitchen where there was a fire, the water in a jar, in which there was a live eel, was frozen to the bottom and I found several small birds frozen to death near my house; they could not have died for want of food, the frost having been but of one day's continuance.
> But the effect much to be regretted, is, that it destroyed almost all the orange trees in the country; I lost three hundred bearing trees, and an olive tree of such a prodigious size, that I thought it proof against all weathers; it was near a foot and half

diameter in the trunk, and bore many bushels of excellent olives every year.

This frost happened on the 7th of February 1747; and the winter having been mild with us till then, the juices were so far risen that the orange trees were ready to blossom; under which circumstances that frost burst all their vessels, for not only the bark of all of them were split, and all on the side next the sun.

Last year, however, many of them shot up again from the root, and I have measured many shoots, which were twelve to fifteen feet in height, and of a tolerable thickness!—a surprising instance of vegetation in a few months and though about the first week of January in this winter we had a pretty smart frost of two or three days continuance, with some snow, it did not injure the tenderest shoots; but a month after we had another smart frost, when the juices were rising, and that has quite killed most of the shoots.[11]

[1] J. Glen, *Description*, 19.
[2] *Idem.*
[3] J. Winthrop, Ms. Met. Obs. 1742–1779 (Harvard); *Boston News-Letter*, 11 Feb 1748.
[4] Alcee Fortier. *A history of Louisiana.* New York, Manzi, Joyant & Co., 2, 12.
[5] D. M. Ludlum. *Early American Winters: 1821–1870.* (In press.)
[6] U. S. Dept. Commerce, Weather Bureau. *Local climatological data with comparative data. 1964. Charleston, South Carolina.* Asheville, N. C., 1965. 2.
[7] J. Lining; L. Chalmers.
[8] George Milligen-Johnston. *A short description of the province of South-Carolina with an account of the air, weather, and diseases at Charles-Town.* London, 1770. Reprint *Colonial South Carolina.* Chapman J. Milling, ed. Columbia, S. C., Univ. South Carolina Press, 1951. 106.
[9] Alexander Hewatt. *An historical account of the rise and progress of the colonies of South Carolina and Georgia.* London, 1779.
[10] *S. Car. and Amer. Gen. Adv.* (Charleston), 19 Jan 1780; David Ramsay. *The history of South Carolina from its first settlement to 1808.* Charleston, 1809. Reprint: Spartanburg, S. C., The Reprint Co., 1960. (1858 ed.) 2, 30.
[11] J. Glen, *Description*, 17–19.

## COLD WAVES IN 1766 AND 1768

The concluding third of the 18th Century brought several instances of severe winter conditions to Southern areas. It is not clear whether these were indicative of a new climate trend setting in, or whether our documentation becomes more complete as the colonies grew in population and affluence. Contemporary accounts suffered from lack of any continuous temperature records. Not until the last decade of the century were thermometers read on a regular basis in the Deep South. Evidence of particularly cold periods in 1766 and 1768, however, was put down by contemporary writers.

### 1766

A documented cold wave at Charleston occurred early in January 1766. The *Journal of Ann Manigault* contained the following:

Jan. 4. Cloudy cold day. Snowed very hard at night.
5. Exceedingly cold. Sometimes snow, wind and drizzly.
6. Very cold and clear.[1]

John Bartram of Philadelphia, a pioneer American naturalist, happened to be in the South at this time. He had stopped at Charleston for some days and made a few notes about the climate and weather of the region, as was his wont. He noted that snowstorms were not unknown and snow could lie for two to three days, but "this is uncommon."[2] On the days of extreme cold in January 1766, Bartram was on the St. Johns River south of Lake Georgia in northeastern Florida. His diary entry, dated Clement's Bluff, January 3d, related:

Clear cold morning; thermometer 26. Wind NW. The ground was froze an inch thick on the banks: this was the fatal night that destroyed the lime, citron, and banana trees in Augustine, many curious evergreens up the river, that were near 20 years, and in a flourishing state.[3]

A later climatologist of Jacksonville assigned a reading of 20° to the local scene for 3 January 1766, a figure which would place the day among the ten coldest in the past 200 years at the Florida city. He stated that the orange trees were not destroyed, but most tender products did perish.[4]

[1] Extracts from the journal of Ann Manigault. *The S.C. Hist. & Gen. Mag.* (Charleston), 20–3 (July 1919), 209.
[2] John Bartram. Diary of a journey through the Carolinas, Georgia, and Florida. Francis Harper, ed. *Trans. Amer. Philo. Soc.* (Phila), ns. 33–1 (1942). 20.
[3] *Ibid.*, 39.
[4] T. Frederick Davis. Climatology of Jacksonville, Florida, and vicinity. *Monthly Weather Review,* (Wash., D.C.). 23 (Sept. 1895), 337.

### 1768

The winter of 1768 (probably 1767–68) was included in the group of three early winters in Louisiana that killed the orange trees.[1] Dr. John Monette in his manuscript physical history of the Mississippi Valley supplied more details of this winter though he did not divulge his sources.² On January 17–18 ice was seen floating in the Mississippi River at Natchez, and at New Orleans ice formed several yards from the shore while the orange trees were killed. Confirmation of the degree of cold sufficient to form ice and kill citrus trees came from Dr. J. Lorimer who chanced to have a thermometer at the British outpost of Pensacola in West Florida.³ Lorimer took thrice daily observations, and somehow a record of these for 1768 found its way to the American Philosophical Society in Philadelphia where they were published in the *Transactions* for the year 1771. The lowest reading of +17° came presumably in the January cold wave that Dr. Monette had mentioned.

[1] Alcee Fortier. *History of Louisiana*. New York, Manzi, Joyant & Co., 1904.
[2] John Monette Mss. 4–6, 321. (Clements, Univ. of Mich.)
[3] Extracts of a letter from Dr. J. Lorimer of West Florida to Hugh Williamson, M.D., Pensacola, 7 Jan 1769. *Trans. Amer. Phil. Soc.* (Phila.). 1–2 (1771), 251.

## CITRUS FREEZES OF WINTER 1771–72 IN THE DEEP SOUTH

Louisiana historians have included the winter of 1772 (presumably 1771–72) in their lists of severe seasons, although local details were always lacking. From other sources we learn that conditions proved hard on citrus in all the Deep South. Bernard Romans in *A concise history of East and West Florida* (1776) mentioned apple and pear trees being killed in West Florida in the winter of 1771–72, but again gave no dates or details.¹ Thomas Jefferson stated in his *Garden Book* that orange trees in South Carolina died from the cold in 1771 (presumably December of that year).²

A document containing some meteorological detail pinpointed one of the severely cold periods at the close of December 1771 in Savannah:

> Savannah, 29 Dec. 1771—I believe that I mentioned in my last that we have had 4 or 5 days of the most severe weather I ever knew in Georgia, and perhaps anywhere else, however. I am sure I found it so. It began with a cold rain, which soon turned into a frozen sleet, afterwards snow, and which froze so intensely, that for 2 or 3 days, the boys were sliding upon the sundry streets and squares of this town. You will say this was an unusual phenomenon in this climate, and if it had continued much longer, it probably would have produced fatal consequences among our Negroes.³

Toward the end of January 1772 the great snowstorm raged over North Carolina and Virginia of which Thomas Jefferson, George Washington, and others left full accounts. The circulation stirred up by this tempest opened the way for Arctic air streams to penetrate into the Southland. The Journals of David Taitt on 3 February 1772 related: "This morning we had some snow and a very hard frost."⁴ Taitt wrote from the Escambia River about four days travel (50 miles) north of Pensacola in southern Alabama. At Charleston the always-too-brief pen of Ann Manigault informed: "Feb. 7—Very cold weather."⁵

[1] Bernard Romans. *A concise history of East and West Florida*. New York, 1776, 10.
[2] *Thomas Jefferson's Garden Book 1766–1824*. Edwin M. Betts, ed. Phila., The American Philosophical Society, 1944. 78.
[3] The letters of Hon. James Habersham, 1756–1775. *Coll. Ga. Hist. Soc.* 6 (1904), 159.
[4] Journal of David Taitt. *Travels in the American Colonies*. Newton D. Mereness, ed. N. Y., The Macmillan Co., 1916, 498.
[5] Jour. Ann Manigault, 21, 59.

## THE WASHINGTON & JEFFERSON SNOWSTORM

George Washington maintained a separate diary at various times during his private and public careers which he called "An account of the weather." The first entries of this type appeared in January 1767, and the last was penned almost a third of a century later on the day preceding his death in December 1799.¹ Washington's chief concern with the weather related directly to its effect on his agricultural interests. When away from his beloved plantation at Mt. Vernon, he usually requested his overseer to send a weekly summary of recent weather conditions so that he could judge its effect on the progress of his crops. Many of these diaries have been preserved in the Library of Congress though they were not published when the great mass of Washingtoniana was collected and printed at the first president's bicentennial in 1932. Many important meteorological events were witnessed and described by Washington, and his statements on these give the facts an air of authenticity.

Fortunately for the climatological history of the District of Columbia area, our first president-to-be was home at Mt. Vernon in late January 1772 when the greatest snowstorm in the history of the middle and lower Potomac Valley occurred. His diary entries from January 26th to 29th supply a graphic account of the event:

January 26—Raw, cold, and cloudy with the wind tho not much of it Northerly

January 27—A snow which began in the night and was about 5 or 6 inches deep this morning kept constantly at it the whole day with the wind hard and cold from the northward

January 28—The same snow continued all last night and all this day with equal violence the wind being very cold and hard from the Northward drifting snow into banks

January 29—Fine pleasant morning without any wind—but before 11 o'clock it clouded up & threatened snow all the remaining part of the day—being full three feet deep everywhere already [2]

In his regular diary Washington described the day of the 27th as "dreadfully bad" and complained that he was confined to his home on both the 27th and 28th. The following day he related that "with much difficulty rid as far as the Mill, the snow being up to the breast of a Tall Horse everywhere." [3] In a subsequent letter, dated 21 February, Washington wrote: ". . . would be shut up for ten or twelve days, by the deepest snow which I suppose the oldest living ever remembers to have seen in this country." [4]

Evidence from other sources has been gathered to indicate that George, indeed, was not telling a lie about the storm or the depth of the snow. The *Maryland Gazette* of Annapolis, the nearest newspaper published to present-day Washington, commented on 30 January 1772:

> The winter has in general been very mild until Sunday evening last when it began to snow, which continued without intermission until Tuesday night. Yesterday morning we had again the appearance of fine moderate weather, but in the evening it began to snow very fast which continued all night; tis supposed the depth where not drifted is upwards of three feet, and it is with utmost difficulty people pass from one house to another.[5]

To the south at Williamsburg the deep snow prevented many of the county burgesses from reaching the Virginia colonial capital, so the meeting of the General Assembly had to be postponed.[6] The local *Virginia Gazette* complained about the stoppage of the postal service from the North; it was not until 5 March, five weeks after the storm, that it was able to carry news from a northern source.[7]

Our southernmost check-point for the storm is Bethabara, North Carolina, near present-day Winston-Salem. The Moravian Brethren had established an outpost there in the 1750's and chronicled all the important events, meteorological and otherwise, which befell their frontier community. The Bethabara Diary indicates that rain commenced about 0900 on 26 January 1772 and turned to snow in the evening. Snow fell all the following day, piling up a cover of six inches; toward night clearing set in and it froze.[8] Thus, precipitation commenced in North Carolina about twelve hours before it reached Mount Vernon in northern Virginia, a distance of about 250 miles.

That the storm reached westward to the Blue Ridge Mountains of Virginia is well-known to anyone who has visited Monticello and read the historical marker on Jefferson's honeymoon cottage. The owner of that grand weather observation point had been married on New Year's Day of 1772. After a leisurely journey from Charles City during which they stopped with friends along the way, Jefferson and his bride neared their home on the afternoon of the 26th. Most biographers state that Jefferson arrived at Monticello on 25 January. In view of the above meteorological evidence, it appears that he returned from his honeymoon late on the 26th, the evening of the day on which the big snow commenced. A light fall had started and soon so increased in intensity that the bridal couple were forced to abandon their carriage at Blenheim, about eight miles from Monticello, and to pursue the remainder of the way on horseback over a mountain trail, all the while the storm increased in fury making progress very difficult. As his daughter in later years related, "they arrived late at night, the fires all out and the servants retired to their houses for the night. The horrible dreariness of such a house, at the end of such a journey, I have often heard both relate." [10]

In his *Garden Book* entry for 26 January Jefferson made note: "the deepest snow we have ever seen. in Albemarle it was about 3. f. deep." [11] In later years he referred to this storm several times as exceeding anything that he recorded in his regular *Weather Memorandum Book,* which commenced in 1776 with the purchase of a thermometer on 1 July at Philadelphia.[12]

The writer happened across another reference to this storm which confirms the measurement of Washington and Jefferson and also indicates that the snow pattern was quite similar to that of the "Knickerbocker" storm of 1922.* In the columns of the Philadelphia *United States Gazette* for 27 June 1818 appeared a letter recalling big storms and severe winters of the past. It was written by a resident of Winchester, Virginia, at the northern head of the Shenandoah Valley, and originally appeared in the *Winchester Gazette*. For 1772 the correspondent remembered:

> The fall of this present winter until the 27th January, the most pacific winter ever known since the memory of man. On the 27th and 28th of this month there fell a snow exceeding all ever known for the space of a hundred years. I measured it and it was 2 feet 9 inches deep.[13]

* The Knickerbocker Storm, Washington's greatest of the modern era, deposited a 28-inch blanket on 27–28 January 1922, exactly 150 years to the day after the Washington & Jefferson Storm. It was so named from the collapse of the overburdened roof of the Knickerbocker Theater which killed more than 100 movie patrons.

Contemporary weather reports from farther north indicate that the snow canopy of 1772 was much like that of 1922 in that the very deep snowfall did not reach much farther north than the Mason-Dixon Line. Good instrumental records for 1772 are at hand for Philadelphia. At 0900 on the 27th of January the temperature was 18°, wind northeast, and barometer 30.50 inches—it commenced to snow an hour later. After a stormy night the snow had ceased to fall by 0900 on the 28th, but the total snow accumulation was not considered noteworthy.[14]

[1] George Washington. Ms. Account of the weather 1772. (LC.)
[2] Idem.
[3] *The diaries of George Washington. 1748–1799.* John C. Fitzpatrick, ed. Boston & New York, Houghton Mifflin Co., 1925. **2**, 52.
[4] *The writings of George Washington.* John C. Fitzpatrick, ed. Wash., D.C., GPO, 1931. **3**, 79.
[5] *Md. Gaz.* (Annapolis), 30 Jan 1772.
[6] *Va. Gaz.* (Williamsburg), 6 Feb 1772.
[7] *Ibid.*, 5 March 1772.
[8] *Moravians in N.C.*, **2**, 669.
[9] T. Jefferson. Ms. Weather memorandum book. (LC.)
[10] *The domestic life of Thomas Jefferson.* Sarah N. Randolph, ed. N.Y., Harper & Bros., 1871. 44–45.
[11] T. Jefferson, *Garden Book*, 33.
[12] T. Jefferson. Ms. Weather memorandum book.
[13] *Winchester* (Va.) *Gazette* in *U.S. Gaz.* (Phila.), 27 June 1818.
[14] Thomas Coombe. Ms. Register of the weather Anno 1772. (Amer. Phil. Soc.)

## SNOWY MARCH IN MARYLAND: 1772

Charles Carroll, a signer of the Declaration of Independence, lived at Carrollton in Howard County, Maryland, for most of his life. In his autobiographical notes he left a very informative account of the three major snowstorms which swept the Middle Colonies and New England in March of 1772, prolonging an already severe winter to the very start of spring:

> March 11. It began to snow this morning between 4 & 5 a Clock, I measured it a 9 a Clock in one of our walks & it was 9 inches deep so that for the time it must have fallen in more abundance than the *great snow* in January. It is now 12 a clock and it continues to snow, but moderately with an appearance of its ceasing.
> March 17. It snowed here the 12th & 13th. I sent my man into the woods to measure the snow and found it to be 17 inches deep.
> I may say that the Planters here have lost two months work, & I apprehend the loss in stock of all sorts will be great.
> March 20. Snow again yesterday & continued to this time (1100)—wind NE. Little of fall of 11th gone. I think with this addition it is at least 20 inches deep. It has been warm from the 10th. It ceased to snow about 2 a clock.[1]

[1] Carroll Papers. *Md. Hist. Mag.* 14–2 (June 1919), 138–39.

## COLD SABBATH IN FEBRUARY 1773

The Arctic air mass which produced one of Ezra Stiles three coldest days of the century in New England also swept southward on the wings of a snowstorm to strike Charleston a wintry blow.[1] The *South Carolina Gazette* took notice of the sudden descent of winter and then its rapid retreat, following the same pattern that occurred in the North at this time:

> Charleston—On Sunday and Monday the 21st and 22d past we have had the greatest fall of snow here that has been known by any person living. The mercury on Fahrenheit's thermometer fell so low as to 19 degrees. We had some warm weather since, and yesterday was like a May Day.[2]

Ann Manigault also left short testimony to her double hardship during these days:

> Feb. 21. A very bad day, sleet and a little snow.
> 22. A deal of snow all day, high wind and extremely cold.
> 23. A very cold day.
> 24. A very bad day. . . . Such deep snow that we could not bury her until the 24th.
> 25. Bad days.
> 26. " "
> 27. A fine day.[3]

Writing in the same year about conditions in Georgia, Sir James Wright stated briefly:

> In January, February, March common winter weather and sometimes intensely cold and the mercury in the thermometer has been down at 20, but usually from 25 to 30.[4]

[1] Ezra Stiles. Ms. Thermo. Reg. (Yale.)
[2] *S.C. Gaz.*, 1 March 1773.
[3] *Jour. Ann Manigault*, 21, 62–63.
[4] Report of Sir James Wright on the condition of the province of Georgia, on 20th Sept. 1773. *Coll. Ga. Hist. Soc.* **3** (1873), 159.

## WHITE RAIN IN FLORIDA DURING 1774

The year 1774 was famous in Florida for a snowstorm—the only such instance mentioned by early Anglo-Saxon writers until the year 1800. John Lee Williams, the historian of Florida's colonial and territorial days, with true Chamber of Commerce euphemism, referred to "an extraordinary white rain" which spread over an unspecified part of the peninsula on an unspecified day in 1774:

> In 1774, there was a snow storm, which extended over most of the Territory. The ancient inhabitants still speak of it as an extraordinary white rain. It was said to have done little damage.[1]

The only other contemporary reference to winter conditions in the region, so far uncovered, appeared in a diary entry at Ebenezer, Georgia, on 20 November 1774: "Last night the ice froze to the depth of a fingerbreadth and now a few flakes of snow and cold rain are falling which is something very unusual here."[2]

[1] John L. Williams. *The territory of Florida: or sketches of the topography, civil and natural history, of the country, the climate, and the Indian tribes, from the first discovery to the present time, with a map, views &c.* N. Y., A. T. Goodrich, 1837, 17.
[2] *Journal of Henry Muhlenberg*, **2**, 625.

## THE SNOW CAMPAIGN OF DECEMBER 1775

The first military action of the War of the Revolution in the Southern Colonies consisted of some skirmishing toward the end of 1775 between the recently mobilized Carolina and Georgia militia and small bands of British and Tories. The final phase of this action became known ever afterwards as "The Snow Campaign,"[1] when a pre-Christmas storm dropped a remarkably deep snow cover over the interior of the Southern Colonies, matching in depth anything occurring in the modern records of the Weather Bureau for the area.

"On the 23d, Col. Thompson with his detachment and prisoners, returned to Col. Richardson's camp; when it commenced snowing which continued without intermission for thirty hours, covering the ground generally two feet deep."[2] This statement by John Drayton in his *Memoirs of the American Revolution* supplied the main facts known about the event. The camp was located at the Great Cane Brake on the Reedy River in western South Carolina. Confirmation of the dating and of the severity of the event can be found in the Moravian *Diary* entry for December 23d: "The stormy weather continued, and the snow fell 1½ feet deep."[3] Capt. Hugh McCall in his *History of Georgia* (1811) also spoke of the storm as extending into his state with a very deep blanket of white, presumably in the upcountry:

> On the night of the 25th was a great fall of snow, supposed to be deeper on the ground, than what had ever been witnessed in the southern provinces. In Georgia it was generally eighteen inches deep; and from this circumstance it was called the *snow campaign*. The troops having no tents, and generally, not well provided with thick clothing, suffered severely. When the Georgia troops were discharged, they had to march one hundred miles knee deep in the snow.[4]

The snowfall was probably confined to the Piedmont region where temperature conditions were just right for frozen precipitation. This storm system most likely was one and the same that brought a welcome Christmas Eve snow in the Albany, New York, area where young Henry Knox was struggling to bring the captured Ticonderoga cannon over the hills to assist in the siege of Boston. He reported a snowfall of two feet by Christmas Day—apparently this storm was a snow producer of the first rank.

John Drayton related that for seven days following Christmas the Carolina and Georgia troops marched on snow, but on the eighth day a cold rain mixed with sleet fell, resulting in a thaw and freshets as the heavy ground snow melted.[5] Thomas Jefferson, then at Monticello in Virginia, also took notice of the wintry conditions existing throughout the South at this time: ". . . in December 1775 & January 1776 there was a frost of four or five weeks duration, the earth being frozen like a rock the whole time. This killed all the olives."[6]

[1] Hugh T. Lefler and Albert R. Newsome. *The History of a Southern State. North Carolina.* Chapel Hill, Univ. North Carolina Press, 1963. 198.
[2] John Drayton. *Memoirs of the American Revolution.* Charleston, A. E. Miller, 1821. **2**, 135.
[3] *Moravians in N. Car.*, **2**, 908.
[4] Hugh McCall. *The history of Georgia, containing brief sketches of the most remarkable events up to the present day (1784).* Savannah, 1811–16. Reprint: Atlanta, A. B. Caldwell, 1909, 295.
[5] J. Drayton. *Memoirs*, 132.
[6] T. Jefferson. *Garden Book*, 77.

## WINTER OF INDEPENDENCE: 1776–77

Thomas Jefferson, after penning the Declaration of Independence at Philadelphia, had taken his newly-purchased thermometer and his weather register back to Monticello in west-central Virginia where he kept a faithful watch on the weather. His *Garden Book* contained an entry for March 10th summarizing the past winter:

> the fall of last year was fine. the first snow fell 20th December, but did not lay a day. the day before Christmas the weather set in cold. Christmas night a snow fell 22 I. deep and from that time till the 7th March was the coldest weather & upon the whole the severest winter remembered. from the 20th December to the 6th March fell ten snows to cover the ground, and some of them deep. the 9th of March I think was the first rain of this year. the rivers all that time so low that there could be no water for transportation above the falls. the 10th March is the first day we can do any thing in the garden. Scarse any appearance of vegetation yet.[1]

The big event of the winter came on Christmas Day 1776. As far south as central North Carolina the Moravians at Salem reported "shoe-top" snow on Christmas night, and at Freidberg nearby the depth amounted to "more than a foot."[2] Thomas Jefferson related in his manuscript Weather Book that a deep snow of 22 inches visited the area on Christmas night, and later referred to this storm which "fell in one night 24 inches deep." Jefferson's thermometer read 23.5° at 0915 and 30° at 1500 on Christmas Day, good snow-making conditions.[3]

Another witness of the storm was Nicholas Cresswell, a British prisoner passing his captivity at Pennroyal Hill, Frederick County, in extreme northwestern Virginia. His journal for December 26th noted: "The snow fell last night two feet thick. This is the greatest fall of snow I have seen in this country."[4]

The Christmas storm in Virginia, of course, was the same one of which another native son took advantage to cover his crossing of the Delaware River and the advance on Trenton that stormy night.

The Moravians agreed with Jefferson that this had been a hard winter. The *Diary* commented on the 6th of March: "This is the fifth snow of the winter and almost no one can remember such a winter in Carolina."[5] A later entry summed up: "We had an unusually long, hard winter which in some places killed the buds on the fruit trees, and did much damage to the grain planted in the fall."[6]

[1] T. Jefferson. *Garden Book*, 70.
[2] *Moravians in N. Car.*, **3**, 1109.
[3] T. Jefferson. Ms. Weather memorandum book. (LC.)
[4] *The journal of Nicholas Cresswell, 1774–1777*. N. Y., The Dial Press, 1924, 178.
[5] *Moravians in N. Car.*, **3**, 1143.
[6] *Ibid.*, **3**, 1136.

## THE HARD WINTER OF 1780 IN THE SOUTH

### CHESAPEAKE BAY AND VIRGINIA

The greater part of Chesapeake Bay froze over. It was reported to be solid from the head near Elkton as far south as the mouth of the Potomac River. Sleighs went from Baltimore to Annapolis on ice thought to be from 5 to 7 inches thick, and loaded vehicles crossed from Annapolis to the Eastern Shore via Kent Island, "which has not be known before by our oldest inhabitants, nor has the like happened, we believe, in the memory of man."[1]

In the lower bay the ice appeared solid "almost to the Capes," the *Virginia Gazette* reported.[2] The York River could be crossed between York and Gloucester, "an instance which is not remembered by the oldest person now living."[3] Six loaded wagons traversed the James River near Warwick Point in the vicinity of Williamsburg.[4] All waterways surrounding the port of Norfolk were firm enough to support the crossing of American soldiers on foot: Hampton, Newport News, Portsmouth, and Norfolk were joined by a natural ice bridge.[5] Many ships were lost in the bay when the thaw loosed grinding ice floes. Jefferson declared that such an extensive freeze of the tidal waters had not occurred previously, not even in the famous Hard Winter of 1740–41.[6]

The only Southern temperature readings now preserved appeared in the *Virginia Gazette* in January. These were only fragments, not including the days of severest cold in late January. No doubt, the readings were made on a thermometer belonging to Rev. James Madison, president of William and Mary College, who had participated in simultaneous observations with Jefferson in 1777.[7] Nothing was known about the exposure of the instrument, and there was no attempt to achieve a minimum reading. From the low of +6° registered at 0730 on January 13th, it would be safe to assume an absolute reading of about zero at Williamsburg as the coldest reached there during the Hard Winter of 1780. The persistency of the westerly flow combined with the snow-covered and ice-locked conditions of the surrounding terrain would exclude the usual maritime influences normally present in the area. Another set of readings taken at Hanover, Virginia, just north of Richmond, gave a figure of +9° as the low on the 13th, but these appear to have been taken at a sheltered location. For the first three weeks of January they gave an average 0730 reading of 22.5°:

|        | 0730 | Noon | 1500 | Wind |
|--------|------|------|------|------|
| Jan. 7 | 15°  | 18°  | 20°  | NW   |
| 8      | 14   | 16   | 18   | NW   |
| 9      | 16   | 20   | 23   | WbyN |
| 10     | 27   | 29   | 31   | W    |
| 11     | 33   | 34   | 34   | SW   |
| 12     | 26   | 22   | 16   | W    |
| 13     | 6    | 16   | 17   | NW   |
| 14     | 10   | 16   | —    | W[8] |

## North Carolina

In the interior of North Carolina near Winston-Salem the Moravian Brethren felt the rigors of the Hard Winter. "The past winter was unusually severe, and no one remembers such continuous cold and so much snow," declared Rev. Frederic Marshall in the *Diary*.[9] "In addition the last harvest had been rather poor, and finally there was a great rise in prices," the *Diary* continued.[10] Though no thermometer was at hand, an account of all the principal weather events in the small frontier community of Salem gave a graphic picture of the rugged conditions in December, January and February 1779–80:

### December 1779

5. The first snow of the season fell last night, though not deep.
13. Yesterday there was a thunderstorm and a wind like a tornado which blew down various fences and roofs. The wind changed to the north and today is very cold.
14. The wind blew hard during the night and it is colder than is usual even in midwinter.
17. It froze last night, and the east wind brought rain and glaze ice, which continued all day.
20. For three days it has grown continually colder; no one remembers such a long cold spell at this time of the year.
22. It moderated today with wind from the south.
27. This afternoon it began to snow, and continued late into the night.
30. The weather was mild and rainy.[11]

### January 1780

2. For snow fell all last night and continued today, clearing up toward evening with a cold west wind . . .
3. The wind was from the north-west, and it was very cold. . . .
5. The wind was from the west today, and especially toward evening it blew heavily and brought a bitter cold.
6. On account of the intense cold, which must be the worst of the winter, the singstude was omitted.
7. The second service was omitted because it remained as cold as yesterday, with a strong wind from the west-north-west. Dr. Johan Krause came from Steiner's mill and reported that not only had the water-wheel frozen fast, which has never happened before, but the ice had also sprung the wheel. . . .
8. The severe cold continues.
10. For today it has alternately snowed and rained, with wind from the south-east.
11. The weather cleared with the wind from the north and west, and in the following night it froze.
12. The wind changed to north-west, and all day the sun was unable to thaw the ground. Many people declare that it was the coldest day we have had this winter.
14. The weather has moderated somewhat.
17. The weather has been moderate for some days, but this afternoon a strong wind from the north-west brought with it a piercing cold.
22. The bitter cold has moderated a little.
24. This morning it snowed a little, and tonight the northeast wind has again made it very cold.
30. For several days the weather has been milder, and today the ice and snow have melted rapidly.

### February 1780

5. Since yesterday the wind has been from the north, so it is cold again, and does not thaw much during the day.
7. Shortly before noon a hard storm of rain and sleet came up from the east, and continued all day and into the night. . . .
8. The weather has cleared up cold from the north-west.
10. This is the first warm and pleasant day of the winter, with wind from the south.
11. It rained all day, with a south wind, and melted practically all the ice and snow, and began to thaw the earth which had been frozen a foot deep. Toward evening there was a thick fog, and during the night it did not freeze for the first time this winter.
15. It was rainy all day.
16. The wind today was from the north-west, and during the following night it froze.
18. The weather was pleasant; toward evening it clouded up, and did not freeze.
22. It rained all day. During the night a heavy storm came up from the north-west, and toward morning it froze.
23. There was a sharp wind from the north-west all day, it was bitterly cold.
24. It is a little less cold today.
26. Last night it did not freeze; toward evening there was a little warm air.
28. The weather was spring-like.[12]

Along the tidewater of North Carolina the *State Records* revealed that Albemarle Sound froze over solidly. This prevented boats passing, but opened the way for the militia to move quickly north on foot.[13]

## South Carolina

Firsthand documents for this period in South Carolina dealing with anything but the deteriorating military situation were few. The only continuous diary of the period, that of Ann Manigault, related that on 29 January the weather had been "very cold since Dec. 20," but gave no details.[14] A mention of the existing severe conditions appeared in the *South Carolina and American General Gazette* on 19 January 1780, and this comprised the only press notice of contemporary Charleston meteorological conditions:

> Since the middle of last month, the weather has been more severe than can be remembered by the oldest inhabitant. The mercury during the greatest part of the above period has been below 30° and frequently as low as 17°. In the back country there has been an extraordinary fall of snow, and we are informed several rivers are frozen over.[15]

## Georgia

The diary of Capt. Hinrichs, a Hessian mercenary recently arrived in Savannah, gave brief details as to the winter's effect at that port then in British hands: "According to the account of a thirty-year old inhabitant of Savannah this winter has been the coldest experienced. There has been ice in the rooms at night and once it even snowed a little during the day—unheard of things in this part of the country."[16]

## The Old Southwest

Two parties taking part in the exploration and settlement of the uplands of the southern Appalachians were caught by the early onset of severe winter conditions and forced to establish winter quarters in extreme western North Carolina. The Donelson party in December on their way to found a settlement on the Cumberland River at the present site of Nashville were forced to halt by "a most excessive frost" on the upper Holston River in Hawkins County northeast of the present location of Knoxville and to wait until late February before resuming the trip into the interior.[17] It was said that cattle were driven across the frozen river near Nashville this winter at latitude 36°N.[18]

Another party, which had been surveying the boundary between Virginia and North Carolina, was caught by the widespread early freeze near the Kentucky border, forcing them to "lay still" from 6 January until 13 February.[19] The significant meteorological details from their daily journal follow:

### December 1779

2. Windy and showers of snow latter part of the day cloudy.
4. Snow tonight.
5. Snowing, lay still.
6. Cloudy, lay still.
9. A hard wind tonight.
11. Rain tonight.
12. Much rain today, all day. Lay still.
13. Cloudy and some showers of snow. A cold night.
14. A very cold day, but clear. An excessive cold night.
15. Cold and cloudy. A little snow tonight.
16. Lay still all day.
17. Misty all day.
24. Rather cloudy.
25. Christmas Day. Rather cloudy.
27. Cloudy & misty or little rain.
28. Same.
29. Saw the Sun a little tho not enough to take a good observation.
30. Cloudy & a little snow.
31. Clear and cool.

### January 1780

1. Snow tonight.
2. Cloudy & some snow.
3. Clear & very cold tonight.
4. The ice was so bad coming down the river we could only reach our Sunday's night camp.
6. Cold to such a degree the river froze over, and continued froze over till Sunday 9th Jany. 1780 when Major Bledsoe crossed over on it to go to Prices.
13. There was no appearance of a thaw.
27. No appearance of a thaw yet.

### February 1780

7. Snow a little last night & today.
9. The weather had moderated a little.
10. An appearance of a thaw coming. Rain tonight a little.
12. River rose much.
13. This morning the ice broke and we launched our canoe.[19]

## Louisiana

Charles Gayarre, the outstanding mid-nineteenth century historian of Louisiana, wrote that in 1780 the lower Mississippi River Valley experienced "a winter more rigorous than had ever been known."[20] Though only seventy years had passed, Gayarre could supply no details except for repeating the general complaint of the populace of hard times. Among many causes was mentioned the unprecedented cold. Fortunately, one surviving document throws some light on the severity of conditions. William Dunbar, a Scottish gentleman of unique scientific attainments, was then residing on a primitive plantation at Richmond, near Baton Rouge. He entered the following in his 1780 diary notes:

> January 24th. The weather during this month has been so excessively cold that the Negroes have not been able to do much labour & moreover have been almost all sick.

February 4th. The weather has continued excessively cold untill within these few days, the winter upon the whole has been the coldest ever known; the River has been covered with ice drifting down & in some places it has been found to frooze entirely across which in the Lat. 30°30′ is something very surprising & has perhaps never been heard of before; at present it is becoming a little milder but we apprehend a return to Cold weather, the season being not yet passed.[21]

[1] *Va. Gaz.*, 5 Feb. 1780.
[2] *Ibid.*, 29 Jan 1780.
[3] George Meriwether to George R. Clark, Louisa, 24 Jan 1780. *Coll. Ill. State Hist. Soc.* (Springfield), 8 (1912), 383–84.
[4] *Va. Gaz.*, 22 Jan 1780.
[5] *Ibid.*, 5 Feb 1780.
[6] T. Jefferson, Ms. Weather memorandum book.
[7] *Va. Gaz.*, 15 Jan 1780.
[8] *Idem.*
[9] *Moravians in N. Car.*, 4, 1900.
[10] *Idem.*
[11] *Ibid.*, 3, 1320–21.
[12] *Ibid.*, 4, 1520–28.
[13] James Long to Gov. Caswell. *State Records N. Car.* 15, 318.
[14] Jour. Ann Manigault. *S.C. Hist. Gen. Mag.*, 21, 119.
[15] *S.C. and Amer. Gen. Adv.* (Charleston), 19 Jan 1780.
[16] Diary of Capt. Hinrichs. *The siege of Charleston.* B. A. Uhlendorf, ed. 151–53.
[17] Voyage of the Donelson Party 1779–80. *Early travels in the Tennessee Country 1540–1800* Samuel C. Williams, ed. Johnson City, Tenn., The Watauga Press, 1928. 223.
[18] *Idem.*
[19] The journal of Daniel Smith. *Tenn. Mag. Hist.* (Nashville). 1–1 (March 1915), 57–60.
[20] Charles Gayarre. *Hist. of La.*, 2, 153.
[21] *Life, letters and papers of William Dunbar.* Mrs. Dunbar Rowland, ed. Jackson, Miss., Miss. Hist. Soc., 1930. 70–71.

## THE LONG FREEZE-UP OF 1784

The winter of 1783–84 achieved lasting memory in the Southland for long continuance of cold, extremely heavy snowstorms, and a disastrous January thaw and a March break-up which caused great floods and severe damage from the falls line to tidewater. In the Piedmont of North Carolina the snow season commenced early. On both the 21st and 22d of December 1783 heavy snow fell, and there were additional storms to maintain the snow cover and to make travelling very difficult at Christmas holiday time.[1] January, opening very cold, produced a substantial snowstorm on the 9–10th that served as a preliminary for one of the greatest of Southern snowstorms.[2] On the 18–19th, "two feet of snow" fell at Salem, North Carolina, and the following northwest wind blew at gale force on the 19th to pile the snow into huge drifts. "The oldest Brother in North Carolina does not remember such a storm," the Moravian *Diary* declared.[3]

### VIRGINIA

The storm struck hard in southern Virginia. The *Richmond Gazette* reported that people, unable to travel or trade, had perished from famine in the southern parts of the section, so deep was the snow.[4] There were no actual measurements or estimates of the snow depths in Virginia or elsewhere in North Carolina except in the Salem area. The only temperature check on storm conditions was made at Williamsburg, Virginia, where Rev. James Madison's thermometer indicated 26° on the 18th and 38° on the 19th—it appeared likely that Williamsburg was in the warm sector of the storm on the 19th, as the next day, the 20th, the mercury had descended to 18°.[5]

The impact of the storm at a point in Cumberland County, Virginia, about 35 miles west of Richmond, was caught by Henry Skipworth in a letter to Thomas Jefferson:

Hors du Monde, January 20, 1784
Your favor reached me last evening, preceding the most tremendous snow storm this country has ever experienced since my remembrance. It commenced about seven at night, and never ceased until the evening of the present day about four O'Clock. It is impossible to say what the depth of the snow is, since from the wind it is exceedingly irregular, in some places scarsely any in others dangerously deep; its surface is a beautiful representation of a troubled water; Prior to this we have had for four weeks a severe frost, variegated with all the snows, hails rains &c. incident to such a season, so that the industrious of this country begin almost to despond, and those whose crops of grain were short absolutely to despair.[6]

George Washington had returned to Mt. Vernon to spend the Christmas season and enjoy the subsequent winter at home, but found the elements uncooperative. On January 14th he wrote: "The torpid state into which the severity of the season has thrown things"—on 22 January: "We have been so fast locked in snow and ice since Christmas"—on 18 February: "The intemperance of the weather, and the great care which the post riders seemed disposed to take care of themselves, while it continued severe; prevented your letter of the 13th of last month from reaching my hands till the 10th of this"—and on March 5th: "arrived at this Cottage on Christmas eve, where I have been locked up ever since in frost and snow."[7]

James Madison had returned to his home at Orange in central Virginia and found some blessing in being snowbound. He wrote to Thomas Jefferson on 11 February:

> We have had a severer season and particularly a greater quantity of snow than is remembered to have distinguished any preceding winter. The effect of it on the price of grain and other provisions is much dreaded. It has been as yet so far favorable to me that I have pursued my intended course in law reading with fewer interruptions than I had presupposed.[8]

Thomas Jefferson, too, complained of the delays in the mail from his post at Annapolis, Maryland, where he was preparing for his diplomatic post abroad. On 16 January he wrote: "The Southern post, which had not come in for three weeks past, surprised us by his arrival today."[9] Jefferson, as usual, had his trusty thermometer with him, placed "at the north side of the wall." During the early January cold wave he noticed the following morning readings from the 7th to 10th: +4°, +1°, 0°, and 0°. Later in the month the mercury was "in the ball" on the 15th, 16th, 28th, and 30th.[10] Jefferson continued to pursue his search for more data on the Virginia climate. Writing to Rev. James Madison at William and Mary College at Williamsburg, he attempted to revive the series of simultaneous observations carried on in 1777 and 1778. The reply revealed the difficulties in carrying on scientific investigations in the immediate post-war period:

> Williamsburg, Jan. 22, 1784
> I did not receive your favour of the 24th Dec. until last post. I immediately looked out for a thermometer and obtained one which appears very sensible to Heat or Cold, tho' it is so constructed that I cannot ascertain the accuracy of the division by plunging it into boiling water; this appears of consequence especially when we keep correspondent observations. I shall observe the time you mention, and send at present, as it may be of some gratification, an account of the severity of the season my morning observations from the 16th until this date. viz. 14°, 16½°, 26°, 38°, 18°, 18°, 25°. In order to observe the greatest cold, I expose the thermometer to the night air. It either stands out all night, or lies in an open window. The remainder of the day it is also as much exposed as it prudently can be, on the occasion of meeting with some accident—for it is borrowed. I mention this, because, both ought to be treated in the same manner. I wish we had (a) barometer but there is no possibility of getting one here at present. The British robbed me of my thermometer and barometer. We have sent to England and expect a return by this spring.[11]

The severe cold at the turn of the year sealed most of the harbors serving Chesapeake Bay. Baltimore closed on the 2d of January and was not to open again until March 25th, and then only with the assistance of some ice cutting. An historian of Baltimore has written:

> The winter of 1783–84 proved exceedingly severe; the bay was closed by ice almost to the mouth of it, and the harbor which closed on the 2d of January, was not clear to admit vessels until the 25th of March—nor then, but with much labor in cutting passages—which was sixteen days later than in 1780. At both periods much injury was sustained by the shipping in the bay and on the coast, and considerable sums were collected to relieve the poor.[12]

At Annapolis all communications by land and sea closed with the great snowstorm of the 18–19th. The *Maryland Gazette* on the 29th complained that no mails had been received for eight days. Early in February the columns contained accounts of maritime losses to the icy sheath covering Chesapeake Bay: a large ship sunk at Barnwell's Ferry, two small ships lost on their way to Portsmouth, and six sail cast ashore in the James River amidst ice floes.[13] The first packet since late January arrived at Annapolis on March 5th though destined for Baltimore.[14] For most of March Annapolis continued to serve as the port of entry for vessels destined for Alexandria or Baltimore. In the south of the bay area the Elizabeth River at Norfolk was frozen over.[15]

The season was marked by two spectacular ice break-ups. A great January thaw occurred just four days after the deep snow of the 18–19th. At Salem, North Carolina, the melting commenced on the 23d with the waters reaching a peak the next day.[16] At Richmond the breaking of an ice jam in the James River on the night of the 24th caused extensive damage.[17] The scene was relayed to Jefferson by Benjamin Harrison:

> Council Chamber (Richmond?), Jan. 30, 1784.
>
> The weather here has been for four weeks a few days excepted as severe as we have known for many years, and we have at the present little prospect of its growing better. The earth being covered with a very deep snow and the wind to the westward great damage has been done to the shipping in every part of the river, five sail of sea vessels that were at Rockets are driven by the ice up Gilly's creek very near the road and it is feared most of them will be lost and Overtons mill is totally destroyed, a few days quick thaw has given us these specimens of the mischief ice assisted by a current is capable of doing and has filled the inhabitants of the lower town and Rockets with dreadful apprehensions of their houses being overwhelmed by it if the weather should break up with another quick thaw.[18]

The final break-up of the ice-locked rivers did not commence until mid-March. The editor of the *Virginia Journal and Alexandria Gazette* took notice of the event occurring on March 15th:

> Sunday last the ice in the river Potomack began to break up, and on Monday ran very rapid exhibiting an appearance of such vast bodies of ice and timber as was never before known by the oldest

inhabitants here. Our apprehensions for the shipping, wharves, and stores were great, but luckily neither have received much damage, and we are in hopes the river will soon be clear.

We hear that much damage has been done at Georgetown by the breaking of the ice in this river.[19]

The frigid air masses of January and February extended their influence far southward. Even the harbor of Charleston, South Carolina, was reported "having produced ice strong enough for skating on, which is very uncommon there," so said a skipper who brought his vessel from Charleston into Egg Harbor, New Jersey, being unable to get into Delaware Bay on account of ice conditions.[20] This outstanding Charleston event has not been confirmed from a local source as the press was in a state of disarray at this time in the recently evacuated city.

## NORTH CAROLINA

The Moravians at their outposts in the Winston-Salem area of west-central North Carolina provide the best documentation for the impact of the severe winter on the people still in the throes of recovery from the disruptions of war. All entries are taken from the Bethabara diary unless otherwise noted:

### January 1784

5. For several days the weather has been cloudy and rainy, very unpleasant and unwholesome. Yesterday and today we had storms, with thunder, lightning and rain.
6. It rained all night and until eight o'clock this morning; the creeks will be high.
9. It was very cold. (Salem).
10. Because of a snow storm there was no evening service. (Salem.)
10. It began to snow.
11. The weather was very unfriendly, with rain which froze during the morning and continued most of the day; toward evening it snowed.
11. Because of a cold rain and much sickness there were only two meetings. (Salem.)
12. The weather was cold.
14. The weather was foggy.
18. Toward evening and during the night two feet of snow fell. (Salem.)
18. About three o'clock it began to snow, and when we arose on
19. Monday, the snow was very deep. Road opening was the chief work of the day, and as the wind blew the snow about like a cloud many places had to be cleared two or three times.
19. This was followed by a hard storm from the northwest, with snow flurries. The oldest Brother in North Carolina does not remember such a storm. In spite of it two boys came from Bethabara for the postponed celebration of Boys' Covenant Day. (Salem.)
20. In the southwest a comet was seen; it did not have a long tail. (Salem.)
20. During the night the strong wind ceased.
22. Toward evening it rained heavily so that no service could be held.
23. The rain continued until about noon, melting most of the snow. In the evening there was no meeting because of the wet and muddy roads.
23. Last night and today the snow melted quickly in a warm south wind, raising the streams. (Salem.)
24. The water was high yesterday, but rose still further today and then began to fall.
26. The weather was penetratingly cold.
27. The strong northwest wind made it so cold the people thought it had never been so cold before.

   Several hogs were killed for household use, and the workers suffered much from the intense cold.
30. The cold continues, though without the wind.
31. It began to rain and snow, and was very cold.

### February 1784

2. It was rainy today.
3. Yesterday it cleared up cold, and so continued today, with a strong northwestwind.
5. Between seven and eight o'clock in the evening it began to snow.
7. The cold was penetrating, but there was no wind.
11. The weather was cloudy, with some sleet. . . . No service could be held because of the weather.
12. The weather cleared up toward noon.
22. Toward evening it rained and snowed at the same time, and no service could be held.
24. Soon thereafter it began to snow, continuing until
25. In the afternoon.
28. The weather cleared very cold.
29. As the cold and the strong northwest wind continued, there was only one meeting in the morning.

### March 1784

2. The garden was dug and some seeds were sown.
6. In the morning it began to snow, falling more heavily in the afternoon and until some time during the night.
7. The sun began to shine and melt the snow.
8. The weather was unpleasant, and in the evening it began to rain.
9. Most of the snow disappeared in last night's rain.
13. It was cloudy and rainy.
14. The weather was clear but the water high.
16. Today there were unusually many people here, moving from Virginia [to Kentucky and Tennessee]. They had much to say about the extraordinary winter.
17. There was a very high wind from the northwest, and below the mill fire broke out in the bush, and came across the mill road.
20. The cold wind which began yesterday was more penetrating today.

20. We went to Salem. It was intensely cold, with a penetrating wind, such as could not be expected at this season. (Friedberg.)
21. Because of the weather only twenty persons came, and the meeting was held in the school-room. (Friedberg.)
21. The evening meeting was dropped because of a snow storm. During the night there was a hard frost which injured the peach trees. (Salem.)
21. It snowed from early in the day until afternoon.
22. The sun melted the snow which fell yesterday.
27. The men began to sow oats.
29. During these days it became apparent that the unusual cold of the 22d injured the peach buds, which had not yet bloomed. (Bethania.)
30. This morning before day was a storm, and about six o'clock a strong wind began to blow from the west, continuing all day.

### April 1784

1. Today the first fish were brought from the Yadkin for sale.[27]

## LOUISIANA

There are only two instances in recorded meteorological history of ice floes passing out of the mouth of the Mississippi River at 29°N and being met by ships another degree to the southward in the open Gulf of Mexico. These occurred in February 1899 during the greatest of modern Arctic outbreaks to penetrate the South and in February 1784 during a cold period that must have exceeded anything that even the Hard Winter only four years previously had produced in southern Louisiana.[22]

Again our historical references for the region and season are only two. In January Don Esteban Miro wrote in a dispatch of "the inconvenience of the hour and the heavy snow."[23] Apparently a snowy January was followed by a severely cold period in early February as a second contemporary document related:

> On the 13th of February, 1784, the whole bed of the river, in front of New Orleans, was filled up with fragments of ice, the size of most of which was from twelve to thirty feet, with a thickness of two to three. This mass of ice was so compact, that it formed a field of four hundred yards in width, so that all communication was interrupted for five days between the two banks of the Mississippi. On the 19th, these lumps of ice were no longer to be seen. "The rapidity of the current being then at the rate of two thousand and four hundred yards an hour," says Villars, "and the drifting of the ice by New Orleans having taken five days, it follows that it must have occupied in length a space of about one hundred and twenty miles. These floating masses of ice were met by ships in the 28th degree of latitude.[24]

[1] *Moravians in N. Car.,* **5**, 1988.
[2] *Ibid.,* **5**, 2011.
[3] *Idem.*
[4] *Va. Gaz.* (Richmond), 14 Feb 1784.
[5] J. Madison to T. Jefferson. *Wm. & Mary. Quar.* (Williamsburg.) 2d ser., **5**–2 (April 1925), 79
[6] *The papers of Thomas Jefferson,* **6**, 472.
[7] *The writings of George Washington,* **27**, 297, 312, 315, 333.
[8] *T. Jefferson.* **6**, 537.
[9] ——. **6**, 468.
[10] ——. Ms. Weather memorandum book. (LC.)
[11] ——. **6**, 507.
[12] Thomas W. Griffin. *Annals of Baltimore.* Balto., W. Woody, 1821.
[13] *Md. Gaz.* (Annapolis), 5, 12 Feb 1784.
[14] *Ibid.,* 11 March 1784.
[15] *Public Ledger* (Norfolk), 1 Feb 1815.
[16] *Moravians in N. Car.,* **5**, 2047.
[17] *Va. Gaz.,* 31 Jan 1784.
[18] T. Jefferson. **6**, 512.
[19] *Va. Jour. & Alexandria Adv.,* 18 March 1784.
[20] Phila., 26 Feb, in *Md. Gaz.,* 18 March 1784.
[21] *Moravians in N. Car.,* **5**, 1988–
[22] U. S. Dept. Agri. *Report for February 1899. Louisiana Section of the Climate and Crop Service of the Weather Bureau.* New Orleans, 1899. **4**–2 (Feb 1899), 8.
[23] Caroline Burson. *The stewardship of Don Esteban Miro, 1782–1792.* New Orleans, American Printing Co., 1940, 196.
[24] Villars' dispatch, 25 Feb 1784, in Charles Gayarre, *Hist of La.,* 163. John L. C. Andreassen. Mississippi River ice at New Orleans. *La. Hist. Quar.* **21**–2 (April 1938), 349–53. Berquin-Duvallon. *Vue de la colonie espagnole du Mississipi, ou des provinces de Louisiane et Floride Occidentale, en l'annee 1802.* Paris, 1803, 78.

## THE SNOWY TURN OF THE CENTURY AT CHARLESTON AND SAVANNAH

David Ramsay in his impressive *History of South Carolina* (1809) took notice of the wintry events marking the decade of the 1790's at Charleston:

> On December 31, 1790, wind N.E. a severe snow storm began in Charlestown which continued for twelve hours. In consequence of which the streets were covered with snow from two to four inches deep. Another took place on the 28th of February 1792, wind N.W. which continued for several hours, and till it covered the ground five or six inches. Similar snow storms fell in January 1800, and were thrice repeated in twenty-three days, and amounted in the whole to more than ten inches. But these phenomena are rare.

From records presently available, it appeared that no major snowstorm had occurred at Charleston since

1773, but residents of the city near the turn of the century were to see four seasons with snowstorms in excess of anything that had occurred there previously or would occur in the modern period since the Weather Bureau commenced keeping records in 1871. All the events can be documented from contemporary press accounts.

### 1790

Charleston:

> Accounts from Charleston say, that on Dec. 31st. they had an uncommon fall of snow in that city. It began about four o'clock in the morning and continued about 12 hours. In most streets, the snow lay four to six inches deep; and what was remarkable and almost without precedent in the city of Charleston, two sleighs were driven about the city with velocity and ease. *Penna. Jour.* (Phila.), 26 Jan 1791

Savannah:

> Dec. 30—Snow storm at Savannah. Ezra Stiles. Ms. Met. Obs. (Yale.)

Midway, Georgia, 30 miles southwest of Savannah:

> On the 31st a snow storm began five minutes before 8 a.m. and continued till 11; but did not whiten the ground. *Mem. Amer. Acad. Arts & Sci.,* 3–2 (1815), 108.

### 1792

Charleston:

> Yesterday (28 Feb.) there was a heavy fall of snow in this city; it was succeeded by a shower of hail about two in the afternoon, and continued till near six o'clock in the afternoon. *City Gazette and Daily Advertiser* in *Penna. Jour.* (Phila.), 21 March 1792.

> On Wednesday last (Feb. 29) as two waggons were going over the Ashley Bridge, it suddenly gave way, owing to the great weight of snow which had collected upon it. . . . *City Gaz.,* 2 March 1792.

### 1800

The month of January 1800 proved the snowiest of all months at Charleston and Savannah and deserves a chapter of its own. Refer to page 158 for a full account.

### 1803

Savannah:

> Snow Storm—On Tuesday last [15 Feb.], we had a considerable fall of snow, which still remains upon the ground. The old and the young on this occasion equally experienced an irresistible impulse to taste the "joys of sleighing," and the "ambling pad ponies" of our city, have sorely paid for this freak of the climate. *Columbian Museum and Savannah Advertiser,* 18 Feb 1803; also *Courier* (Charleston) 23 Feb 1803.

South Carolina:

> Snow fell in February. Robert Mills. *Statistics of South Carolina.* Charleston, Hurlburt and Lloyd, 1826. 448.

The *Courier* made no mention of snowfall at Charleston, though it did carry the above note about Savannah.

(See page 206 for accounts of February 1803 snowstorm in North Carolina and Virginia.)

## TWO LEGENDARY SNOWSTORMS: 1790 & 1798

During the Southland's snowy ten years at the close of the 18th Century two snowstorms occurred whose descriptions indicate each to have been in excess of anything known in these localities since. These are here labeled legendary since our recent historical search has failed to turn up sufficient firsthand data to substantiate the contemporary claims. These reputed events have been included in these pages for two reasons: first, they have been mentioned previously by good authorities— and, second, in the hope that a more thorough quest by local historians may uncover confirming evidence as to their actual circumstances.

### THE NEW BERN STORM OF 30 DECEMBER 1790

The diary of Ezra Stiles of Yale College contained the following entry immediately after 31 December 1790: "Snow four feet deep at New Bern, N. C., after snow storm of 48 hours; which extended from Georgia to Boston."

That a storm did occur at this time was well documented. On the 30th snow fell at Savannah, Georgia, and at nearby Midway sufficient to whiten the ground. At Charleston the depth estimates in the press ran 4 to 6 inches. Snow also fell at Philadelphia and at New Haven on 31 December and at Salem, Massachusetts, on 1 January. So a worthy example of a northeaster must have swept up the length of coast on these days.

There was no newspaper published at New Bern in 1790–91 although there had been an active press there earlier and would be another later. A search of other North Carolina newspaper files has proved unrewarding. New Bern then served as the cultural center of North Carolina society and possessed a local scientific society. Most probably the reference originated in a letter sent from a member of the intellectual community at New Bern to Ezra Stiles, a leading figure in educational circles in the North.

The mention of snow four feet deep in coastal North Carolina, of course, must cause the raising of a few critical meteorological eyebrows. Perhaps the informant referred to the deepest drift. In the records of the U. S. Weather Bureau, snowfall figures have been maintained from 1885 to the present. During this time the heaviest single storm snowfall in North Carolina occurred on 2 March 1927 when 31 inches fell within 24 hours at Nashville, some 85 miles northwest of New Bern. In this storm New Bern received only 6 inches of snow, though a shift of the storm track southward a hundred miles could conceivably have buried New Bern with similar amounts received to the north. But nothing in North Carolina records, early or modern, can match the amounts attributed to New Bern in 1790.

## THE GREAT NORFOLK SNOW— 16 FEBRUARY 1798

The *New York Spectator* on 3 March 1798 carried the following dispatch from Norfolk, Virginia, dated 17 February: "Yesterday (16th) and last night we had the greatest fall of snow ever experienced here—it is now, in many places, upwards of six feet deep." No doubt, this originated in the issue of the *Norfolk Herald* for 17 February 1798, (No. 705 should have been published that day), but no copy of this particular issue has been uncovered by our researches.

This minute press notice apparently gave rise to the later legendary magnitude of the storm. It so happened that Noah Webster served as editor of the *New York Spectator,* and it was known that he had discussions with Comte de Volney concerning the American climate, and much of the material appearing in the latter's book (1804) was gained from these exchanges. Another press appearance of the storm took place in David Warden's *History of the United States* (1819), a widely-circulated book for its time, being translated into French and going through several English editions. Dr. Charles F. Brooks in his study of American snowfall in 1914 again repeated and added to the legendary depths of this storm. In a conversation with the writer before his untimely death, Dr. Brooks recalled that his source had been Volney.

A search for contemporary material to confirm Volney's statement as to 40 inches of snow falling at Norfolk in February 1798 has turned up nothing conclusive. It is known that a very heavy snowstorm did affect a strip of northeastern North Carolina on the date. The *North Carolina Journal* at Halifax, about 85 miles west-southwest of Norfolk, reported the storm: "On Friday (16th) we had a heavier fall of snow than has been known for many years past—it measured on a level about 16 inches."

Other weather observers noticed the storm: the Moravians at Salem in western North Carolina, Col. James Madison at Orange in west-central Virginia, and George Washington at Mt. Vernon in northern Virginia. But none of these made any mention of unusual severity or accumulations. No other press available to the writer in North Carolina or Virginia carried news about the snowstorm. Nor have any diaries for the area been found that might confirm or deny the legendary nature of this storm.

A check of later Norfolk records and press has revealed nothing to match the reputation of the 1798 storm. On 16–18 March 1841 a very heavy snow fell measuring 30 inches deep, "as was ascertained by measurements in enclosures where it was not affected by the wind," according to the local *Beacon*. At nearby Fort Monroe the Medical Corps rain gage collected 2.20" of water, but made no snowfall measurement. In the modern Weather Bureau period from 1871 to the present, the heaviest snow at Norfolk occurred on 26–28 December 1892 when 18.6 inches were measured.

For those who might like to delve deeper into the history of the event, all references so far located are reproduced below:

### Norfolk Snow—1798

Sometimes this wind itself gives evident proofs of it in its course, by covering the seashore with snow, which does not extend ten miles from it. This occurred at Norfolk on the 14th of February 1798, when in a single night more than 40 inches of snow fell in that city and its environs, with a north-east wind; while five and twenty miles inland it had not even rained, and the wind was rather north-west, as several newspapers observed. Volney (1804), 171.

On the 14th of February 1798, more than 40 inches fell, during the prevalence of this wind, at and around the city of Norfolk, while at a distance of twenty-five miles in the interior, when the wind at the same time, blew in a north-west direction, there was neither snow or rain. David Warden, *History of the U.S.* (1819), **1**, 156.

Norfolk, Virginia, 17 Feb: Yesterday (16th) and last night we had the greatest fall of snow ever experienced here—it is now, in many places, upwards of six feet deep. *Norfolk Herald,* 17 Feb, in *N.Y. Spectator,* 3 March 1798.

Halifax, North Carolina, 19 Feb: On Friday last (16th) we had a heavier fall of snow than has been known for many years past—it measured on a level about 16 inches. In consequence of which, we presume, that mail due on Saturday evening has not arrived. *North Carolina Journal* in *City Gazette & Daily Advertiser* (Charleston, S. C.), 7 March 1798.

Orange, Virginia, 16 Feb: Sunrise 29°, wind east, ground covered with snow. 1400—36°. 1600—35°, wind northeast, cloudy. (No measurable precipitation appeared in records from 13th to 19th). Col. James Madison. Ms. Met. Obs. (Amer. Phil. Soc.)

Bethabara, North Carolina: February 1798

13. We had a rather hard storm, with rain and hail mixed. Next day it cleared cold.
18. It snowed and sleeted, continuing through the next day, There being a cold wind from the northwest. *Records of the Moravians*, 6, 2615.

Mount Vernon, Virginia: February 1798

13. A sprinkle of snow fell last night—Wind at NE—raw and threatening a fall of [     ] all day—returned home Mer. 30 at night.
14. About an inch deep of snow fell last night—weather cloudy and cold—25 in the morning. Clearing [     ] Mer. 33 at night
15. Clearing morning—wind [     ] at NW & mer at 24—in evening at 32—at highest 36
16. Cloudy & wind Northwesterly & mer. at 30 in the morning—North easterly afterwards —mer. 28 at night and at 32 the highest —cloudy most part of the day. George Washington. Ms. Account of the weather, 1798. (LC.)

Farther back in history are others. At Norfolk, Va., for example, old records tell of a fall of 60 inches February 4, 1798, followed 10 days later by another of 40 inches. Charles F. Brooks, *Why the Weather*, 2d ed. (1938), 223.

## COLD WAVES IN 1796-97

The coldest period in the records of both Dr. Robert Wilson of Charleston (1791–1812) and James Kershaw of Camden (1791–1815) came in December 1796, and another almost equal frigid period followed two weeks later in January 1797.[1] Dr. Wilson's thermometer, "in his house suspended in an open passage about ten feet from the floor," dropped to +17° on both the 23d and 24th of December. This comprised the lowest point reached in the period of the Medical Society's records to 1808, according to historian Ramsay who had inspected the complete manuscript. At Camden the mercury dropped to +9° on James Kershaw's thermometer. This figure would be reached again on 22 January 1810 during the Southern aftermath of the Arctic blast on Cold Friday in New England, but no lower reading was reached at Camden throughout the span of records covering 1791–1802; 1808–1815.

The onset of the cold at Camden in December 1796 dropped the mercury from 70° at noon of the 21st to 30° next morning, and to +9° on the second morning. The two following days were authentic ice days with the noon readings rising only to 22° and to 25°. The morning temperature on the 24th stood at +13°, and on Christmas morning edged up farther to 21°. A reading of 40° at noon Christmas Day gave some relief, though still a very chilly figure for the season and the region. Next morning it was down to 24°, the fifth consecutive below-freezing morning. James Kershaw indicated "hard frost" on these days in his notes.

Two weeks later the mercury dropped to +19° on the 8th of January and to +17°, the month's minimum, on the 9th. Some snow fell on the 7th and sleet on the 10th, but thereafter more seasonable conditions prevailed in South Carolina.

The Moravian *Diary*, as usual, revealed some details as to conditions in the vicinity of Winston-Salem in western North Carolina. A thermometer had been procured in 1788 so that exact measurements of the cold could be made:

Dec. 23. The cold has been rather piercing for some days, and today there was a strong wind from the north-west and the cold was greater than one expects in this climate. At sunrise the Fahrenheit thermometer stood at two degrees below zero; during the middle of the day it did not rise above sixteen degrees. In the evening it was again very cold, though the sharp wind had died down.

Dec. 24. It was very cold during the night, and at sunrise the thermometer was at three degrees below zero. The cold forced its way into the houses so that in the cellars the milk, beer, and other food froze. In the afternoon the cold moderated so that our little children could attend their Christmas Eve service at five o'clock.[2]

Colonel James Madison, father of the future president, recorded a low of zero in December 1796 and −1° in January 1797. The observations were made at his home, Montpelier, near Orange in west-central Virginia. The winter was not particularly snowy there; his records showed only 18.25 inches compared to an 8-year average of 23.5 inches.[3]

One other scrap of data indicated a temperature of +4° at Columbia, South Carolina, in December 1796, said to have been the coldest experienced at the South Carolina capital in a record extending from 1796 to 1818.[4]

The non-instrument diary of Col. John Sevier, then living near Knoxville in Tennessee, gave an almost daily account of the snows and cold of December and the cold snap early in January:

### November 1796

27. Very cold, snowed at night.

### December 1796

1. Cold & snowy day.
6. Cold & some snow.
7. Very cold & flying snow.
8. Snowed in the night.
9. Very cold.
10. Some milder weather.
11. Very cold.
12. Cold & clear.
13. Rained.
15. Very pleasant day.
16. Rained
17. Fine & cold.
18. Rained in morning.
19. Cold.
21. Snowed & rained.
22. Extremely cold froze very hard the river across & all the small streams.
23. Very cold.
24. Very cold.
25. Very cold.
26. Cold.
28. Very cold.
29. Very cold.
30. Very cold.
31. Very cold.

### January 1797

1. Some m. [more] moderate
2. Very cold.
3. ditto flying snow.
4. A little rain & freeze at night.
6. Very cold.
7. Snowed.
8. Very cold.
9. Clear & some more moderate.
10. Rained very much in the night and turned warm.
11. Cloudy & windy the weather moderate.
12. Very warm & pleasant.

[1] D. Ramsay. *Hist. S. Car.*, 2, 52–53; James Kershaw. Ms. Met. Records at Camden, S. C. (NA.)
[2] *Moravians in N. Car.*, 6, 2565.
[3] T. Jefferson, Ms. Weather memorandum book.
[4] *National Intelligencer* (Wash., D.C.), 3 Oct 1818.
[5] Journal of Gov. John Sevier. *Tenn. Mag. Hist.* (Nashville). 6–1 (April 1920), 193.

## RECORD SOUTHERN SNOWS IN 1800

Noah Webster remarked in his diary notes for 1803 that during the past three winters much more snow had fallen in the Southern States than up North.[1] His statement was well borne out by testimony of weather registers, diaries, and newspaper accounts as to the coincidence of several most unusual snowstorms in the Deep South. In fact, conclusive evidence pointed to the winter of 1799–1800, the ultimate of the century

and of this section, as the snowiest ever experienced along the South Atlantic seaboard—both Charleston and Savannah measured individual snowstorms and seasonal snows totals unequalled in either early or recent records.

## VIRGINIA

Future President James Madison, writing to Vice President Thomas Jefferson from his home near Orange in the Rapadan country of north-central Virginia on 14 February 1800, declared: "for two weeks or more, snow on the ground from 15 to 20 inches deep, which has blockaded every body within his own doors." He added another bit of wintry information in a message of 15 March: "Ground has been covered with snow for 6 weeks, still a remnant around."[2] The weather records maintained by Madison's father indicated the winter of 1800 as the snowiest in his 8-year span of snow reports. He measured 38.6 inches this season against an average of only 23.5 inches.[3]

## NORTH CAROLINA

Farther south in central North Carolina, the Moravians had much to relate about the identical snowstorms of early February and early March that the Madisons had experienced:

Bethania:

Feb. 2. Snow fell so heavily today and during the night that the oldest inhabitant said they had never seen anything like it in North Carolina. A strong wind piled the snow into drifts, which were more than three feet deep in places. The roads were so blocked that near neighbors had difficulty in opening them one to another. On the 3d school was suspended, and evening meetings could not be held throughout the entire month.[4]

Salem:

Feb. 2. Snow began this morning about eight o'clock and grew worse steadily, continuing until the next day at noon. The snow was so deep that the oldest inhabitant in this neighborhood said that he had never seen one like it. During the following night it stormed, and by morning the drifts were five or more feet deep. In the bushes, where the wind could not pile it, it was about one foot and a half deep.

3. Brethren and Sisters had plenty to do all morning, for the snow had sifted through the single, tile roofs, and lay a foot deep on the floors of the houses, and that had to be cleared away and the necessary paths dug. At the end of the month there was still much snow on the north side of hills.[5]

Friedberg:

Feb. 3. In the morning the snow was eighteen to twenty inches deep.[6]

Bethabara:

Feb. 2. There was a heavy snow.

5. Dr. Hessler went to Salem this morning, but because of the deep snow and uncleared roads he reached there too late for the Conferenz.

15. It had been cold and wet all this week.

28. Yesterday afternoon it began to rain, and continued today, snow mixed with the rain.

Mar. 8. Yesterday and today snow fell about a foot deep.[7]

Salem:

March 7. In the afternoon it began to snow, and continued all the next day. This time the snow was eight inches deep.[8]

## SOUTH CAROLINA

Henry Ravenel in his personal diary related that Charleston in the winter of 1799–1800 underwent four unusual snowstorms, each with sufficient depth to cover the ground. The largest quantity, which he estimated at 6 to 7 inches at his country seat near Berkeley, fell on the 9th and 10th of January.[9] The Charleston press took notice of the extraordinary event—the *State Gazette* under the headline, "SNOWSTORM,'" commented:

The weather has been uncommonly cold for the last two days; and we witnessed yesterday, for the first time these eight years, a very severe snow storm.[10]

The *City Gazette* was able to supply more meteorological details:

On Thursday evening last a severe gale came on from the North-east, attended with sleet and snow, which lasted until Friday night, at 12 o'clock; during this period a fall of snow took place, of eight inches depth on a level. A snow of this depth has not been known in this city for many years past. We do not learn of any damage being done by the gale.[11]

Inland at Camden in northeastern South Carolina on 10 January, James Kershaw noted "hard snow all day" with northeast wind, but did not given any measurement.[12] Perhaps he was on the northern border of this particular snowbelt as the Moravians to the north did not mention snow at this time, while to the south in Georgia the storm assumed its greatest fury. Kershaw's thermometer at the three observations on the 10th read: 30°, 34°, and 29°, sufficient to produce satisfactory conditions for a snow-covered ground. He also observed "hard snow all day" on the 23d with temperatures at 27°, 35°, and 32°—this was probably one of the falls mentioned by Ravenel near Charleston. The Kershaw thermometer reached its January nadir of 23° (only 0800 readings taken) on the 29th.

The wintry spell continued over into the first days of February. After a cold day on the 1st with the mercury hovering near freezing all day, sleet commenced at noon of the 2d, the temperature being at 35°. This turned to a mixture of sleet and snow in late evening, and to "heavy snow" at night, the reading now 30°. No actual measurement of the accumulation of this storm of the 2–3d appeared in Kershaw's records, but the fall ranged from 18 to 20 inches in central North Carolina and in southern Virginia. The wind at Camden on the 2d came from the northeast placing the storm track offshore, but close enough to place the Piedmont in the heavy snow canopy.

## GEORGIA

The snowstorm of 9–10 January 1800 in coastal Georgia developed into the greatest in the entire history of the region. The reported depths far exceeded any other storm in either the early or modern records of coastal stations to the north in South Carolina or to the south in Florida. Only the highest elevations of the Southern Appalachians far inland have experienced amounts in recent times equal to those reported in 1800 at sea level in latitude 32°N. The storm is most remarkable in view of the modern record (1871-present) of only 2.0 inches in a single storm as observed by the U. S. Weather Bureau.[13]

Abiel Holmes, son-in-law of Ezra Stiles and father of Oliver Wendell Holmes, spent some of his early years on a Georgia plantation about 25 miles southwest of Savannah. A friend of his from there supplied some vital information about the great snow:

> During seven winters, I never saw the ground whitened with snow but on the tenth of January, 1800, there fell at Savannah the deepest snow, accompanied with the severest cold, ever remembered in the lower parts of Georgia. By a letter from an intelligent friend, dated Midway, 17 February, 1800, I was informed, that the snow had been three feet deep in particular places, and from sixteen to eighteen inches on a level. A sleet, the same winter, loaded the trees with ice from Broad river (South Carolina) toward the Savannah, a space of ten or fifteen miles, and made great devastation in the forests.

The intensity of the storm was confirmed by the *Columbian Museum and Savannah Advertiser* three days after the end of the 36-hour fall:

> A snow storm, accompanied with a high wind, commenced in this city last Thursday evening, the 9th inst and continued all that night, Friday and Friday night incessantly, until Saturday morning, which left the snow above 18 inches deep, and is not half dissolved yet, although it has been clear sunshining warm weather ever since. Hasty made sleighs were common in the streets and going out of the city, which were never known or seen here before, and the oldest inhabitant, since the first settlement of the colony, says tho' there have been several snows, none of them were so deep as this.[16]

The absence of any evidence of additional snowfalls at Savannah, such as were experienced in the Carolinas, suggested that the snow belt in late January and early February lay farther to the north and did not extend to coastal Georgia, but the one storm there would serve for a lifetime.

## FLORIDA

The January 1800 storm also produced the deepest snowfall known to have fallen in Florida.[17] It may be that some part of interior northwest Florida, escaping official scrutiny, could have received five inches or more in the great February 1899 storm, but no report has been uncovered to confirm this. Thus, the five inches or more that fell on January 10th (the actual amount that members of Andrew Ellicott's surveying party found alongside their blankets on the next morning) must be considered the deepest snow ever measured near Florida.[18] Ellicott, most fortunately for meteorological historians, had the habit of being on the spot when the weather elements raged. At this time he was running the Florida-Georgia border for the Federal Government. His troop were camping at Point Peter near the mouth of the St. Marys River across the river from Florida, then Spanish territory. Ellicott's journal, as usual, was informative as to current meteorological conditions:

### January 1800

10. Thermometer 37° at sunrise, rose to 40°—Snow and hail the whole day! which continued until 10 o'clock in the evening when the thermometer fell to 32°, the wind shifted to N.W. and it became clear at midnight.
11. Thermometer 28° at sunrise, rose to 40°—Snow five inches deep.
12. 34° at sunrise—rose to 67°.[19]

Perhaps the snow fell much deeper than the five inches remaining on the ground the next morning. Certainly with the mercury above freezing during part of the snow period, there must have been much settling of the wet pack during that period and the night. The measurement of five inches as a minimum, however, remained the only way to judge this historic storm.

Ellicott's Journal also carried an account of a freeze on 19–20 February 1800 when there was a "smart frost," water congealed nine feet from the fire, and ice formed 1/6 of an inch thick.[20]

## TENNESSEE

Col. Sevier, again, made brief notes about the weather near Knoxville during this memorable winter:

### December 1799

30. Snow was 6 inches deep & snowed in the morning, very cold, cleared up in the evening.
31. Clear & windy. snowed.

### January 1800

1. Cold.
2. Clear and cold.
3-10. Clear & cold.
11. Clear & cold a little moderate
12. Warm & pleasant
13. Warm & pleasant
14. Warm & pleasant pleasant for the season.
15. Warm & cloudy.
16. Warm & cloudy. Rained in night.
17. Rainy & stormy & snowed four inches deep by evening.
18. Cleared & pretty cold.
19. Moderate.
20. Clear & windy.
21. Clear, cold & windy.
22-24. Clear, cold & windy.
25. Clear, cold & windy. Some little rain in evening.
26. Very cold.
27. Cloudy & cold.
28. Cloudy morning & cold.
29. Cloudy. Snowed in the night.
30. Snowed in the morning.
31. Warm & pleasant.

### February 1800

1. Snowed.
2. Snowed & very cold.
3. Cloudy & cold.
4. Cold day.
5. Snowed part of day.
6. Pleasant day.
7. Pleasant day.
8. Snowed & very cold.
9. Very cold, snowed & some rain.
10. Some snow & very cold.
11. Very cold & some snow.
12. A fine day.
13. Snowed in morning & most of day (not very cold).
14. Cold rain & some snow & hail.
15. Cloudy & very cold. Snowed. Cleared up in the night.
16. Clear day & pleasant.
17. Very fine day.
18. Very fine day.[21]

## MISSISSIPPI & LOUISIANA

Snow fell at New Orleans on the morning of 2 February 1800, according to Berquin-Duvallon, a visitor, in his *Vue de la colonie* (1803).[22] He stated that this was the first snowfall in 20 years, but this was incorrect since snow had fallen in 1784, as well as in the severe winter of 1780. No newspapers for February 1800 are extant from a New Orleans press so details are lacking of the event. But from Natchez, Mississippi, some 135 miles to the northwest, we have a wealth of material as William Dunbar had commenced his series of meteorological observations at The Forest about six miles from Natchez. His notes show a rather snowy period persisting from 31 January to 2 February:

| | | | |
|---|---|---|---|
| Jan. 31. | 29°<br>N 1<br>Snow | 32.5°<br>NE 2<br>Snow | 32°<br>NE 1<br>Rain |
| Feb. 1. | 32°<br>NE 1<br>Rain freezing | 30°<br>NE 1<br>Hail & sleet freezing | 30°<br>NE 1<br>Fine rain freezing |
| 2. | 27°<br>N | 32.5°<br>N 1<br>Cloudy & a little snow[23] | 32°<br>NE<br>Snow |

The above would indicate that a trough of low pressure persisted to the south of Natchez during the three days, probably located in the Gulf of Mexico, and gave birth to the cyclonic disturbance which moved northeastward giving the Carolinas their heavy snow on the 2d and 3d. Dunbar's description of the unusual snow follows:

*Remarks transcribed from the general daily Journal.*

### January

This month has been attended with more regular continued cold than is usual in this climate, with a smaller proportion of rain, which fell in moderate quantities on 7 or 8 different days; on the 31st. we were presented with a beautiful appearance. As the rain and sleet fell, the branches of trees were enveloped in a thin sheet of ice, and from every minute protuberance or angle depended an elegant christalization, which altogether produced an enchanting effect, giving to the trees the appearance of the most resplendent blossoms. Many large limbs were broken down with the weight of the ice.

### February

2d. This morning the ground is covered with snow, and the trees beautifully spangled with ice. At 10 o'clock the snow begins to melt away, although the sun is yet veiled in clouds. The snow to the depth of two inches is speedily thawed, in exposed situations; but remains all day on dry grass, chips and other bad conductors of heat, to the north of buildings, trees &c. but no where on the bare ground.

3d. This morning the ground is white with snow, and the trees completely glazed. One would suppose himself rather in Canada than in lat. 31°.—The sun peeps out, and a moment is granted to admire the most enchanting of pictures—The eye is dazzled with the prospect of myriads of gems, beautiful beyond imagination, with which the whole forest is decked, reflecting a combination of the most vivid colours from the facets of the icy chrystalizations—but another moment, and all is dissolved. From the dreary depth of winter we emerge at once to the enjoyment of the delicious softness of a morning in May.[25]

1. N. Webster, *Notes*, 1, 560.
2. J. Madison to T. Jefferson. Orange, Va., 14 Feb 1800. *Letters and other writings of James Madison*. Phila., J. B. Lippincott & Co., 1856. 2, 156.
3. J. Madison to T. Jefferson. Orange, Va., 15 Mar 1800. *ibid.*, 2, 158.
4. T. Jefferson. Ms. Weather Memorandum Book.
5. *Moravians in N. Car.*, 6, 2660.
6. *Ibid.*, 2643.
7. ———, 2661.
8. ———, 2659.
9. ———, 2644.
10. Extracts from the diary of Henry Ravenel of Berkeley, quoted in U. S. Dept. of Agri., *Climate and Crops, South Carolina Section*, Feb 1899, 3.
11. *S.C. State Gaz. and Timothy's Daily Adv.* (Charleston), 11 Jan 1800.
12. *City Gaz. and Daily Adv.* (Charleston), 13 Jan 1800.
13. J. Kershaw. Ms. Met. Obs.
14. U. S. Dept. Commerce, Weather Bureau. *Local climatological data with comparative data. 1964. Savannah, Georgia*. Ashville, N. C., 1965.
15. Abiel Holmes. *American Annals*. Cambridge, Mass., W. Hilliard, 1805. **2**, 409; *Mem. Amer. Acad. Arts Sci.* (Boston), 3–2 (1815), 109.
16. *Columbian Museum and Savannah Adv.*, 14 Jan 1800.
17. David Ludlum. Extremes of snowfall in the U. S. *Weatherwise* (Boston), **15**–6 (Dec 1962), 247.
18. *The journal of Andrew Ellicott . . . 1796–1800 . . . likewise a great number of thermometrical observations*. Phila., Fry, 1814. Appendix, 121.
19. *Idem.*
20. Andrew Ellicott. Astronomical and thermometrical observations made on the boundary between the United States and His Catholic Majesty. *Trans. Amer. Phil. Soc.* 5 (1802), 281.
21. Jour. Gov. Sevier, *Tenn. Mag. Hist.*, **6**-1 (1920), 22–24.
22. Berquin-Duvallon. *Vue de la colonie espagnole du Mississippi*, 77.
23. William Dunbar. Ms. Met. Obs. (Miss. Archives.)
24. *Trans. Amer. Phil. Soc.*, 6–1 (1801–04), 40.
25. *Ibid.*, 44.

## THE CLOSE OF THE EIGHTEENTH CENTURY—CLIMATE CHANGE?

The subject of climate change has always fascinated scientific man and also unscientific men. Great have been the arguments, especially in the early years of our country, despite the almost complete lack of scientific data upon which to base a judgment. But with the coming of meteorological measurements and continued observations over the years, the beginnings of a foundation upon which to build hypotheses were at hand. One of the first to treat the subject was Dr. Hugh Williamson who read a paper before the American Philosophical Society on 17 August 1770: "An attempt to account for the change of climate which has been observed in the Middle Colonies in North America." This was published in the first volumes of the *Transactions* in 1771. Through this and several later reprints in magazines, Williamson's ideas received a wide circulation among thinking men.

Williamson stated without substantiating evidence that the winters were now less severe and the summers warmer than in the earlier part of the century. This he ascribed to the cutting down of the forests and the multiplication of open fields since bare ground would absorb and retain more heat than forested terrain. This, in turn, ameliorated the cold of the northwest wind which was the instigator in cooling the climate. No attempt at statistical analysis was made since such data did not exist.

Among the followers of the Williamson theme was Thomas Jefferson who gave the concepts concrete form in his *Notes on the State of Virginia,* mostly composed in 1781. This "most important scientific and political book written by an American before 1785" spread the Williamsonian ideas far and wide:

A change in our climate however is taking place very sensibly. Both heats and colds are become much more moderate within the memory even of the middle-aged. Snows are less frequent and less deep. They do not often lie, below the mountains, more than one, two, or three days, and very rarely a week. They are remembered to have been formerly frequent, deep, and of long continuance. The elderly inform me the earth used to be covered with snow about three months in every year. The rivers, which then seldom failed to freeze over in the course of the winter, scarcely ever do do now. This change has produced an unfortunate fluctuation between heat and cold, in the spring of the year, which is very fatal to fruits. From the year 1741 to 1769, an interval of twenty-eight years, there was no instance of fruit killed by the frost in the neighborhood of Monticello. An intense cold, produced by constant snows, kept the buds locked up till the sun could obtain, in the spring of the year, so fixed an ascendency as to dissolve those snows, and protect the buds, during their development, from every danger of returning cold. The accumulated snows of the winter remaining to be dissolved all together in the spring, produced those overflowings of our rivers, so frequent then, and so rare now.

David Ramsay in his *History of South Carolina* (1809) apparently drew from his own experiences in writing the following summary of recent meteorological events:

It is remarkable that oranges, though plentiful forty or fifty years ago, are now raised with difficulty. Once in every eight or ten years a severe winter destroys the trees on which they grow. Of this kind were the winters of 1776, 1779, 1786, and 1796.

Ramsay must have referred to the seasons of 1776–77, 1779–80, 1786–87, and 1796–97, as evidence at hand pointed to all of these as containing at least one severely cold spell. Jefferson had supplied evidence of the rigorous conditions in 1776–77, and the Hard Winter of 1780 needed no documentation, so secure was its place in American meteorological history. Both 1786–87 and 1796–97 contained cold waves that drove the mercury to the lowest points reached since the cold of 1748 and 1752.

Another contemporary view on the subject was contained in William Dunbar's letter to Thomas Jefferson in 1801:

*General remarks respecting the winds, weather, &c.*

It is with us a general remark, that of late years the summers have become hotter and the winters colder than formerly. Orange trees and other tender exotics have suffered much more in the neighbourhood of New Orleans within these 4 or 5 years than before that period; the sugar cane also has been so much injured by the severity of the frosts of the two last winters, as greatly to discourage the planters, whose crops, in many instances, have fallen to one third or less of their expectations. In former years I have observed the mercury of the thermometer not to fall lower than 26 or 27°, but for a few years past, it has generally once or twice in the winter fallen as low as from 17 to 20°. and on the 12th. of December 1800 as above noticed it was found sunken to 12°. which has hitherto no parallel in this climate, indicating a degree of cold which in any country would be considered considerable, and probably may never be again produced by natural means in lat. $31\frac{1}{2}°$.

As this apparent alteration of climate has been remarked only for a few years and cannot be traced up to any visible natural or artificial change of sufficient magnitude, it would be in vain to search for its physical cause. Doctor Williamson and others have endeavoured to show that clearing, draining and cultivation, extended over the face of a continent, must produce the double effect of a relaxation of the rigours of winter, and an abatement of the heats of summer; the former is probably more evident than the latter, but admitting the demonstration to be conclusive, I would enquire whether a partial clearing extending 30 or 40 miles square, may not be expected to produce a contrary effect by admitting with full liberty, the sunbeams upon the discovered surface of the earth in summer, and promoting during winter a free circulation of cold northern air.

# THE EARLY NINETEENTH CENTURY IN THE NORTHEAST

The Great Coastal Storm and Deep Snow of Late Winter in 1802 165

The Widespread May Snow in 1803 ........................ 167

The Snowy Late Winter in 1804 ........................... 168

New England's Snow Hurricane of 1804 .................... 169

The Severe Winter of 1805 ................................ 170

The Forty-Eight Hour Snow at New York in 1805 ............ 172

The Late Starting Winter of 1807 ......................... 174

April Fools' Day Morning in 1807 ......................... 175

Cold Friday in New England—19 January 1810 .............. 179

Two Cold Storms and a Hard Winter: 1811–12 .............. 182

The Heavy May Snow of 1812 .............................. 187

The Severe Cold of 1815 and Hard Winter on Cape Cod ........ 188

June Snows of 1816 ...................................... 190

The Wintry February in 1817 ............................. 194

An Old-Fashioned Winter in 1819–20 ...................... 196

# THE GREAT COASTAL STORM AND DEEP SNOW OF LATE WINTER 1802

The first part of winter in 1801–02 had been mild and pleasant with little snow, in fact, the least wintry season since the Revolution. Noah Webster at New Haven noticed violets blooming, tulips germinating, and grass starting in January.[1] At Albany no ice formed on the Hudson River strong enough to bear a team for crossing and only 1.25 inches of snow fell during December and January.[2] At Newbury, Massachusetts, the ice on the Merrimac River moved with the ebb and flow of the tide, a very unusual January event.[3]

The first three weeks of February brought alternate periods of frost and mild weather, but none of the extremes usually associated with the New England winter. Sunday, February 21st, was "remarkably calm and pleasant" at Cambridge with the mercury climbing to 47° and the smoke rising straight up.[4] Even though it was the Sabbath, a number of ships at Salem took advantage of the favorable weather and put to sea. They were given Godspeed by many Sunday strollers who crowded the wharves and walks around the harbor.[5]

This situation is what is known in Yankee dialect as a "weather breeder." At the very time that the New England population was basking in the sunlight and looking forward to an early spring, a developing coastal storm was sweeping the Carolina seaboard area and spreading a canopy of cloud and precipitation northeastward.[6] The rain reached the Nation's Capital by 1730 and by 2200 a "boisterous storm" was raging.[7] The disturbance raced rapidly northeastward, with precipitation having changed to snow in southern New Jersey, commencing at New York City by 2300, at New Haven by midnight, and at Boston only an hour later—a very swift movement.[8] Its progress northward up the Hudson Valley was less rapid, reaching Poughkeepsie by 0400 and Albany a little before daybreak.[9] This timetable indicated that the main force of the storm would be expended along the coastal sections of southern New England.

The facts and figures for this meteorological event were gathered by Hon. Samuel Latham Mitchill, professor at Columbia College, U. S. Senator from New York, and editor of the *Medical Repository,* a New York publication which served as the leading journal for scientific matters of the early 1800's. Mitchill's article bore the title: Account of a North-east Storm, or Memorandum towards a Theory of the Winds in the Region between the Gulf-Stream and the great Range of Mountains.[10] Mitchill found confirmation of the earlier theory of Franklin and Evans as to the northeastward movement of storms which had originated to the southward along the South Atlantic coast, despite their seemingly opposing surface headwinds.

Dawn of the 22d of February came with all of southern and central New England locked in a furious northeast snowstorm. At Cambridge the day was described by President Webber, Harvard's current weatherman: "A severe snow storm continued through the whole of the 22d. The falling snow was very thick; the wind very strong and somewhat to the E of N, but appearing to me, by the college wave, to be nearer to the N than N.E." His colleague, Prof. Waterhouse, when communicating with Prof. Mitchill in New York, thought the storm was "the longest if not the severest storm I ever knew."[11] And so it was. It rated among the *great* snowstorms of the hill country of southern and eastern New England and also among the notable northeasters that have spread havoc and destruction along the coastline.

President Timothy Dwight of Yale College, who also took an avid interest in the weather and served as one of our first meteorological historians, stated that the snow depth in 1802 would have been equal to the memorable February 1717 storms if there had not been a considerable amount of hail (sleet) mixed with the falling flakes.[12] But, as our account of that memorable storm has shown, some sleet did fall in 1717, as it appears to do eventually in all such storms when a very intense circulation from the relatively warm Atlantic Ocean is generated and sustained for an extended period.

U. S. Senator William Plumer of New Hampshire, long a weather-watcher as well as able politician and prosperous farmer, has left a graphic account of the snow accumulation near his home at Epping, located near Exeter about 15 miles from the sea:

### February 1802

22. Wind NE & high—fell 16″ of snow, much drifted.
23. Wind NW & high, snow blew much, road almost impassable, banks of snow some places 5 to 8 feet deep—cold.
24. Epping to Brunswick & Exeter—wind W, fair & cool—roads impassable—obliged to ride and walk through fields & pastures—near half the ground bare.
25. Wind NE–E–SE snowed all day and night—much snow fell—moon quartered.
26. Wind E–SE–N and high—snowed all day, snow much drifted—roads absolutely impassable—thawed some.
27. Wind E–NE–snowed some, rained a little. There is now four feet and a half of snow on the

ground—some banks 12 feet deep—no traveling but with snow shoes, cold, sun has not been seen but one day this week.

28. Wind NE–N–cloudy cold, snowed all day—fences all buried beneath the snow—no traveling.

**March 1802**

1. Wind NE, cloudy, cold, thawed some—sun did not shine—snowed in evening—fourteen men & 20 oxen all the day broke through the snow only 1¼ mile and made a bad path.
2. Wind E—cloudy, moderate rain most of day, snow disappeared very fast—thawed all night.[13]

In central Massachusetts at Rutland, a rural diarist, Seth Metcalf, noted among the events of 1802: ". . . I would take notis of a Snow that fell the Last Week of February which fell more than four feet Deep with exceeding High wind. . . ."[14] Also in central Massachusetts at Worcester, Isaiah Thomas gave confirmation as to the snow depth: "Feb. 28—Snow fell 3½ feet on a level, mail due this office on 25th, arrived only this evening, three days late."[15] These figures all refer to new snowfall since the ground was bare or practically so when this great storm commenced.

In southern New Hampshire the *Concord Courier* complained on March 4th that there had been no southern or eastern mails in 10 days, or since the commencement of the great snow. Even along the immediate seaboard prodigious amounts fell as the *New Hampshire Gazette* at Portsmouth related:

### THE STORM

On Thursday last, the snow began to come down; on Friday it fell in amazing quantities, and by Saturday morning the streets, roads, etc. were nearly impassable. The oldest persons in this town, have no recollection of so large a body of snow, at any one period. It is nearly 3 feet on a level; and the drifts are from 6 to 10 feet deep. The air has felt ever since as if impregnated by additional snows. Saturday, Sunday and Monday we had more or less and appearances indicate another heavy storm. The wind blew strong at dew[sic] East—The swell of the sea was prodigious, and we anticipate melancholy news from Eastern coasts and elsewhere, of shipwrecks, loss of lives, etc.[17]

Among the ships which set sail from Salem on that delightful Sunday were three full-rigged East-Indiamen, the *Ulysses, Brutus,* and *Volusia,* bound for French and Mediterranean ports. The rising storm, catching the ships about midnight, drove them back toward the dangerous shoreline as the northeasterly gale increased in fury. Their captains fought desperately to save their vessels. The *Ulysses* and *Volusia,* in attempting to reach the haven of Cape Ann, were forced onto the shoals of Cape Cod off Truro; fortunately both ships were carried over the bar, well toward the beach. At low tide the crews were able to make their ways to safe ground without the loss of a single life. The *Brutus* was not so fortunate. She fought the storm all day, but was constantly forced back toward the shore where she finally struck after dark only about two miles from the other wrecks. Though carried over the bar, the *Brutus* began to split in two; the crew was barely able to scramble over the fallen main mast into shallow water. Soon they found themselves on land, but soaked and exhausted from their ordeal. They were uncertain of their location, shivered in near-zero temperatures, and had more than a foot of deep snow to trudge through. During the following night of horror the famished men wandered over the sand hills between Truro and Provincetown in search of shelter. One by one the exhausted men fell down in the snow and death came quickly from freezing: nine perished including the captain, only five survived. The people of Salem were plunged into great apprehension for the fate of the three ships, knowing that they had been exposed to the severest type of northeaster that the Atlantic could raise. Lacking means of communication such as telegraph or radio, it was not until March 4th that the suspense was lifted and the varying fates of the vessels revealed to the families and friends of crewmen at home.[18]

[1] N. Webster, *Notes,* **1**, 557.
[2] *Annals of Albany,* **3**, 319.
[3] Joshua Coffin. *History of Newbury, Mass.* 273.
[4] *Medical Repository* (New York), **5**, (1802), 468.
[5] Sidney Perley. *Historic Storms of New England.* 161.
[6] *Med. Rep.,* **5**, 467.
[7] *Idem.*
[8] *Idem.*
[9] *Idem.*
[10] *Ibid.,* 465–68.
[11] *Ibid.,* 467.
[12] Timothy Dwight. *A statistical account of New Haven.* New Haven, Walter Steele, 1811. 60.
[13] William Plumer. Ms. Met. Obs., (Harvard).
[14] *Journal of Seth Metcalf,* 24.
[15] The diary of Isaiah Thomas. *Proc. Amer. Antiq. Soc.* ns. **26**, (April 1916), 64.
[16] *The Courier* (Concord), 4 March 1802.
[17] *New Hamp. Gaz.* (Portsmouth), 2 March 1802.
[18] Sidney Perley, 162–67.

# THE WIDESPREAD MAY SNOW IN 1803

A small barometric depression moved eastward from Kentucky across Virginia and then apparently headed northeastward somewhat parallel to the coastline on 7–8 May 1803. It produced the first measurable May snow at seaboard locations since the famous event in May 1774. The snow canopy did not reach northern New York State or northern New England. The cut-off line probably ran close to Albany and the northern Massachusetts border. Winds at all points in the snow area were first northeast, then shifting to northwest. Thunder and lightning were reported in the Philadelphia area as a change-over from rain to snow took place early in the morning of the 8th. Since trees were in leaf at southern locations considerable damage occurred, especially to the susceptible poplars which lined many of the main streets of Philadelphia. The occasion was made memorable by the appearance of sleighs in Hudson Valley towns and in Massachusetts. Maximum depths appeared to have been about six inches, though hill locations may have received more. The early history of the storm in the Ohio Valley is presented on page 227. Its progress through the Northeast can best be followed through the many press accounts describing the unusual event:

(All references to 8 May unless otherwise indicated)

**District of Columbia,** Washington:
Early May—We have experienced for several days an unprecedented coldness of weather; having had the uncommon spectacle of snow in May, and ice of considerable thickness having formed for several successive nights. *Nat. Int.* (Wash., D. C.), 13 May 1803.

**Pennsylvania,** Philadelphia:
7 May—temperature 38° at 0700, ice in country; 8th—37° at 0700, north east great snow storm in night thunder. The trees torn to pieces. Rittenhouse family. Ms. Met. Obs. (Amer. Phil. Soc.).

**New Jersey,** Elizabeth, Union Co.:
Snow covered the ground between 0400 and 0500. *Amer. Adv.* (Phila.), 12 May 1803.

............ Belleville, Essex Co.:
This morning cut a mess of asparagus—the beds covered with snow. Gerard Rutgers. Ms. Diary. (Rutgers Univ.).

**New York,** New York City:
A considerable fall of snow this morning, the weather during the remaining part of the day cold and disagreeable. Henry Laight. Ms. Met. Obs. (NA).

....................:
On Saturday morning (7th) frost was so severe as to form ice the thickness of a dollar—yesterday (8th) there was a fall of snow for several hours. *Amer. Adv.* (Phila.), 11 May 1803.

............, Poughkeepsie, Dutchess Co.:
Snow several inches deep—sleighs gliding through the streets. *The Barometer* (Poughkeepsie) in *Amer. Adv.,* 17 May 1803.

............, Hudson, Columbia Co.:
Friday night 6th severe frost—Sunday (8th) considerable fall of snow. *The Balance* (Hudson), 10 May 1803.

**Connecticut,** New Haven, New Haven Co.:
A fall of snow to the depth of two to three inches, & had the ground been frozen, the depth would have been six inches. Noah Webster, *Notes,* 1, 561.

............, Hamden, New Haven Co.:
Two inches—very snowy morning—snow melts before night. J. Alling. *Weather Register,* 59.

............, Haddam, Middlesex Co.:
Very rainy. It snowed considerably. In some places the snow is six inches deep. 10—some snow that fell on the 8th remaining. T. Robbins. *Diary,* 1, 195.

**Massachusetts,** Springfield, Hampden Co.:
Three inches snow on the average. *Springfield Spy* in *Amer. Adv.,* 19 May 1803.

............, Princeton, Worcester Co.:
Snow 0600 to 1800. People went visiting in sleighs. *Columbian Centinel* (Boston), 14 May 1803.

............, Waltham, Middlesex Co.:
9 May—Snow covered hills. 28°. Charles Fisk. *Boston Transcript* in *U. S. Reg.* (Phila.), 9 June 1841, 366.

............, Boston, Suffolk Co.:
In this town and vicinity a large quantity of snow fell, and it is feared much damage has been done to early vegetation. *Boston Weekly Magazine,* 14 May 1803.

....................:
In this town we had no very great falls of snow, but on Sunday night considerable ice was made. *Columbian Centinel,* 14 May 1803.

............, Lynn, Essex Co.:
Snow for 7 hours, one inch deep—apple trees in blossom. A. Lewis. *History of Lynn,* 228.

............, Salem, Essex Co.:
The rain began this day at eight & the snow at eleven & it snowed throughout the day. W. Bentley. *Diary,* 3, 22.

....................:
Temperature at four stated observations: 42°, 34°, 35°, 33°. E. Holyoke. *Met. Jour.,* 153.

# THE SNOWY LATE WINTER OF 1804

Snowy winters came back in vogue in 1804 though the season proved a late starter. Noah Webster at New Haven noted its general character.

From January to late March, generally cold winter, & frequent snows which accumulated to 4 feet depth. The first week of March fell a great snow, & until late March the snow was three feet deep in the country generally. More snow than since 1780, fodder scarse by reason of the drouthe of last summer, & in the interior many cattle died.[1]

Late February and early March brought three major snowstorms in one week—the one-two-three punch for which New England can be famous at this time of year. These storms, however, appear to have been unlike the famous triple blows in the seasons of 1717 and 1802 in that the deep snowfalls were not confined to a section of New England, but reached westward to cover Pennsylvania and New York as well.

Dr. Bentley with his diary and Dr. Holyoke with his meteorological instruments were on hand to record the events as they took place at Salem:

## February 1804

18. The first pleasant day of the season.
23. Several vessels went out this day but returned soon enough to escape the storm which began this afternoon & continued with snow and high wind till next day.[2]

| Sunrise | Noon | Sunset | 2200 |
|---|---|---|---|
| 24° | 27° | 27° | 27° |
| Fair | Snow | Snow | Snow |
| 29.67" | | | 29.30"[3] |

24. The storm continues with unabated violence & the fence near our house, above six feet high, is covered with the drifts which are forced against it. In January we had snow 8 times, rain 6 times, hail once & thunder twice.

| 21° | 14° | 11° | 9° |
|---|---|---|---|
| Snow | Snow | Snow | Snow |
| 28.98" | | | 29.15" |

25. The storm continued until last night at midnight. The quantity of snow in Town is much beyond any for many years. The roads at present impassable. One Southern and two Eastern mails are due. Yesterday the mail stage driver in a single sleigh forced through after a struggle for a whole day. This day we heard of no passenger. It is undoubtedly the deepest snow I have ever seen in Salem. The banks before our house were six feet in drifts & that height at a mean throughout the town, & few places were left entirely bare. At 1400 on Friday was the thickest flight of snow I ever saw. We are still shut up.
28. We have not time to clear our roads before we have snow again. After a cloudy day at one it began to snow & continued but not with violence, through the remainder of the day. Dr. Holyoke had a fall on the ice yesterday which rendered him senseless.

| 20° | 31° | 32° | 31° |
|---|---|---|---|
| Cloudy | Snow | Snow | Snow |
| 29.97" | | | 29.83" |

29. It snowed in the morning & the sun broke out. Glass just above the freezing point.

| 27° | 34° | 30° | 23° |
|---|---|---|---|
| Snow | Fair | Fair | Fair |
| 29.92" | | | 30.03" |

## March 1804

1.

| 31° | 37° | 32° | 32° |
|---|---|---|---|
| Cloudy | Snow | Cloudy | Cloudy |
| 29.99" | | | 29.74" |

2. The travelling remains bad and dangerous & the snow continues to fall. Our harbor has not been frozen so our navigation has been open.

| 34° | 33° | 33° | 29° |
|---|---|---|---|
| Snow | Snow | Snow | Snow |
| 29.47" | | | 28.95" |

3. Some of the stages did return after attempting the Turnpike, & the Marblehead stage did not get through.

| 19° | 28° | 18° | 12° |
|---|---|---|---|
| Cloudy | Fair | Fair | Fair |
| 29.09" | | | 29.13" |

At Boston the press declared the storm of the 23–24th "as severe a snow storm as has occurred in 10 years."[4] The Ames Diary spoke of conditions south of Boston around Dedham on Feb. 29th: "Country encumber'd with more Snow & road blocked more than for above 30 years past, travel totally obstructed in many places & more snow still falls 2 and 4 March."[5] At New Haven Thomas Beers measured the snow of the 28–29th and found 16 inches of new snow, and on the 4th reported: "a great body of snow on ground."[6]

Inland areas also received great falls. President Day, probably relying on press reports, wrote: "In the first part of this month, the depth of the snow, between this State and Canada, was from four to six feet."[7] Around Albany the snow lay three feet on a level on March 5th, and three mails were due from New York City—"circumstances unknown to the oldest inhabitants."[8] The *Hudson Balance* reported: "On Friday we had a most abundant fall of snow in this vicinity. Its average depth was upwards of two feet."[9] In Vermont the bridge between Hanover and Norwich was crushed by the weight of the massive accumulation.[10] And at Bennington on April 4th the crust of the snow would bear the weight of horses and loaded sleighs.[11] Around the Philadelphia area "the deepest snow remembered for some years past" had fallen on February 23d and on the 24th, a "deep snow on the ground." Press reports indicated "medium depth of snow in winter 2 feet."[12]

The snow cover remained in eastern Massachusetts throughout March. The Ames diary on March 31st declared: "Cold as January—freezes the road in daytime. Winter still holds on 1 April. Roads still blocked to Abner Smith's the travel in diverse places is thro' fields & that is difficult. Sleys run until 21st (March) and then Wheels cannot get through many banks. Road from Capt. Jon Richards's by J. Wilson's totally obstructed to End of this month."[13]

[1] N. Webster, *Notes,* **1,** 562.
[2] W. Bentley, *Diary,* **3,** 76.
[3] E. Holyoke. Met. Jour. *Mem. Amer. Acad. Arts & Sci.* Ns. **1,** (1833), 151.
[4] Boston, 25 Feb, in *N.Y. Post,* 3 March 1804.
[5] The Ames Diary. *The Dedham Hist. Reg.* **13,** (1902), 26.
[6] T. Beers, Ms. Met. Jour., (Yale).
[7] J. Day, Ms. Met. Jour., (Yale).
[8] *Annals of Albany,* **3,** 327.
[9] *The Balance* (Hudson), 6 March 1804.
[10] *Boston Weekly Mag.,* 31 March 1804.
[11] *Ibid.,* 21 April 1804.
[12] S. Hazard, Effects of climate, *Penna. Reg.,* **2,** 382.
[13] Ames Diary, 26.

# NEW ENGLAND'S SNOW HURRICANE OF 1804

The major meteorological event in the opening years of the Nineteenth Century developed when a severe coastal disturbance, probably of hurricane origin, reached full fury over southern New England during the daylight hours of 9 October 1804.[1] It struck massive blows at Connecticut and Massachusetts points resulting in extensive structural damage. The intense circulation caused gale force winds to sweep the area from the Hudson Valley in New York eastward to the Maine and Massachusetts coasts and beyond. The great atmospheric currents involved brought down a bitterly cold air stream from Canada of record frigid severity for the early season as the intense disturbance, supplied with copious amounts of moisture and meeting below-freezing temperatures, produced an exceptionable early season snowstorm. "Such an event is very remarkable—the only one I have found recorded," confided meteorological historian, Noah Webster.[2]

The early fall season of 1804 had been cold. A September snow spread over the highlands of New York and western New England as early as the autumnal equinox. Timothy Dwight, the peripatic Yale president, had noticed a snowstorm in the vicinity of Marcellus, Onondaga County, New York, on 20 September.[3] Again late on the 8th of October another cold rain set in when Dwight tarried at Bemis, near Rochester, in New York, and on the 9th he witnessed "a considerable flight of snow, which, however, dissolved as it fell."[4] This appeared to be the western fringe of the severe storm then raging along the southern New England coastline.

The coastal disturbance passed very close to New York City, south of Poughkeepsie, north of New Haven, and probably right over Boston, between noon to late afternoon of the 9th.[5] The advance circulation had already triggered a vast precipitation shield over all of New England except central and northern Maine. In Vermont the storm commenced as snow. In the upper Connecticut Valley at Lunenburg the day received long remembrance as Dr. Hiram A. Cutting related in his interesting "Natural History of Essex County":

> October 9, 1804 brought with its dawn a great snow storm. The weather had been cloudy and extremely cold for the season for a number of days; and on the morn of this day it commenced snowing, and continued until full 20 inches of snow had fallen.[6]

The contemporary press and later many New England town histories gave special coverage to this unique event. The *Vermont Journal* told of snow depths of three to four feet on the heights of land along the crest of the Green Mountains[7]; and at Goffstown, in the highlands of central New Hampshire, the town historian mentioned snow falling two feet deep at this usually snowy spot where northeast winds, meeting the highlands, were forced to rise and intensify the precipitation process.[8] At Hanover in the Connecticut Valley the snow on the evening of the 9th measured six inches, and great damage to orchard trees still in leaf resulted.[9] A good account of the storm and its destructive effects came from the pen of the editor of the *Political Observatory* at Walpole, Cheshire County in southwestern New Hampshire, who proved a very weather-conscious newsman in devoting space in two issues to the storm story:

### EXTRAORDINARY SNOW STORM

On Tuesday last (9th instant) about the middle of the forenoon, the weather suddenly changed from temperate rain, to a storm of snow, attended with thunder and violent wind on the high lands—the storm continued with some intermissions till Wednesday morning. It is judged that the mean depth which fell was from 15 to 18 inches. Contiguous to the river, it dissolved rapidly, yet repeatedly measured from 4 to 5 inches, and covered the ground for more than 30 hours. On the hills it was blown considerably into drifts, which in places covered the fences and blocked up the roads. The eastern stage could not run, & the mail was conveyed on horseback. Great damage was done to fruit trees and timber than was ever known to be sustained in one year since the settlement of the country. Their foliage found a lodgment for the adhesive snow, which broke many branches by its weight, and the wind lending its aid leveled many a trunk with the earth.— The western mail had not arrived when this paper went to press. Nor have we received papers from the eastern part of the state. . . . To enliven the gloom of the scene, sleighs ran briskly during the continuance of the snow in this village.

*Political Observatory* (Walpole, N. H.),
13 October 1804.

### OF THE SNOW STORM

Accounts from every direction prove the destructive effect of the late storm of snow, particularly on timber and fruit trees. So wide and severe a havoc was never before made in this part of the county. We have seen the devastation in some of the orchards nearly equal to that of a tornado; Scarsely a tree remains uninjured; many have left but here and there a solitary branch, and some are rent through the length of their trunks and prostrated each way on the earth. The damage to one individual's orchard in this town is estimated at 300 dollars. Others have suffered to a considerable amount. The quantity of fruit must be lessened for years to come, which is more unhappy as there is but a small supply of cider the present season.

On the height of land in Vermont, the snow was 3 feet in depth: and on less elevated parts in that and this state it was from 2 to 2½ feet, of which a considerable portion has since continued, covering potatoes in the earth and a part of the corn so that it is impossible to gather those crops.

*Political Observatory* (Walpole, N. H.),
20 October 1804.

In western Massachusetts press reports mentioned depths from 24 to 30 inches on the western slopes of the Berkshires. Snow fell on both sides of the Hudson River on the highlands, though apparently none stuck in the valley floor.[10] In the Catskills some of the towns to the westward experienced 12 to 18 inches of snowfall, and the mountain tops continued white six days later.[11] There was sleighing at New Lebanon, New York, in the Berkshires on the Massachusetts border.[12]

As to the southern extent of the snowfall in New England, we are indebted to Noah Webster in relating that the hills around Woodbridge, near New Haven, Connecticut, just north of the Yale Bowl where the Wilbur Cross Parkway tunnels through West Rock, were whitened by the snow.[13] Inland at Litchfield three inches were reported, and at the higher elevation of Goshen just to the north 12 inches fell.[14] As in the north, elevation proved the determining factor in temperature conditions and therefore in the depth of snow. To illustrate the combination of meteorological elements available for concocting such a severe storm, President Day's thermometer at New Haven read 38° on the evening of the 9th and 3.66 inches of rain had fallen during the storm period.[15] A short distance to the north, this produced an excessive snowfall.

In eastern New England no snow reports came from Providence, Boston, or Worcester. Temperature conditions there, in and to the south of the track and closer to maritime influences, did not permit the formation of frozen precipitation.[16]

[1] *Violent Storm.* (Broadside). Boston, 15 Oct 1804?.
[2] N. Webster. *Notes,* 1, 563.
[3] T. Dwight. *Travels,* 4, 33.
[4] *Ibid.,* 94.
[5] New England's Snow Hurricane of 1804. David M. Ludlum. *Early American Hurricanes,* 35–38.
[6] H. A. Cutting. Natural History of Essex County, Vermont. A. Hemenway. *Vermont Historical Gazetteer,* 1-10, (Oct 1868), 1052.
[7] *Vermont Journal* (Windsor), 16 Oct 1804.
[8] George P. Hadley. *Hist. of Goffstown,* 1, 554.
[9] *Dartmouth Gazette* (Hanover, N. H.), 12 Oct 1804.
[10] *Boston Weekly Magazine,* 27 Oct 1804.
[11] Catskill, 15 Oct, in *N. Y. Post,* 19 Oct 1804.
[12] *Hudson Balance,* 16 Oct 1804.
[13] N. Webster. *Notes,* 1, 563.
[14] J. Day. Ms. Met. Obs. (Yale).
[15] *Idem.*
[16] D. Ludlum. 38.

# THE SEVERE WINTER OF 1805

The first severely cold winter in the Nineteenth Century occurred in 1804–05 when a cold December was followed by an icy and snowy January, and these conditions continued through the first ten days of February. A continuing thaw then routed the hold of winter, ending the excellent sleighing of six weeks duration and soon unlocking the rivers from their icy fetters.

The season at Philadelphia had been described as "variable and peculiar, intense cold, deep snow, hail, sleet, high wind, and heavy rain."[1] In short, the month contained everything possible in a winter season. In addition, January 1805 won the title of being the snowiest month of early record in the New York City and lower Connecticut area. At Hamden near New

Haven a total of 57 inches of snowfall was measured by Jeremiah Alling who maintained a meteorological register from 1785 to 1810 and published his observations in an interesting booklet.[2] The snowy January also appeared in the records of Professor Day with 43 inches of January snowfall measured on the campus of Yale College.[3] In the New York City area there were seven distinct snowstorms in December and January with a total of 60 inches, according to a later press notice quoting an unknown contemporary weather observer.[4] The climactic storm of the month came on the 27th and 28th of January when a forty-eight hour snow brought from 20 to 24 inches to the city already under a massive blanket from previous falls, especially one a week before on the 20–21st. Noah Webster at New Haven took note of the wintry conditions:

January 1805—Winter commenced about the middle of December & was severe from the 20th with good sleying. It continued with severe & steddy cold through January and most of February. . . . The snow of January 1805 was about three feet deep. This was the severest winter since 1780. But the snow left the earth in March in good season and Spring was early. I cut asparagus on the 14th of April, 9 days earlier than last year.[5]

Temperatures in January ran well below normal throughout the Northeast: New Haven −3.1 degrees following a December with a −2.3 degree deficit.[6] Yet there were no severely cold polar outbreaks. The lowest mark reached at New Haven was −6°, at Salem −3°, and at New York City −3°.[7] There were reports from interior western Connecticut of −19°, but these marks are normal for a colder than usual January.[8] The first three weeks of the month did exhibit some steadiness in the cold that prepared the way for the grand freeze-up of the mighty Hudson River at New York just at the time of the month when the January thaw should be expected. Henry Laight's records show +40° as the maximum during the period 1–23 with only four days of noontime mercury above freezing. The final week ran relatively warm with thawing weather except for the period of the big snowstorm on the 27th and 28th. The monthly maximum at New York reached 45° on the 30th, at New Haven 47.5°, and at Salem, Mass. 44°.[9]

Henry Laight, New York's weatherman since 1788, made full notes of the winter's events:

### December 1804

15. Snow about 6 inches.

### January 1805

1. Deep snow.
3. Excellent sleighing.
4. The coldest night since 23 Dec. 1796 at which time the mercury was 1°—next morning 0°. −2° at 11 P.M.—+8° next morning at 8.
6. A cake of ice lodged in East River between this city and Brooklyn—by which many persons crossed the river.
10. Early in the day it began to snow & continued so to do till sunset from which time it hailed until the next morning—Snow and hail about 8 inches.
18. The sleighing continued fine until this time.
20. Violent snow storm & heavy gale from NE—The streets are almost impassable from the great fall of snow.
22. Extremely cold—wood $8. per load.
23. This day & yesterday several persons crossed the Hudson from the State Prison to Hoboken.
26. It began to snow in the evening of this day and continued until the evening of the 28th without any interruption—48 hours. So much snow has not fallen at one time for a great number of years. Pine St., Cedar St., Liberty St., and many narrow streets are altogether impassable for sleighs on account of the great depth of the snow.
31. Excellent sleighing during the whole of this month.

### February 1805

14. Heavy rain almost all day—a sensible impression is made on the snow.[10]

A weather observer who contributed a regular column to the Boston *Monthly Anthology,* probably located near the Harvard campus at Cambridge, also left some notes on the major events:

### December 1804

9–10. 2 to 3 inches snow.
12. moderate snow.
14. 0° at sunrise—barometer 30.50".
15–16. snow, hail, rain.
24–25. snow storm.
29. snow and rain—barometer 28.80" at 2200.

### January 1805

2. snow A.M.
3–4. snow—very high wind—snow & rain 4th—29.30".
5. snowed moderately all day.
7. snowed till noon—frozen mist P.M.
8. hail, then rain, thaws 40°.
10. snow after 1500.
13. some rain 39°.
18. great thaw 41°.
19. snow 1100–1500.
20. snow after 1400.
21. snow & hail A.M.—rain P.M.—29.00" at 1400.
23. 0° at 0800.
27. Snow storm. Wind moderate until near sunset, when it rose very much.

| Hamden, Conn. | |
|---|---|
| Nov. 14 | 1.0″ |
| Dec. 3 | 1.5 |
| 7 | .75 |
| 12 | 4. |
| 15 | 3. |
| 24 | 12. |
| 29 | 4. |
| | 25.25 |
| Jan. 2 | 4. |
| 3 | 1. |
| 4 | 4. |
| 5 | 3. |
| 10 | 2. |
| 11 | 3. hail |
| 13 | 4. |
| 19 | 3. |
| 20 | 3. |
| 21 | 12. |
| 27 | 10. |
| 28 | 8. |
| | 57. |
| Feb. 7 | 3.00 |
| 19 | .75 |
| 28 | 1. |
| | 4.75 |

None listed in March or April[12]

28. Storm continued all day. Between 2 P.M. and 4 P.M. rain, although temperature did not rise. Snow afternoon.
29. Snow most of day. Wind moderate.

**February 1805**

5. +6° at 0800.
8. great thaw 34°.
9. 38°.
10. 40°.
11. 54°.
12. 50°.
13. 49°.[11]

The snowfall record at Hamden in southern Connecticut showed many small snows with two major storms: 15 inches on the 20–21st and 18 inches on the 27–28th. The figures, in general, agree with those of President Day, but run about 20 per cent higher as might be expected in the generally hilly country back from the shore of Long Island Sound.

[1] S. Hazard. Effects of climate. *Penna. Reg.* **2**, 383.
[2] J. Alling. *Register of the Weather.* 64.
[3] J. Day. Ms. Met. Obs. (Yale).
[4] *N. Y. Gazette,* 2 March 1833.
[5] N. Webster. *Notes,* **1**, 564.
[6] J. Day.
[7] J. Day; E. Holyoke; H. Laight. Ms. Met. Jours.
[8] *New York Post,* 19 Jan 1805.
[9] See #7.
[10] H. Laight.
[11] *Monthly Anthology and Boston Review.* 2-1, (1805) 2.
[12] J. Alling, *Register,* 64.

## THE FORTY-EIGHT-HOUR-SNOW AT NEW YORK IN 1805

The climatic event of the wintry season of 1804–05, generally agreed to have been unequaled in severity since the Hard Winter of 1780, enveloped the New York area on the evening of January 26th when the first flakes of one of the city's greatest snowstorms commenced to filter down. A deep blanket of undetermined depth already covered the ground, and rivers and harbors were so choked with ice that navigation was at a stand.

New York's longtime weatherman, Henry Laight, described the storm scene in his notes:

Jan. 26, 1805—It began to snow in the evening of this day and continued until the evening of the 28th without interruption—48 hours. So much snow has not fallen at one time for a great number of years. Pine St., Cedar St., Liberty St. and many narrow streets are altogether impassable for sleighs on account of the great depth of the snow.[1]

The *New York Post* on the 28th noticed the continuing storm: "It is now nearly forty-eight hours since the snow storm which yet rages with undiminished violence and with increasing severity has been begun."[2] And next day followed: "The present fall of snow is probably greater than ever known in the latitude of New York. It began to snow at 8 o'clock Saturday evening and continued without intermission till Monday 5 in the afternoon—held up a little—then recommenced and continued till about 8 in the evening. It can be said that it snowed forty-eight hours, a continuance not to be paralleled in the memory of any man living."[2]

There does not exist a day-by-day snow depth record for New York City for this season. In later years a writer in summarizing the high points of this winter stated: "In December and January there were seven distinct falls of snow, one of which lasted 48 hours, and during which the snow fell two feet on a level. The whole quantity of snow this winter exceeded 60 inches on a level, but there were occasional rains and thaws, its average depth was never more than between 2 and 3 feet."[4] At a nearby point in New Jersey the Scudder family's diary contained the following passage for their residence at Springfield, a snow pocket against Watchung Mountain, only a dozen miles from New York City: "Jan. 28—At night the Snow fell about 3 feet deep which make about 4 feet on a level with the overnight, with a −25° noticed at the sunrise observation. Prof. Cleaveland's reading during this intensely cold period follow:

|  | Min. | Max. |
|---|---|---|
| Jan. 20. | −19° | +19.5° |
| 21. | −5.5 | +23.5 |
| 22. | −20.25 | +6.5 |
| 23. | −30. | +24. |
| 24. | +11. | +26.5 |
| 25. | +7.75 | +23.5 |
| 26. | −13.5 | −4.5 |
| 27. | −29.75 | +9.5 |
| 28. | −1.5 | +35.[2] |

These low readings were confirmed by marks elsewhere. From Hallowell in Maine, the report of −34° on the 27th was considered the lowest thermometer ever reached in the United States up to that time, and drew notice in the publications of the American Philosophical Society.[3]

In eastern Massachusetts the extreme degree reached in Maine was not achieved, but the 26th stood as a zero day in many places. At Cambridge the three readings on the 26th were: −16°, −1°, and −9.5°, for what appeared to be an authentic zero day though a registering thermometer was not in use.[4] At Andover, some 15 miles to the north, the three readings that day were: −18°, −6°, and −9°, for an average of −11°.[5]

The month of February was an in-and-out affair, with two severe cold waves separated by marked thaws, a situation leading to disastrous consequences. The January cold wave had stopped the Delaware at Philadelphia on January 14th. The river held firm until the warm spell in early February when the river drove on the 3d. Arctic blasts soon congealed the river again on the 7th, only to have the mid-February thaw free the river so that vessels could sail seaward.[6]

February 1807 was the month noted for the famous Cold Friday in the Midwest and Upper South when a cold air mass drove down the eastern reaches of the Mississippi Valley and penetrated deep into the Southland with a degree of cold that would not be matched again until the Great Arctic Outbreak of 1835.[7] Since the main stream of the invading cold air remained west of the Appalachians, temperatures in the Northeast did not fall as low as they had in the previous month. Nevertheless, most of the East was treated to sub-zero conditions that set the stage for the spectacular ice break-up in mid-month. At Brunswick, Maine, the coldest February mornings were the 8th and 9th with −12° and −18.5°, though on neither day did the mercury remain below zero all day.[8] Down at Cambridge, Massachusetts, one February morning had a −11° and one afternoon an even zero, but this did not constitute a zero day either.[9] At New Haven the lowest read −3.5° on the 8th.[10]

[1] W. Bentley, *Diary*, 3, 272–75.
[2] Parker Cleaveland. Ms. Met. Obs., (Bowdoin).
[3] D. N. Collin. Extract of a letter relative to the great cold in January 1807, at the town of Hallowell, in the District of Maine, Mass. *Trans. Amer. Phil. Soc.* 6-2, (1809), 401–02.
[4] *Mem. Amer. Acad.*, 3-2 (1815), 378.
[5] *Ibid.*, 408.
[6] S. Hazard. Effects of climate, *Penna. Reg.*, 3, 383.
[7] D. M. Ludlum. *Early American Winters: 1821–1870.* (In press.)
[8] P. Cleaveland.
[9] *Mem. Amer. Acad.*, 3-2, 378.
[10] J. Day. Ms. Met. Obs.

## APRIL FOOLS' DAY MORNING IN 1807

From Illinois to New England early risers on the morning of 1 April 1807 were greeted by a deep white mantle, in many places of record depth for so late in the season. The storm commenced in the lower Ohio Valley late on the evening of 30 March, and then spread rapidly eastward during the night reaching the Middle Atlantic coast by daybreak and covering all New England by nightfall. The snowfall at eastern points continued well into the first day of April. This storm has been accorded the distinction of being the greatest late-season snow event of our period in the Northeast, both in regard to amount of snow dropped in a single storm over a vast geographic area and to the final accumulations on the ground at the conclusion of a week's continuance of precipitation.

Available wind data indicated that this was not a coastal disturbance such as usually produces heavy snows in the Northeast. Midwestern reports show the center of the disturbance as probably moving northeastward from the Tennessee Valley: the track taking the center across western Virginia and eastern Pennsylvania, then just north of New York City, and through southern New England, still pursuing a northeasterly direction. The center must have deepened considerably over Pennsylvania and New York as the intense circulation drew in vast quantities of Gulf of Mexico and Atlantic Ocean moisture. The trajectory put all the highlands of the Northeast in the belt of heaviest snow: the Allegheny Mountains in central Pennsylvania, the Poconos of northeast Pennsylvania, the Catskills of New York, and the Berkshire, Green, and White Mountains of New England—all received about the maximum precipitation that a cold season situation can produce.

The westernmost report came from Vincennes on the Illinois-Indiana border where eleven inches of snow were on the ground at the conclusion of the fall on the 30th.[4] Five inches fell at Gnadenhutten in east-central

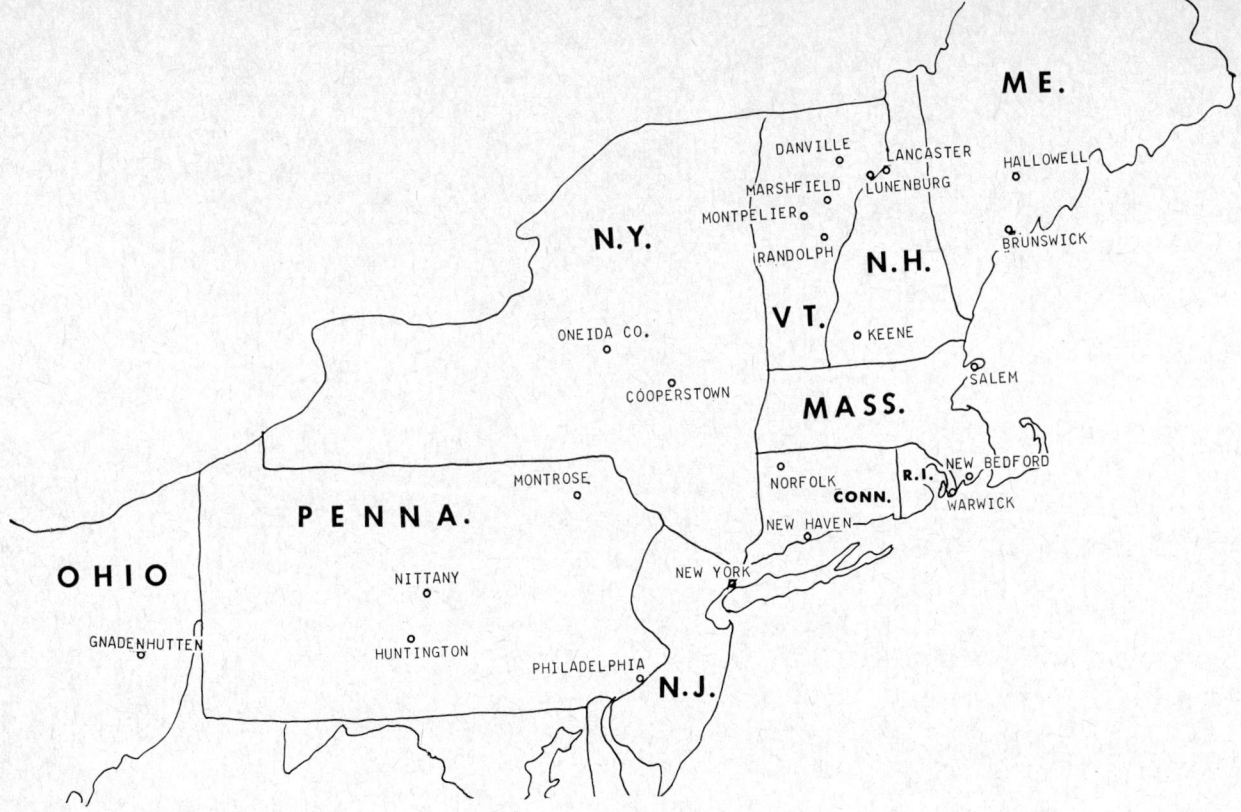

Ohio on the night of the 30–31st, with the temperature just at freezing.[2] In Pennsylvania the increased moisture supply turned the heavy snow into excessive falls as mountain barriers lay across the line of air flow from the east and northeast, thus stimulating the snow-making mechanism. From Huntington in central Pennsylvania a press dispatch related that the storm "commenced at 2100 Monday evening [30th] and ended at 0700. Next morning was nearly three feet deep."[3] That this was an overnight snowburst of the greatest intensity was confirmed by a letter extract from Centre County near the elevated location where Pennsylvania State University is now located:

> On the night of the 30th, and the forenoon of the 31st of March, there fell in this county the most prodigious quantity of snow remembered by the oldest persons here. It appears by actual measurement in different parts of Nittany Valley, that toward evening of the 31st, the snow was on an average, from three to three feet six inches deep in the valley, and on mountains it is certainly twice that depth.[4]

Northward over the Poconos of northeastern Pennsylvania even greater depths accumulated. At Montrose near Scranton the total cover on April 1st reached 52 inches in the middle of the village.[5] It was the same scene in New York State where previously there had been an extensive, deep snow cover. In Oneida County just west of Utica, in the famous lakes snow-belt, a local historian measured the snow on April 7th: "in the forest where not drifted and found it 4½ feet deep."[6] Another resident of the same area moved into a new house on April 1st and recalled that the snow surrounding the new abode was five feet deep.[7] To the eastward the editor of the *Otsego Herald* at Cooperstown described the local scene:

> The snow, in this place, is rising two feet deep on a level, the greater part of which fell day before yesterday, accompanied by high winds. Yesterday the wind roared in the forests similar to the sound of a great cataract—the air was alternately filled with snow, and transient gleams from the sun. We do not recollect so great a body of snow on the ground, at this season of the year, since 1772. As snow, at this time, is the property called the poor men's manure, we hope it will prove propitious, but we fear the consequences of a flood.[8]

### South of the Center's Track

The storm center passed close to both Philadelphia and New York City where shifting gales at both locations caused considerable damage to structures and high tides did injury to shipping and shore installations. Peter Legaux near Philadelphia noticed a low barometer reading of 28.57″ (uncorrected?) at the time of the wind shift from "easterly to westerly."[9] At New York City the barometer read 28.75″ two hours before the wind shift from southeast to southwest.[10] These two extremely low barometric readings are indications that the center reached below 28.75″ and close to the lowest ever achieved at this season of the year. Six inches of snow fell at New York City before the wind shift raised the temperature and turned the thick snow to rain.[11] The *New York Post* described the storm scene on the 31st in New York Harbor:

> THE GALE.—Yesterday morning at 2 o'clock, a gale commenced from ENE. with a heavy fall of snow, and continued till about 11, blowing most of the time from East. About 12 o'clock the wind fell to a moderate breeze, and immediately veered round to SSW. blew fresh from that quarter till 3 in the afternoon, when the wind commenced a gale from WNW. It is a remarkable fact, that the tide, at eleven o'clock, was from 12 to 18 inches higher than it has been known by the oldest inhabitants—from this time the water fell, though it was not time for high water till past three o'clock!—Many cellars were filled, and considerable property damaged. During the gale, the brig *Signal Pole,* was blown down, and three schooners were driven from their anchors, and lodged on the mud-flats on the Jersey side, opposite the city; one of which is the *Cornelia* from St. Thomas. We have reason to fear, that the vessels on the coast, both those bound in as well as those which recently sailed, have suffered. The ships *Frances,* [Capt.] Brain, from Greenock; and *Four Sisters,* Lathain, from Ireland; both rode out the gale, the former in the East, and the latter in the North River. The brig *Almira,* from Savannah, was safe at anchor in the Narrows yesterday at one o'clock. Eight or nine sail of vessels went down on Monday morning, and all went to sea except the ships *Native* and *Milford,* and the brig *Mars,* for Amsterdam—they anchored in the Bay, within the Hook.
>
> Amidst the bustle along the Docks, in securing vessels and getting out fenders, were seen hundreds with their dogs, killing rats, which had been routed by the high tide. Hardly a terrier in the city was unemployed; and we may safely say, that not less than one thousand rats were destroyed on the east side of the town. Though this remark may, by some, be considered unworthy of notice, it will be of use, if a proper use is made of it—that is, by removing the carcases of the animals before the sun operates upon them.
>
> During the height of the gale, several flocks of wild geese passed over the city, from the sea shore—whence they no doubt had been driven by the severity of the storm.
>
> It is also remarkable, that many Robins lodged in the rigging of the vessels at our docks, some of which were driven by the wind with such velocity against the masts and spars of vessels, that they fell down dead.
>
> Since writing the above, we learn by the Union pilot-boat, which left the Hook at 12 o'clock, that two ships were ashore about 7 miles to the westward of the Hook, one of which had lost two masts, and the other came in from sea during the gale in the morning—probably one of the ships that went out the preceding day. There was also a large ship ashore outside, about 4 miles south of the light house, supposed from her appearance, to be an Indiaman.
>
> From the violence of the gale yesterday afternoon, from W. and WNW. we are afraid that the vessels which rode out the easterly wind in the Bay, in the morning, went ashore, or put to sea.—

At New Haven a violent gale arose from the northeast on the night of the 30th with snow, sleet, and finally rain. At noon of the 31st the Yale barometer read 28.75″, indicating a depression of the greatest intensity.[13] The tide mounted very high, and a veer of the wind to southeast kept the water in the harbor until 1400 when a sudden shift of the gale to southwest permitted the tide to fall considerably. Much damage, however, had already been done to Long Wharf. On land part of the steeple of the West Haven Meeting House blew down, a victim of the raging winds.[14] In the vicinity of Warwick, Rhode Island, several houses were unroofed and scarcely a barn or shed escaped without some damage.[15] Part of the important bridge at New Bedford on Buzzards Bay was carried away at the height of the blow with damage estimated at the not inconsiderable figure of $8,000.[16]

### North of the Center's Track

Weather-watching Thomas Robbins happened to be at his father's home in northwest Connecticut during this stormy week. He related that the snow was "nearly two feet deep in the woods" when the storm of the 31st commenced, which he described as "a very violent snow-storm."[17] Robbins' testimony as to the deep snowfall in northwestern Connecticut had significance as demonstrating that the storm center passed south of that point, otherwise there would have been some rain mixed with the later snow as there had been at coastal points to the south.

The farther northward one progressed in New England the heavier the snowfall became. In southwestern New Hampshire in the Keene area the new snow on the 31st was estimated at 12 inches and the cover at the end of the week's snow activity at 18 inches. The winds in Cheshire County had been violent, unroofing some buildings and blowing down others. No wind direction was given at Keene, but again the mention of snow and no rain tended to indicate a southward passage of the low center.[18]

It was in the hill country of northern New England that the snowfall reached its greatest intensity and that the total snow cover approached record proportions, if it did not establish all-time figures. When writing his "Natural History of Essex County" in the 1870's, Dr. Hiram Cutting of Lunenburg in northeastern Vermont singled out this storm for special mention:

> There was on the last day of March a great snow storm accompanied with a very high wind—such a wind as is seldom known. It blockaded the roads so that they were not passable for some days. On

the first day of May (April ?) the snow would average 4⅓ feet deep, and the weather cold and forbidding—yet warm days soon came and crops came forth with great rapidity, and it is seldom that a better harvest is gathered than in that year.[19]

The editor of the Danville *North Star* on April 7th took measure of the snow situation:

> The unusually severe storm of last week, blocked up the roads to such a degree, that they are in many places in this vicinity impassable with horses or sleighs. ... We presume there never was such a time known here at this season of the year. The snow is considered to be five feet deep on a level, in many places covering the fences, and rendering it extremely difficult to travel unless it is with snow shoes.[20]

Over at the newly established capital of Montpelier, the editor of the *Vermont Precursor* commented in like vein:

> On Tuesday last (March 31st), there was a snow storm, the most driving we have had this winter, though not cold, the mercury in the Thermometer being at the freezing point. It snowed most of Friday and Saturday (April 3d & 4th). The snow is now near four feet deep in the streets and common roads on a level. So much snow on the ground at this time of year in this place, it is said, has never been known before, since the country has been settled.[21]

The editor of the *Dartmouth Gazette* apologized for the lack of news content stating that the Boston mail has been unable to get through:

> For coldness the past winter has been almost without a parallel. March, too, has been unequaled for snowstorms and severity of weather. Last Tuesday [31st] the snow fell 8 or 10 inches, and the Tuesday [24th] preceding about a foot in depth. It is now computed to be upwards of 4 feet deep in the woods and on low ground.[22]

In New Hampshire at Lancaster schoolmaster Adino Brackett entered the following in his diary: "March 31—began to snow in the morning—continued to April 5—it measured yesterday 3 feet 9 inches deep."[23] At Marshfield in central Vermont, Joshua Perkins, also measuring the snow when he commenced sugaring on April 4th, found the depth to be 54 inches.[24] Over in Maine at tidewater the great storm deposited a wet pack of 20 inches at Gardiner.[25]

The editor of the Randolph *Weekly Wanderer* well expressed the feelings of his fellow Vermonters at the inforced isolation caused by the huge snow blanket:

> Snow! Snow! Snow! On Tuesday morning the 31st of March we were visited by a snow storm which continued with little intermission till Friday morning, four days: during this time the snow fell about two and a half feet—which, with the snow on the ground before the storm, made about six feet upon a level, in the woods, and more than four feet in open land. The fences in many places were entirely covered, the tops of the posts could not be seen. On Saturday the fourth inst. it was a gloomy sight indeed to behold such a body of snow on the ground. We have since, however, been visited with the sun, for a few days, which has lessened the snow considerably. For a fortnight we did not receive any mail from the southward, in consequence of the great snow; there has been very little passing.
> 
> We think our readers will ask no other apology from us for getting out no paper last week. (Dated Randolph, 13 April 1807.)[26]

Rev. Thomas Robbins at his father's home at Norfolk, high in the hills of northwestern Connecticut, penned the following impressions:

### March 1807

5. rode to Goshen and returned in a sleigh
12. good sleighing
14. Last night a hard snow. At least a foot deep, supposed to be the deepest we have had this winter.
16. We have had snow steadily for four months, and the most of the time very cold
21. very good sledding
23. A great and general scarcity of hay
25. Last night a hard storm of snow
28. very good sleighing
30. The snow in the woods nearly two feet deep
31. A very violent snow-storm.

### April 1807

1. Cold and tedious. The snow flew very violently all day. No person scarsely goes out
2. Was out with most people the most of the day breaking paths. The snow between three and four feet deep. It snowed some.
4. This week has been more tedious, snowy, and blustery than any one in the past winter. It snowed every day but one. Some people are wholly out of hay
5. Warm and pleasant
6. The snow settles pretty fast
7. More snow here than at Winchester. I am persuaded I never saw such a quantity of snow and such drifts about my father's as now.
9. In the morning the sleighing is tolerable
11. The snow thaws very fast, and the ground begins to appear
12. People came here to meeting, some in sleighs, *Nov 16th,* and I believe there has been one or more every Sabbath since.
13. It snowed most of the day.
15. Sleighing about gone.
19. Very warm I took off my outside coat.

### May 1807

1. Snow appears in a few places, though it has gone wonderfully for 3 weeks.

[1] David Thomas. *Travels through the western country in the summer of 1816.* Auburn, David Rumsey, 1819. 109.

[2] John Heckewelder. Ms. Met. Obs., (Amer. Phil. Soc.).
[3] *Democratic Press* (Phila.), 13 April 1807.
[4] *Ibid.*, 22 April 1807.
[5] *Independent Volunteer* (Montrose, Pa.) in *U. S. Gazette* (Phila.), 20 Jan 1836.
[6] Pomroy Jones. *Annals and recollections of Oneida County*. Rome, N. Y., the author, 1851.
[7] Henry A. Ward. *Annals of Richford, N. Y.*, 4.
[8] *Otsego Herald* (Cooperstown, N. Y.), 2 April 1807.
[9] Peter Legaux. Ms. Met. Obs., (Amer. Phil. Soc.).
[10] J. Day. Ms. Met. Obs.
[11] *N.Y. Post*, 31 March 1807.
[12] *American Register* (Phila.), 1, 24–25.
[13] J. Day.
[14] New Haven, 7 April, in *The Berkshire Reporter* (Pittsfield), 18 April 1807.
[15] *Medical & Agricultural Register* (Boston), April 1807, 255.
[16] New Bedford dispatch in *Vt. Jour.* (Windsor), 27 April 1807.
[17] T. Robbins. *Diary*, 1, 319–22.
[18] *N.H. Sent.*, 4 April, in *Green Mountain Patriot* (Peacham), 14 April 1807.
[19] H. A. Cutting. Natural History of Essex County. Abby Hemenway, ed. *Vermont Historical Gazetteer*, 1, (1862), 1056.
[20] *North Star* (Danbury, Vt.), 7 April 1807.
[21] *The Precursor* (Montpelier), 6 April 1807.
[22] *Dartmouth Gazette* (Hanover, N. H.), 3 April 1807.
[23] Adino Brackett. Ms. Diary, (N. H. Hist. Soc.).
[24] Hemenway. 4, 203.
[25] John W. Hanson. *Hist. of Gardiner, Maine*. 282.
[26] *Weekly Wanderer* (Randolph), 13 April 1807.

## COLD FRIDAY IN NEW ENGLAND—19 JANUARY 1810

The most celebrated cold wave in the eyes of early New England historians occurred on 19 January 1810. Its just fame rested not so much on the extremities reached, though they certainly deserve respect, but for the speed of the mercury's descent overnight and the fierce west-northwest and northwest gales that spread death and destruction across the countryside during the daylight hours of that sad Friday.

The season previously had been remarkably mild without a day of tolerable sleighing. The only snowstorm worthy of the name had occurred in late November. Dr. Holyoke's thermometer at Salem descended in December only as low as +8° and in the first half of January only to +14°; so, with winter half over and the ground bare, people were looking forward to spring activities.[1]

On the very afternoon that a most vigorous cold front was sweeping southeastward into northern New York and northern Vermont, farmers in the vicinity of Portsmouth, New Hampshire, were seen plowing in the fields as southwesterly breezes raised the thermometer in the afternoon of the 18th to 42°.[2] The ground there remained free of snow as it had for many weeks. That evening a light rain fell gently and people went to bed without making the usual preparations for a wintry night. Shortly before midnight a sharp cold front raced into the coastal areas of central New England with an almost immediate wind shift from southwest to northwest. Arctic air replaced the balmy air from the south. The northwesterly flow mounted soon to gale force as colder and colder blasts of the most frigid type swept across the countryside. In a few short minutes the scene had been changed from January thaw conditions to those of the deepest Arctic.

Charles Peirce, who served as Portsmouth's weatherman for 15 years, left a record of the events on the famous day and for the equally cold three days following. At daybreak on Friday, 19 January 1810, his thermometer read −7°, down 49 points from the previous evening, and the mercury continued its descent during the day despite the warming efforts of the sun. By 1200 it reached −12°—off 54 degrees in 12 hours. By 1500 it read −13°, and next morning the nadir of −14° was achieved.[3]

It was the same story up and down the coast. Prof. Cleaveland at Brunswick, Maine, saw his instrument drop from 41° at noon on the 18th to −10.25° at 0830/19th. His barometer at the early morning observation read 29.20″ with a northwest gale raging, so

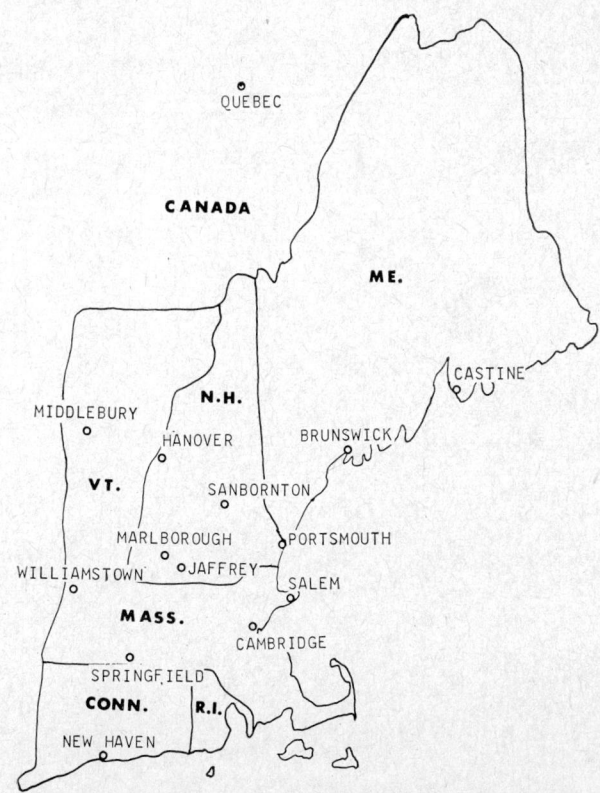

the glass must have been on the rise from a lower point. Dr. Holyoke at Salem recorded a temperature drop from 41° at noon/18th to an even zero at 0800/19th. During the day his mercury climbed only one notch to +1° at both noon and 1500, and then commenced a descent to −5° in late evening.[4] At Cambridge it was even colder on Abiel Holmes' thermometer: −5°/0730, −2°/1200, −2°/1400, −5°/1500, and −7°/1930—certainly chill enough to keep the freshmen from loitering around Harvard Square.[5] From our best informants, the mercury at Boston climbed just to the +1° mark in early afternoon, spoiling the chance of a record zero day, but still containing a chill factor to satisfy the most avid winter sports fan.[6]

Minimum temperatures across central New England were remarkably uniform on Cold Friday, attesting to the homogenous character of the air mass. Middlebury in western Vermont registered −13.5°; while down in Massachusetts, Williamstown in the west had −14° and Worcester in the center had −12°; figures along the coast were: Portsmouth −14°, Brunswick −10°, Cambridge −8°, Boston −6°, and Salem −5°.[7] Some of these figures were achieved on the morning of the 20th when it was only slightly colder than at noontime of the 19th, the hour when the core of the coldest air appeared to be over eastern New England.

Another temperature check uncovered for northern New England appeared in the *Dartmouth Gazette* in February 1817 with the statement: "on the morning of the famous cold Friday the mercury stood at 17 or 18 below 0 at this place."[8] A contemporary historian of Maine gave the low figure for that state as −15° or −16°. At Castine in the District of Maine the mercury plummeted 44 degrees in 8 hours when the cold front struck.[9]

An interesting indication of the suddenness of the mercury's fall and its penetrating quality came in a notice in the *New Hampshire Sentinel,* the press at Keene, Cheshire County, in southwestern part of the state:

Marlborough (Cheshire County):
The transition from temperate to cold, within 24 hours past has exceeded any meteorological observation within my recollection for fifteen years past—at 11 o'clock on the morning of the 18th inst. the thermometer in a N.W. room, no fire in the adjoining rooms—stood at 51° above 0—at 10 o'clock on the morning of the 19th day, 8° below 0—at 11 o'clock 12° below—63° difference in temperature.[10]

The general meteorological situation that set the stage for the great Arctic outbreak on 19 January can be deduced from available meteorological registers at New York, New Haven, New Bedford, Salem, and Brunswick. No reports have been found which would give a clue to wind behavior or movement of the barometer from either interior New York or northern interior New England. It is obvious that a trough of low pressure, probably oriented north-south, moved across New England from west to east on the afternoon and evening of the 18th as the southerly flow, above normal temperatures, and decreasing barometric pressure from south to north indicated. Probably an intense low center followed the familiar track through the St. Lawrence Valley with a trough of low pressure trailing southward. Imbedded in this trough was a cold front separating greatly contrasting air masses.

The degree of severity of the Arctic air mass when in its source region in central Canada cannot be determined with precision since no thermometer reports have been uncovered for northern New York or southern Ontario along the assumed trajectory of the invading air stream. We do know that the mercury sank to −26° on 20 January 1810 at Quebec—equal to the lowest reading there in the decade 1801–10.[11] This does give an indication of the coldness of the air mass. A search of Canadian newspapers for the period revealed no contemporary mention of any weather phenomena at the time, but a later reference appeared in a discussion of severe winters of the mid-century by Captain J. H. Lefroy of the Toronto Observatory:

Of the former character may have been that of 1809–10, which by this rule should fall in a warm group, although it will long be remembered by the old inhabitants of Canada, for the memorable *black night,* the 18th January, 1810, in which the temperature changed in a few hours from a high thermometer, with rapid thaw, warm and congenial sunshine, to the most intense frost, producing distress and devastation unparalleled in their recollection. There are probably in existence some precise notes taken on this remarkable occasion, but I have not been able to hear of them.[12]

Why the otherwise mild season of 1809–10 produced only one such frigid air mass, and this such an extreme one, must remain unanswered until the mysteries of meteorology are unraveled in full by some super computer mind of the future.

Nor do we, in the absence of hourly observations, possess adequate information as to the timing of the arrival of the cold front. It would appear to have been oriented on a north-south line as the northwest blasts reached Washington "in the evening."[13] The front had passed New York and New Haven by the 2100 observation as the thermometer at each place was dropping rapidly.[14] The historian of Sanbornton, New Hampshire, the scene of the Cold Friday tragedy, gave the time of arrival of the cold blasts as nine in the evening. Charles Peirce at Portsmouth, in the same state but to the southeast, indicated the wind shift about midnight.[15] By daybreak the cold air had assumed complete charge of all New England with the temperature everywhere at zero or below. The degree of cold achieved in coastal New England assumed all the more remarkable status in view of the complete lack of snow cover. None existed at New Haven, Worcester, or Portsmouth, and only a hard, icy base in the interior.[16]

Down in central Connecticut, Rev. Thomas Robbins was abroad in the cold and recorded the event in his January diary:

19. I think I never saw so few people in the streets at Hartford. Not a team to be seen. I was very cold.
20. Tremendous cold. No person scarsely goes out.
23. The river, which was perfectly clear last Thursday, shut over on Friday (the 19th) night, and is now in the best condition for crossing. People crossed on Saturday. The ground is wholly bare.[17]

At New Haven the thermometer on the Yale campus followed suit of those in more northerly locations. It had fallen from 42° at noon/18th to 25° by 2100. Next morning it stood at zero and rose only to +3° in early afternoon before slumping down to −4° in the evening.[18]

New York City remained well east of the main channel of cold flow. The mercury on Henry Laight's thermometer touched an even zero on the 19th for the lowest reached during the four-day cold wave—his maximum on the same day rose to +8°.[19] The accompanying gale struck a damaging blow at the shipping in the harbor which had been breasting a moderate southwest wind when the blasts from the northwest struck. The steamship *Raritan* sank at its wharf, and most of the small vessels drove ashore. Many chimneys throughout the city tumbled in the "complete hurricane from N.W., N.N.W., and N."

The cold blast had reached Washington in late afternoon of the 18th and so high did the gale rage around the Capitol building that Congress had to adjourn its evening session.[21] The cold air did not spread southward immediately, but seemed to be held by a front through Virginia. Thomas Jefferson's thermometer read +16° on the 19th, but gradually dropped on successive days to 14° on the 20th, 9.75° on the 21st, and to +5.5° on the 22d.[22] Farther south in North Carolina the Moravians at Winston-Salem experienced an even zero on the morning of the 22d, and it was down to +9° at Camden in northeastern South Carolina.[23] By this time New England thermometers had commenced to recover some of their poise and head upwards.

Residents of Springfield in west-central Massachusetts noticed a strange phenomenon as the cold northwesterly gale passed over the still unfrozen waters of the Connecticut River:

A very singular appearance was exhibited in Springfield on Friday, the 19th ulto. The thermometer standing at 0°, and two degrees above, with the wind very high at N.N.W. The river furnished an appearance of heavy fog passing rapidly down it. On an appearance so extraordinary, examination was made and it was found that the wind took up small particles of water and carried them up into the atmosphere, and was immediately congealed into fine snow, and arose some as much as 40 feet above the surface of the water. Its commencement was about Meridian and continued through the day, but most conspicuous at two P.M. Several very aged people living in this vicinity, do not remember ever seeing the like appearance.[24]

On the meteorological score, Cold Friday certainly deserved distinctive rating. And it also achieved prominence from the economic distress caused across the New England countryside when roofs, sheds, barns, and even houses were blown down by the blasts out of the northwest. Part of the roof of the Meeting House at Jaffrey in southern New Hampshire was blown off by the gale and several dwelling houses in the community received structural damage.[25] Perhaps the nearby presence of Mt. Monadnock funneled the air flow through the village with a venturi effect.

But it was from a family tragedy at Sanbornton in east-central New Hampshire that Cold Friday reached beyond the commonplace and achieved an unforgettable status, forever afterwards arousing human compassion in the minds and hearts of all mothers and fathers who heard of the sad fate of the Ellsworth children in the gale and snow that day.[26] Under the bold headline of "Melancholy," the story appeared in the *New Hampshire Patriot* soon afterwards and was republished far and wide, more so than any other non-political event of the period.[27] Thus, Cold Friday entered the folklore of America, and whenever bitter gales out of the northwest suddenly descended on the countryside, the chilling tale of the three little Ellsworth children was retold many times as family groups huddled in front of the fireplace.[28] *

* For full account of the Cold Friday tragedy, see A Winter Anthology at end of volume.

[1] E. Holyoke, Ms. Met. Obs.
[2] *N. H. Gazette* (Portsmouth), 20 Jan 1810.
[3] *Idem.*
[4] P. Cleaveland. Ms. Met. Obs., (Bowdoin).
[5] Abiel Holmes. Ms. Met. Obs., (Library of Congress).
[6] Boston *Daily Adv.,* 2 Feb, in *N. Y. Spectator,* 8 Feb 1815.
[7] C. Dewey. Ms. Met. Obs., (Williams); P. Cleaveland; I. Thomas, *Diary; N. H. Gaz.,* 23 Jan 1810; E. Holyoke; F. Hall, *Literary & Philosophical Repository* (Middlebury, Vt.), 397.
[8] *Dartmouth Gazette* (Hanover), 19 Feb 1817.
[9] Williamson. *History of Maine,* 1, 100; G. A. Wheeler, *History of Castine,* 53.
[10] *N. H. Sentinel* (Keene), 27 Jan 1810.
[11] Table 4, showing the extremes of heat and cold at Quebec, for eleven years, from 1800–1810 inclusive,

from the Appendix to Smith's *History of Canada* in *The British American Journal,* Jan 1848, 229.
[12] Capt. J. H. Lefroy. On the winter of 1851–52 in Canada. *The Upper Canada Medical Journal,* 1–2, (May 1852), 47–48.
[13] Washington dispatch in *Columbian Centinel* (Boston), 27 Jan 1810.
[14] Henry Laight. Ms. Met. Obs., (N. Y. Hist. Soc.).
[15] *N. H. Gaz.,* 23 Jan 1810.
[16] J. Day. Ms. Met. Obs., (Yale); I. Thomas, *Diary,* 84; *N. H. Gaz.,* 3 Feb 1810.
[17] T. Robbins. *Diary,* 1, 425.
[18] J. Day.
[19] H. Laight.
[20] *Amer. Register* (Phila.), 7, 165.
[21] T. Jefferson. Ms. Weather Book, (Lib. of Congress).
[22] *Moravians in N. C.,* 7, 3107.
[23] James Kershaw. Ms. Weather Diary, (NA).
[24] Springfield dispatch in *N. H. Patriot* (Concord), 13 Feb 1810.
[25] *N. H. Sent.,* 24 Jan 1810.
[26] Sidney Perley, *Historic Storms of New England,* 180–82; *N. H. Hist. Soc. Coll.,* 5, (1837), 77–78; *Merry's Museum* (Boston), 33, 5–7, Jan 1857.
[27] *N. H. Patriot,* 6 Feb 1810.
[28] *Eve. Traveller,* 20 Jan 1857.

## TWO COLD STORMS AND A HARD WINTER: 1811–12

### LONG ISLAND

The remarkable snow-storm of Dec. 23rd, 1811, was the most destructive of both life and property of any that is known to have occurred on the northern shore. The preceding day was remarkably warm and fair. The change took place suddenly in the night, the mercury falling almost to zero. A snow-storm commenced, accompanied with a tremendous wind, which lasted without intermission for 24 hours. Between 50 and 60 vessels foundered in the Sound, or were driven on the north shore of the island in that terrible night. In some cases, the entire crews perished, while in others, those who survived, were objects of greater commiseration than the dead, being horribly frozen. The writer can speak with entire confidence on this subject, as he was an eyewitness to some of the ravages of that awful tempest. About 20 perished within 10 miles of his residence, 4 of whom, from one vessel, he assisted in burying, on Christmas day; and in administering of the necessities of 3 wretched survivors of the same crew. The bodies taken up from the shore were completely covered with ice of an inch in thickness, through which the features of the face appeared in all the ghastliness of death. The storm will never be forgotten by the last survivor of that generation. And no man that spent that day as the writer spent it, will ever hear that *always* unappropriate compliment, *"a merry Christmas,"* without conscious pain.[1]

The Day-Before-Christmas Storm of 1811 along the shores of Long Island Sound possessed all the elements which would now qualify for the designation of "Eastern blizzard"—near-zero temperatures, gale force winds, and thick, driving snow. The same combination struck on 26 December 1778 in the Hessian Storm, on 18–19 January 1857 in the Cold Storm, and on 12–13 March 1888 in the Great Blizzard.

Fortunately, the disturbance on 24 December 1811 had its historian in the person of Dr. Samuel Latham Mitchill, the New York educator and scientist, sometime U. S. Senator and Congressman, longtime editor and contributor to scholarly journals, who was once described by a colleague as "a walking Library of Congress." Mitchill took a particular interest in meteorology, and occasionally produced studies of particular storms, such as the Great Snowstorm of February 1802

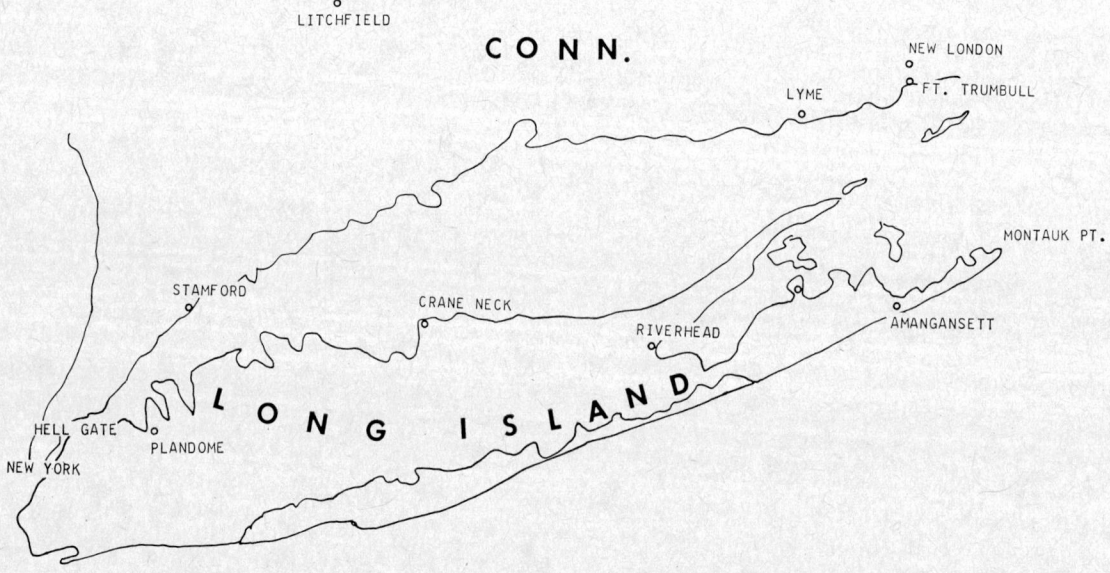

sudden end to the terrour of winter & to all its horrours. We fear for dams, floods, & for the traveling & roads.[33]

Concord, New Hampshire, 31 March: Cold Winter—We believe there has not been within the recollection of the oldest inhabitants a winter in which the cold has been so severe and of such long continuance. Even now sleighing is good in the interior of the state, and the Merrimack is in most places passable on the ice.[34]

[1] Nathaniel S. Prime. *A history of Long Island.* N. Y. & Pittsburgh, R. Carter, 1845. 39–40.
[2] Samuel L. Mitchill. The history of that extensive commotion. . . . *Trans. Lit. Phil. Soc. N. Y.,* (1815), 331–340.
[3] *Ibid.*
[4] H. Laight. Ms. Met. Obs., (N. Y. Hist. Soc.).
[5] thru [10]. S. Mitchill.
[11] J. Day. Ms. Met. Obs., (Yale).
[12] N. Webster. *Notes,* 2, 172.
[13] J. Day.
[14] J. Day. *N. Y. Post,* 31 Dec 1811; *Col. Cent.,* 26 Dec 1811; P. Cleaveland. Ms. Met. Obs., (Bowdoin).
[15] E. Holyoke. *Met. Jour,* 170; W. Bentley. *Diary,* 4, 74.
[16] J. Day; T. Robbins. *Diary,* 1, 479.
[17] *Ibid.,* 1, 479.
[18] *N. H. Sentinel* (Keene), 28 Dec 1811.
[19] I. Thomas, *Diary,* 127.
[20] *Col. Cent.,* 7 Jan 1812.
[21] Henry P. Hedges. *A history of the town of East-Hampton, N. Y.* Sag Harbor, J. H. Hunt, 1897. 154.
[22] *N. Y. Post,* 30 Dec 1811.
[23] Benjamin Harwood. Ms. Diary, (Bennington Museum).
[24] Adino Brackett. Ms. Diary, (N. H. Hist. Soc.).
[25] H. Laight.
[26] C. F. in *Col. Cent.,* 6 Jan 1836.
[27] *Portsmouth Oracle* in *N. H. Sent.,* 1 Feb 1812.
[28] Abiel Holmes. Ms. Met. Obs., (Lib. Cong.).
[29] *Col. Cent.,* 1 Feb 1812.
[30] J. Day.
[31] T. Robbins. *Diary,* 1, 479.
[32] E. Holyoke.
[33] W. Bentley. *Diary,* 4, 87.
[34] N. H. Patriot (Concord), 31 March 1812 in Nathaniel Bouton, *The History of Concord,* 354.

## THE HEAVY MAY SNOW OF 1812 IN THE NORTHEAST

The spring of 1812 was probably the most retarded of our period. On 30 April, Rev. William Bentley summed up the situation: "We cannot refuse to notice an uncommon backward spring. Not a flower to be seen this Maying which the eye could anticipate for the pleasure next morning. We just begin to collect dandelions for the table & as yet there are few. Ice is seen this week & all the snow is not dissolved upon our hills. It is a Canada season, winter & summer, but no spring. A strange contrast to the heat of last summer." The month of May brought little change: a heavy snowstorm during the first week, a *much below* month with the average 5.9 degrees under normal at New Haven, and no apple blossoms until June 1st, the latest date of the century.

As a northeaster swept up the coast on 3–4 May 1812, the heavy rain became mixed with snow in the Philadelphia area and became all snow in the vicinity of New York and northeastward. Amounts varied from light slush to a heavy covering up to 12 inches deep on the interior highlands. Our best meteorological reports came from New Haven where Prof. Day had all of his instruments in operation:

|  | 0700 | 1200 | 2100 |
|---|---|---|---|
| May 3. | 42° | 48° | 40° |
|  | 29.95″ | 29.90″ | 29.90″ |
|  | NE | N | NE |
|  | Rain | Rain | Cloudy |
| 4. | 35° | 32° | 34° |
|  | 29.85″ | 29.78″ | 29.60″ |
|  | NE | NE | NE |
|  | Snow | Snow | Snow |
| May 5. | 37° | 51° | 47° |
|  | 29.60″ | 29.65″ | 29.70″ |
|  | NW | NNW | NNW |
|  | P. Clo. | Clear | Clear |
| 6. | Apricots blossomed | | |

Precipitation: 3d—.31″
4th .78″ Mostly melted snow.

### 1812

(All references to 4 May unless otherwise indicated)

**Pennsylvania,** Philadelphia:
Rain and snow. S. Hazard. *Register of Penna.,* 2, (1828), 25.

............, Spring Mill, Montgomery Co.:
Rain, frost, & hail all day. NE wind. Peter Legaux. Ms. Met. Obs. (Amer. Phil. Soc.).

**New York,** New York City:
Violent snow from 1000 to 1500—34°, 36°, 35°. Henry Laight. Ms. Met. Obs. (N. Y. Hist. Soc.).

**Connecticut,** New Haven:
It snowed all day. Noah Webster. *Diary,* 2, 174.

............, East Windsor, Hartford Co.:
4th—It snowed hard all day. 5th—The snow went off. 7th—snow is to be seen on mountains. T. Robbins. *Diary,* 1, 513.

**Massachusetts,** Millbury, Worcester Co.:
A snow storm continued for twenty-five hours during which 12 inches of snow fell, some remaining until the 11th. *History of Millbury,* 86.

............., Waltham, Middlesex Co.:
A remarkable snow storm all day and night, from NNE. Probably nine inches fell. Some remaining on the ground until the 9th. Charles Fisk. *Boston Transcript* in *U. S. Reg.* (Phila.), 9 June 1841.

............., Boston, Suffolk Co.:
Four inches of snow fell. John Gorham, M.D. Met. Obs. *New Eng. Jour. Med. & Surgery.* 1-4 (July 1812).

............., Lynn, Essex Co.:
Snow all day and night, 8 inches deep. A. Lewis. *History of Lynn,* 235.

............., Salem, Essex Co.:
Snow 6 inches deep. 5th—The earth covered with snow this morning. W. Bentley. *Diary,* 4, 95.

**New Hampshire,** Keene, Cheshire Co.:
Snow commenced Monday forenoon, lay 10 to 12 inches deep on high lands Tuesday morning. *N. H. Sentinel* (Keene), 9 May 1812.

............., Epping, Rockingham Co.:
4th—snowed all the day, 33°, 34°, 32°. 5th—the snow that fell yesterday and today was equal to one foot if it had not dissolved as it fell. 33°, 40°, 39°. William Plumer. Ms. Met. Obs. (Harvard).

**Maine,** Brunswick, Cumberland Co.:
Snow one inch. 33°, 40.5°, 38°. Rain at 1400. Total .81". Parker Cleaveland. Ms. Met. Obs. (Bowdoin College).

## THE SEVERE COLD OF 1815 AND HARD WINTER ON CAPE COD

The last day of January 1815 had the distinction of being the coldest day at Salem since Dr. Edward Holyoke commenced his second, improved series of weather records in 1786. From a morning low of −9°, his thermometer rose only to −3° at noontime, and then sank by sunset again to −9°. There came a slight recovery to −7° by the 2200 observations.[1] Since Holyoke did not possess a registering thermometer, there existed no record of the actual maximum in the afternoon, but from other readings throughout eastern New England it appeared quite likely that the high did not exceed zero and, thus, this might be an authentic zero day. At suburban Waltham Charles Fisk included 31 January 1815 in his list of five such zero days in the span of years from 1812 to 1835.[2]

The deep plunge of the mercury had been well prepared by the extremely cold air mass moving into the Northeast on the 26th. Salem had the following 0800 readings daily from January 27th through February 1st: 0°, +1°, +1°, 0°, −9°, and +3°—these far outdid the famous Cold Friday period five years previously. Fisk at Waltham had −5° on the 28th and −15° on the 31st. In downtown Boston an interesting thermometer record appeared in the *Daily Advertiser* showing that the lowest readings on the 31st were reached between 1900 and 2100, after which the mercury commenced to rise as it had at Salem.[3] The core of the cold air must have been over eastern Massachusetts in early evening. Other press figures for Boston gave the minimum at −12°, a reasonable figure in view of the Salem and Waltham reports.[4]

North of Boston equally severe conditions prevailed. At Portsmouth the local *Oracle's* thermometer registered −13°, both in the morning and evening of the 31st. At noon, however, it had climbed to an even zero, but soon commenced descending to −13°, maintained from 2000 to 2200, when a rise commenced.[5] Prof. Cleaveland's thermometer at Brunswick, Maine, read −24° at sunrise of the 31st and climbed only to −4° by early afternoon—his only zero day in this winter.[6]

Down in Connecticut at Windsor, Thomas Robbins had a similar thermal experience: −2° at sunrise of the 31st, +2° at noon, −7° at sunset, and −8° at 2000, the hour when most of eastern New England also experienced its lowest reading. "The sun shone, but obscurely. I think I never saw a colder day," Robbins entered in his diary.[7]

New York City became virtually icebound at the end

of January as Long Island Sound closed at Sands Point, interdicting traffic from New England, and the Hudson River and East River on each side of Manhattan Island were so choked with ice as to prevent any boats crossing. The southern mail on the 30th, after battling the floes for six hours, finally sank, though the mail carrier was rescued. Thereafter, the southern mail moved across the open bay below Governor's Island, entailing a considerable delay in circling the city and approaching from the east by way of Brooklyn. Full navigation did not resume until mid-month.[6] The Delaware at Philadelphia closed on January 30th, and not until February 21st did ferries to the New Jersey shore break through. The river drove on March 5th opening navigation to the sea.[9]

The winter of 1814–15 struck especially hard at the southern shore of New England and the islands from Long Island to the tip of Cape Cod. Frederick Freeman, the able historian of Cape Cod writing in 1860, singled out this season as being especially severe, and newspaper editors in the 1850's would hark back to January and February 1815 as a winter comparable with the snows and cold of the mid-fifties.[10]

The forces of nature struck a major blow early in the season when a coastal disturbance caused one of the major shipping disasters of the period. Nathaniel Prime has left an account:

> The loss of *H. B. M. Sloop of War Sylph* was one of the most disastrous shipwrecks that ever occurred on the L. I. coast. She came on shore near Southampton, in a snowstorm, Jan. 16th, 1815. Out of a crew of 117 men, only 6 survived. This lamentable event took place just one month before the news of peace arrived. The fact of its being an enemy's ship, and one, in particular, that had previously been a great annoyance to our coasting vessels, prevented the public sympathy from being excited to as great a degree as might have been the case under different circumstances. But no human aid could avail the hapless crew, who perished beneath the fury of the tempest and the waves.

Temperature records maintained at New Haven and New Bedford indicated greater departures from normal for the months of January and February 1815 than elsewhere in the Northeast. Apparently trough conditions existed not far offshore to maintain a northerly circulation into the coastal regions most of the time. New Bedford had minus departures for the three winter months of: −2.9°, −1.8°, and −3.7°; and at New Haven the figures ran: −2.2°, −2.2°, and −4.0°. The mercury was continuously below freezing at New Haven from the 22d of January through the 1st of February. And at New Bedford the mercury read below 32° on every morning of February, and for three weeks from 26 January to 16 February managed to remain below 34°. Thus, the heavy snows which fell at New Bedford on January 17–18th, 22d, and February 4th, 6th, and 18th were little diminished by Old Sol.[12]

The bitter cold wave at the end of January brought amazing low readings to southeastern New England. Samuel Rodman at New Bedford had commenced his great meteorological records in 1812. Though continued in the family through 1905, no day in that almost century of thermometer readings could match those obtained on 31 January. The four readings were: −5°, −2°, −5°, and −9°.[13] The local *New Bedford Mercury* on 3 February took notice of the cold:

> The weather has been unusually inclement for several days past. Yesterday (Tuesday) the mercury in the thermometer was down to 10° deg. below cypher; a degree of cold not experienced here for several years past. The harbour is completely frozen over to Long Island.[14]

With Nantucket Sound and surrounding waters nearly solidly congealed, the air flow was little modified when it reached the outer islands. Obed Macy, the historian of early Nantucket writing in 1835, experienced the cold of January 31st and February 1st: "On the first of the second month, 1815, the weather was remarkably cold. The thermometer was eleven degrees below zero, lower by several degrees than had ever before been known." [15]

No account of snow depths on Cape Cod were maintained, though it was always later referred to as the year of the deep snow. At New Haven 15 inches fell in January and 23 inches in February. Samuel Rodman, though not a snow-measurer, indicated very heavy amounts of precipitation in the snow periods of February: 1.20 inches on the 18th (all snow) and .80 inches on the 24–25th (a mixture of snow and rain).[16]

[1] E. Holyoke. *Met. Jour.*, 177.
[2] *Col. Cent.*, 6 Jan 1836.
[3] *Boston Daily Adv.*, 2 Feb, in *N. Y. Spectator*, 8 Feb 1815.
[4] *Col. Cent.*, 1 Feb 1815.
[5] *Portsmouth Oracle*, 4 Feb 1815.
[6] P. Cleaveland, Ms. Met. Obs., (Bowdoin).
[7] T. Robbins. *Diary*, 1, 618.
[8] *N. Y. Spectator*, 30 Jan & 3 Feb 1815; R. S. Guernsey. *New York City during the War of 1812–15.* N. Y., C. L. Woodward, 1895. 2, 454.
[9] S. Hazard, Effects of climate, *Penna. Reg.*, 2, 384.
[10] Frederick Freeman. *History of Cape Cod*. Boston, Geo. C. Rand & Avery, 1858.
[11] Nathaniel S. Prime. *History of Long Island*, 41.
[12] J. Day. Ms. Met. Obs. (Yale); S. Rodman, Ms. Met. Obs. (Harvard).
[13] S. Rodman.
[14] *New Bedford Mercury*, 3 Feb 1815.
[15] Obed Macy. *History of Nantucket*. Boston, Hilliard, Gray & Co., 1835. 211.
[16] J. Day, S. Rodman.

## JUNE SNOWS OF 1816*

*Melancholy Weather—On the night of the 6th water froze an inch thick—on the night of the 7th and the morning of the 8th, a kind of sleet or exceeding cold snow fell, attended by high wind, and measured in places where it drifted 18 to 20 inches in depth. Saturday morning (8th) the weather was more severe than it generally is during the storms of winter. It was indeed a gloomy and tedious period. North Star* (Danville, Caledonia Co., Vermont), 15 June 1816.

The year 1816 has ever been of almanac fame as the "Year without a Summer." It comprised a backward spring with record late snows, a cold and dry summer featuring light frosts in July and August, and a droughty early fall that culminated in a killing frost before the end of September—in all, a most distressing season for the rural economy of northern New York and northern New England.

The most spectacular meteorological events of the unusual season came at an end of the first week of June when snow fell to considerable depths over the highlands of New York, Vermont, New Hampshire, and Maine, and flurries reached to the coast and southward. Actually, there were two distinct snow periods: the first during daylight hours of Thursday, the 6th, when a steady rain gradually changed to intermittent snowfall; the second on the night of the 7–8th when a second impulse of cold air triggered moderate to heavy snow that lay all day at higher elevations of northern New England with snow squalls spreading on the morning of the 8th eastward to the seacoast of Maine, New Hampshire, and northern Massachusetts, and southward into the Berkshires of northwestern Connecticut and to the high elevations in the Catskills of New York.

The events of these days have been well described in the diaries of two farmers who were engaged in outdoor work during the wintry spell—Benjamin Harwood at Bennington, in southwestern Vermont, and Joshua Whitman at North Turner in west-central Maine:

### Bennington, Vermont

June 6. It had rained much during the night and this morning the wind blew exceedingly high from NE raining copiously, chilling and sharp gusts. About 8 A.M. began to snow—continued more or less till past 2 P.M. The heads of all the mountains on every side were crowned with snow. The most gloomy and extraordinary weather ever seen.

* This section considers only the June snowfall phase of the "Year without a Summer"—the other events of the spring, summer, and fall of this remarkable season will be treated, we hope, in a future publication.

June 7. In ploughfields and other parts the surface of the ground was stiff with frost—the leaves of the trees were blackened—past 6 in the morning a wash-tub full of rain water was scum'd with ice, snow remained on Sandgate and Manchester Mountain past noon or as late as that. Wind extremely high night & day and the cold abated but little in the P.M. Father & Mr. Brown rode till noon hunting sheep—mended fences with greatcoat & mittens on.

June 8. The awful scene continued. Sweeping blasts from North all the forepart of the day, with light snow squalls. More clear P.M.—no snow—wind not so high—but held cold. Were principally engaged in digging stone. So cold in the morning that we were absolutely compelled to send for our mittens and wear them till near noon-day.

June 9. Frosty morning, perfectly clear all day, dry chilling N wind.

June 10. Another frost, cold day, indeed obliged to thrash our hands while hoeing. Corn, which had been up a few days badly killed—difficult to see it—gloomy weather.

June 11. Frosty morning, but fine day.

June 12. Warm & smoky—signs of rain.

### North Turner, Androscoggin Co., Maine

June 6. Some showers and cold N.W. wind, some squalls of snow, I pile, etc.

June 7. Cloudy and very high and cold N.W. winds, with some squalls of snow. I pile for planting etc.

June 8. Cloudy and very cold N.W. wind. Some snow for three hours—very uncomfortable weather vegetation gains but little. All travellers need great coats and mittens. I presume the oldest person now living knows of no such weather the 8th of June. Many of the leaves of the trees are blown off and to pieces by the roughness of the weather. I continue piling for planting.

June 9. Cloudy and very cold N.W. wind. Apple trees in bloom.

June 10. Fair and very cold in the morning. It has frozen very hard for four nights past. Many birds die with the cold. The ground freezes and is raised by the frost. I began to plant my corn.

The meteorological situation attending the early June snow period can be reconstructed from a study of the records of the "college system" which had reporting stations on campuses at Middlebury in western Vermont, Williamstown in northwestern Massachusetts, New Haven in southern Connecticut, and Brunswick in east-central Maine.[3] Also helpful were the regular observations of Dr. Edward A. Holyoke of Salem, Samuel Rodman at New Bedford, and Charles Fisk at Waltham—all in the Bay State.[4] Thrice daily observations were usually taken of temperature, wind direction, and sky conditions. Barometric observations were also made at all except Williamstown, Middlebury, and Waltham.

## WEDNESDAY—5 JUNE 1816

An analysis of the observations in early June suggests the passage across all of New England of a deep trough of low pressure, entering from the west after 2100/5th and clearing the southeastern Maine coast about 0800/6th. To the east of the approaching trough on Wednesday, the 5th, the mercury, under the urging of a strong southern flow, reached normal warm sector heights: Williamstown 83° at noon, New Haven 79° at 1400, and Brunswick 76° at the same hour.[5] These cannot be considered the maximums as registering thermometers were not generally in use at this time. A thunder shower occurred at Williamstown soon after noon, dropping the mercury to 69° at 1400, but this would seem to have been an air mass shower or perhaps a squall line type, rather than a true frontal-induced storm, as the mercury remained at relatively high levels during the first part of the night: 69° at 2100.

## THURSDAY—6 JUNE 1816

A new air mass, however, had reached Williamstown by the time of the first observation on Thursday, the 6th. The mercury went down to 45°, and the day was described in the meteorological register as "a cold rainy day from N.W.—not much rain & wind & very chilly."[6]

Morning temperatures on the 6th in central New England remained at seasonable early June levels (Salem 57° and Brunswick 44°), but these were the highs for the day as the steady northwesterly flow drove the mercury lower and lower throughout the daylight hours. It was still raining at the morning observation on the 6th at Williamstown, Salem, and Brunswick and continued to do so sporadically at these points during the day—described at Salem as "rainy, cool, damp."[7]

In the highlands of interior northern New York and northern New England, however, the rain changed to a wet snow in the morning: at 0730 at Elizabethtown in northeastern New York, about 0800 at Bennington in southwestern Vermont. At Bangor in eastern Maine the change-over did not come until mid-afternoon. Montpelier on the plateau of north-central Vermont had snow all day, apparently a wet one falling on moist ground as no accumulations were spoken of.[8] Other high elevations in the Green Mountain State received a light snowfall which became more intermittent as the day progressed. But in the valleys and lower elevations only flakes of snow were mentioned, suggesting a mixture of rain and some kind of frozen precipitation such as often occurs in these localities on early spring days. Only on higher elevations did snow whiten the ground on the 6th.[9]

## THE EXTENT OF SNOWFALL

The snow flakes on the 6th fell over a wide area from the highlands of western New York and northwestern Pennsylvania northeastward to Maine and the St. Lawrence Valley of Canada.[10] At Geneva, New York, "a considerable quantity of snow fell on Thursday morning," and in Oneida County there long existed a fireside story of school children being caught in the snow of June 6th.[11] The Catskills of southeastern New York were covered by an inch of white this day. The flakes reached down to within 10 miles of tidewater on the Hudson River, but no snow reports at valley locations such as Albany have been noticed.[12]

To the north, Elizabethtown in Essex County near northern Lake Champlain had a three-hour snowfall on the morning of the 6th, followed by intermittent snow showers throughout a blustery day.[13] Along the St. Lawrence Valley, closer to the air mass source region, more rigorous conditions prevailed. Montreal had snow squalls on both the 6th and 8th, while in the vicinity of Quebec City the accumulations from the 6th to 10th totaled 12 inches with drifts reaching to the axel trees of carriages.[14] The editor of the *Montreal Gazette* took notice of the unusual events:

> Extraordinary Season.—Our co-temporaries, as well as ourselves, took some notice of the backwardness of last month. Since the beginning of the present month the weather has been alarmingly unpropitious. Last Sunday and Monday, it was rather mild, Tuesday was cold, attended with some rain; Wednesday was hot and sultry; Thursday exceedingly cold, some snow fell between 11 A.M. & 1 P.M. Yesterday the frost was sharp, ice as thick as a dollar, which has injured tender as well as hardy plants. Such an alarming season loudly demands the attention of the husbandman to provide against an impending scarsity. [15]

Down in central Maine the editor of the *Bangor Register* supplied some interesting details of the storm period under the head—Curiosity:

> In this town, June 5, a very warm rain commenced, and continued until past the middle of the 6th, the night was so warm that one blanket was sufficient to keep a person comfortable. Between two and three o'clock P.M. on the 6th, snow began to fall in beautiful large flakes, some of which as they struck the ground covered spots two inches diameter. The snow continued to fall one hour and a half.[16]

All day the 6th temperatures tumbled as the cold flow from the northwest brought truly Arctic air of record late-season severity over New England. It appeared quite likely that Hudson Bay remained frozen over as the spring season had been notoriously backward. Smaller lakes north of the St. Lawrence River continued frozen until late June, according to the *Quebec Gazette*.[17] On the morning of June 7th at Chester in south-central Vermont ice formed to the thickness of a half-dollar on bodies of standing water, and in northern sections of the state it froze an inch thick.[18] Prof. Frederick Hall at Middlebury College in Vermont registered a June low of an even 32°, indicative of conditions at lower levels in northern New England.[19] The 33° figure reached at Waltham, only nine miles west of Boston, also demonstrated what readings must have been at higher elevations to the northward.[20] The evidence of ice formation and of laying snow confirmed that in the highlands the mercury at the ground level dropped several degrees below the freezing point.

## THE WEATHER MAP SITUATION

The occurrence in June of measurable snow and freezing conditions over the highlands of New England constituted an outstanding event, indeed. The meteorological situation that could produce this must meet the following conditions. The source region of the air mass in Canada must have been either snow covered or ice covered so that an initial low thermal content of the atmosphere would be assured, and the dome of cold air must have been very deep to maintain its energy on the southward journey. The terrain over which the air stream moved must have been conditioned by the backward spring conditions, with ground and water surfaces remaining relatively cool, so modification of the air would be held to a minimum.

The actual weather map situation over New England would require a cold northerly stream of unstable air to follow cyclonically-curved streamlines of flow. Such air tends to create and maintain cloud cover in daytime when passing over hilly or mountainous areas, thus lessening solar influences and preserving the original cold content of the air masses involved. Convergence of the air flow around a cyclonic center to the north or northeast was indicated; shower-type precipitation often occurs in this situation. A weather map of the period would probably show a low pressure center moving from the upper Great Lakes region east-northeastward just north of the St. Lawrence Valley with a deep trough trailing southward in which was imbedded a vigorous cold front. The storm center probably stalled for many hours when in the vicinity of the Quebec-Labrador border as it came under the influence of a blocking anticyclone to the northeastward in the Greenland and Iceland area. No doubt, an upper-air vortex existed over Quebec a short distance to the westward of the surface low, in an excellent position to continue and to reinforce the northwesterly flow for the next four days from the cold Hudson Bay source region.

The key to the continuance of the rain/snow situation over the Northeast after the 6th can be found in the behavior of the barometer at Brunswick, Maine, during the remainder of the 6th and on the 7th. It was here that the pressure fell the lowest, according to our rather limited reports from United States points. It rose very gradually on the morning of the 6th, from the low position in the vicinity of 29.18″ to 29.43″ by the evening of the 7th.[21] The slow rise would indicate a stalling and a deepening of the storm center to the north in Canada. No doubt, the deep trough, tied to the low center to the north, slowed its easterly progress after passing off the coast, when the whole system felt the blocking influence of an anticyclonic ridge somewhere east or northeast in the Atlantic Ocean. Thus, a strong northwest flow continued for the next four days as the strong pressure gradient was maintained between the Hudson Bay region and the trough feature just east of the New England coast.

## FRIDAY–SATURDAY—7–8 JUNE 1816

Late on the 7th barometers slowed their gradual climbs, temperatures did not fall as low as they had the previous night, and the wind at New Haven, at least, shifted from northwest to west.[22] These were indications that a second front, the leading edge of a colder, reinforcing air mass was to pass through the area on the night of the 7–8th. Its journey southeastward occasioned a second, heavier snow period as additional unstable air poured over the hills and mountains. The Danville editor in northern Vermont spoke of a "kind of sleet or exceeding cold snow" on the night of the 7–8th, and the ground remained white all day the 8th at Montpelier from the previous night's snowfall. In the highland near the Vermont capital the drifts were "more than a foot" and near Williamstown and Cabot in the Green Mountain State a letter claimed a depth of 18 inches where drifted.[23]

At Lunenburg in the northeastern section of the state in the bottom of the upper Connecticut River Valley, Dr. Hiram Cutting, a careful observer of nature, reported a depth of five inches, and at Lancaster nearby in New Hampshire Adino Brackett recorded: "6th, snowed in considerable quantities. 7th also snow. 8th snow. This is beyond anything of the kind I have ever known."[24] Evidence pointed to the ground being covered all day Saturday, 8th June, at towns and villages in the northern Vermont highlands, in the upper Connecticut Valley, northern New Hampshire, and probably in northwestern Maine, though no reports have been found from this remote section.

At lower elevations only flurries or snow showers, as they are now properly designated, were observed. At low-lying Middlebury in the Champlain Valley, Prof. Hall noted only "a few flakes fell on both June 6th and 8th in the village." At Bennington, Harwood made mention of no snow laying in the valley, though it covered the higher mountains each day, and a similar report came from Williamstown in Massachusetts just to the south. The Windsor *Vermont Journal* in the middle Connecticut Valley also reported snow on Mt. Ascutney as clinging to the foliage, but none accumulated along the river. Nor did the *Dartmouth Gazette* carry any evidence of snow at Hanover also in the trough of the Connecticut Valley. The *New Hampshire Sentinel* at Keene in the extreme southwestern part of the state, in mentioning the widespread storm reports, stated "some fell in this vicinity on the 7-8th," but did not indicate whether at valley or hillside locations.[25]

The question arose as to how far south did the snow extend on this historic June occasion. Noah Webster established the fact that no measurable snow fell at Amherst in north-central Massachusetts, but "on the hills 30 to 40 miles north and west, snow fell for several hours." Both Isaiah Thomas at Worcester and Rev. Thomas Robbins at East Windsor, Connecticut, gave the same testimony for their locations. There was one report of snow on an unspecified day at Plymouth in the hills of Litchfield County in northwestern Connecticut, an area often susceptible to early and late snows.[26]

In eastern New England the snow squalls of the 8th penetrated south and east of the hill country as cold, turbulent air was carried from Vermont and New Hampshire by the vigorous northwesterly flow. A report of "flakes of snow" came from the Waltham weatherman in suburban Boston on the 8th, and Dr. Holyoke recorded a "flight of snow" at Salem the same day. The *Salem Gazette* backed this up: "at 10 o'clock on Saturday, we had a slight snow."[27]

Down East in Maine the diary evidence of Joshua Whitman has been considered as to snow squalls on both the 6th and 7th at North Turner, and on the 8th "some snow for three hours." At Brunswick on the immediate coast snow appeared in Prof. Cleaveland's record book on the 8th, and at Hallowell in the same vicinity "enough to whiten the ground" descended on both the 6th and 8th. At Portland there were snow squalls on Saturday morning, the 8th, with the air temperature dropping to 34° and ice forming on puddles in the streets. Governor Plumer also noticed "a little snow" at Concord in southern New Hampshire on both the 6th and 8th. Thus snow actually was seen in the air in the month of June at sea level at latitude 42° 30' north, and it whitened the ground at high elevations as far south as 42° north.[28]

The remainder of the summer of 1816 lies beyond the scope of this article and this volume. Although many almanacs state that snow fell in every month of 1816, no authentic account of snowfall in July or August has been uncovered in this research. There were frosts in both months as far south as Pennsylvania and New Jersey, those on August 21st and 29th did some damage to tender crops. Both months averaged about five degrees below normal in New England, and the lack of warm nights retarded the development of the corn crop. This delayed its maturing until a killing frost on September 27th cut off all prospects of even a small crop in northern New England. The failure of the corn crop, upon which most farmers depended for their breadstuff, caused extreme hardship in the more northerly located farming communities as a severer than normal winter in 1816–17 dragged on and the threat of semi-starvation became a reality.

---

MISCELLANY.

*For the CENTINEL.*

MR. RUSSELL,

IF you think it would be gratifying to many of your numerous readers to see a correct statement of the weather during the inconstant and particoloured month of June, the following observations are humbly submitted to your disposal, by Yours, CURIOSUS.

| Day of month | Least heat, at sunrise | Greatest heat, at 3 P.M. | Remarks. | Winds. |
|---|---|---|---|---|
| 1 | 46 | 87 | Clear. | S.W. |
| 2 | 60 | 80 | Fair. Cloudy. | S.W.E. |
| 3 | 59 | 72½ | Fair. | N.W. |
| 4 | 40 | 67½ | Fair, Slight Frost. | E. |
| 5 | 60 | 90½ | Fair, Thundershower. | S.W. N.W. |
| 6 | 57 | 43 | Rain, strong wind, and snow in many places. | N.W. |
| 7 | 35 | 57 | Clear. Frost. | N.W. |
| 8 | 58 | 53 | Cloudy. Flakes of snow. | N.W. |
| 9 | 37 | 65 | Clear. Frost. | N.W. |
| 10 | 33 | 59½ | Clear. Water froze. | N.E. |
| 11 | 36 | 68 | Clear. Frost. | E. |
| 12 | 48 | 80 | Clear. | S.W. |
| 13 | 56 | 78½ | Fair. Cloudy. | E. |
| 14 | 53 | 76 | Cloudy. Thun. shower. | E. |
| 15 | 53 | 63 | Cloudy. | N.E. |
| 16 | 51 | 63 | Fair. | N.E. E. |
| 17 | 48 | 60 | Cloudy. | N.E. |
| 18 | 49 | 58 | Very rainy. | N.E. |
| 19 | 57 | 86 | Clear. Thunder. | S.W. |
| 20 | 54 | 78 | Clear. | N.W. N. |
| 21 | 47 | 83½ | Clear. | S.W. |
| 22 | 62 | 93½ | Clear. Smoky. | W. |
| 23 | 69 | 99 | Clear. Smoky. | W. N. of W. |
| 24 | 70 | 98 | Clear. | W. S.W. |
| 25 | 72 | 57 | Cloudy. Rainy. | N.E. |
| 26 | 51 | 66 | Cloudy. Clear. | E. |
| 27 | 52 | 64½ | Foggy. Showery. | S.W. |
| 28 | 62 | 81 | Th. shower. Fair P.M. | S.W. |
| 29 | 56 | 74½ | Cloudy. Fair | N.N.W. |
| 30 | 73 | 73 | Fair. | N.E. E. |

10th day, least heat 33°, (lower than was every known here before in June.) The greatest heat 99°—Difference of extremes 66°. Greatest change in 36 hours, from 5th at 3 o'clock, to 7th at sunrise, 55°. Mean heat 62.1–7°, deduced from the extremes.

For the same month last year, the least heat was 47°—The greatest heat 93°. Mean heat 68°.

*Waltham, July* 1, 1816.

[1] Willis I. Milham. The year 1816—The causes of abnormalities. *Monthly Weather Review* (Wash., D. C.). **52**-12 (Dec 1924), 563. Joseph B. Hoyt. The cold summer of 1816. *Annals of the Association of American Geographers.* **48**-2 (June 1958), 118–131.
[2] Benjamin Harwood. Ms. Diary. (Bennington Museum); *Maine Farmer,* 21 March 1840, 82.
[3] *The Literary and Philosophical Repository* (Middlebury, Vt.), May 1817, 434.
[4] E. Holyoke. Ms. Met. Obs. (Harvard); S. Rodman. Ms. Met. Obs. (Harvard); C. Fisk in *Col. Centinel* (Boston), 6 July 1816.
[5] J. Day. Ms. Met. Obs. (Yale); P. Cleaveland. Ms. Met. Obs. (Bowdoin); *Mem. Amer. Acad.* **4**-2 (1821), 338.
[6] Chester Dewey. Ms. Met. Obs. (Williams College).
[7] J. Day; E. Holyoke; P. Cleaveland.
[8] *Vermont Watchman* (Montpelier), 11 June 1816; Waterbury, Vt., 9 June, in *N. Y. Spectator,* 29 June 1816.
[9] *Lit. & Phil. Rep.,* May 1817, 434.
[10] W. J. McKnight. *A pioneer outline history of northwestern Pennsylvania.* Phila., J. B. Lippincott, 1905. 366.
[11] *Geneva* (N. Y.) *Gazette* in *N. Y. Spectator,* 19 June 1816; Pomroy Jones. *Annals & recollections of Oneida County,* 79.
[12] *N. Y. Post,* 13 June 1816.
[13] *Albany Adv.,* 22 June 1816, in J. B. Hoyt, 120.
[14] *Quebec Gazette,* 6 & 13 June 1816; *Quebec Mercury,* 7 June 1816.
[15] *Montreal Gazette,* 8 June 1816.
[16] *Bangor* (Me.) *Register* in *Dartmouth Gazette* (Hanover, N. H.), 19 June 1816.
[17] *Quebec Gazette,* 27 Sept 1816.
[18] *Dart. Gaz.,* 19 June 1816; *North Star* (Danville, Vt.), 15 June 1816.
[19] *Lit. & Phil. Rep.,* May 1817, 434.
[20] C. Fisk in *Col. Cent.,* 6 July 1816.
[21] P. Cleaveland.
[22] J. Day.
[23] *Vt. Watchman,* 11 June 1816; *North Star,* 15 June 1815; *N. Y. Spectator,* 29 June 1816.
[24] Hiram Cutting. Natural History of Essex Co. A. Hemenway. *Vermont Historical Gazetteer.* **1**, 1056; Adino Brackett. Ms. Diary, (N. H. Hist. Soc.).
[25] *Lit. & Phil. Rep.;* W. Harwood; C. Dewey. *Vt. Journal* (Windsor) in *Dart. Gaz.,* 19 June 1816; *N. H. Sentinel* (Keene), 15 June 1816.
[26] N. Webster. *Notes,* **2**, 178; I. Thomas. *Diary,* 316; T. Robbins. *Diary,* **1**, 670.
[27] E. Holyoke. *Salem Gaz.;* 11 June 1816; *Col. Cent.,* 6 July 1816.
[28] *Maine Farmer,* 21 March 1840; *Nat. Int.* (Wash., D. C.), 20 June 1816; P. Cleaveland; William Plumer. Ms. Met. Obs. (Harvard).

# THE WINTRY FEBRUARY OF 1817

A wintry seven weeks period extended from mid-January to the first days of March in 1817 during which there occurred a sufficiency of events to please any weather fan: four major cold waves, record extreme cold with the mercury congealing near tidewater, the coldest average February in the contemporary record books, a major northeaster with the lowest barometric pressures so far observed, and an amazing out-of-season thunder and lightning storm that raged for four hours over points in central New England.

The early part of this winter had continued the delightful, almost Indian Summer weather of the late fall of 1816, a welcome relaxation in the elements in view of the adversities of the previous spring, summer, and early fall. Even after New Year's Day conditions continued pleasant and sunny in eastern Massachusetts with the mercury climbing into the 40's on eight of the first ten days of January.[1] Rev. Robbins at East Windsor, Connecticut, observed on the 10th that the December frosts were mainly out of the ground.[2]

The mild spell, however, was destined for a quick, spectacular ending as a major circulation change commenced on the 12th when a cold anticyclone pushed frigid air into New England on the wings of a northwest gale. The core of the cold air took an easterly track over New England with the main stream of densest air passing over the District of Maine to inaugurate a memorable winter there. Very low temperatures were registered on the morning of the 15th: Gardiner down to −32°, and Hallowell to −34°, an "enormous cold morning"—"probably the greatest cold ever registered in the United States."[3] At Brunswick, where we have the excellent daily records of Prof. Parker Cleaveland, the mercury dropped below zero on three successive mornings from the 13th through the 15th of January.[4]

Following the initial cold wave of the season, temperatures relaxed on the 16th and 17th as a strong southerly flow prevailed in advance of a marked trough of low pressure advancing from the west on the heels of the retreating anticyclone. This set off light snows and rains on the 17th across New England which reached a spectacular climax during the night of the 17–18th when the mixing air masses triggered a winter thunderstorm of unusual duration and geographical extent. Noticed from Williamstown in the Berkshires to Boston on the seaboard, the pyrotechnics continued in some places as long as four hours and were especially remarked for the brilliance of the white lightning.[5] The following impulse of cold air turned the light rains into flaky snow which clung to trees and objects to create a winter wonderland scene the next morning. The spectacular flashes of lightning did contain some damaging strokes causing fires in Massachusetts and southern New Hampshire. The Fitzwilliam area in the southwestern part of the Granite State suffered the greatest losses with at least six strikes made within the town. The newly erected Meeting House received a direct hit on its protective lightning rods which kindled a fire on the ground in shavings left underneath the structure by carpenters. The building was consumed by the flames, along with the residence of Colonel Robinson in the same town.[6]

From the meteorological view, the most interesting aspect of the thunderstorm concerned the occurrence of St. Elmo's Fire in the Vermont hills near Andover while a heavy snow was falling.[7] A full account of this will be found in A Winter Anthology at the conclusion of this work. Following the passage of the front, a three-day gale swept the New England countryside, reminiscent of the tempestuous wind seven years before on the same dates, Cold Friday of 1810, though the degree of cold accompanying the blasts this time ran much warmer.

A second major cold outbreak of the season occurred on the 26th. Brunswick, Maine, experienced six consecutive mornings with the mercury below zero. The 29th proved the coldest when the season's low of $-21°$ was registered on the Bowdoin campus at tidewater.[9] It ran even colder inland at Gardiner on the Kennebec River where a $-40°$ reading obtained, the degree of cold authenticated by the exposure of a bowl of quicksilver which quickly congealed.[10] Both Hanover, New Hampshire, and Windsor, Vermont, in the Connecticut Valley reached $-30°$ on the morning of the 29th, but this time the cold air did not penetrate into southern New England.[11] No report of the severity of the cold in extreme northern New York State or northern New England has come to hand.

January snowfall after the 15th generally proved adequate for sleighing in interior New England, though coastal areas had to wait until the 24th for sufficient cover. At Brunswick, 24.5 inches fell during the month, and at North Turner, Androscoggin Co., 21 inches insured good conditions.[12]

February 1817 averaged one of the coldest months of record in all corners of New England. At Brunswick, Maine, it ran 7.4 degrees below normal and followed a January which had a deficit of 4.6 degrees.[13] At New Haven the minus departure was 8.6 degrees, for the coldest February since the commencement of monthly records in 1780, and not to be exceeded until February 1836.[14] Similar departures were registered at Williamstown ($-7.6$ degrees) and at New Bedford ($-6.3$ degrees).[15] There were three principal cold periods: from the 4th to 6th, 11th to 17th, and 25th to 28th. Only one brief warm period occurred, from the 21st to 23d.

The first cold spell dropped the mercury quickly to below-zero regions, but it as rapidly rebounded. At Williamstown an advective blast contracted the mercury to $-14°$ by the morning of the 5th. It remained below the zero mark all day, but by next noontime had soared into the high 20's.[16] At Waltham near Boston the 5th was a bitter day with readings: $-11°$, $+6°$, $-2°$, but by 1400/6th the reading ran up to $+28°$.[17]

The major cold outbreak of the winter and the spell that insured the month its reputation for coldness struck late on the 13th after a brief afternoon thaw. The thermometer at Williamstown went below zero early on the 14th, remaining in this depressed state until late forenoon of the 16th. The daylight periods of the 14th and 15th were as cold as had been observed at Williamstown since 1796: 14th, $-7.6°$, $-8°$, $-16°$; and 15th, $-20°$, $-5°$, and $-5.6°$.[18] Eastward at Waltham the advancing cold air mass poured in all day the 14th, driving the mercury steadily downward despite the efforts of the sun: $+5°$, $-5°$, and $-15°$ — as spectacular a reversal of the normal diurnal temperature trend as a Bostonian ever witnesses. The Hub City did not experience an authentic zero day at this time nor on the following day, the 15th, which had a morning minimum of $-14°$, but an afternoon maximum of $+8°$.[19] At Cambridge, Prof. Farrar observed $-18°$ on the morning of the 15th, the coldest in Harvard records stretching back to 1790.[20] There were credible press reports of $-20°$ from other points around suburban Boston.[21]

The cold of 14–15 February seemed even more intense in New York State. A congenial group of thermometer watchers in Whiteborough, Oneida County, decided to stay up all night to see how low their instrument would fall. Apparently either fatigue or the spirits of the affair overcame them at 0300/15th when their glass read $-35.5°$, so they decided to be done with their foolishness and crawl into a nice warm bed.[22] At Sackets Harbor at the northeastern end of Lake Ontario a figure of $-32°$ was noted.[23] In New Hampshire the college thermometer at Hanover sank down to $-30°$ again, the lowest reading on the scale of the instrument.[24] No doubt, the mercury congealed at many of the cold pockets throughout northern New York and New England near sunrise on 15 February 1817.

Winter's most striking blow was yet to come. So far the season had been a snowy one with frequent light to moderate snow after the 15th of January, but no great storm of driving snow to block up the roads and to cancel out the excellent conditions for doing business that the even snow cover had provided until one of the major depressions of our period swept up the Atlantic seaboard and across all southern and eastern New England. Captain Brantz at Baltimore on the 24th noticed a "violent storm from NE and NW with constant driving snow."²⁵ In New England it combined gale-force winds, thick snow, and falling temperatures in a degree unmatched since 1811. From the meteorological reports at New Bedford, Salem, and Brunswick, it appeared that the storm center moved very close to Cape Cod and remained well enough inshore to spread a heavy snow canopy over much of the interior and most of the coastal section from Boston northeastward. New Bedford had heavy rain, strong northerly winds, and a rapidly falling barometer on the morning and afternoon of the 24th. The glass stood at 29.35″ at sunrise, but by early evening was down to 28.70″, a very low figure for a coastal disturbance. In all, 1.52 inches of precipitation fell, mostly rain in the morning, but included some snow in late afternoon and evening.²⁶

Dr. Holyoke's barometer at Salem sank to 28.79″, the lowest he had observed since the commencement of such records in 1786.²⁷ Snow commenced at Boston at 0200 and continued to fall all day the 24th and until early morning on the 25th.²⁸ Twelve inches were measured at Waltham and 10 inches at Williamstown.²⁹ In New Hampshire at Epping the depth reached 14 inches, the maximum figure reported anywhere.³⁰ To the north at Brunswick the new fall amounted to only seven inches. This mighty storm raised the February total at Waltham to 36.5 inches, at Epping to 39.5 inches, at Brunswick to 27 inches, and at North Turner to 24 inches, to push seasonal totals well toward record amounts.³¹ Temperatures after the shift of winds to northwest on the 25th dropped off gradually to reach −2° at Brunswick and +10° at Waltham.

Another 8-inch snow on March 2d and an additional 6 inches on the 19th continued the deep snow cover at Brunswick past the vernal equinox. At North Turner, Joshua Whitman added 25 inches in March and 7 inches in April, for a grand seasonal total of 119 inches, the highest in his span of snowfall measurements from 1812 to 1840.³² This figure, however, would be greatly exceeded in the famous Down East Winter of 1843.

In retrospect, the cold and snows of January, February, and March led historian William Williamson to single out the winter of 1816–17 in Maine as one of the hardest in many years.³³ Others judged it the most severe since that of 1783–84, always a landmark for extreme conditions in the Northeast.³⁴ Proof of the degree of severity lay in the crossing of the wide Penobscot by heavy teams, a feat that had not been achieved "since the cold winters of the American Revolution."³⁵

[1] *Col. Cent.*, 2 Feb 1817.
[2] T. Robbins. *Diary*, **1**, 695.
[3] W. Bentley. Ms. Met. Notes, 57-4, (Amer. Antiq. Soc.); *Nat. Int.* (Wash., D. C.), 25 Jan 1817.
[4] P. Cleaveland. Ms. Met. Obs., (Bowdoin).
[5] C. Dewey. Ms. Met. Obs., (Williams); I. Thomas, *Diary*, 340.
[6] *N. H. Sentinel* (Keene), 25 Jan 1817; John F. Norton. *The history of Fitzwilliam, N. H. from 1752 to 1887.* N. Y., Burr Printing House, 1888. 195.
[7] John Farrar. An account of a singular electrical phenomenon, observed during a snow storm accompanied with thunder. *Mem. Amer. Acad. Arts & Sci.* **4-1**, (1821), 98.
[8] I. Thomas. 340.
[9] P. Cleaveland.
[10] *Amer. Jour. Sci.* (New Haven), **31**, (Jan 1837), 161.
[11] W. Bentley. 57-4.
[12] P. Cleaveland; *Maine Farmer*, 29 Aug 1840, 266.
[13] P. Cleaveland.
[14] J. Day. Ms. Met. Obs., (Yale).
[15] C. Dewey; S. Rodman. Ms. Met. Obs., (Harvard).
[16] C. Dewey.
[17] *Col. Cent.*, 2 March 1817.
[18] C. Dewey.
[19] *Col. Cent.*, 2 March 1817.
[20] *Boston Journal*, (1823–24), 492.
[21] Abiel Holmes. Ms. Met. Obs., (Lib. of Cong.).
[22] *Medical Repository*, (1818), 92.
[23] *Niles National Register* (Balto.), Supp. Vol. 15, 16.
[24] *Idem.*
[25] L. Brantz. Ms. Met. Obs., (NA).
[26] S. Rodman. Ms. Met. Obs., (Harvard).
[27] E. Holyoke. Ms. Met. Obs.
[28] *Col. Cent.*, 25 Feb 1817.
[29] *Ibid.*, 2 March 1817; C. Dewey.
[30] William Plumer. Ms. Met. Obs., (Harvard).
[31] C. Fisk, W. Plumer, P. Cleaveland, C. Whitman in *Maine Farmer*, 29 Aug 1840.
[32] C. Whitman.
[33] William Williamson. *History of Maine*, **1**, 100.
[34] *Col. Cent.*, 22, 25 Feb & 15 March 1817; Diary of Jeremiah Weare, Jr. *New Eng. Hist. Gen. Reg.* (Boston), **66**, (1912), 315.
[35] *Col. Cent.*, 22 Feb 1817.

## AN OLD-FASHIONED WINTER 1819–20

"The winter has been more uniform & like an old fashioned winter, than any that has occurred in many years, tho not so severe as the years 1739–40 [1740–41?] & 1779–80," wrote John Pintard at New York City on 29 January 1820.¹ Noah Webster from his observation post at Amherst in west-central Massachusetts agreed on the character of the season: "Winter began rather earlier than for some years past. Two or three violent storms. In Jan. & Feb. the snow in New England was from three to four feet deep. A few days of severe cold, & the cold was continued for about five weeks with little intermission."² At East Windsor in Connecticut, a short distance north of Hartford, Rev. Thomas Robbins caught the essentials of the winter in his diary:

### December 1819

22. Very pleasant and good riding.
24. Wet and rainy.
26. The morning very cold. Thermometer at 8°.
27. This morning at 15°.
28. 22° . . . Very windy and tedious.
29. 18° Severe cold . . . The ground very hard frozen.
30. 10° . . . The afternoon we had a violent snow-storm. Severe cold for snow.
31. 8°. The snow is nearly a foot deep, but much drifted. Very windy and tedious. The snow flies very much . . . with regard to weather for this year there has been but a small portion of wet, and very little cloudy weather. I think I never knew so pleasant a season. God is supplying us with unmerited favors.

### January 1820

1. Severe cold. Morning 11° below zero. Several degrees colder than any time last winter. It rose during the day to about 20°.
2. This morning 12° below zero. It rose very slowly . . . The cold was very severe.
3. 10° . . . I fear my green trees are much injured by the frost.
4. This morning 15° . . . It thaws some.
5. 14°.
6. 23°.
7. 10° below zero.
8. The weather mild and pleasant. The snow thaws.
10. The sleighing is poor.
11. Last night we had a good deal of snow . . . The weather is moderate.
12. Good sleighing.
13. Excellent sleighing and crossing the river. This morning 14°.
14. 8°. My best orange-tree was hurt last night.
15. 15°.
16. Good sleighing and good meeting . . . this morning 8°.
17. We had a hard storm of snow and rain. It was quite violent.
19. 14° . . . Severe cold.
20. Excellent sleighing. This morning 2° below zero.
21. The late storm was very severe at New Haven.
22. Early in the morning, and most of the forenoon, it snowed hard. My thermometer yesterday morning was 2° below zero; today it was 15° . . . The new snow, I think, is six or seven inches.
23. About 10°.
24. Morning 15°. In the evening it was at 6° . . . Cold and tedious.
25. 19° . . . Very pleasant for winter.
26. Weather quite moderate . . . It snowed some.
27. The thermometer rose to about 50°. The sleighing very fine. There is a heavy body of snow on the ground.
29. The thermometer goes but little below the freezing point.
30. Thermometer was at about 50°.
31. Last night it snowed. Quite blustering.

### February 1820

1. Very cold and tedious . . . Thermometer in the morning 2°, and at two o'clock 11°. Much colder in the middle of the day than any one this year.
2. Morning 4° . . . The roads are drifted. Severe cold.
3. It snowed and rained considerably.
4. Weather moderate. The snow is covered with a very sharp crust.
5. This morning was 8° below zero. Last night it grew cold very much.
6. Last evening at 12°, and this morning at sunrise 38°. The eaves run. It thawed much all day. Rose to 50°.
7. Morning 38°. It snowed and thawed all day.
8. Morning 8°; but it rose above 40°.
9. It snowed steadily all day. We have an immense body of it on the ground.
10. Worked shoveling snow. 2° . . . Returned in the evening in a very thick snow-storm. Had difficulty in keeping the road. Not very cold.
11. The snow of last night is perhaps a foot deep, and much drifted. People are out generally breaking roads. It is said there is more than three feet on the ground, and very heavy. Morning 5°, but rose to 40°.
12. 14°, and rose to 40°. The roads in many places are said to be impassable.
13. Rose to 60°. It thaws, and the snow settles very much. The walking is so bad that I had no conference.
14. The thermometer goes very little below the freezing point. It rose about 50°.
15. The sleighing is very bad. It thaws very much, and the snow is very deep.
16. It rained a good deal. We had a number of showers. Got considerably wet. The mass of snow retains the water; the streams do not rise much. The water in the road in many places is quite deep . . . Yesterday at 60°, today above 50°.
17. Quite rainy . . . Got my feet very wet.
18. The water seems to get into the ground, which is a great favor in its present dry state.
23. The sleighing grows poor.
24. Had to cross at Hartford.
25. The snow wastes but slowly.
26. The sleighing is poor.
27. Wet and some of the time it rained hard . . . There is a great deal of water on the ground.
28. Rode to Hartford in a carriage. We might have gone much better in a sleigh. There is still a great body of snow.
29. Last night it became cold. Morning 20°.

### March 1820

25. About 70°. The snow goes off very fast.
26. Rose to 83°. In the afternoon wore no out coat. The ground settles remarkably fast. We have rode to meeting twelve Sabbaths in succession, with a plenty of snow; it is now good going with a carriage.[3]

[1] Noah Webster, *Diary*, 2, 182.
[2] John Pintard, *Coll. N.Y. Hist. Soc.* 70 (1937), 264.
[3] T. Robbins, *Diary*, 1, 805–14.

# THE OLD SOUTH IN THE EARLY NINETEENTH CENTURY

Two Early Weathermen at Old Natchez ..................... 199

Winter Highlights at Natchez: 1799–1820 .................. 203

Winters with the Moravians in North Carolina: 1803–1820 ..... 206

Cold Friday of 1807 in the South .......................... 209

Thomas Jefferson and Virginia Winters: 1810–1816 .......... 211

# TWO EARLY WEATHERMEN AT OLD NATCHEZ

Most of the region known as Mississippi became part of the United States of America in 1783 in accordance with the terms of the Treaty of Paris. The area had been claimed and occupied at times by the colonial powers of France, Great Britain, and Spain, and finally by the new State of Georgia. A territorial government of the United States was established in 1798, though the population remained sparse and economic activity rudimentary. It was not until the population surge westward following the conclusion of the War of 1812 that Mississippi became qualified for admission to the union as a state (1817).

In this remote frontier district, inhabited mainly by Indians and frequently a pawn in diplomatic and military struggles, one might not expect to find two well-educated men, versed in science, who distinguished themselves especially in the pursuit of meteorology. They were William Dunbar (1749–1810) of "The Forest" and Winthrop Sargent (1753–1820) of "Grove Plantation" and later "Glo'ster Place," whose home sites lay within three miles of each other just south of the river port of Natchez. Thanks to their native intelligence, formal training, and regular habits of observation, meteorological records of good quality were maintained for the Natchez area during the period from August 1798 through December 1819, a span of two decades during which many interesting wintry weather events occurred.

## William Dunbar: 1749–1810

William Dunbar, the heir to a distinguished title though he never appeared to have assumed it, was born in Scotland of noble ancestry in 1749, the youngest son of Sir Archibald Dunbar.[1] He was educated in Edinburgh and later studied mathematics and astronomy in London. Of delicate constitution as a youth, he came to America seeking renewed health in 1771. After entering the trading business in Philadelphia, he took a journey down the Ohio and Mississippi Rivers in 1773 and decided to settle in the vicinity of Baton Rouge, then part of British West Florida. During the turmoil attending the Revolutionary War, his plantation was twice plundered by armed bands and his labor force dispersed by a slave insurrection. At this early date Dunbar's scientific interests were illustrated by his possession of a thermometer. His diary entry for 8 January 1777: "This morning a black frost. 20½° Fahrenheit's Thermomr." [2]

In addition to the ravages of war, the Louisiana and West Florida region experienced two severe hurricanes in 1779 and 1780. Dunbar happened to be in New Orleans at the time of the occurrence of the first, and from his personal observations of the passage of the great disturbance he reasoned that the center of a tropical storm consisted of a relatively calm vortex around which a circular system of winds whirled and that the whole body had a forward motion. This correct view of the structure of a tropical storm system was unique, though a similar surmise had been made contemporaneously by an Englishman, James Capper, from experiences over the years with Bay of Bengal cyclones in India. In an historical coincidence that often has marked research in science, both men announced their findings to a scientific audience in the same year of 1801.[3]

Dunbar's thermometer and other scientific equipment had been dispersed when his plantation was plundered by warring forces, and such articles could not be replaced at the time in that remote part of the world. Not until the Spanish authorities employed him to establish the international boundary in 1798 were the proper instruments for scientific pursuits in his hands. Dunbar commenced a series of regular meteorological observations on 1 February 1799, and a manuscript record of these for the next 11 years has been preserved.[4] The site was now in the United States in Mississippi Territory at "The Forest," his plantation located nine miles south of Natchez and four miles east of the Mississippi River, in the extreme southwest corner of the present state. Dunbar took thrice daily observations of temperature, barometric pressure, wind direction, precipitation, and state of sky. There were very few omissions until his fatal illness commenced in the month of March 1810. Occasional monthly notes and comments, especially in wintertime, gave valuable data as to the frequency and severity of frost, ice, and snowfall in early Mississippi.

When U. S. Commissioner Andrew Ellicott came down the Mississippi River to survey the border between Spanish and United States territory, he made the acquaintance of Dunbar, and they spent many mutually rewarding hours discussing scientific matters of the day. Dunbar had developed a facile method of calculating longitude without resort to a chronometer, and this greatly simplified frontier survey work.[5]

As part of his duties in surveying the border between Spanish West Florida and Mississippi, Dunbar submitted a summary: "Report of William Dunbar to the Spanish Government at the conclusion of his services in locating and surveying the thirty-first degree of latitude."[6] Going far beyond astronomical calculations, this gave a rather full discussion of the flora and fauna of the largely unknown region. In other papers Dunbar summarized his study of the local Indians, making valuable contributions to an understanding of their speech and methods of communication. Upon Ellicott's recommendation, Dunbar was elected to membership in the American Philosophical Society in Philadelphia. Then commenced a friendly, enlightened correspondence with Thomas Jefferson, president of the United States and also president of the American Philosophical Society.[7] He had written Jefferson as early as 14 July 1800 with a summary of his meteorological observations and some views on the nature of the Mississippi climate. Many of Dunbar's original papers during the next decade were published in the *Transactions* of the Society. His biographer claimed that Dunbar made more such contributions in the next ten years than any other American writer.[8]

When Thomas Jefferson sought to explore the newly-acquired Louisiana Territory, he secured the assistance of Dunbar to accompany expeditions to traverse the Washita River region of Arkansas in 1804–05 and the Red River region farther southwest. Dunbar's full diary of the first expedition has been preserved.[9] In this he gave a good meteorological accounting of this memorable winter in the Old Southwest, and it makes interesting reading when compared with the meteorological notes of the Lewis & Clark Expedition wintering at the same time in the Mandan country of the Dakotas. Both these pioneer accounts of the winter climate of the West will be found in the concluding section of this work: A Winter Anthology.

Dunbar made two meteorological contributions to the *Transactions of the American Philosophical Society*. The first was contained in a letter to Thomas Jefferson, dated 22 August 1801, from which extracts were read to the Society on 18 December 1801 and published in the 6th volume appearing in 1804.[10] The second communication covering his observations in 1801, 1802, and 1803 apparently went directly to the Society and was read on 6 April 1804. This, too, received space in the 6th volume. No other printed records or extracts from Dunbar's meteorological observations have come to light, but very fortunately a manuscript copy of his records has been preserved in the Mississippi Department of Archives and has been used extensively in the summary of Natchez winter weather from 1799 to 1823 that follows.

Dunbar's first communication to Philadelphia contained information as to winter conditions in the lower Mississippi Valley:

> Before the close of November we are reminded of the approach of winter by a few cold mornings and evenings and sometimes nipping frosts, which exhibit their destructive power, first, in the vallies by killing tender plants, while those on the adjoining hills retain sometime longer their bloom and verdure. This effect is to be accounted for by the greater specific gravity of the condensed freezing air, which runs off on all sides from elevated situations into the nearest vallies, there forming a mass of great extent, while the hills are supplied with air less dense and warmer from a superior stratum of the atmosphere. The influence of this cause is so great at the first approaches of winter that a difference of 10°. of Farenheit's scale has been noted at the short interval of 3 miles in the direction of East and West; one position overlooking the great valley of the Mississippi 30 miles wide, while the other was in the interior, environed by forests. On the morning of the 13th, November 1799 the thermometer stood in the first situation at 42°. and in the latter at 32°.

\* \* \* \* \*

> The winds of this country are extremely variable in the winter season, seldom blowing above three days successively from the same point; the north-west wind brings us the severest cold. It may be considered as a general rule during winter, that all winds blowing from the east to the meridian bring rain, and those from the west dry weather; the east and south east winds are most abundantly charged with moisture, as the opposite points are always the driest; the north-east wind during this season is moist chilly and disagreeable, but seldom prevails for any length of time: the north-wind brings (though rarely) sleet or snow.—After 2, 3 or 4 days of damp cloudy or rainy weather, it suddenly clears up with a cold north-west wind, which blows frequently with great force during the first and sometimes part of the second day of the change, the nights being generally calm; after a like period of fair weather, of which the two first days are clear and freezing, and the other two fine mild and agreeable with a morning's hoar frost, it revolves again into the same circle of damp and rainy weather. This may be considered as the general revolution of the winter season, but with many exceptions. The frequent and rapid

changes in the state of the weather, during the winter in this climate furnish an excellent opportunity of verifying the vulgar opinion of the moon's pretended influence at her conjunctions, oppositions and quadratures; but truth compels me to say (what probably may be said of many similar persuasions) that after a continued and scrupulous attention to this object, I have not discovered any such regularity of coincidence, which might justify the reverence with which those traditional maxims are at this day received by all these whose minds are not expanded by the lights of philosophy.

With the month of February our spring season may be said to commence and southerly winds prevail, as if propitious nature was inclined to facilitate the operations of the husbandman, by carrying off the superabundant moisture with which the surface of the earth is drenched after the winter rains. This salutary effect is much more apparent on the flat lands of lower Louisiana than with us. Those regular gales are also peculiarly favourable in facilitating the ascent of the commercial boats, which at this season, with commencement of the annual inundation, perform their yearly voyage to the Spanish settlements in the higher parts of Louisiana.

### Winthrop Sargent: 1753–1820

Winthrop Sargent first appeared on our meteorological scene during the great early December snowstorms in 1786 when he first commenced jotting thermometer readings in his diary.[12] He had been graduated from Harvard College in 1771 and later participated in the war rising to the rank of major. After the cessation of hostilities, he turned his interests westward, first becoming secretary to the governor of the Old Northwest Territory, General Arthur Sinclair, and then, along with many fellow New Englanders, he became active in the Ohio Company in its quest to establish settlements in the new lands.[13]

Sargent continued to carry a thermometer with which he took daily observations whether at home or abroad on his many travels. From 1 September 1788 to 31 May 1791 he made thrice daily observations, mainly at Marietta, the seat of early government and settlement on the Ohio River.[14] In addition to temperature, they contained wind data, force and direction, and general comments. These observations comprised the first regular information on climatic conditions in the Ohio Country. Excerpts were transmitted to the American Philosophical Society in 1789 and later were deposited in the American Academy of Arts and Sciences, and thus were known to scientific men. The observations continued, though not without breaks, until late in the decade of the 1790's. Some of these have been preserved in the fragments of Sargent's diary which have survived, and a general summary of winter conditions based on a Sargent memorandum appeared in Daniel Drake's *Notices concerning Cincinnati* in 1810.[15]

In 1798 Sargent, in true frontier fashion, migrated again to the new Mississippi Territory in the lower part of the valley where he served as the first territorial governor of the newly-organized district. His unwavering adherence to the Federalist cause brought him into much political bickering with the rising Republican opposition, and after the Jeffersonian triumph in the election of 1800 he failed to secure reappointment, though he made strenuous efforts to obtain this. Bitterly disappointed, he then turned his attention to developing his plantation, land speculation, and the pursuit of scientific interests, mainly in connection with meteorology and river hydrology.[16]

Sargent had succeeded in transporting his thermometer by boat all the way from Ohio to Mississippi as his new meteorological diary commenced in August 1798. Apparently now shunning the Republican-dominated American Philosophical Society, Sargent sent his meteorological observations back home to Federalist Boston where they were published in the *Memoirs* of the American Academy of Arts and Sciences.[17] Brief summary tables covering the years 1798 to 1808 at Natchez appeared in 1809. These contained annual maximums and minimums of temperature, monthly precipitation, and number of days with no rain and number of days with rain or snow. The dates of first and last frosts, along with snowfall occurrences, were included. A second summary, confined to the month of December 1811, described meteorological conditions preceding and after the great earthquake occurrences of that month in the middle Mississippi Valley. These were published in the volume of the *Memoirs* for 1815.[18]

Sargent continued his observations almost to the conclusion of the second decade of the 19th Century as his manuscript diary confirmed. Occasional summaries appeared in the local press such as the *Natchez Intelligencer* and the *Mississippi Republican*, and these were also issued separately as broadsides.[19] An interesting and extremely valuable account of the rise and fall of the Mississippi River covering the period from 1798 to 1818 also appeared in the frontier press to preserve an account of Old Man River's doings during this early period.[20] And most fortunate for historians of the early Mississippi climate, Sargent permitted Dr. A. Perlee, who made a study of the yellow fever epidemics at Natchez in 1817 and 1819, to make use of his temperature and precipitation statistics from 1810 to 1819, and these were appended at the end of Perlee's article appearing in the *Philadelphia Journal of the Medical and Physical Sciences* in 1821.[21] Thus, only the year 1809 of Sargent's 22-year record of the Natchez weather scene are not now currently available for the student wishing to study the monthly variations of temperature and precipitation in early Mississippi. Winthrop Sargent died on 3 June 1820 in his 66th year while seeking medical succor at New Orleans.

The following tables give a good comparison of the relative severity of winters at Natchez. The first series from 1799 to 1810 were taken from William Dunbar's manuscript record book. The second series from 1810 to 1819 are based on Winthrop Sargent's summary appearing in the *Philadelphia Journal of the Medical and Physical Sciences* in 1821. Only fragments of Sargent's records survive in his diary. For the only two months for which the records overlap, Dunbar's averages for January and February ran one full degree lower than Sargent's.

|  | Dec. | Jan. | Feb. | Mar. | Mean 3 months Dec.–Feb. |
|---|---|---|---|---|---|
| 1798–99 |  |  | 48 | 52 |  |
| 99–00 | 47 | 44 | 43 | 59 | 44.7 |
| 1800–01 | 47 | 51 | 58 | 61 | 51.9 |
| 01–02 | 49 | 55 | 59 | 62 | 54.3 |
| 02–03 | 47 | 47 | 52 | 62 | 48.7 |
| 03–04 | 53 | 46 | 53 | 53 | 50.5 |
| 04–05 | 51 | 48 | 50 | 59 | 49.7 |
| 05–06 | 59 | 53 | 59 |  | 57.0 |
| 06–07 | 48 | 43 | 47 | 50 | 46.0 |
| 07–08 | 52 | 43 | 58 | 61 | 51.0 |
| 08–09 | 61 | 41 | 55 | 60 | 52.3 |
| 09–10 | 46 | 52 | 53 |  | 50.3 |
| 10–11 | 52 | 52 | 49 | 64 | 51.0 |
| 11–12 | 53 | 46 | 51 | 62 | 50.0 |
| 12–13 | 47 | 43 | 49 | 70 | 48.3 |
| 13–14 | 50 | 47 | 59 | 56 | 52.0 |
| 14–15 | 44 | 48 | 50 | 65 | 47.3 |
| 15–16 | 52 | 44 | 55 | 64 | 50.3 |
| 16–17 | 56 | 50 | 50 | 63 | 52.0 |
| 17–18 | 51 | 48 | 47 | 55 | 48.7 |
| 18–19 | 50 | 58 | 60 | 61 | 56.0 |
| 19–20 | 52 |  |  |  |  |

[1] *Life, letters, and papers of William Dunbar of Elgin, Morayshire, Scotland, and Natchez, Mississippi. Pioneer scientist of the Southern United States.* Compiled and prepared from the original documents for the National Society of Colonial Dames in America. Mrs. Dunbar Rowland (Eron Rowland). Jackson, Mississippi, Press of the Mississippi Historical Society, 1930, 9–15.

[2] *Ibid.*, 40.

[3] D. M. Ludlum. *Early American Hurricanes*, 65–66.

[4] W. Dunbar. Ms. Met. Obs. (Miss. Archives.)

[5] Andrew Ellicott. Astronomical and thermometrical observations made on the boundary between the United States and His Catholic Majesty. *Trans. Amer. Phil. Soc.* 5 (1802), 203.

[6] D. Rowland. *Life, letters, papers*, 78–99.

[7] T. Jefferson to W. Dunbar, Washington, 12 Jan 1801. *Ibid.*, 111.

[8] *Ibid.*, 11.

[9] *Discoveries made in exploring the Missouri, Red River, and Washita by Captains Lewis and Clark, Doctor Sibley, and William Dunbar, Esq. with a statistical account of the countries adjacent. With an appendix by Mr. Dunbar.* Natchez, A. Marschalk, 1806, 113–64; Reprint: D. Rowland, 216–320.

[10] Extract of a letter from William Dunbar, Esq. of Natchez, to Thomas Jefferson, President of the Society. Natchez, 22 Aug 1801. *Trans. Amer. Phil. Soc.* 6–1 (1801–04), 40–42.

[11] William Dunbar. Monthly and annual results of meteorological observations made by (1801–03) Wm. Dunbar, Esq. at the Forest, 4 miles east of the River Mississippi. . . . *Trans. Amer. Phil. Soc.* 6–1 (1804), 188–89.

[12] Winthrop Sargent. Ms. Diary. (Mass. Hist. Soc.)

[13] Benjamin H. Pershing. Winthrop Sargent. *Ohio Archeological and Historical Quarterly.* 33–3 (July 1924), 237–81.

[14] Sundry Met. Obs., Marietta, Ohio. Read, 21 Aug 1789. *Proc. Amer. Phil. Soc.* 22–3 (1884), 174. Winthrop Sargent. Ms. Observations with Fahrenheit thermometer at the sun's rising, setting and 2 o'clock P.M., made at Marietta in the County of Washington and Territory of the United States N.W. of the River Ohio—Lat. 39° 23′ North. September 1, 1788-May 31, 1791. (Amer. Acad. Arts Sci., Harvard.)

[15] Daniel Drake. *Notices concerning Cincinnati.* Cincinnati, John W. Brown & Co., 1810.

[16] *Encyclopedia of Mississippi History.* Dunbar Rowland, ed. Madison, Wis., Selwyn A. Brant, 1907. 2, 594–609.

[17] Winthrop Sargent. Meteorological observations at Grove Plantation, five miles south of Natchez. 1798–1808. *Mem. Amer. Acad. Arts Sci.* 3–1 (1809), 113–115.

[18] Winthrop Sargent. Account of several shocks of an earthquake in the southern and western parts of the United States. *Ibid.,* 3–2 (1815), 350–60.

[19] Hon. Winthrop Sargent, Natchez. Respecting the quantity of rain in that country in 1814. Communicated for the *Natchez Intelligencer*, No. 2. Broadside. McMurtrie Biblio. T 50. Originally published in *Natchez Intelligencer* between 1 Aug and 5 Sept 1815. Copy in Amer. Antiq. Soc. (Worcester). No issue of the *Natchez Intelligencer* prior to its merger with the *Washington* (Miss.) *Republican* on 17 Nov 1815 is known to exist. Meteorological Observations of Col. Winthrop Sargent. *Washington Republican and Natchez Intelligencer,* 24 Jan 1816.

[20] Details of the rise and fall of the Mississippi river at Natchez landing, for more than 20 years, by a gentleman who arrived there in August 1798, and has been since resident in its vicinity. *Mississippi Republican* (Natchez) 10 Jan 1819?, in *Nat. Int.* (Wash., D.C.), 16 March 1819. Also issued as broadside, McMurtrie Biblio. T 75. Copies in Amer. Antiq. Soc. (Worcester) and Amer. Phil. Soc. (Phila.)

[21] A. Perlee. An account of the yellow fever of Natchez, as it prevailed in the autumn of 1817 and 1819. *The Phila. Jour. Med. and Phy. Sci.* 3 (1821), 17.

# WINTER HIGHLIGHTS AT NATCHEZ: 1799–1820

**A February Snow in 1799**—February was a cold month. There were nine mornings with temperatures 32° or below, and on two days the mercury did not rise above freezing. Snow fell during the morning and afternoon of the 21st, depth not mentioned. On that morning the thermometer stood at 19 ¾°, the low for the season.

**The cold Winter of 1800**—The three winter months averaged 44.2 degrees for the coldest winter during the span of Dunbar's records from 1799 to 1810. February, as throughout the rest of the South, proved the coldest month with an average of 42.5°. It had been introduced by a wintry period featuring sleet, glaze, and snow from 31 January to 2 February. On the morning of the 3d, "The Forest" was covered with a two-inch thickness of icy mass and the trees were "beautiful to the eye." December had 10 mornings below freezing, January 11, and February 8, for a record total of 29 cold mornings. The lowest readings this winter reached 21.5° on 3 January and 25° on 3 February.

**The coldest day: 12 December 1800**—This became a progressively warmer winter after a very cold commencement. The first freeze occurred on November 20th, and there followed four more freezing mornings from the 21st to 24th: lowest 22° on the 22d, a very low reading for November. Then succeeded an outstanding Arctic outbreak in the first half of December. On the 12th the mercury descended to +12° at "The Forest" and to +11° at Grove Plantation. This resulted in the coldest morning in the early Natchez experience of Dunbar and Sargent. Light snow had fallen on the 11th as the mercury sank from a morning 37° to an evening 20°, and it remained below freezing all day on the 12th (max. 32°), and on the 13th rose from a morning 17° to an afternoon 49°, to end the cold wave. The rest of the winter ran very warm.

**Icy mornings in January 1804**—After a string of relatively mild winters, the forces of the North returned in January 1804 with the coldest month since 1800. There were 14 mornings with freezing or below in January, though no day qualified as a true ice day. Dunbar's lowest of 25° came on the 25th at the conclusion of a three-day ice period when ponds and bayou froze over to a good thickness. February averaged a little below normal, and March introduced a snowstorm on the 1st that fell in the morning with temperatures just above freezing—no accumulation being mentioned. Then followed a March cold wave which drove Sargent's thermometer down to 20°, an unusually low March reading.

**Wintry January 1805**—There were 16 mornings with below freezing weather at The Forest. From January 1 to 6th, it continued below freezing every morning (lowest 22° on 2d). From the 10th to 15th only the 13th rose above freezing at 0600 (min. 17° on 12th; Sargent had 21°)—mercury fell from 71° at 1500/9th to 27° at 0600/11th. This cold period had been introduced by a real snowstorm on the morning of the 10th. Dunbar recorded 0.84" of precipitation which would give about 8.5" of snow, though he did not actually record a depth measurement. Temperatures this day were 27°, 39°, 31° at the three observation times. In his remarks were the following: "Ice a foot and a half thick in a barrel. 15th Snow not yet melted on the north side of the house and the ice an inch and a half thick at 9 P.M." The month concluded with another cold spell having consecutive freezing mornings from the 25th to 29th (min. 20°) on 27th.

**A cold wave in January 1806**—An Arctic air mass swept into southern Mississippi early in January. On the 8th the mercury read 17°, 30°, and 20° for an authentic ice day, and on the morning of the 9th it stood at 13°, short of Dunbar's all-time record. Ice formed to a thickness of ¾ of an inch. It became cold again on the morning of the 17th with a 17° reading, but thereafter conditions relaxed to a normal Mississippi winter.

**The snowy and cold winter of 1807**—Snow fell twice in December to introduce the most eventful of early Mississippi winters. On the 2d an inch came, and on the 11th "a little snow in the evening." On January 17th snow fell to a depth of 2" to introduce a severely cold spell with three ice days. On the morning of the 19th, with radiation conditions at an optimum, the mercury descended to +9° at 0600. Winthrop Sargent's thermometer nearby read +13° the same morning. This cold period contributed to making January 1807 an equal as the second coldest first month in the record book at The Forest (43°).

After a period of relaxation the spectacular Cold Friday air mass rushed into the region on the night of 5–6 February. The mercury at 1500/5th stood at 71° with a south wind blowing under a cloudy sky. It rained at 2100 with the wind now at north, and the mercury slumped to 62°, still near normal for a February evening. Next morning, however, the north wind blew at force 3 ("A very strong wind") and kept up all day. The mercury at 30° read 41 degrees down from the previous afternoon and continued to slump all day reading 26° at noon and 18° in mid-evening. Next morning the nadir of +9° was reached, a figure equal to the lowest ever achieved in Dunbar's span of records. The daylight of the 7th proved a bitter one at Natchez as it did throughout all the South—the thermometer read +9°, +27° and +23° at the three observations. Winthrop's thermometer read a low of +12° on the morning of the 7th.

**1809: The Coldest January and the Great Snowstorm**—With only three of 93 observations missing, January 1809 easily qualified as the coldest single calendar month in Dunbar's records having an average of 41°, or 6.5 degrees below normal. There were 16 ice mornings and seven ice afternoons, a record number. The mercury remained continuously below freezing from 2100/2d to 1500/7th, and again from 1500/28th to 1500/31st. The lowest occurred on the 6th with a reading 13°. The main event came at the commencement of the late January cold spell. Dunbar's entry read:

> Jan. 28, 1809—Began to snow at 11 o'clock and snowed all day. 29th continued to snow all day. at 4 P.M. the snow measured 6 ½ inches and as it rather inclined to thaw than freeze, there may have been two inches lost by thawing. The snow was found at last to amount to ten inches in level places upon bad conductors of heat.

|          | 0600   | 1500   | 2100   |
|----------|--------|--------|--------|
| Jan. 28. | 36°    | 32°    | 30°    |
|          | 30.12" | 29.98" | 29.98" |
|          | N      | N      | N      |
|          | Cloudy | Snow   | Snow   |
| Jan. 29. | 31°    | 32°    | 32°    |
|          | 29.72" | 29.72" | 29.72" |
|          | N      | N      | N      |
|          | Snow   | Snow   | Snow 1.00" |

**The final winter at The Forest**—Dunbar continued his records through March 1810. The final winter produced 13 cold mornings in December with a lowest temperature of 15°. His January records were of interest in illustrating the failure of the Cold Friday in New England air mass to affect the lower Mississippi Valley. On the morning of the 22d the mercury ran down to 22°, but this seemed relatively mild compared with other air streams which had roared directly down the channel of the Mississippi River from Canada in 1800, 1807, and 1809. A late touch of winter appeared in Dunbar's final month of meteorological records:

> The Forest
> March 12, 1810
> At half past 9 P.M. a hail storm; some of the hail stones were an inch in diameter. They appeared to be composed of snow in the heart, covered with layers of ice. Some of them remained on the ground until ten o'clock the next morning. In some parts of the country they are said to have been as large as hen's eggs. (Temperature was 62° at 2100/12th and 35° at 0600/13th—thunder and lightning had accompanied the hailstorm and cold front passage.)

**The Cold and Snow of the year 1812—**

No winter had passed away in the preceding 14 years, in which the earth had not been whitened with snow; remaining not unfrequently, for several days in the shade; and upon the 28th and 29th January 1809, we had full eight inches on a level. Upon the 10th of January 1812, we had an equal quantity; and increased, twenty miles south, to a foot, 'though forty miles N.E. there was not four inches. . . . The lowest state of the thermometer in 1812 was January 21st and December 12th, mercury at 20 degrees. Upon no other days of the year has it been equally low. *Winthrop Sargent.*

A general snowstorm swept over the lower Mississippi Valley and the middle Gulf Coast on 10 January 1812. William Darby, an early writer about the region, described the occurrence when in south-central Louisiana some 80 miles southwest of Natchez: "I once, in January 1812, witnessed a snow at Opelousas 11 inches deep, which did not entirely disappear in less than 7 or 8 days." The wintry conditions also extended to the coast as J. Blakely writing from Mobile, Alabama, on 28 February 1812 noted: "During the last winter we have had one snow two or three inches deep, some of which was on the ground for three days. We have had much cold weather this winter, several times ice half an inch thick."

The cold also impressed Amos Stoddard who published a descriptive and historical study of Louisiana in 1812: "It has been observed that, of late years in this quarter, the summers have been warmer, and the winters colder, than formerly. Orange trees, and other tender exotics were once cultivated here to some advantage; but, for some years past, they have suffered from frosts. In former years, the mercury never fell below twenty-six degrees; latterly it has sunk to seventeen and in December 1800 to twelve degrees."

Sargent made record of the occurrence of unusual vernal frosts on 4th and 5th of May, "uncommonly late," and also early autumnal visitations on the 27th of October, though it was not until November 19th that vegetation in the cotton fields received a full check. It will be recalled that the summer of 1812 proved exceptionally cold in the North with a major snowstorm on 4–5 May and corn not maturing before the frosts came. Both May 1812 and October 1812 were the coldest such months in Sargent's records.

**The Coldest January in 1813**—The coldest month in the span of Sargent's records came in January 1813 with a mean temperature of 43°. On the night of the 27th of January sleet and snow sufficient to whiten the ground occurred. The coldest morning of the season came on January 5th with a reading of 14°. The winter of 1813 ranked first in the decade for continued coldness, a *below* average December being followed by *much below* Januarys and Februarys.

**Cold December in 1814**—This month averaged only slightly warmer by one degree than the exceptionally cold January of 1813. It was colder by three degrees than any other December in the decade with an average of 44°. Fortunately, a surviving fragment of Winthrop's diary for his Mississippi years covered this period; the following extracts portray this wintry 12th month:

Nov. 30. Considerable white frost.
Dec. 1. White frost.
  2. White frost.
  14. 30°.
  15. White frost.
  19. First ice at Gloster Place.
  20. Considerable ice and white frost this morning. Temp. during day: 22°, 52°, 42°.
  21. Considerable white frost and ice this morning. Day fair and light SE wind. 30°, 59°, 56°.
  22. Some little sunshine, generally cloudy. Rain and thunder afternoon with light wind SE before noon, northerly afternoon. Rain 150/225th inch. 56°, 66°, 62°.
  23. Some rain last night—day cloudy. Some rain and light variable wind. Rain 63/225th inch. 61°, 56°, 52°.
  24. Some little sunshine—snowing frequently in the day but ground not whitened—moderate northerly wind. Some rain last night. 63/225th. 33°, 36°, 33°.
  25. Frost and ice. Day fair and moderate northerly wind. 20°, 40°, 32°.
  26. 20°, 48°, 44°. Frost and ice. Sunshine before, cloudy afternoon and rain in evening. 32/225th.
  27. 29°, 58°, 47°. Frost and ice. Day fair and light northerly wind.
  28. 27°, 62°, 51°. Frost and ice. Day fair and light easterly wind.
  29. 40°, 48°, 44°. Some little sunshine before noon, cloudy afternoon and snowing at evening with light, moderate NE wind. 6/225th.
  30. 26°, 38°, 30°. Frost and ice. Day fair and moderate. NE wind. Snowing late at night. Snow fast disappeared—probably four inches—gave of water 38/225th.
  31. 24°, 42°, 37°. Frost and ice. Fair and moderate wind. Ohio said to be closed by ice.

William Darby in Louisiana at this time made mention of the season: "In the last days of December 1814, the ponds and lagoons around New Orleans were frozen so as to admit half-grown boys to skate or play on the ice."

**A Snow in 1816**—The winter of 1815–16, unlike conditions along the Atlantic seaboard, produced some cold weather. At Natchez the January average of 44° was only one degree higher than the lowest in the Sargent record books. A moderate snowstorm occurred on January 13th with 3 ¾" being measured on boards and 2½" on the ground by Dunbar's successor. No account of this snow was available from Sargent's records. The conditions at The Forest follows:

| | | | |
|---|---|---|---|
| Jan. 12 | 32° | 35° | 28° |
| | Cloudy | Snow | Snow |
| | NW | N | N |
| | 30.03" | 30.08" | 30.08" |
| Jan. 13 | 25° | 29° | 26° |
| | Cloudy | Cloudy | Cloudy |
| | N | N | M |
| | 30.08" | 30.10" | 30.16" |

**The Coldest Winter at Natchez: 1817–18**—The winter season of 1817–18 at Natchez produced the coldest two consecutive months in the Sargent records, and nothing in the earlier Dunbar span in the first decade of the century could match the long continuance of frosty conditions. January averaged 48° and February 47°. These were followed by the coldest March in the period of record when 55° was registered for a very backward spring.

Though the details of the Sargent records have not been preserved, the Dunbar family manuscript exists for this period and lends a firsthand account of the main events of the season:

### December 1817

3. A considerable frost and ice. 28°.
4. Frost.
5. Frost. 31°.
7. Slight frost. 37°.
14. Ice. 29°.
15. 19°.
19. Slight frost. 30°.
20. A considerable frost and ice. 23°.

### January 1818

4. A considerable frost. 22°.
10. —, 55°, 41°.
11. 21°, 27°, 23°.
12. Ice on the pond 1½" thick—18°, 22°, 16°.
13. A considerable hoar frost with ice very thick. 15°, 30°, 19°.
14. 14°, 37°, 23°.
16. 29°, 63°, 49°.
31. 26°.

### February 1818

4–10. Pretty considerable hoar frost each morning.
4.  28°, --, 43°
5.  28°, 42°, 33°.
6.  28°, 52°, 29°.
7.  24°, 55°, --.
8.  23°, --, 35°.
9.  25°, 46°, 24°.
10. 27°, --, 46°.

March 1818, not to be outdone by the successive cold spells in each of the three preceding months, produced the major event of the winter and caused the editor of the *Mississippi Republican* at Natchez to take notice of the untoward happenings:

### FALL OF SNOW

This winter has been the most severe, of any known to the oldest inhabitants of the place for twenty-four years past. A greater quantity of rain has fallen, the cold more regular, and the ice thicker. The 2d instant the day was clear and rather warm, but became cloudy toward evening and continued dark all night, the wind blowing from the North-East, and on the morning of the 3d, a little before day-light, commenced a fall of snow which continued for several hours but began to clear away about 12 o'clock the wind hauling round to North West. *Mississippi Republican* (Natchez), 5 March 1818.

A snowstorm occurred at New Orleans on 12 January 1818. The wind shifted at 0400 to the northwest, and then rain, sleet and snow followed. It was one inch deep by 0900, and two sleighs appeared from nowhere and were driven about the streets, much to the amazement and delight of the residents. The mercury dropped to 27° by evening and next morning stood at 18°.

## WINTERS WITH THE MORAVIANS IN NORTH CAROLINA:: 1803–1820

### 1803

The month of February and the first days of March were wintry in the Southland as described elsewhere. The *Moravian Diary* chronicled the principal events at Salem:

Feb. 6. We had a very cold rain from the northeast which froze on the ground and covered everything with glaze ice. This lasted all day, and services could not be held in any of our congregations, for no one could leave the house without danger. Toward evening the wind changed to southwest, and it began to thaw.

7. After the cold of yesterday it has turned warm, with storms and heavy rain. The Wach rose nearly as high as some years ago when Br. Hall lost his life. (Jan. 17, 1796.)

13. A hard rain.

16. Last night and today snow fell twelve to eighteen inches deep which is rather unusual here in North Carolina.

25. After very warm and fine spring weather it today turned very cold and snowed.

Mar. 2. The coldest morning of the winter. The Fahrenheit thermometer stood at 6° above zero.

17. Tonight and last night there was a hard frost, the thermometer fell to 27°. Apple and peach blossoms, many garden vegetables, also the wheat, were badly damaged.

Raleigh, North Carolina:

The heaviest storm of snow fell in this part of the country on Tuesday and Wednesday last (15–16th) that has been experienced for many years. It is supposed to have been from 18 inches to 2 feet deep on the level; and having had frosts every night since, a considerable quantity of snow yet remains. The roads have been and remain almost impassable for carriages. On this account, no mail (except one from the southward on Wednesday morning) has arrived here since our last publication. This failure of mails will account for the barrenness of today's paper, with respect to news. *Raleigh Register and North Carolina Weekly Advertiser,* 22 Feb 1803.

Richmond, Virginia:

Since last Saturday [12 Feb.] there has been a most tremendous storm of rain and snow, than has been experienced at Richmond in many years. It began to rain about seven in the evening, and continued without intermission until Sunday night; by which time Mayos bridge was rendered impassable. The rain was succeeded by a severe frost on Monday and Tuesday.—On Wednesday [16th] about 4 in the morning, the fall of snow commenced, which endured all that day, accompanied by a violent gale of wind from the north-west. Richmond, 2/18, in *N.Y. Post,* 28 Feb 1803.

### 1804–05

In northerly climes the winter of 1804–05 was considered the severest since the famous Hard Winter of 1780 and the Long Winter of 1784. Accounts of prevailing conditions may be found in the sections devoted to the Northeast and the Old Northwest. That similar weather prevailed throughout the Upper South was readily evident from pertinent selections in the diaries of Salem and Bethabara:

Dec. 13. We had the first snow that lay on the ground. *Salem.*

20. It began to snow again and continued all night, so that at the places where the wind did not pile it up it was 15 or 16 inches deep.

23. It began to snow again. *Bethabara.*

24 Because of the deep snow many of our members and their children living out of town were unable to come to the Christmas Eve services, which we regretted. It was two feet deep here, and in the neighborhood of Salisbury it was three feet and more. The teamsters who had gone to Fayette and Petersburg brought back their horses during these days, leaving their wagons at Fayette and on the road. *Salem.*

Jan. 1. There was an unusually heavy snow today.

10. Last night and today we had heavy rain so that most of the snow melted. In the morning there was rather sharp lightning and thunder, with another thunderstorm toward evening. Streams rose, bridges and fences were torn away, and much damage done to mills and the like. Men could not remember such a sudden flood in years.

11. In the morning the Wach at Salem nearly as high, and nearly as far out of its banks, as nine years ago when Br. Hall lost his life in it. With clear weather and a cold wind from the northeast it soon began to fall.

Jan. 12. This morning the thermometer was 8° above zero.

13. The congregation meeting was held in the afternoon at four o'clock because of the sleet and slippery streets.

15. The roads having become passable many wagons and travelers came through, and it began again to be lively in town.

16. We had the pleasure of receiving a number of packages of Nachrichten and other papers from Barby, brought by a wagon from Petersburg which had been detained about thirty miles from here for a number of weeks by the snow.

Jan. 20. Today we had a hard storm, so that no evening service could be held. Indeed they must be omitted for the entire week, first because of the astonishing cold, and then the thaw which rendered the streets of the town almost impassable. *Bethania*.

20. New snow fell today. *Salem*.

22. This morning it was most unusually cold for this climate. At sunrise the thermometer stood at 12½° below zero. *Bethania*.

22. We had the coldest day of the winter; this morning the Fahrenheit thermometer stood at 8° below zero. The oldest inhabitant could not remember such a degree of cold. *Salem*.

27. The monthly English meeting at Friedland was not held for it rained and snowed almost all day, and in the country congregations in general few came to service.

Feb. 3. The weather was cold and stormy.

4. This morning the thermometer stood at 9° above zero.

10. This was the first clear Sunday this year.

## 1807

(See **Cold Friday in the South**.)

## 1809–10

The winter of the famous Cold Friday in the North showed similar characteristics in the South. There was only one severe spell separating two rather mild periods in early and late winter. The storm front sweeping the New York and New England countryside on Jan. 19th struck into west-central North Carolina a few hours earlier, if we may believe contemporary evidence. Unfortunately, we do not have any actual temperature readings, but it was quite evident that the cold air mass had lost its severest sting in passing over ground without snow cover. Nevertheless, the wind remained very potent and did much damage in the Moravian settlements:

Jan. 18. We had a severe storm, which began in the morning and continued into the night. The wind was so high that on the hills great stretches of fence were blown down. In town bricks were blown from chimney-tops and many shingles were torn from older roofs. *Bethania*.

Jan. 21. It was very cold.

Jan. 21. Because of the extreme cold, very few members came to Sunday services. That evening, also the 22d & 23d, there could be no meetings because of the cold. .... *Bethabara*.

## 1811–12

A cold season prevailed in North and South alike. It was memorable for the 30-day period following the severe cold storm of 23 December 1811 along the southern New England shore and Long Island. The mercury plunged to low levels during the storm, and henceforth Arctic air masses dominated the scene throughout January. Chesapeake Bay froze over more solidly than at any time since the freeze-up of February 1784. The weather summaries at the Moravian settlements reflected the cold conditions in January and also tallied two April snowstorms, a warning perhaps a cold spring would turn into a cold summer, to make up a remarkably cold calendar year:

Dec. 27. There was the first snow of the winter; the evening meeting was dropped.

Jan. 10. Toward evening it snowed, so the evening meeting must be omitted.

11. In the morning the thermometer stood at zero. *Salem*.

19. Snow and rain began yesterday afternoon and continued during the night and until ten o'clock this morning. In the evening in the tenth hour it stormed and rained. *Bethania*.

April 2. In the afternoon we had a snowstorm, which is unusual at this season. Toward evening it turned to rain. *Salem*.

13. It snowed for several hours, which seldom occurs at this time of year.

April 2. The weather was very raw, and in the afternoon it snowed until the ground was covered. *Bethania*.

13. This afternoon it snowed for some hours, and the roofs were covered, which is unusual here. The weather cleared in the afternoon. *Bethania*.

## 1812–13

The winter season of 1812–13 commenced early and continued well into February:

Dec. 11. The weather has been very cold, and colder since last night, when we had the first snow of winter. *Salem*.

27. Because of the astonishing cold the evening meetings were omitted to the close of the year. *Bethania*.

Jan. 2. The singstunde was omitted because of the cold.

7. During the night we had a severe windstorm.

12. The cold was intense, and this morning the Fahrenheit thermometer stood at six above zero. During the next days it fell to two above zero.

14. Because of snow flurries there could be no service. *Salem*.

14. We had the first snow of this year. *Bethabara*.

16. We had the coldest morning of this winter. The thermometer stood at two degrees below zero. *Bethania*.

19. There could be no prayer meeting because of a storm with a heavy fall of snow. *Salem*.

28. Last night and during this morning there was again a heavy fall of snow, which measured eight inches deep, and hindered the meeting.

28. All day it snowed steadily, lying nine inches deep, which is unusual in this climate. When it cleared a family drove to Salem in a sleigh, which has never before been done here. Because of the deep

snow and the drifts several feet high no service could be held in Bethania during the latter part of the week. *Bethania.*

29. The evening meeting was omitted because the snow lay twelve inches deep, no proper paths had been dug, and it was very cold. *Bethabara.*

31. From early morning it snowed again, covering the roads just made with several inches of snow.

Jan. 31. To the snow still on the ground more was added, for more fell during the night and continued all day. The falling snow and the lack of paths prevented the holding of the Sunday services. In general this month has been marked by cold and snow such as we have not had for many years. The widest streams were frozen over, and only lack of the necessary equipment prevented everybody from going sleigh-riding, which some were able to arrange to do. During the snow a number of deer were killed.

Feb. 2. No one came to service because the streets in the village are so bad. *Bethabara.*

9. This afternoon we had another snow storm.

19. This afternoon it began to snow again and continued until the following morning, attaining a considerable depth.

19. There was a high wind in the afternoon it began to snow, and continued until the following morning, lying eight or nine inches deep. *Bethania.*

21. Because of the deep snow few came to service. *Bethabara.*

23. Because of the snow and high water the post failed to arrive for the second time this winter.

Mar. 6. After a number of clear, warm days we had a cold rain.

## 1814–15

Dec. 25. We could have no evening service, as it snowed from the forenoon until in the night, and lay several inches thick. *Bethania.*

25. . . . but all had to leave in the afternoon in thick snow. *Friedburg.*

25. In the latter half of the day a considerable amount of snow fell. *Salem.*

25. Soon after this service it commenced to snow heavily and continued until late at night. On the following days no services could be held on account of the cold and the bad roads. *Bethabara.*

Jan. 13. Last night it began to snow, and continued until the ninth hour this morning. It is very cold. *Bethabara.*

22. During the night snow fell, which melted today, making roads wet and slippery. All through the week it was unusually cold for this climate, and the roads were coated with ice. *Bethania.*

22. The weather is piercingly cold, and last night we had snow. *Salem.*

Feb. 4. Late last evening it began to rain, continuing until this morning, and the snow which has been on the ground for fourteen days was finally melted. *Bethania.*

Feb. 7. We had another snow. *Salem.*

14. This morning snow fell again. *Salem.*

21. During the last days the rain and snow have covered everything thickly with glaze ice. *Bethania.*

24. It snowed and sleeted the greater part of the day, and turned very cold. *Salem.*

## 1816–17

Jan. 11. It was colder than it has been this winter, with a very raw northwest wind. *Bethabara.*

13. Last night there was a hard freeze, and this morning the thermometer stood at 15° above zero.

18. Last night the first snow of the winter fell, and today and during the following night it was piercingly cold, with a high wind. *Salem.*

19. This morning the thermometer stood at 1° above zero.

23. It rained and snowed in turn, and froze, so that the roads were slippery. *Bethabara.*

30. The services were omitted because of intense cold.

Feb. 3. Last night the first considerable snow of the season fell. *Salem.*

3. It snowed last night, and did not melt much during the day because of the cold northwest wind. *Bethabara.*

5. Yesterday was very cold, and today a fairly deep snow fell on top of that which fell day before yesterday.

13. The cold and the strong wind from the northwest were very piercing this week.

16. The unusually severe cold has moderated a little today.

Feb. 23. Because of a storm with mingled rain, snow, and sleet, which was followed by very stormy weather which lasted until the evening of the 24th, when the wind finally died down.

Mar. 2. The cold and the raw wind from the northwest still continue.

3. The weather was somewhat milder during the day, but the nights continue to be very cold.

21. During this week it froze very hard at night.

25. Since yesterday the weather has been warm, and today 83°.

28. It rained, and then from half past one in the afternoon until during the night it snowed steadily, which has not happened during the winter.

30. This was a real winter day. It snowed from morning to evening, and during the afternoon the snow fell so heavily that had not the ground been wet from the preceding rain this would probably have been the deepest snow of the winter. Even as it was the snow lay so deep that it was not all melted three days later when it turned warm. *Bethania.*

## 1817–18

Raleigh, North Carolina:
Last Friday to Saturday (30–31 Jan.), "although falling on ground both warm and wet, it covered the ground to a depth of 12 inches." *Raleigh Minerva,* 6 Feb, in *Courier* (Charleston), 10 Feb. 1818.

Camden, South Carolina:
The snow lay 9 or 10 inches deep. *Camden Gazette,* 7 Feb, in *Courier,* 12 Feb 1818.

Camden, South Carolina:
Jan. 30–31. Hail & snow.
Feb. 1. 18°    James Kershaw, Ms. Met. Obs. (NA).

#### 1818–19

Fayetteville, North Carolina:
Dec. 18. Snow fell 15 inches deep. *Courier* (Charleston), 24 Feb 1818.

#### 1819–20

Nov. 30. Since Sunday it has been cool, and today was colder than it has been this fall; this morning the thermometer stood at 15°. *Bethabara*.

Dec. 2. It was very cold and stormy.

13. It rained a good deal, especially during the evening, and on the 14th there was no service on account of the cold.

17. Today it snowed continuously, beginning in the early morning, and on the 18th there was more snow mixed with rain, and the roads were so bad that it was impossible to travel on foot.

20. This was a very cold day.

21. This morning the thermometer was 19° above zero.

25. After the Christmas Eve lovefeasts last evening it rained heavily for an hour. Today was clear but rather cool.

30. At daybreak it began to snow and continued all day, then cleared with the wind from the northwest, and was very cold. The snow was about a foot deep.

30. Snow began at daybreak and continued until evening, lying six to eight inches deep. *Bethania*.

Dec. 31. Because of the deep snow, which had not melted at all, and the bitter cold, some of the members, especially those living outside the town, were unable to attend the services. *Bethabara*.

Jan. 1. There was no other service because of the extreme cold; the thermometer stood between 8° and 10° below zero.

3 & 4. The great cold continued. On the 3d the thermometer stood at 3° below zero, and the next day it was 4° below zero.

5. The extreme cold broke, and on this and the following days was quite pleasant.

9. In the following days of the week no evening meetings could be held, partly because of the cold and partly because of the bad roads. It rained off and on during the latter half of the week, and on the 14th it snowed heavily from early morning to noon, then it rained but did not melt the snow. On the 15th it was milder and the snow disappeared.

16. Sunday. Early in the afternoon it began to snow, then there was rain mixed with hail which continued until the next day, and everything was covered with glaze ice, until it cleared and turned warmer. During the week it rained and snowed intermittently.

23. Before dawn it began to snow, and continued without intermission until the middle of the afternoon. The snow lay about nine inches deep.

24. This morning the thermometer stood at 6° above zero; and in the morning of the 25th it was only 2° above. However, on the latter day the snow began to melt on the south side of the houses, and continued to disappear slowly during the following days which were milder.

Jan. 28. It rained from early morning throughout the day.

30. Last night it rained, and again this afternoon, so that all the streams were swollen, the meadows were under water, and the roads as bad as possible.

Feb. 3. Last night it began to rain, and continued through the day and following night, then cleared very cold.

16. For some days the weather has been unusually warm for this time of year, and there have been storms in the evenings. The one today was accompanied by heavy rain.

25. In the evening there was a hard storm, but with little rain; but much rain fell on the next day, during another storm.

27. Since the storm yesterday it has been rather cool, raw and windy, and this weather continued for several days. There was also much hoarfrost, for the wind always died down after midnight and did not rise again until morning.

Mar. 2. A hard storm from the northwest, which began yesterday, continued all day and late into the night, and even in the houses it was impossible to keep warm. On the 3d the thermometer fell to 10° below zero, and the windows were covered with ice. All day it was piercingly cold.

4. Yesterday was mild, and today it rained constantly.

7. Yesterday was mild, but during the night there was a terrible storm with cold rain which lasted until the morning of the 10th when it cleared up cold.

14. Yesterday was a rainy day, and the rain continued until this afternoon. It was followed by a terrible wind which blew from the southwest and then from the northwest. During the afternoon it became unusually strong, and did not fall until during the night. Many fruit trees, and also trees in the forests, were torn up by the roots, fences were blown down, shingles were torn from various roofs, and other damage was done here and there. During the following days the weather was again fairly pleasant.

Mar. 22. Last night it snowed and sleeted a little, and there was a hard frost. It did the same on the 23rd, but the following days were pleasantly warm.

Apr. 3. Easter Monday. It was an unfriendly, raw day, and in the morning it snowed a little.

10. This morning the ground was white with frost, and the thermometer stood at 22° above zero.

## COLD FRIDAY OF 1807 IN THE SOUTH

"The season of 1807 was the coldest ever known here," wrote J. F. H. Clairborne in his *Mississippi as a province, territory and state* (1880). Though not completely correct in this statement, the winter of 1806–07 contained a number of interesting weather events and gave the impression of extreme severity so that its reputation lingered on.[1] The principal event came with an outbreak of bitterly cold Arctic air that made history in the Midwest as well as in the South. "Cold Friday" became a household phrase south of the Ohio River as well as it did to the north.² Interest in the affairs of the Old Southwest had been heightened at this time by the presence of Aaron Burr, then engaged in allegedly traitorous activities. Federal authorities pursued Burr and his party through Mississippi and Alabama during the wintry days of January and February. The great amount of space devoted in the local presses to this story excluded notes about the severity of the weather, so this often fruitful source of meteorological information proved disappointingly thin for the weather historian in this instance.

All three winter months of 1806–07 at Natchez averaged below normal in the Dunbar records. In fact, only the cold season of 1799–1800 averaged colder during the first decade of the century. December had 13 mornings with below-freezing conditions with the lowest 20° on the 13th. January was still colder on the average, having 11 below-freezing mornings and three consecutive ice days on the 17, 18, and 19th. During this wintry period two inches of snow fell at Natchez and the mercury descended to +9° on the 19th, the lowest so far in the local meteorological records.³ The cold and snow at this period covered a vast part of the Southland. Augusta, Georgia, had a six-inch snowfall which lay for several days as the ensuing cold wave dropped President Meig's thermometer on the University of Georgia campus at Athens to +2°, also a new low mark for the record period there commencing in 1801.⁴ The *Augusta Chronicle* commented on the severity of conditions: "On Saturday morning last (17th) it began to snow in this place, and continued till Sunday; considering the latitude, a considerable quantity fell; on Sunday night a very hard frost set in, which still continues; in the upper parts of Georgia, we understand that there has been a very heavy fall of snow."⁵

The principal event of the winter, however, came at the end of the first week in February, a favorite time for record cold in the South. The same Arctic outbreak that made history in Ohio and Kentucky on February 6th roared southward over Tennessee and into all parts of the South later that day and on the 7th. Though meteorological details are scarce, we have sufficient evidence at hand to judge the severity of the cold and the sting of the gales that preceded and accompanied the arrival of the cold air mass.

It so happened that Dr. John R. Bedford of Rutherford County on the Cumberland River near Nashville embarked on one of his periodic trips to New Orleans. Fortunately for us, he decided to while away his idle hours by keeping a diary of events on the voyage:

> Thursday, 5th. Set out early with the prospects of making New Madrid [Missouri, almost opposite Kentucky-Tennessee border] . . . proceeded without difficulty within five miles of New Madrid, when tempestuous wind forced put in. It continued without abatement till night—encamped on the beach with prospects of setting out early in the morning, by which time the wind might probably abate.
>
> Friday, 6th. Wind very high, without any sensible abatement, coming from the north, continued till dusk of evening, too late to make any progress—moved our encampment on the bank above in the midst of a very thick and lofty cane, which was a great protection from the north wind that yet continued with little abatement—cold almost insupportable—wind abated about 8 o'clock in the night—were therefore sure of proceeding in the morning.
>
> Saturday, 7th. The intense severity of the weather yesterday and last night froze the water to an extraordinary degree—far beyond what is usual in this latitude, viz. 30°30′. The Mississippi was blocked up from bank to bank with thick and extensive cakes of floating ice—which rendered the river impassable by crafts of any kind, great or small. We had therefore no other prospects but to remain in statu quo this day out at least—how much longer could not be anticipated—but hope, ever accomodating to our will and wishes, pointed to the shortest possible time and flattered us with a departure tomorrow morning. Stuck close to the fire the whole of this day, moving to the river at intervals, with anxious looks on the ice, which seemed to come thicker and thicker, if possible.
>
> Sunday, 8th. Weather and ice as yesterday—no prospect of departure this day—but surely tomorrow. This day spent as yesterday—moved camp about twenty or thirty yards for the greater convenience of getting wood—having consumed all adjacent to the other.
>
> Monday, 9th. Weather moderated and the quantity of ice diminished—but yet unsafe to proceed—have great hopes tomorrow.
>
> Tuesday, 10th. Cut through the ice that blocked us up, about forty feet and set out, under great dread and alarm at the floating ice that yet continued pretty thick—floated only 3 miles and, alas! stuck fast on a large sand-bar 2½ miles above New Madrid. . . . Neglecting to secure our canoe when found, no means were left us to gain the shore. Slept above deck without a shelter. In the night came a cold rain, to which were every how exposed—were wet under and above.
>
> Wednesday, 11th. Still raining, rose from our lodging, having a buffalo rug and blankets under the two blankets above, wet, cold and with heavy hearts and sad fears, not knowing when relief could be obtained. [They were rescued that day by two men coming over from the main shore in a canoe which transported the party to New Madrid.] ⁶

Meteorological data for the February period were scanty. The *Impartial Review* of Nashville, publishing on the 7th, reported the mercury at the Tennessee capital down to −5° on the 6th, and still at zero by 1000 on the 7th when the press was locked up. The writer did not know the cause of the atmospheric upheaval, "whether it was the late congress of the climates or a more general cause."[7]

Southward in the lower Mississippi Valley at Arkansas City, Mr. Treat registered a February low of +3°, presumably on the 6th or 7th. This was the same degree of cold he had experienced in January 1805.[8] Farther south at Natchez, Winthrop Sargent saw his thermometer descend to +12°, one degree lower than it had been in January 1807 and one degree higher than his all-time low mark achieved in December 1800.[9] William Dunbar's thermometer at The Forest apparently dropped to +9°, though the manuscript is blotted and the figure possibly could be +19°.[10] Dunbar has left a full meteorological account of the cold wave which indicated that the cold air mass was losing some of its sting in its passage over bare ground, yet the northerly gale blowing all day at Dunbar's next to highest wind force must have created a memorably bitter day in the lower Mississippi country. Dunbar's record for these days follows:

|         | 0600 | 1500 | 2100 |
|---------|------|------|------|
| Feb. 5— | 46°  | 71°  | 62°  |
|         | South | South | North |
|         | Cloudy | Cloudy | Rain |
| 6—      | 30°  | 26°  | 18°  |
|         | North 2 | North 3 | North 3 |
|         | Cloudy | Clear | Clear |
|         | Precipitation 0.30". | | |
| 7—      | 9°?  | 27°  | 23°? |
|         | North | North | North |
|         | Clear | Very clear | Clear |
|         | Precipitation 0.30". | | |
| Feb. 8— | 18°  | 43°  | 32°  |
|         | North | North | North |
|         | Clear | Clear | Clear |
| 9—      | 36°  | 70°  | Missing[9] |
|         | Cloudy | | |
|         | East | East | |

In Louisiana, William Darby reported the frost on February 7th severe to the coast of the Gulf. The horned cattle suffered greatly with about one-quarter dying, but horses and mules escaped harm.[10] In Alabama a meteorological historian, writing in 1890, declared that February 7th was known in that state as "Cold Friday," though he did not substantiate this with an exact reference or contemporary quotation.[12]

[1] John F. H. Clairborne. *Mississippi as a province, territory, and state, with biographical notices of eminent citizens.* Jackson, 1880. Reprint: Baton Rouge, La., La. State Univ. Press, 1964.
[2] "Wetumpka," *Alabama Hist. Quar.* 4 (1942), 57; Alabama Dept. Agri., *Annual Report, 1890*, 51.
[3] William Dunbar. Ms. Met. Obs. (Miss. Dept. Archives.)
[4] Josiah Meigs in *Nat. Int.* (Wash., D. C.), 25 Feb 1807.
[5] *Augusta* (Ga.) *Chronicle*, 24 Jan 1807.
[6] Dr. John R. Bedford. A tour in 1807 down the Cumberland. *Tenn. Hist. Mag.* 5-1 (April 1919), 58–59.
[7] *Impartial Review* (Nashville), 7 Feb 1807.
[8] T. Jefferson. Ms. Weather memorandum book.
[9] Winthrop Sargent. Meteorological observations, communicated for the *Natchez Intelligencer*, No. 2. *Natchez Intelligencer*, August (n.d.) 1815.
[10] W. Dunbar. Met. Obs.
[11] William Darby. *View of the United States, historical, geographical, and statistical.* Phila., H. S. Tanner, 1828, 78.
[12] *Ala. Agri. Rt. 1890*, 51.

# THOMAS JEFFERSON AND VIRGINIA WINTERS: 1810–1816

Thomas Jefferson always maintained an avid interest in snowfall through his personal experiences and from a professional concern. He had witnessed two of Virginia's greatest all-time snowstorms while at home in the early years at Monticello: the "Washington & Jefferson Storm" when returning with his bride from an extended honeymoon trip in January 1772, and the "Battle of Trenton Storm" on Christmas Day of 1776.[1] He observed and commented on the relative severity of the Hard Winter of 1780 when governor at Williamsburg and of the rigorous season of 1784 while at Annapolis preparing to go abroad as representative of his country at the Court of France.[2]

In later years, when President of the United States in the new capital at Washington from 1801 to 1809, he found time from his onerous duties to observe each snowfall and to compile a record of its depth and duration, from which he was able to construct a statistical table that can be very helpful today in judging changes in climate trends from the early 19th Century to the present day. Certainly, Jefferson was the first Federal official at Washington to make meteorological observations and thus qualified for the nomination as the first "chief" of a Federal weather bureau. When making his retirement journey in March of 1809 from Washington to his beloved Monticello, he endured "one of the most disagreeable snowstorms as I was ever in."[3]

Jefferson commenced his first thermometer record at Philadelphia on 1 July 1776, the day before the Continental Congress accepted his draft of the Declaration of Independence. Most appropriately, he paid merchant Sparhawk the sum of £3-15 for the instrument

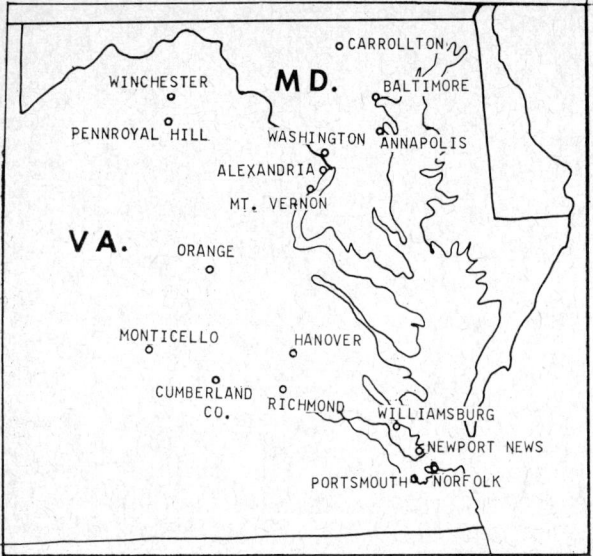

on the celebrated July 4th and carefully noted the readings for that day. Unlike many subsequent anniversaries, it was a comfortable day in the Quaker City with the afternoon temperature in the mid-70's. He also purchased a barometer on the 8th for the sum of £4-10.[4] Thereafter, whether at his Monticello home, in the governor's office at Williamsburg, abroad in France as ambassador, as Secretary of State in Philadelphia, or in the Presidential chair at Washington, he was seldom without a thermometer and seldom failed to note its daily readings. These have been preserved in his *Weather Memorandum Book,* now in the manuscripts division of the Library of Congress.

As early as 1777 Jefferson had carried on a series of simultaneous weather observations with Rev. James Madison, the scientifically-minded president of William and Mary College at Williamsburg, and he employed these in composing the celebrated *Notes on the State of Virginia* in 1781.[5] Later he purchased the only thermometer then available in Philadelphia for transmission to Isaac Zane for thermometric observations in the far western part of Virginia on the Ohio River where little was known of climatic conditions.[6] Early in 1784 he wrote to another James Madison, the future president, at his home in west-central Virginia:

> I wish you had a thermometer. Mr. Madison of the college and myself are keeping observations for a comparison of climate. We observe at sunrise and at 4 o'clock P.M. which are the coldest and warmest points of the day. If you could observe at the same time it would show the difference between going north and northwest on this continent. I suspect it would be colder in Orange or Albemarle than here.[7]

Apparently a thermometer soon became available as an interesting series of meteorological observations was commenced late in 1784 at Montpelier, the Madison home near Orange, Virginia. Thus, while Jefferson remained out of the country on diplomatic missions or in the Middle States carrying out the duties of Secretary of State or Vice-President, members of the Madison family kept tab for him on Virginia weather events for the span of years from 1784 to 1802. These records now rest in the American Philosophical Society in Philadelphia, the thoughtful gift of Dolly Madison after her husband's death in 1836.

From years of rural living Jefferson was well acquainted with the general features of his native climate. In his *Notes on Virginia,* though based on meager meteorological data, he had commented on the salubrity and attractiveness of its atmospheric locale. When in Vermont experiencing the rigors of a New England spring in 1791, he confided in a letter to his daughter:

> On the whole, I find nothing anywhere else, in point of climate, which Virginia need envy to any part of the world. . . . When we consider how much climate contributes to the happiness of our conditions, by the fine sensation it excites, and the productions it is parent of, we have reason to value highly the accident of birth in such a one as that of Virginia.[9]

Again, when writing Comte de Volney in 1797, Jefferson declared: ". . . indeed my experience in different parts of America convinces me that these mountains are the Eden of the U. S. for soil, climate, navigation and health." [10] But the Sage of Monticello always yearned for more specific data that could be reduced to orderly statistics.

When once again in residence on his hilltop far from the Federal political battlefields, Jefferson turned his attention to improving his properties and agricultural products. Deeming a study of the local climate essential to this, he instituted a series of regular meteorological observations commencing in 1810 and faithfully continued through 1816. At the conclusion of the seven years' record, he was able to compose a *Memorandum of Climate,* comprising a series of tables showing maximum, minimum, and mean temperatures for each month, total precipitation by months, prevailing wind direction, and barometric activity, along with much phenological material.[11] His winter records indicated the earliest frost and first snowfall in the autumn along with the last frost and latest snowfall in the spring. There were also tables of seasonal snowfall and the number of days each winter that snow lay on the ground. At the commencement he described the dimensions of a new snow gage specially constructed to handle frozen precipitation. The regular series of observations in the *Weather Memorandum Book* close with the end of 1816, but there were additional fragments of similar records as late as 1825 and the first half of 1826, indicating that weather-watching continued but perhaps not on such a systematic basis. In fact, the last rainfall entry was dated 29 June 1826, less than a week prior to Jefferson's death on 4 July 1826, at the age of 83, a half century after the memorable day in Philadelphia when he commenced thermometer watching.

The portions of the *Memorandum on Climate* pertinent to our study of Virginia winter conditions follow. These also contain portions of the Madison family records which Jefferson dutifully copied in his notebooks:

Thomas Jefferson's

## MEMORANDUM OF CLIMATE

### Monticello: 1810–1816

1817, January. Having been stationary at home since 1809, with opportunity and leisure to keep a meteorological diary, with a good degree of exactness, this had been done: and, extracting from it a term of seven years complete, to wit from January 1, 1810, to December 31, 1816, I proceed to analyze it in the various ways, and to deduce the general results, which are of principal effect in the estimate of climate. The observations, three thousand nine hundred and five, in the whole, were taken before sunrise of every day; and again between three and four o'clock P. M. On some days of occasional absence they were necessarily omitted. In these cases the averages were taken from the days of the same denomination in the other years only, and in such way as not sensibly to affect the average of the month, still less that of the year, and to be quite evanescent in their effect on the whole tenor of seven years.

The table of thermometrical observations, shews the particular temperature of the different years from 1810 to 1816 inclusive. The most interesting results, however, are that the range of temperature with us may be considered as within the limits of $5\frac{1}{2}°$ and $94°$ of Fahrenheit's thermometer; and that $55\frac{1}{2}°$ degrees as its mean and characteristic measure. These degrees fix the laws of the animal and vegetable races which may exist with us; and the comfort also of the human inhabitant, so far as depends on his sensations of heat and cold. Still it must be kept in mind that this is but the temperature of Monticello; that in the northern and western parts of the State, the mean and extremes are probably something lower, and in the southern and eastern, higher. But this place is so nearly central to the whole State, that it may fairly be considered as the mean of the whole.

A Table of Thermometrical Observations, Made at Monticello, From January 1, 1810, to December 31, 1816

| | 1810 | | | 1811 | | | 1812 | | | 1813 | | | 1814 | | | 1815 | | | 1816 | | | Mean of each Month |
|---|---|---|---|---|---|---|---|---|---|---|---|---|---|---|---|---|---|---|---|---|---|---|
| | Min. | Mean | Max. | Min. | Mean | Max. | Min. | Mean | Max. | Min. | Mean | Max. | Min. | Mean | Max. | Min. | Mean | Max. | Min. | Mean | Max. | |
| Jan. | $5\frac{1}{4}$ | 38 | 66 | 20 | 39 | 68 | $5\frac{1}{2}$ | 34 | 53 | 13 | 35 | 59 | $16\frac{1}{2}$ | 36 | 55 | $8\frac{1}{2}$ | 35 | 60 | 16 | 34 | 51 | 36 |
| Feb. | 12 | 43 | 73 | | | | 21 | 40 | 75 | 19 | 38 | 65 | 14 | 42 | 65 | 16 | 36 | 57 | $15\frac{1}{2}$ | 41 | 62 | 40 |
| Mar. | 20 | 41 | 61 | 28 | 44 | 78 | $31\frac{1}{2}$ | 46 | 70 | 28 | 48 | 71 | $13\frac{1}{2}$ | 43 | 73 | 31 | 54 | 80 | 25 | 48 | 75 | 46 |
| April | 42 | 55 | 81 | 36 | 58 | 86 | 31 | 56 | 86 | 40 | 59 | 80 | 35 | 59 | 82 | 41 | 60 | 82 | 30 | 49 | 71 | $56\frac{1}{2}$ |
| May | 43 | 64 | 88 | 46 | 62 | 79 | 39 | 60 | 86 | 46 | 62 | 81 | 47 | 65 | 91 | 37 | 58 | 77 | 43 | 60 | 79 | $61\frac{1}{2}$ |
| June | 53 | 70 | 87 | 58 | 73 | 89 | 58 | 74 | $22\frac{1}{2}$ | 54 | 75 | 93 | 57 | 69 | 87 | 54 | 71 | 88 | 51 | 70 | 86 | 72 |
| July | 60 | 75 | 88 | 60 | 76 | $89\frac{1}{2}$ | 57 | 75 | 91 | 61 | 75 | $94\frac{1}{2}$ | 60 | 74 | 89 | 63 | 77 | 89 | 51 | 71 | 86 | 75 |
| Aug. | 55 | 71 | 90 | 59 | 75 | 85 | 61 | 71 | 87 | 62 | 74 | 92 | 56 | 75 | 88 | 58 | 72 | 84 | 51 | 73 | 90 | 73 |
| Sept. | 50 | 70 | 81 | 50 | 67 | 81 | 47 | 68 | 75 | 54 | 69 | 83 | 52 | 70 | 89 | 45 | 61 | 82 | 54 | 63 | $90\frac{1}{2}$ | 67 |
| Oct. | 32 | 57 | 82 | 35 | 62 | 85 | 39 | 55 | 80 | 32 | 53 | 70 | 37 | 58 | 83 | $38\frac{1}{2}$ | 59 | 76 | 37 | 57 | 73 | 57 |
| Nov. | 27 | 44 | 69 | 32 | 45 | 62 | 18 | 43 | 76 | 20 | 48 | 71 | 23 | 47 | 71 | 20 | 46 | 70 | 24 | 46 | 71 | $45\frac{1}{2}$ |
| Dec. | 14 | 32 | 62 | 20 | 38 | 49 | 13 | 35 | 63 | 18 | 37 | 53 | 18 | 38 | 59 | 12 | 36 | 57 | 23 | 43 | 69 | 37 |
| Mean of clear weather | | 55 | | | 58 | | | 55 | | | 56 | | | $56\frac{1}{2}$ | | | $55\frac{1}{2}$ | | | $54\frac{1}{2}$ | | $55\frac{1}{2}$ |

An Early American Observatory—Thomas Jefferson's Monticello

It is a common opinion that the climates of the several States, of our Union, have undergone a sensible change since the dates of their first settlements; that the degrees both of cold and heat are moderated. The same opinion prevails as to Europe; and facts gleaned from history give reason to believe that, since the time of Augustus Caesar, the climate of Italy, for example, has changed regularly, at the rate of 1° of Fahrenheit's thermometer for every century. May we not hope that the methods invented in later times for measuring with accuracy the degrees heat and cold, and the observations which have been and will be made and preserved, will at length ascertain this curious fact in physical history?

Within the same period of time, about fifty morning observations, on an average of every winter, were below the freezing point, and ten freezing days for the average of our winters.

It is generally observed that when the thermometer is below 55°, we have need of fire in our apartments to be comfortable. In the course of these seven years, the number of observations below 55°, was as follows:

| | | |
|---|---|---|
| In 1810— | 195 mornings and | 124 afternoons |
| '11 | 176 | 102 |
| '12 | 209 | 137 |
| '13 | 197 | 123 |
| '14 | 190 | 127 |
| '15 | 189 | 116 |
| '16 | 172 | 116 |
| Average | 190 | 120 |

Whence we conclude that we need constant fires four months in the year, and in the mornings and evenings a little more than a month preceding and following that time.

The first white frost in

1809–10 was October 25, the last April 11
'10–11            18,            Mar. 19
'11–12            21,            April 14
'12–13             9,
'13–14            22,            April 13
'14–15            24,            May 15
'15–16            26,            April 3
'16–17             7,              " 12

But we have seen in another period a destructive white frost as early as September.

Our first ice in

1809–10 was in Nov. 7, the last April 10
'10–11    "    Oct. 24,   "    Mar.  8
'11–12    "    Nov. 15,   "    April 12
'12–13    "     "   13,   "    Mar. 25
'13–14    "     "   14,   "     "   17
'14–15    "     "    9,   "     "   22
'15–16    "     "   13,   "     "   19
'16–17    "     "    7,   "     "   20

The quantity of water (including that of snow) which fell in every month and year of the term was as follows.

|      | 1810  | 1811  | 1812   | 1813   | 1814   | 1815  | 1816  | Average of every Month |
|------|-------|-------|--------|--------|--------|-------|-------|------------------------|
| Jan. | 1.873 | 3.694 | 3.300  | 1.735  | 4.179  | 6.025 | 4.86  | 3.656 |
| Feb. | 4.275 | 2.351 | 4.060  | 1.763  | 3.760  | 5.90  | 2.205 | 3.473 |
| Mar. | 3.173 | 2.295 | 3.090  | 1.750  | 4.386  | 2.96  | 2.825 | 2.926 |
| Apr. | 4.750 | 4.342 | 2.228  | 3.685  | 5.471  | 1.35  | 3.52  | 3.595 |
| May  | 2.124 | 3.779 | 14.761 | 2.670  | 7.134  | 2.57  | 6.19  | 5.604 |
| June | 5.693 | 5.574 | 5.565  | 0.799  | 3.450  | 2.94  | 0.33  | 3.470 |
| July | 5.729 | 8.206 | 2.025  | 3.319  | 13.654 | 7.59  | 4.63  | 6.565 |
| Aug. | 1.883 | 5.969 | 8.963  | 3.920  | 3.370  | 3.48  | 0.85  | 4.062 |
| Sept.| 4.908 | 2.923 | 0.630  | 14.224 | 6.834  | 2.32  | 9.91  | 5.964 |
| Oct. | 0.731 | 7.037 | 5.184  | 4.264  | 2.632  | 0.73  | 3.23  | 3.401 |
| Nov. | 6.741 | 0.781 | 1.187  | 3.932  | 4.794  | 2.09  | 0.96  | 2.926 |
| Dec. | 0.333 | 0.5   | 1.232  | 6.658  | 1.259  | 3.55  | 0.36  | 1.556 |
| Average of a year | 42.033 | 47.451 | 53.025 | 45.719 | 60.923 | 41.505 | 39.87 | 47.218 |

From this table we observe that the average of the water which falls in a year is $47\frac{1}{4}$ inches, the minimum $41\frac{1}{2}$, and the maximum 61 inches, from tables kept by the late Col. James Madison, father of the President of the United States, at his seat about [?] miles from Monticello, from the year 1794 to 1801 inclusive, the average was $43\frac{1}{4}$ inches, the minimum $35\frac{3}{4}$ inches, and the maximum 52 inches.

During the same seven years there fell six hundred and twenty two rains, which gives eighty nine rains every year, or one for every four days; and the average of the water falling in the year being $47\frac{1}{2}$ inches, gives fifty three cents of an inch for each rain, or ninety three cents for a week. Were this to fall regularly, or nearly so, through the summer season, it would render our agriculture most prosperous, as experience has sometimes proved.

Of the three thousand nine hundred and five observations made in the course of seven years, two thousand seven hundred and seventy six were fair; by which I mean that the quarter part of the sky was unclouded. This shows our proportion of fair weather to be as two thousand seven hundred and seventy six to one thousand one hundred and twenty nine, or as five to two, equivalent to five fair days to the week. Of the other two, one may be more than half clouded, the other wholly so. We have then five of what observing astronomers call "observing days" in the week; and of course a chance of five to two of observing any astronomical phenomenon which is to happen at any fixed period of time.

The snow of Monticello amounted to the depth in

1809–10 of $16\frac{1}{4}$ in. and covered the ground 19 days
'10–11  "  $31\frac{3}{4}$           "                31  "
'11–12  "                            "                11  "
'12–13  "  35                        "                22  "
'13–14  "  $13\frac{1}{4}$           "                16  "
'14–15  "  $29\frac{3}{4}$           "                39  "
'15–16  "  23                        "                29  "
'16–17  "  $19\frac{1}{4}$           "                19  "
           ———                                       ——
Average—$22\frac{1}{2}$                              22

Which gives an average of $22\frac{1}{2}$ inches in a year, covering the ground twenty two days, and a minimum of eleven inches, and eleven days, and a maximum of thirty five inches and thirty nine days. According to Mr. Madison's tables, the average of snow, at his seat, in the winters from 1793 to 1801–2 inclusive, was $23\frac{1}{4}$ and the minimum $10\frac{5}{8}$ and maximum, $33\frac{1}{2}$ inches, but I once (in 1772) saw a snow here three feet deep.

The course of the wind having been one of the circumstances regularly observed, I have thought it better, from the observations of the seven years, to deduce an average for a single year and for every month of the year. This table accordingly exhibits the number of days in the year, and in every month of it, during which each particular wind, according to these observations may be expected to prevail. It will be for physicians to observe the coincidences of the diseases of each season, with the particular winds then prevalent, the quantities of heat and rain, &c.

|      | N. | N.E. | E. | S.E. | S. | S.W. | W. | N.W. | Total |
|------|----|------|----|------|----|------|----|------|-------|
| Jan. | 4  | 1    | 1  | 1    | 5  | 7    | 5  | 7    | 31    |
| Feb. | 3  | 3    | 1  | 1    | 4  | 6    | 4  | 6    | 28    |
| Mar. | 5  | 3    | 2  | 2    | 6  | 5    | 3  | 5    | 31    |
| Apr. | 4  | 2    | 3  | 2    | 7  | 6    | 2  | 4    | 30    |
| May  | 5  | 2    | 1  | 1    | 6  | 6    | 4  | 6    | 31    |
| June | 5  | 2    | 1  | 1    | 4  | 6    | 5  | 6    | 30    |
| July | 6  | 2    | 1  | 1    | 6  | 5    | 5  | 5    | 31    |
| Aug. | 6  | 3    | 1  | 2    | 3  | 6    | 4  | 6    | 31    |
| Sept.| 6  | 5    | 1  | 2    | 4  | 4    | 3  | 5    | 30    |
| Oct. | 5  | 2    | 1  | 1    | 5  | 5    | 5  | 7    | 31    |
| Nov. | 7  | 2    | 1  | 1    | 5  | 5    | 5  | 7    | 30    |
| Dec. | 5  | 2    | 1  | 1    | 5  | 5    | 5  | 7    | 31    |
| Total| 61 | 29   | 15 | 16   | 60 | 66   | 47 | 71   | 365   |

## Montpelier, Orange, Orange County, Virginia

The following data are found in Jefferson's manuscript Weather Memorandum Book and are appended here since they cover an earlier period than his Monticello record. The Montpelier observations were made by Col. James Madison and the Washington snowfall record by Jefferson, himself, when occupying the Presidency.

Temperature

|      | Min. | Max. |
|------|------|------|
| 1785 | 22   | 88½  |
| 86   | 27   | 91   |
| 87   | 20   | 91   |
| 88   | 1¾   | 88   |
| 89   | 2    | 96   |
| 90   | 2    | 93   |
| 91   | 10   | 93   |
| 92   | 0    | 103  |
| 93   | 13   | 96   |
| 94   | 11   | 95   |
| 95   | 8    | 94   |
| 96   | 0    | 93   |
| 97   | −1   | 100? |
| 98   | M    | 97 (page torn) |
| 99   | M    | 93 ( " " ) |
| 1800 | 12   | 97   |
| 01   | 10   | 96   |

From 1785 to 1787 the thermometer was probably located inside in a passageway; afterwards in the open air.

|         | Snowfall |
|---------|----------|
| 1793–94 | 35.75    |
| 94–95   | 14.31    |
| 95–96   | 23.35    |
| 96–97   | 18.35    |
| 97–98   | 15.25    |
| 98–99   | 33.12    |
| 99–00   | 38.56    |
| 1800–01 | 10.12    |
|         | 23.5     |

## Washington, D. C.

Snowfall*

|         | Depth | Days on ground |
|---------|-------|----------------|
| 1802–03 | 10″   | 8              |
| 03–04   | 21    | 23             |
| 04–05   | 19.5  | 10             |
| 05–06   | 4.5   | 2              |
| 06–07   | 8     | 7              |
| 07–08   | 21    | 18             |
| 08–09   | 17.5  | 34             |
|         | 14.5  | 16             |

* For comparison, the Weather Bureau record at 24th & M Streets (1887–1949) averaged 20.4″ annually and the modern record at National Airport (1943–1965), 16.9″.

[1] T. Jefferson. Ms. Weather memorandum book.
[2] T. Jefferson. *Notes on the State of Virginia*, William Peden, ed. Chapel Hill, Univ. North Carolina Press, 1955. 78.
[3] T. Jefferson to J. Madison, Monticello, 17 March 1809. *The writings of Thomas Jefferson*. Andrew A. Lipscomb, ed. Wash., D. C., The Thomas Jefferson Memorial Assoc., 1903, **12**, 266.
[4] T. Jefferson. *Garden Book*, 69.
[5] A letter from J. Madison, esquire, to D. Rittenhouse, esquire. William and Mary College, Virginia, Nov 1779. *Trans. Amer. Phil. Soc.* **2** (1786), 141–58.
[6] T. Jefferson to Isaac Zane, Phila., 8 Nov 1783, *The papers of Thomas Jefferson*, **6**, 347.
[7] T. Jefferson to J. Madison, Annapolis, 20 Feb 1784. *Ibid.*, **6**, 545.
[8] Ms. James Madison [Sr.] at his plantation. Met. Obs., 1784–1802. (Amer. Phil. Soc.)
[9] T. Jefferson to Martha Randolph, Lake Champlain, 31 May 1791. Henry S. Randall. *Jefferson*, quoted in *Garden Book*, 157–58.
[10] T. Jefferson to C. F. C. Volney, 9 April 1797, quoted in *Garden Book*, 255.
[11] Ms. Weather memorandum book. (Lib. Cong.); *Garden Book*, 622–28; *Va. Lit. Museum* (Charlottesville), 24 June 1829. 1–2, 26–29.

## 1784

## ON A LADY THROWING SNOW-BALLS

By a Young Gentleman

Poet's Corner

*New York Independent Gazette,* 29 January 1784

To the bleak winds, on barren
    sands,
  While Delia dares her charms expose,
To missive globes with glowing hands
  She forms the soft descending snows.

The lovely maid, from ev'ry part
  Collecting moulds with nicest care,
The fleaks, less frozen than her heart,
  Less than her downy bosom fair.

On my poor breast her arms she tries,
  Levell'd at me, like darted flame
From Jove's red hand, the pellet flies,
  As swift its course, as sure its aim.

Cold, as I thought, the fleecy rain,
  Unshock'd I stood, nor fear'd a
    smart;
While latent fires, with pointed pain,
  Shot through my veins, and pierc'd
    my heart.

Or with her eyes she warms the snow,
  (What coldness can their beams
    withstand?)
Or else (who would not kindle so?)
  It caught th'infection from her hand.

So glowing seeds to flints confin'd
  The Sun's enlivening heat conveys;
Thus iron to the load-stone join'd,
  Usurps its pow'r and wins its praise.

So strongly influent burn her charms,
  While heav'n's own light can scarce
    appear;
While winter's rage his rays disarms,
  And blasts the beauties of the year.

To ev'ry hope of safety lost,
  In vain we fly the lovely foe;
Since flames invade, disguis'd in frost,
  And Cupid tips his shafts with snow.

# EARLY WINTERS IN THE OLD NORTHWEST: 1780–1820

The Hard Winter of 1779–80 in the West ..................... 219

The Long Winter of 1784 at Detroit ........................ 222

Early Winters in the Ohio Valley ........................... 223

The Ohio Country Controversy: 1781–1810 ................... 231

The Winters of the War of 1812 ........................... 233

The Cold and Snow of Winter in 1818 ...................... 237

# THE HARD WINTER OF 1779–80 IN THE WEST

There were few Americans west of the Appalachian Mountains to record the rigors of the winter of 1779–80. George Rogers Clark's men held the westernmost position having seized Kaskaskia in southern Illinois and later captured Vincennes in southern Indiana. But no meteorological record has been uncovered from either of these posts to define the winter's weather events, though a thermometer had been in use at the former in the previous summer.[1]

The British held Detroit and all Lake Erie. Fortunately, the log of the crew of H.M.S. Welcome has survived to give a very brief sketch of the daily weather, though the author went into no details and did not possess a thermometer.[2] The general trend of events coincided with Col. Fleming's account to the southeastward and with other Eastern weather registers.

Back at Fort Pitt, the American military outpost at the juncture of the Alleghany and Monongahela Rivers at the present site of Pittsburgh, Col. Broadhead in a brief dispatch to General Washington gave a thumbnail impression of the winter:

> Such a deep snow and such ice has not been known at this place in the memory of the eldest natives; Deer & Turkies die by hundreds for want of food, the snow on the Alleghany & Laurel hills is four feet deep.[3]

The only non-military settlements in the Ohio Valley were located in Kentucky County of Virginia. Here a few pioneers had moved in during the years of the Revolutionary War, eager to leave the troubles of the old colonies and to turn the sod of the rich blue grass region. In fact, Daniel Boone, having just traced the Wilderness Trail from Virginia proper into the new country, was engaged in building his first cabin at Boonesboro on the Kentucky River in the fateful month of April 1775.

The State of Virginia soon took steps to exercise authority over the new settlements as more and more settlers poured into the region. It was in pursuit of this authority that Colonel William Fleming (1729–1795) spent the winter of 1779–80 in Kentucky holding courts of justice. Fortunately for this study, Colonel Fleming, unlike most Virginians, kept a diary, and from his manuscript we can now draw a very vivid picture of conditions on the frontier in this most rigorous of all winters.[4] The following extracts contain all entries of meteorological significance:

## COLONEL FLEMING'S DIARY

Kentucky County, Virginia

### November 1779

28. . . . it rained last night which was the first rain we have had since coming into this country this night there fell a snow and so dark on the 29th that was bad travelling. . . .

### December 1779

3–4. It continued excessive cold.
5. a storm of snow fell and the Kentucky rose.
6. . . . continued cold with snow. The Inhabitants avered that they never knew so severe weather at that season the winter generally setting in about Christmas and continuing about 6 weeks.
7. the storm abating.
11. it rained hard in the night.
12. showery all day in the evening lightning and thundered in the night a violent storm of wind rain, and snow.
13. windy and cold.
14. Cold and cloudy with some snow the night excessively cold hard frost.
15. Cloudy but fair.
16. it rained in the morning and froze as it fell. . . .
17. ground covered with rain and snow—the weather very severe, it snowed a little in the night.
18. the weather severely cold and cloudy. . . .

19. clear frosty and very cold.
20. the frost continues severe . . . the river has rose considerably from Snow Rain and transient thaws toward their head, the Kentucky had been full of ice for two days but was closed up this Evening and frozen over.
22. The morning of the 22nd which was moderate Clear and Sunshine.
25. The Frost still continuing I crossed the Kentucky on the Ice and found it one hundred yards over opposite the Fort.
26. Clear and moderate.
27. Morning over east trail snow and then rain.
29. . . . it seemed to relent and thaw but continued very cold and in the night snowed we put our horses over the Kentucky on the ice and the 31st left Boonesburg for Elkhorn.

### January 1780

1. The frost continued but a clear sun shine day. . .
2. A snow fell last night and continued Snowing this morning.
3. and all day the snow 12 Inches deep Cold and Piercing.
4, 5, 6. the cold continued intense.
9. The Weather continued in the day Clear and Freezing in the night is severely cold as ever I felt it in America the people at this place all sickly from colds the hardships they endured in the Journey and the Change of Air the most of the settlers moving from South Carolina two young men died yesterday. The frost had penetrated fourteen inches into the ground as we found by the opening of the graves.
10. In the night it snowed and continued snowing in the morning of the 10th so that it was five inches deep on the old snow continued to snow buisily all day.
11. clear above head.
12–18. the frost still continues clear in the day and cold.
19. so excessively cold we were afraid of being frost bit the night violently cold.
20. the frost still continues.
24. crossed Kentucky on ice . . . this day so exceeding cold I had one of my toes bit with frost and some of my fingers frozen.

[no weather entries—Col. Fleming holding court]

### February 1780

6. The frost still continuing, the Kentucky was frozen two feet thick of Ice but the night of the 6th it turned cloudy rained a little which turned to snow, in the morning the snow was two inches thick on the old snow the wind Easterly and continues to snow.
7. very dark cold cloudy
8–9. clear and moderate in the night of the 9th it rained and continued the 10th to rain gently the snow melted and the thaw continuing the earth began to uncover the 11th 12th.
13. the thaw continued gentle till the 23rd it froze at night and thawed in the day, when it rained in the night and snowed all day the wind N.W. the 24th it froze hard the 25th Do the 26th more moderate.
29. it rained in the evening and all night.

### March 1780

1. it hailed and snowed by turns.
7. it thundered and rained, the creeks were high the 8th it snowed the 12th.
14. Monday night there was a smart white frost succeeded by a warm clear day.
16. it snowed a little in the night and very cold in the morning of the 17th—which was cold . . . 18th continued cold and in the night it snowed and covered the ground.
19. continued cold though the snow soon melted.
20. Last night it was cold and froze hard, the effects of the severe winter was now sensibly felt, the earth for so long a time being covered with snow and the water entirely froze, the Caine almost all killed, the Hogs that were in the country suffered greatly, being frozen to death, in their beds, the deer likewise not being able to get either water or food, were found dead in great numbers, tirkies dropt dead of(f) their roosts and even the Buffalos died starved to death, the vast increase of people, near three thousand that came into this Country with the prodigious losses they had their cattle and horses, on their Journey, and the severity of the winter after they got here killings such numbers, all contributed to raise the necessaries of life to a most extravagant price.

### April 1780

6. Corn fell from $150 a bushel to $40 when the first boats came down the Ohio.

## NEAR DETROIT, CANADA

Logs of *H.M.S. Welcome* and *H.M.S. Hope.*

The Pinery near Fort Sinclair on the Grand River.

### November 1779

27. Wind S.W. moderate breeze frosty weather.
28. Wind W. moderate breeze cold weather.
29. Wind S. fresh breezes cold frosty weather.
30. Wind S.E. moderate weather.

### December 1779

1. Wind variable with flying showers of snow toward the evening.
2. Wind N. & N.W. fresh breezes with constant snow all this day, people repairing their hutt & fitting a load tackle, being prevented by the weather from working at the new house.
3. Wind N.W. frosty weather.
4. Wind N. frosty weather.
5. Wind N.E. fresh breezes frosty weather.
6. Wind N.W. frosty weather.

7. Wind N. light breezes with flying showers of snow.
8. Wind S.E. fresh breezes & soft weather.
9. Wind S. soft weather.
10. Wind S.S.E. fresh breezes with constant snow all this day . . . afternoon no working by reason of the great fall of snow.
11. Wind N. fresh breezes frosty weather.
12. Wind N.W. fresh gales & flying showers of snow all this day . . . no work in the woods.
13. Wind S.W. moderate weather.
14. Wind W. hard frosty weather.
15. Wind S.W. frosty weather with little snow.
16. Wind W.S.W. hard frosty weather, a deal of ice running in the Grand River.
17. Wind N.W. hard frosty weather. The Grand River taken all over this day.
18. Wind N.W. fresh breezes cold frosty weather
19. Wind N.W. cold frosty weather . . . no work in the woods this day.
20. Wind W.N.W. frosty weather.
21. Wind N.W, moderate weather
22. Wind N.W. mild weather.
23. Wind W. moderate weather.
24. Wind W. mild weather.
25. Wind S.W. mild weather. No work in the woods this day being Christmas
26. Wind S.W. moderate weather . . . no work in the woods this day.
27. Wind S.W. frosty weather.
28. Wind W. frosty weather.
29. Wind W. frosty weather.
30. Wind variable frosty weather with flying showers of snow
31. Wind W. frosty weather.

## January 1780

1. Wind W. cold weather with a little snow—This day no work done.
2. Wind W. frosty weather & snow . . . no other work done.
3. Wind W. frosty weather.
4. Wind W. frosty weather with little snow in the evening.
5. Wind W. frosty weather with snow all this day.
6. Wind W.N.W. frosty weather.
7. Wind N.W. frosty weather.
8. Wind W. frosty weather.
9. Wind S.W. mild weather.
10. Wind S.W. mild weather with a little snow.
11. Wind W. blowing weather with flying showers of snow.
12. Wind W. frosty weather.
13. Wind N.W. frosty weather.
14. Wind N. frosty weather.
15. Wind S.W. fresh breezes with flying showers of snow.
16. Wind S. mild weather.
17. Wind S.W. moderate weather.
18. Wind S.W. frosty weather.
19. Wind S.E. frosty weather with snow.
20. Wind S.W. frosty weather.
21. Wind S.E. fresh breezes.
22. Wind S.E. moderate weather.
23. Wind E mild weather, no work done this day.
24. Wind S.E. moderate weather.
25. Wind S. blowing weather.
26. Wind S. fresh breezes.
27. Wind S. fresh breezes with snow.
28. Wind S.W. blowing weather.
29. Wind W. moderate weather.
30. Wind W. mild weather.
31. Wind W. cold frosty weather.

## February 1780

1. Wind N. fresh breezes with flying showers of snow.
2. Wind S. blowing weather.
3. Wind S.E. with a little snow in the evening.
4. Wind E. moderate weather.
5. Wind N. frosty weather.
6. Wind N. mild weather.
7. Wind N. mild weather with snow in the evening.
8. Wind N. with snow.
9. Wind N. blowing weather.
10. Wind N.E. blowing weather.
11. Wind N.E. blowing weather.
12. Wind N. frosty weather.
13. Wind N. fine weather.
14. Wind N.E. with a little snow.
15. Wind E fresh breezes.
16. Wind E. mild weather.
17. Wind N. frosty weather.
18. Wind W. moderate weather.
19. Wind W. mild warm weather.
20. Wind W. mild weather.
21. Wind S.W. soft weather.
22. Wind S.W. fresh breezes with snow.
23. Wind W. frosty weather.
24. Wind N.W. frosty weather.
25. Wind W. mild weather.
26. Wind W. mild weather.
27. Wind W. soft weather.
28. Wind N.W. frosty weather.
29. Wind S.W. soft warm weather.

## March 1780

7. Wind S. with constant rain all day . . . afternoon no work by reason of the great rain.
8. Wind S. mild weather with a little rain.
16. Wind N.W. frosty weather—No work done this day being held for St. Patrick's Day.
17. Wind N.W. frosty weather—Manual baking, no work done by the others except grinding axes.
18. Wind W. with a little snow—in the forenoon no work done.

## April 1780

14. Wind W. fresh breezes with flying showers of snow. (Last mention of snow falling.)
16. Wind S. mild weather . . . This afternoon Mr. Inglis with 4 seamen arrived in a boat from Detroit to join our party. (First mention of open navigation.)
20. Wind E. blowing weather—The Grand River full of ice.
23. The River full of ice.

30. Wind E. cloudy weather with rain ... The Grand River full of ice.

**May 1780**

1. Wind variable with lights airs. The River quite full of ice.
7. Wind E. cloudy weather with rain—the Grand River quite full of ice.
11. Wind E. mild warm weather ... the Grand River quite full of ice.

[1] T. Jefferson. *Notes on the state of Virginia*, 75.
[2] Ms. Log book. *H.M.S. Welcome.* Capt. Alex Harrow. (Burton Coll., Detroit Public Library).
[3] Col. Daniel Broadhead to George Washington, Fort Pitt, Feb. 11, 1780. *Penna. Archives*, 12 (1855), 206.
[4] Colonel William Fleming's journal of travels in Kentucky 1779–1780. *Travels in the American Colonies.* Newton D. Mereness, ed. N. Y., The Macmillan Co., 1916, 617.

## THE LONG WINTER OF 1784 AT DETROIT

One of the severest winters of the century followed immediately on the close of the War of the Revolution. Some contemporary witnesses thought conditions even more rigorous than during the two landmark winters of 1740–41 and 1779–80. For the western country, then inhabited mainly by Indians and soldiers, we have a satisfactory meteorological report for the entire season of 1783–84 at Detroit, then still in British hands. Dr. George C. Anthon, presumably with His Majesty's troops, had succeeded in transporting a thermometer to that remote location undamaged and from 1781 to 1786 recorded the doings of the weather with a daily diligence. And equally as remarkable, this record has been preserved over the years so that we can today gain an insight in what was truly an outstanding winter for the lower Great Lakes area.[1]

Winter set in just before Christmas after a mild first 20 days of December. Snow fell during the afternoon of the 20th with falling temperatures. Some frosty mornings followed until the 23d when the mercury remained below freezing all day from a +19° start. Christmas Day brought "heavy snow all day" with the temperature at 21°, 25°, 24° and wind out of the north. The mercury dropped to the month's low of +1° on the 28th with the glass continuously below freezing from the 27th to the end of the year. The final day produced "snow all day."

A warmer spell introduced the New Year: 3d—"pleasant & thaw, 38°," 4th—"rain all day, sharp frost at night," 5th—"high wind & snow," 6th—"thaw & rain P.M. high wind hard frost: 34°, 36°, 19°." Then commenced as wintry a spell as the Detroit area has witnessed, before or since. The mercury slid below freezing on the afternoon of the 6th, and thereafter only one day in January registered above the freezing mark—the 22d with 33° and a heavy snow fell all that day.

The thermometer on the morning of the 7th of January was down to −7° and a high wind out of the west-southwest brought "exceeding cold" which closed the Detroit River firmly. The mercury struggled up to zero by 1200, but next morning declined to −14° and on the 9th to −15°. There followed a brief relaxation from zero readings until the 14th when another cold term produced three successive mornings with −9°, −12°, and −15.5°. After two days of higher readings, three more consecutive below-zero mornings followed on the 19–21st: −1°, −8°, and −3°. The 22d witnessed "heavy snow all day" with wind northeast. A comet in the southeast was visible from the 20th to 24th.

The worst, however, was yet to come. A strong southwest wind following the heavy snow of the 22d introduced much colder air into the region. The mercury dropped below zero on the afternoon of the 24th, then followed six successive mornings of bitter cold. Here is the record of Dr. Anthon:

**January 1784**

|  | 0700 | 1200 | 2000 |  |  |
|---|---|---|---|---|---|
| 24. | 13° | 17° | −3° | WSW | Fair very cold, comet appeared in SW, last time here |
| 25. | −15 | 2 | 0 | SW | Excessive cold. Fair & clear day |
| 26. | −3 | 16 | −5 | W | Cloudy small snow. P.M. fair, very cold |
| 27. | −18 | 16 | 2 | SW | Excessive cold. Serene weather |
| 28. | −17 | 3 | −1 | SSW | Excessive cold. P.M. Cloudy & snow |
| 29. | −16 | 21½ | −7 | SW | Excessive cold. Clear day |
| 30. | −17 | 13 | 14 | SW | Excessive cold. P.M. Cloudy & snow |
| 31. | 20 | 28 | 28 | N | Cloudy & snow |

During the first two days of February the Detroit area succeeded in getting into the warm sector of a disturbance. A heavy snow on the 1st, turning into rain, continued into the next day. A thaw prevailed all morning with the mercury reaching 51° at noontime. As the cold front came through, a southwest gale raged with rapidly falling temperature bringing the reading to −3° by the evening of the 3d. Another two weeks of tough winter weather followed with no thaw until the 17th. There were nine mornings in February with the 0700 reading at zero or lower. The coldest mornings were the 8th and 9th with −12° on each occasion. The last zero of this series came on the morning of the 18th, but by noon the reading had soared to +38° and the back of the cold wave had been broken.

The last days of February had frosty mornings, but usually a thaw in the afternoon. Snow fell on the 22d and 26th to an undetermined depth. Another cold wave struck on the 28–29th driving the mercury to +12° on the 28th and way down to −10° on the 29th (perhaps a date record) as a northwest wind brought "exceeding cold, clear weather." Two back-to-back, below-zero mornings of −6° and −4° on the 4th and 5th of March concluded the series of 23 such mornings during this frigid winter. The early March cold had been preceded by "much snow" on the 2d and 3d. A manuscript note in the Burton Collection indicated a snow depth at Detroit of four feet on March 6th, and the ice on Lake St. Clair was three feet thick.

The early March cold spell was succeeded immediately by a warm period. From −4° at 0700 on the 5th, the thermometer rebounded to 39° at noontime —"fair pleasant day much thaw." The following days had "much thaw" and "great thaw." The 9th was "a very pleasant warm day, much thaw," and on the 10th the mercury stood at 56° at the noon reading. The remainder of the month had typical mid- and late-March types. There were only five more days with noontime readings below freezing. Morning temperatures ran in the teens from the 17th to 23d; the lowest reading sank only to +12° on the 21st. There were eight days with snow, but except that of the 2–3d these were all indicated as light. On the 22d the river was crossed on a sledge. (There was no date given for the opening of the river, but a series of overnight thaws set in on April 3d with the mercury in the high 40s and low 50s.) A hard gale took place on the 5th which would have assisted the break-up of the ice fields.

An additional note about the ice break-up in the rivers of western Pennsylvania has been found in the manuscript records of John Fitch, an early surveyor of lands bordering the Ohio River. His account told of the ice driving on the Monongahela on March 10th and on the Yougiogheny the next day. A great fresh occurred on the 15th as the crest of the two rivers joined in swelling the Ohio River.[3]

[1] George C. Anthon, M.D. A meteorological journal kept at Detroit, Upper Canada, (now in the Michigan Territory) from Aug. 1781 to May 1786 inclusive. (N. Y. Hist. Soc.).
[2] Ms. note in Burton Collection. (Detroit Public Library).
[3] John Fitch. Ms. Accounts 1784–1791. John Fitch Papers II-35-D,4. (Lib. Cong.).

## EARLY WINTERS IN THE OHIO VALLEY

Little was known about the climate of the country north of the Ohio River until after the War of the Revolution. It had been the domain of Indian tribes, many of whom were hostile to the colonists along the seaboard, and this enmity was generously subsidized by those in possession of the Great Lakes region and the St. Lawrence Valley outlet, first by the French until 1759 and thereafter by the British. The land had been traversed on military campaigns and by an occasional trader or missionary, but there were no permanent settlers until 1788, aside from a few squatters in the extreme southeast along the great river. Following the organization of the territory under the Northwest Ordinance of 1787, a group of enterprising New Englanders formed the Ohio Company and established the first going settlement at Marietta, at the junction of the southeast-flowing Muskingum River and the Ohio River, some 125 miles down-stream from Pittsburgh.

Thomas Jefferson took an early interest in seeking more knowledge about meteorological conditions west of the mountains. His curiosity about differences in the climate of the eastern and western slopes had been aroused when compiling his *Notes on the State of Virginia* in 1781. He had suggested that every county in Virginia be provided with a thermometer and that a daily record of maximum and minimum temperatures be maintained, so that accurate data on climate differences could be studied. The turmoil attending the Revolutionary War prevented the fulfillment of this visionary plan, but in November of 1783 Jefferson wrote that he had procured the only available thermometer in Philadelphia and was sending it to Isaac Zane who lived in the western part of Virginia then bordering the Ohio River. Zane's family, prominent in the area for many years, were remembered in history by the naming of Zane's Island at Wheeling, Zanesville in central Ohio, and Zane's Trace which blazed the way across southern Ohio to northern Kentucky. No record has been uncovered as to the results of this early thermometric mission into the West.

Another early student of climate conditions in the western country was surveyor John Fitch who has left a manuscript diary, now in the Library of Congress, which described occasional weather events in the mid-1780's.

The group of settlers organized by the Ohio Company of New England, arriving at Marietta on 8 April 1788, found the fields green with verdure and the season well advanced. Not considering their change in altitude and perhaps the recent arrival of a new air mass, they were much impressed by the contrast of these conditions with the harshness of the weather in the highlands of western Pennsylvania which they had just departed. From this they derived an erroneous view of the softness of the Ohio Valley climate which was to affect climatological thinking for many years to come.

The first possessor of a thermometer in Ohio whose daily records have been preserved to the present day was Winthrop Sargent (1753–1820), the secretary of the Northwest Territory under General Arthur St. Clair, the first governor. Sargent, a graduate of the Class of 1771 at Harvard, also held a position in the Ohio Company. Among other officials in the Company was Rev. Manasseh Cutler who had previously maintained good meteorological records at Ipswich in northeastern Massachusetts during the early 1780's. Perhaps it was Cutler who stimulated Sargent in his lifelong devotion to meteorological investigation. In 1789 Sargent sent a communication to the American Philosophical Society presenting his daily thermometer record for the autumn and winter of 1788–89 which elicited the comment from the reader: "It appears that the changes of the weather, marked by the thermometer, are sudden and extraordinary." Another communication from Sargent on meteorological matters found its way to the American Academy of Arts and Science at Boston. Covering the period from 1 September 1788 to 31 May 1791, it comprised the best document on the early Ohio winter climate.

Another early meteorological register was maintained at Fort Washington, now the site of Cincinnati. Two fragments of this covering the years 1790 and 1791 have survived. One including a study of the rise and fall of the Ohio River was transmitted to the American Philosophical Society by Judge George Turner and another now resides among the General Josiah Harmar manuscripts in the Clements Library of the University of Michigan. Both are useful in establishing some of the facts about the winter of 1790–91.

The interest of medical men in weather conditions was early demonstrated in the U. S. Army. An early meteorological record was maintained in 1795 at Fort Defiance in extreme northwestern Ohio by Dr. Joseph Gardner Andrews. This may be considered the forerunner of the extensive series of observations to be made during the first half of the 19th Century by surgeons of the Army Medical Corps at their far-flung posts around the periphery of the country. Though no instruments were available at Fort Defiance at this early date, the record was faithfully kept and provided a good description of the freeze-up and thaw at this American outpost. Another early military contributor to meteorological knowledge was the controversial General James Wilkinson who has been accused of engaging in many shady deals while serving as the ranking officer in the U. S. Army. Wilkinson received the post of Detroit from the British in 1796 and apparently found a thermometer there as he later transmitted a thermometric register made there and on a voyage to Mackinac.

Some early observations in the far Northwest had been communicated to Philadelphia by Peter Pond who partially explored the headwaters of the Mississippi River in 1790; these readings, however, were taken in summertime and do not contribute to a knowledge of the winter climate. Another explorer carrying a thermometer was Andrew Ellicott. His party surveying the western and southern borders of the United States camped at the confluence of the Ohio and Mississippi Rivers during December 1796 and January 1797 and very conveniently registered the degree of cold in this most bitter winter of the decade of the 1790's.

By the year 1800 the characteristics of Ohio air masses were being tested at additional places. Colonel Return Jonathan Meigs, a leading figure in territorial days in Ohio, had two thermometers at Marietta "which he attended to." Our informant for this bit of information was John Gottlieb Ernestus Heckewelder (1743–1823), who, as a missionary of the Moravian Church, served both his Indian wards and the U. S. Government well in the difficult days of racial conflict in the early Ohio country. Heckewelder resided at Gnadenhutten on the Tuscarawas River in east-central Ohio during the first years of the 1800's. For a number of years he possessed a thermometer and kept a daily weather diary. His records from 1800 are extant. These provide the best contemporary source of data as to the nature of Ohio winters for the period prior to 1815, but the record does not seem to have been known to contemporary writers concerned with the history and geography of the region.

The distinction of being the first to undertake a study of the climate of the Ohio Valley and its influence on the inhabitants must deservedly be accorded to Daniel Drake (1785–1852), an early Cincinnati physician and educator with wide-ranging interests. Drake set forth his views on the climate of the region based on original observations in two early volumes: *Notices concerning Cincinnati* (1810) and *Picture of Cincinnati* (1815). Much later in a partially posthumous work he summarized his lifetime experience in *A Systematic Treatise . . . on the Principal Diseases of the Interior Valley of North America* (1850, 1854).

During the first decade of the 19th Century, Drake gathered together all the meteorological data available about the Ohio River country. His principal reliance about early Ohio winters came from a now unlocated memorandum from Winthrop Sargent. This apparently covered the years up to 1798 when Sargent went down river to the new Mississippi Territory. Only parts of Sargent's diary after 1791 have survived, so the use of the memorandum by Drake has preserved information that otherwise would have been lost to historians. Drake classified the winters from 1785 to 1810 as mild, normal, or severe. The following discussion of early Ohio winters depends, in the main, on Drake's outline, though many additional details have been culled from a multitude of sources to enlarge Drake's rather scanty outline:

### 1785–91

All the winters from 1785 to 1791 in the Ohio Country were mild, according to Drake's information.[1] There were several brief cold snaps and two or three deep snowstorms, but the duration of wintry conditions was short, and this apparently led many new settlers into a misconception as to the true nature of the Ohio Valley winter. The journal of John Matthews told of an 18-inch snowfall on 5 December 1786, "which I am informed by the inhabitants is very remarkable for this season and is seldom deeper through the course of the winter."[2] General Harmar also witnessed a major snowstorm for the area on 18 February 1791 at Cincinnati when 11 inches fell, "by far the most that has fallen at one time during the winter or since the settlement of this place."[3] The same storm reached Marietta about noon of the 18th and continued through the rest of the day and night. Next morning Winthrop Sargent noted in his diary: "Snow is 12 inches deep this morning on a level—cloudy day."[4]

[1] Daniel Drake. *Notices concerning Cincinnati.* Cinn., 1810. Reprint: *Quar. Pub. Hist. and Phil. Soc. Ohio,* **3**–1 (Jan-Mar 1908), 18–19; also Microcard library.
[2] Journal of John Matthews. *Ohio in the time of the Confederation.* Archer B. Hulbert, ed. Marietta, Marietta Hist. Comm., 1918, 211.
[3] Daniel Britt and George Turner. Meteorological observations. Fort Washington. 1790–91. *Trans. Amer. Phil Soc.,* **4** (1799), 329–47.
[4] Winthrop Sargent. Ms. Met. Obs. (Harvard).

### 1791–92

The first season that could be classified with the rigorous winters of the Revolutionary period or compared with the severity of a normal New England winter commenced in early December 1791. Press reports from Pittsburgh told of very deep snows to the westward in Ohio. Depths of 24 inches were mentioned on the upper Muskingum and at Marietta, the two principal places of settlement at this early date.[1] The winter regime extended over southwestern Ohio also, Cincinnati reporting a total snowfall of 24 inches in January and the mercury dropping to $-7°$ on the 23d.[2] The Ohio River at Wheeling, where the main road for westbound pioneers crossed the river barrier, provided a frozen surface for 40 days permitting loaded wagons to cross from side to side over Zane's Island.[3] As a result of the freeze-up of waterways, it was regarded locally as the severest winter since the Hard Winter of 1780.[4]

[1] *Pittsburgh Gazette* in E. Stiles, Ms. Met. Obs. (Yale).
[2] Judge George Turner of the Western Territory. *Proc. Amer. Phil. Soc.,* **22**–3 (1885), 174.
[3] William Darby. *The emigrant's guide to the western and southwestern states and territories.* N. Y., Kirk & Mercein, 1818, 237.
[4] *Idem.*

### 1792–96

For the next four-year span, Drake listed the winters of 1792–93 and 1795–96 as definitely mild in Ohio, as they were on the Atlantic seaboard, and the back-to-back seasons of 1793–94 and 1794–95 ran close to average with no outstanding winter events.[1] We have a detailed account of conditions in west-central Ohio for the winter of 1794–95 as the post surgeon at Fort Defiance kept a daily tab on the weather, though he lacked any instruments.[2] This early interest of military medical men in weather conditions reflected the general concern of doctors with climate conditions as one of the mainsprings of disease.

[1] D. Drake. *Cincinnati,* 18–19.
[2] A surgeon's mate at Fort Defiance. The journal of Joseph Gardner Andrews for the year 1795. Richard C. Knopf, ed. *The Ohio Hist. Quar.,* **66**–1, 2, 3, (Jan-July 1957), 57–86, 159–186, 238–268.

### 1796–97

The winter proved exceedingly rigorous with a period of Arctic cold extending from early December to the end of January. Fortunately, we have good documentation for the intensity of the two cold waves, for astronomer Andrew Ellicott was then descending the Ohio River on a Federally-sponsored expedition to determine the western and southern boundaries of the United States. Soon after mid-December he camped at the junction of the Mississippi and Ohio rivers close to the site of present-day Cairo, Illinois. It was his custom to take frequent thermometer readings and to note the major weather incidents of the day. His entry for 22 December related that both rivers had been closed by ice during a solstice-timed onset of winter. On that day a "keen north wind" kept the mercury close to the zero mark: 0800 $-5°$, 1400 $+1°$, and 2100 $-5°$. Next morning, with clear skies and wind out of the northwest, the mercury commenced the day even lower: 0800 $-7.5°$, 1000 $-6°$, 1200 $+1°$, and 2000 $+7°$—apparently surveyor Ellicott did not get out of his blankets earlier or he might have had an even lower reading.[1] The severe cold was also noted to the east for the *Kentucky Gazette* at Lexington marked readings of −13° and −12° on the 23d and 24th of December 1796.

Ice conditions proved troublesome along the Ohio River this winter. Ellicott stated that the Ohio at Cairo remained closed for a full 30 days until January 20th. The junction of the Alleghany and the Monongahela rivers at Pittsburgh was blocked by ice jams much longer, from 20 November to 30 January, and at Cincinnati the river remained closed for about the same duration as at Cairo.[3] The editor of the *Kentucky Gazette* complained that the Ohio mail had been interrupted for a period of 11 weeks. As we shall hear time and again, it was always considered the prerogative and duty of the opposition press to blame the current Washington administration of the postal system for all untoward meteorological events that stopped the normal dispatch of the mails.

Francis Bailey related in his account of travels in the area that the Ohio River had been frozen over for 10 days previous to December 20th when the ice measured a thickness of nine inches, inclosing firmly the "Kentucky boats" of a number of emigrants. Heavy rains fell and the voyagers hoped for a quick release. But a subsequent harder freeze in early January, when the mercury dropped to −17°, held them tight until the ice bridge broke up "with a noise like thunder," carrying many of the boats along with their occupants to destruction.[5]

The second major cold wave of the winter struck at the end of the first week in January. Drake told of the frigid Arctic air mass dropping the mercury at Cincinnati to −18°—a record up to then and unsurpassed there until the Great Arctic Outbreak of February 1835.[6] Down in Kentucky, 35 miles to the south of Cincinnati, Dr. Doniphan's thermometer went down to −14°.[7] Surveyor Ellicott, ice-bound and still camped at the junction of the Mississippi and Ohio, experienced the second cold wave and this time he was out of his blankets at sunrise for a more representative reading:

| | | | |
|---|---|---|---|
| Jan. 7 | −7° at sunrise; | −5° at 0900; | +19° in P.M. |
| Jan. 8 | −7° at sunrise; | +29° in P.M.; | +10° at 1900. |
| Jan. 9 | −3° at sunrise; | +42° in P.M.[8] | |

In the dozen winters from 1798 to 1810, Drake considered five seasons as severe and four as notably mild. The severe periods were also placed in the same category along the Atlantic seaboard: 1798–99, 1803–04, and 1804–05, 1806–07, and 1808–09. Outstanding for lack of wintery qualities, four were numbered: 1799–1800, 1801–02, 1805–06, and 1809–10—again in close agreement with our previous classification of winters in the Northeast.[9]

[1] Andrew Ellicott. *Trans. Amer. Phil Soc.*, 5 (1802), 164.
[2] *Kentucky Gaz.* (Lexington), 24 Dec 1796.
[3] W. Darby. *Emigrant's guide*, 237.
[4] *Ky. Gaz.*, 20 Dec 1797.
[5] Francis Bailey. Journal of a tour in 1796–97. Richard H. Collins, ed. *History of Kentucky*, 1, 395.
[6] Drake, 18–19.
[7] *Idem.*
[8] A. Ellicott, ap. 7–8.
[9] Drake, 18–19.

## A Mild Winter: 1801–02

The soft winter conditions in 1801–02 caused comment at both Pittsburgh and White River Mission in Indiana. The diary maintained at the latter has the following entries:

Jan. 18. The weather this month is as nice as in spring.
Feb. 9 . . . as the weather is very beautiful and springlike. . . .
Mar. 2 The weather was as beautiful as in spring; in fact, we suffered little from the cold this winter, in that it was generally cold only for a few days at a time. As to snow, we hardly have any. The climate here is quite different from that below, in that the weather sometimes changes two or three times a day.

At Pittsburgh the press took notice of the open winter on January 8th: "Our days are as warm as the latter end of April and but little frost at nights."[2]

[1] Lawrence H. Gipson. *The Moravian Indian mission on White River*. Indianapolis, Indiana Hist. Comm., 1938, 142, 151.
[2] *Pitts. Gaz.*, 8 Jan 1802.

## The Uneven Winter of 1802–03

Though Drake did not include this season among his list of severe winters, it contained several noteworthy weather events, mainly recorded for us by the missionary observers at White River and at Gnadenhutten on the Tuscarawas River.

The Indiana diary told the story of December succinctly:

Dec. 1. It began to snow and continued till the 3d, so that the snow lay a foot deep in the woods. Then it froze hard so that the deep snow not only remained but it was very cold as well.
12. The cold has increased so that everything in our room was frozen solid.
15. It began to snow hard again and the snow lay 1½ft. deep on the level.
27. Rain and the ice on the White River broke up.

The Gnadenhutten record for eastern Ohio conditions did not commence until an entry on December 14th informed: "snow'd hard from midnight to noon 10 inches deep." Next morning the temperature was down to −6° and on the following morning to −8°. The 16th, described as having a "sharp & piercing wind," was truly a cold day with readings of −8° at 0700, only +7° at 1300, and +4° at 1700. Another bitter day followed on the 17th—"snowy morning from east & snows all day." Not until the 19th did the mercury rise above freezing; thereafter, a marked thaw took place as the Indiana record reflected. The only relapse occurred on Christmas Day when a morning reading of +8° shot up to +34° just after noon. On the day of the ice break-up on the White River, the 27th, the Gnadenhutten thermometer registered a very warm +64°.[2]

January was an in-and-out month. The mercury on Heckewelder's thermometer dropped to −2° on the 29th, though it had been as high as +56° on the 12th. The only substantial snow brought three inches on the 3d.

February witnessed a return to severe conditions with two marked cold spells. On the 4th the thermometer on the Tuscawaras in east-central Ohio dropped to −12° and rose only to +11° during the day. But the outstanding wintry spell of the season came from the 12th to 18th. During the night of the 12–13th two inches of snow fell, and then another storm during the afternoon and evening dropped seven inches more. A northwest wind drove the mercury on the morning of the 14th down to +1° at 0700 (a registering thermometer probably would have caught zero or lower). The cold spell with nighttime radiation working at an optimum continued five mornings:

| Feb. 14 | + 1° | +24° | +20° |
| 15 | −11° | +21° | +19° |
| 16 | + 2° | +30° | +25° |
| 17 | − 2° | +40° | +32° |
| 18 | + 9° | +44° | +39° |

Though another snow of three inches fell on the 24th, spring came on fast during early March and reigned through April to set the stage for the final wintry event of the season.

[1] L. Gipson. *White River,* 202–04.
[2] John Heckewelder. Ms. Met. Obs. (Amer. Phil. Soc.).

### The May Snow of 1803

A remarkable cold spell struck the Ohio Country during the first week of May 1803 bringing a severe frost which killed early blooming fruit and covered the terrain with an out-of-season white mantle. Our westernmost report came from White River Mission in central Indiana: "This week we had very cold weather. During the night from the 6th to the 7th (of May) it snowed, and on the morning of the 7th there were six inches of snow on the ground, but it did not last long. Meanwhile everything that we had planted in our garden and had already come up, was frozen." By the 9th an improvement had set in: "The weather became warm once more and we could resume our necessary field work."[1]

The snow area included much of Kentucky also. Richard Collins, the historian of early days in the Blue Grass State, recorded the snow occurrence on May 5th in the western counties giving the depth as four inches. Hard frosts followed on the next three nights. Apples, already advanced to the size of "ounce bullets," were destroyed.[2]

The width of the snow belt through the Ohio Valley was quite narrow. It had a northeastern orientation as a small low, probably moving at a rather slow pace, crossed southern Kentucky and northern Virginia. At Athens in southeastern Ohio the snow began to fall before 1000 on the morning of the 6th and by night had completely covered the ground. The severe frost following that night killed all fruit buds—"not a peach or apple grew in southern Ohio, that year, except a few on the islands in the Ohio River."[3]

The records at Gnadenhutten, 75 miles north of Athens, do not mention any snowfall, though a severe freeze blighted the area.[4] The mercury on the morning of May 3d had been down to +20° and on the morning of the 4th to +32°—rain, however, fell that evening and continued into the next day with mild conditions. The 6th, with the thermometer at +34°, +45°, and +39°, was described as "a cold day, hard frosty morning." This was the day and evening on which the snowstorm swept up the Ohio Valley from the southwest. Next morning, the 7th, found the Gnadenhutten thermometer at +24° and the 1300 reading at +44°. And the three following mornings, 8th through 10th, each had a morning reading of exactly +25°, and conditions described as "hard frost." On the 9th the mercury at noontime rebounded to 62° and on the 10th to 82°. It seems quite apparent that Heckewelder's thermometer was directly exposed to both the sun's influence and also to open sky radiative conditions at night. This would account for the excessive daily ranges such as from 25° to 82° on the 10th and from 37° to 88° on the 11th.

The northeastward-trending snow belt moved from Ohio into Pennsylvania generally following the track of the present Pennsylvania Turnpike. The ground in northwestern Pennsylvania already had been covered by a fall of four to six inches on the 4–5th.[5] Apparently the cold rain recorded at Gnadenhutten on these days fell as four inches of snow at Beaver in extreme western Pennsylvania on the Ohio River and as six inches at Bradford in the hills close to the New York border as the Ohio Valley storm expanded its snow canopy northward.[6] To the eastward the southern boundary of the snowfall can be delineated, as Philadelphia had a substantial amount on the night of the 7-8th, but Washington, D.C. received only a little.[7]

[1] L. Gipson. *White River*, 227.
[2] R. Collins. *Hist. Kentucky*, 1, 399.
[3] Charles M. Walker. *History of Athens County, Ohio.* Cinn., R. Clarke & Co., 1869, 577-78.
[4] J. Heckewelder. Ms. Met. Obs.
[5] Joseph H. Bausman. *History of Beaver County, Penna. N. Y.* The Knickerbocker Press, 1904. 11.
[6] *History of Bradford County, Pennsylvania.*
[7] *National Intelligencer* (Wash., D.C.), 13 May 1803. David Rittenhouse. Ms. Met. Obs. (Amer. Phil. Soc.).

## Two Severe Winters 1803-04

A major snowstorm struck the missionary post on White River on 21-23 January 1804 and should rate among the deepest ever to visit the central Indiana country:

> January: On the 21st it began again to snow hard and kept it up day and night until the 23d, so that the snow was over two feet deep. 30th. The weather moderated today, which was the first time in a month. We were very glad because we were quite worn out from chopping so much wood and at the same time freezing.[1]

The same storm brought hardship to the New England and Pennsylvania settlers who had recently come to the parts of northeastern Ohio known as New Connecticut and the Western Reserve. Rev. Thomas Robbins, who has previously supplied notes on the vagaries of central Connecticut winters, was living at this time at Poland in Trumbull County on the Ohio-Pennsylvania line where he was serving as a missionary seeking to bring the light of the Gospel to the infidels around him. As usual, he made careful observations on weather conditions: Jan. 23—"yesterday and last night a great fall of snow. It is now more than two feet deep on a level. More than has ever been known here. Very cold." On the 24th: "It has snowed nearly every day for three weeks . . . extreme cold." On February 4th: "The creeks now generally hard froze."[2]

There followed some relaxation of the severe conditions as Robbins wrote on the 16th: "Very pleasant weather." On the 18th: "The snow appears to be wasting away by the gentle heat of the sun." On the 22d: "We have had very pleasant weather for near a fortnight; it now comes on cold."

As often happens after a warm February, March turned wintry: 3d "extreme cold." And on the 4th: "Yesterday and today the coldest days we have had this winter."[3]

[1] L. Gipson. *White River*, 274-76.
[2] Thomas Robbins. *Diary*, 1, 245-49.
[3] *Idem.*

## 1804-05

This winter has generally been considered the most rigorous as a whole since the famous Hard Winter of 1780. At its close in February, the editor of the *Kentucky Gazette* invoked the testimony of those time-honored witnesses: "The oldest inhabitants in this country do not recollect a winter so severe as the present."[1] The rough conditions extended along the eastern seaboard with the Hudson River at New York City frozen over in late January and a massive 48-hour snowstorm raging on the 27-28th, thought to rate among the great in the city's history. Testimony as to the frigidity of invading air masses from Canada had been afforded by Captains Meriwether Lewis and William Clark who spent this winter at Fort Mandan in Dakota where their thermometer sampled the extreme readings experienced in this severe winter on the open Plains.[2]

The Heckewelder thermometer readings in Ohio have been fortunately preserved by a bit of luck, and they give good evidence of the nature of the winter there. Though the full manuscript record for this period does not commence until February, Heckewelder forwarded the extreme readings on his thermometer in a letter to Philadelphia where they were published soon afterwards in Barton's *Medical and Physical Journal*[3]:

| | |
|---|---|
| Dec. 19 | $-15°$ |
| 20 | $-8°$ |
| Jan. 1 | $+2°$ |
| 2 | $+8°$ |
| 14 | Thaw |
| 21 | $-15°$ |
| 22 | $+7°$ |

The main channel of cold air this season apparently lay well to the east of Ohio as conditions proved more severe at comparable latitudes over the Middle Atlantic States and New England. The widespread extent of the rigorous conditions was exemplified by a Quebec dispatch: "The present winter since a few days before Christmas has been one of the most severe experienced for a great many years back.—snow at present about seven feet deep in the woods where it does not drift— usually about 4-5 feet in middle of March."[4]

A spectacular thaw took place in mid-February to mark the close of winter. From the 18th to the end of February the Heckewelder thermometer reached above freezing every day. The sugar maples commenced to run on the 24th; next day with "fine sunshine" the ice went out of the Muskingum River as the mercury climbed to 55°.[5] The break-up on the Ohio came in spectacular fashion. The *Kentucky Gazette* carried an account in the February 15th issue. The ice broke on the 10th, and on one of the following days the editor reported he saw descending amidst the ice floes: eight flat boats, four keel boats, ten ferry boats, between 60 and 80 canoes, and one house. Three families from Virginia and Maryland were reported lost when a boat overturned—in all, the editor counted 31 emigrants drowned during these days in the treacherous icy water.[6]

Rev. Thomas Robbins in northeastern Ohio again suffered through a hard winter, such as he had previously complained about in Connecticut. On January 7th his diary gave testimony: "The snow is two feet to two and a half feet deep." On the 11th: "The weather very severe. Equal to any that we have had." On the 19th: "Extreme cold." And on the 21st: "Most extreme cold. Froze one of my ears."[7]

A January thaw then set in shortly with rain on the 24th and 25th: "The snow thaws and the streams rise very fast." It seemed "very comfortable winter weather" on the 28th and "warm" on the 31st. Though there came a number of thaws in February, the deep snow went off slowly. On the 13th the ground showed for the first time since December 2d, but not until March 5th could Robbins report the snow entirely gone after the long winter siege.[8]

[1] *Ky. Gaz.*, 15 Feb 1805 in *Conn. Courant* (Hartford), 6 Mar 1805.
[2] *The journals of the expedition under the command of Capts. Lewis and Clark.* Nicholas Biddle, ed. Phila., 1814. Reprint: New York, The Heritage Press, 1962.
[3] *Phila. Med. & Phy. Jour.*, 2-1, (1805), 143.
[4] *Quebec Gazette* in *Boston Weekly Magazine*, 6 April 1805.
[5] J. Heckewelder.
[6] *Ky. Gaz.*, 15 Feb 1805.
[7] T. Robbins. *Diary*, 1, 247-51.
[8] *Idem.*

## A Snowy October in 1805

The White River Mission diary noticed:

Oct. 25. While busy with potato digging this afternoon, it began to snow hard.

26. It still continued to snow so that it looks as it does in mid-winter. The Indians were frightened on account of it. They said they had never seen the like, this time of year, in this place. . . . Later on we heard that in Fort Wayne, which is three days journey north of us, that the snow had been a foot deep on the day mentioned.[1]

In northwestern Pennsylvania close to the Ohio line, Rev. Robbins then at Mercer also experienced the October snowfall. His diary noted on the 24th: "Quite cold and stormy. It snowed most of the day." And the 27th: "The snow in the morning about three inches deep and most of it continued through the day."[2]

[1] L. Gipson, 387.
[2] T. Robbins, 1, 269.

## The Eventful Winter of 1806–07

This season provided four outstanding meteorological events: (1) A severe cold wave in January, (2) the famous Midwest Cold Friday of 6 February, (3) The first stages of the Great April Fool's Snowstorm in the Northeast, (4) and one of the most backward springs during this period.

The month of December produced some cold mornings at the Tuscarawas settlements, but no severely cold days. On the 7th the mercury was down to +14° and the next morning at an even zero. On the 14th the Heckewelder records indicate a low of −8°, followed by readings of +14° on the two following days. The rest of the month was quite mild—Christmas Day had a morning +34° and an afternoon +64°. We have no exact information about precipitation conditions during this month.[1]

New Year's Day opened with the mercury at zero, "a very cold morning," according to Heckewelder. Seasonable temperature and light snows followed with flocks of robins being reported among the snowflakes. After snow on the 14th and 15th a severe cold wave descended on the area.

The record follows:

|  | Sunrise | 1400–1500 | Sunset |  |
|---|---|---|---|---|
| Jan. 16 | 17° | 20° | 18° | Inch and half snow. Dark day |
| 17 | − 3° | 25 | 20 | Cloudy day |
| 18 | − 2° | +11 | +17 | Clear & cold excessive |
| 19 | −17° | +19 | +14 | Excessive cold. Clear forenoon, cloudy afternoon. |
| 20 | − 3° | +35 | +32 | Clear morning. Afternoon strong S.W. wind. Air somewhat smoky. |

## Cold Friday in the West—6 February 1807

Cold Friday of 1807 in the Midwest has often been confused with the New England Cold Friday of 1810. Many writers of Yankee origin when compiling local histories of the Ohio and Kentucky areas have thought of the two as the same event, as occurring on identical days. Hence much confusion as to the dating and the actual happenings have entered local tradition. For the meteorologist, however, the Heckewelder records clearly establish the date as 6 February 1807 and supply valuable data as to the circumstances.

Dr. Samuel P. Hildreth, the historian of pioneer days in Ohio and long the weatherman at Marietta, gave testimony when recalling the day: "I was then practising medicine at Belpre (on the Ohio near Marietta) and have cause to remember it; for on riding a few miles that morning, one of my ears was badly frosted. The Ohio River from being filled with floating ice the day before, was so frozen firmly in one night that loaded teams crossed the next day on its surface."[2]

Historian Richard Collins also devoted considerable space to Cold Friday in his *Historical Sketch of the Climate of Kentucky:*

> On two occasions, only, since the commencement of the present century, the mercury has been caused to sink sixty degrees within twelve hours by these cold winds. The first occurred on the evening of the 6th of February, 1807, which was Thursday [incorrect; 6th was Friday]. At nightfall, it was mild, but cloudy; after night it commenced raining, with a high west wind. The rain soon changed to snow, which continued to fall rapidly to the depth of six inches; but the wind, which moved at the rate of a hurricane, soon lifted and dispersed the clouds, and, within the short space of twelve hours from the close of a very mild Thursday, all Kentucky was treated to a gentle rain, a violent snow-storm, and a bright, sunshiny morning, so bitterly cold that by acclamation it was termed "Cold Friday." [3]

Fortunately, the Heckewelder records are complete for this period and provide a good scientific sounding of the intensity of the famous frigid air mass that swept out of the Great Lakes area and across Ohio and Kentucky that day.[4] The total descent of the mercury at Gnadenhutten amounted to 59 degrees, and this bears out Collins' statement, though this remarkable descent did not actually occur within the space of 12 hours. The 6th of February was truly a zero day. Very likely Cold Friday was a zero day throughout all Ohio except possibly along the lee shore of Lake Erie where some modification of the air in crossing the lake usually occurs. Heckewelder's full record for the period of extreme cold follows:

|  | Sunrise | 1400–1500 | Sunset |  |
|---|---|---|---|---|
| Jan. 31 | 20° | 31° | 24° | Snow 2½ inches. Cloudy day. |
| Feb. 1 | − 7 | 34 | 20 | Cold morning. Clear day. Cloudy evening. |
| 2 | 23 | 22 | 17 | High west wind, blows hard evening. |
| 3 | 0 | 27 | 20 | Clear afternoon. Cloudy afternoon. |
| 4 | 7 | 22 | 16 | Cloudy morning. Clear afternoon. |
| 5 | 1 | 28 | 29 | Dark morning. Snows in afternoon one inch. |
| 6 | −11 | − 6 | −11 | Storm all day. West wind. |
| 7 | −10 | + 7 | + 5 | Dark cold day. |
| 8 | − 8 | 23 | 13 | Fine clear morning & day. |
| 9 | −10 | 32 | 27 | Fine day. *Was coldest night.* |
| 10 | 20 | 41 | 34 | Cloudy morning. Fine Day. Thaws. |

At Cincinnati the Mansfield records showed the mercury descending to −11° at the time of the February cold, and we assume that this occurred on 6 February.[5] This was not as low as reached in 1797 during a night of intense radiation, but is about the lowest level the mercury can reach at the Queen City under an advective cold wave situation.

The prolonged cold period caused extreme ice jam conditions in the Niagara River at the exit of Lake Erie. Ice bridges formed on which horses and loaded wagons could cross.[6] This situation was unknown before and would not occur again until the severe winter of 1821.

### The End of March Snow in 1807

The third major event of the winter came in late March to prolong an already lengthy winter. This was a storm of great stature that spread a mantle of record depth for so late in the season from the Mississippi River to New England and beyond. Our most southwesterly report came from Vincennes in southern Indiana where David Thomas in his *Early Travels in Indiana* stated: "In the remarkable snow of 3 mo. 31, 1807, it was about eleven inches deep. No snow in the area for the previous eight years had exceeded five inches in depth." [7]

The Heckewelder weather diary contained a complete report on the stormy conditions that prevailed in east-central Ohio as March turned into April:

| March 28 | 24° | 49° | 43° | Thunders and rains hard all afternoon. |
|---|---|---|---|---|
| 29 | 47 | 37 | 32 | Rains, river rises, stormy day. |
| 30 | 19 | 35 | 32 | Snow in the afternoon. River rises. |
| 31 | 24 | 33 | 29 | 5 inches snow. Stormy day. |
| April 1 | 17 | 44 | 33 | Snow melts. Sugar sap runs some. |
| 2 | 28 | 31 | 27 | Snows from N.E. 2 inches. |
| 3 | 18 | 34 | 29 | Snows one inch. |
| 4 | 24 | 39 | 34 | Fine day. Snow melts. |
| 5 | 15 | 46 | 39 | Fine day. Sugar sap runs very well. |
| 6 | 31 | 52 | 42 | Fine day. Saps runs well.[8] |

The snowstorm gained momentum as it raced northeastward and drew Atlantic moisture into its circulation. Also a leeshore snowburst mechanism came into operation along the borders of Lake Ontario. Snowfalls became excessive in the hills of western New York where there already had been great depths on the ground from February and March snow. Pomroy Jones in his nostalgic *Annals of Oneida County* related that the snow about Annsville measured five feet deep when Elias Brewster moved his family to the locality on 1 April 1807. The author, measuring the snow cover in the forests around his home on 7 April, found the ground buried under four and a half feet of compact snow.[9] In St. Lawrence County the spring of 1807 was long remembered as an especially backward season, followed by a cold summer in which little corn ma-

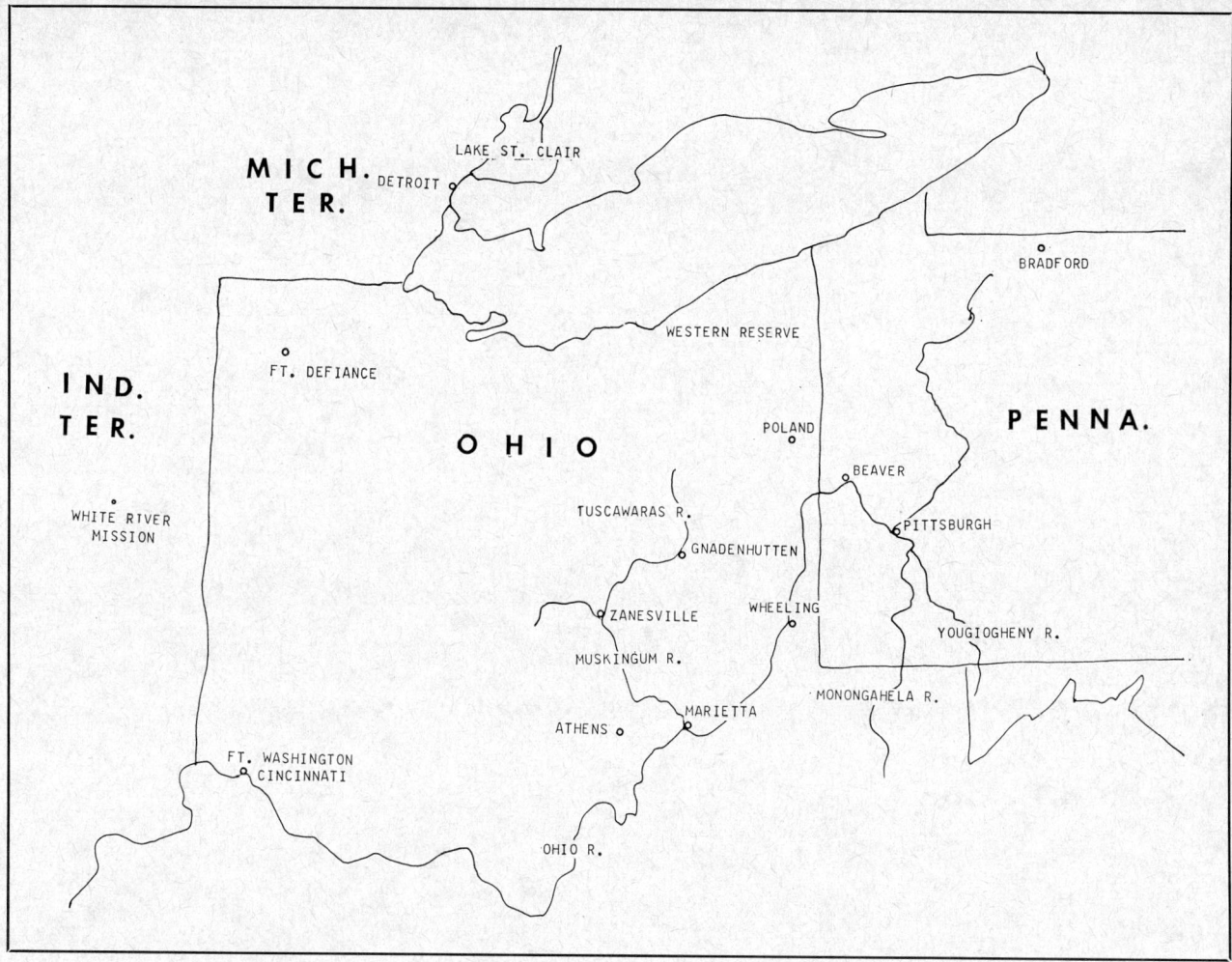

tured.[10] In fact, this year inaugurated a series of cold summers that would not end until the near-disastrous season of 1816. Of this series of cold crop years, those of 1807, 1812, and 1816 were the standouts.

Back in Ohio the Heckewelder records show May as a cold month with the mercury below freezing at sunrise on seven mornings. On the 3d the temperature stood at 19°, a "very hard frost" occurred, and as late as the 19th the mercury dropped down to 29° with a frost. The "Ice Saints of May" reigned from the 7th to 12th with only one morning above freezing.[11]

Even as the summer solstice approached, winter gave up its grip reluctantly. Snow banks were still remaining in May in northern sections, and ice floating in waterways in early June. Residents along the Niagara River reported ice to be seen in the river on June 4th, and the last floes did not disappear in Buffalo Harbor until the 6th though navigation had opened on June 1st.[12]

[1] George W. Mindling. *Weather headlines in Ohio.* Columbus, Ohio State Eng. Exp. Station—Bulletin No. 120, 1944.

[2] Samuel Hildreth. *The Medical Repository* (New York). 6 (1809), 360.

[3] Richard H. Collins. Historical sketch of the climate of Kentucky. *Hist. of Ky.,* 1, 394.

[4] J. Heckewelder, Ms. Met. Obs.

[5] Jared Mansfield. *Med. & Agri. Reg.* (Boston). Sept 1807, 335.

[6] *Nat. Int.,* 26 Jan 1821.

[7] David Thomas. *Travels through the western country in 1816.* Auburn, N. Y., David Rumsey, 1819, 109.

[8] J. Heckewelder, Ms. Met. Obs.

[9] Pomroy Jones. *Annals and recollections of Oneida County.* Rome, N. Y., 1851. 74.

[10] *N. Y. Regents, Annual Report 1852,* 367.

[11] J. Heckewelder.

[12] Franklin B. Hough. *Results of Met. Obs . . . Academies in N.Y. State.* Albany, Weed, Parsons and Co., 1872, 2, 370.

## THE OHIO COUNTRY CONTROVERSY: 1781–1810

What was the nature of the climate in the country west of the Alleghany Mountains? Was it warmer than along the Atlantic seaboard? This posed a question that intrigued many men of the Revolutionary era, among them Thomas Jefferson. Arguments pro and con were to spark many lively exchanges in the press and to enliven many discussions at scientific meetings for years to come. No doubt, the prevailing favorable view of the question had something to do with generating the Ohio Fever which raged throughout the older states along the Atlantic seaboard in the first decades of the new century.

Though Jefferson traveled no more than 50 miles west of his beloved Monticello in central Virginia, he constantly sought for information as to conditions in the vast territory that his native state claimed extending westward to the Mississippi River and northward to the Great Lakes. He questioned all travelers from the region as to the facts of climate, among other geographical subjects, and he searched the literature for clues. When later in position to do so, he sent several well-equipped scientific expeditions beyond the Mississippi River into the newly-purchased Louisiana Territory with a study of meteorological conditions high on the agenda of mission.

Jefferson composed his famous *Notes on the State of Virginia* in the early 1780's. Here he attempted to describe the geography, flora, fauna, and human resources of his native colony and state. These discussions appeared first in a Paris edition of 1785 and a London edition soon followed.[1]

Though apparently not widely circulated in America, the ideas expressed therein about the climate of the Ohio Country received extensive dissemination 15 years later when Constantin Francois de Chasseboeuf, Comte de Volney, published an account of his sojourn in the United States between October 1795 and June 1798 during which he actually traveled westward from Washington to Vincennes on the Wabash in Indiana.[2] Volney was well aware of Jefferson's ideas from reading *Notes on the State of Virginia,* through a letter on the subject from Jefferson in January 1797, and as a result of personal conversations in the summer of 1797 when Volney visited Monticello on his western trip.

Here are Jefferson's words on the subject that touched off the controversy destined to rage for many years:

> In an extensive country, it will of course be expected that the climate is not the same in all its parts. It is remarkable that, proceeding on the same parallel of latitude westwardly, the climate becomes colder in like manner as when you proceed northwardly. This continues to be the case till you attain the summit of the Alleghany, which is the highest land between the ocean and the Mississippi. From thence, descending in the same latitude to the Mississippi, the change reverses; and, if we may believe travellers, it becomes warmer there than it is in the same latitude on the sea side. Their testimony is strengthened by the vegetables and animals which subsist and multiply there naturally, and do not on our sea coast. Thus Catalpas grow spontaneously on the Mississippi as far as the latitude of 37°. and reeds as far as 38°. Perroquets even winter on the Sioto, in the 39th degree of latitude. In the summer of 1779, when the thermometer was at 90° at Monticello, and 96 at Williamsburgh, it was 110°. at Kaskaskia.[3]

Volney expanded on this Jeffersonian surmise. His work published in 1804 contained the following opinion:

> The climate of the basin of the Ohio and of the Mississippi is less cold by three degrees of latitude than that of the Atlantic Coast. . . . This is one of those singularities, that deserves so much the more attention, as I do not know that it has been described with all its circumstances.[4]

Yet Volney made use of no essential new material except to enumerate other plants found in Ohio. He had attempted to gather information on the winds and weather in America through a circular letter in the press, but this apparently elicited little of real meteorological value.[5] He employed the published writings of Dr. Benjamin Rush of Philadelphia and Prof. Samuel Williams of Vermont, neither of whom had ever visited Ohio.[6] Some of his material came from a "literary gentleman" in New York City, presumably Noah Webster, then the weather-conscious editor of the *Herald*.[7]

To back up his argument, Volney referred to the cultivation of cotton at Cincinnati and Vincennes and the presence in this area of the catalpa, sassafras, papaw, and Illinois nut. In order to determine the reasons for the supposed greater warmth, Volney sought to make an investigation of "the complete system of currents of air, that prevail throughout the year in the United States." He concluded that there was a much greater prevalence of southerly winds in the Mississippi and Ohio Valleys than along the Atlantic seaboard where he had often observed northeasterly currents dominating. But, according to Volney, this zonal difference ended at the Great Lakes because north of that physiographic feature his evidence pointed to the interior of Canada as being colder than the seaboard. Volney gave no reason for the circulation system he had described.[8]

Volney's ideas received surprisingly wide circulation in the young nation eager to learn about itself. A writer in 1808 in the New York *Medical Repository,* one of the leading scientific journals of the day, echoed Volney in his paper: "The Geological, Topographical and Medical Information concerning the Eastern Part of Ohio.":

> Our climate is much more mild in the same degree of latitude, than eastward of the Alleghany Mountains. This is caused by the winds which are mostly up the river, or from southward or westward. (See Volney's account of this country.) I have rarely known a north-east storm here; that unfriendly wind seems to know that its bounds are the Alleghany Mountains.[9]

The first refutation of the ideas publicized by Volney came in 1810 from the Cincinnati physician and geographer, Daniel Drake, in his *Notices Concerning Cincinnati*. Here he stated:

> From which it appears that the opinion concerning the greater heat of this climate [Ohio Valley], first expressed by our late illustrious President [Jefferson], afterwards glanced at by Loskiel [*History of the Missions*], and since supported and extended by Mr. Volney, is not, at least, in its full extent correct. The former published his celebrated NOTES, at a time when but obscure accounts respecting this country had been received; the latter traveled here in 1796, and therefore should have possessed more correct information. He however seems to have been sometimes misled by a favorite and ingenious, but not unexceptionable hypothesis.[10]

William Darby in *The Emigrant's Guide to the Western and Southwestern States and Territories* (1818) also questioned the authenticity of Volney's views.[11] After spending a number of years about the lower Mississippi Valley covering some 20,000 miles afoot, Darby published a detailed, though primitive, geography containing both physical and economic information. Thoroughly familiar with the Ohio Valley country, he once referred to Volney's "innoxious vulgar error" concerning the climate of the region.[12]

The subject later received the attention of Dr. Lewis C. Beck of the Albany Institute who explored the subject in depth in a paper, read on 1 September 1823, before the meeting of the Institute. This comprised a distinguished group of men who played an important part in medical and scientific discussions of the day. They were especially concerned with meteorology, and numbered among their members at this time Joseph Henry, the emerging physicist, who was to play a leading role years later in the actual climatological exploration of the Mississippi Valley. Beck's paper was entitled: "An Examination of the Question, whether the Climate of the Valley of the Mississippi, under similar parallels of latitude, is warmer than that of the Atlantic Coast." Taking up all the evidence submitted by Volney, he disposed of each by making use of materials recently published on the specific subjects.[13]

As late as the 1840's Samuel Forry still combated Volney's idea. *The Climate of the United States and its Endemic Influences* (1843) formed the first scientific attempt to describe the climate of the U. S. by making use of the observations of the surgeons at the military posts throughout the country. "Written more than 40 years ago, when this savant made a flying visit through our country," Forry wrote about Volney's book, "it is still quoted by every writer on this topic. So barren of precise data, in truth is this work, that the author's only instrumental observations consist of a few thermometrical results obtained from a literary gentleman in New York, for which even he made no acknowledgment."[14]

Lorin Blodget apparently put the subject finally to rest in 1857 in his *Climatology of the United States,* long the authority on such matters:

> The early distinction between the Atlantic States and the Mississippi has been quite dropped, as the progress of observation has shown them to be essentially the same, or to differ only in unimportant particulars.

*****

The Ohio Valley at Cincinnati, the Atlantic coast at Norfolk, and the interior of New York at Rochester, may each be swept over by some general change,— of pressure, temperature, winds, or rain,—and influenced as uniformly as if they were all located within a circuit of a hundred miles.[15]

[1] Thomas Jefferson. *Notes on the State of Virginia.* Paris, 1785; London, 1787; Phila., 1788.
[2] Constantin Francois Chassebouef Comte de Volney. *View of the climate and soil of the United States of America.* London, J. Johnson, 1804.
[3] Thomas Jefferson. *Notes on the State of Virginia.* W. Peden, ed. Chapel Hill, Univ. North Carolina Press, 1955, 75.
[4] Volney, 146–47.
[5] N. Webster. *Notes,* 1, 406.
[6] Samuel Williams. *The natural and civil history of Vermont.* Walpole, N. H., I. Thomas & D. Carlisle, 1794.
  Benjamin Rush. *Medical inquiries and observations.* Phila., T. Dobson, 1796.
[7] *Volney,* 146–47.
[8] *Idem.*
[9] *Medical Repository* (N. Y.). **6** (1809), 351.
[10] Daniel Drake. *Notices concerning Cincinnati,* 15–17.
[11] W. Darby. *Emigrant's guide,* 147; 230–51.
[12] ———, *View of the U.S., historical, geographical, and statistical.* Phila., H. S. Tanner, 1828, 380.
[13] *Trans. Albany Institute.* 1 (1830), 34–54.
[14] Samuel Forry. *The climate of the United States and its endemic influences.* N. Y., J. & H. G. Langley, 1842.
[15] Lorin Blodget. *Climatology of the U.S.,* 126, 134.
  Emmet F. Horine. *Daniel Drake (1785–1852) Pioneer physician of the Midwest.* Phila., Univ. of Penna. Press, 1961, 101–02.

## THE WINTERS OF THE WAR OF 1812

The War of 1812 must have been equally as unsatisfactory to the participants as it has been to its historians. The same may be said for its meteorology. There appeared to have been no weather records made in the field or even close to the scene of hostilities. In fact, it was the lack of such that stimulated Surgeon General James Tilton in 1814 to issue a directive that all post surgeons maintain a "diary of the weather" and forward these quarterly to Washington.[1] Thus was inaugurated the first Federally-sponsored attempt to gather facts about the weather and climate of the United States.

Our reliance for information about weather conditions during these winters must be placed on sketchy diary information, a few general dispatches, and two meteorological registers maintained at some distance from the operations. The scene of winter campaigning in 1812–13 and 1813–14 stretched from the Detroit area at the western end of Lake Erie eastward to the northern end of Lake Champlain in New York State. The final months of the war comprising the first part of the winter of 1814–15 produced no campaigning in the North, though the soldiers were still in the field on the alert until news of the peace arrived in February 1815. The winter season of 1814–15 developed into a severe one, equal to the winter of 1811–12 which had preceded the opening of hostilities. It was fortunate for the troops opposing each other in the North that they had not been called into the field a year earlier nor required to continue active campaigning during the severe days of January and February 1815.

Of the meteorological registers which have survived, one was of particular value in describing conditions in the western theater of operations. At Beersheba, in Tuscawaras County of east-central Ohio, located about 80 miles south of Cleveland and Lake Erie, the records originally commenced by John Heckewelder at the Moravian settlements were continued by G. G. Miller and periodically transmitted to the Moravian headquarters at Bethlehem, Pennsylvania, and eventually found their way to the library of the American Philosophical Society in Philadelphia.[2] These observations sampled the same air masses and general weather conditions that the troops operating in the winter of 1812–13 some 150 miles to the northwest of Beersheba experienced.

The temperature conditions marked by the Miller records can be considered close approximates to conditions existing along Lake Erie, but precipitation amounts, especially snowfall depths, might vary greatly. The general weather map situations for the area would be the same with both points experiencing related passages of cold fronts and cyclonic storms.

The Canadian campaign in the summer and fall of 1812 produced a series of American disasters. First the U. S. post at Machilimackinac Island in the Northwest fell. Then General Hull surrendered Detroit without firing a shot. Fort Dearborn at the head of Lake Michigan was the next to go. To retrieve the situation, General William Henry Harrison took command of the Northwest Army in the autumn with the express orders to take Detroit. A force was assembled near Toledo at the western end of Lake Erie to move forward toward Detroit, but while enroute the plodding advance guard became ambushed and decisively defeated by the energetically-led British who had sortied from their frontier base at Fort Malden across the river from Detroit. The affair took place at Frenchtown on the Raisin River not far from present-day Monroe, Michigan. This setback coupled with an adverse turn of the weather caused an abandonment of the American plans, and the entire force fell back to the main base at Ft. Meigs near the mouth of the Maumee River.

### Winter Weather: 1812–13

The general weather conditions during the preparation for this drive can be gathered from the Beersheba weather records. December 1812 was a generally cold month. Winter had set in on the 9th when a northwest wind brought some snow and freezing temperatures: down to +5° on the 10th and consistently below freezing until the 16th when a "snow of some inches" fell. Another cold front arrived on the 19th bringing "stormy, snow shower, with great storm from NW in P.M." The mercury stood at +10° on the 20th and at +8° on the 21st. The cold spell continued with only slight moderation through the 28th when another cold air mass brought the morning reading to +7°. But then a thaw came on with the mercury rising into the 50's on 30 and 31 December and on the 1st of January.

Colder air returned on the 2d (25°), sinking the mercury eventually down to +5° on the 5th. Another energetic cold air mass invaded on the afternoon of the 7th (+9°) and morning of the 8th (−10°). "A great snowstorm" raged on the afternoon of the 9th. Still another Arctic outbreak followed on the 10th with −1° and on the 11th to −17°—"clear and windy"—certainly a wintry ten-day period.

Conditions moderated after this with seasonable temperatures for five days. Then came a string of thawing afternoons from the 16th to the 22d with the mercury generally in the upper 30's or low 40's. On the day of the ambush battle at Frenchtown the Beersheba conditions were: "+8°, 45°, 28°—clear, windy, hazy." A marked frontal system moved across the area on the 24th. The mercury shot up to 62° accompanied by phenomena described as: "stormy, thunder, fog, hard rain P.M." Next day it rained hard, then sleeted, and the ice on the Tuscarawa River broke up, having been solid since mid-December. The close of January brought a return to wintry conditions: deep snow on the 26th, mercury at −3° on the 27th and at −10° on the 30th. On the final day it "snowed all day and some at night."

February 1813 produced much warmer conditions than January. In fact, there were only three days on which a thaw did not occur in the afternoon. These were the 1st, 13th, and 15th. The lowest reading of 7° came on the 16th. The principal cold spell held from the 13th to the 19th, during which morning readings were well below freezing, but afternoon conditions were generally moderate. The mercury soared to 62° on the last day of February. There were no severe storms of snow this month as there had been in January.[3]

### The Advance on Detroit: January 1813

The progress of the American Army toward Detroit had been assisted by the cold and snow cover of December, but the end-of-year thaw greatly hampered the advance. General Harrison in early January referred to: "A most unfortunate rain which has broken up the roads so as to render them impassable for the Artillery altho it is fixed on sleds—The whole train is stopped 25 miles from this (Hdq. of the N.W. Army)—I have reason to believe that the Miami River has broken up."[4]

At mid-month he advised Washington: "Our hopes were again checked by a general thaw succeeded by a very deep snow when the ground was in a soft state. . . . It is however cold again & we calculate upon being able to use with effect the sleds in considerable number of which I had caused to be prepared."[5]

The snow was stated to be about 8 inches deep on 14 January, and much of this remained on the ground for the next week. In fact, the deep snow at the ambush was credited with hindering the escape of the defeated troops[6]—some 500 Americans were taken prisoners and some 400 were either killed or massacred by the British and Indians in the disaster. The February thaw put an end to any attempts to retaliate. A dispatch of 10 February from Dover, Ohio, stated: "The weather is very unfavorable—the rivers are nearly impassable and the roads are breaking up."[7]

The ending of winter conditions led General Armstrong to remark on 5 March 1813: "It would appear that Malden (opposite Detroit in Ontario) can only be successfully approached by the route you are now upon, at two seasons of the year—Mid-winter & mid-summer. The former is gone, and to wait for the latter would be hardly less disastrous than defeat itself."[8]

### Western New York State: 1813–14

The American forces fought on the defensive at the western end of Lake Erie during spring and summer of 1813 until events took a dramatic turn. It had become readily evident that control of Lake Erie dictated control of the land. Accordingly, a number of shipwrights had been sent to the vicinity of Erie, Pennsylvania, through the deep snows of February and March which had piled up along the lee shores of the lake. By mid-summer their ships were ready for combat. Admiral Perry's decisive—"we have met the enemy

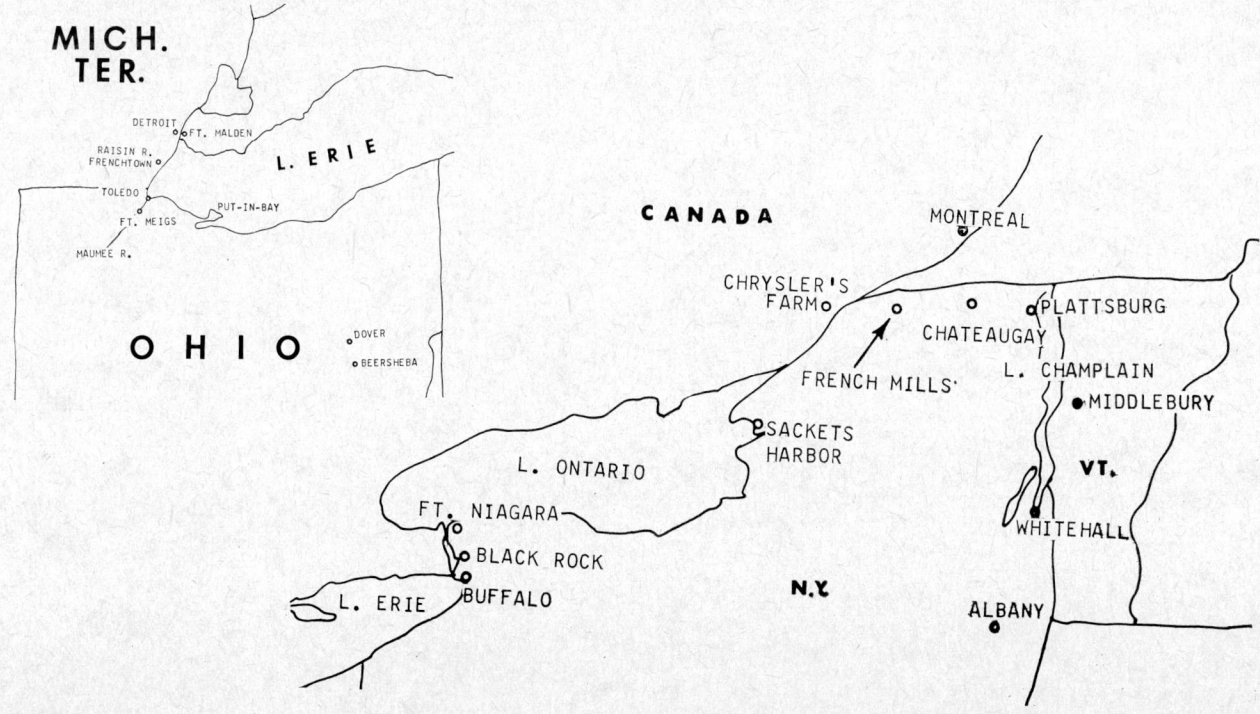

and they are ours"—victory over the British fleet occurred at summer's end on 10 September 1813. This forced the British to evacuate Detroit and Malden at the western end of the lake and to fall back to the Niagara frontier area at the western end of Lake Ontario. Here the British did some successful raiding around the time of the winter solstice, seizing Fort Niagara from the Americans on 18 December and burning Buffalo and Black Rock on 29–30 December. The weather proved favorable during both these operations.

Winter made an early fling in the season of 1813–14 when in late November and early December the temperature dropped to +8° on both the 29th of November and on the 3d of December. These were the readings at Beersheba, Ohio, some 250 miles southwest of the scene of the December skirmishes. But thereafter, a southerly circulation prevailed, and an open midwinter ensued. On the day of the loss of Fort Niagara, the thermometer in Ohio read 36°, 42°, and 36° with no cold weather either before or after. From the 23d of December to the 29th, the mercury rose into the 40's every afternoon, and on the 28th, when Buffalo was seized, read: 36°, 48°, and 42°. There were no severe storms during December.[9]

January continued to enjoy the mild regime. The temperature did not drop below +10° on the Ohio thermometer again until the very last day of the month. January had some snows, but none marked as severe or deep. February commenced cold at the start, but then another very warm period followed, reaching 65° on the 19th. A cold wave at the end of February caused the only below-zero reading of the winter (−2° on 1 March). But it soon warmed again and March closed with a 76° reading.[10]

## Northern New York State: 1813–14

Farther east the Americans planned an ambitious campaign for the fall and winter. A general advance on Montreal was ordered with General Wilkinson proceeding from the eastern end of Lake Ontario at Sackets Harbor down the St. Lawrence, while General Wade Hampton was to move northward from the Plattsburg area on Lake Champlain. Wilkinson left his base on 17 October with 8,000 men. His advance guard of about 2,000 men was checked on 11 November by a smaller British force of 800 at Chrysler's Farm on the north side of the St. Lawrence about 90 miles from Montreal. Hampton moved northwestward in anticipation of a juncture with Wilkinson's forces, but did not push very energetically. He halted after fighting an indecisive affair with smaller British forces at Chateaugay. When he received news of Wilkinson's check, Hampton abandoned his advance and fell back toward Plattsburg. In turn, when informed of this, Wilkinson quickly decided on 13 November to go into winter quarters at French Mills on the Salmon River. Thus ended the venture, and the troops commenced preparations for what a northern winter might bring. "On the arrival of the army at French Mills, the weather became intensely severe and remained so till the 23d January," we are informed by an early historian of the area.[11]

Our checkpoint for meteorological conditions in this theater of operations was supplied by Prof. Frederick Hall of Middlebury College in Vermont. Situated on the eastern side of Lake Champlain about 45 miles southeast of Hampton's camp at Plattsburg and about 120 miles from Wilkinson's camp, Hall's thermometer sampled the same air masses as passed over the two camps of Americans in northern New York. Prof. Hall maintained his records at Middlebury from 1812 at least until 1817. He published these in the local periodical, *The Literary and Philosophical Repertory,* which he edited. Middlebury College also served as the center for a collection of meteorological reports from other colleges such as Williams, Yale, Harvard, and Bowdoin—these were also published from time to time.[12] Here was an early effort by individuals to set up a weather reporting system.

In the Champlain Valley a mild open winter prevailed in 1813–14 as in Ohio. Winter set in on December 20th at Middlebury.

January 1814 produced only four mornings with below zero-temperatures, and February had a like number. The coldest period came at the very end of January and during the first days of February. The mercury dipped to −12° on 31 January and to −10° on both the 3d and 4th of February. The latter was the only zero day of the winter with three readings of −10°, −6°, and −10°. After the 10th of February the mercury did not descend below +10° and was generally above freezing each afternoon. Readings made at Albany by Dr. Eights agreed that this had been a mild season with a winter's minimum only −6° registered there.[12]

## The Final Half-Winter: 1814–15

It was fortunate for the troops that there was no campaigning in the North during the winter of 1814–15, for it proved a severe season. Winter set in on December 20th with the arrival of an Arctic air mass which dropped the mercury to +11° on the 20th and to −6° on the 21st. It continued cold through the end of the year except for a brief thaw on 28–29 December. The Albany thermometer went down to +2° for its December low. The frozen surface of Lake Champlain posed a threat to the American fleet wintering at Whitehall at the southern extremity. Fears were expressed in the press that the enemy might make an incursion over the ice in an attempt to destroy the vessels, but this did not materialize.[13]

Dr. James Mann, a prominent surgeon of Massachusetts serving with the American forces, concluded his survey of disease as related to climatic conditions with the following weather summary plus some philosophical thoughts:

> The weather during the past winter was very changeable. After a very cold period in the month of January, and during part of the month of February, the transition from cold to very warm, was sudden. This month anticipated spring, so as to dissolve the ice in the fresh ponds in the country. The change again was so great in the month of March, from very pleasant to severe cold, that these ponds were again frozen; and during the last month, the daily transitions of weather were great; and these sudden variations continued into May. These transitions are believed to have been one cause of this epidemic. To search for remote predisponent causes, floating on the wings of the wind, is like building castles in the air. Atmospheric influences, independent of hot and dry, cold and wet, are out of the bounds of our circumscribed knowledge, and were we able to comprehend their nature, could we by any means control their powers, so as to obviate their effects upon the human constitution? [14]

[1] Thomas G. Mower. *N.Y. Jour. Medicine*, 2 (1844), 135; E. E. Hume. The foundations of American meteorology by the U. S. Army Medical Department. *Bulletin of the history of medicine.* (Balto.) 8 (1940), 202–38.
Joseph H. Hagerty. Dr. James Tilton: 1745–1822. *Weatherwise* (Boston), 15-3 (June 1962), 124.
[2] John Heckewelder and G. G. Miller. Ms. Met. Obs. (Amer. Phil. Soc.).
[3] *Idem.*
[4] William H. Harrison. Hdq. N.W. Army, Portage River, 15 miles from Miami Rapids. Jan. 1813. *Document transcriptions of the War of 1812 in the Northwest.* Richard C. Knopf, ed. Columbus, The Ohio Historical Society, 1957, 1, 38.
[5] *Ibid.*, 1, 30.
[6] *Ibid.*, 2, 235, 19.
[7] *Ibid.*, 1, 240.
[8] *Ibid.*, 1, 83.
[9] J. Heckewelder and G. G. Miller.
[10] *Idem.*
[11] Franklin B. Hough. *A history of St. Lawrence and Franklin Counties.* Albany, Little & Co., 1853, 648.
[12] *Trans. Albany Institute*, 3.
[13] *Vermont Mirror* (Middlebury), 21 Dec 1814, in *N.Y. Spectator*, 4 Jan 1815.
[14] James Mann. *Medical sketches of the campaign of 1812, 13, 14.* Dedham, Mass., H. Mann & Co., 1816, 310.

## THE COLD AND SNOW OF WINTER IN 1818

"Everyone says it was a cold winter, and some of the older inhabitants say they never experienced a colder," reported the *Detroit Gazette*. "The weather that may properly be called winter has continued nearly four months. It commenced about the 20th of November and ended about the 10th of March. At four times the mercury fell below zero; on the 21st of December it was 10° below; on the 12th of January it was 4° below; on the 9th of February 13° below, and on the 23d of the same it was 12° below. . . . Our first shower of snow was on the 18th of November, but the ground was not covered until the 7th of December, and the greatest depth of snow was about ten inches, which we are informed by the old inhabitants was deeper than ordinary. . . ." [1] The shores of the Great Lakes were commencing to receive American emigrants after the terms of the Treaty of 1815 had settled at one time both the Indian and British problems, but little was known definitely as to the nature of the winter climate of this inviting region.

The upper Ohio Valley also experienced as wintry a spell of weather as could be remembered—general opinion agreed that the Old Northwest had not undergone such extreme conditions at any time since the country was first settled in 1788. Dr. Hildreth at Marietta described the severe snowstorm of February 3d: "it commenced during the night and continued for 12 hours during which 26 inches fell on the level." This was 10 to 12 inches deeper than had fallen at the Ohio River village to the knowledge of the settlers, and to this day has been equaled only by the Great Appalachian Storm in late November of 1950 in this part of the Valley. The wind in the 1818 storm came from northeast and east, indicating the passage of the center southward, probably across Tennessee and North Carolina. Its track carried the belt of heavy snow into Virginia also. The winds increased to gale force as the deepening storm center "turned the corner" near Norfolk and came roaring up the Atlantic seaboard as a violent northeaster. Petersburg in southern Virginia experienced 18 inches, and Norfolk press accounts referred to "hurricane winds." [3] There were no other snow depth reports from the Ohio Valley, but we do know that Hudson in the Western Reserve measured a cover of 20 inches on the ground this month. [4]

Following the deep snow, the circulation stirred up by the developing storm drew severe Arctic air into the Midwest—the deep snow cover assisted the radiative process to create some very low temperature readings. At Marietta the mercury chilled to −20° on the morning of the 9th, and at 0630 on the next morning slumped further to −22°. [5] This compared closely with the all-time low of −24° reached at Marietta in January 1852. Dr. Hildreth related that the intense cold caused snapping of trees, killed the peach orchards, and destroyed the branches of the sassafras and spice bushes. The rare spectacle of Arctic sea smoke was noticed steaming above open holes in the river ice. The Ohio at Marietta had been closed to navigation for four weeks at this time.[6]

At Chillicothe farther downstream the thermometer at the U. S. Land Office descended to $-10°$, $-21°$ and $-11°$ on the 9th, 10th, and 11th at observations taken 15 minutes before sunrise. "An awful silence reigned," noted observer Williams. "The air was as still as though it were congealed into a solid mass."[7] Vincennes, Indiana, registered $-16°$.[8]

Extreme cold readings were reported from northern sections also. At Green Bay, Wisconsin, a reading of $-35°$ in February chilled the soldiers at Fort Howard.[9] At Montreal successive readings of $-31°$, $-32°$, and $-29°$ concluded what had been a very bitter January there.[10] In southwestern Pennsylvania a figure of $-26°$ was reported in Fayette County and a $-24°$ at Meadville in the northwest, according to the press.[11]

[1] *Detroit Gazette,* 10 April 1818.
[2] S. Hildreth. *Amer. Jour. Sci.,* **11**–2 (Oct. 1826), 232.
[3] *Nat. Int.,* 16 & 19 Feb 1818.
[4] S. Hildreth. *Amer. Jour. Sci.,* **49**–2 (Oct. 1845), 283.
[5] *Ibid.,* **30**–1 (July 1836), 56.
[6] *Ibid.,* **11**–2 (Oct. 1826), 232.
[7] *Niles Weekly Register* (Balto.), Supp. No. 15 (1818), 5.
[8] David Thomas. *Travels through the western country,* 107.
[9] *Detroit Gaz.,* 3 April 1818.
[10] Montreal press in W. Plumer, Ms. Met. Obs. (Harvard).
[11] *Huntington* (Pa.) *Gaz.,* 5 Mar 1818.

## ON THE SUPPOSED CHANGE IN THE TEMPERATURE OF WINTER

### Noah Webster

(Read before the Connecticut Academy of Sciences, 1799, with Supplementary Remarks, written and read before the Academy in 1806).

It is a popular opinion that the temperature of the winter season, in northern latitudes, has suffered a material change, and become warmer in modern, than it was in ancient times. This opinion has been adopted and maintained by many writers of reputation; as the Abbe Du Bois, Buffon, Hume, Gibbon, Jefferson, Holyoke, Williams; indeed, I know not whether any person, in this age, has ever questioned the fact.[1]

* * * * *

From all I can discover, in regard to the seasons, in ancient and modern times, I see no reason to conclude with Dr. Williams,\* that the heat of the earth is increasing. It appears that all the alterations in a country, in consequence of clearing and cultivation, result only in making a different distribution of heat and cold, moisture and dry weather, among the several seasons. The clearing of lands opens them to the sun, their moisture is exhaled, they are more heated in summer, but more cold in winter near the surface; the temperature becomes unsteady, and the seasons irregular. This is the fact. A smaller degree of cold, if steady, will longer preserve snow and ice, than a greater degree, under frequent changes. Hence we solve the phenomenon, of more constant ice and snow in the early ages; which I believe to have been the case. It was not the degree, but the steadiness of the cold which produced this effect. Every forest in America exhibits this phenomenon. We have, in the cultivated districts, deep snow to-day, and none to-morrow; but the same quantity of snow falling in the woods, lies there till spring. The same fact, on a larger scale, is observed in the ice of our rivers. This will explain all the appearances of the seasons, in ancient and modern times, without resorting to the unphilosophical hypothesis of a general increase of heat.[2]

\* Dr. Samuel Williams, former professor and weather observer at Harvard, migrated to Vermont in 1788 and wrote a chapter on the American climate in *The natural and civil history of Vermont (1793)*.

* * * * *

From a careful comparison of these facts, it appears that the weather, in modern winters, is more consistent, than when the earth was covered with wood, at the first settlement of Europeans in the country; that the warm weather of autumn extends further into the winter months, and the cold weather of winter and spring encroaches upon the summer; that the wind being more variable, snow is less permanent, and perhaps the same remark may be applicable to the ice of the rivers. These effects seem to result necessarily from the greater quantity of heat accumulated in the earth in summer, since the ground has been cleared of wood, and exposed to the rays of the sun; and to the greater depth of frost in the earth in winter, by the exposure of its uncovered surface to the cold atmosphere.

But we can hardly infer, from the facts that have yet been collected, that there is, in modern times, an actual diminution of the aggregate amount of cold in winter, on either continent.[3]

[1] Noah Webster. *A collection of papers on political, literary, and moral subjects.* New York, Webster & Clark, 1843. 119.
[2] *Ibid.,* 148.
[3] *Ibid.,* 162.

# A WINTER ANTHOLOGY

The Governour's Discomfiture: 1705 .......................... 241

A Winter Tragedy in New York Bay: 1705/06 ............... 241

The Great Snow of 1717
    John Winthrop: The Prodigious Storms of Snow ............ 242
    Cotton Mather: An Horrid Snow ......................... 243

A Sermon Preached at Naraganset, March 15th. A.D. 1740, 1. .. 244

A Winter at Philadelphia with Peter Kalm: 1749–50 .......... 245

St. John de Crèvecoeur: A Snow Storm as it Affects the American Farmer 1778 ......................................... 247

Observations on Snow: 1789 ................................ 251

With Lewis and Clark at Fort Mandan: 1804–05 .............. 252

With William Dunbar on the "Washita River" to the Hot Springs of Arkansas: 1804–05 ................................ 262

Cold Friday in New Hampshire: 19 January 1810 ............. 268

Springtime at Quebec: 1816 ................................ 268

The Luminous Snowstorm: January 1817 ..................... 270

The New Haven, Connecticut, Temperature Record: 1780–1870 .. 272

A Connecticut Snowfall Record: 1779–1820 ................... 278

# A WINTER ANTHOLOGY

## 1705
### THE GOVERNOUR'S DISCOMFITURE
Samuel Sewall

> Samuel Sewall (b. Bishopstoke, England; d. Boston, Mass., 1730). Born of New England parents, Sewall returned with his family to Boston c. 1661 and graduated from Harvard, 1671. Active in politics, he held many legislative and judicial posts in the colony throughout his life. He is remembered chiefly as a writer for his diary which covers the period 1674–1729 with a gap of about eight years, 1677–85. It is an incomparable picture of the mind and life of a New England Puritan and his society in this period. Most of the important meteorological and natural events of his lifetime are mentioned in the entries.
>
> Source: Diary of Samuel Sewall 1674–1729. *Collections of the Massachusetts Historical Society* (Boston). Ser. 5, **5**–**7** (1878–82).

Thorsday, Jan$^y$. 11$^{th}$. The Gov$^r$ and his Lady essaying to come from Charlestown to Boston in their Slay, 4 Horses, two Troopers riding before them, First the Troopers fell into the water, and then the Gov$^r$ making a stand, his four Horses fell in, and the Two Horses behind were drown'd, the Slay pressing them down. They were pull'd up upon the Ice, and there lay dead, a sad Spectacle. Many came from Charlestown with Boards, planks, Ropes &c. and sav'd the other Horses. Tis a wonderfull Mercy That the Gov$^r$, his Lady, Driver, Postilion, Troopers escaped all safe.

January, 19. 170$\frac{5}{6}$ The Gov$^r$ coming to Town, the way being difficult by Banks of Snow, his Slay was turn's upon one side against the Fence next Cambridge, and all in it thrown out, Governour's Wigg thrown off, his head had some hurt; and my Son's Elbow. The Horses went away with the foundation and left the Superstructure of the Slay and the Riders behind.

## 1705/06
### A WINTER TRAGEDY IN NEW YORK BAY
*The Boston News-Letter*

> *The Boston News-Letter* was the first newspaper in the British North American Colonies to appear on a continuous basis. Aside from an eight-month hiatus in 1709, it appeared under varying titles regularly from *24 April 1704* to at least *29 February 1776*, ultimately becoming a war casuality. A Micro Print edition of all known copies has been made by the American Antiquarian Society of Worcester, Massachusetts, and has been made available to other libraries and students. The following excerpt also was produced in the publications of the New Jersey Archives: *Documents relative to the colonial history of New Jersey. Newspaper extracts*. William Nelson, ed. 1st. ser., **11** (1894), 14–15.
>
> Source: *The Boston News-Letter*, Dec. 31 to Jan. 7, 1705/06. **6**, No. 90.

*New-York, December* 24. On the 19th. instant, The Private Ship of War call'd the Castle Del Key of 130 Tons, 18 Guns. Capt. Otto Van Tyle [1] Commander, Sailed from Jakques Bay (about 10 Miles from hence) and in going down towards Sandyhook with an easy Gale of Wind, She struck upon the East bank and stuck there; They sent some of their men on Shoar in their Canoo for boats to assist them, but that night a hard Gale of Wind Sprung up between W. & N.W. and Froze very hard, the Ship began to fill with Water: A Sloop and large Boat was sent down, but it Friezing and blowing so hard, they would not venture to relieve them, for fear of running the same fate of being a ground, and so Froze or Drowned: The next Morning the Gale continued hard all day, and the men were all alive upon the Deck and in the Shrouds, the Sea beating over them: And on Fryday Morning the Wind abating, a Boat went on board and found but 4 of the men alive; The Captain and all the rest being Froze and Drowned, there was 145 men on board when She Sailed, who all perished but 13, & 132 dyed in this deplorable manner. Here are Widows Lamenting the loss of their Husbands and Parents their Children: Tis said about 80 or 90 of the men were English, Scotch and Irish, and the rest of Dutch Parentage, most born in this Country.

[1] Otto Van Toyle or Van Tayl or Van Tyle had been captured and imprisoned in 1699 as one of Capt. William Kidd's men, but released without bail, to the alarm of the honest merchants and skippers.—(*N. Y. Col. Docs.*, IV, 551, 623). He now turns up again as the commander of a privateer. *Doc. Col. Hist. N. J.* 11 (1894), 15.

## 1717

# THE PRODIGIOUS STORMS OF SNOW

John Winthrop

John Winthrop (b. Boston, 26 August 1681; d. Sydenham, Kent, England, 1 August 1747), was a great grandson of John Winthrop, first governor of Massachusetts Bay Colony and a cousin of Harvard's John Winthrop who distinguished himself in several fields of science while holding the Hollis Professorship in Mathematics and Natural Philosophy. The writer of the following letter was known, genealogically, as John Winthrop, F.R.S., to distinguish him from others of the same name. Apparently his only achievement in life was his election to the Royal Society of London in 1734 in recognition of his gift of a collection of zoological, mineralogical, and botanic items of American origin. Most of his youth and middle age were spent in the New London, Connecticut, area where his family possessed large landholdings. After many political and legal battles, he removed to England where he spent his later years.

Source: Copy of a letter from the Hon. John Winthrop, Esq. of New-London, to the Rev. Dr. Mather, of Boston. New-London, Sept. 12, 1717. *Collections of the Massachusetts Historical Society* (Boston). 2 (1793), 12–13.

*New-London,* Sept. 12, 1717.

SIR,

Being from home the last post day, when your letter arrived here, I am now to thank you for it, and to make answer to what you demand of me. The observations I made of the prodigious storms of snow, in the doleful winter past, are many. But I shall mention but two at this time, and they are these. That the snow spangles which fell on the earth, appeared in large sexangular forms. *Seu nivem sex radiatem; et stellas has niveas observavi prout astrologi vulgo adspectum depingunt sextilem.*\* The other is, that, among the small flock of sheep, that I daily fold in this distant part of the wilderness, (for I am a poor shepherd) to secure them from the wild rapacious quadrupeds of the forest; after the unusual and unheard of snows, the aforesaid animals from the upland parts of the country, were, in great numbers forced down to the sea side among us, for subsistence, where they nested, kenelled and burroughed in the thick swamps of these ample pastures, nightly visiting the pens and yards for their necessity, &c. And the ewes big with young being often terified and surprised, more especially with the foxes, during the deep snows; it had such impression on them, that the biggest part of the lambs they brought forth in the spring, are of Monsieur Reynard's complexion and colour, when their dams were all either white or black. The storm continued so long and severe, that multitudes of all sorts of creatures perished in the snow drifts. We lost at the island and farms, above eleven hundred sheep, besides some cattle and horses, interred in the snow. And it was very strange that twenty-eight days after the storm, the tenants at Fisher's Island, pulling out the ruins of one hundred sheep, out of one snow bank in a valley, (where the snow had drifted over them sixteen feet) found two of them alive in the drift, which had lain on them all that time, and kept themselves alive by eating the wool off the others, that lay dead by them: As soon as they were taken out of the drift they shed their own fleeces and are now alive and fat; and I saw them at the island the last week, and they are at your service.

The storm had its effect also on the ocean: The sea was in a mighty ferment, and after it was over, vast heaps of the enclosed shells came ashore, in places where there never had been any of the sort before. Neptune with his trident, also, drove in great schools of porpoises, so that the harbour and river seemed to be full of them; but none of these came on shore, but kept a play day among the disturbed waves. As for the golden fleece—the hider and his partner intended to settle in your town after they had made a few more wreck voyages, and have come back undiscovered like trading men, as I was told by my author. And as to my informer, he was always plotting and contriving how to accomplish your business, without discovering it to any more; but he was so needy that I believe he had never so much money together to carry him down, and keep him there any time for the purpose; and a few weeks before he died, he was proposing to me for a new trial and discovery of the thing. Sir, what I know about it I have truly, faithfully, and ingeniously communicated to you, and hope, by some means or other, you may in time be the better for it. I thank you for your publications, I have mentioned to my honest neighbour Timothy the reprinting them, without mentioning your name in the matter, encouraging him to the work, by the quick vent of so large a number of the first impression.

I have given a dose of your febrifu gium to one of the town, which I hope, has cured him of a malignant fever, and it is an excellent remedy *ob dolorem lienis*. I am indebted for your mentioning my name inter F. R. S.* at Gresham; I am an obscure person, less than the poorest of your servants, and not fit to stand before princes, but am contented to lie hid among the retired philosophers.

     I am &c  JOHN WINTHROP
To the Rev. Doctor Cotton Mather.

* This appointment afterwards took place.

# 1717
## AN HORRID SNOW
Cotton Mather

---

Cotton Mather (b. Boston, Mass., 1662/63; d. Boston, 1727/28), Puritan clergyman, scholar, author. In addition to his well-known theological writings and his massive introspective diary, Mather took upon himself the task of reporting to the Royal Society in London many scientific and pseudoscientific happenings in America. Henry Thoreau considered the following letter on the Great Snow of 1717 as Mather's supreme contribution to the intellectual world. The letter forms part of the Mather manuscript collection in the archives of the Massachusetts Historical Society. It was published several times in the early Ninteenth Century. Parts of the letter were frequently quoted by New England newspaper editors as background material whenever a big snowstorm occurred. The letter was addressed to Dr. John Woodward of the Royal Society of London.

Source: Mather Mss. fols. 52–53. 26th article in 1717. Massachusetts Historical Society; see John Warner Barber, *Incidents in American History; being a selection of the most important and most interesting events which have transpired since the discovery of America, to the present time*, New York, Geo. F. Cooledge & Brother, 1847. 68–71.

---

BOSTON, 10th Dec. 1717.

Tho' we are gott so far onward as the beginning of another winter, yett we have not forgott y<sup>e</sup> last, which at the latter end whereof we were entertained & overwhelmed with a Snow, which was attended with some Things, which were uncommon enough to afford matter for a letter from us. Our winter was not so bad as that wherein Tacitus tells us that Corbulo made his expedition against the Parthians, nor that which proved so fatal to y<sup>e</sup> Beasts & Birds in y<sup>e</sup> days of y<sup>e</sup> Emperor Justinion, & that the very Fishes were killed under y<sup>e</sup> freezing sea, when Phocas did as much to y<sup>e</sup> men whom Tyrants treat like y<sup>e</sup> Fishes of y<sup>e</sup> Sea. But y<sup>e</sup> conclusion of our Winter was hard enough, and was too formidable to be easily forgotten, & of a piece with what you had in Europe a year before. The snow was y<sup>e</sup> chief Thing that made it so. For tho' rarely does a Winter pass us, wherein we may not say with Pliny, *Ingens Hyeme Nivis apud nos-copia,* yet our last Winter brought with it a Snow, that excelled them all. The Snow, 'tis true, not equal to that, which once fell & lay twenty Cubits high, about the Beginning of October, in the parts about y<sup>e</sup> *Euxine Sea,* Nor to that which y<sup>e</sup> *French Annals* tell us kept falling for twenty Nine weeks together. Nor to several mentioned by *Bœthius,* wherein vast numbers of people, & of Cattel perished, Nor to those that *Strabo* finds upon *Caucasus* & *Rhodiginus* in *Armenia*. But yett such an one, & attended with such circumstances, as may deserve to be remembered.

On the twentieth of the last *February* there came on a *Snow,* which being added unto what had covered the ground a few days before, made a thicker mantle for our Mother than what was usual: And y<sup>e</sup> storm with it was, for the following day, so violent as to make all communication between y<sup>e</sup> Neighbors every where to cease.—People, for some hours, could not pass from one side of a street unto another, & y<sup>e</sup> poor Women, who happened in this critical time to fall into Travail, were putt unto Hardships, which anon produced many odd stories for us. But on y<sup>e</sup> *Twenty fourth* day of y<sup>e</sup> Month, comes *Pelion upon Ossa:* Another Snow came on which almost buried y<sup>e</sup> Memory of y<sup>e</sup> former, with a Storm so famous that Heaven laid an Interdict on y<sup>e</sup> Religious Assemblies throughout y<sup>e</sup> Country, on this Lord's day, y<sup>e</sup> like whereunto had never been seen before. The Indians near an hundred years old, affirm that their *Fathers* never told them of any thing that equalled it. Vast numbers of Cattel were destroyed in this Calamity. Whereof some there were, of y<sup>e</sup> Stranger sort, were found standing dead on their legs, as if they had been alive many weeks after, when y<sup>e</sup> Snow melted away. And others had their eyes glazed over with Ice at such a rate, that being not far from y<sup>e</sup> Sea, their mistake of their way drowned them there. One gentleman, on whose farms were now lost above 1100 sheep, which with other Cattel, were interred (shall I say) or *Innived,,* in the Snow, writes me word that there were *two Sheep* very singularly circumstanced. For no less than eight and twenty days after the Storm, the People pulling out the Ruins of above an 100 sheep out of a Snow-Bank, which lay 16 foot high, drifted over them, there was two found alive, which had been there all this time, and kept themselves alive by eating the wool of their dead companions. When they were taken out they shed their own Fleeces, but soon gott into good Case again. *Sheep* were not y$^e$ only creatures that lived unaccountably, for whole weeks without their usual sustenance, entirely buried in y$^e$ Snow-drifts.

The *Swine* had a share with y$^e$ *Sheep* in strange survivals. A man had a couple of young *Hoggs,* which he gave over for dead, But on the twenty seventh day after their *Burial,* they made their way out of a *Snow-Bank,* at the bottom of which they had found a little Tansy to feed upon. The *Poultry* as unaccountably survived as these. Hens were found alive after seven days; Turkeys were found alive after five and twenty days, buried in y$^e$ Snow, and at a distance from y$^e$ ground, and altogether destitute of any thing to feed them. The number of creatures that kept a *Rigid Fast,* shutt up in Snow for divers weeks together, & were found alive after all, have yielded surprizing stories unto us.

The Wild Creatures of y$^e$ Woods, y$^e$ outgoings of y$^e$ Evening, made their Descent as well as they could in this time of scarcity for them, towards y$^e$ Sea-side. A vast multitude of Deer, for y$^e$ same cause, taking y$^e$ same course, and y$^e$ Deep Snow Spoiling them of their only Defence, which is to *run,* they became such a prey to these Devourers, that it is thought not one in twenty escaped. But here again occurred a Curiosity. These carniverous Sharpers, & especially the Foxes, would make their Nocturnal visits to the Pens, where the people had their sheep defended from them. The poor Ewes big with young, were so terrified with the frequent Approaches of y$^e$ Foxes, & the Terror had such Impression on them, that most of y$^e$ *Lambs* brought forth in the Spring following, were of Monsieur *Reinard's* complexion, when y$^e$ Dam, were either *White* or *Black.* It is remarkable that immediately after y$^e$ fall of y$^e$ Snow an infinite multitude of *Sparrows* made their Appearance, but then, after a short continuance, all disappeared.

It is incredible how much damage is done to y$^e$ *Orchards,* For the Snow freezing to a Crust, as high as the boughs of y$^e$ trees, anon split y$^m$ to pieces. The Cattel also, walking on y$^e$ crusted Snow a dozen foot from y$^e$ ground, so fed upon y$^e$ Trees as very much to damnify them. The Ocean was in a prodigious Ferment, and after it was over, vast heaps of little shells were driven ashore, where they were never seen before. Mighty shoals of Porpoises also kept a play-day in the disturbed waves of our Harbours. The odd Accidents befalling many poor people, whose Cottages were totally covered with y$^e$ Snow, & not y$^e$ very tops of their chimneys to be seen, would afford a Story. But there not being any relation to philosophy in them, I forbear them.

And now *Satis Terris Nivis.* And there is enough of my Winter Tale. If it serve to no other purpose, yett it will give me an opportunity to tell you That nine months ago I did a thousand times wish myself with you in *Gresham Colledge,* which is never so horribly snow'd upon. But instead of so great a Satisfaction, all I can attain to is the pleasure of talking with you in this Epistolary way & subscribing myself.

    Syr Yours with an affection
     that knows no Winter
      COTTON MATHER

---

### 1741

## A SERMON PREACHED AT NARAGANSET. MARCH, 15th. A.D. 1740, 1.

### James MacSparran, D.D.

---

James MacSparran (b. probably County Derry, Ireland, 1693; d. South Kingston, R.I., 1757), first came to America about 1718. Refused ordination because of Cotton Mather's enmity, he returned to England and was ordained in the Church of England in 1720. He returned to America as a missionary for the Society for the Propagation of the Gospel in Foreign Parts. Settling at Narragansett, R.I., in April 1721, he became an able and respected churchman. A man of literary ambition, he published in addition to several sermons an interesting collection of letters to friends in the home country. This appeared in 1753 under a Dublin imprint with the impressive title: *America dissected, being a full and true account of all the American Colonies, shewing the intemperance of the climates, excessive heat and cold, and sudden violent changes of weather, terrible and mischievous thunder and lightning, bad and unwholesome air, destructive to human bodies.* Despite the pertinent connotation of the title, very little of climatological value appeared in the body of the text. He apparently exhausted his knowledge of the subject in the sub-title.

Source: *A sermon preached at Naraganset. March, 15th. A.D. 1740,1.* By James MacSparran, D.D. Newport: Printed by the Widow Franklin, under the Town School House, 1741. Copy in John Carter Brown Library, Brown University, Providence, Rhode Island.

* * * * *

Thirdly, we are warn'd also, by the uncommon Inclemencies of a Cold and long Winter.

The Elements have been arm'd with such piercing cold, and suffocating Snows, as if God intended the Air that he gave us to live and breath in, should become the Instrument to execute his Vengeance on us, for our Ingratitude to his Goodness, and our Transgression of his Law. We may contemplate to our Comfort, the Wisdom and Power of God, in the Beautiful Structure of the Heavens, and his wise sorting of the Seasons, for the Benefit and Delight of Man. But as no human Skill can count the number of the Stars nor call them by their Names; so it exceeds the utmost Art of Astronomy to account for either extreme Heat, or extreme Cold; otherwise than by the Distance or Nearness of the Sun; which yet we see have Variations and Vicissitudes that do not always correspond to that Cause. It is no small Comfort to consider God's Care to provide food for the Beasts of the Field, and the Fowls of the Air, and to supply their starving Importunity. And our Gratitude grows, as we are assured all this is ultimately intended, as a Kindness and Bounty for the Sons of Men. But how of late has the Grasier groan'd to see the Severity of the Season; to hear his Herds and his Flocks making Mean for their Meat; and after a few fruitless Complaints, uttered in acents peculiar to their Kind, drop down and die, and disappoint the Increase and Expectation of the Spring?

With what amazement do we behold, and can ill endure God's sudden and intolerable Cold, that proceeds from the breath of his Nostrils! The Snow that looks so White, Innocent and Light, as if it could bear down and oppress nothing; yet we see it hides and covers the Earth, from the warmth and sight of the Sun; and thus also does the Ice turn Rivers into Rocks, and the Sea (as it were) into dry land. We see the fluid Element, which yielded to the smallest force, become so hard and rigid, that it resists the Impression of the Travellers Foot, and the weight of Beasts and Burdens, with a firmness superior to the driest Land, *boreas* has so far enter'd into the Chambers of the South, that he hath Sealed up the Sun, and intercepted his dissolving Influence; and Southern Snows are signs, of that Planets impotent Efforts to regain his usurp'd Dominions. The great Luminary that rules the Day, has now advanced and display'd his Banner on this side the Line; yet so faint are his Armies, tho' innumerable, and each Atom harness'd in Fire, that they cannot force the Frost to give ground, nor dissolve the Intrenchments of Snow. No Arm that is not Almighty, can melt or open what *Orion* has shut up, bound in his Bands, and hardned; or freeze and make fast, what the *Pleiades* have loosed and softned; the first, being the Constellation; which in the Omnipotent's Hands, begets and begins the Winter; as the other are the Orbs, that attend the advancing Spring.

Would we therefore be reliev'd from the Burden and Inconvenience of the Winter, and refreshed with the blessed Breathings and Benefits of the Spring; we must propitiate the God, *who alone can loose the Bands of Orion and drove down the sweet Influences of the Pleiades. Feb. 38. 31.* It may be the Advances of the Vernal Heat, to sooth our Sorrows, invite us to sing and say, in the Language of *Solomon's Song, Chap. 2, 11. 12. Lo the Winter is past the Rain is over and gone. The Flowers appear on the Earth, the time of the singing of Birds is come, and the Voice of the Turtle is heard in our Land.* Yet how many sad Remembrances do still remain, to remind us of the past Winter? The Husbandman and the Mariner, the Rich and the Poor have already sensibly felt its Effects; and tho' the dissolved Rivers have opened their Mouths, return'd to their Channels, and offer their usual Administrations to Navigation, Fishing and Commerce; yet alas! are not the Cattle now corrupting in the Fields, which we expected to have eaten or exported next Autumn; and that, after they have consumed most part of the Corn, that might have maintain'd us to that Time.

* * * * *

## 1749-50
## A PHILADELPHIA WINTER
Peter Kalm

Peter Kalm (b. Province of Angermanland, Sweden, 1716: d. Abo in Swedish Finland, 1779). A naturalist who had traveled extensively in Russia and eastern Europe, Kalm arrived in Philadelphia on 15 September 1748. He visited in Pennsylvania, New York, New Jersey, and southern Canada, though his base was always Philadelphia. He was the first to publish a worthwhile description of Niagara Falls. While in America, he maintained a good set of meteorological observations. He departed for Europe on 13 February 1751 after a stay of 29 months. The account of his American experiences was first published at Stockholm in three volumes from 1753 to 1761: *En Resa til Norra America*. Several German editions soon appeared, and one of these was translated into English appearing in 1770–71: *Travels into North America*, John Reinhold Forster, trans., Warrington, printed by William Eyres. The current edition employed contains some additional manuscript material discovered later.

Source: *Peter Kalm's Travels in North America*. Adolph B. Benson, ed. New York, Wilson-Erickson Inc., 1937.

### December the 11th

The Cold. It is now becoming quite cold. Yesterday especially it felt very penetrating, in particular when walking against the wind. All small streams and inlets are now covered with ice so that one can pass over on most of them without danger. The Schuylkill River was well frozen too. On the Delaware River there was so much ice that it was completely frozen this morning near the city. Yet the ice was very thin and disappeared as soon as the tide appeared. Otherwise there drifted so much ice in the river that at Gloucester's Ferry it was impossible to cross with a horse. One could now cross only in small boats between the pieces of ice. People who had brought wood to town on boats expected to leave them and return by the highway. Ships that intended to sail hastened down the river before they would be frozen fast, and those only half loaded began to consider remaining where they were over winter, wherefore some took their boats into dock or to some safe place where it would be protected from the ice, both now and in the spring. The price of wood went up rapidly, because before that one had been able to buy a cord of hickory for 22 shillings, but now it had gone up to from 25 to 27 shillings per cord, and even then one had to hurry and take it lest it be snapped up by someone else. Oak wood rose from 16 to 19 and 20 shillings per cord, and one was glad to get it at that price. All wood bought now was green, cut this fall, for although the country people cut much wood in the spring and summer, which they let dry and cart into town in the early autumn, it is bought up at once by the wealthy and thoughtful, who then get their supply at a lower price. Later only green wood can be found on the market.—The following days the weather changed and became milder, so that by the 13th of December there was hardly a piece of ice to be seen near the Gloucester ferry; it had either melted or been carried away by the water.

### December the 21st

The Shortest Days. We were now passing through that time of the year when the northern hemisphere has its shortest days. But we learned that there was a large difference in this respect between the Old and the New Sweden. The sun rose here at 7:15 and set at 4:45. It was possible to read a book without artificial light at seven in the morning and five in the afternoon. But it was very dark at six, both morning and night, and before 7 A.M., and after 5 P.M. it was almost impossible to read by natural light. The frost had not yet had any serious results, for the ground was bare everywhere; but little snow had fallen so far, and what little had come had melted the same day it came, or the day after. The River was still open, and the smaller streams that had been covered with ice a little more than a week before had by the sunshine and recent rains been cleared of the ice again. This neighborhood now had about the appearance of a Swedish countryside in the beginning of October. The cattle went outdoors continually seeking their food, and but little was fed them at home. It may be seen from the meteorological notes that, with few exceptions, the weather had for a long time been fair and pleasant.

### December the 22nd

Weather Forecast. To-day and for a couple of days following the sunsets colored the clouds in the west red. Mr. Turner, a merchant, said that in this city (Philadelphia) it meant fair weather for the next day, perhaps for several days, with relatively high temperatures. No winds followed as in the old countries.

### December the 28th

The cold now became noticeably severe; the wind that blew was biting, and the River full of floating ice. A ship went down the River this morning, but encountered so much ice that it was compelled to turn back and either postpone the trip until a milder temperature should drive away the ice, or until spring.

### December the 29th

Season Forecast. In the above-mentioned *Gazette* I read the following: "Annapolis in Maryland, October 25. We are told by people from the back parts of this province, that they have had great numbers of Bears and other wild beasts, come down among them this fall; which they look upon as a certain token of an approaching hard winter."

### January the 2nd, 1750

The cold was now quite severe. The Delaware River had yesterday been covered by ice near Philadelphia, and to-day the whole river was full of boys, girls and older people moving about upon it, the majority of them skating. But at Gloucester the River was still open, because it is narrower there and the current therefore swifter. On the third of the month several shoppers walked over the River, but on the fifth a large part of it was so open again that horses were being carried across in boats.

### January the 9th

The Delaware River was now frozen in most places at Philadelphia. For the last three days there had been a large number of young men and boys on the ice, some walking but most of them skating. There was still an open place here and there in the middle of the River; nevertheless, to-day at eleven I saw a man successfully driving a horse and sleigh on the ice directly in front of the city. The next day was mild and beautiful, when a section of the ice before the town suddenly broke up and began to move downstream. There were a good many people on this piece of ice: booths had been set up to sell brandy and such things to the skaters, and now they all found something else to do besides enjoying themselves. People rushed away precipitiously, and fortunately all of them reached *terra firma* safely. The ice remained, but for a few days no one dared go out on it. There had been some people on the other side of the river starting to cross when the ice began to loosen, but these were obliged to turn back. In the 13th of this month the river was wholly open again so that ships could move in and out. The English youth is very found of skating, and so are men of thirty years or over. Men of all classes have a passion for this sport. They would sometimes go three or four miles to reach a place where the ice was safe. Sheltered spots were flooded with men skaters, but I saw no women on the ice here.

## 1778

### A SNOWSTORM AS IT AFFECTS THE AMERICAN FARMER

St. John de Crèvecoeur

---

Michael-Guillaume Jean de Creve Coeur, known as St. John de Crèvecoeur, (b. near Caen, France, 1735; d. Sarcelles, France, 1813) came to Canada with General Montcalm in 1759. After traveling through the colonies for several years after the war, he engaged in farming and observing the American scene in Orange County and in the Mohawk Valley of New York from 1769 to 1780. After a brief visit to France, he returned to New York City to serve as French consul from 1783 to 1790. It was during the decade of the 1770's that he composed his famous *Letters from an American Farmer* which was first published at London in 1782. The above letter-essay did not appear until the expanded, three volume French edition was issued at Paris in 1787 under the title: *Lettres d'un cultivateur Americain*. The "Description d'une chute de neige. Dans le pays des Mohawks, sous le rapport qui intéresse le cultivateur Americain" occupied pages 289–314 in volume one. It was dated, Germanflats (N.Y.), 17 January 1778. This particular letter did not appear in English until 1925.

Source: *Sketches of Eighteenth Century America by St. John de Crèvecoeur*. H. L. Bourdin, R. H. Gabriel, and S. T. Williams, eds. New Haven, Yale University Press, 1925. 39–50.

---

Germanflats [Herkimer County],
17 January 1778

No man of the least degree of sensibility can journey through any number of years in whatever climate without often being compelled to make many useful observations on the different phenomena of Nature which surround him; and without involuntarily being struck either with awe or admiration in beholding some of the elementary conflicts in the midst of which he lives. A great thunderstorm; an extensive flood; a desolating hurricane; a sudden and intense frost; an overwhelming snowstorm; a sultry day,—each of these different scenes exhibits singular beauties even in spite of the damage they cause. Often whilst the heart laments the loss to the citizen, the enlightened mind, seeking for the natural causes, and astonished at the effects, awakes itself to surprise and wonder.

Of all the scenes which this climate offers, none has struck me with a greater degree of admiration than the ushering in of our winters, and the vehemence with which their first rigour seizes and covers the earth; a rigour which, when once descended, becomes one of the principal favours and blessings this climate has to boast of. I mean to view it as connected with the welfare of husbandry; as a great flood of congealed water sheltering the grass and the grains of our fields; and overwhelming men, beasts, birds living under the care of man. [He] in the midst of this sudden alteration has to provide food and shelter for so many animals, on the preservation of which the husbandman's welfare entirely depends. This single thought is really tremendous: from grass and pastures growing in our meadows and in our fields; from various other means by which the tenants of our farms lived before, they must suddenly pass to provenders, to grains, and to other resources gathered by Man when the face of the earth teemed with a luxuriant vegetation.

'Tis at this period that the functions of a great farmer become more extended and more difficult. 'Tis from his stores that all must draw their subsistence. He must know whether they will be sufficient to reach the other end of the wintry career. He must see whether all have a sufficient quantity daily delivered to them; whether each class is properly divided; whether water can be procured; what diseases and accidents may happen. These are a few sketches of that energetic circle of foresight, knowledge, and activity which fill the space of five months; to which you must add the care of a large family as to raiment, fuel, and victuals.

The tenants of his house, like the beasts of his farm, must now depend on the collected stores of the preceding season, sagaciously distributed and prepared by the industry of his wife. There lies the "aurum potabile" of an American farmer. He may work and gather the choicest fruits of his farm, but if female economy fails, he loses the comfort of good victuals. He sees wholesome meats, excellent flours converted into indifferent food; whilst his neighbour, more happy, though less rich, feeds on well-cooked dishes, well-composed puddings. For such is our lot: if we are blessed with a good wife, we may boast of living better than any people of the same rank on the globe.

Various tokens, long since known, guide the farmer in his daily progress and various occupations from the autumnal fall of the leaves. If he is prudent and active, he makes himself ready against the worst which Nature can give. Sheds, stables, barn-yards, partitions, racks, and mangers must be carefully reviewed and repaired; the stores of corn-stalks, straw, and hay must be securely placed where neither rain nor snow can damage them.

Great rains at last replenish the springs, the brooks, the swamps, and impregnate the earth. Then a severe frost succeeds which prepares it to receive the voluminous coat of snow which is soon to follow; though it is often preceded by a short interval of smoke and mildness, called the Indian Summer.* This is in general the invariable rule: winter is not said properly to begin until these few moderate days and the rising of the waters have announced it to Man. This great mass of liquid once frozen spreads everywhere natural bridges; opens communications impassable before. The man of foresight neglects nothing; he has saved every object which might be damaged or lost; he is ready.

The wind, which is a great regulator of the weather, shifts to the northeast; the air becomes bleak and then intensely cold; the light of the sun becomes dimmed as if an eclipse had happened; a general night seems coming on. At last imperceptible atoms make their appearance; they are few and descend slowly, a sure prognostic of a great snow. Little or no wind is as yet felt. By degrees the number as well as the size of these white particles is increased; they descend in larger flakes; a distant wind is heard; the noise swells and seems to advance; the new element at last appears and overspreads everything. In a little time the heavy clouds seem to approach nearer the earth and discharge a winged flood, driving along towards the southwest, howling at every door, roaring in every chimney, whistling with asperous sound through the naked limbs of the trees; these are the shrill notes which mark the weight of the storm. Still the storm increases as the night approaches, and its great obscurity greatly adds to the solemnity of the scene.

\* This is the earliest known usage of the term Indian Summer in its meteorological connotation. Crèvecoeur's manuscript, though composed in 1778, was not published in full until 1787.

Sometimes the snow is preceded by melted hail which, like a shining varnish, covers and adorns the whole surface of the earth of buildings and trees; a hurtful time for the cattle which it chills and oppresses. Mournful and solitary they retire to what shelters they can get, and, forgetting to eat, they wait with instinctive patience until the storm is over. How amazingly changed is the aspect of Nature! From the dusky hues of the autumnal shades, everything becomes refulgently white; from soft, miry roads, we pass all at once to solid icy bridges. What could an inhabitant of Africa say or think in contemplating this northern phenomenon? Would not it raise in his mind a greater degree of astonishment than his thunder-storms and his vertical suns?

A general alarm is spread through the farm. The master calls all his hands; opens the gates; lets down the bars; calls and counts all his stock as they come along. The oxen, the cows, remembering ancient experience, repair to the place where they were foddered the preceding winter; the colts wild, whilst they could unrestrained bound on the grassy fields, suddenly deprived of that liberty, become tame and docile to the hands which stroke and feed them. The sheep, more encumbered than the rest, slowly creep along, and by their incessant bleating show their instinctive apprehension; they are generally the first which attract our attention and care. The horses are led to their stables; the oxen to their stalls; the rest are confined under their proper sheds and districts. All is safe, but no fodder need be given them yet; the stings of hunger are necessary to make them eat cheerfully the dried herbage and forget the green one on which they so lately fed. Heaven be praised, no accident has happened; all is secured from the inclemency of the storm. The farmer's vigilant eye has seen every operation performed; has numbered every head; and as a good master provided for the good welfare of all.

At last he returns home loaded with hail and snow melting on his rough but warm clothes; his face is red with the repeated injury occasioned by the driving wind. His cheerful wife, not less pleased, welcomes him home with a mug of gingered cider; and whilst she helps him to dried and more comfortable clothes, she recounts to him the successful pains she has taken also in collecting all her ducks, geese, and all the rest of her numerous poultry; a province less extensive indeed but not less useful. But no sooner this simple tale is told than the cheerfulness of her mind is clouded by a sudden thought. Her children went to a distant school early in the morning whilst the sun shone, and ere any ideas were formed of this storm. They are not yet returned. What is become of them? Has the master had tenderness enough to tarry awhile and watch over his little flock until the arrival of some relief? Or has he rudely dismissed them in quest of his own safety?

These alarming thoughts are soon communicated to her husband who, starting up in all the glow of paternal anxiety, orders one of his negroes to repair to the schoolhouse with Bonny, the old faithful mare, who, like his wife, by her fecundity has replenished his farm. 'Tis done: she is mounted bare-back and hurried through the storm to the schoolhouse, at the door of which each child is impatiently waiting for this paternal assistance. At the sight of honest Tom, the negro, their joy is increased by the pleasure of going home on horseback. One is mounted before and two behind. Rachel, the poor widow's little daughter, with tears in her eyes, sees her playmates, just before her equals, as she thought, now provided with a horse and an attendant,—a sad mortification. This is the first time she ever became sensible of the difference of her situation. Her distressed mother, not less anxious to fetch her child, prays to heaven that some charitable neighbour may bring her along. She, too, has a cow to take care of; a couple of pigs hitherto tenderly fed at the door; three or four ewes, perhaps, demanding her shelter round some part of her lonely log-house. Kind heaven hears her prayers. Honest Tom lifts her [Rachel] up and, for want of room, places her on Bonny's neck; there she is upheld by the oldest boy. Thus fixed with difficulty, they turn about and boldly face the driving storm; they all scream and are afraid of falling; at last they clinch together and are hushed. With cheerfulness and instinctive patience, Bonny proceeds along, and, sensible of the valuable cargo, highly lifting her legs, she securely treads along, shaking now and then her ears as the drifted snow penetrates into them.

A joyful meeting ensues. The thoughts of avoided danger increase the pleasure of the family. The milk-biscuit, the short-cake, the newly-baked apple-pie are immediately produced, and the sudden joy these presents occasion expels every idea of cold and snow. In this country of hospitality and plenty it would be a wonder indeed if little Rachel had not partaken of the same bounty. She is fed, made to warm herself; she has forgot the little reflections she had made at the school-house door; she is happy, and to complete the goodly act, she is sent home on the same vehicle. The unfeigned thanks, the honest blessings of the poor widow, who was just going to set out, amply repays the trouble that has been taken; happy wages of this charitable attention.

The messenger returns. Everything is safe both within and without. At that instant the careful negro, Jack, who has been family employed in carrying wood to the shed that he may not be at a loss to kindle fire in the morning, comes into his master's room carrying on his hip an enormous back-log without which a fire is supposed to be imperfectly made and to be devoid of heat. All hands rise; the fire is made to blaze; the hearth is cleaned; and all the cheerful family sit around. Rest after so many laborious operations brings along with it an involuntary silence, even among the children who grow sleepy with their victuals in their hands, as they grow warm. "Lord, hear, how it blows!" says one. "My God, what a storm!" says another. "Mammy, where does all this snow come from?" asks a third. "Last year's storm, I think, was nothing to this," observes the wife. "I hope all is fast about the house. How happy it is for us that we had daylight to prepare us for it."

The father now and then opens the door to pass judgment, and to contemplate the progress of the storm: "'Tis dark, 'tis pitch-dark," he says; "a fence four rods off cannot be distinguished. The locust-trees hard by the door bend under the pressure of the loaded blast. Thank God, all is secured. I'll fodder my poor cattle well in the morning if it please Him I should live to see it." And this pious sentiment serves him as a reward for all his former industry, vigilance, and care. The negroes, friends to the fire, smoke and crack some coarse jokes; and, well-fed and clad, they contentedly make their brooms and ladles without any further concern on their minds. Thus the industrious family, all gathered together under one roof, eat their wholesome supper, drink their mugs of cider, and grow imperceptibly less talkative and more thoughtless, as they grow more sleepy. Now and then, when the redoubled fury of the storm rattles in the chimney, they seem to awake. They look at the door again and again, but 'tis the work of omnipotence; it is unavoidable; their neighbours feel it as well as themselves. Finally they go to bed, not to that bed of slavery or sorrow as is the case in Europe with people of their class, but on the substantial collection of honest feathers picked and provided by the industrious wife. There, stretched between flannel sheets and covered with warm blankets made of their own sheep's wool, they enjoy the luxury of sound, undisturbed repose, earned by the fatigues of the preceding day. The Almighty has no crime to punish in this innocent family; why should He permit ominous dreams and terrific visions to disturb the imaginations of these good people?

As soon as day reappears, the American farmer awakes and calls all his hands. While some are busy in kindling the fires, the rest with anxiety repair to the barns and sheds. What a dismal aspect presents itself to their view! The roads, the paths are no longer visible. The drifted snow presents obstacles which must be removed with the shovel. The fences and the trees, bending under the weight of snow which encumbers them, bend in a thousand shapes; but by a lucky blast of wind they are discharged, and they immediately recover their natural situation. The cattle who had hitherto remained immovable, their tails to the wind, appear strangely disfigured by the long accession and adherence of the snow to their bodies. On the sight of the master, suddenly animated, they heavily shake themselves clean, and crowd from all parts in expectation of that fodder which the industry of Man has provided for them. Where their number is extensive, various and often distant are their allotments, which are generally in the vicinity of the stacks of hay. In that case, when the barn-yard work is done, the farmer mounts his horse, followed by his men armed with pitch-forks. He counts again the number of each sort, and sees that each receives a sufficient quantity. The strong are separated from the weak, oxen with oxen, yearlings with yearlings, and so on through every class. For cattle, like men, conscious of their superior force will abuse it when unrestrained by any law, and often live on their neighbour's property.

What a care, what an assiduity does this life require! Who on contemplating the great and important field of action performed every year by a large farmer, can refrain from valuing and praising as they ought this useful, this dignified class of men? These are the people who, scattered on the edge of this great continent, have made it to flourish; and have without the dangerous assistance of mines, gathered, by the sweat of their honest brows and by the help of their ploughs, such a harvest of commercial emoluments for their country, uncontaminated either by spoils or rapine. These are the men who in future will replenish this huge continent even to its utmost unknown limits, and render this new found part of the world by far the happiest, the most potent as well as the most populous of any. Happy people! May the poor, the wretched of Europe, animated by our example, invited by our laws, avoid the fetters of their country, and come in shoals to partake of our toils as well as of our happiness!

The next operation is to seek for convenient watering-places. Holes must be cut through the ice; 'tis done. The veteran, experienced cattle lead the way, tread down the snow, and form a path; the rest soon follow. Two days' experience [teaches] them all the way to this place as well as the station they must occupy in their progress thither; the stoutest marching first and the weakest closing the rear. The succeeding operations with regard to the preservation of the cattle entirely depend on the judgment of the farmer. He knows, according to the weather, when it is best to give them either straw, corn-stalks, or hay. In very hard weather they are more hungry and better able to consume the coarse fodder; corn stocks are reserved for sheep and young cattle; hay is given to all in thaws.

Soon after this great fall of snow the wind shifts to the northwest and blows with great impetuosity; it gathers and drives the loose element. Everything seems to be involved a second time in a general whirlwind of white atoms, not so dangerous indeed as those clouds of sand raised in the deserts of Arabia. This second scourge is rather worse than the first, because it renders parts of the roads seemingly impassable. 'Tis then that with empty sleighs the neighbourhood gather, and by their united efforts open a communication along the road. If new snow falls, new endeavours must be made use of to guard against the worst of inconveniences. For, to live, it is necessary to go to market, to mill, to the woods. This is, besides, the season of merriment and mutual visiting. All the labours of the farm are now reduced to those of the barn; to the fetching of fuel and to cleaning their own flax. The fatigues of the preceding summer require now some relaxation. What can be more conducive to it than the great plenty of wholesome food we all have? Cider is to be found in every house. The convenience of travelling invites the whole country to society, pleasure, and visiting. Bees are made, by which a number of people with their sleighs resort to the inviter's house, and there in one day haul him as much wood as will serve him a whole year. Next day 'tis another man's turn; admirable contrivance which promotes good-will kindness, and mutual assistance. By means of these associations often the widows and orphans are relieved.

After two or three falls of snow the weather becomes serene though cold. New communications are opened over lakes and rivers and through forests hitherto impassable. The ox rests from his summer labour, and the horse amply fed now does all the work. His celerity is strengthened by the steel shoes with which his hoofs are armed; he is fit to draw on the snow as well as on the ice. Immense is the value of this season: logs for future buildings are easily drawn to the saw-mills; ready-piled stones are with equal ease brought to the intended spot; grain is conveyed to the different landings on our small rivers, from whence in the spring small vessels carry it to the sea-port towns, and from which again larger ones convey it away to the different marts of the world. The constancy of this serenely cold weather is one of the greatest blessings which seldom fails us. More to the southward their winters are often interrupted by thaws and rains which are unfavourable to transportation as well as to the cattle. [This is] a happy suspension of toils and labours; happy rest without which the vegetation of our cold climates would soon be exhausted. On the other hand, 'tis an expensive season in every respect: nothing profitable can be done, and clothes of the warmest sorts must be provided for everyone. Great parts of the profits of summer are expended in carrying a family through this wintry career,—but let not that reflection diminish our happiness! We are robust, healthy, and strong; the milder climates of the South have nothing that can compensate for these advantages. It is true that the class of men who work for the farmers have less employment, but nevertheless they live with comfort and in such abundance as is proportioned to their situation; everyone has bread and meat. As for the real poor, we have none in this happy country; those who through age and infirmities are past labour, are provided for by the township to which they belong. Such are the Mohawk and Canadian winters. . . . A long ramble like this through a cold Canadian storm requires rest, silence, and sleep. After so long an excursion we may with propriety wish each other good night.

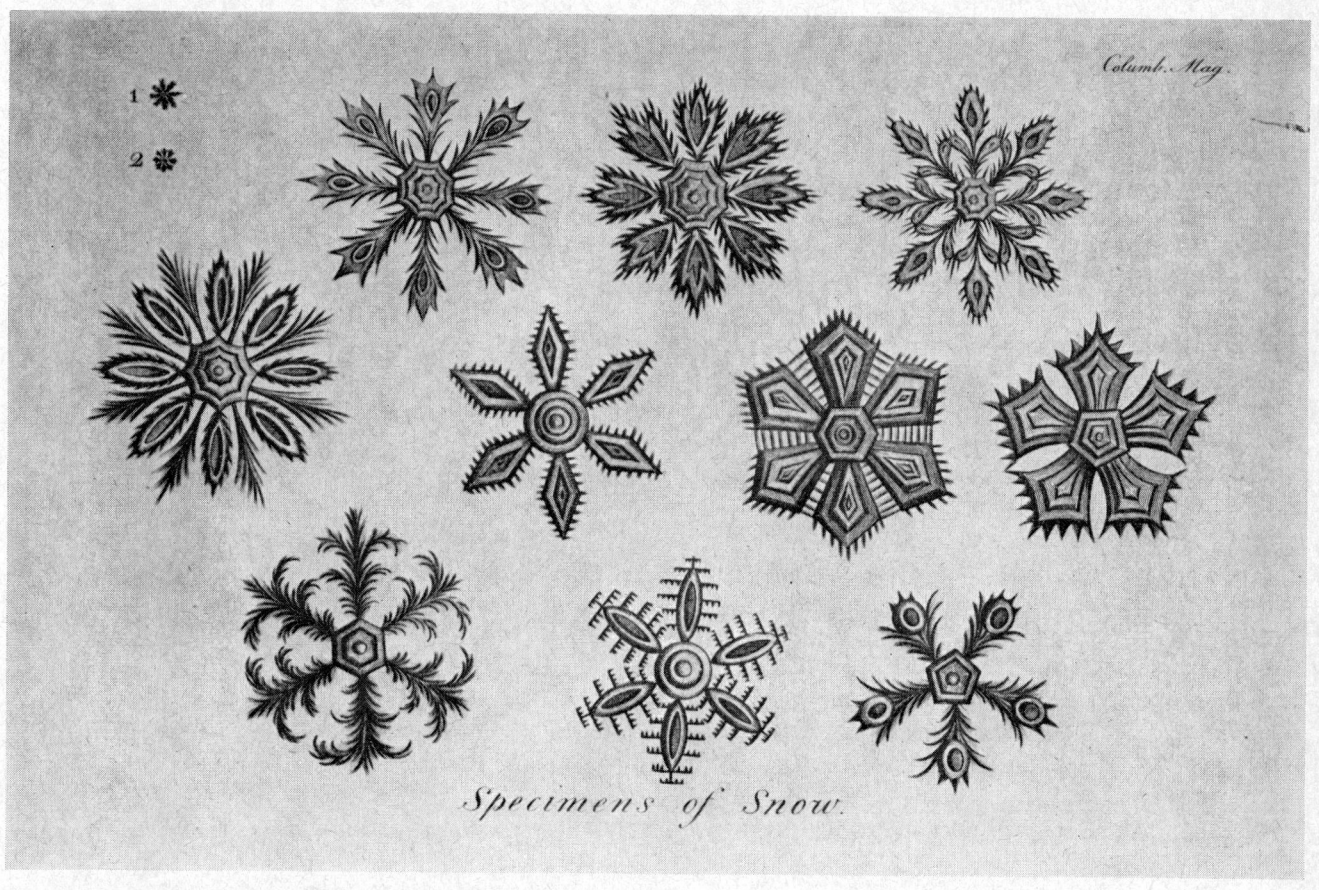

*Specimens of Snow.*

1789

## OBSERVATIONS ON SNOW

(Illustrated by a Beautiful Engraving)

*The Columbian Magazine, or monthly miscellany, containing a view of the history, literature, manners & character of the year 1789* (Philadelphia). 3-3 (March 1789), 180–81.

SNOW is a meteor formed by the freezing of the vapours of the atmosphere, and being crystalized, as it were, differs from hail and hoar-frost. A flake of snow is composed of a number of distinct parts which, in their descent towards the earth, happen to meet and adhere together; and thus, like a drop of rain, or a hail-stone, the flakes are larger or smaller, according to the accession of parts coming into contact. A warm current of air crossing the passage of snow, softens the descending particles, and renders them susceptible of adhesion; hence the flakes are encreased in size; an atmosphere thoroughly cold has a contrary tendency; and hence the snow falls in small and distinct congelations. The particles of snow are formed of fine shining spicula, which, diverging from a common center, run into an endless variety of beautiful figures. We have said that a flake is composed of several distinct parts: those parts, when viewed through a glass, will appear to be severally complete in themselves, but generally of different configurations. If we look at a number of flakes together, we shall then perceive an astonishing variety of these configurations; many of them so admirably beautiful, so exquisitely contrived, as to mock all attempts to explain or delineate them. A warmth in the atmosphere, the action of the sun's rays, or the blowing of the wind, will often blunt the points or break off the finer parts of snow, so as to give an appearance of irregularity or imperfection: but such appearances always proceed from one or other of these adventitious causes, and not from any defect in the natural configuration of the parts.—Nature is ever steady to her purpose.

The best time for observing snow, is immediately after it has fallen, when the air is dry, cold and calm. It was in this state of the weather, at an early period of the late winter, when the specimens annexed (for which we are indebted to the ingenuity of mr. Thomas Bedwell) were delineated, by means of a pretty good glass: the snow was at that time of a fine and remarkably bright kind. Fig. 2 and 3 represent, in their natural sizes, as they appeared to the naked eye, two of those particles of which snow-flakes are formed: the ten larger figures express similar parts, as they appeared when viewed through a magnifier: but the configurations of others were varied almost to infinity; and yet it was plain that all those varieties belonged to as many classes, in which no difference was perceivable in their respective configurations. Many of those were of exquisite beauty, far surpassing these on the plate; but they were so delicately fashioned, so complicated, and the spicula so inimitably interwoven, as to baffle every attempt to trace them with the pencil.

In the course of the same winter similar observations were occasionally made in Philadelphia, on different falls of snow. Appearances were always the same, except in one instance, where the snow fell large and fleecy: these flakes showed few or none of the characters which distinguished the small ones in other observations; they appeared to be rather a confused blend of parts, exhibiting neither beauty nor variety of configuration—but this, we conceive, may be accounted for from reasons already assigned.

It may be amusing to those who have not turned their investigations towards the nature of snow, to be told, that every particle of it is formed of firm ice; and yet it floats, like the lightest substances, on the air: this is owing to the excess of its surface, in comparison to the matter contained under it; as gold itself, the heaviest of metals, may be extended in surface, till it will ride upon the least breath of air.

## 1804–05

## WITH LEWIS AND CLARK AT FORT MANDAN, DAKOTA, LOUISIANA TERRITORY

### Diary of Meriwether Lewis

Meriwether Lewis (b. Albemarle County, near Charlottesville, Virginia, 1774; d. central Tennessee 1809) was selected in 1803 by his friend, Thomas Jefferson, to lead the exploring expedition to the Missouri River and the Pacific Northwest. Lewis selected Captain William Clark (b. Caroline County, Virginia, 1770; d. St. Louis, Missouri, 1838) as his associate in guiding the expedition. Among other things, they were given the mission of describing:

Climate, as characterized by the thermometer, by the proportion of rainy, cloudy, and clear days; by lightning, hail, snow, ice; by the access and recess of frost; by the winds prevailing at different seasons; the dates at which particular plants put forth, or lose their flower or leaf; times of appearance of particular birds, reptiles, or insects.

The expedition left a point near St. Louis on 14 May 1804 and reached the Mandan area in central North Dakota, a distance of 1600 miles, late in October. The erection of winter quarters commenced on 2 November 1804 at a site on the Missouri River near present-day Bismarck and adjacent to several Indian villages. The site was called Fort Mandan. Meteorological observations were taken at least twice a day with thermometer and visual observation. These continued through 5 September 1805 when the thermometer was broken. Thereafter, winds and weather only were observed.

The following extracts from the Lewis diary contain all entries of meteorological significance from 2 November 1804 until the party departed northwestward with the spring ice breakup. Some supplementary material, where not repetitive, has been added and placed in italics for identification. These have been extracted from comments in the regular meteorological journal. The full thermometrical tables are appended at the end.

The Lewis diary first appeared in full in 1814 with the publication of:

*History of the expedition under the command of Captains Lewis and Clark, to the sources of the Missouri, thence across the Rocky Mountains and down the River Columbia to the Pacific Ocean. Performed during the years 1804–5–6. By order of the Government of the United States.* Prepared for the press by Paul Allen, Esquire. In Two volumes. Philadelphia: Published by Bradford and Inskeep; and Abm. H. Inskeep, New York. J. Maxwell, Printer. 1814.

This was based mainly on the diary maintained by Lewis with supplements of similar material from the field notes of Captain Clark and information from other participants. Nicholas Biddle made a narrative from the rather verbose and disjointed original material, and the text was seen through the press by editor Paul Allen. The original manuscript is now in the library of the American Philosophical Society. The complete text included two meteorological items: "Thermometrical observations, showing also the rise and fall of the Mississippi (Missouri); appearances of weather, winds, &c. commencing at the mouth of the river" and "Remarks and Observations."

Source: *The Lewis and Clark expedition. By Meriwether Lewis. The 1814 edition, unabridged.* Introduction by Archibald Hanna. Philadelphia and New York, J. B. Lippincott Company, 1961.

## November 1804

2. ... the wind was from the southeast, and the weather being fine a crowd of Indians came down to visit us.
3. *Wind blew hard all day.*
4. ... the day was clear and pleasant, but last night was very cold and there was a white frost.
5. The weather is cloudy and the wind moderate from the northwest
6. At Daylight, Tuesday 6th, the clouds to the north were darkening and the wind rose high from the northwest at eight o'clock, and continued cold during the day.
7. The day was temperate but cloudy and foggy. ... *A few drops of rain this evening; saw the aurora-borealis at 10 P.M.; it was very brilliant in perpendicular columns, frequently changing position.*
8. The morning again cloudy ... the frost this morning was very severe, the weather during the day cloudy and the wind from the northwest ... great numbers of wild geese are passing to the south. ... *Since we have been at our present station, the river has fallen 9 inches.*
9. *Very hard frost this morning.*
10. We again had a raw day, a northwest wind, but rose early in the hopes of finishing our works before the extreme cold begins. ... Large flocks of geese and brant, and also a few ducks are passing towards the south.
11. The weather is cold.
12. The last night had been cold and this morning we had a very hard frost; the wind changeable during the day, and some ice appears on the edges of the river; swans too are passing to the south.
13. At half past ten ice began to float down the river for the first time. ... It snowed all day and the air was very cold.
14. The river rose last night half an inch, and is now filled with floating ice. This morning was cloudy with some snow.
15. The morning again cloudy, and the ice running thicker than yesterday, the wind variable. ... The swans are still passing to the south.
16. We had a very hard white frost this morning, the trees are all covered with ice, and the weather cloudy.
17. Last night was very cold, and the ice in the river is thicker than hitherto. *The frost of yesterday remained on the trees until 2 P.M. when it descended like a shower of snow; swans passing from the north.*
18. To-day we had a cold windy morning.
18. The ice continues to float in the river, the wind high from the northwest, and the weather cold.
20. We this day moved into our huts which are now completed. This place which we call Fort Mandan, is situated in a point of low ground, on the north side of the Missouri, covered with tall and heavy cotton wood. ... The latitude by observation is 47° 21' 47", and the computed distance from the mouth of the Missouri sixteen hundred miles. *Little soft ice this morning; the boat in much danger from ice, &c.*
21. The weather was this day fine: the river clear of ice and rising a little: we are now settled in our new winter habitation, and shall wait with much anxiety the first return of spring to continue our journey.
22. The morning was fine, and the day warm.
23. Again we had a fair and warm day, with the wind from the northeast: the river is now at a stand having risen four inches in the whole.
24. The wind continued from the same quarter and the weather was warm.
25. The weather is still fine, warm and pleasant, and the river falls one inch and a half.
26. We now completed our huts, and fortunately too, for the next day, Monday, November 26th, before daylight the wind shifted to the northwest, and blew very hard, with cloudy weather and a keen cold air, which confined us much and prevented us from working. The night continued very cold, and, Tuesday 27th, the weather cloudy, the wind continuing from the northwest and river crowded with floating ice.
27. The river fell two inches to-day and the weather became very cold.
28. About eight o'clock last evening it began to snow and continued till daybreak, after which it ceased till seven o'clock, but then resumed and continued during the day, the weather being cold and the river full of floating ice. ... The river fell one inch today.
29. The wind is again from the northwest, the weather cold, and the snow which fell yesterday and last night is thirteen inches in depth. The river closed during the night at the village above, and fell two feet; but this afternoon it began to rise a little.*
30. He [Captain Clark] then crossed the river on the ice and returned on the north side to the fort. The day as well as the evening was cold, and the river rose to its former height.

\* Snowfall records have been maintained at Bismarck since 1885. The former record for the heaviest 24-hour snowfall (13.5 inches on 26–27 March 1950) was broken on 3 March 1966 when 15.5 inches fell. This was also the greatest single storm record with 22.4 inches on 2–4 March 1966. The deepest snow cover of record, 22 inches, existed on 8 March 1897.

## December 1804

1. The wind was from the northwest.
2. The latter part of the evening was warm, and a thaw continued till the morning, when the wind shifted to the north.
3. The morning was fine, but in the afternoon the weather became cold with the wind from the northwest.
4. The wind continues from the northwest, the weather cloudy and raw, and the river rose one inch.
5. The morning was cold and disagreeable, the wind from the southeast accompanied with snow; in the evening there was snow again and the wind shifted to the northeast.
6. The wind was violent from the north northwest with some snow, the air keen and cold. At eight o'clock A.M. the thermometer stood at ten degrees above 0, the river rose an inch and a half in the course of the day.
7. The wind still continues from the northwest and the day is very cold. . . . The river closed opposite the fort last night, (with ice) an inch and a half in thickness. In the morning the thermometer stood at one degree below 0. Three men were badly frostbitten in consequence of their exposure.
8. The thermometer stood at twelve degrees below 0, that is at forty-two degrees [sic] below the freezing point: the wind was from the northwest . . . the cold, too, was so excessive that the air was filled with icy particles resembling a fog, and the snow generally six or eight inches deep and sometimes eighteen, in consequence of which two of the party were hurt by falls, and several had their feet frostbitten. *The ice one and a half inches thick on the part that had not previously frozen; the buffaloe appear.*
9. The wind this day was from the east, the thermometer at seven degrees above 0, and the sun shone clear: two chiefs visited us, one in a sleigh drawn by a dog and loaded with meat.
10. He (Capt. Clark) had spent a disagreeable night on the snow, with no covering but a small blanket, sheltered by the hides of buffalo they had killed. We observe large herds of buffalo crossing the river on ice, the men who were frostbitten are recovering, but the weather is still exceedingly cold, the wind being from the north, and the thermometer at ten and eleven degrees below 0; the rise of the river is one inch and and half.
11. The weather became so intensely cold that we sent for all the hunters who had remained out with captain Clark's party, and they returned in the evening several of them frostbitten. The wind was from the north and the thermometer at sunrise stood at twenty-one below 0, the ice in the atmosphere being so thick as to render the weather hazy and give the appearance of two suns reflecting each other. The river continued at a stand.
12. The wind is still from the north, the thermometer being at sunrise thirty-eight degrees below 0. . . . We measured the river on ice, and find it five hundred yards wide immediately opposite the fort.
13. Last night was clear and a very heavy frost covered the old snow, the thermometer at sunrise being twenty degrees below 0, and followed by a fine day. The river falls.
14. The morning was fine, and the weather having moderated so far, that the mercury stood at 0. . . . Notwithstanding the snow we were visited by a large number of Mandans. *Captain Clark set out with a hunting party on the ice with sleighs.*
15. The wind being from the north, the mercury at sunrise eight degrees below 0, and the snow of last night an inch and a half deep.
16. The morning is clear and cold, the mercury at sunrise 22° below zero.
17. The weather today was colder than any we had experienced, the thermometer at sunrise being 45° below zero, and about eight o'clock it fell to 74° below the freezing point.* [sic].
18. The thermometer at sunrise was 32° below 0. The Indians had invited us yesterday to join their chase to-day, but the seven men we sent returned in consequence of the cold, which was so severe last night that we were obliged to have the sentinel relieved every half hour. The northwest traders however left us on their return home.
19. The weather moderated, and the river rose a little, so that we were enabled to continue the picketing of the fort. Notwithstanding the extreme cold, we observe the Indians at the village engaged out in the open air at a game which resembled billiards.
20. The wind was from the N.W. the weather moderate, the thermometer 24° above 0 at sunrise.
21. The day was fine and warm, the wind N.W. by W.
22. [No weather entry].
23. The weather was fine and warm like that of yesterday.
24. The day continued warm and pleasant. . . . We this day completed our fort.

* Temperature records have been maintained at Bismarck since 1875. The coldest reading of −45° was observed on two occasions; 13 January 1916 and 16 February 1936. Thus, the mark observed by Lewis & Clark would equal the modern record though exposure conditions may have differed.

25. . . . and the next morning being Christmas, Tuesday 25th, we were awakened before day by a discharge of three platoons from the party. We had told the Indians not to visit us as it was one of our great medicine days; so that the men remained at home and amused themselves in various ways, particularly with dancing in which they take great pleasure. The American flag was hoisted for the first time in the fort; the best provisions we had were brought out and this, with a little brandy, enabled them to pass the day in great festivity.
26. The weather is again temperate.
27. A little fine snow fell this morning and the air was colder than yesterday, with a high northwest wind. *The trees are all white with the frost which attached itself to their boughs.*
28. The wind continued high last night, the frost severe, and the snow drifting in great quantities through the plains. *It blew very hard last night; the frost fell like a shower of snow.*
29. There was a frost fell last night nearly one quarter of an inch in depth, which continued to fall till the sun had gained some height: the mercury at sunrise stood at 9° below zero.
30. The weather was cold, and the thermometer 20° below 0.
31. During the night there was a high wind which covered the ice with hillocks of mixed sand and snow; the day however was fine.

## January 1805

1. The new year was welcomed by two shots from the swivel and a round of small arms. The weather was cloudy but moderate; the mercury which at sunrise was at 18°, in the course of the day rose to 34° above 0: toward evening it began to rain, and at night we had snow, the temperature for which is about 0° [sic].
2. It snowed last night.
3. Last night it became very cold, and this morning we had some snow. *The snow is nine inches deep.*
4. The morning was cloudy and warm, the mercury being 28° above 0: but towards evening the wind changed to northwest, and the weather became cold.
5. We had high and boisterous winds last night and this morning.
6. A clear morning with high wind. *At 12 o'clock today two luminous spots appeared on each side of the sun, extremely bright.*
7. The weather was again clear and cold with a high northwest wind, and the thermometer at sunrise 22° below 0: the river fell an inch.
8. The wind was still from the northwest, the day cold. *The snow is now ten inches deep, accumulating by frosts.*
9. The weather is cold, the thermometer at sunrise 21° below 0. Kagohami breakfasted with us, and captain Clark with three or four men accompanied him and a party of Indians to hunt, in which they were so fortunate as to kill a number of buffalo: but they were incommoded by snow, by high and squally winds, and by extreme cold: several of the Indians came to the fort nearly frozen, others are missing, and we are uneasy, for one of our men who was separated from the rest during the chase has not returned.
10. In the morning, however, he came back just as we were sending five men in search of him. The night had been excessively cold, and this morning at sunrise the mercury stood at 40° below zero, or 72° below the freezing point. He had, however, made a fire and kept himself tolerably warm. A young Indian, about thirteen years of age, also came in soon after. His father who came last night to inquire after him very anxiously, had sent him in the afternoon to the fort: he was overtaken by the night, and was obliged to sleep on the snow with no covering except a pair of antelope skin moccasins and leggings and a buffalo-robe: his feet being frozen we put them into cold water, and gave him every attention in our power. About the same time an Indian who had also been missing returned to the fort, and although his dress was very thin, and he had slept on the snow without a fire, he had not suffered the slightest inconvenience. We have indeed observed that these Indians support the rigors of the season in a way which we had hitherto thought impossible.
11. Like that of yesterday the weather today was cold and clear the thermometer standing at 28° below 0.
12. The weather continues very cold, the mercury at sunrise being 20° below 0. *Singular appearance of three distinct Halos or luminous rings about the moon appeared this evening at half after nine, P. M. and continued one hour; the moon formed the centre of the middle ring, the other two of which lay north and south of the moon, and had each of them a limb passing through the moon's centre, and projecting north and south, a semidiameter beyond the middle ring, to which last they were equal in dimensions, each ring appearing to extend an angle of fifteen degrees of a great circle.*
13. We have a continuation of clear weather, and the cold has increased, the mercury having sunk to 34° below 0.

14. The weather was more moderate to-day, the mercury being at 16° below 0, and the wind from the S.E. We had however some snow, after which it remained cloudy.
15. The morning is much warmer than yesterday, and the snow begins to melt, though the wind after being for some time from the S.E. suddenly shifted to N.W. Between twelve and three o'clock A.M. there was a total eclipse of the moon, from which we obtained part of the observation necessary for ascertaining the longitude. *A total eclipse of the moon last night visible here, but partially obscured by the clouds.*
16. The party who went down with the horses for the man who was frostbitten returned, and we are glad to find his complaint not serious.
17. The day was very windy from the north; the morning clear and cold, the thermometer at sunrise being at 0.
18. The weather is fine and moderate.
19. Another cloudy day. *Ice now three feet thick on the most rapid part of the river.*
20. The day fair and cold.
21. The weather was fine and moderate.
22. The cold having moderated and the day pleasant, we attempted to cut the boats out of the ice, but at the distance of eight inches came to water, under which the ice became three feet thick, so that we were obliged to desist.
23. The cold weather returned, the mercury having sunk 2° below 0, and the snow fell four inches deep. *It frequently happens that the sun rises fair and in about fifteen or twenty minutes it becomes suddenly turbid, as if the moon* [sic] *had some chemical effect on the atmosphere.*
24. The day was colder than any we have had lately, the thermometer being at 12° below 0.
25. The thermometer was at 25° below 0, the wind from N.W. and the day fair, so that the men were employed in preparing coal (charcoal), and cutting the boats out of the ice.
26. A fine warm day.
27. Another warm and pleasant day: we again attempted to get the boat out of the ice.
28. The weather today is clear and cold: we are obliged to abandon the plan of cutting the boat through the ice, and therefore had another attempt the next day.
29. . . . by heating a quantity of stones so as to warm the water in the boat, and thaw the surrounding ice: but in this too we were disappointed, as all the stones on being put into the fire cracked into pieces: the weather warm and pleasant.
30. The morning was fair, but afterwards became cloudy.
31. It snowed last night, and the morning is cold and disagreeable with a high wind from the northwest. *The snow fell two inches last night.*

## February 1805

1. A cold windy day.
2. The day is fine.
3. The weather is again pleasant.
4. The morning fair and cold, the mercury at sunrise being 18° below 0, and the wind from the northwest.
5. A pleasant fair morning with the wind from the northwest.
6. The morning was fair and pleasant, the wind N.W.
7. The morning was fair and much warmer than for some days, the thermometer being at 18° above 0, and the wind from the S.E.
8. A fair pleasant morning, with S.E. winds. *The black and white speckled woodpecker has returned.*
9. The morning was fair and pleasant, the wind from the S.E.
10. A slight snow fell in the course of the night, the morning was cloudy, and the northwest wind blew so high that although the thermometer was 18° above 0, the day was cooler than yesterday, when it was only 10° above the same point.
11. We sent down a party with sleds, to relieve the horses from their loads; the weather fair and cold, with a N.W. wind.
12. The morning was fair though cold, the mercury being 14° below 0, the wind from the S.E.
13. The morning was cloudy, the thermometer at 2° below 0, the wind from the southeast.
14. Last night the snow fell three inches deep; the day, however, fine.
15. The morning was fine and cool, the thermometer being at 16° below 0. In the course of the day one of the Mandan chiefs returned from captain Lewis's party, his eye-sight having become so bad that he could not proceed. At this season of the year the reflection from the ice and snow is so intense as to occasion almost total blindness. This complaint is very common, and the general remedy is to sweat the part affected by holding the face over a hot stone, and receiving the fumes from snow thrown on it.
16. The morning was warm, mercury at 32° above 0, the weather cloudy.
17. The weather continued as yesterday, though in the afternoon it became fair: several of the Indians who went with captain Lewis returned, as did also one of our men, whose feet had been frostbitten.
18. The morning was cloudy with some snow, but in the later part of the day it cleared up.

19. The weather was clear and warm, the wind from the south.
20. The day was delightfully fine; the mercury being at sunrise 2° and in the course of the day 22° above 0, the wind southerly.
21. We had a continuation of the same pleasant weather.
22. The morning was cloudy and a little snow fell, but in the afternoon the weather became fair.
23. The day is warm and pleasant.
24. The weather is again fine.
25. The day was exceedingly pleasant.
26. The weather is again fine.
27. The weather continues fine.
28. The day is clear and pleasant.

### March 1805

1. The day is fine.
2. The day is fine, and the river begins to break up in some places, the mercury being between 28° and 36° above 0, and the wind from the N.E. *The snow has disappeared in many places, the river partially broken up.*
3. The weather pleasant, the wind from the E. with clouds; in the afternoon the clouds disappeared and the wind came from the N.W. . . . A flock of ducks passed up the river to-day.
4. A cloudy morning with N.W. wind, the latter part of the day clear.
5. About four o'clock in the morning there was a slight fall of snow, but the day became clear and pleasant with the mercury 40° above 0.
6. The day was cloudy and smoky in consequence of the burning of the plains by the Minnetarees; they have set all the neighboring country on fire in order to obtain an early crop of grass which may answer for the consumption of their horses, and also an inducement for the buffalo and other game to visit it. . . . The river rose a little and overran the ice, so as to render the crossing difficult.
7. The day was somewhat cloudy, and colder than usual; the wind from the northeast.
8. The day cold and fair with a high easterly wind.
9. The morning cloudy and cool, the wind from the north.
10. A cold windy day.
11. The weather was cloudy in the morning and a little snow fell, the wind then shifted from southeast to northwest and the day became fair. It snowed again in the evening.
12. . . . was fair with the wind from the northwest. *Snow but slight, disappearing to-day.*
13. We had a fine day, and a southwest wind. . . . The river rose a little to-day, and so continued.
14. The wind being from the west, and the day fine.
15. The day is clear, pleasant and warm. We take advantage of the fine weather to hang all of our Indian presents and other articles out to dry before our departure.
16. The weather is cloudy, the wind from the southeast.
17. A windy but clear and pleasant day, the river rising a little and open in several places.
18. The weather was cold and cloudy, the wind from the north.
19. Some snow fell last night, and this morning was cold, windy, and cloudy. *But little snow, not enough to cover the ground. Collected some roots, herbs and plants, in order to send by the boat, particularly the root said to cure the bite of a mad dog and rattlesnake.*
20. The morning was cold and cloudy, the wind high from the north, but the afternoon pleasant.
21. *Some ducks in the river opposite the fort.*
22. This was a clear, pleasant day, with the wind from the S.S.W.
23. The weather was fine, but in the evening we had the first rain that had fallen during the winter.
24. The morning cloudy, but the afternoon fair, the wind from the N.E. We are employed in preparing for our journey. This evening swans and wild-geese flew towards the N.E. *But little snow.*
25. A fine day, the wind S.W. The river rose nine inches and the ice began breaking away in several places, so as to endanger our canoes which we are hauling down to the fort. *A flock of swan returned to-day.*
26. The river rose only half an inch, and being choked up with ice near the fort, did not begin to run till towards evening. This day is clear and pleasant. *Some geese pass today.*
27. The wind is still high from the S.W.: the ice which is occasionally stopped for a few hours is then thrown over shallow sandbars when the river runs. *The first insect I have seen, was a large black gnat to-day; the ice drifting in great quantities.*
28. The day is fair. Some obstacle above has prevented the ice from running. Our canoes are now nearly ready, and we expect to set out as soon as the river is sufficiently clear to permit us to pass. *Ice abates in quantity, wind hard, river rises thirteen inches, and falls twelve inches.*
29. The weather clear, and the wind from N.W. The obstruction above gave way this morning, and the ice came down in great quantities; the river having fallen eleven inches in the course of the last twenty-four hours. *A variety of insects make their appearance, as flies bugs, &c.*
30. The day was clear and pleasant, the wind N.W. and the ice running in great quantities.

31. Early this morning it rained, and the weather continued cloudy during the day; the river rose nine inches, the ice not running as much as yesterday. Several flocks of ducks and geese fly up the river.

### April 1805

1. This morning there was a thunderstorm, accompanied with large hail, to which succeeded rain for about a half an hour. We availed ourselves of this interval to get all the boats in the water. At four o'clock P.M. it began to rain a second time, and continued till twelve at night. With the exception of a few drops at two or three different times, this was the first rain we have had since the 15th of October last. *The cloud came from the west, and was attended by hard thunder and lightning. I have observed that all thunderclouds in the western part of the continent, proceed from the westerly quarter, as they do in the Atlantic states. The air is remarkably dry and pure in this open country; very little rain or snow, either winter or summer. The atmosphere is more transparent than I ever observed it in any country through which I have passed.*
2. The wind was high last night and this morning from N.W. and the weather continued cloudy.
3. The weather is pleasant, though there was a white frost and some ice at the edge of the water. We were all engaged in packing up our baggage and merchandise.
4. The weather is clear and pleasant, though the wind is high from the N.W. *Observed a flock of brant passing up the river to-day: the wind blew very hard, as it does frequently in this quarter. There is scarcely any timber to break the winds from the river, and the country on both sides being level plains, wholly destitute of timber, the winds blow with astonishing violence, in this open country, and form a great obstruction to the navigation of the Missouri, particularly with small vessels, which can neither ascend nor descend should the wind be the least violent.*
5. Fair and pleasant, but the wind high from the northwest.
6. Another fine day with a gentle breeze from the south.
7. We left the fort with fair pleasant weather though the northwest wind was high, and after making four miles encamped on the north side of the Missouri, nearly opposite the first Mandan village.

## LEWIS & CLARK THERMOMETRICAL OBSERVATIONS

| Day of the month | Therm. at sun-rise | Weather | Wind | Therm. at four o'clock | Weather | Wind | River r. and f. | River Feet | River Inches |
|---|---|---|---|---|---|---|---|---|---|
| 1804 | Deg. | | | Deg. | | | | | |
| Oct. 5 | 36 a. | f. | N.W. | 54 a. | f. | N.W. | | | |
| 6 | 43 a. | f. | N.W. | 60 a. | f. | N.W. | | | |
| 7 | 45 a. | c. | S.E. | 58 a. | f. | S.E. | | | |
| 8 | 48 a. | f. | N.W. | 62 a. | f. | N.W. | | | |
| 9 | 45 a. | c. | N.E. | 50 a. | c. a. r. | N. | | | |
| 10 | 42 a. | f. a. r. | N.W. | 67 a. | f. | N.W. | | | |
| 11 | 43 a. | f. | N.W. | 59 a. | f. | N.W. | | | |
| 12 | 42 a. | f. | S. | 65 a. | f. | S.E. | | | |
| 13 | 43 a. | f. | S.W. | 49 a. | c. a. r. | S.E. | | | |
| 14 | 42 a. | r. | S.E. | 40 a. | r. | S.E. | | | |
| 15 | 46 a. | f. | N. | 57 a. | f. a. r. | N.W. | | | |
| 16 | 45 a. | c. | N.E. | 50 a. | f. | N.E. | | | |
| 17 | 47 a. | f. | N.W. | 54 a. | f. | N.W. | | | |
| 18 | 30 a. | f. | N.W. | 68 a. | f. | N.W. | | | |
| 19 | 43 a. | f. | S.E. | 62 a. | f. | S. | | | |
| 20 | 44 a. | f. | N.W. | 48 a. | f. | N. | | | |
| 21 | 31 a. | s. | N.W. | 34 a. | s. | N.W. | | | |
| 22 | 35 a. | c. a. s. | N.E. | 42 a. | c. | N.E. | | | |
| 23 | 32 a. | s. | N.W. | 45 a. | c. | N.E. | | | |
| 24 | 33 a. | s. a. f. | N.W. | 51 a. | c. a. s. | N.W. | | | |
| 25 | 31 a. | c. | S.E. | 50 a. | c. | S.E. | | | |
| 26 | 42 a. | f. | S.E. | 57 a. | f. | S.E. | | | |
| 27 | 39 a. | f. | S.W. | 58 a. | f. | S.W. | | | |
| 28 | 34 d. | f. | S.W. | 54 a. | f. | S.W. | | | |
| 29 | 32 a. | f. | S.W. | 59 a. | f. | S.W. | | | |
| 30 | 32 a. | f. | S.W. | 52 a. | f. | S.W. | | | |
| 31 | 33 a. | f. | W. | 48 a. | f. | W. | | | |
| Nov. 1 | 31 a. | f. | N.W. | 47 a. | f. | N.W. | | | |
| 2 | 32 a. | f. | S.E. | 63 a. | f. | S.E. | | | |
| 3 | 32 a. | f. | N.W. | 53 a. | f. | N.W. | | | |
| 4 | 31 a. | f. | N.W. | 43 a. | c. | W. | | | |
| 5 | 30 a. | c. | N.W. | 58 a. | c. | N.W. | | | |
| 6 | 31 a. | c. | S.W. | 43 a. | c. | W. | | | |
| 7 | 43 a. | c. | S. | 62 a. | c. | S. | | | |
| 8 | 38 a. | c. | S. | 39 a. | c. | W. | | | |
| 9 | 27 a. | f. | N.W. | 43 a. | f. | N.W. | | | |
| 10 | 34 a. | f. | N.W. | 36 a. | c. | N.W. | | | |
| 11 | 28 a. | f. | N.W. | 60 a. | f. | N.W. | | | |
| 12 | 18 a. | f. | N. | 31 a. | f. | N.E. | | | |
| 13 | 18 a. | s. | S.E. | 28 a. | c. a. s. | S.E. | f. | | 1½ |

| Day of the month | Therm. at sun-rise | Weather | Wind | Therm. at four o'clock | Weather | Wind | River r. and f. | River Feet | River Inches |
|---|---|---|---|---|---|---|---|---|---|
| 1804 | Deg. | | | Deg. | | | | | |
| Nov. 14 | 24 a. | s. | S.E. | 32 a. | c. a. s. | S.E. | r. | | 1 |
| 15 | 22 a. | c. | N.W. | 31 a. | c. a. s. | N.W. | r. | | ½ |
| 16 | 25 a. | c. | N.W. | 30 a. | f. | S.E. | r. | | ¼ |
| 17 | 28 a. | f. | S.E. | 34 a. | f. | S.E. | r. | | ¼ |
| 18 | 30 a. | f. | S.E. | 38 a. | f. | W. | r. | | ½ |
| 19 | 32 a. | f. | N.W. | 48 a. | f. | N.W. | r. | | 1 |
| 20 | 35 a. | f. | N.W. | 50 a. | f. | W. | r. | | 1½ |
| 21 | 33 a. | c. | S. | 49 a. | f. | S.E. | r. | | |
| 22 | 37 a. | f. | W. | 45 a. | f. | N.W. | r. | | ½ |
| 23 | 38 a. | f. | W. | 48 a. | f. | N.W. | | | |
| 24 | 36 a. | f. | N.W. | 34 a. | f. | N.W. | | | |
| 25 | 34 a. | f. | W. | 32 a. | f. | S.W. | | | |
| 26 | 15 a. | f. | S.W. | 21 a. | f. | W. | | | |
| 27 | 10 a. | f. | S.E. | 19 a. | c. | S.E. | f. | | 3 |
| 28 | 12 a. | s. | S.E. | 15 a. | s. | E. | f. | | 4 |
| 29 | 14 a. | c. a. s. | N.E. | 18 a. | f. | W. | f. | | 2½ |
| 30 | 17 a. | f. | W. | 23 a. | f. | W. | f. | 2 | |
| Dec. 1 | 1 b. | f. | E. | 6 a. | f. | S.E. | r. | | 1 |
| 2 | 38 a. | f. | N.W. | 36 a. | f. | N.W. | r. | | 1 |
| 3 | 26 a. | f. | N.W. | 30 a. | f. | N.W. | r. | | 1 |
| 4 | 18 a. | f. | N. | 29 a. | f. | N. | r. | | 1 |
| 5 | 14 a. | c. | N.E. | 27 a. | s. | N.E. | | | |
| 6 | 10 a. | s. | N.W. | 11 a. | c. a. s. | N.W. | | | |
| 7 | 0 a. | f. | N.W. | 1 b. | c. | N.W. | r. | 2 | ½ |
| 8 | 12 b. | s. | N.W. | 5 b. | f. a. s. | N.W. | | | |
| 9 | 7 a. | f. | E. | 10 b. | f. | N.W. | | | |
| 10 | 10 b. | c. | N. | 11 b. | c. | N. | r. | | ½ |
| 11 | 21 b. | f. | N. | 18 b. | f. | N. | f. | | ½ |
| 12 | 38 b. | f. | N. | 16 b. | f. | N. | | | |
| 13 | 20 b. | f. | S.E. | 4 b. | c. | S.E. | | | |
| 14 | 2 b. | c. | S.E. | 2 a. | s. | S.E. | f. | | 1 |
| 15 | 8 b. | c. a. s. | W. | 4 b. | c. a. s. | W. | | | |
| 16 | 22 b. | f. | N.W. | 4 b. | f. | N.W. | f. | | 1 |
| 17 | 45 b. | f. | N. | 28 b. | f. | N. | r. | | 3 |
| 18 | 32 b. | f. | W. | 16 b. | f. | S.W. | r. | | 1 |
| 19 | 2 b. | c. | S.W. | 16 a. | f. | S. | r. | | 1 |
| 20 | 24 a. | f. | N.W. | 22 a. | c. | W. | r. | | 2 |
| 21 | 22 a. | f. | N.W. | 22 a. | c. | N.W. | r. | | 2 |
| 22 | 10 a. | f. | N.W. | 23 a. | f. | N.W. | r. | | 2½ |
| 23 | 18 a. | c. | S.W. | 27 a. | c. | W. | f. | | 1 |

| Day of the month | Therm. at sun-rise | Weather | Wind at sun-rise | Therm. at four o'clock | Weather | Wind at four o'clock | River | | |
|---|---|---|---|---|---|---|---|---|---|
| | | | | | | | r. and f. | Feet | Inches |
| 1804 | Deg. | | | Deg. | | | | | |
| Dec. 24 | 22 a. | s. | S.W. | 31 a. | c. a. s. | W. | f. | | 2½ |
| 25 | 15 a. | s. | N.W. | 20 a. | c. a. s. | N.W. | f. | | 1 |
| 26 | 18 a. | c. | N.W. | 21 a. | f. | N.W. | | | |
| 27 | 4 b. | c. | N.W. | 14 a. | c. | N.W. | | | |
| 28 | 12 a. | f. | N. | 13 a. | f. | N.W. | r. | | 2½ |
| 29 | 9 b. | f. | N. | 3 a. | f. | N. | r. | | 1 |
| 30 | 20 b. | f. | N. | 11 b. | f. | N. | r. | | ½ |
| 31 | 10 b. | f. | S.E. | 12 a. | c. | S.W. | r. | | 1½ |
| 1805 | | | | | | | | | |
| Jan. 1 | 18 a. | s. | S.E. | 34 a. | f. | N.W. | r. | | 1 |
| 2 | 4 b. | s. | N.W. | 8 b. | f. a. s. | N. | | | |
| 3 | 14 b. | c. | N. | 4 b. | s. | S.E. | | | |
| 4 | 28 a. | c. a. s. | W. | 4 b. | c. | N.W. | r. | | 2½ |
| 5 | 20 b. | c. | N.W. | 18 b. | s. | N.E. | r. | | 2 |
| 6 | 11 b. | c. a. s. | N.W. | 16 b. | f. | N.W. | r. | | 3 |
| 7 | 22 b. | f. | N.W. | 14 b. | f. | W. | f. | | 1 |
| 8 | 20 b. | f. | N.W. | 10 b. | f. | N.W. | r. | | 1 |
| 9 | 21 b. | f. | W. | 18 b. | f. a. c. | N.W. | | | |
| 10 | 40 b. | f. | N.W. | 28 b. | f. | N.W. | | | |
| 11 | 38 b. | f. | N.W. | 14 b. | f. | N.W. | f. | | ½ |
| 12 | 20 b. | f. | N.W. | 16 b. | f. | N.W. | r. | | 1 |
| 13 | 34 b. | f. | N.W. | 20 b. | f. | N.W. | | | |
| 14 | 16 b. | s. | S.E. | 8 b. | c. a. s. | S.E. | | | |
| 15 | 10 b. | f. | E. | 3 a. | c. | S.W. | r. | | 1 |
| 16 | 36 a. | c. | W. | 16 a. | f. | S.W. | r. | | 2½ |
| 17 | 2 b. | c. | W. | 12 b. | f. | N.W. | | | |
| 18 | 1 b. | f. | N.W. | 7 a. | f. a. c. | N.W. | f. | | 1 |
| 19 | 12 a. | c. | N.E. | 6 b. | f. | N.W. | r. | | 1 |
| 20 | 28 a. | f. | N.E. | 9 b. | c. | S.E. | r. | | ½ |
| 21 | 2 b. | c. | N.E. | 8 a. | f. | S.E. | | | |
| 22 | 10 a. | f. a. h. | N.W. | 19 a. | c. | N.W. | r. | | 1¾ |
| 23 | 20 b. | s. | E. | 2 b. | c. a. s. | N. | f. | | 2½ |
| 24 | 12 b. | c. | N.W. | 2 b. | f. | N.W. | r. | | ¼ |
| 25 | 26 b. | f. | N.W. | 4 b. | f. a. c. | W. | | | |
| 26 | 12 a. | c. | N.E. | 20 a. | f. a. c. | S.E. | | | |
| 27 | 20 a. | c. | S.E. | 16 a. | c. | N.W. | r. | | 2 |
| 28 | 2 b. | f. | N.W. | 15 a. | f. | S.W. | | | |
| 29 | 4 a. | f. | S.W. | 16 a. | f. | W. | r. | | ½ |
| 30 | 6 a. | c. | N.W. | 14 a. | c. | N.W. | r. | | 1 |
| 31 | 2 b. | c. a. s. | N.W. | 8 a. | f. a. c. | N.W. | f. | | 1 |

| Day of the month | Therm. at sun-rise | Weather | Wind at sun-rise | Therm. at four o'clock | Weather | Wind at four o'clock | River | | |
|---|---|---|---|---|---|---|---|---|---|
| | | | | | | | r. and f. | Feet | Inches |
| 1805 | Deg. | | | Deg. | | | | | |
| Feb. 1 | 6 a. | c. | N.W. | 16 a. | f. | N.W. | r. | | 2½ |
| 2 | 12 b. | f. | N.W. | 3 a. | f. | S. | f. | | 1 |
| 3 | 8 b. | f. | S.W. | 2 a. | f. | W. | | | |
| 4 | 18 b. | f. | N.W. | 9 b. | f. | W. | | | |
| 5 | 10 a. | f. | N.W. | 20 a. | f. | N.W. | r. | | 1 |
| 6 | 4 b. | f. | N.W. | 12 a. | f. | W. | r. | | ½ |
| 7 | 18 a. | f. | S.E. | 29 a. | c. | S. | r. | | ½ |
| 8 | 18 a. | f. | N.W. | 28 a. | c. | N.E. | f. | | 1 |
| 9 | 10 a. | f. | S.E. | 33 a. | c. | S.E. | | | |
| 10 | 18 a. | c. a. s. | N.W. | 12 a. | c. | N.W. | | | |
| 11 | 8 b. | f. | N.W. | 2 b. | f. | N.W. | | | |
| 12 | 14 b. | f. | S.E. | 2 a. | f. | W. | | | |
| 13 | 2 b. | c. | S.E. | 10 a. | c. | N.W. | f. | | 1 |
| 14 | 2 a. | c. a. s. | N.W. | 2 b. | f. | N.W. | | | |
| 15 | 16 b. | f. | S.W. | 6 b. | f. | W. | | | |
| 16 | 2 a. | f. | S.E. | 8 a. | f. | W. | f. | | 1 |
| 17 | 4 a. | c. | S.E. | 12 a. | f. | N.W. | | | |
| 18 | 4 a. | s. | N.E. | 10 a. | f. | S. | | | |
| 19 | 4 a. | f. | S.E. | 20 a. | f. | S. | | | |
| 20 | 2 a. | f. | S. | 22 a. | f. | S. | | | |
| 21 | 6 a. | f. | S. | 30 a. | f. | S. | | | |
| 22 | 8 a. | c. | N. | 32 a. | c. a. r. | | | | |
| 23 | 18 a. | f. | N.W. | 32 a. | f. | W. | r. | | ½ |
| 24 | 8 a. | f. | N.W. | 32 a. | f. | W. | | | |
| 25 | 16 a. | f. | W. | 38 a. | f. | N.W. | | | |
| 26 | 20 a. | f. | N.E. | 31 a. | f. | N. | | | |
| 27 | 26 a. | f. | S.E. | 36 a. | f. | E. | f. | | ½ |
| 28 | 24 a. | f. | E. | 38 a. | c. | S.E. | | | |
| Mar. 1 | 28 a. | c. | W. | 38 a. | f. | N.W. | | | |
| 2 | 28 a. | f. | N.E. | 36 a. | f. | N.E. | r. | | 1½ |
| 3 | 28 a. | c. | E. | 39 a. | f. | N.W. | | | |
| 4 | 26 a. | f. | N.W. | 36 a. | f. | N.W. | | | |
| 5 | 22 a. | f. | E. | 40 a. | f. | N.W. | | | |
| 6 | 26 a. | c. | E. | 36 a. | f. | E. | r. | | 2 |
| 7 | 12 a. | f. | E. | 26 a. | c. | E. | r. | | 2 |
| 8 | 7 a. | c. | E. | 12 a. | f. | E. | r. | | 2½ |
| 9 | 2 a. | c. | N. | 18 a. | f. | N.W. | r. | | 2 |
| 10 | 2 b. | f. | N.W. | 12 a. | f. | N.W. | r. | | 3½ |
| 11 | 12 a. | c. | S.E. | 26 a. | f. a. c. | N.W. | r. | | 4½ |
| 12 | 2 b. | f. a. s. | N. | 10 a. | f. | N.W. | r. | | 5 |

| Day of the month | Therm. at sun-rise | Weather | Wind at sun-rise | Therm. at four o'clock | Weather | Wind at four o'clock | River r. and f. | Feet | Inches |
|---|---|---|---|---|---|---|---|---|---|
| 1805 | Deg. | | | Deg. | | | | | |
| Mar. 13 | 1 b. | f. | S.E. | 28 a. | f. | S.W. | r. | | 3½ |
| 14 | 18 a. | f. | S.E. | 40 a. | f. | W. | | | |
| 15 | 24 a. | f. | S.E. | 38 a. | f. | W. | f. | | 1 |
| 16 | 32 a. | c. | E. | 42 a. | c. | W. | f. | | 3 |
| 17 | 30 a. | f. | S.E. | 46 a. | f. | S.W. | r. | | 2 |
| 18 | 24 a. | c. | N. | 34 a. | c. | N. | f. | | 1 |
| 19 | 20 a. | c. a. s. | N. | 31 a. | f. | N.W. | r. | | 1 |
| 20 | 28 a. | c. | N.W. | 28 a. | f. | N.W. | r. | | 3 |
| 21 | 16 a. | c. | E. | 26 a. | s. & h. | S. | | | |
| 22 | 22 a. | f. a. s. | S. | 36 a. | f. | S.W. | f. | | 4 |
| 23 | 34 a. | f. | W. | 38 a. | c. a. r. | N.W. | f. | | 4 |
| 24 | 28 a. | c. a. s. | N.E. | 30 a. | c. a. s. | N. | r. | | 1 |
| 25 | 16 a. | f. | E. | 32 a. | f. | S. | r. | | 5 |
| 26 | 20 a. | f. | S.E. | 46 a. | f. | W. | r. | | 4½ |
| 27 | 28 a. | f. | S.E. | 60 a. | f. | S.W. | r. | | 9 |
| 28 | 40 a. | f. | S.E. | 64 a. | f. | S.W. | r. | | 1 |
| 29 | 42 a. | f. | N.W. | 52 a. | f. | N.W. | f. | | 11 |
| 30 | 28 a. | f. | N.W. | 49 a. | f. | N.W. | r. | 1 | 1 |
| 31 | 35 a. | c. a. r. | S.E. | 45 a. | c. | S.E. | r. | | 9 |
| April 1 | 33 a. | c. | N.W. | 43 a. | c. a. t. | W. | f. | | 11 |
| 2 | 28 a. | c. a. r. | N.W. | 38 a. | f. a. c. | W. | f. | | 5 |
| 3 | 24 a. | f. | N. | 44 a. | f. | N. | f. | | 4 |
| 4 | 36 a. | f. | S. | 55 a. | f. | N.W. | f. | | 4 |
| 5 | 30 a. | f. | N.W. | 39 a. | f. | N. | f. | | 2 |
| 6 | 19 a. | f. | N. | 48 a. | c. | N.W. | f. | | 1 |
| 7 | 28 a. | f. | N. | 64 a. | f. | S.W. | r. | | 2 |
| 8 | 19 a. | f. | N.W. | 56 a. | f. | N.W. | f. | | 2 |
| 9 | 38 a. | f. | S.E. | 70 a. | f. | S.W. | f. | | ½ |
| 10 | 42 a. | f. | E. | 74 a. | f. | S.W. | r. | | ¾ |
| 11 | 42 a. | f. | N.W. | 76 a. | f. | W. | f. | | ½ |
| 12 | 56 a. | f. | N.W. | 74 a. | c. r. t. l. | W. | r. | | ½ |
| 13 | 58 a. | f. | S.E. | 80 a. | f. | S.E. | f. | | 1 |
| 14 | 52 a. | c. | S.E. | 82 a. | f. | S.W. | f. | | ¾ |
| 15 | 51 a. | f. | E. | 78 a. | f. | S.W. | f. | | ½ |
| 16 | 54 a. | f. | S.E. | 78 a. | f. | S. | f. | | ½ |
| 17 | 56 a. | f. | N.E. | 74 a. | c. | N.W. | f. | | ½ |
| 18 | 52 a. | f. | N.E. | 64 a. | c. | N. | | | |
| 19 | 54 a. | c. | N.W. | 56 a. | c. | N.W. | | | |
| 20 | 40 a. | c. | N.W. | 42 a. | c. a. s. | N.W. | | | |
| 21 | 28 a. | f. | N.W. | 40 a. | c. | N.W. | f. | | ½ |

## 1804-05

# WITH WILLIAM DUNBAR ON THE WASHITA RIVER TO THE HOT SPRINGS OF ARKANSAS

### Journal of a Voyage by William Dunbar

> William Dunbar (b. Thunderton, Elgin, Scotland, 1749; d. near Natchez, Miss., 1810), planter, explorer, scientist. A younger son of Sir Archibald Dunbar, he came to America in 1771. After a journey down the Ohio and Mississippi rivers in 1773, he settled on a plantation near Baton Rouge in then British West Florida, later transferred to Spanish control. After the turmoil of the Revolutionary years, he moved into the United States near Natchez. Always concerned with scientific pursuits, he served the Spanish as surveyor of the U.S. border and compiled valuable notes on the natural and aboriginal history of the region. At Jefferson's behest, Dunbar undertook the exploration of the Washita River and the Arkansas Hot Springs, located about 45 miles southwest of Little Rock. He maintained good meteorological records at Natchez from 1799 to 1810 and contributed many original papers to the *Transactions of the American Philosophical Society* in Philadelphia.
>
> The Washita expedition left St. Catherines Landing near Natchez on 16 October 1804, arrived near Hot Springs on 6 December, commenced the return trip on 8 January 1805. Dunbar left the party on 17 January and traveled overland arriving at Natchez on 26 January. On 15 January the party viewed the same lunar eclipse mentioned in the Lewis and Clark diary at Fort Mandan, Dakota.
>
> The above extracts contain all items of meteorological interest in Dunbar's daily journal. The winter season of 1804–05, a particularly severe one nationwide, set in on 30 November. The low temperature and snow depths are near the records for the area as revealed by modern records.
>
> Dunbar's journal first appeared in print in shortened form at Natchez in 1806 along with a brief account of the Lewis and Clark expedition. His complete manuscript was delivered to the American Philosophical Society library in 1817. It was not published in full until 1904.
>
> Source: Journal of a voyage. Commencing at St. Catherines landing, on the East bank of the Mississippi, proceeding downwards to the mouth of the Red river, and from thence ascending that river, the Black river and the Washita river as high as the Hot Springs in the proximity of the last mentioned river. Manuscript in the library of the American Philosophical Society. Published in full in: *Documents relating to the purchase and exploration of Louisiana*. Boston and New York, Houghton, Mifflin and Company, 1904. 189 pp.

### November 1804

29. Therm. 72° river water 62°—Cloudy—wind South, blew strong all night. . . . Therm. at 8 p.m. 52°. Extremes 52°–76°. . . . The weather clears up and begins to grow cold, we expect a northwester in the morning.

30. Therm. in air 38°, in river water 60°—river rises 19 inches—clear calm. . . . The wind from North and N.W. opposed us most of the day, so that our progress was not rapid. . . . Therm. at 3 p.m. 57°.

### December 1804

1. Therm. in air 32°, in river water 54°. Clear—calm—river fallen 18 inches. The morning was cold and damp. . . . Therm. at 8 p.m. 35°. Extremes 32°–58°.

2. Therm. in air 30°, in river water 50°. Clear—calm—river fallen 4 inches. . . . Therm. at 8 p.m. 38°. Extremes 30°–59°.

3. Therm. in air 38°—in river water 48°—clear—calm—river fallen 8 inches . . . it was now night, the stars were visible, the water was cold, and altho' the weather was not freezing, it was far from being mild, the therm. being at 45° . . . we are encamped under the incessant roar of the cataracts which resembles nothing so much that I have heretofore witnessed, as the horrid din of a hurricane at New Orleans in the year 1779. . . . Therm. at 8 p.m. 44°—Extremes 38°–59°.

4. Therm. in air 36°, in river water 48°—clear—calm—river fallen 2 inches. . . . Therm. at 8 p.m. 36°—Extremes 36°–50°.

5. Therm. in air 23°, in water of river 47°—very serene—calm—river risen 2 inches. The morning tho' cold was agreeable, the air being very dry. . . . Therm. at 8 p.m. 38°. Extremes 23°–56°.

6. Therm. in air 45°, in river water 48°—cloudy—light wind at S.W. river fallen 2 inches. . . . This morning the Weather being cloudy we apprehended rain, but hoped to reach the 'fourche of Calfat' (Caulker's creek) the point which is to terminate our navigation & encamp before bad weather . . . soon after we arrived it began to rain, we were however tented before it commenced. Therm. 8 p.m. 56°. Extremes 54°–67°.

7. Therm. before sun-rise 38°, in river water 47°. Cloudy—Wind N.W., river risen 4 inches. . . . Therm. at 3 p.m. 50°—the weather cleared up about 9 p.m. and became very serene and cool with wind at N.W.

8. Therm. in air 10°, in river water 43°—very se-

rene—light wind at N.W. river risen 4 inches. We found the weather this morning extremely cold, the therm. having fallen lower, than we expected in this latitude, particularly at the present early period of the winter season; it is perhaps to be ascribed to the elevation of the country and the neighbourhood of mountains: as we have no barometer with us to indicate the pressure of the atmosphere, we shall when we get to the hot spring, ascertain the degree of the thermometer at which water boils, from which scientific men may draw their own conclusions respecting the elevation of the land. . . . The Therm. at 3 p.m. 47°. We may prepare for another cold night: a flock of swans passed us to day. . . . The Therm. at 8 p.m. 26°; very serene and calm, the stars shown with uncommon lustre: in an hour more the face of the heavens changed, a general cloud produced an intense darkness; the therm. rose to 36° and we expected snow or rain; after midnight notwithstanding, the clouds were dissipated, the face of heaven recovered its brightness & the Stars shone with undiminished splendor. Extremes of the therm. 10°–47°.

9. Therm. in the air 19°, in river water 41° very serene—Wind moderate at N.W. river risen 2 inches. . . . Therm. at 8 p.m. 28°. Extremes 19°–42°.
10. Therm. 26°—very serene. Wind moderate at N.W.—We spent a cold night in our new lodgings. . . . the day proved serene and fine. . . Therm. at 8 p.m. 28°. Extremes 26°–50°.
11. Thermometer before sun-rise 48°. Wind S.E. The weather changed very much in the night; it became much warmer and the heavens were overcast witth one general cloud; the air was still damp and penetrating. . . . At 3 p.m. the thermometer rose to 59° and in the evening at 8 fell to 50°, the weather still being disagreeable and cloudy. . . . No change in the appearance of the weather at bed-time. Extremes of the therm. 48°–59°.
12. Thermometer before sun-rise 36°. The weather has become colder, but still continues overcast, damp and disagreeable, the wind being about north, a few drops of rain fell last evening & during the night. As it still continues cloudy, no astronomical observations could be made. . . . Therm. at 8 p.m. 36°. Extremes 36°–50°.
13. Therm. before sunrise 26°. Wind north. The weather still continues cloudy, dark and disagreeable. Notwithstanding the late severity of the weather, we found along the ridge a considerable number and some variety of plants in flower, & others retaining their verdure. We found indeed the ridge much more temperate than the valley: When we left the valley it was extremely damp, cold and penetrating; upon ascending the ridge, the atmosphere became dry & mild. . . . Therm. at 8 p.m. 30°. Extremes 26°–40° wind North.
14. Therm. 28°. Wind N.E. Cloudy, dark, cold and sleet—This morning has made no improvement on the weather; rain & sleet fell in the night & the ground is hard frozen.

The day continues to drip a little from time to time, being still dark, damp, and disagreeably cold. Therm. at 8 p.m. 32°. Extremes 28°–40°. We have news from the Sargeant that the river has fallen 5 feet.
15. Therm. 26°. Wind N.W. strong. The morning was cloudy, but less dark and disagreeable than the day before. The air became drier and the clouds were dissipating by 9 & 10 o'clock. . . . Therm. at 3 p.m. 32°, at 8 p.m. 30°.
16. Therm. 21°. Wind moderate N W this morning is cold but promises fine weather, the wind nevertheless arose at 9 o'clock & continued to blow strong all day . . . and in the Evening between 10 & 11 o'clock, the Therm. being at 22° perfectly serene and calm. . . . Therm. at 8 p.m. 22°. Extremes 21°–34°.
17. Therm. before Sun rise 26° wind moderate N.W. The morning is bright & promises a fine day . . . but we were disappointed, the evening become hazy, the Stars frequently obscured, and a large halo with a broad white brim appeared around the moon. The night became cloudy & some drops of rain or sleet fell. appearance of bad weather for to morrow. Therm. at 8 p.m. 28°. Extremes 26°–42°.
18. Therm. 34° wind north, Cold, damp, disagreeable. The appearance of the weather prevents Dr. Hunter from making another excursion to day, some rain fell in the night, but the aspect of this morning bespeaks snow or sleet. . . . The day continues dark, cloudy & rainy: in the afternoon it begun to hail & in the evening it snowed pretty fast; about 8 p.m. it was 3 inches thick; Therm. at the same hour 32°. Extremes 32°–36°.
19. Therm. 30° wind in the valley West, but changeable; This morning we have a full prospect of a northern winter, the ground is covered 4 inches with snow and it continues from time to time to fall, tho' not remarkably fast, the eves of our Cabin hang with beautiful icicles, which we have the pleasure of admiring thro' the logs as we sit by the fireside: out-door business being out of the question . . . the same state of the weather continues, the therm. at 3 p.m. being at 30° and

at 8 p.m. 28° at bed time the weather still continues dark and threatening more snow.

20. Therm. 30° wind in the valley west. There appears over head driving light clouds from the N.W. The snow continues lying on the ground, the night was very cold, but has greatly softened toward morning, from appearances we expect a thaw, it becomes a little clearer. The Dr. and myself both a little indisposed probably from cold & wet feet and the inclemency of the weather; after breakfast, some hopes of the clouds dissipating. The Sun has shown himself thro' the veil of clouds for a moment. Prepare for observation but disappointed the heavens are again completely veiled in clouds and a thaw comes on, the Therm. at 36° at 3 p.m. . . . Therm. at 10 p.m. 32°. The weather continues cloudy & the snow lies upon the ground the thaw having stopped.

21. Therm. 32° Wind N. No favorable change as yet in the weather; cloudy, damp, dark & cold, the snow still lies upon the ground, so that the Dr. is unable to undertake another more considerable excursion as he intended. We were in hopes of making another set of astronomical observations for the long. of this place but as the time is now much advanced we shall be desirous of getting away as soon as the weather permits the transport of our baggage:—in the meantime the Doctor is desirous of making another excursion while we are preparing to move: observed a spot of ground on the same side of the creek with the hot Springs, covered with herbage which had not lost but partially its verdure; upon this spot no snow lay, it appeared to thaw as soon as it lay, altho' on other places even very near some of the hot springs the snow remained undissolved; as soon as the weather permits I shall examine this ground and ascertain the temperature which resists the rigours of winter: what a fine situation for a green or hot house, where at a small expence all the tropical fruits may be propagated. Therm. at 3 p.m. 36° it has rained a little we were in hopes of seeing the snow carried away, that it might afterwards become dry undeer foot. . . . Therm. 8 p.m. 31°.

22. Therm. 31° wind N. dark & cloudy, the Snow continues upon the ground. without any prospect of favorable change; after breakfast it began to rain, the water the rain froze as it fell upon the branches of the trees, many limbs broke down around us in consequence of the weight of the Ice adhering to them; we are still confined within doors by the inclemency of the weather which greatly retards us, so that we cannot even prosecute our intended researches respecting the hot springs. . . . The Therm. at 3 p.m. 36°. The day continues unfavorable & keeps dropping rain from time to time, yet the snow does not melt: The temperature of the hot springs remains the same as in the former trial & the temperature of boiling water was ascertained to be 212°; hence it appears that this place is not elevated so as sensibly to alter the pressure of the atmosphere, otherwise water would boil at a smaller temperature. . . . Therm. 8 p.m. 34° Snow falls again this Evening—no prospect of a change.

23. Therm. before sunrise 30°. Wind N.W. by the clouds. blow down the valley reflected from the side of the hill N.N.E.; this morning some appearance of a change. The clouds (scudding from the N.W.) begin to dissipate, the blue celestial Sky appears in several parts of the heavens. The snow still lies partially on the ground—but we hope it will soon dissolve as the Sun appears. . . . The Therm at 3 p.m. was 44° and at 8 p.m. 38°.

24. Therm. before sunrise 32° Wind moderate from N.W. Some prospect this morning of a favorable change, the moon is visible, and the Sun yet behind the hill, announces his approach with a bright blase: prepare for observation . . . at noon obtained a good altitude for the Sun but soon afterwards it became cloudy, so that we got no corresponding altitudes for the regulation of the watch. . . . Therm. 8 p.m. 34°. Extremes 32°–45°.

25. Therm. 34° Wind N.W. Cloudy—The state of the heavens did not admit of any astronomical observations in the morning; it cleared away before noon, so that we had a good meridian of the Sun, which was scarcely over when the clouds again overspread the face of heaven, & it rained a part of the afternoon: the present being Christmas Day, we indulged the men with a holy-day, for which object they had hoarded up their rations of whiskey, to be expended in merriment on this occasion, which terminated with inebriety but no ill consequences ensued. We mused ourselves with farther experiments on the hot waters; the conduct of analysis being left to Doctor Hunter as a professed Chemist, the results will be hereafter given. Thermom. at 8 p.m. 44°. Extremes 34°–51°.

26. Therm. 34°. Wind N.W. clear. prepare for observation. . . . The afternoon being cloudy prevented taking the correspondent equal altitudes for the regulation of the watch. Therm. 8 p.m. 44°. Extremes 34°–50°.

27. This morning being fine Doctor Hunter prepared to make his long meditated excursion of 3 or 4 days into the mountains, which the unfavorable state of the weather has hitherto prevented: the therm. stood at 26° before sun rise, and the face of the hill and creek were shrouded in condensed vapor. . . . Took a set of observations for equal altitudes, but we were again disappointed in observing the corresponding afternoon observations by the intervention of clouds. . . . Therm. at 8 p.m. 38°. Extremes 26°–45°.
28. Therm. 34° Wind S.W.—Cloudy—appearance of rain or snow. . . . A considerable quantity of snow fell while we were engaged on the survey and after our return. Thermometer at 8 p.m. 30°. Extremes 30°–34°—at 3 p.m. 32°.
29. Therm. 25°. Wind at N.W. strong all night, some flying clouds appear in the morning . . . it began to snow at 10 o'clock, but did not continue; the weather continued cloudy, but the exercize of walking rendered the temperature (tho' cold) very agreeable. . . . At 8 p.m. the therm. was down at 24°.—the wind blew strong all the afternoon, but fell calm by night.
30. Therm. in air 9°, in river water 36°—wind very light at N.W. This morning & the night past are the coldest we have experienced this winter. . . . The Sky was most serenely clear this day, its color over head was that of the darkest prussian blue and during last night the stars shown with uncommon lustre. . . . This evening some light clouds appeared about the sun-setting, which is an indication of change of weather; we now anxiously expect rain, as we wait only for the first rise of the river to go down with safety over the falls and rapids; 5 or 6 feet perpendicular will be sufficient. At night the atmosphere became again extremely bright—at 8 p.m. the therm. at 21°. Extremes 9°–38°—It became very cold at 10 p.m.
31. Therm. in air 29°, in river water 36°—Wind S.E. During the night the Weather altered greatly; the temperature was much molified and the stars disappeared; in the morning one general cloud enclosed the horizon, and from the damp penetrating chilliness of the morning we look for snow: ordered setting poles to be made & every thing to be prepared for the first favorable moment to depart. The day continued cloudy, & in the afternoon the therm. having risen to 32° it began to snow and continued all day and part of the night.

## January 1805

1. This morning the thermometer was at 26°—It had ceased snowing in the night but recommenced after day light; the snow was sounded and found in most places to be 11 to 13 inches; we are in hopes that the melting of this snow united to the rain which will probably accompany the thaw, will be sufficient to take us down in safety; being desireous however of ascertaining what aid we had to expect from the snow, I made the following experiment—I took a Cylindric Kettle 10 inches deep & having by sounding found a flat piece of snow of the same depth, I pressed down the Kettle bottom upwards perpendicularly to the ground; I was thus enabled to return the Kettle completely filled with its column of snow, and having thawed it gradually to the temperature of 33° I found the water to measure exactly 1.07 inches, that is, 9.346 inches of snow will yield one inch of water in the circumstances above mentioned; it is observable that the snow fell lightly without wind, it is therefore probable that the proportion of ten to one may be adopted as a general standard to be varied according to circumstances. The snow continued frozen all day, and the therm at 3 p.m. did not fall below the freezing point and in the evening at 8 p.m. it was fallen to 18°.
2. Thermometer in air 6° in river water 32°. Calm—The night proved extremely cold; large fires with all the covering that could conveniently be used were necessary to render our situation comfortable in a bad tent negligently chosen at New Orleans. The sun arose bright and shone with splendor upon the surface of the snow which covered every object upon the ground; the river alone presented a bleak appearance with a condensed vapor floating upon its surface; the temperature of the river was at the freezing point; a kettle of water being brought up to Camp and placed on the ground four feet from a large fire, its surface began immediately to shoot into icy chrystalizations.—Our hunts are tolerably successful, bringing in every day abundance of Venison and Turkies.—The day became pleasant and agreeable, the temperature at 3 p.m. being 45°, and at 8 p.m. the thermometer fell to 32°.
3. Thermometer in air 22°, in river water 34°—wind moderate at N.W. The atmosphere became cloudy in the night and we looked confidently for a change in the weather, but this morning it has become serene and fine; the vicissitudes of the weather have of late been frequent, a change is now extremely desirable but the season seems

obstinately bent against all change. The day became pleasant and of an agreeable temperature, the thermometer at 3 p.m. being 48° and at 8 in the evening 30°.

4. Thermometer in air 22°, in river water 36°—Calm—during the night it became cloudy, not a star was to be seen but before morning it cleared away & became perfectly serene and cloudless. The day proved fine, the sky overhead of a bright but deep prussian blue, the temperature mild, the thermometer at 3 p.m. being up to 50°. In the afternoon the Doctor made an excursion upon the river to examine some neighbouring hills: I continued to bring up and arrange my Journals. The evening was fine, the thermometer at 8 p.m. was at 32°—no favorable appearance yet of rain to raise the river; the snow is disappearing without producing any beneficial effect: we continue here as prisoners, waiting for what is usually called bad weather, to bear us away from this place.

5. Thermometer in air 22°, in river water 36°. Wind N.W. The atmosphere became cloudy in the night, but was perfectly serene and clear at daybreak, so that we have no near prospect of our departure. The day became fine and seemed to invite us to recommence astronomical observations. . . . Wind S.E.

The day continued fine and of mild temperature; some few clouds keep up our hopes of a change—Thermometer at 8 p.m. 28°—Extremes 22°–55°.

6. Thermometer before sun-rise in air 28°, in river water 38°. This morning proved cloudy contrary to expectations and revived our hopes of a change of weather favorable to our descent: This state of the atmosphere continued all day; from time to time there was a little light rain or mist. The rain increased a little after dark, but still very light: the snow now seems melted away to about one fifth or sixth of the original quantity; we began to apprehend that the whole would disappear without any influence upon the river, but now it has risen about 12 inches. Thermometer at 8 p.m. 44°. Extremes 28°–50°.

7. Thermometer in air 64°, in river water 44°. Last night it rained by intervals, so little indeed that a cylindric vessel placed to receive it, did not contain enough to be measured. During the night the temperature was extremely warm, and the weather continues to be cloudy, but not very dark, so that our prospect of rain is not flattering; the river has nevertheless risen 18 inches since last night, which has no doubt been caused by the melting of the snows. The sun shows himself at intervals between the clouds: it became so warm that we dined abroad under the shade of lofty pine and oak trees, upon the wild game of the forest and the river, such as Venison, wild Turkey, bear, Cygnet &c: The thermometer at the hour of dinner was at 75° which at this season produces the sensation of a summer's sun of 90°; the river continues to rise, and we have taken the resolution to wait the present state of the weather and to set out at all events; if there be not water enough to go over the falls with safety by the oar, we shall pass along by letting ourselves down by the help of a rope, step by step, until the danger is passed. Thermometer at 8 p.m. 38°. Extremes 38°–78°. In the evening the river continues to rise.

8. Thermometer in air 28°, in river water 46°. Last night was cloudy, moist and cold, the river rose considerably in the night; we suppose it to be about six feet perpendicular, higher than the level of the river when we came up, we now think ourselves secure of going down with speed and safety . . . Thermometer at 8 p.m. 37°. Extremes 28°–37°. It rained lightly after we encamped, which rendered the flat ground of our encampment very wet and the wood difficult to burn.

9. Thermometer in air 42°, in river water 44°—The river fallen about six inches. During the night it rained by intervals, but very lightly, the air was moist and cold. . . .

The day continued dark, cloudy & cold with the wind at North; at 11 a.m. it began to snow and hail with rain by intervals . . . toward evening it began to clear away; and soon after we encamped the sky became serene. . . . Thermometer at 8 p.m. 24°, Extremes 24°–42°. At 3 p.m. 36° The moon and stars shown with uncommon lustre.

10. Thermometer in air 23°, in river water 42°—river fallen 7 inches. The faces of the heavens changed much in the night, it became extremely dark and cloudy, and this morning the wind was at north; it is cold, damp and penetrating; the river fallen seven inches during the night. After setting out the clouds began to dissipate & the sun to shew himself, a very agreeable sight to travellers in cold & unpleasant weather; it continues nevertheless cold all day, the sun not possessing power to soften the rigorous cold which prevailed, the thermometer not rising above the freezing point from morning until night. . . . Thermometer at 8 p.m. Extremes 19°–32°. The Moon & Stars shine with uncommon splendor.

11. Thermometer in air 11°, in river water 39°. River fallen 4½ inches. Wind moderate at North. The

morning is fine, the sky perfectly serene, but the air very cold and penetrating. . . .

The weather continued clear & very cold all day, we landed at the Cadaux to make a fire and dine, the Thermometer at 3 p.m. 32° at 8 p.m. it fell to 26°.

12. Thermometer in air 20°, in river water 40°—river risen an inch. Much vapor ascending from the river. Part of the night was cloudy and this morning the heavens are not entirely cloudless, we therefore expect an approaching change of weather. The air is damp and penetrating so that it continues yet very cold on board the boat; as the day advanced, it proved more cloudy and disagreeable and altho' at 3 p.m. the thermometer was found at 43°, the sensation of cold to the human body was greater than in dry air at 22°—the face of the heavens was overspread with clouds & the atmosphere extremely moist. . . . The Thermometer at 8 p.m. 30°.

13. Thermometer in air 27°, in river water 40°—river risen 1½ inches—Calm. The morning very fine and the atmosphere dry, consequently the temperature not cold to the human body. These two mornings the river has risen without rain for several days past. . . .

This morning no condensed vapor was visible on the surface of the river, yesterday it was considerable; hence it appears that 13° difference of temperature (the river being highest) does not condense vapor with sufficient rapidity to render it visible, altho' 20° are more than are necessary; it must not be omitted to be mentioned that this morning the atmosphere was extremely dry, and therefore greedy of moisture, and yesterday it was very moist, and consequently not disposed to dissolve water rapidly. The day proved cool, tho' not disagreeably so; the wind in the afternoon N.E. and air moist. . . . Thermometer at 8 p.m. 30°. Extremes 27°–53°.

14. Thermometer in air 23°, in river water 40°—river risen 1½ inch. Wind very light at N.W. The atmosphere is dry and the temperature to the human body seems not very cold; there is a thin condensed vapor upon the surface of the river, the difference of temperature between the river water and the air being this morning 17°; yesterday the atmosphere being nearly in the same state 13° were insufficient to render the vapor visible. If our hygrometers were instruments of less dubious nature, and capable of indicating by a scale the absorbing, disolving or attracting power of the atmosphere for water, without being influenced by heat or cold we should then be able to determine a priori at what difference of temperature between water and air corresponding to a given degree of the hygrometer, ascending vapor will be visibly condensed.

The day continued fine and of an agreeable temperature; at 3 p.m. the thermometer was at 53°, at 8 p.m. 32°. An eclipse of the moon will take place this night after midnight, we prepare to observe it; regulated the watch as near as possible to the apparent time at the setting of the Sun; to-morrow we shall give an account of our observations, the sky is perfectly serene.

15. Thermometers in air 30°, in river water 40°—no vapor visible on the surface of the river: river risen 1½ inch—wind light at S.E. cloudy . . . the commencement of the Eclipse was not correctly noted, occasioned by the very strong effect of the penumbra in our perfectly serene & clear sky. . . . I am rather disposed to say a quarter of a minute [error], for the transparency of the atmosphere was as perfect as can ever be expected in situations not more elevated than ours.

This morning the heavens are veiled by clouds; during the night the thermometer was down to 28° with a pure serene sky and the atmosphere so dry that the cold was not very sensible; this morning with a higher temperature and moist air, it is very cold and penetrating. . . . The moon and stars shine with a mild lustre, no appearance of change in the weather notwithstanding the increased temperature of the atmosphere. Thermometer at 8 p.m. 43°.

16. . . . in river water 41°—river risen 1¼ inches: . . . proceeding from atmospheric moisture, being very different from what we see arising out of the river under considerable difference of temperature—Arrived at the Post of Washita about noon—The day proved very fine and warm, the thermometer at 3 p.m. being at 65° and at 8 p.m. it remained at 60°. Found all well at the post—no news of any importance.

17. Thermometer in air 60°; in river water 44°—river risen one inch. Wind at S.W.—very clear during the night but cloudy this morning. . . .

## COLD FRIDAY IN NEW HAMPSHIRE: 19 JANUARY 1810

The following account, appearing in the *New-Hampshire Patriot* of Concord on 6 February 1810, contained the first public news of the Cold Friday tragedy at Sanbornton, New Hampshire, on 19 January 1810. All subsequent retellings appear to have been based on this single newspaper story.

### MELANCHOLY!

A more extraordinary and distressing scene, than was experienced in Sandbornton [sic] in the late tremendous storm of wind is seldom known. The sufferers are David Brown, Jeremiah Elsworth and his family.

On Friday morning the 19th ult. Mr. Elsworth arose about an hour before sunrise; some part of the house was soon burst in by the violence of the wind. Being apprehensive that the whole house would be soon torn to pieces, and that the lives of the family were in danger, Mrs. E. went into the cellar, taking her youngest child, which she had dressed, with her, leaving her two other children in bed. Mr. E. attempted to go to the nearest neighbor which was to the north, for assistance; but the wind was so strong against him that he found it impracticable. He then set out for the nearest the other way, which is one fourth of a mile, and arrived about sunrise at Mr. Brown's, when his feet were considerably frozen, and he so overcome by the cold, that he did not dare, and Mr. Brown thought it not advisable for him, to return. But Mr. Brown took his horse and sleigh, and went with all possible speed to save the woman and her children from impending destruction. When he arrived, he found Mrs. E. and one child in the cellar, and the other two in bed, whose clothes the wind had blown away, so they could not be dressed. Mr. Brown put a bed into the sleigh, put the children upon it, and covered them over with bedclothes. Mrs. E. also got into the sleigh; but they advanced no more than six or eight rods before the sleigh was blown over, and the children and bed scattered by the wind. Mrs. E. held the horse, while Mr. B collected the children and the bed, and put them into the sleigh again. Mrs. E. then concluded to make her escape on foot; but before she arrived at the house, she was so overcome by the cold, that she found it impossible to walk any farther. She made a stop, concluding that she must then perish. She soon made another attempt by crawling on her hands and knees; in which manner she arrived at Mr. B's house; but was so altered in her looks, that her husband did not know her. He concluded twice to go to the assistance of Mr. B. and his children; but his wife persuaded him not to venture, telling him that Mr. B and her children would certainly perish, and that, if he ventured, he must perish too; and she wished him to stay with her, for she expected to be a corpse herself before night. Mr. B having put the children into the sleigh the second time, proceeded but two or three rods before the sleigh was blown over, and torn to pieces, the bed and children driven to some distance. He then collected them once more, laid them on the bed and covered them over; and then called for help—but to no purpose. Knowing that the children must soon perish in that situation, whose distressing shrieks then pierced his heart, he attempted to carry them all on his shoulder, wrapped in a coverlet; but was soon blown down, and the children taken from him by the violence of the wind. Finding it impossible to carry them all, he left the youngest, which happened to be dressed, by the side of a large log, and attempted to carry the other two in the same manner; but was soon stopped as before. He then took the two, one under each arm, with no other clothing than their shirts. In this manner, though he was blown down once in a few rods, he arrived at the house, in about two hours from the time he left it. The children, though frozen stiff, were alive, but died in a few minutes. Mr. B's hands and feet were badly frozen, and he very much chilled, so that he could not return to fetch the child he had left.

Who can suppress a sympathetic tear, when he considers their wretched, distressing situation? Three so frozen, that they could not leave the house, two dead, and one out in the open world, exposed to all the severity of the weather!

At one o'clock a neighbor came in. Having no hope that the child, which was left, was living, they thought it advisable to send in the first place for a doctor, who arrived about half an hour before sunset. No other person had then arrived: but some came in in a short time. They then went in search of the child left, who was found and brought in dead. Thus the bereaved, distressed parents are left childless.

*New-Hampshire Patriot* (Concord), 6 Feb 1810

## 1816

## SPRINGTIME AT QUEBEC

**Quebec Gazette, 30 May 1816**

**Extraordinary Season.**—After the frost in the week from the 12th to the 19th inst. the weather became mild and dry, with the wind for some days at north-east. At one time, the wind having changed to the south-west, the thermometer rose to 75, and the air, as is usual in

June, was loaded with the smoke of the burning forests. On Sunday last it began to rain, with an easterly wind; the next morning there was fog and a gentle rain. On Tuesday afternoon the wind came from the north west, and blew strong during the night. Yesterday morning there was ice of about a quarter of an inch in thickness, and a slight fall of snow! This morning there also fell some snow, and at eight o'clock the thermometer stood nearly at the freezing point.

The rain of Sunday, and the mild weather of Monday gave a new spring to vegetation. The wheat and the pease, just above the ground, had a most promising appearance; and the meadows and pasture ground were in deep verdure. The blossoms of the wild fruit trees were ready to open, & the buds of the large forest trees were just expanding into leaves. The effect of so severe a frost on this state of vegetation is not known.

The last spring and the present are certainly the most backward of any for the last 25 years.

### Quebec Gazette, 6 June 1816

We are happy in being able to state, that the late Frost has not had any very injurious effect on vegetation. A few fine days, and the present rains, have restored the young crops to all their former vigor. The gardens alone have materially suffered.

### Quebec Gazette, 13 June 1816

**More Extraordinary Weather.**—From eleven o'clock 'till half-past twelve, this day, the 6th June, there has been an uninterrupted fall of Snow in this City.

We noticed in this paper of Thursday last, the 6th instant, the extraordinary circumstance of a fall of snow, of upwards of an hours' duration, on that day. Since that time the weather has presented more permanent and extraordinary features of severity. On the afternoon of the 6th, when the clouds cleared away, the tops of the mountains to the north of the city were perceived to be covered with snow, the most distant apparently to the depth of a foot. On the 7th there was a slight fall of snow during the whole day, the thermometer constantly standing at the freezing point. At half past ten o'clock at night, the roofs of the houses and squares of the town, were completely covered with snow; and the next morning, the 8th, it was observed that the whole of the surrounding country was in the same state, having, within twelve days of the summer solstice, the appearance of the middle of December. A gentleman who was on Friday on the south shore, about fifteen miles back from the St. Lawrence, found banks of snow up to the axeltrees of his carriage, and a drift as in the midst of winter. On the 8th, snow continued to fall at intervals, in different parts of the country. It again snowed on the 9th. From the 6th to the 10th it froze every night. On the 7th the ground in exposed situations, became hard with the frost in the day-time. The wind was constantly strong from the north-west, driving before it an immense mass of lowering clouds, which constantly concealed the sun: it was not until Sunday afternoon that they finally began to clear away. It was then discovered, that though the snow which fell on the night of the 7th had disappeared in the vicinity of the city early on the following day, the tops of the mountains to the north and south still remained covered with snow. On the west side of the Chaudiere, large tracks of cleared land were still covered, and continued so on Monday. We are informed that, in that quarter, the snow lay for some time about a foot in depth.

Among the many unusual circumstances which accompanied a state of weather so entirely unexampled in the memory of the inhabitants or in the annals of the country, we have to notice that, on Thursday, great numbers of birds, which are never found but in the distant forests, resorted to the city, and were to be met with in every street, and even among the shipping. Many of them dropped down dead in the streets, and many were destroyed by thoughtless or cruel persons. The swallows entirely disappeared for several days. Some descriptions of trees began to shed their leaves, withered before they were half expanded. In the country, numbers of sheep newly shorn were killed by the cold. The prudent farmer housed his cattle for several days. In almost every house the stoves were heated as in winter.

The mischief done to the crops in this neighborhood, we flatter ourselves, is not nearly so great as might have been apprehended. The snow on Friday night protected them against one of the severest frosts. If vegetation had been further advanced, it probably would have suffered more. The buds of the orchard trees were hardly opened. In exposed situations, the forest trees have suffered considerably, though the leaves were not half opened. The gardens, and such wild fruit trees as were in blossom, have suffered severely.

Last year was one of the most backward ever before known in the country: on the 4th of June, the trees were not in full leaf. At present, the 21st, they are not so forward as they were last year on the 4th. We have had only five or six days in which the thermometer has risen above 60° of Fahrenheit. In respect to the backwardness of the season, we find the same complaints extend throughout all the northern section of the United States. On the 15th of May, it froze in Virginia and Pennsylvania. About the same time they complain of the cold on the Mississippi and Missouri, and along the Ohio. Lake Erie was not cleared of ice until about the 10th of May. Along the whole course of the St. Lawrence, and even to Halifax, the complaints are the same.

Under circumstances so unfavorable to the productions of the earth throughout so great an extent of country, precautions against scarcity cannot be too strongly recommended. We have a few days remaining, during which potatoes, barley and turnips, may be sown with hopes of their coming to maturity. Nothing which may provide sustenance for man and beast ought to be neglected, though we may yet be blessed with a more favourable year than is indicated by present appearances.

## 1817

## THE LUMINOUS SNOWSTORM

An account of a singular electrical phenomenon, observed during a snow storm accompanied with thunder.

### BY JOHN FARRAR,

PROFESSOR OF MATH. AND NAT. PHIL. IN THE UNIVERSITY AT CAMBRIDGE.

*Memoirs of the American Academy of Arts and Sciences, 1821.*

On the evening of the 17th of January 1817, there was a remarkable thunder-shower, which extended through a great part of the United States. It took place about the same time at Brunswick, in the District of Maine, at Boston and Williamstown, at Andover, Vermont, at Philadelphia, and at Savannah, Georgia. At Boston and several places in the interior, there was rain and snow; at other places only snow, and this in great quantity and accompanied with almost incessant thunder and lightning. There were other electrical appearances also, that were particularly remarkable.

The following is taken from the meteorological register of Professor Cleaveland.

"In the earlier part of the evening, the wind was blowing from the N. E. and the thermometer descended to 17.5°. But after a short calm, the wind suddenly changed to S. E. attended at first by snow and rain and flashes of lightning. The thermometer rose rapidly, while the barometer fell to 28.89. At this time three persons crossing the bridge over the Androscoggin, observed the borders of their hats to be luminous, and when they held up their hands covered with woollen gloves, the ends of their fingers were also luminous. These appearances were observed on the bridge only."

I am informed also by another observing and intelligent gentleman,* who had collected a number of facts relating to this extraordinary phenomenon, from persons in whom he placed the highest confidence, that at Williamstown, it was seen by a physician on the ears and hair of his horse's head, on the whip of a young man who accompanied him, and on the hat of a gentleman, who, in attempting to brush it off, saw it extend itself over the greater part of his hat; and that at Williamstown, Vermont, it was observed by a company of fourteen persons, as they were returning from a religious meeting, on horses, bushes, fences, logs, and on each other. In one instance a quantity of logs and brush appeared perfectly luminous. The preacher broke off several boughs, on the ends of which the fluid rested. In several cases when he presented his hand, the fluid hissed with the appearance and noise of the electric spark. At this time, it snowed very fast, at the rate, as was supposed, of 6 inches in an hour; the lightning was frequent, and the thunder heavy. At Williamstown it rained principally, and also at Brattleborough. But from Adams through Wilmington to Brattleborough it snowed with great rapidity.

A still more particular account of these electrical appearances was communicated to me in a letter from a young gentleman,† a member of Union College, Schenectady, who was at this time residing at Andover, Vermont, and was a witness of what he relates. The following is his statement.

"In the evening of the 17th of January 1817, as I was returning from a neighbour's house in company with another young man, between the hours of ten and eleven, we observed that the snow was falling very fast, and that there were frequent flashes of lightning. The singularity of the last-mentioned appearance, at that season of the year, particularly attracted our attention. After noticing it for some minutes, we passed on, and when at the distance of a few rods, we observed an appearance of light or fire upon the tops of the stakes in the fence and bushes by the side of the way. The novelty of these appearances rendered them, in our opinion, worthy of particular attention. And the probability of their soon disappearing made us more anxious that there might be others to witness the same fact. We accordingly called the people who were in a neighbouring house; but instead of the lights disappearing, they seemed to shine with additional brightness, and to appear where they were unobserved before; on our hats, on our hair, when our heads were uncovered, and on a woollen mitten, when held above our heads. These lights appeared on all substances, which extended to any considerable distance above the surface of the ground,

---

* Professor Dewey of Williams College.

† Joel Manning, jun.

and approached to a point; but they had not all the same form. For the most part the light appeared like a spark or star, but in some instances it resembled a blaze, in form of an inverted cone of about two inches in height, and three fourths of an inch in diameter at the base. These blazes emitted a hissing sound resembling that of the water in a tea-kettle just before it boils, which could be heard distinctly at the distance of six or eight feet. After viewing them for some time, we proceeded homewards, and in passing over ground somewhat higher, found this appearance to increase, so that our hats and shoulders were almost covered with the lights; and when we spit, the small particles of saliva, when at a little distance from the mouth, assumed a shining appearance. After going about fifty or sixty rods, we came to the side of a lot of standing timber, where these appearances were not to be seen, except on the tops of some high apple trees on the other side of the road. The falling of the snow, and the height prevented our ascertaining whether there were lights on the tops of the forest trees. We did not leave the standing timber, until we had come down on low ground, where we saw no lights until we got home. About twelve o'clock, we returned to the place where we first saw the lights. The snow was yet falling very fast, and there appeared to be still more of the before-mentioned lights; but we saw no blazes.

"Where these lights were seen, was a tongue of elevated land, extending from the north, down between two quite small branches of Williams' river. The whole length of way we travelled that evening was about a mile. Where we first saw the lights, was very near the top of this ridge of land, descending steeply to the east, for about a hundred rods to a small stream, not sufficient to turn a mill, and to the west, with a more gradual descent, for a mile to another stream a little larger. There are no very considerable streams in this vicinity.

"The wind was not strong, but a light breeze blowing from the northeast, and the weather was not so cold as usual for that season of the year. The flashes of lightning, when we first observed them, which was a little past ten o'clock, were very frequent four or five in a minute; but the claps of thunder were seldom, and these appeared to be at a distance, and not heavy. But the flashes of lightning soon became less frequent, more vivid and more usually attended with thunder. About twelve o'clock, there was a number of very sharp flashes of lightning, attended with quite heavy thunder.

"The above-mentioned blazes of light were precisely like the appearance upon a wire, in a dark room, overcharged with positive electricity. All that I can say of the circumstances necessary to produce these blazes is, that we observed them on stakes in the fence higher than other substances near them, and extending to a considerable depth in the ground, and when they were removed, the blazes disappeared, and were succeeded by stars."

Appearances similar to the above, it is said, were observed a few years ago at Colchester, Connecticut, and on the 10th of March 1817, at Shelburn, Hampshire County, Ms. During a thunder storm at the latter place, a light appeared on a well-pole when elevated. Upon its being drawn down, the light gradually diminished, and at length entirely vanished. When the pole was raised again, it reappeared.

[The storm was the subject of another brief article. In the hill country of southern Vermont the displays of St. Elmo's Fire were noticed in Andover, Jamaica, Wardsborough, Dover, Somerset, Stratton, and Newfane: On luminous appearances in the atmosphere. By J. A. Allen, A.M., lecturer on chemistry in Middlebury College. *American Journal of Science* (New Haven). 4-2 (1822), 341–42.]

# THE NEW HAVEN, CONNECTICUT, TEMPERATURE RECORD: 1870–1870

### New Haven, Connecticut

| | Mean Temperature, °F. | | | | Departure from normal, °F. | | | |
|---|---|---|---|---|---|---|---|---|
| | Dec. | Jan. | Feb. | Mar. | Dec. | Jan. | Feb. | Mar. |
| 1780–81. | 32.4 | 34.0 | 33.5 | 38.5 | +2.0 | +7.2 | +5.1 | +2.8 |
| 82. | 31.6 | 24.9 | 26.9 | 35.0 | +1.2 | −1.9 | −1.5 | −0.7 |
| 83. | 31.1 | 26.1 | 32.4 | 36.0 | +0.7 | −0.7 | +4.0 | +0.3 |
| 84. | 29.8 | 21.2 | 20.6 | 34.3 | −0.6 | −5.6 | −7.8 | −1.4 |
| 85. | 29.2 | 23.9 | 27.2 | 31.1 | −1.2 | −2.9 | −1.2 | −4.6 |
| 86. | 31.3 | 24.4 | 30.0 | 41.1 | +0.9 | −2.4 | +1.6 | +5.4 |
| 87. | 26.1 | 27.7 | 28.2 | 39.2 | −4.3 | +0.9 | −0.2 | +3.5 |
| 88. | 31.3 | 25.6 | 26.8 | 37.4 | +0.9 | −1.2 | −1.6 | +1.7 |
| 89. | 29.6 | 29.4 | 24.1 | 37.8 | −0.8 | +2.6 | −4.3 | +2.1 |
| 90. | 36.2 | 33.3 | 31.1 | 36.9 | +5.8 | +6.5 | +2.7 | +1.2 |
| 91. | 22.6 | 28.0 | 25.8 | 42.2 | −7.8 | +1.2 | −2.6 | +6.5 |
| 92. | 31.9 | 21.0 | 26.7 | 38.4 | +1.5 | −5.8 | −1.7 | +2.7 |
| 93. | 28.8 | 30.6 | 29.0 | 38.2 | −1.6 | +3.8 | +0.6 | +2.5 |
| 94. | 30.6 | 29.0 | 27.4 | 38.2 | +0.2 | +2.2 | −1.0 | +2.5 |
| 95. | 38.2 | 26.2 | 27.6 | 34.9 | +7.8 | −0.6 | −0.8 | −0.8 |
| 96. | M | 30.1 | 28.6 | 34.1 | M | +3.3 | +0.2 | −1.6 |
| 97. | 26.6 | 24.5 | 34.9 | 38.1 | −3.8 | −2.3 | +6.5 | +2.4 |
| 98. | 25.9 | 28.9 | 26.8 | 37.8 | −4.5 | +2.1 | −1.6 | +2.1 |
| 99. | 24.7 | 28.1 | 26.3 | 31.3 | −5.7 | +1.3 | −2.1 | −4.4 |
| 1799–1800. | 31.3 | 26.9 | 29.2 | 36.3 | +0.9 | +0.1 | +0.8 | +0.6 |
| 1800–01. | 35.2 | 28.7 | 29.4 | 41.0 | +4.8 | +1.9 | +1.0 | +5.3 |
| 02. | 35.1 | 35.6 | 28.4 | 38.2 | +4.7 | +8.8 | 0.0 | +2.5 |
| 03. | 31.1 | 27.9 | 33.6 | 37.5 | +0.7 | +1.1 | +5.2 | +1.8 |
| 04. | 37.8 | 24.5 | 29.8 | 35.8 | +7.4 | −2.3 | +1.4 | +0.1 |
| 05. | 28.1 | 23.7 | 30.5 | 40.4 | −2.3 | −3.1 | +2.1 | +4.7 |
| 06. | 39.6 | 27.6 | 34.4 | 31.9 | +9.2 | +0.8 | +6.0 | −3.8 |
| 07. | 31.0 | 25.5 | 28.5 | 33.0 | +0.6 | −1.3 | +0.1 | −2.7 |
| 08. | 37.5 | 26.4 | 32.0 | 38.7 | +7.1 | −0.4 | +3.6 | +3.0 |
| 09. | 34.3 | 24.8 | 25.8 | 35.2 | +3.9 | −2.0 | −2.6 | −0.5 |
| 10. | 36.7 | 28.0 | 32.7 | 35.6 | +6.3 | +1.2 | +4.3 | −0.1 |
| 11. | 31.5 | 27.2 | 27.3 | 39.4 | +1.1 | +0.4 | −1.1 | +4.7 |
| 12. | 30.3 | 24.2 | 27.0 | 31.2 | −0.1 | −2.6 | −1.4 | −4.5 |
| 13. | 30.6 | 23.4 | 27.3 | 32.4 | +0.2 | −3.4 | −1.1 | −3.3 |
| 14. | 30.0 | 25.3 | 29.6 | 32.9 | −0.4 | −1.5 | +1.2 | −3.8 |
| 15. | 28.2 | 24.6 | 24.4 | 35.6 | −2.2 | −2.2 | −4.0 | −0.1 |
| 16. | 28.8 | 23.0 | 28.4 | 32.4 | −0.6 | −3.8 | 0.0 | −3.3 |
| 17. | 30.6 | 25.0 | 19.8 | 32.4 | +0.2 | −1.8 | −8.6 | −3.3 |
| 18. | 30.6 | 25.2 | 20.6 | 34.3 | +0.2 | −1.6 | −7.8 | −1.4 |
| 19. | 25.6 | 30.5 | 31.5 | 29.9 | −4.8 | +3.7 | +3.1 | −5.8 |
| 20. | 30.4 | 22.6 | 30.6 | 33.9 | 0.0 | −4.2 | +2.2 | −2.8 |
| 21. | 28.0 | 19.1 | 31.2 | 33.9 | −2.4 | −7.7 | +2.8 | −1.8 |
| 22. | 28.4 | 23.4 | 27.7 | 40.3 | −2.0 | −3.4 | −0.7 | +4.6 |
| 23. | 30.9 | 27.9 | 22.1 | 33.9 | +0.5 | +1.1 | −6.3 | −1.8 |
| 24. | 32.9 | 31.8 | 29.8 | 35.9 | +2.5 | +5.0 | +1.4 | +0.2 |
| 25. | 35.9 | 29.0 | 31.1 | 40.8 | +5.4 | +2.2 | +2.7 | +5.1 |
| 26. | 30.0 | 26.5 | 31.6 | 35.1 | −0.4 | −0.3 | +3.2 | −0.6 |
| 27. | 31.4 | 22.1 | 29.8 | 36.9 | +1.0 | −4.7 | +1.4 | +1.2 |
| 28. | 34.2 | 32.5 | 38.1 | 38.8 | +3.8 | +5.7 | +9.7 | +3.1 |
| 29. | 36.2 | 27.8 | 22.0 | 32.4 | +5.8 | +1.0 | −6.4 | −3.3 |
| 30. | 38.6 | 25.6 | 26.4 | 39.1 | +8.2 | −1.2 | −2.0 | +3.4 |
| 31. | 34.4 | 23.2 | 24.6 | 41.2 | +4.0 | −3.6 | −3.8 | +5.5 |
| 32. | 17.4 | 26.2 | 27.9 | 36.7 | −13.0 | −0.6 | −0.5 | +1.0 |
| 33. | 31.7 | 30.5 | 25.9 | 33.4 | +1.3 | +3.7 | −2.5 | −2.3 |
| 34. | 30.8 | 25.5 | 34.0 | 37.4 | +0.4 | −1.3 | +5.6 | +1.7 |
| 1834–35. | 28.4 | 25.2 | 23.5 | 32.3 | −2.0 | −1.6 | −4.9 | −3.4 |

### New Haven, Connecticut

| | Mean Temperature, °F. | | | | Departure from normal, °F. | | | |
|---|---|---|---|---|---|---|---|---|
| | Dec. | Jan. | Feb. | Mar. | Dec. | Jan. | Feb. | Mar. |
| 1835–36. | 23.5 | 24.3 | 17.9 | 30.3 | −6.9 | −2.5 | −10.5 | −5.4 |
| 37. | 27.9 | 20.1 | 26.6 | 33.2 | −2.5 | −6.7 | −1.8 | −2.5 |
| 38. | 29.7 | 34.9 | 23.3 | 39.0 | −0.7 | +8.1 | −5.1 | +3.3 |
| 39. | 26.4 | 26.2 | 30.1 | 36.8 | −4.0 | −1.6 | +1.7 | +1.1 |
| 40. | 31.7 | 19.2 | 32.5 | 37.3 | +1.3 | −7.6 | +4.1 | +1.6 |
| 41. | 29.6 | 31.1 | 26.7 | 37.3 | −0.8 | +4.3 | −1.7 | +1.6 |
| 42. | 34.3 | 32.6 | 36.6 | 42.8 | +3.9 | +5.8 | +8.2 | +7.1 |
| 43. | 27.1 | 31.4 | 19.4 | 33.1 | −3.3 | +4.6 | −9.0 | −2.6 |
| 44. | 29.1 | 19.5 | 31.4 | 39.8 | −1.3 | −7.3 | +3.0 | +4.1 |
| 45. | 30.2 | 30.3 | 28.6 | 39.8 | −0.2 | +3.5 | +0.2 | +4.1 |
| 46. | 25.3 | 29.3 | 24.5 | 38.6 | −5.1 | +2.5 | −3.9 | +2.9 |
| 47. | 29.1 | 28.3 | 28.1 | 33.0 | −1.3 | +1.5 | −0.3 | −2.7 |
| 48. | 36.5 | 31.2 | 27.3 | 33.8 | +6.1 | +4.4 | −1.1 | −1.9 |
| 49. | 36.2 | 23.0 | 22.4 | 38.0 | +5.8 | −3.8 | −6.0 | +2.3 |
| 50. | 30.7 | 30.7 | 31.9 | 35.6 | +0.3 | +3.9 | +3.5 | −0.1 |
| 51. | 28.7 | 29.5 | 32.0 | 38.5 | −1.7 | +2.7 | +3.6 | +2.8 |
| 52. | 24.9 | 23.6 | 29.0 | 35.5 | −5.6 | +3.2 | +0.6 | −0.2 |
| 53. | 39.2 | 28.3 | 32.1 | 39.4 | +8.8 | +1.5 | +3.7 | +3.7 |
| 54. | 31.3 | 27.6 | 28.5 | 36.2 | +0.9 | +0.8 | +0.1 | −0.5 |
| 55. | 26.7 | 31.4 | 23.6 | 34.5 | −3.7 | +4.8 | −4.8 | −1.2 |
| 56. | 33.6 | 19.1 | 24.5 | 30.8 | +3.2 | −7.7 | −3.9 | −4.9 |
| 57. | 27.8 | 17.4 | 34.7 | 33.8 | −2.6 | −9.4 | +6.3 | −1.9 |
| 58. | 36.1 | 34.7 | 25.4 | 34.3 | +5.7 | +7.9 | −3.0 | −1.4 |
| 59. | 30.7 | 25.8 | 30.7 | 40.3 | +0.3 | −1.0 | +2.3 | +4.6 |
| 60. | 27.5 | 29.0 | 27.6 | 39.7 | −2.9 | +2.2 | −0.8 | −4.0 |
| 61. | 27.0 | 27.3 | 34.3 | 38.2 | −3.4 | +0.5 | +5.9 | +2.5 |
| 62. | 33.6 | 26.8 | 28.9 | 36.0 | +2.2 | 0.0 | −0.5 | +0.3 |
| 63. | 32.1 | 32.9 | 30.1 | 31.1 | +1.7 | +6.1 | +1.7 | −4.6 |
| 64. | 29.5 | 27.5 | 30.8 | 37.0 | −0.9 | +0.7 | +2.4 | −1.3 |
| 65. | 29.5 | 22.6 | 27.7 | 40.6 | −0.9 | −4.2 | −0.7 | +4.9 |
| 66. | 34.0 | 24.8 | 29.8 | 34.6 | +3.6 | −2.0 | +1.4 | −1.1 |
| 67. | 30.2 | 20.7 | 34.4 | 34.0 | −0.2 | −6.1 | +6.0 | −1.7 |
| 68. | 25.4 | 24.1 | 22.8 | 36.5 | −5.0 | −2.7 | −5.6 | +0.8 |
| 69. | 27.0 | 31.7 | 31.9 | 33.2 | −3.4 | +4.9 | +3.5 | −2.5 |
| 1869–70. | 31.8 | 34.1 | 28.5 | 33.1 | +1.4 | +7.3 | +0.1 | −2.6 |

Source: Elias Loomis and H. A. Newton. On the mean temperature, and on the fluctuations of temperature at New Haven, Conn., *Trans. Conn. Acad. Arts and Sciences*. 1–1 (1866), 200–223.

Alexis Caswell. Results of meteorological observations made at Providence, R. I., extending over a period of forty-five years, from December, 1831, to December, 1876. *Smithsonian Contributions to Knowledge. 24.* Washington, The Smithsonian Institution, 1885. 13.

Note. No satisfactory set of records for the years 1866–70 for New Haven or southern Connecticut have been located. The figures employed by Kirk and by Clayton, as well as other SI and SG records for southern Connecticut, have certain obvious errors which distort the monthly and seasonal averages. It was found that in both the early and the modern period the records for Providence, R. I., and New Haven show close agreement. The Providence record of Prof. Caswell 1831–65 was compared with the New Haven record 1831–65 and the following monthly variations found: Dec. +1.2°, Jan. −0.1°, Feb. +1.0°, and March +2.1°. These differences were added to the Providence record and employed in the above table for the years 1866–70. For the modern period (1930–60) the Providence (airport) record shows even smaller differences from the New Haven (airport) record: −0.1°, −0.7°, −0.2°, and −0.8°.

## New Haven, Connecticut
## Relative Coldness

| | Percentile* | | | | Graphic** | | | |
|---|---|---|---|---|---|---|---|---|
| | Dec. | Jan. | Feb. | Mar. | Dec. | Jan. | Feb. | Mar. |
| 1780–81. | 74 | 95 | 89 | 75 | + | ++ | ++ | + |
| 82. | 67 | 33 | 32 | 38 | + | – | – | N |
| 83. | 59 | 44 | 86 | 49 | N | N | + | N |
| 84. | 39 | 9 | 5 | 34 | N | – – | – – | – |
| 85. | 33 | 22 | 34 | 5 | – | – | – | – – |
| 86. | 64 | 26 | 66 | 96 | + | – | + | ++ |
| 87. | 11 | 58 | 46 | 83 | – – | N | N | + |
| 88. | 63 | 42 | 31 | 63 | + | N | – | + |
| 89. | 37 | 75 | 14 | 79 | – | + | – | + |
| 90. | 91 | 94 | 75 | 57 | ++ | ++ | + | N |
| 92. | 2 | 64 | 22 | 98 | – – | N | – | ++ |
| 92. | 72 | 8 | 28 | 73 | + | – – | – | + |
| 93. | 29 | 82 | 57 | 72 | – | + | N | + |
| 92. | 52 | 73 | 38 | 71 | N | + | N | + |
| 95. | 96 | 45 | 41 | 37 | ++ | N | N | – |
| 96. | 51 | 77 | 54 | 31 | N | + | N | – |
| 97. | 13 | 28 | 97 | 67 | – – | – | ++ | + |
| 98. | 9 | 69 | 29 | 65 | – – | + | – | + |
| 99. | 4 | 65 | 24 | 7 | – – | + | – | – – |
| 1799–1800. | 62 | 52 | 58 | 52 | N | N | N | N |
| 1800–1801. | 85 | 68 | 59 | 95 | ++ | + | N | ++ |
| 02. | 84 | 99 | 48 | 69 | + | ++ | N | + |
| 03. | 58 | 62 | 91 | 64 | N | N | ++ | + |
| 04. | 95 | 27 | 65 | 46 | ++ | – | + | N |
| 05. | 23 | 21 | 69 | 92 | – | – | + | ++ |
| 06. | 99 | 57 | 95 | 8 | ++ | N | ++ | – – |
| 07. | 57 | 39 | 52 | 17 | N | N | N | – |
| 08. | 94 | 48 | 84 | 77 | ++ | N | + | + |
| 09. | 82 | 32 | 21 | 41 | + | – | – | N |
| 10. | 93 | 63 | 88 | 45 | ++ | N | ++ | N |
| 11. | 66 | 53 | 37 | 85 | + | N | – | + |
| 12. | 45 | 24 | 33 | 6 | N | – | – | – – |
| 13. | 47 | 18 | 36 | 14 | N | – | – | – |
| 14. | 42 | 37 | 61 | 15 | N | – | N | – |
| 15. | 24 | 29 | 15 | 44 | – | – | – | N |
| 16. | 28 | 15 | 47 | 13 | – | – | N | – – |
| 17. | 48 | 34 | 3 | 12 | N | – | – – | – – |
| 18. | 49 | 36 | 4 | 33 | N | – | – – | – |
| 19. | 8 | 81 | 78 | 1 | – – | + | + | – – |
| 20. | 46 | 13 | 71 | 28 | N | – – | + | – |
| 21. | 22 | 3 | 76 | 27 | – | – – | + | – |
| 22. | 25 | 17 | 43 | 91 | – | – | N | ++ |
| 23. | 56 | 61 | 7 | 26 | N | N | – – | – |
| 24. | 75 | 89 | 64 | 47 | + | ++ | + | N |
| 25. | 86 | 72 | 74 | 94 | + | + | + | ++ |
| 26. | 41 | 49 | 79 | 39 | N | N | + | N |
| 27. | 65 | 11 | 63 | 56 | + | – – | + | N |
| 28. | 79 | 91 | 99 | 78 | + | ++ | ++ | + |
| 29. | 89 | 59 | 6 | 11 | ++ | N | – – | – – |
| 30. | 97 | 41 | 35 | 82 | ++ | N | – | + |
| 31. | 83 | 16 | 18 | 97 | + | – | – | ++ |
| 32. | 1 | 47 | 44 | 54 | – – | N | N | N |
| 33. | 69 | 79 | 23 | 23 | + | + | – | – |
| 34. | 55 | 38 | 92 | 62 | N | N | ++ | N |
| 1834–35. | 26 | 35 | 12 | 9 | – | – | – – | – – |

## New Haven, Connecticut
## Relative Coldness

| | Percentile* | | | | Graphic** | | | |
|---|---|---|---|---|---|---|---|---|
| | Dec. | Jan. | Feb. | Mar. | Dec. | Jan. | Feb. | Mar. |
| 1835–36. | 3 | 25 | 1 | 2 | – – | – | – – | – – |
| 37. | 21 | 6 | 26 | 22 | – | – – | – | – |
| 38. | 38 | 98 | 11 | 81 | N | ++ | – – | + |
| 39. | 12 | 46 | 68 | 55 | – – | N | + | N |
| 40. | 68 | 4 | 87 | 61 | + | – – | ++ | N |
| 41. | 36 | 84 | 27 | 59 | – | + | – | N |
| 42. | 81 | 92 | 98 | 99 | + | ++ | ++ | ++ |
| 43. | 17 | 86 | 2 | 19 | – | + | – – | – |
| 44. | 32 | 5 | 77 | 88 | – | – – | + | ++ |
| 45. | 43 | 78 | 53 | 87 | N | + | N | ++ |
| 46. | 6 | 74 | 17 | 76 | – – | + | – | + |
| 47. | 31 | 67 | 45 | 16 | – | + | N | – |
| 48. | 92 | 85 | 35 | 25 | ++ | + | N | – |
| 49. | 88 | 14 | 8 | 66 | ++ | – | – – | + |
| 50. | 53 | 83 | 82 | 43 | N | + | + | N |
| 51. | 27 | 76 | 83 | 74 | – | + | + | + |
| 52. | 5 | 19 | 56 | 42 | – – | – | N | N |
| 53. | 98 | 66 | 85 | 84 | ++ | N | + | + |
| 54. | 61 | 56 | 51 | 51 | N | N | N | N |
| 55. | 14 | 87 | 13 | 35 | – | ++ | – – | – |
| 56. | 77 | 2 | 16 | 3 | + | – – | – | – – |
| 57. | 19 | 1 | 96 | 24 | – | – – | ++ | – |
| 58. | 87 | 97 | 19 | 32 | ++ | ++ | – – | – |
| 59. | 54 | 43 | 72 | 89 | N | N | + | ++ |
| 60. | 18 | 71 | 39 | 86 | – | + | N | + |
| 61. | 16 | 54 | 93 | 68 | – | N | ++ | + |
| 62. | 76 | 61 | 55 | 48 | + | N | N | N |
| 63. | 73 | 93 | 67 | 4 | + | ++ | + | – – |
| 64. | 35 | 55 | 73 | 58 | – | N | + | N |
| 65. | 34 | 12 | 42 | 93 | – | – – | N | ++ |
| 66. | 78 | 31 | 62 | 36 | + | – | N | – |
| 67. | 44 | 7 | 94 | 29 | N | – – | ++ | – |
| 68. | 7 | 23 | 9 | 53 | – – | – | – – | N |
| 69. | 15 | 88 | 81 | 21 | – | ++ | + | – |
| 1869–70. | 71 | 96 | 49 | 18 | + | ++ | N | – |

\* Percentile. The 90 winter months of the same name from 1780–81 to 1869–70 have been rated according to relative coldness: from 1 for the coldest to 99 for the warmest. Since only 90 seasons are considered, numbers divisible by ten from 10 to 100 have been eliminated to maintain the percentile distribution.

\*\* Graphic: ++ = much above normal, 12½%  
          + = above " 25%  
          N = normal " 25%  
          – = below " 25%  
         – – = much below " 12½%

## New Haven, Connecticut
### Relative Coldness

|  | Percentile* | | | | Graphic** | | | |
|---|---|---|---|---|---|---|---|---|
|  | Coldest Single Month | Two Consecutive Months | Three Months Dec.–Feb. | Four Months Dec.–Mar. | Coldest Single Month | Two Consecutive Months | Three Months Dec.–Feb. | Four Months Dec.–Mar. |
| 1780–81. | 97 | 97 | 94 | 96 | ++ | ++ | ++ | ++ |
| 82. | 45 | 34 | 42 | 31 | N | – | N | – |
| 83. | 58 | 69 | 69 | 65 | N | + | + | N |
| 84. | 12 | 1 | 2 | 2 | – – | – – | – – | – – |
| 85. | 38 | 27 | 24 | 12 | N | – | – | – – |
| 86. | 41 | 52 | 51 | 69 | N | N | N | + |
| 87. | 77 | 49 | 33 | 51 | + | N | – | N |
| 88. | 51 | 32 | 37 | 42 | N | – | – | N |
| 89. | 32 | 38 | 31 | 36 | – | N | – | – |
| 90. | 95 | 94 | 92 | 92 | ++ | ++ | ++ | ++ |
| 91. | 24 | 25 | 8 | 34 | – | – | – – | – |
| 92. | 15 | 14 | 21 | 25 | – | – | – | – |
| 93. | 91 | 84 | 65 | 71 | ++ | + | N | + |
| 94. | 76 | 65 | 58 | 66 | + | N | N | N |
| 95. | 61 | 51 | 81 | 73 | N | N | + | + |
| 96. | 89 | 93 | 72 | 61 | ++ | ++ | + | N |
| 97. | 28 | 16 | 34 | 41 | – | – | – | N |
| 98. | 47 | 43 | 13 | 23 | N | N | – – | – |
| 99. | 34 | 22 | 5 | 3 | – | – | – – | – – |
| 1799–1800. | 65 | 58 | 59 | 52 | N | N | N | N |
| 1800–01. | 87 | 75 | 79 | 88 | ++ | + | + | ++ |
| 02. | 84 | 95 | 91 | 94 | + | ++ | ++ | ++ |
| 03. | 82 | 85 | 78 | 83 | + | + | + | + |
| 04. | 44 | 55 | 76 | 72 | N | N | + | + |
| 05. | 35 | 41 | 38 | 55 | – | N | – | N |
| 06. | 75 | 92 | 96 | 87 | + | ++ | ++ | ++ |
| 07. | 55 | 53 | 49 | 35 | N | N | N | – |
| 08. | 67 | 78 | 87 | 91 | + | + | ++ | ++ |
| 09. | 46 | 28 | 48 | 47 | N | – | N | N |
| 10. | 79 | 88 | 89 | 86 | + | ++ | ++ | + |
| 11. | 72 | 56 | 55 | 67 | + | N | N | + |
| 12. | 39 | 25 | 41 | 18 | N | – | N | – |
| 13. | 29 | 29 | 32 | 21 | – | – | – | – |
| 14. | 52 | 59 | 47 | 32 | N | N | N | – |
| 15. | 43 | 19 | 14 | 19 | N | – | – | – |
| 16. | 27 | 37 | 26 | 17 | – | – | – | – |
| 17. | 9 | 6 | 7 | 5 | – – | – – | – – | – – |
| 18. | 14 | 8 | 11 | 11 | – | – – | – – | – – |
| 19. | 56 | 76 | 63 | 28 | N | + | + | – |
| 20. | 23 | 46 | 45 | 27 | – | N | N | – |
| 21. | 5 | 19 | 18 | 15 | – – | – | – | – |
| 22. | 33 | 36 | 23 | 44 | – | – | – | N |
| 23. | 19 | 24 | 28 | 22 | – | – | – | – |
| 24. | 93 | 91 | 86 | 85 | ++ | ++ | + | + |
| 25. | 92 | 86 | 93 | 95 | ++ | + | ++ | ++ |
| 26. | 68 | 67 | 67 | 58 | + | + | + | N |
| 27. | 17 | 42 | 44 | 46 | – | N | N | N |
| 28. | 98 | 98 | 99 | 98 | ++ | ++ | ++ | ++ |
| 29. | 16 | 21 | 52 | 29 | – | – | N | – |
| 1829–30. | 53 | 39 | 74 | 82 | N | N | + | + |

\* Percentile. The 90 winters from 1780–81 to 1869–70 are rated according to relative coldness, from 1 for the coldest to 99 for the warmest. Since there are only 90 winters, numbers divisible by 10 have been omitted to maintain the percentile distribution.

\*\* Graphic. ++ = Much above normal, 12½%  
+ = Above " 25%  
N = Normal " 25%  
– = Below " 25%  
– – = Much below " 12½%

## New Haven, Connecticut
### Relative Coldness

| | Percentile* | | | | Graphic** | | | |
|---|---|---|---|---|---|---|---|---|
| | Coldest Single Month | Two Consecutive Months | Three Months Dec.–Feb. | Four Months Dec.–Mar. | Coldest Single Month | Two Consecutive Months | Three Months Dec.–Feb. | Four Months Dec.–Mar. |
| 1830–31. | 26 | 13 | 36 | 56 | − | −− | − | N |
| 32. | 2 | 4 | 3 | 7 | −− | −− | −− | −− |
| 33. | 63 | 68 | 66 | 53 | N | + | N | N |
| 34. | 54 | 63 | 75 | 74 | N | N | + | + |
| 35. | 36 | 18 | 15 | 9 | − | − | − | −− |
| 36. | 3 | 3 | 1 | 1 | −− | −− | −− | −− |
| 37. | 11 | 11 | 6 | 6 | −− | −− | −− | −− |
| 38. | 21 | 72 | 57 | 68 | − | + | N | + |
| 39. | 62 | 44 | 39 | 38 | N | N | N | N |
| 40. | 6 | 26 | 43 | 48 | −− | − | N | N |
| 41. | 69 | 74 | 61 | 64 | + | + | N | N |
| 42. | 99 | 99 | 97 | 99 | ++ | ++ | ++ | ++ |
| 43. | 8 | 31 | 17 | 13 | −− | − | − | −− |
| 44. | 7 | 17 | 25 | 43 | −− | − | − | N |
| 45. | 86 | 79 | 68 | 78 | + | + | + | + |
| 46. | 42 | 48 | 19 | 26 | N | N | − | − |
| 47. | 81 | 62 | 46 | 33 | + | N | N | − |
| 48. | 73 | 77 | 84 | 84 | + | + | + | + |
| 49. | 18 | 7 | 29 | 37 | − | −− | − | − |
| 50. | 94 | 89 | 82 | 77 | ++ | ++ | + | + |
| 51. | 85 | 73 | 73 | 76 | + | + | + | + |
| 52. | 31 | 15 | 12 | 16 | − | − | −− | − |
| 53. | 83 | 87 | 95 | 97 | + | ++ | ++ | ++ |
| 54. | 78 | 64 | 62 | 62 | + | N | N | N |
| 55. | 37 | 61 | 35 | 24 | − | N | − | − |
| 56. | 4 | 2 | 9 | 4 | −− | −− | −− | −− |
| 57. | 1 | 5 | 16 | 14 | −− | −− | −− | −− |
| 58. | 48 | 82 | 83 | 81 | N | + | + | + |
| 59. | 59 | 71 | 64 | 79 | N | + | N | + |
| 60. | 66 | 54 | 27 | 49 | N | N | − | N |
| 61. | 64 | 45 | 53 | 59 | N | N | N | N |
| 62. | 57 | 47 | 56 | 54 | N | N | N | N |
| 63. | 96 | 96 | 98 | 93 | ++ | ++ | ++ | ++ |
| 64. | 74 | 66 | 88 | 89 | + | N | ++ | ++ |
| 65. | 22 | 23 | 22 | 45 | − | − | − | N |
| 66. | 49 | 57 | 71 | 57 | N | N | + | N |
| 67. | 13 | 33 | 54 | 39 | −− | − | N | N |
| 68. | 25 | 12 | 4 | 8 | − | −− | −− | −− |
| 69. | 71 | 81 | 77 | 63 | + | + | + | N |
| 1869–70. | 88 | 93 | 85 | 75 | ++ | ++ | + | + |

**Note.** Coldest Single Month: How the coldest month in each winter compared with the coldest month in other winters.
Two Consecutive Months: How the combined average of Dec. and Jan. or Jan. and Feb. compared with the coldest similar periods in other winters. March not considered here.
Three Months: The combined average of Dec., Jan., and Feb. compared with similar periods in other winters.
Four Months: The combined average of Dec., Jan., Feb., and March compared with similar periods in other winters.

## New Haven, Connecticut
## Maximum and Minimum Temperatures, °F.

|  | Dec. | Jan. | Feb. | Mar. | Max. Jan.–Feb. | Min. Dec.–Mar. |
|---|---|---|---|---|---|---|
| 1780-81. | 50/6 | 57/13 | 54/0 | 59/19 | 57 | 0 |
| 82. | 50/8 | 51/−5.5 | 53/2 | 63/10 | 53 | − 5.5 |
| 83. | 59/9 | 51/−7.5 | 54/−13 | 66/5 | 54 | −13 |
| 84. | 57/6 | 45/−2.2 | 45/−10 | 62/−5 | 45 | −10 |
| 85. | 53/−2 | 49/−0.7 | 54/7 | 51/8 | 54 | − 2* |
| 86. | 56/5 | 57/−4 | 50/5 | 75/17 | 57 | − 4 |
| 87. | 46/−7 | 51/4 | 52/2 | 61/17 | 52 | − 7* |
| 88. | 55/12 | 46/4 | 45/0 | 60/9 | 46 | 0 |
| 89. | 54/−6 | 46/6 | 47/−12 | 55/9 | 47 | −12 |
| 90. | 54/16 | 56/12 | 49/4 | 60/5 | 56 | 4 |
| 91. | 45/−8 | 50/1 | 48/1 | 63/14 | 50 | − 8* |
| 92. | 49/8 | 49/−8 | 46/8 | 62/22 | 49 | − 8 |
| 93. | 47/9 | 54/9.5 | 50/8 | 71/7 | 54 | 7** |
| 94. | 50/3 | 57/9 | 49/3 | 70/5 | 57 | 3 |
| 95. | 59/18 | 50/1 | 47/0 | 63/16 | 50 | 0 |
| 96. | M | 50/−6 | 51/2 | 57/6 | 51 | − 6 |
| 97. | 49/−6 | 50/−10 | 52/15 | 58/14 | 52 | −10 |
| 98. | 51/1 | 48/8 | 50/−1 | 64/18 | 50 | − 1 |
| 99. | 49/−3 | 49/−4 | 47/2 | 59/4 | 49 | − 4 |
| 1799-1800. | 45/9 | 48/0 | 50/3 | 61/6 | 50 | 0 |
| 1800-01. | 61/8 | 45/0 | 66/0 | 60/22 | 66 | 0 |
| 02. | 57/10 | 57/13 | 60/−2 | 64/16 | 60 | − 2 |
| 03. | 59/1 | 53/4 | 64/6 | 71/3 | 64 | 1* |
| 04. | 60/13 | 45/0 | 57/8 | 64/5 | 57 | 0 |
| 05. | 54/−1 | 48/−6 | 58/4 | 74/16 | 58 | − 6 |
| 06. | 61/20 | 57/−3 | 66/10 | 60/8 | 66 | − 3 |
| 07. | 52/7 | 52/−2 | 52/−3.5 | 53/11 | 52 | − 3.5 |
| 08. | 56/22 | 52/3 | 63/9 | 63/14 | 63 | 3 |
| 09. | 57/7 | 54/−3 | 56/−9 | 63/7 | 56 | − 9 |
| 10. | 68/4 | 54/−7 | 68/3 | 56/17 | 68 | − 7 |
| 11. | 49/10 | 50/4 | 48/2 | 72/10 | 50 | 2 |
| 12. | 56/0 | 42/−6 | 51/5 | 62/0 | 51 | − 6 |
| 13. | 52/9 | 49/−8 | 42/2 | 62/8 | 49 | − 8 |
| 14. | 48/11 | 40/1 | 48/4 | 66/5 | 48 | 1 |
| 15. | 49/6 | 45/−7 | 41/3 | 59/13 | 45 | − 7 |
| 16. | 50/10 | 45/−6 | 52/0 | 60/5 | 52 | − 6 |
| 17. | 56/10 | 48/−4 | 44/−12 | 48/8 | 48 | −12 |
| 18. | 52/3 | 43/0 | 50/−5 | 58/13 | 50 | − 5 |
| 19. | 47/0 | 56/5 | 60/10 | 50/9 | 60 | 0* |
| 20. | 55/8 | 40/−2 | 49/1 | 68/3 | 49 | − 2 |
| 21. | 45/7 | 47/−12 | 46/7 | 58/11 | 47 | −12 |
| 22. | 46/6 | 53/−10 | 52/2 | 63/21 | 53 | −10 |
| 23. | 63/6 | 47/4 | 46/−2 | 60/0 | 47 | − 2 |
| 24. | 52/6 | 52/6 | 52/0 | 58/17 | 52 | 0 |
| 25. | 54/14 | 48/10 | 51/4 | 69/21 | 51 | 4 |
| 26. | 50/−10 | 52/−14 | 56/−15 | 54/14 | 56 | −15 |
| 27. | 55/2 | 45/−7 | 49/−2 | 63/14 | 49 | − 7 |
| 28. | 55/8 | 53/6 | 60/14 | 69/13 | 60 | 6 |
| 29. | 60/1 | 46/−2 | 40/−2 | 69/10.5 | 46 | − 2 |
| 30. | 61/12 | 48/−5 | 54/−3 | 71/17 | 54 | − 5 |
| 31. | 55/5 | 57/−8 | 45/5 | 62/18 | 57 | − 8 |
| 32. | 44/−11 | 55/−2 | 58/−6 | 60/9 | 58 | −11* |
| 33. | 49/11 | 64/1 | 50/6 | 64/−6 | 64 | − 6** |
| 34. | 46/9 | 57/2 | 57/6.5 | 62/18 | 57 | 2 |
| 1834-35. | 56/−6 | 49/−24 | 57/−5 | 58/−9 | 57 | −24 |

\* Dec.
\*\* Mar.
M: Missing (Dec. 1795)

## New Haven, Connecticut
## Maximum and Minimum Temperatures, °F.

|  | Dec. | Jan. | Feb. | Mar. | Max. Jan.–Feb. | Min. Dec.–Mar. |
|---|---|---|---|---|---|---|
| 1835–36. | 43/−9 | 44/−2 | 45/−8 | 52/7 | 45 | − 9* |
| 37. | 51/−1 | 45/−4 | 45/−1 | 56/5 | 45 | − 4 |
| 38. | 60/4 | 56/10 | 48/7 | 61/20 | 56 | 4* |
| 39. | 48/2 | 51/−2 | 49/4 | 66/7 | 51 | − 2 |
| 40. | 55/5 | 42/−11 | 57/−4 | 71/14 | 57 | −11 |
| 41. | 53/4 | 50/−12 | 54/3 | 67/12 | 54 | −12 |
| 42. | 59/6 | 52/4 | 60/12 | 71/16 | 60 | 4 |
| 43. | 45/10 | 55/−6 | 42/−3 | 49/8 | 55 | − 6 |
| 44. | 45/4 | 44/−5 | 53/5 | 62/13 | 53 | − 5 |
| 45. | 53/0 | 48/4 | 58/−1 | 76/18 | 58 | − 1 |
| 46. | 52/1 | 54/0 | 48/−2 | 66/8 | 54 | − 2 |
| 47. | 56/6 | 53/2 | 50/−2 | 55/11 | 53 | − 2 |
| 48. | 63/1 | 49/−6 | 49/1 | 61/7 | 49 | − 6 |
| 49. | 56/3 | 47/−6 | 47/−6 | 66/16 | 47 | − 6 |
| 50. | 51/6 | 53/13 | 55/1 | 61/8 | 55 | 1 |
| 51. | 52/4 | 53/0 | 50/1 | 68/19 | 53 | − 5* |
| 52. | 51/−5 | 51/−4 | 50/2 | 57/10 | 51 | − 4 |
| 53. | 55/16 | 47/7 | 49/10 | 61/12 | 49 | 3* |
| 54. | 50/3 | 48/3 | 48/8 | 64/17 | 48 | 3 |
| 55. | 47/3 | 53/7 | 41/−16 | 54/15 | 53 | −16 |
| 56. | 56/9 | 38/−8 | 45/0 | 46/3 | 45 | − 8 |
| 57. | 51/−2 | 39/−18 | 67/3 | 57/2 | 67 | −18 |
| 58. | 57/8 | 53/10 | 48/0 | 64/0 | 53 | 0 |
| 59. | 56/6 | 46/−14 | 54/3 | 58/10 | 54 | −14 |
| 60. | 60/−4 | 48/−1 | 49/−4 | 63/19 | 49 | − 4 |
| 61. | 42/5 | 43/−4 | 51/−9 | 69/8 | 51 | − 9 |
| 62. | 55/8 | 45/5 | 44/10 | 50/20 | 45 | 5 |
| 63. | 57/0 | 55/7 | 50/−7 | 52/6 | 55 | − 7 |
| 64. | 55/3 | 52/−2 | 48/−4 | 55/14 | 52 | − 6* |
| 1864–65. | 55/−6 | 45/−3 | 51/0 | 62/17 | 51 | − 3 |
| 1865–66.** | 56/10 | 44/−17 | 54/−1 | 55/12 | 44 | −17 |
| 67.** | 58/−3 | 34/−5 | 51/10 | 58/14 | 51 | − 5 |
| 68.** | 51/3 | 41/6 | 47/−1 | 56/1 | 47 | − 1 |
| 69.** | 48/7 | 49/7 | 60/13 | 61/5 | 60 | 7 |
| 1869–70.** | 53/11 | 50/10 | 51/8 | 48/16 | 51 | 8 |
|  | 68/−11 | 64/−24 | 68/−16 | 76/−9 | 68 | −24 |

* December.
** Record for 1865–66 to 1869–70 is for Providence, R. I. No satisfactory record for New Haven for these years has been located.

# A CONNECTICUT SNOWFALL RECORD: 1779-1820

## NEW HAVEN
### Tutor Atwater at Yale College

|  | O | N | D | J | F | M | A | M | Season |
|---|---|---|---|---|---|---|---|---|---|
| 1779-80 | — | 11 | 48 | 18.5 | 7.5 | 10 | — | — | 95.0 |
| -81 |  |  |  |  |  |  |  |  | 25.0 |

Snowstorms of 10 inches or more at New Haven in 1779-80:

| 1779, 18 Dec. | 17″ |
| 1779, 28 Dec. | 18″ |
| 1780, 3 Jan. | 12″ |

Snowstorms of 10 inches or more at Hamden from 1785-86 to 1809-10:

| 1786, 2 April | 12″ | 1796, 20 Jan. | 12″ |
| 1786, 5 Dec. | 20″ | 1801, 6 March | 10″ |
| 1786, 9 Dec. | 17″ | 1802, 22 Feb. | 18″ |
| 1792, 19 Jan. | 12″ | 1804, 23 Jan. | 10″ |
| 1792, 7 Feb. | 10″ | 1804, 24 Dec. | 12″ |
| 1792, 24 Nov. | 13″ | 1805, 21 Jan. | 15″ |
| 1793, 12 Feb. | 10″ | 1805, 28 Jan. | 18″ |
| 1795, 13 March | 10″ | 1807, 13 March | 10″ |
| 1796, 17 Jan. | 12″ |  |  |

## HAMDEN
### Jeremiah Alling

|  | O | N | D | J | F | M | A | M | Season |
|---|---|---|---|---|---|---|---|---|---|
| 1785-86 | — | 1.5 | 12 | 4.5 | 23 | 4 | 12 | — | 57.0 |
| -87 | 4 | 6 | 44 | 15.5 | 13 | 15 | T | — | 97.5 |
| -88 | — | — | 13.5 | 14 | 9 | .5 | — | — | 37.0 |
| -89 | — | 1 | 11 | 28 | 10 | 1 | 3 | — | 54.0 |
| -90 | — | — | 10 | 12 | 12.5 | 18.5 | 1 | — | 54.0 |
| -91 | — | 7 | 18 | 20 | 17 | 1 | — | — | 63.0 |
| -92 | T | 4 | 6.5 | 20 | 12 | 5 | — | — | 47.5 |
| -93 | — | 13 | 7 | 8 | 18 | 5.5 | — | — | 51.5 |
| -94* | 1 | 2.5 | 22 | 15 | 10.5 | T | — | — | 51.0 |
| -95 | — | 3 | 1 | 10 | 14 | 19.5 | — | — | 47.5 |
| -96 | — | — | 8 | 26.5 | 17 | 12 | — | — | 63.5 |
| -97 | — | — | 8.5 | 5.5 | 3.5 | 4 | 3 | — | 24.5 |
| -98 | — | 1.5 | .5 | 14 | 8 | T | T | — | 24.0 |
| -99 | T | 12 | 24 | 13 | 24 | 11.5 | T | 1 | 85.5 |
| 1799-1800 | — | T | 6 | 1 | 13.5 | 12 | T | — | 32.5 |
| 1800-1801 | — | 8 | 1.5 | 7 | 16 | 10 | T | — | 42.5 |
| -02 | — | 1 | 3 | T | 21 | T | — | — | 25.0 |
| -03 | — | 2 | 4 | 10.5 | 9.5 | 9 | 4 | 2 | 41.0 |
| -04 | — | T | 4 | 18 | 17 | 14 | — | — | 53.0 |
| -05 | — | T | 25 | 57 | 5 | — | — | — | 88.0 |
| -06 | — | T | T | 30 | 4.5 | 16 | 1 | — | 51.5 |
| -07 | — | T | T | 2.5 | 16.5 | 15 | 1 | — | 35.0 |
| -08 | — | .5 | 1.5 | 14.5 | 3.5 | 3 | T | — | 23.0 |
| -09 | — | T | 5 | 17 | 17 | 9.5 | T | — | 48.5 |
| 1809-10 | — | 11 | 6 | 2 | T | 6 | M | M | 25.0 |

* On 17 January 1794, Alling's record read: "in Sandisfield, Mass. from Dec. 7, 1793 until Feb. 13, 1794." It is not clear whether the snowfall record for 1793-94 was made by someone else at Hamden or by Alling at Sandisfield, Mass.

## NEW HAVEN
### President Day at Yale College

|  | O | N | D | J | F | M | A | M | Season |
|---|---|---|---|---|---|---|---|---|---|
| 1803-04 | M | M | M | 9 | 13 | 11.2 | — | — | 33.2 |
| -05 | — | T | 29.7 | 43.5 | 3.5 | — | — | — | 76.7 |
| -06 | — | .5 | ? | 31 | 4 | 15 | 1 | — | 51.5 |
| -07 | — | — | 10 | 1 | 10 | 16 | — | — | 37.0 |
| -08 | — | .2 | .5 | 15 | 5.5 | 2 | — | — | 23.2 |
| -09 | — | — | 4 | 18 | 20 | 10 | — | — | 52.0 |
| -10 | — | 10.5 | 6.5 | 4 | — | 5 | — | — | 26.0 |
| -11 | .5 | 5 | 10 | 8.5 | 26.5 | 4 | 4 | — | 58.5 |
| -12 | — | .5 | 12.5 | 9.5 | 8 | 2.5 | 3 | 6 | 42.0 |
| -13 | — | — | 3 | 23 | 9 | 3 | — | — | 38.0 |
| -14 | — | 9 | 3 | 6.5 | 10 | 5.5 | T | — | 34.0 |
| -15 | — | .5 | 3.5 | 15 | 23 | 3 | — | — | 45.0 |
| -16 | — | — | 9 | 20 | .5 | 13 | 1 | — | 43.5 |
| -17 | — | — | — | 14 | 25 | 2.5 | — | — | 41.5 |
| -18 | — | — | — | 15 | 10 | 6.5 | — | — | 31.5 |
| -19 | — | — | 11 | 7 | 14 | 20 | — | — | 52.0 |
| 1819-1820 | — | .2 | 1.8 | 19 | 19 | 8 | 1 | — | 49.0 |

Snowstorms of 10 inches or more at New Haven from 1804 to 1820:

| 1804, 2 March | 10″ | 1813, 15 Jan. | 10″ |
| 1805, 21 Jan. | 14″ | 1815, 1 Jan. | 10″ |
| 1805, 27 Jan. | 16″ | 1815, 18 Feb. | 10″ |
| 1806, 22 Jan. | 11″ | 1816, 12 Jan. | 11″ |
| 1807, 13 March | 12″ | 1817, 17 Feb. | 10″ |
| 1808, 15 Jan. | 10″ | 1819, 13 March | 11″ |
| 1809, 5 Feb. | 12″ | 1820, 10 Jan. | 10″ |
| 1811, 8 Feb. | 12″ | 1820, 10 Feb. | 20″ |

## HARTFORD
### Connecticut Courant (Hartford)

|  | O | N | D | J | F | M | A | M | Season |
|---|---|---|---|---|---|---|---|---|---|
| 1817-18 |  |  |  |  |  |  |  |  | 26.0 |
| -19 |  |  |  |  |  |  |  |  | 38.0 |
| -20 |  |  |  |  |  |  |  |  | 85.0 |
| -21 |  |  |  |  |  |  |  |  | 90.0* |

* This represents the maximum seasonal snowfall in the record extending from 1817-18 to 1840-41.

# THE SOURCES OF WINTRY DATA

One cannot compile a bibliography on the subject of American winters since individual works do not exist. To the writer's knowledge, there has been no book, or even an article, depicting the meteorological characteristics of the many aspects of winter weather over a substantial period of years for the Nation as a whole. Perhaps the closest approach to such was Sidney Perley's *Historic Storms of New England* (1891), which did include descriptions of outstanding winters, though for a restricted area and containing little scientific information.

The main sources of wintry data must be found in the wealth of contemporary newspapers, magazines, and diaries existing for the period prior to 1820. There are excellent guides to the locations of these; without the long labors of the compilers of the three volumes listed here the research for this work could not have progressed as it has, and its publication would certainly have been posthumous:

Charles S. Brigham. *History and bibliography of American newspapers 1690–1820.* 2 vols. Worcester, American Antiquarian Society, 1947.

Edna Brown Titus, ed. *Union list of serials in libraries of the United States and Canada.* 3 ed. 5 vols. New York, The H. W. Wilson Co., 1965.

William Matthews. *American Diaries: An annotated bibliography of American diaries prior to . . . 1861.* Berkeley, Univ. of California Press, 1945.

During the period under survey no government service existed for collecting weather observations although the need of such was being recognized at the end of the period. The Medical Corps of the U. S. Army (1814) and the U. S. National Land Office (1817) did issue instructions for maintaining meteorological registers. Though little significant data was gathered prior to 1820, these did plant the seed that would eventually, in fifty years, result in the formation of a national weather bureau. Thus, the many meteorological registers employed in this work were made by private individuals, completely lacking in uniform method and content. The following listing is not intended to be a complete inventory of weather records in the period prior to 1820. Rather, only records which have proved most useful in describing more than a single event in our winter weather history. Fragmentary records and those describing only a single event or season have been referenced in the chapter citations throughout the volume.

Several guides to early meteorological records have been compiled, and those listed below proved the most helpful:

Lorin Blodget. *Climatology of the United States and the temperate latitudes of the North American continent.* Phila., J. B. Lippincott and Co., 1857. 536 pp.

U. S. Signal Service. *Index of meteorological observations in the United States from the earliest records to January, 1890.* Washington, Signal Office, 1891.

The National Archives. Ms. Inventory of packages among unpublished hydrologic data in attic of Smithsonian Institution observed and listed by Mr. C. S. Jarvis, Mr. H. S. Schrieber, and Mr. R. W. Ellis, May 3, 1937. 10 pp.

The National Archives. *List of climatological records in the National Archives.* Special List No. 1. Prepared in the Division of Agricultural Department Archives by Lewis J. Darter, Jr. Washington, 1942. 160 pp.

James M. Havens. *An annotated bibliography of meteorological observations in the United States 1731–1818.* Florida State University, Dept. of Meteorology. Technical Report No. 5 Tallahassee, 1956. 31 pp.

## THE NORTHEAST

### Maine

Bangor: 1816–1907. *Opening and closing of navigation of the Penobscot River, Maine. 1816–1907.* Broadside.

Brunswick: 1807–52. Parker Cleaveland. Ms. Met. Jour. (Bowdoin).

Bucksfield: Zadoc Long's Journal. A. Cole and C. Whitman. *A history of Bucksfield, Me.* Bucksfield, 1915. 469–508

Dennysville: 1816–49. Mean temperature. *U. S. Patent Office Report, 1850.* 305.

Gardiner: 1785–1913. B. H. Wentworth. *Chart of Maine winters.* Broadside.

Norway: 1800–40. Joshua Whitman. Summary Notes. *Maine Farmer,* 21 Mar 1840, 82.

Portland: 1722–87. *Journals of Rev. Thomas Smith, and the Rev. Samuel Deane.* Portland, 1849.

——: 1816–52. Portland Observatory. Ms. temperature record. (Maine Hist. Soc.).

Turner: 1810–46. A. Barton. Summary. *American Almanac, 1848.* 93.

### New Hampshire

Bedford: 1754–88. *The diary of Matthew Patten.* Concord, 1903. 545 p.

Bristol: 1785–1899. Richard W Musgrove. *History of the town of Bristol, N.H.* Chap. 44.

Dover: 1758–86. Jeremy Belknap. Ms. Met. Obs. (Hist. Soc. Mass.).

Epping: 1796–1823. William Plumer. Ms. Met. Obs. (Harvard).

Goffstown: 1763–1918. G P. Hadley. *History of the town of Goffstown.* 1, 554–57.

Hampton Falls: 1747–1811. Journal of Deacon David Batchelder. Warren Brown. *History of the town of Hampton Falls.* Concord, 1900.

Hopkinton: 1775–1869. C. C. Lord. *Life and times in Hopkinton, N.H.* Chap. 71.

Lancaster: 1807–17. Ms. diary of Adino Brackett (N. H. Hist. Soc.).

Portsmouth: 1799–1813. Charles Peirce. Met. Obs. (occasional press summaries). *Portsmouth Journal*.

Rockingham County: 1737–72. Ms. diary of Rev. William Parsons (N. Y. Pub. Lib.).

Stratham: 1739–1803. Samuel Lane. *A journal for the years 1739–1803*. Concord, 1937. 115 pp.

### Vermont

Bennington: 1805–37. Benjamin Harwood. Ms. Diary (Bennington Museum).

Burlington: 1803–08. Daniel C. Sanders. Monthly mean temps. Zadock Thompson. *History of Vermont*. Burlington, 1842. 9–10.

Middlebury: 1810–17. Frederick Hall. Met. obs., summary tables. *Literary & Philosophical Repertory* (Middlebury), 1812–17.

Rutland: 1789–95. Samuel Williams. 1789. Z. Thompson, *Hist. Vermont;* 1790–91, Ms. Met. Obs. (Harvard); 1795, *The Rural Magazine & Vt. Repository* (Rutland), 1795.

### Massachusetts

Andover: 1782–1829. Abiel Abbott. *History of Andover from its first settlement to 1829*. Andover, 1829.

Boston: 1811–13+. John Gorham. Met. Obs. *N.E. Jour. Med. & Surgery*.

——: 1818–48. Enoch Hale. Ms. Met. Obs. (Amer. Acad., Harvard).

Cambridge: 1742–79. John Winthrop. Ms. Met. Obs. (Harvard).

——: 1781–89. Edward Wigglesworth. Ms. Met. Obs. (Harvard) and printed summaries, *Boston Magazine*.

——: 1790–1821. Samuel Webber and John Farrar. *Mem. Amer. Acad.* 3 (1815), 361–98; *American Almanac* (1837), 176; *Boston Recorder* (1821).

——: 1795–1829. Abiel Holmes. Ms. Met. Obs. (Lib. Cong.).

Charlestown: 1786–1802. Joseph Barrell. Account of rain, &c. *Mem. Amer. Acad.* 3–2 (1815), 113–15.

East Bridgewater: 1806–69. Leonard Hill. *Meteorological and chronological register*. Plymouth, 1869. 396 pp.

Ipswich: 1781–83. Manasseh Cutler. Met. Obs. *Mem. Amer. Acad.* 1 (1785), 336–71.

Salem: 1754–85. Edward A Holyoke. Ms. Met. Obs. (Harvard).

——: 1786–1829. E. A. Holyoke. Ms. Met. Obs. (Harvard).

——: 1786–1829. E. A. Holyoke. A meteorological journal. *Mem Amer. Acad.* ns.1 (1833), 107–216.

——: 1785–1817. William Bentley. *Diary*. 4 vols.

——: 1804–14. William Bentley. Ms. notes on met. events (Amer. Antiq. Soc.).

Waltham: 1774–76. Jacob Cushing. Ms. monthly met. summaries. (Amer. Acad., Harvard).

——: 1806–41. Charles Fisk. Summaries met. obs. *Columbian Centinel* and Boston *Transcript*.

West Millbury: 1801–47. Elijah Water. Weather notes. *History of Millbury*. Millbury, 1915.

Williamstown: 1816–38. Chester Dewey, etc. Ms. Met. Obs. (Williams).

——: 1811–1949. Willis Milham. *Meteorology in Williams College*. Williamstown, 1950. 40 pp.

### Rhode Island

Newport: 1763–76. Ezra Stiles. Ms. Thermo. Reg. (Yale).

——: 1817–56. —— Taylor. Monthly summaries (Nat. Arch.).

### Connecticut

Joseph M. Kirk. *The weather and climate of Connecticut*. Hartford, 1939. 242 pp.

Ellington: 1817–47. John Hall. Ms. Met. Obs. (Yale).

Hamden: 1785–1810. Jeremiah Alling. *A register of the weather*. New Haven, 1810. 80 pp.

Hartford: 1816–52. Hoadley or Turner?. Ms. Met. Obs. (Conn. Hist. Soc.).

New Haven: 1780–95. Ezra Stiles. Ms. Thermo. Reg. (Yale).

——: 1788–91; 1796–1805. Isaac Beers and Hezekiah Howe. Ms. Weather diary (Yale).

——: 1804–20. Jeremiah Day. Ms. Met. Obs. (Yale).

——: 1821–70. Alfred Monson. Ms. Weather diary (Yale).

——: 1778–1865. Meteorology of New Haven. E. Loomis and H. Newton. *Trans. Conn. Acad.* 1–1 (1866), 194–246.

Thompson: 1771–1888. J. A. Wheelock and family. Record of coldest days. *Mon. Wea. Rev.* 16–5 (May 1888), 129.

East Windsor, etc.: 1794–1854. *Diary of Thomas Robbins, D.D.* 2 vols.

### New York

E. T. Turner. The climate of the state of New York. Albany, 1894. 440 pp.

*Results of a series of meteorological observations . . . from 1826 to 1850*. Franklin B. Hough, ed. Albany, 1855. 499 pp.

*Results of a series of meteorological observations . . . from 1850 to 1871*. Franklin B. Hough, ed. Albany, 1872. 406 pp.

New York City: 1788–1836. Henry Laight. Ms. Met. Obs. (copy). (Nat. Arch. & N. Y. Hist. Soc.).

——: 1789–1831. Notices of the winters at New York for the last 42 years. *Albany Daily Advertiser* in *Amer. Quar. Jour. Agri. and Sci.* 1 (1845), 347.

### New Jersey

Belleville: 1803–29. Gerard Rutgers. Ms. Book of meteorological observations, January 1803–December 1829 (Rutgers).

Morristown: 1783–95. Diary of Joseph Lewis. *Proc. N. J. Hist. Soc.* 59–3 (July 1941), 155 passim.

### Pennsylvania

Bradford: 1777–1900. Clement F. Heverly. *History of Bradford County*.

Philadelphia: 1681–1842. John F. Watson. *Annals of Philadelphia and Pennsylvania in the olden time*. Phila., 1856, 2, 347–69.

——: 1681–1828. Samuel Hazard. Effect of weather on climate.

——: 1770–78. Thomas Coombe. Ms. Met. Obs. (Amer. Phil. Soc.).

——: 1775–78. Phineas Pemberton. Ms. Met. Obs. (Amer. Phil. Soc.).

———: 1788–1805. David Rittenhouse and family. Ms. Met. Obs. (Amer. Phil. Soc.).
———: 1813–46. Charles Peirce. *A meteorological account of the weather in Philadelphia*. Phila., 1847. 300 pp.
Spring Mill (near Norristown): 1786–1828. Peter Legaux for the Penna. Vine Co. Ms. Met. Obs. (Amer. Phil. Soc.).
York: 1801–08. Robert Cathcart. Ms. weather diary (York Co. Hist. Soc.).

## THE OLD SOUTH

### Maryland

Baltimore: 1817–24. Lewis Brantz. Monthly summary broadsides (Md. Hist. Soc.).

### District of Columbia

Washington: 1801–09. Thomas Jefferson. Ms. Weather Book (Lib. Cong).
———: 1816–33. Josiah Meigs, etc. Columbian Institute. Monthly summaries in press. *National Intelligencer*.
———: 1818–25. John Quincy Adams. Ms. weather diary (Mass. Hist. Soc.).

### Virginia

Monticello: 1774–1826. Thomas Jefferson. Ms. Weather Book (Lib. Cong.).
Montpelier, Orange: 1785–1818. James Madison, Sr. and family. Ms. Weather records (Amer. Phil. Soc.).
Mount Vernon: 1767–99. George Washington. Ms. Account of the weather (Lib. Cong.).

### North Carolina

Salem and vicinity: 1756–1836. *Records of the Moravians in North Carolina*. 8 vols.

### South Carolina

Camden (near): 1791–1802; 1808–15. James Kershaw. Ms. Met. Obs. (copy) (Nat. Arch.).
Charleston: 1737–61. John Lining et al. Summary met. obs. Robert Aldredge. Ms. Weather observers and observations at Charleston, South Carolina, 1670–1871 (Weather Bureau Library).

### Alabama

Thomas M. Owens. *History of Alabama*. Chicago, 1921. 1, 279–83.
Patrick H. Mell. *Climatology of Alabama*. Agri. Exp. Station, Auburn. Bulletin No. 18. Ns. (Aug 1890). 73 pp.

### Mississippi

John Monette. Ms. History of the Mississippi Valley (Clements Lib., Univ. Mich.).
Natchez: 1798–1820. Winthrop Sargent. Summary met. obs. *Mem. Amer. Acad. Arts Sci.* 3–1 (1809), 113–15; *Natchez Intelligencer* 1814–20; *Phila. Jour. Med. and Phy. Sci.* 3 (1821), 17.

Natchez: 1799–1810. William Dunbar. Ms. Met. Obs. (Miss. Hist. Soc.); *Trans. Amer. Phil. Soc.* 6–1 (1804), 40–42 and 188–89.

### Louisiana

Louisiana: 1810–56. Edward Hall Barton. *Report to the Louisiana Medical Society on the meteorology, vital statistics, and hygiene of the State of Louisiana*. 1850–57.
Monroe: 1811–50. Judge H. Bry. Weather diary. Fenner. *Southern Medical Reports*. 2, 165.

### Arkansas

Arkansas: 1819–79. W. C. Hickmon. Weather extracts from *Arkansas Gazette*. *Mon. Wea. Rev.* 48–8 (Aug 1920), 447.
Arkansas: 1805–08. John B. Treat. Ms. Met. Obs. (Amer. Phil. Soc.).

### Tennessee

Knoxville (near): 1790–1815. Journal of John Sevier. *Tenn. Mag. Hist.* 5–1 (April 1919), 192–93 passim.

### Kentucky

Lawrence Young? Historical sketch of the climate of Kentucky. Richard H. Collins. *History of Kentucky*. Covington, Ky., 1874. 1, 394–401.

## THE OLD NORTHWEST

### Ohio

Ohio State Board of Agri. Meteorology of Ohio. *12th Annual Report, 1857*. Also *13th Report, 1858* and *22d Report, 1867*.
William H. Alexander. *A climatological history of Ohio*. Columbus, Eng. Exp. Station, Ohio State Univ., 1923.
George W. Mindling. *Weather Headlines in Ohio*. Ohio State Eng. Exp. Station, Bulletin No. 120. Columbus, 1944.
Cincinnati: 1814–48. Farmers College, College Hill. Ms. Met. Obs. summary. (Nat. Arch.).
Gnadenhutten: 1800–14. John Heckewelder et al. Ms. Met. Obs. (Amer. Phil. Soc.).

### Michigan

Detroit: 1781–86. George C. Anton. Ms. Met. Journal (N. Y. Hist. Soc.).
Sault Ste. Marie: 1812–42. Henry R. Schoolcraft. *Personal memoirs of a residence of thirty years*. Phila., 1851.

### Wisconsin

Eric R. Miller. A century of temperature in Wisconsin. *Trans. Wis. Acad. Sci., Arts, Letters*. 23 (1927), 165–77.

# INDEX OF PLACES

Albany, N. Y. 79, 147, 165, 168, 191, 236
Amherst, Mass., 193
Annapolis, Md., 44, 47, 50, 61, 65, 115, 148, 152, 246
Athens, Ga., 210

Baltimore, Md., 115, 148, 152, 195
Bangor, Me., 191
Baton Rouge, La., 19, 150–151
Bennington, Vt., 73, 80, 185, 190–192
Bethabara, N. C. *See* Winston-Salem, N. C.
Boston, Mass., 13, 16, 89, 96–97, 194–196, 241; Cold Days, 77, 78, 80, 82; Cold Friday, 180; Day Before Christmas Storm, 183, 185; Hard Winters, 49–51, 113–114, 116–117, 186; Hessian Storm, 110–111; Long Winter, 75; snows, 41, 42, 44–45, 46–47, 55, 62, 63, 70, 71, 136, 155, 167, 168–169, 188, 190, 192, 193, 243–244
Bismarck, N. D., 253, 254, 257, 258, 260
Brunswick, Me., 174, 175, 179, 180, 188, 190, 191, 192, 194, 196

Cairo, Ill., 225, 226
Cambridge, Mass., 17, 25, 27, 55, 56, 60, 61, 63–64, 73, 89–90, 142, 195; Cold Days, 78, 79, 80; Cold Fridays, 175, 180; Hard Winters, 41, 48, 186; Hessian Storm, 109–110; snows, 45, 60, 68, 70, 71, 82, 165, 173
Camden, S. C., 157, 159–160
Charleston, S. C., 35, 141, 142, 143–144; Cold Sabbath, 146; Great Carolina Gale, 183; Hard Winters, 50, 139, 140, 150; snows, 154–155, 157, 159
Chester, Vt., 191–192
Cincinatti, O., 225, 226, 230, 232, 233
Concord, Mass., 89–90, 96, 97
Concord, N. H., 16, 96, 97, 187, 193
Connecticut Valley, 135, 169, 177–178, 192; floods of 1740–41, 48–49
Cooperstown, N. Y., 176

Delaware Valley, 27–28, 31
Detroit, Mich., 222, 224
Dover, N. H., 16, 17, 24, 41–42, 89, Cold Days, 78; snows, 66, 68, 80, 81, 82–83

Elizabeth, N. J., 167
Exeter, N. H., 165–166

Fort Mandan, N. D., 228, 253, 257, 258–260

Gnadenhutten, O., 226, 227, 228, 229, 230, 231

Halifax, N. C., 156
Hamden, Conn., 70, 73, 170. *See also* New Haven
Hampton Falls, N. H., 56, 75
Hampton Roads, Va., 134, 148
Hanover, N. H., 169, 178, 195
Hartford, Conn., 65, 74; Cold Days, 79, 80; Hard Winter, 115, 116, 117, 120–121, 124, 126, 128; snows, 61–62, 64, 68, 70–71, 185

Ipswich, Mass., 108–111, 137

Jacksonville, Fla., 143
Jamestown, Va., 32–35

Keene, N. H., 75, 177, 180, 185, 188, 193
Knoxville, Tenn., 157–158, 160–161

Lancaster, N. H., 75, 192
Lancaster, Pa. *See* Philadelphia

Lexington, Ky., 226
Lexington, Mass., 89–90
Long Island, N. Y., 22, 27, 49, 98, 172, 186, 189; Hard Winters, 51, 116; ice, 47, 65; snows, 134, 182–185

Malone, N. Y., 185, 186
Marietta, O., 224, 225, 229, 237–238
Martha's Vineyard, Mass., 4
Middlebury, Vt., 190–192
Mobile, Ala., 204
Monhegan Island, Me., 7
Monticello, Va., 89, 145, 147–148, 162; snows, 83, 98; Washington and Jefferson Storm, 213–215
Montpelier, Vt., 178, 191–192
Montreal, 7, 191–192
Morristown, N. J., 72, 134–135; Cold Days, 79; Hard Winters, 112, 122–124, 127, 129–130, 131, 133; snows, 65, 68, 70; Washington's accounts, 122 ff., 129 ff.
Mount Vernon, Va., 83, 151, 156, 157

Nantucket, Mass., 71, 111, 116, 189
Nashville, Tenn., 150, 156, 210
Natchez, Miss., 144, 161, 199, 200, 201, 211; weather tables, 202, 203, 206, 210
New Bedford, Mass., 180, 189, 195, 196; snows, 177, 185, 190
New Bern, N. C., 155–156
New Haven, Conn., 21, 22, 65, 66, 69, 71, 72, 107, 136 ff., 170–172, 186, 187, 189, 195; April Fool's Day Storm, 177; Cold Days, 78 ff.; Cold Fridays, 175, 180–181; Hard Winters, 50, 112 ff., 120–121, 124, 126, 128, 130, 132; Hessian Storm, 109; Long Winter, 74–75; snows, 68, 70, 71, 73, 81, 155, 165, 167 ff., 173, 184–185, 190–191
New London, Conn., 49, 52, 79, 113, 134; snows, 42 ff., 56, 59, 183–184, 242–243
New Orleans, La., 144, 161, 163, 199, 201, 205, 206, 210
Newport, R. I., 47, 49, 50, 61, 65, 113, 185; Cold Days, 78, 79; Hessian Storm, 109–111; snows, 46, 63, 70, 71, 134
New York, N. Y., 7, 16, 28, 42, 46, 47, 61, 65–66, 73, 74, 135 ff.; April Fool's Day Storm, 183; Cold Days, 77 ff.; Cold Fridays, 180–181; Hard Winters, 50, 111, 114 ff., 122–123, 125, 127, 129; 131, 133; Hessian Storm, 109; Severe Winter, 170–172; snows, 44, 46–47, 49, 61, 82, 134–135, 165, 167 ff., 173, 187; Winter Tragedy, 241–242
Norfolk, Va., 73, 148, 156, 157, 237
North Turner, Me., 190, 196

Orange, Va., 65, 151, 152, 157, 159, 212, 251

Philadelphia, Pa., 18, 41, 46–47, 61, 64 ff., 70, 73–74, 89, 101, 102 ff., 136, 146, 189, 245–247; April Fool's Day Storm, 176; Cold Days, 79 ff.; Cold Friday, 175; Great Snow, 43–44; Hard Winters, 49–50, 114, 115, 117; Long Winter, 75; meteorological report, 99–100; snows, 49, 60 ff., 70, 80 ff., 100, 155, 167 ff., 187
Plymouth, Mass., 4, 7–8, 9 ff., 14
Portland, Me., 47–48, 60–61, 62, 72, 89; Hard Winter, 48, 50; Long Winter, 75; snows, 56, 68–69, 75, 81, 193
Port Royal, N. S., 4–5
Portsmouth, N. H., 45, 63–63, 116, 166, 186, 188, 179, 180
Poughkeepsie, N. Y., 80, 83
Princeton, N. J., 114
Provincetown, Mass., 8–9

Quebec, 11, 180, 191–192

Raleigh, N. C., 206, 208
Richmond, Va., 65, 149, 152, 206
Rutland, Vt., 73, 80

## INDEX OF PLACES

Sagadahoc, Me., 6, 32
Ste. Croix Island, N. B., 3–4
Salem, Mass., 61, 63, 71, 73, 74, 89–90, 96, 97, 174, 188, 196; Cold Days, 78–80, 188, 193; Cold Friday, 179–180; Day Before Christmas Storm, 184; Great Snow, 45; Hard Winters, 113 ff., 120, 121, 126, 128; Hessian Storm, 109; Long Winter, 75; Severe Winter, 171; snows, 55, 56, 70, 80–81, 155, 165, 168, 173, 190, 191
Sanbornton, N. H., 67, 180–181
Savannah, Ga., 140–141, 144, 150, 155, 159, 160
Scranton, Pa., 176
Springfield, Mass., 181
Stratham, N. H., 55, 78

Trappe, Pa., 66–67, 99–100, 101–102, 107–108, 134, 136; Hard Winter, 113–114, 122–123, 125, 127, 129, 131, 133; Hessian Storm, 109; snows, 70
Trenton, N. J., 211

Utica, N. Y., 176

Valley Forge, Pa., 100–102
Vincennes, Ind., 230 ff., 238; April Fool's Day Storm, 175
Walpole, N. H., 169–170, 174
Washington, D. C., 145 n, 180, 181, 183, 215, 228; snows, 165, 167
Weare, N. H., 52, 75
Westborough, Mass., 56 ff., 114, 120–121, 124, 126–128, 130, 132
Williamsburg, Va., 108, 115, 145, 148, 151, 152
Williamstown, Mass., 80, 190–192, 194–196
Winchester, Va., 145
Winston-Salem, N. C., 66, 73 n, 81, 89, 135, 147 ff., 153–154, 156, 157, 159, 206–209; Cold Friday, 181; Hard Winter, 149; snows, 151; Washington and Jefferson Storm, 145
Worcester, Mass., 174, 193

York, Me., 75, 82

# INDEX OF PEOPLE

Ainslee, Thomas, 92, 93–95
Alling, Jeremiah, 70, 81, 171, 173
Anthron, Dr. George C., 222–223
Ashe, Thomas, 35
Atwater, Tutor, 114, 120–122

Belknap, Jeremy, 66, 68
Bentley, Rev. William, 73, 74, 75, 81, 187; diary, 83; snows, 173–174
Brackett, Adino, 178, 185–186, 192
Bradford, William, 7–8, 11
Brickell, John, 139

Carroll, Charles, 146
Catesby, Mark, 36
Champlain, Samuel de, 3, 4, 9
Chalmers, Dr. Lionel, 140, 142
Clap, President, 50, 77, 78
Clark, William, 228, 252, 253, 255
Clayton, Rev. John, 33–34
Cleaveland, Prof. Parker, 174–175, 179–180, 188, 193, 194
Collins, Richard, 227, 230
Coombe, Thomas, 89, 101, 102–107
Crèvecoeur, St. John de, 34, 65 n, 247–251
Cushing, J., 71, 83, 117
Cutler, Manasseh, 83, 108, 136, 137, 224; Cold Days, 78; Hessian Storm, 110–111
Cutting, Dr. Hiram A., 169, 177–178, 192

Darby, William, 204, 205, 211, 232
Day, President Jeremiah, 83, 168, 171, 172, 173, 186; Day Before Christmas Storm, 184–185; May snow, 187
Douglass, Dr. William, 45, 46, 76, 77
Drake, Daniel, 201, 224, 225, 226, 232
Dunbar, William, 161, 163, 199 ff., 210–211

Ellicott, Andrew, 160, 224, 225, 226

Falckner, 31–32
Farrar, Prof., 73, 186, 195
Farmer, John, 16, 24
Felt, J. B., 26, 63, 80
Fisk, Charles, 186, 188, 190
Fleming, Col. William, 219–222

Gaine, Hugh, 100, 115, 122–123, 135, 136
Glen, Gov. James, 141–143

Hall, Prof. Frederick, 192
Harwood, Benjamin, 185, 190–192
Haskell, Caleb, 93–95
Hazens, James M., 29–30
Heckewelder, John Gottlieb Ernestus, 224, 227, 228 ff., 233
Hempstead, Joshua, 43–45, 52–54, 56–59
Hildreth, Dr. Samuel P., 229, 237, 238
Hiltzheimer, Jacob, 79, 82
Holm, John Campanius, 29, 30–31
Holmes, Rev. Abiel, 160, 180, 186
Holyoke, Pres. Edward A., 45, 56, 63, 70, 73, 76, 78, 90, 96, 97, 109, 116, 117, 168, 190, 193, 196; Cold Friday, 179; Cold Winter, 186; Day Before Christmas Storm, 184; diary, 79–83; Forty-eight Hour Snow, 173; Hard Winter, 113–114

Hull, John, 16, 22–24
Jefferson, Thomas, 65, 83, 89, 98, 115, 147, 151, 152, 163, 200, 211–215, 223; Cold Friday, 181; Garden Book, 144, 148; Hard Winter, 112; memoranda, 212, 213–215; Washington and Jefferson Storm, 145, 211; Williamson theme, 162
Josselyn, John, 13, 14, 33

Kalm, Peter, 18, 39, 41, 245–247

Laight, Henry, 73, 171, 172, 181, 183, 185, 187
Lane, Samuel, 55, 78, 83–87, 89 n
Lawson, John, 36, 139
Lewis, Joseph, 65, 70, 72, 79
Lewis, Meriwether, 200, 228, 252, 253–257, 258–260
Lining, Dr. John, 50, 139–140, 141–142

MacSparran, Rev. James, 49–50, 244–245
Macy, Obed, 116, 189
MacKenzie, Frederick, 110, 115, 134
Madison, James, 65, 151–152, 156, 159
Madison, Rev. James, 148, 151–152, 157, 214, 215
Manigault, Ann, 143–144, 146, 150
Mather, Rev. Cotton, 17, 26, 42, 43, 47, 243–244
Mitchell, Dr. Samuel Latham, 82, 165, 182–184
Monette, Dr. John, 143–144
Montresor, Capt. John, 102–103, 105–107
Moravian Brethren. *See* Winston-Salem, N. C.
Muhlenburg, Rev. Henry M., 65, 66–67, 99, 100, 101–102, 136; Hard Winter, 113–114; Hessian Storm, 109; journal, 61, 102–107, 122–123, 125, 127, 129, 131, 133

Norris, Isaac, 41, 80, 84

Parkman, Rev. Ebenezer, 47, 48, 49, 114; diary, 55–59, 120–121, 124, 126–128, 130, 132
Patten, Matthew, 68, 71, 89, 134, 135; diary, 81 ff.
Pemberton, Phineas, 99, 100
Peirce, Charles, 179–180, 186
Pike, Rev. John, 16, 17, 22, 24–27, 40–41, 42, 80
Plumer, Sen. William, 165–166
Preston, John, 56, 80, 81

Ramsay, David, 142, 154, 157, 162–163
Rittenhouse, David, 74, 79, 80, 120, 129, 131, 167
Robbins, Thomas, 83, 178, 181, 186, 188, 193, 194, 228, 229; Day Before Christmas Storm, 185
Rodman, Samuel, 189, 190

Sargent, Winthrop, 72, 199, 201–202, 203 ff., 224–225; Cold Friday, 211
Sewall, Judge Samuel, 16, 26, 47, 241; diary, 17–18, 24, 27, 41, 42, 46, 77, 80; Great Snow, 43
Smith, Capt. John, 7, 32–33
Smith, Rev. Thomas, 47, 48, 52, 56, 61, 62, 66, 68, 69, 72, 89, 90, 93, 134, 136; Hard Winter, 116; journal, 81; snows, 68–69, 71
Stephens, Col. William, 141
Stiles, Rev. Ezra, 48, 50, 63, 65, 66, 73, 81, 100, 107, 109, 136, 155, 156, 160; Cold Days, 76 ff.; Hard Winter, 113, 117; snows, 69, 70
Stoudt, John J., 103–105
Strachey, William, 6, 32
Strong, Rev. Nathan, 17, 69

284

Thacher, Dr. James, 107, 108, 114
Thomas, Isaiah, 166, 174, 185

Volney, Comte de Constantin Francois de Chasseboeuf, 231–232

Washington, George, 83, 100, 113, 114, 116, 151, 156–157; Washington and Jefferson Storm, 144–146
Webber, Pres. Samuel, 73, 165
Webster, Noah, 15, 16, 65, 66, 70, 74, 79, 158, 165, 168; Long Winter, 74–75; snows, 71, 169, 170, 173, 184, 193

Whitman, Joshua, 190, 192, 196
Wigglesworth, Prof. Edward, 70, 71
Williamson, William, 66, 196
Wilson, Samuel, 35–36
Winthrop, John, 12, 13, 14, 18–22, 33, 82, 173
Winthrop, Prof. John, 50, 56, 60, 61, 77, 78, 89–90, 96, 97, 142, 204–205, 242–243; Great Snow, 45; Hessian Storm, 109–110; snows, 63–64
Wood, William, 10, 12, 13–14

Zane, Isaac, 212, 223